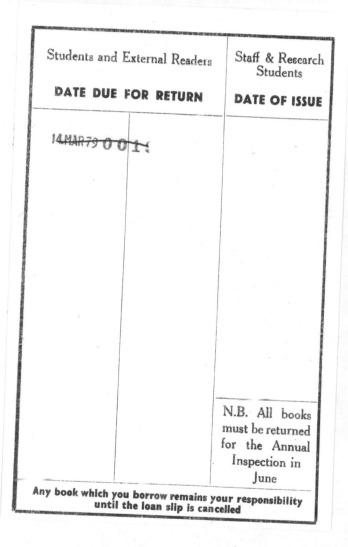

☆

CROFTS AMERICAN HISTORY SERIES

Dixon Ryan Fox, General Editor

☆

THE

# Roots of American Civilization

*A HISTORY OF AMERICAN COLONIAL LIFE*

*BY*

*CURTIS P. NETTELS, Cornell University*

☆ ☆
☆

*APPLETON-CENTURY-CROFTS, INC.*
*New York*

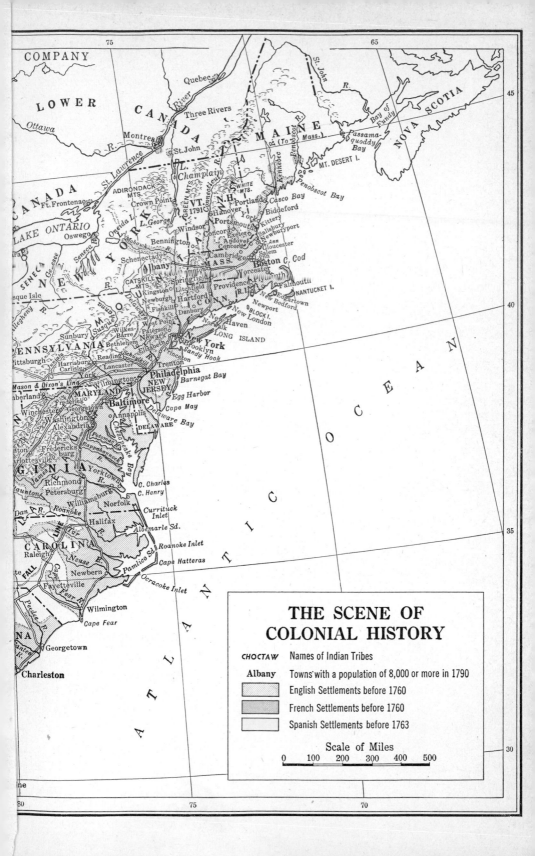

THE SCENE OF
COLONIAL HISTORY

CHOCTAW  Names of Indian Tribes

Albany  Towns with a population of 8,000 or more in 1790

English Settlements before 1760

French Settlements before 1760

Spanish Settlements before 1763

Scale of Miles

0   100   200   300   400   500

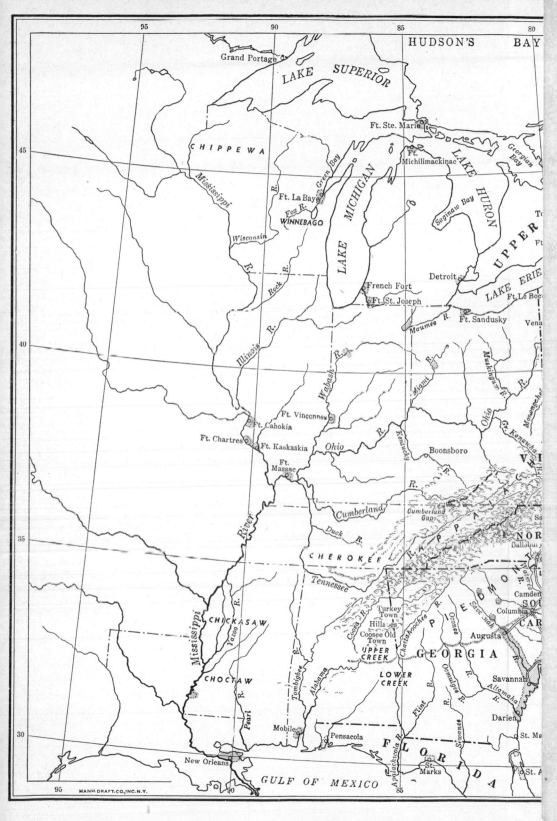

*To*

ELSIE PATTERSON NETTELS

# EDITOR'S FOREWORD

"THE basic institutions of American government and the prevailing philosophy of today were shaped in large measure during the colonial period." With this striking summary statement Professor Nettels begins his chapter on government and religion, but its application will be recognized in every part and phase of his book; wherefore it is properly entitled *The Roots of American Civilization*.

If it could be assumed that the number of people involved in a transaction, either in the cause or in the immediate effect, should be taken as an index of its comparative historical importance, then of course colonial history would sink into insignificance. But the few men who start an enterprise may be more significant than the vast number who carry it on long afterwards. The pioneer is immensely important; his ideals and his purposes may prove to be as fundamental influences in conditioning the lives of a people many generations later as the geographical facts of rivers and soils and mountains or those strong new economic forces which have come with changes in the form and character of work. As the twig is bent, runs the old adage, so grows the tree. Of course, the changing winds may alter its shape somewhat in later years, but the original bent continues to account for much of its peculiarity. America is what it is, partly, at least, because men like John Winthrop, William Penn, John Wise, John Peter Zenger, Thomas Jefferson, and George Washington were what they were. Conjecturing the viewpoint of historians two or three centuries hence is a hazardous business, but it seems safe to say that any one of these men was more important because he lived in the colonial period than he would have been if he had lived in the twentieth century.

It would certainly be a mistake to assume, too, that colonial history is a "dead" subject, that productive research in that field, largely speaking, has been finished. Put an able, industrious mind to work on the first half of our life as Americans, judged by years, and you will get as fresh and novel a history as you will get from the same kind of mind set to the second half. Professor Nettels' book is a proof of it, if there were nothing more at hand. Scholars have discovered as much about the America of the seventeenth and eighteenth centuries in the past forty years as they knew before that time. The astonishing number of books published in this field during the nineteen-thirties, which the author here cites, illustrates how the fruitful work proceeds. The identification and analysis of economic forces, of group rivalries, of stirring ideas, of the fundamental reasons why wars were fought and won or lost in that period, has gone on and is going on with constantly increasing result. The discovery that there was a British colonial policy maturing through many vicissitudes from the days of Elizabeth to those of George III, and of some of the factors that made its execution difficult, indeed impossible, is the work of men who for the most part are still alive.

But in no other single volume, I believe, has so much of this modern scholarship been laid under contribution, or its results so clearly analyzed and fused into so coherent an account, informed throughout by the author's own original investigations, as in the book before us. Its main thesis is the emergence and definition of social classes in colonial America, with their respective economic foundations and their social and political conflicts. There were aristocratic tendencies flowing from a persistent tradition and from personal and family ambition; there were democratic tendencies encouraged by American environment; and the two could not work together in peace. Neither could imperial and local interests. These conflicts insisted upon expression not only in politics, but also in religion, military administration, education, and, indeed, in every phase of popular culture.

This, however, is not to say that every event, every policy, every life is interpreted in terms of this conflict. It is well to have a thesis, if it is come by after long, industrious, and honest study of the data, but it is not well to attempt to jam everything into its pattern and to reject as unimportant all that does not contribute to its argument. The process of colonization is considered as a challenge to intelligence and courage, those of statesmen and promoters on the one hand and those of colonist families on the other. All took a risk, and in large part their hopes were joined. "Plantations," remarked Lord Bacon, "are amongst ancient, primitive and heroic works." No reader of these pages can escape vicarious thrills as he follows the first strike into the wilderness on a strange continent. The life of a people, however, holds abundant interest even when it is not thrilling. Curtis Nettels, I believe, has given us a fuller, clearer picture of the common day of American colonials than is to be found in other one-volume histories, and has done so in a rational order of treatment so often missed by writers on the social scene.

Reference has been made to the colonial people. There are obvious inherent difficulties in treating thirteen colonies as one people, though we may realize that they were much alike and undergoing similar experiences. Despite these difficulties the author has made a notable contribution in attempting to view them as a whole rather than in a series, and reflective readers will remark with satisfaction how well he has succeeded. Certain social or political phenomena appeared in one colony before they did in another; in consequence chronology is less regarded here than logical arrangement.

The author has designed a scheme of references to make additional reading as attractive and convenient as possible. Instead of the usual consolidated bibliography at the back of the book, so dismaying to the average reader, he has introduced occasional citations and counsel after appropriate paragraphs of the text, where they may satisfy awakened curiosity, and, at the chapter's end, a more extended note, listing books in designated parts which deal with the subject at hand, a few atlas maps of special application, and with cautious restraint some source materials that the ordinary reader might actually desire to read; here and there, for the benefit of more hearty appetites he discusses specialized, "technical" works, which are not recommended for the many. Much care has been given to these devices to lure the reader into further inquiry; from them he will be aware of at least some of the material that lies behind the present volume, and occasionally he will be tempted, beyond the resistance of our common natural indolence, to explore a few parts of it for himself.

DIXON RYAN FOX

# PREFACE

HISTORY is man's guide to action in the present and future. And such action is certain to be most constructive when it is informed by an understanding of the problems and conditions which, having emerged slowly from the past, mold and limit the activities of today and tomorrow. Those who know the circumstances of their country's development and who understand the elements of its civilization will be the ones best qualified to meet present issues with decision, intelligence, and economy of effort.

Such is the conception of the uses of history that underlies this book. My effort has been to understand and to describe the essentials of American society as they have appeared in the course of its development. One who studies the colonial period is continually pulled in two directions: toward the time that has passed since then, that one may relate colonial origins to contemporary trends; and toward the remote past, that one may understand the sources of those enduring influences which have outlived the colonial period. For this reason I have emphasized the European background of American history— not for itself, but in order to explain the forces that have made the United States what it is today.

It is impossible to acknowledge all intellectual debts incurred in preparing this book. Among those who have read parts of the manuscript and have saved me from errors are Dean G. C. Sellery and Professor Robert L. Reynolds of the University of Wisconsin, Professor Marcus W. Jernegan of the University of Chicago, Mr. Louis M. Hacker of Columbia University, Dr. Dixon Ryan Fox, President of Union College, and Dr. Carl Bridenbaugh of the Massachusetts Institute of Technology.

To the University of Wisconsin I am indebted for the aid of research assistants and the opportunity for four months of uninterrupted study, both of which were made possible by grants from research funds. I have also profited from studies of several graduate students in American history at Wisconsin, particularly those of John M. Weidman, Bertha M. Hamilton, George T. Hunt, Merrill M. Jenson, Milton Longhorn, Alexander C. Kern, Leo Wearing, Katherine Ragen, Emil F. Heintz, Clarence M. Weiner, Raymond Plath, Marion Hoffman Gottfried, William Marsh, and Ruth Dunham.

The eight original population maps printed in the text were prepared by Mr. H. R. Friis, to whom I am deeply obliged for his generous permission to include them in this book.

CURTIS P. NETTELS

# TABLE OF CONTENTS

xiii

# LIST OF MAPS AND ILLUSTRATIONS

# ☆ I ☆

## FACTORS IN THE EXPANSION OF EUROPE

THE United States which we know today is the product of two principal forces. One—the immigration of many European peoples—introduced a variety of European ideals, customs, and racial characteristics.[1] Yet European cultural traits have not remained distinctly European in their American setting; they have been greatly modified by the second factor, the environment of the new country—natural resources, the climate, the lie of the land. The history of the United States is a story of the impact of a rich and undeveloped continent upon transplanted European ideas and ways of life. The outcome is a social order in many ways similar to European societies, yet possessing an unmistakably American character.

### THE NORSE REVIVAL IN EUROPE

After the barbarian invasions in Europe had prostrated the Roman empire, a state of lethargy and economic stagnation settled upon the peoples of Western Europe. Among the forces which finally aroused them from this slumber was an infusion of vital energy from the northern kingdoms of Denmark, Norway, and Sweden. The consolidation of the Norse people into these three kingdoms, accomplished between 900 and 1050, was accompanied and followed by tidal waves of expansion and conquest, motivated at first by lust for plunder, and later by hunger for more fertile lands. To the east the Northmen established a kingdom in Russia, and reached Constantinople, where they became a symbol of military power. To the south, they conquered Normandy in France and twice overran large parts of England. Their descendants, the Normans, aided in the reconquest of Spain from the Moors, made settlements in southern Italy and Sicily, and seized outposts in northern Africa. Westward, the Northmen subdued Ireland and discovered and colonized Iceland and Greenland. Then, between

[1] The best survey of the early European background for the general student is Edward P. Cheyney's *The Dawn of a New Era* (New York, 1936)—a book that combines learning, breadth of view, insight, and literary charm.

I

986 and 1003, two Norwegians, Biarni Heriulfson and Leif Ericsson, on separate voyages, reached the shores of America somewhere between Labrador and Cape Cod. Several later voyages failed to accomplish an intended colonization of "Vinland," the wooded, vine-covered shore which Leif Ericsson first explored.[2]

In retrospect, the Northmen are less important for their discovery of America than for the mighty impetus they gave to the renewal of European life. It is likely that the knowledge of their discovery was lost to most of Europe, and that it did not contribute to the final opening of the New World. But as pioneers in seafaring, shipbuilding, and colonization, they entered the main stream of European expansion. They were the first to build vessels which could safely ride the turbulent waters of the Atlantic. Their conquests, affording a thousand contacts of kinship within the known world, led to an expansion of trade which helped to dissolve the isolation in which the villagers of Western Europe had previously lived. Prodigious was the energy of the Northmen, while their capacity for political leadership and their genius for organization and assimilation were unexcelled. Their zeal for Christianity was blended with an ardor for military renown and a primitive reverence for sacred sites and objects. They felt that their church should be a militant warrior chastising its enemies in glorious physical combat and redeeming the holy places of the faith. In consequence, the descendants of Northmen who settled in Europe became the foremost leaders of the Crusades.[3]

### EUROPE AND THE ORIENT

These pilgrimages of the twelfth and thirteenth centuries—inspired by curiosity, by religious fervor, and by love of glory, plunder, and adventure—supplied another powerful force to break the shell of isolation which had encased the people of early medieval Europe. The armies of crusaders voyaging to Palestine gave a tremendous stimulus to the building of ships. New transports had to be constructed, and when crusading activity subsided, such vessels were used in ordinary trade. Merchants of Italian cities like Genoa and Venice grew rich upon the profits of transporting and provisioning the warrior pilgrims; capital for commerce thus accumulated in the northern

[2] A scholarly study is Geoffrey M. Gathorne-Hardy's *The Norse Discoverers of America* (Oxford, 1921). An older work of merit is Joseph Fischer's *The Discoveries of the Norsemen in America* (London, 1903). An especially good treatment is William Hovgaard, *The Voyages of the Norsemen* . . . (New York, 1914).

[3] Charles H. Haskins, *The Normans in European History* (Boston, 1915), is a model of historical writing.

Mediterranean towns. In Syria and Egypt the crusaders beheld rare and costly articles of the Orient—spices, fine cloth, and precious stones —and new visions of wealth and splendor opened before the West. Likewise, European merchants came into contact with the terminal cities on the routes of oriental trade. There they later established trading posts in order to obtain the precious commodities of the East.[4]

The products which came from Arabia, India, Ceylon, China, and the Spice Islands wrought a transformation of European life. Before 1100, living conditions had been extremely mean and hard. The arts of cooking and preserving food were little known. Even at the tables of the nobles the fare was monotonous and coarse. It is not strange, then, that the Europeans relished the spices of the Orient—pepper, nutmeg, cinnamon, ginger, cloves, and mace. Such seasoning made stale food more palatable in the days before refrigeration. The nobles likewise welcomed the elegant fabrics of the East which satisfied the craving for display to set apart the noble from the lowly serf. Oriental rugs and carpets—then as now the best in the world—beautiful chinaware, fine glass, tapestries, diamonds and pearls from India and rubies from Ceylon—all these brought a glow of warmth and color into a previously drab existence. Perfumes provided a crude but welcome substitute for baths. And there were soothing drugs—camphor, medicinal rhubarb, and musk, and opium, the only drug then known which deadened pain.[5]

These oriental goods could be carried great distances because they were abundant and cheap in the East and scarce and expensive in the West. All were of slight weight and bulk; this made long-range transportation possible. They were brought to Europe over three principal routes of trade. One led from Japan and China by way of the China Sea, or from the Spice Islands—athwart the equator—and past the rich East Indies, to the port of Malacca, a great center where Chinese merchants met Arab and Indian traders from the West. Thence the goods were conveyed by sea to Calicut in India; then across the Arabian Sea and by way of the Red Sea to Alexandria. The second or central route touched at points along the western coast of India and led to Ormuz in the Persian Gulf. Next the goods went by Bozra and the Tigris River to Bagdad, whence some were taken by caravan to Jaffa or Antioch. To Trebizond on the Black Sea other wares were

---

[4] *The Crusades*, by Richard A. Newhall (New York, c. 1927), is the best brief discussion for the general reader.
[5] Clive Day's *History of Commerce* (New York, 1936) discusses medieval trade admirably in chapters 9–14.

4 THE ROOTS OF AMERICAN CIVILIZATION

carried north from Bagdad. The third route began near Peking, and crossed the inland provinces of China and Turkestan to the Caspian Sea. Thence it proceeded through Tabriz to the Black Sea and across to Constantinople.

At Alexandria, Antioch, and other terminals of these three routes the trading towns of France and Spain and particularly of Italy established business headquarters called *fondachi*. These consisted of warehouses, market places, offices, churches, dwellings, and baths. The traders bought from native princes the privileges of self-government and protected trade. Their business was to obtain the incoming oriental wares and to reship them to their home cities, such as Pisa, Genoa, or Venice.[6]

These cities in the late Middle Ages came to resemble trading corporations, in which the merchants controlled the government for their own advantage. All Venetian traders were required to send to Venice the wares they purchased in the East. These were to be stored in warehouses and exported only on government license. After 1300, fleets of vessels with galley convoys were fitted out and dispatched for trade with Western Europe. The "Flanders fleet" usually made a yearly voyage to Spain, Portugal, France, Britain, and Flanders. The expense was borne and the profit made by the Venetian merchants. Oriental goods were also carried to northern Europe by German traders who traveled by the Danube and the Rhine, or through towns brought into new importance, like Augsburg and Nuremberg, and over the Alpine passes to Venice. The great distributing agency in northwestern Europe was the Hanseatic League—an association of German towns which included Lübeck, Hamburg, and Bremen. These towns had banded together to secure outside commercial privileges for their traders. The Hanseatic merchants bought their oriental wares in Italy, Antwerp and other towns, and at fairs in Western Europe. Then they supplied the markets of England, Russia, Poland, Scandinavia, and Germany. They also set up trading agencies abroad, with special privileges and protection. In London, the Hanse merchants were called Easterlings, and their walled settlement on the Thames was known as the Steelyard. The word *sterling* survives as a tribute to the quality of the silver money current among the Easterlings.

Most of the commodities exported from Western Europe to the Orient were raw materials such as quicksilver, tin, copper, lead, amber,

[6] The best one-volume text on its subject is Herbert Heaton's *Economic History of Europe* (New York, 1936). For the Middle Ages see chapters 5–11.

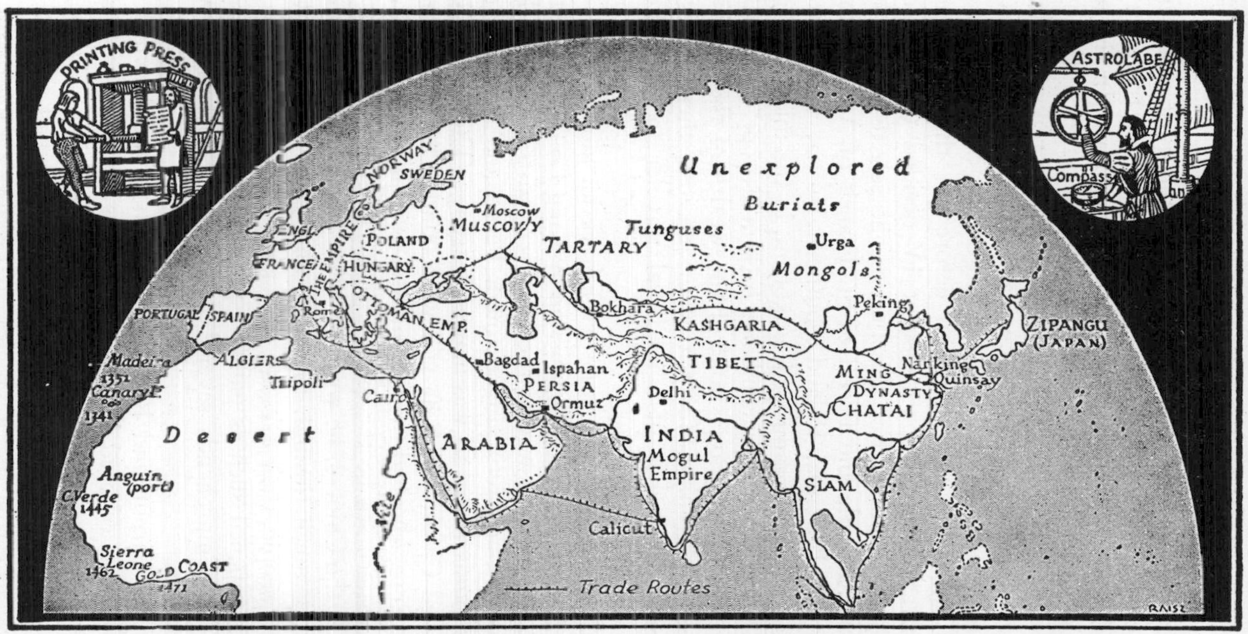
PRINTING PRESS
ASTROLABE
Compass
Unexplored
Buriats
Tunguses
Urga
Mongols
TARTARY
Moscow
MUSCOVY
NORWAY
SWEDEN
ENGL.
POLAND
FRANCE
THE EMPIRE
HUNGARY
PORTUGAL
SPAIN
Rome
OTTOMAN EMP.
ALGIERS
Tripoli
Cairo
Madeira
1351
Canary I.
1341
Desert
Anguin (port)
C. Verde
1445
Sierra Leone
1462
GOLD COAST
1471
Bagdad
Ispahan
PERSIA
Ormuz
ARABIA
Bokhara
KASHGARIA
TIBET
Delhi
INDIA
Mogul
Empire
Calicut
Peking
MING
DYNASTY
CHATAI
Nanking
Quinsay
SIAM
ZIPANGU
(JAPAN)
Trade Routes
RAISZ

*From Wertenbaker and Smith's "The United States of America."* © *Charles Scribner's Sons.*

MEDIEVAL TRADE ROUTES TO THE ORIENT

and tar, and manufactured goods like woolen cloth. Gold and silver money also flowed from west to east.[7]

The regeneration of commerce stirred anew the spirit of adventure and the quest for knowledge, and eased the path for travelers who sought a fuller understanding of the mysterious East. In the meantime great events were stirring there. Between 1206 and 1227 occurred the conquests of the Mongols under their renowned leader, Genghis Khan. Soon afterward the Tartars invaded Armenia and southern Russia, and in 1241 one of their generals captured Budapest. Christian Europe was terror-stricken before the threat of another barbarian invasion, and Pope Innocent IV decided to send ambassadors to the great khan. For this purpose he selected one John of Plano Carpini, disciple and friend of St. Francis of Assisi, who proceeded through Bohemia, Poland, southern Russia, and Turkestan and met the khan at his camp at Karakorum, in the midst of oriental splendor. Two years later Carpini was back in Europe. His carefully written accounts of his travels told of the wealth of the Orient and pictured the opportunities for Christian missions there. This was the first recorded journey of a medieval traveler to the unknown East.

A few years later, in 1253, another Franciscan monk, William de Rubruquis, was sent on a similar mission by King Louis IX of France. Going to Karakorum by way of the northern coasts of the Black Sea and the Caspian, and returning through Persia and Syria, he spent two years in lands where all was new and strange. The description he wrote included China, which he said was bounded by an eastern sea. Previously, Europeans had thought of Asia as an indefinite land mass. Could this eastern sea be the same that stretched away to the west of Spain? Of the Chinese, he wrote: "These Cathayans are little fellows, speaking much through the nose, and, as in general with all those eastern people, their eyes are very narrow. . . . They do their writing with a pencil such as painters paint with, and a single character of theirs comprehends several letters, so as to form a whole word." [8]

The fame of Carpini and Rubruquis and the wonders which they related were soon eclipsed by the adventures experienced and the marvels described by the greatest of medieval travelers, Marco Polo. In 1260, the father and uncle of young Marco had set out from

[7] A good brief introductory sketch is Laurence B. Packard's *The Commercial Revolution* (New York, c. 1927).

[8] For a collection of excellent recent studies of the medieval background of discovery see Arthur P. Newton (ed.), *Travel and Travellers of the Middle Ages* (New York, 1926).

Constantinople on a trading voyage which finally carried them to the court of Kubla Khan. Here they were well received and allowed to return to Venice with a commission to ask the pope to send a hundred wise men to instruct the Mongolians in Western arts and the Christian faith. When the Polo brothers went forth again to China in 1271 they took the enterprising Marco with them. Three and a half years elapsed before they reached the court of Kubla Khan. Marco speedily won the confidence of the great ruler, who made him governor of a great Chinese city and sent him on diplomatic missions to eastern Tibet, Cochin China, and India. Having accumulated a fortune, Marco returned to Venice in 1295. Captured soon afterward in a war between Venice and Genoa, he was clapped into prison by the Genoese. There he dictated the famous narrative of his travels, *The Book of Ser Marco Polo concerning the Kingdoms and Marvels of the East.*[9]

What a panorama of wonders this remarkable book unfolded! It was the first account "to reveal China in all its wealth and vastness, its mighty rivers, its huge cities, its rich manufactures, its swarming population, the inconceivably vast fleets that quickened its seas and inland waters." Into the city of Peking entered every day a thousand cartloads of silk; there stood the palace of the Great Khan, with its walls and ceilings of gold and its banquet hall large enough to accommodate six thousand guests. Japan, or Cipangu, appeared as a very large island, rich in "rose-tinted pearls" and precious stones. There were the pearls and diamonds, the spices, the cotton, the indigo, and the dyestuffs of India, the golden pagodas of Burma and the rubies of Ceylon. In the eastern sea lay hundreds of small islands, every one of which produced "valuable and odorous woods, and gold and gems, and all manner of spices pepper as white as snow, and also the black kind, in great quantity." And from the south came rumors of strange lands—of Abyssinia and Zanzibar and Madagascar —with tales of Negroes and ivory and gold, while from the north came reports of the vast expanse of Siberia, where ranged the dog sledge, the reindeer, and the white bear.

Marco Polo was the first European traveler to traverse the whole length of Asia. The wonders he had seen and the still greater marvels of which he had heard intensified the interest of traders, scholars, and missionaries in the East, and inspired other travelers to journey thither during the next century. His book cast an enduring spell over

[9] C. R. Beazley, "Marco Polo and the European Expansion of the Middle Ages," *Atlantic Monthly*, CIV (Oct. 1909). The latest study, authoritative and readable, is Sir Percy Sykes, *The Quest for Cathay* (London, 1937).

European minds. Printed in 1477, it was read by Columbus and probably inflamed his imagination with a desire to visit wondrous lands. Next to the voyages of Columbus himself, the travels of Marco Polo form the most important chapter in the history of geographical discovery.[10]

## The Renaissance and the Age of Discovery

The extending contacts of commerce and travel helped to prepare the way for another great movement—the Renaissance. This surge of intellectual and artistic energy may be traced in part to the renewed intercourse between Italy and the East which revealed a fuller knowledge of the civilizations of the ancient world. The growth of commerce and industry in towns provided the wealth, the leisure and security necessary for the work of artist and scholar. Italian merchants became promoters of learning, partly in order that they might apply the fruits of knowledge to the advancement of their trade.

Two aspects of the life of the spirit had been prominent before the Renaissance. One was religious faith. The earlier scholars were churchmen who accepted the Scriptures as the revealed word of God. Man attained the truth only when he accepted divine revelation as the premise of his reasoned thought. It is true that after the tenth century, the Greek philosopher, Aristotle, had been widely studied in Latin translations. But Aristotle had expounded the deductive method of logic—reasoning from accepted principles. The medieval school-men were thus able to apply the method of Aristotle to the Bible, taking its teachings as accepted truths to be demonstrated by deductive logic. One would not dare to oppose the Bible with contrary conclusions drawn from personal observations of the natural world.

A second feature of religious life was the ascetic ideal of the monasteries. Man was regarded as a weak and erring creature; his life on earth was a prison of woes; his works of pride and vanity were an abomination in the sight of God. His sinful flesh must be purified by prayerful contemplation of the divine spirit. Through the agency of the Church he might renounce the corruption of the world and enter into the incorruptible and eternal life to come.[11]

One stream of the Renaissance, Humanism, flowed from an ap-

[10] An older coöperative work, the massive *Narrative and Critical History of America* (ed. Justin Winsor, 8 vols., Boston, 1884–89), is still valuable on discovery and exploration. See Vol. I, chapters 1–2.

[11] See an illuminating essay, "The Christian Life," by F. M. Powicke, in *The Legacy of the Middle Ages* (ed. C. G. Crump, Oxford, 1926).

## The Weigher of Gold

This painting by Rembrandt suggests the importance of precious metals
in the seventeenth-century trade of Western Europe.

preciative study of the classics of Greece and Rome. These cultural treasures gave an enlarged view of the dignity of man. He had fashioned exquisite works of art, probed the mysteries of nature, and produced inspiring literature recording heroic deeds and elevated thought. To students of such achievements man did not appear as an unworthy tenant of a corrupting earth. He might at least roughhew the ends of his own destiny, find joy in the cultivation of the arts, and expand the comprehending powers of his mind. By intelligence and effort he might subdue the earth and make it minister to his emotional and intellectual needs. Life should become a blessing to be enjoyed, not a curse to be endured.

In several fields of inquiry the thinkers of ancient Greece had gone beyond the scholars of early medieval Europe. Many of the studies which the Greeks had cultivated—mathematics, astronomy, and geography—were to play important parts in the advancement of science and navigation which led to the age of discovery. For many years the scholars of Europe accepted the classical writers as sources of truth second only to the Bible. But the ancient authorities did not always agree with one another. This led eventually to classifications and comparisons, and to critical appraisals and verifying investigations. Where the Greeks had contented themselves with bold speculative inquiry, the scholars of the late Middle Ages were moved to check with actual measurements. Such advances pointed toward the great era of geographical discovery, whose guiding philosophy was to take nothing for granted but to learn by observation and experience. Moreover, the spirit of Greek philosophers had been distinctly critical. Accordingly, they helped to instruct their later European disciples in the art of examining into the nature of the visible world.[12]

The development of science in Europe took a more practical turn than it had in ancient Greece. The Greek philosophers, living in a society supported by slaves, had been free from the petty cares of daily toil. Breathing a somewhat rarefied intellectual atmosphere, they had dwelt upon the ideal and the abstract. But the European bourgeoisie, not having slaves, became interested in making science do a part of the world's work. Astronomy helped the navigator, geometry was a boon to architects, and arithmetic and algebra (newly derived from Arabian mathematicians), facilitated business and trade. A similar trend was disclosed in scores of inventions introduced in Europe after the twelfth century. Such were magnifying glasses, gun-

[12] Lord Acton's *Lectures on Modern History* (London, 1918) gives a broad view of important themes, emphasizing the influence of ideas. See chapters 1, 3.

powder, compasses, printing presses, bellows, blast furnaces, thermometers, water-power machines, and clocks.[13]

Ancient writers exerted a particularly strong influence upon the study of geography in medieval times. Prior to 1400 the size of the world known to Europeans was smaller than the area still unknown. The continent of Africa, excepting its Mediterranean shore and the valley of the Nile, was as yet a closed book. Europe, north of the Baltic and the Caspian Sea, was another *terra incognita*. Europeans could only estimate roughly the size and relationships of oriental countries. Beyond the Atlantic, shrouded in darkness, lay the two Americas, the Pacific Ocean, and the lands of Australasia.

Lacking first-hand knowledge of much of the world's surface, European scholars could only speculate about its full nature and extent. From the ancient Greeks they derived the idea that the earth is round. This view was commonly accepted by learned men after the time of the Crusades. The Byzantine emperors carried a ball as a symbol of their world dominion; Dante in the *Divine Comedy* pictured the world as a globe; and Columbus later testified that he had always read that ancient geographers had proved the sphericity of the earth.[14]

One of these geographers was Claudius Ptolemy, who lived at Alexandria about 127–151 A. D. His works exerted a stronger influence on medieval scholars than those of any other writer. He conceived the earth as the center of the universe; around it, every twenty-four hours, with incredible speed, revolved the sun and stars, all fixed in a succession of hollow and transparent spheres. He estimated that most of the unknown world consisted of land; hence his "continental theory." In consequence, he exaggerated the size of Asia, and described Africa as extending far to the south and east, joining Asia in a continuous land mass and making the Indian Ocean an inland sea. If these views were correct, the Orient could not be reached from Western Europe by sailing south around Africa. But perhaps one might proceed directly west across the Atlantic.

A greater scientist than Ptolemy, but one less honored in the Middle Ages, was the Greek astronomer, Eratosthenes (276–196 B. C.). His studies convinced him that the unknown parts of the world consisted mainly of water. According to his "oceanic theory," both Eu-

---

[13] Book I of Henry S. Lucas's *The Renaissance and the Reformation* (New York, c. 1934) is a good recent discussion of the Renaissance.

[14] John Fiske's *The Discovery of America* (2 vols., Boston, 1892) begins his history of the colonial period. Not an outstanding historical scholar, Fiske wrote for the general public. His writings are still of interest for their vigorous expression and literary excellence. See Vol. I, chapters 2, 3.

rope at the north and Africa at the south were bounded by immense seas.

Three questions had an important bearing upon geographical discovery. (1) How large was the earth? (2) What was the relation in size of the known world to the unknown? (3) Was there a continuous water passage from west to east? [15]

Although Eratosthenes calculated the earth's circumference at very nearly its true figure, Ptolemy computed it as considerably less than it actually is. Aristotle regarded the earth as a small sphere. Eratosthenes believed that the unknown world covered two-thirds of the earth's surface; the immense extent of the Atlantic made the crossing of it well-nigh impossible. Aristotle, on the other hand, said that the unknown world was so small that a mariner might easily sail from Spain to China. Ptolemy estimated the known world as at least half of the whole. The Roman moralist, Seneca, shared the view of Aristotle. In his play, *Medea*, Seneca said: "And the time shall come when the raging ocean itself, instead of being a limit and an obstacle, shall become a means of communication. The world will thus be thrown open; the pilots of the ocean will discover new worlds, and there shall no longer be a 'remotest Thule' on the map." As the Orient became better known through the medieval travelers, its great extension eastward seemingly reduced in size the ocean supposed to roll between China and the West.

Even though many ancient writers, including Aristotle, Strabo, and Cicero, hinted at the possibilities of the existence of unknown continents beyond the Atlantic, this idea did not strike root in Europe. Africa, Asia, and Europe seemed to be the only habitable parts of the world; the rest was water. If the earth was relatively small, and the unknown world but a fraction of the whole, then there could not be room for other great continents beyond the western sea.[16]

The ideas of Aristotle, Seneca, and Ptolemy appear in the works of two of the foremost European students of geography. One was Roger Bacon, the great Oxford scholar of the thirteenth century. The other was Cardinal Pierre d'Ailly, a fifteenth-century popularizer of other men's ideas and author of the *Imago Mundi*, a series of short treatises devoted partly to cosmography. Both of these writers believed that the known world exceeded half of the earth's surface, and that the Atlantic was but a narrow strip of ocean connecting the

[15] On geographical studies and early discoveries, the outstanding work is C. R. Beazley's *The Dawn of Modern Geography* (3 vols., London and Oxford, 1897–1906).
[16] Medieval conceptions of geography are described in John K. Wright's *The Geographical Lore of the Time of the Crusades* (New York, 1925).

Orient and Spain. Cardinal d'Ailly's *Imago Mundi* may have had a direct influence upon Columbus. He appears to have possessed a copy of the book, which he covered with marginal notes.

Since several of the geographical ideas of the Middle Ages were conducive to exploration in the West, the question arises: Why was the discovery of America so long delayed? Many strange fears held mariners back. Some believed that, if the world was round, Europe must be on top; hence if a vessel went too far "downhill," it might not be able to get back up. At the bottom of the globe, rain would fall away from the land, trees would grow downward, and people and animals would all go tumbling off into space. Even scholars believed that intense heat beat upon the earth at the equator, making it impossible for man to cross the tropics to the southern temperate zone. And there were legends of early voyagers into the unknown who had been forced to turn back because great distances, fruitlessly traversed, had exhausted their ships' supplies.[17]

The progress of the art of navigation eventually helped to dissipate such fears. In the twelfth century, crusaders learned from Arabs the secret of the compass. An iron needle, rubbed with loadstone, was found to point invariably to the north. By 1320, the magnet had been set in a box to indicate directions marked on a card. For a long time, however, the compass was regarded as an instrument of evil spirits, and superstitious mariners would not venture upon vessels where they knew that it was used.

Two devices where employed to determine position at sea—the cross-staff and the astrolabe. Both measured the elevation of stars and indicated the degrees of latitude on metal strips. Ascertaining longitude was a more difficult matter, because the time element entered into the calculation. However, by the fifteenth century clocks had come into use, and tables of data called ephemerides were prepared. If a mariner knew the time of day, and the height of certain stars, by referring these facts to the prepared tables he could readily ascertain degrees of longitude. With the aid of compass, astrolabe, and ephemerides, it became safer for vessels to venture into unknown seas.[18]

Improvements in map making also had an important place in the progress of navigation. Before 1300, maps had been imaginary and crude. They were based on myths and poetical lore and did not even

[17] Joseph Jacobs, *The Story of Geographical Discovery* (London, 1901), is a brief, readable, popular account. For a more extended survey see John N. L. Baker's *A History of Geographical Discovery* . . . (London, 1931).

[18] For a short introductory sketch see James E. Gillespie, *A History of Geographical Discovery* (New York, c. 1933).

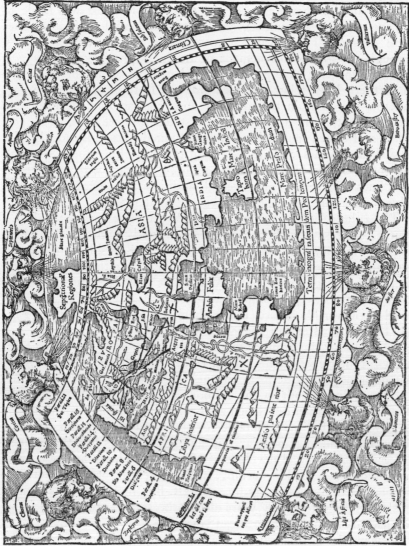

*From Abbott's "The Expansion of Europe."* © *F. S. Crofts & Co.*

This map, entitled *Typus Orbis a Ptol. Descriptus*—the world according to Ptolemy—from an edition of Ptolemy published at Basel in 1540, represents the type of map inherited from Greek geography as re-drawn in the sixteenth century. It is especially interesting on account of the insertion of lines—apparently by the hand of its sixteenth-century owner—of the trade routes.

register all the known facts of the time. Little effort was made to achieve exact measurements, and latitudinal and longitudinal lines were missing. The advance came during the fourteenth century through the gradual refinement of mariners' maps, known as *portolani*. Such maps were probably developed by seamen of the towns of northern Italy. They described only the features of the shore line, but this was done in the minutest and most accurate detail. Exact measurements were attempted on a stated distance scale. The *portolani* still lacked longitudinal and latitudinal lines; instead, they included loxodromes, or lines indicating the prevailing winds. By 1450 the coasts of the known world had been mapped with the utmost care. Such achievement preserved all additions to geographical knowledge for the convenience of explorers of a later day.

The culmination of the map maker's art came in 1492, when a Nuremberg cosmographer, Behaim, constructed the first globe. Made of papier-mâché, with a covering of plaster and outside strips of vellum, and with lettering in colors and gold, it gave the fullest expression to the geographical knowledge of its day. It pictured the unknown ocean between Europe and the Orient as a little more than a third of the earth's surface. It was about this time, also, that maps began to show lines of latitude and longitude.[19]

The way for the explorer was further prepared by improved techniques in the construction of ships. In early medieval times, when the Mediterranean was the main channel of commerce, vessels had been small and light, built in the fashion of an oar-driven galley. The Northmen had then developed a sturdier, larger, more rounded vessel, with a higher mast, suitable for the more tempestuous Atlantic. After 1400 the most popular ship among explorers was the caravel, especially favored and developed in Portugal. The caravel was swift before the wind, quick in turning, well adapted to shallow water, and distinguished by high castles fore and aft. But in spite of the advances in shipbuilding, for many years after 1500 small coasting vessels often had to be employed for ocean voyages.

Perhaps the greatest spur to enterprise along all fronts was given by the invention, about 1450, of movable metal type for the printing press. The writings of geographers and travelers could now be broadcast far and wide at a fraction of the cost of the old laborious method of copying by hand. The tidings of every discovery could be carried quickly and with accuracy into every land. The barriers which had

---

[19] Edward J. Payne's *History of the New World Called America* (2 vols., New York, 1892) devotes Book I to the age of discovery. See pp. 12–112.

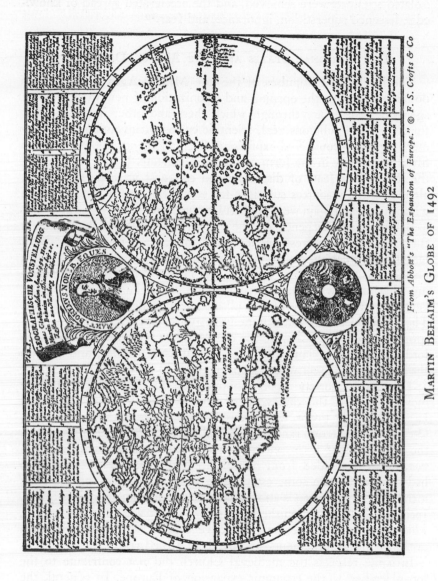

From Abbott's "The Expansion of Europe." © F. S. Crofts & Co

MARTIN BEHAIM'S GLOBE OF 1492

isolated scientists were removed, and the accelerated spread of knowledge lessened superstition, ignorance, and fear.[20]

## THE NATIONAL STATES AND THE AGE OF DISCOVERY

The intellectual impulses of the late Middle Ages in themselves do not account for the opening and colonization of new worlds. Some agency was necessary through which these and other impulses—zest for adventure, religious zeal, scientific curiosity, invention, and commercial profit—could find expression. Such an agency appeared in the fifteenth century in the form of the national state. Under its auspices, the stupendous feats of discovery and conquest were performed. It alone had the resources sufficient for supporting costly enterprises in which success and gain were doubtful in the extreme.

Before the emergence of the nation-state, Europe had been a curious blend of interests, general and local. Each community dwelt largely in isolation, ruled by local lords. But covering all like a blanket was the Universal Church. The Holy Roman Empire, including what are now Germany, Austria, the Netherlands, and Belgium, kept alive the memory of the all-embracing rule of ancient Rome. The common use of Latin united clergy, scholars, and officials. And spreading over Europe were the classes of the feudal order, from the lord who held the land and lived for pleasure, power, and war, to the impoverished serf whose labor maintained the lord's estate.[21]

This feudal society stood in opposition to the forces that were moving toward the discovery of America. Such forces emanated largely from the towns, which were bitter enemies of the feudal lords. Occupying the second rank in medieval society (the Church was first), the nobles looked with contempt upon the bourgeoisie, who were, in fact, often descended from humble itinerant peddlers or serfs who had run away from some estate. The nobles despoiled the traveling merchants of their goods and plundered the inhabitants of the towns. Incessant fighting diminished the security of trade. Surplus wealth, which might have become productive capital, was expended upon castles, armor, tournaments, and bands of armed retainers.

In some respects the medieval Church did not contribute to the forces leading to the economic expansion of Europe. In general, the

[20] A recent coöperative work, *The Pageant of America* (ed. Ralph H. Gabriel, 15 vols., New Haven, 1925–29), is compact, readable, and well-illustrated. The first volume, *Adventurers in the Wilderness* (1925), by Clark Wissler, Constance L. Skinner, and William Wood, devotes chapters 1 and 2 to medieval backgrounds.

[21] Wilbur C. Abbott's urbane and lucid *The Expansion of Europe*, reprinted in one volume (New York, 1929), stresses ideas and politics. See Vol. I, chapters 1–2, 4.

## BOOKMAKING

From the woodcuts of Jost Amman, 1562, illustrating type founding, paper-making, printing, and binding.

writers of the Church approved of feudalism and looked askance upon commerce and finance. Peasants and artisans were the main producers of wealth; trade was a sort of necessary evil. Merchants should be allowed to make only such profit as would reward them for their work. Fair prices ought to govern sales—not the rule of buying low and selling high. Profiteering and monopoly were the offspring of avarice, a deadly sin. Man accumulated riches only at the expense of his fellow man. Money itself was not productive; a lender should not charge interest or "usury" as it was called, especially to the poor. All these ideas were contrary to the spirit of merchant capitalism which animated the growth of medieval trade. The economic activity which was to open and exploit new worlds was based upon credit, interest-taking, monopoly, and a desire for larger gain.[22]

The national states of Europe rose in conjunction with the growth of towns and trade, and at the expense of feudalism and the sway of the Universal Church. Between 1200 and 1600 the modern states of Portugal, Spain, France, England, and Holland were taking form. They developed through the consolidation of a compact territory under a central government. The distinguishing feature of the nation-state was the spirit of patriotism which united people of similar traditions, language, memories, and race.

The enlargement of the royal authority was another tendency at work within the national states. In struggles for supremacy with their feudal lords, the medieval kings were prone to seek alliances with the towns. The burgesses were granted charters of freedom which allowed them to own and dispose of property, to have their own courts and local government, to build walls for their defense, and to be exempt from dues to near-by nobles. In return the townsmen paid the king a regular revenue, granted him extraordinary taxes for emergencies, and put the town militia at his command against the feudal lords.

Secure under such shelter, the towns forged ahead in industry and trade. Freedom, association, and competition all served as spurs to productive work. Permitted to retain most of the property they obtained, the townsmen were impelled to industry and improved techniques. The more ambitious serfs ran away from the manors and became free artisans in towns. Thus the progressive forces of economic life tended to center there. Even after industry in towns had been

[22] The intellectual and political background of the age of discovery is sketched in chapters 1–9 and 11 of Edward M. Hulme's *The Renaissance and the Protestant Revolution* . . . (New York, 1920).

improved by a multitude of inventions, the methods of farming used were still those of ancient times.[23]

Receiving a steady revenue from taxes on commerce and the towns, the kings became less needful of the military aids once given by the nobles. Royal armies of hired troops took form. These could be used, if need arose, against the nobles themselves. The introduction of gunpowder finally unhorsed the feudal knights, while movable cannon battered down their once impregnable walls and castles. With town allies, with enlarged revenues, and with hired troops, the king was able to break the military power of the nobles, and so to unify the state.

An illustration of the alliance of king and merchant appears in the impetus given after 1200 to the study of the Roman law. In the early Middle Ages the canon law had been the principal legal code common to Europe. However, because the Church mistrusted trade, this body of law did not give adequate security to the merchant class. The merchants accordingly promoted the extension of the Roman law, with its well-developed commercial code. This movement received the benediction of the kings, for the Romans had defined the ruler as the source of law. One of the principal cornerstones of the developed nation-state was thus a body of national law formulated by the king and his advisers, which applied to all communities alike.

Equally potent as a nationalizing force was the evolution of vernacular literature and speech. The English language, a mixture of Latin, French, Anglo-Saxon, and Celtic, had achieved mature expression by the time of Chaucer (1340?–1400). Dante (1265–1321) wrote his greatest work in the Italian vernacular. In Spain the language of the people was derived from Castile. This had assumed literary form by 1250, largely through the influence of a poem, *Poema del Cid*. Two principal dialects prevailed in early France, the *langue d'oïl* and the *langue d'oc*, the former becoming the language of the nation as a whole. The emergence of vernacular literature and speech made Europeans conscious of separate identities. Often the awareness of people concerning the differences between themselves and foreigners is a more cohesive force than dimly realized similarities in one another.[24]

Geography also played some part in national unification. The

[23] Henri Pirenne's *Economic and Social History of Medieval Europe* (London, 1936) and *Medieval Cities* (Princeton, 1925) are works of one of the greatest of modern scholars.

[24] Carlton J. H. Hayes, *A Political and Cultural History of Modern Europe* (revised ed., 2 vols., New York, 1936), is an exceptionally good text. See Vol. I, chapter 1 on political backgrounds; chapter 3 on early culture.

English were set apart from the Continent, the Spaniards were isolated by the Pyrenees, and the French were somewhat isolated by the Atlantic, the Pyrenees, and the Alps. In addition, patriotic sentiments were engendered and inflamed by wars to rid native lands of alien foes. The efforts to expel the Moors from Europe aroused and united both Portugal and Spain; French patriotism received its baptism in the long crusade to expel the English invader; and later the Dutch Republic was born in the throes of war with Spain.

All the rising nation-states bordered the ocean highway that disappeared in the unknown west. Remote from the source of oriental goods, they were obliged to buy such products from the Italian cities —and on terms unfavorable to themselves. The prices they paid were high; what they received for their own products seemed too small. They realized that they were paying heavy charges to many middlemen. East of the Mediterranean, where the Arabs had a monopoly of the oriental trade, numerous taxes were levied by rulers on the shipments passing through their lands. Between India and Alexandria, goods moving westward had to pay, at five different ports, a set of duties which quadrupled prices. All the while, the Italian cities prospered through the profits of their merchants and the earnings of their ships which served the West.[25]

The general result of all this was that the western states were confronted with an adverse balance of trade. Their coined money was drained away to Italy and the East. The accumulation of treasure in the Italian towns gave rise to the first medieval banking houses, such as the Bardi, Alberti, and Frescobaldi—firms which received deposits, issued notes, dealt in bills of exchange, and extended credit throughout Europe, thereby adding interest to their earnings in the West. Loans to kings were given in exchange for concessions within the state, or secured by royal taxes due to be collected. Thus, in England, Florentine bankers supplied the money for equipping the early expeditions of the Hundred Years' War.

As the wealth of Europe increased and the products of the East became more widely used, the commercial groups in the nation-states desired to secure a better place in the oriental trade. Unable to dominate the established routes of commerce, they sought to find new routes of their own. This motive guided exploration for nearly two hundred years. Three principal objects inspired the long pursuit. One was the desire of the merchants (who were also manufacturing employers) to retain at home an adequate supply of coin—the very life-

[25] Ferdinand Schevill's *A History of Europe* (New York, 1925) is an excellent summary. See pp. 8–90.

EUROPE
IN 1500

Scale of Miles

0    100   200   300   400

— Boundary of the Holy Roman Empire

SHETLAND IS.

Bergen

Christiania

ORKNEY IS.

HEBRIDES

NORWAY

SCOTLAND

Edinburgh

NORTH

SEA

DENMARK

Copenha

SCHLESWIG

HOLSTEIN

Hamburg

Bremen

Elbe

BRANDENBUR

IRELAND

Dublin

ATLANTIC

WALES

ENGLAND

London

Antwerp

Calais

NETHERLANDS

Cologne

HESSE

HOLY

ROMAN

SAXONY

BOHEM

OCEAN

English Channel

Seine

Paris

Trier

BURG

PALATINATE

EMPIRE

Strassburg

Rhine

BAVARIA

Munich

AUST

Loire

FRANCE

FR. COMTE

SWISS
CONFEDERA-
TION

TYROL

STYR

Bordeaux

Garonne

Grisons

Milan

Turin

SAVOY

MILAN

Venice

VENI

50

50

40

40

60

20

10

0

10

10

Avignon

Rhone

GENOA

FERRARA

ROMAGNA

Oporto

CA

Valladolid

NAVARRE

FLORENCE

ADRI

Lisbon

PORTUGAL

Douro

Ebro

ARAGON

TUSCANY

PAPAL
STATES

CORSICA

Rome

Tagus

Madrid

SPAIN

Barcelona

S

T

I

L

L

E

Guadiana

Valencia

SARDINIA

Naples

N

Guadalquivir

BALEARIC IS.

Granada

GRANADA

MEDITERRAN

Tangier

Cagliari

Palermo

Messina

SICILY

FEZ

ALGERIA

TUNIS

MALTA

MANHATTAN DRAFTING CO.,N.Y.

0

10

blood of industry and trade, far more important in the town economy of that day than in these times of checking accounts and paper money. If a nation could find a new route to the Orient, it would no longer have to pay out profits, freights, and interest to Italian and Arab merchants. Such earnings would go to native merchants, whose stock of capital would remain at home.[26]

Secondly, if a nation-state discovered a shorter and more economical route to the Orient, its merchants would reap the benefits long enjoyed by the Italian cities. The westerners would supply all neighboring lands with oriental wares. Foreigners would thus pay every year a stream of profits, freights, and interest to the fortunate possessor of the better route. The wealth that had made the Italian cities great would fertilize the West. And when a state became the emporium of the oriental trade, its king could play the old game of the eastern princes—that of taxing goods which passed through his domain to other lands.

Outside the five nation-states of France, Spain, Portugal, England, and Holland, social conditions were unfavorable to participation in the enterprise of discovery. The Scandinavian kingdoms were too far removed from the Mediterranean to feel the full impact of the Renaissance. Germany was divided into a multitude of small states, each of which lacked the resources needed for financing visionary schemes. The commercial cities of Germany had not developed under the protection of a powerful king; instead they had been able, through coöperation among themselves, to achieve a virtual independence, and so to delay the final union of the German people. Very much the same thing happened in Italy. Besides, the Italian city-states were exhausted during the fifteenth century by wars against the Turks. And, as beneficiaries of the older routes of trade, the Italians did not feel the urge to find another passage to the Orient which animated the nations in the West.[27]

The discovery of America was a result of the progressive forces at work in medieval times. The rise of commerce stimulated travel and the hope of private gain. Under its invigorating influence, wealth increased, the resources for new enterprise accumulated, and the desire for easier access to oriental products grew apace. The progress of learning tended to dispel the ignorant fear of unknown scenes, and new inventions afforded technical aids for great achievements on the

[26] *The Cambridge Medieval History* (ed. H. M. Gwatkin and J. P. Whitney, 8 vols., Cambridge, 1911–36) contains excellent essays on medieval economy by H. Pirenne and J. H. Clapham (Vol. VI, chapters 14, 15).

[27] Carl Stephenson's *Mediaeval History* (New York, 1935) is comprehensive, well-written, and compact. See chapters 9, 15, 26–28.

ocean. Through the consolidation of the nation-states, local anarchy gave place to internal order, and an effective agency arose to provide support for daring undertakings overseas. One force of earlier days, crusading zeal, survived the transition from medieval to modern times and continued to inspire devout men to conquer distant lands.[28]

[28] Of exceptional value to the general student is E. P. Cheyney's interesting *European Background of American History* (New York, 1904). See chapters 1-3, 6. This book is the first volume of *The American Nation: A History* (ed. A. B. Hart, 27 vols., New York, 1904-08)—a coöperative work that stresses the political aspects of American history.

## BIBLIOGRAPHICAL NOTE

The books cited in the footnotes are guides to reading rather than authorities for statements in the text. The books mentioned are those of fundamental importance or those which are recommended as both reliable and readable.

At the end of the succeeding chapters appear bibliographical notes which serve three purposes: (1) Works previously cited in the footnotes are again listed, with page or chapter references indicating the parts of the work applicable to the chapter in this book. (2) A few collections of sources are given—not as a guide to research in colonial history but merely in order to call attention to accessible sources which will interest the general reader. (3) In some cases separate lists are given of authoritative but specialized books which were written for advanced students.

TEXTS: Acknowledgment is made to the authors of three texts which I have "taught" at one time or another. They are: Marcus W. Jernegan, *The American Colonies* (New York, 1929); Evarts B. Greene, *The Foundations of American Nationality* (New York, c. 1922); and Oliver P. Chitwood, *A History of Colonial America* (New York, 1931).

BIBLIOGRAPHIES: F. Merk, S. E. Morison, A. M. Schlesinger, and P. H. Buck, *The Harvard Guide to American History* (to appear in 1938), will replace the Channing, Hart, and Turner *Guide* of 1912, retaining the same organization.

*The Cambridge History of the British Empire* (ed. J. H. Rose, A. P. Newton, and E. A. Benians, New York, 1929) contains in Volume I (*The Old Empire*) the best bibliography on the imperial aspects of colonial history.

For materials available in 1885 there is no better guide than Winsor's *Narrative and Critical History of America*. The volumes of A. B. Hart (ed.), *The American Nation*, appraise important works published to about 1905. Books on social and economic themes published to 1927 are evaluated in the volumes of *A History of American Life* (ed. A. M. Schlesinger and D. R. Fox, 12 vols., New York, 1927–).

MAPS: *Harper's Atlas of American History*, ably edited by Dixon Ryan Fox (New York, 1920), reprints the maps in the *American Nation* series. For this chapter see pp. 1–2. More comprehensive is the *Atlas of the Historical Geography of the United States* by Charles O. Paullin (ed. J. K. Wright, Washington, 1932). Very important. See plates 1A, 8. William R. Shepherd's *Historical Atlas* (7th ed., New York, 1928) shows particularly well the connections between America and Europe. See 82, 87, 92, 104B–D, 184 for this chapter.

SOURCES FOR CHAPTER I: The first two volumes of A. B. Hart (ed.), *American History Told by Contemporaries* (5 vols., New York, 1897–1926) relate to the colonial period. See Vol. I, pp. 28–34 (Norse). J. Franklin Jameson served as general editor of an important series of source materials, *Original Narratives of Early American History* (19 vols., New York, 1906–17). The first volume, *The Northmen, Columbus and Cabot* (ed. Julius E. Olson and Edward G. Bourne, New York, 1906), contains documents relative to the Norse (pp. 3–74). Arnold W. Lawrence and Jean Young have presented in attractive form the *Narratives of the Discovery of America* (New York, 1931). On the Norse see pp. 3–57. A well-printed collection which celebrates New England and political liberty is *Old South Leaflets* (9 vols., Boston, 1896–1922). There are 222 numbers in all. See nos. 30–32. The standard edition of *The Book of Ser Marco Polo the Venetian* is that of Sir Henry Yule (revised by Henri Cordier, 2 vols., London, 1903). The Everyman's Library edition by John Masefield of *The Travels of Marco Polo* is the most accessible (London, 1908). C. R. Beazley has edited the *Texts and Versions of John de Plano Carpini and William de Rubruquis* for the Hakluyt Society (London, 1903).

# II

# EUROPEAN PIONEERS

## Portuguese Discoveries

First among the nation-states to embark upon a career of discovery was the little kingdom of Portugal. Founded in 1095, its territorial growth completed by 1263, this state in 1383 entered an era of national greatness at the beginning of the reign of John I, a patriot king. The Portuguese were unified and aroused to aggressive action by wars against their Moorish foes. Imbued with a fierce spirit of independence, they maintained their borders against onslaughts of the ambitious rulers of Castile, but the barrier of that powerful neighbor stopped expansion toward the east. The whole length of their land fronted the sea; the rugged coast furnished many splendid harbors and the earliest national center was a port. Hemmed in on land, the Portuguese turned outward upon the Atlantic.[1]

Their genius for seamanship was fostered by the maritime policies of the state. Foreign traders were encouraged to visit Lisbon; treaties of alliance were formed with England in 1294 and 1386; and Genoese seamen were employed to man the Portuguese navy. During the fourteenth century, Portuguese vessels visited the Canary Islands and probably reached the Madeiras and the Azores. Maritime crusades against Moorish pirates stimulated the building of ships. Moreover, the Kings of Portugal coöperated with the native merchant class. Shipbuilders received timber gratis from the royal forests; shipowners were granted a partial exemption from military service; and a coöperative scheme of marine insurance was devised. Lisbon became a bustling town, its harbor fringed with foreign ships and its streets thronged with foreign mariners and traders.

The foremost patron of seafaring in Portugal, Prince Henry the Navigator, became a national figure in 1415. Son of King John I, grandson of Edward III of England, a devout champion of the Church, an ardent student of science, and a practical business man of

---

[1] *The Portuguese Pioneers* (London, 1933), by Edgar Prestage, is an attractive account by a leading authority.

large affairs, Prince Henry devoted his life to one great cause—the
exploration of the western coasts of Africa. The guiding impulse of
his early work was his ardor for the war against the Moors. From
Morocco, Tunis, and Algeria, the Mohammedans had been wont to
launch attacks upon their Christian foes. In Portugal, crusades against
the infidel were the noblest causes in which a Christian could engage.
Prince Henry in 1415 participated in the successful siege of a Moorish
stronghold, Ceuta, and later served as governor of the garrison established there. As a result, he heard reports of the interior of Africa—
of the river Senegal, supposed to traverse the land of Guinea, whose
people were as yet uncontaminated by the Moors. Other rumors
hinted of a Christian country far up the valley of the Nile, the fabled
kingdom of Prester John, who waged a gallant fight against encircling Arabs. And there were tales of a caravan trade into the heart of
Africa by which the Moors enriched themselves with ivory, slaves,
and gold.[2]

Upon these rumors Prince Henry built an imperial design. He
would explore the western shore of Africa and learn how far the
power of the Moors extended toward the south. Then he would find
the land of Guinea, Christianize its people, and unite them in the war
against the Moors. If he gained the realm of Prester John, he would
obtain a new ally; then after forming a Christian power in the heart
of Africa, he might strike the Moors from the south and drive them
from their strongholds on the northern coast. In consequence the inland trade which the Saracens had carried on with the Sudan would
be diverted by an ocean route to Lisbon.

The lure of science also animated Prince Henry's work. Eager for
knowledge for its own sake, he sought to learn by observation the
truth about the unknown world. Probably he hoped his explorations
would open a new passage to the East. In Africa Portugal might
achieve a career of imperial greatness such as she could never realize
in Europe.

Appointed governor for life of the southern province of Portugal,
Prince Henry built a small town, Villa do Infante, on the tip of Cape
St. Vincent—an ideal point for vessels sailing to the south. Here he
also erected an observatory where he immersed himself in studies of
mathematics and cosmography. He used his personal fortune to equip
expeditions in a systematic course of exploration and to provide his
mariners with the best of instruction, maps, and instruments of navigation. His work was blessed at Rome, when the papacy twice called

[2] C. R. Beazley's *Prince Henry the Navigator* (New York, 1895), a history of Portuguese maritime enterprise, is especially recommended.

upon Christian Europe to join him in a new crusade against the Moors.[3]

Between 1420 and 1431 Prince Henry's mariners rediscovered the Madeira Islands and the Azores. Then, in 1434, the Portuguese sailed beyond Cape Bojador—a feat which carried them for the first time into unknown waters. The following year they made their first landing upon the African coast. Already they had passed the land of the Moors. In 1441, after capturing several natives, they inaugurated the European trade in Negro slaves. A burst of enthusiasm now greeted Prince Henry's schemes, previously considered as devoid of private gain. So lucrative did slave-hunting become that later navigators sent out to discover Guinea preferred to stop and capture natives who might be ransomed by their tribes with ivory and gold or sold elsewhere as slaves. Although Prince Henry condoned slavery as a means of Christianizing the Negroes, he remained interested primarily in discovery. The last achievements of his lifetime were the sighting of Cape Verde in 1446 and the discovery of the Cape Verde Islands in 1455.

After Prince Henry's death in 1460, his work was carried forward by his nephew, King Alfonso V. An expedition in 1471 crossed the equator, and another in 1484 reached the Congo River. Then, in 1486, Bartholomew Diaz rounded the Cape of Good Hope. Motivated by scientific rather than commercial interest, Diaz was seeking the kingdom of Prester John. After reaching the eastern shore of Africa, he was forced to turn back by the fears and weariness of his crew. Only on the return voyage did he realize what he had accomplished; the Orient now seemed within the reach of Portugal. In 1497–98 occurred the memorable voyage of Vasco da Gama to Calicut in India. His return to Lisbon in 1499 with valuable spices and precious stones (which more than paid the expenses of the expedition) announced that Portugal had gained admittance to the oriental trade by a cheap and expeditious route.[4]

The Portuguese now prepared for commercial war with the Arabs who dominated the routes of trade in the Indian Ocean and the Red Sea, and the second Portuguese fleet, under Cabral in 1500, seized and burned several Moorish ships. During the next decade two great admirals, Almeida and Albuquerque, captured the Moorish stations

[3] See two excellent articles on Prince Henry by C. R. Beazley in the *American Historical Review*, XVI (Oct. 1910) and XVII (Jan. 1912).

[4] E. G. Bourne's *Essays in Historical Criticism* (New York, 1901) contains an admirable discussion of Prince Henry.

on the eastern coast of Africa and secured a trading center at Goa on the western coast of India. Then the Portuguese, having gained control of distant Malacca, established themselves, too, in Ormuz at the entrance to the Persian Gulf, thus enabling them to levy duties on the products moving westward over one of the older routes.

These victories ushered in the commercial revolution of the six-teenth century, which transferred the seat of commercial power from the Mediterranean to the West. As Portugal diverted the oriental trade to Lisbon, the Italian cities declined. Eager for a monopoly of this commerce, the Portuguese admitted only their own vessels and merchants to the eastern ports which they controlled. However, by reason of limited commercial resources, the Portuguese could not distribute the oriental wares throughout Europe, and consequently other European traders were permitted to come to Lisbon and purchase goods for exportation. In the north, Antwerp rose to take the place of the free towns of Germany as chief distributor of eastern wares in Western Europe.

In the meantime, Portugal had erected a colonial empire in the eastern Atlantic. During the fifteenth century, the papacy conferred upon Prince Henry the title to all lands lying south of Cape Bojador, and excluded all Christians from settling there unless with his consent. From the Portuguese government he received permission to colonize the Azores, the exclusive privilege of navigating the waters of the western coast of Africa, and the right to receive in full the profits of his ventures. Colonies were founded under his auspices in the Azores, the Madeiras, and the Cape Verde Islands. These supplied Portugal with wine, sugar, cattle, sheep, and lumber. In founding settlements the Portuguese government granted land to leaders who were required to develop its resources, to promote exploration, and to share their profits with the king. To protect themselves, the Portuguese endeavored to suppress the news of their discoveries, and in 1480 King Alfonso V ordered that mariners found on foreign ships in Portugal's new sphere of influence should be thrown into the sea.[5]

Although the most spectacular achievements of Portugal came after the death of Prince Henry, he nevertheless deserves the credit for their success. He presents one illustration of individual influence in history—of a leader who devoted his talent and fortune to one undertaking that proved immensely significant in later times. He in-

[5] Albert G. Keller's *Colonization* (Boston, c. 1908) in chapters 3–8 presents a good summary of Portuguese and Spanish enterprise.

spired his nation with a patriotic enthusiasm for discovery. Likewise, he altered the method of exploration, substituting systematic experimentation in place of the earlier reliance upon the views of ancient writers. Every technical improvement in the art of navigation received his encouraging support. It is probable that his success inspired Columbus with his vision of a western voyage. During the lifetime of Prince Henry the hardest part of the circumnavigation of Africa was achieved. When he died, the Dark Continent had been revealed as a populous, fertile land, rich in opportunities for Christian missions and economic gain.

The activities of Portugal throw light upon the motives which dominated the age of discovery. Formerly it was supposed that the conquests of the Ottoman Turks, their plundering of Mediterranean towns, and their capture of Constantinople in 1453 dammed the older routes of trade, deprived Europe of her usual supply of oriental goods, and so impelled the western states to seek a new approach to the East. This view, however, no longer holds. One of the most important routes—the southern, with its terminus at Alexandria—did not fall under the control of the Turks until their conquest of Egypt in 1517—nineteen years after Vasco da Gama arrived in India. Moreover, Portuguese pioneering began in 1417, long before the Turks were supposed to have choked the older channels of trade. Originally the Portuguese were motivated by religious and scientific interests; the search for a new route was in all probability an afterthought. During the fifteenth century, the prices of oriental spices in Europe actually declined. Had the Turks seriously interfered with the eastern trade, such prices must have risen very sharply in response to added charges or reduced supplies.[6]

It must be concluded that the national states finally undertook the search for a new route, not because the older channels were closed, but because they desired to avoid paying the heavy charges to foreign middlemen. Each state sought independent access to the East. After Portugal opened her route, Spain, France, England, and Holland endeavored for many years to acquire separate routes of their own. It was not a matter of single route—or of the general supply of oriental commodities in the West. Each nation-state desired to have its own approach to the East in order that its payments to foreign middlemen might cease and that its own merchants might reap the profits earned by distributors of oriental wares.

[6] A very significant article is A. H. Lybyer's "Influence of the Rise of the Ottoman Turks upon the Routes of Oriental Trade," *Report*, American Historical Association, 1914, Vol. I.

## THE UNIFICATION OF SPAIN

Many of the impulses which urged Portugal to colonizing activity were likewise powerful in Spain. The way for Spanish enterprise was prepared by the consolidation of many separate kingdoms into a unified state. Prior to 1450, national unity in Spain had not been won. Five distinct kingdoms existed on the Iberian peninsula—Aragon, including Barcelona and Valencia; Castile, which had annexed Leon; the Moorish kingdom of Granada; the independent state of Portugal; the northern kingdom of Navarre. Racially, there were the Spanish descendants of the original inhabitants and of early German invaders, along with a large element of Moors, whose forefathers had overrun the peninsula early in the eighth century. Jews, who had always been encouraged by the Moors, formed another important group. The Spanish Christians were bitterly hostile to both the Jewish faith and the Mohammedanism of the Moors. "Judaizing Christians" were Jews who outwardly conformed to Christian beliefs but in secret continued to practice Jewish rites.

The early monarchies of Aragon and Castile were weakened by the military power of the feudal knights, whose services were so essential in the contest with the Moors. A law unto themselves, the nobles readily defied the king's authority and seized estates from his domain. Centuries of warfare and crusading had given rise to three powerful military orders in Castile—the Knights of Santiago, of Calatrava, and of Alcantara. Possessed of towns and extensive lands, many gained by bequests of the pious, the masters of these orders commanded so many tenants, soldiers, revenues, and honors as to make them rivals of the king.[7]

The royal houses of Aragon and Castile finally welded the Spanish territories into a unified state. In 1469 occurred the marriage of Ferdinand of Aragon and Isabella of Castile. The latter became queen of Castile in 1474; the former, king of Aragon in 1479. Although each kingdom remained legally independent, the two sovereigns effected a common rule. The final territorial consolidation of Spain was accomplished through the conquest of Granada in 1492 and the annexation of southern Navarre in 1512. After the death of Isabella, Ferdinand ruled as regent of Castile. Then, in 1516, the united possessions of the two sovereigns passed into the hands of their grandson, King Charles I of Spain.

Little by little the power of the feudal lords gave way before the

[7] Edward D. Salmon's *Imperial Spain* (New York, c. 1931) is especially valuable for the general reader.

encroachments of the state. After 1480 the two sovereigns destroyed the fortifications of the castles of the nobles and compelled them to disband their knights. Duels and private warfare were proscribed. A middle-class league was used to stamp out lawlessness and crime. This society, the *hermandad*, through coöperation among its widely scattered members, captured criminals and punished with a heavy hand. Ferdinand and Isabella placed their ministers in the offices of

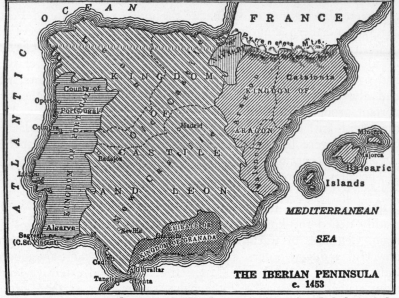

THE IBERIAN PENINSULA
c. 1453

*From Abbott's "The Expansion of Europe."* © *F. S. Crofts & Co.*

this league and used it to subdue the nobles. Royal agents investigated claims to land and confiscated estates once wrested from the Crown. After the nobles were shorn of military power, they were encouraged, by means of titles, honors, and exemption from taxation, to ally themselves with the Spanish court.

Meanwhile the three great military orders were subordinated to the state. Taking for himself the offices of Grand Master in these societies, King Ferdinand practically appropriated their offices and funds. He also sent agents to the towns to assert the royal supremacy over local rights. Gradually a centralized government took form. Its mainspring was a royal council composed principally of lawyers whose training in the Roman law inclined them to assert the absolute power of the state. Out of this body developed several other powerful councils which held the reins of power for the king.

Absolutism assumed its harshest features in religious persecution.

In 1480, the Spanish Inquisition was devised, with papal sanction, to stamp out heresy. The Jews were expelled in 1492—an act that drove from Spain a hundred thousand of their race and persuaded fifty thousand others to embrace the Catholic Church. Then followed a similar expulsion of the Moors. As an agency of the state, the Inquisition labored ceaselessly to uproot heresy and to force all people to accept the king's religion as the national faith.

All these measures made the royal will supreme. The wars against the Moors had unified the Spanish people and subordinated them to the military leadership of the crowns of Aragon and Castile. Final success enhanced the prestige of the two sovereigns and gave them command of the armies and the treasure of their states. Spain soon became the most progressive military power in Europe—the first to organize its army on modern lines. The suppression of the feudal nobles rallied the middle classes to the royal cause. The sovereign power reduced the Spanish parliament, or Cortes, to the impotence of an advisory body which merely ratified the king's commands. By 1500, Spain was ready for expansion overseas. The powerful monarchy could assert its authority over Spanish conquerors and thus extend its arbitrary rule to foreign lands.[8]

## Columbus

Some time between 1446 and 1451 there was born in Genoa, of humble parents, a boy who was destined, some forty-odd years later, to lead Spain upon the path of colonial empire. Having taken to the sea at an early age, the youthful Christopher Columbus was educated in the school of hardship. What he learned of Latin, navigation, and geography was self-taught. About the year 1473, he appeared in Portugal, whence he made a voyage down the African coast to Guinea. Later, in 1477, he visited Iceland. But it has not been proved that while there he ever heard of Leif Ericsson's discovery of Vinland; the sagas which recited the Norse discoveries in the Western World, it happened, were not then current.[9]

By 1484, Columbus had conceived his idea of a western voyage. There are two interpretations of his original aim. One is that he had derived from his study of Aristotle, Ptolemy, and Cardinal d'Ailly

[8] Edward Channing in his *History of the United States* (6 vols., New York, 1905–25) exhibits a mastery of narration, description, and characterization, although his work does not emphasize social forces. See Vol. I, pp. 14–114, on Spain and France.

[9] Clements R. Markham's *Life of Columbus* (London, 1892) presents the most widely held view of Columbus's career. A more formal but equally scholarly biography is Justin Winsor's *Christopher Columbus* (Boston, 1891).

the theory that the western ocean was so small that one might readily sail from Spain to China. Accordingly, he wrote to a Florentine astronomer, Toscanelli, for additional information. Toscanelli sent him a copy of a letter and a map. These described in glowing terms the wealth of the Indies, and indicated that the distance thither across the Atlantic was only about four thousand miles. Fed with these ideas and fired by hope, Columbus sought deliberately to reach the Orient by a western route.

The other view is less flattering to Columbus. While he was sojourning in Portugal, he is supposed to have sheltered a Portuguese mariner who had accidentally discovered a strange land in the Atlantic. This narrative harmonized with contemporary legends of islands in the western sea. To one of these (Antilia), the last Gothic king of Spain had fled before the avalanche of the Moors. Another land, Brazil, was supposed to lie to the west of the British Isles. A third, St. Brandan's, had presumably been peopled in the sixth century by three thousand monks. Columbus must have been familiar with these legends. Was he seeking some such fabled land? If so, the length of his voyage convinced him that he had gone far beyond his intended destination and had accidentally reached the Indies. Either he or his friends then wished to show that he had made his discovery, not by accident, but through design. Thus it is inferred that someone forged the Toscanelli letter to prove that Columbus had acted with a scientific aim.[10]

Whatever his original object, it seems certain that in 1483 or 1484 Columbus asked the King of Portugal to provide the vessels for a voyage, but to no avail. The king was irritated by the boastful manner of Columbus and by his inordinate demands. Moreover, the Portuguese were occupied with their explorations of the African coast. Thereupon Columbus turned to Isabella of Castile. He enlisted the aid of a leader of the Spanish nobles, the Count of Medina-Celi, who later said that he had brought the novel plan before the queen. It was then referred to a committee whose presiding officer believed that the views of Columbus were contrary to the teachings of the Bible. For several years Columbus made fruitless pleas for aid. Even though the queen was favorably disposed, the energies of her court were devoted to a war against the Moors. In a final effort Columbus persuaded a former confessor of the queen to make a fresh appeal. This

[10] Examples of brilliant scholarship are Henri Vignaud's *The Columbian Tradition* (Oxford, 1920) and *Toscanelli and Columbus* (London, 1902)—very important. See also G. E. Nunn's "The *Imago Mundi* and Columbus," *American Historical Review*, XL (Oct. 1934) and his *The Geographical Conceptions of Columbus* (New York, 1924)—important.

coincided with the conquest of Granada early in 1492, and at last the queen was free to act. Accordingly, a commission was issued to Columbus at Santa Fé in April 1492.

Columbus was to be recognized as admiral and governor of the islands and mainlands which he might discover. He was privileged to contribute one-eighth of the money for the voyage and to receive a like share of the profits. Otherwise, after expenses were deducted, a tenth of the proceeds should go to him, and the remainder to the queen. Isabella advanced more than a fourth of the funds, Columbus or his friends contributed an eighth, and the rest was probably lent to Castile by the treasurer of Aragon. During the early summer three vessels were fitted out—the *Santa Maria*, of about one hundred and twenty tons burden, the *Pinta* of fifty tons, and the *Nina* of forty tons. The crew of ninety common sailors was a cosmopolitan lot.[11]

Sailing from Palos on August 3, Columbus proceeded first to the Canary Islands and then took the path of the trade winds to one of the Bahama Islands, which was sighted in the early morning of October 12. But for the fears and opposition of his men, which Columbus tried to quiet with false reports of the distance traveled, the voyage was easily performed. After the initial landing, probably at Watling Island, Columbus pushed on to Cuba, and then discovered Haiti. The former, he thought at first, was Asia; the latter, Japan. At Cuba he sent envoys in search of the court of the great khan of China. Meanwhile, he hunted for some valuable products which might provide a profit for the voyage, or at least give cause for another expedition. Taking along several natives—whom he had named Indians—he returned to Europe, arriving in Portugal in March 1493.

The news of the discovery spread like wildfire. The exaggerated accounts which Columbus related of the wealth of the Indies made him a hero overnight. "From all the neighboring places the people gathered along the highway to see him and the Indians and the other things so novel that he brought . . ." Spanish gentlemen of means and position were eager to share the anticipated spoils of conquest. A fleet of seven vessels was now equipped at Cadiz, whence Columbus with fifteen hundred followers embarked in the autumn of 1493 upon his second voyage. Proceeding by way of the Leeward Islands and Puerto Rico, he planted at Haiti the first Spanish colony in the New World. Next he discovered Jamaica, only to return to

---

[11] Cecil Jane has edited for the Hakluyt Society a handsome collection of *Select Documents Illustrating the Four Voyages of Columbus* (London, 1930, 1933). Volume I contains a splendid essay on the objective of Columbus.

Haiti to find his settlers in revolt. He was then obliged to go back to Spain to answer charges against him which his enemies had carried to the queen.

On his third voyage, in 1498, Columbus reached the mouth of the Orinoco River on the mainland of South America. Such a mighty fresh-water stream, he was persuaded, did not issue from an island. Yet this new land was apparently too far south for Asia; it must be a separate continent, an *otro mundo*. On his last voyage in 1502 he endeavored to sail around the northwestern end of the new continent in order to reach the wealthy parts of Asia. He coasted along Central America between Honduras and Panama, always seeking

> . . . the wealth of Ormuz and of Ind,
> Or where the gorgeous East with richest hand
> Showers on her kings barbaric pearl and gold.

Until his death in 1506 Columbus remained convinced that he had visited the outlying lands of Asia.[12]

The mistakes of Columbus and the defects of his character should not obscure the greatness of his achievement. Vain, boastful, arrogant, and deceitful he certainly was, and in his last years highly visionary; yet his tenacity, courage, hardihood, and independence indicate a man of heroic stature. Although many men had thought that a western voyage was possible, he was the first to venture into perilous seas on the strength of that belief. His success affected profoundly every important phase of later European history.

## PORTUGAL AND SPAIN

When Columbus arrived in Portugal in 1493 and described his first discovery, the Portuguese insisted that he had not reached the Indies but had merely visited lands belonging to them. In 1480, Castile and Portugal had agreed to a treaty which consigned the Canary Islands to Castile, and northern Africa, Guinea, and other western islands in the southern ocean to Portugal. This treaty confirmed earlier grants from the papacy to the two states. It had been the custom in the Middle Ages for the pope to confer title to lands conquered from the infidel. Accordingly, Spain in 1493 felt it necessary to obtain papal sanction to her claims arising from the voyage of Columbus.

[12] *The Discovery of North America*, by Henry Harrisse (London, 1892), is the chief reference work in English of a great French-American scholar.

At this time Spain exerted a strong influence over Pope Alexander VI. It is probable that Spanish officials prepared three decrees which were issued in May and September 1493 by the pope. These decrees provided that a line of demarcation should be drawn through a point a hundred leagues west and south of the Azores and the Cape Verde Islands. As far to the west of this line as the Indies, Spain was to have title to, and a monopoly of the commerce with, the lands she had discovered or might discover, provided they did not already belong to a Christian prince. Portuguese subjects should not pass beyond the line without consent of Spain.

These decrees did not satisfy Portugal because the line was placed too far to the east. An appeal to Spain resulted in the Treaty of Tordesillas (June 7, 1494), which declared that the line should run north and south through a point three hundred and seventy leagues west of the Cape Verde Islands. Not until 1506 did this shift of the line receive papal confirmation. The so-called papal line was in reality a line agreed upon by Portugal and Spain. It did not divide all new territories between the two states; it merely mapped out areas in which discovery would confer title to land. Each state agreed to keep out of the other's sphere of activity.[13]

The wariness of Portugal in demanding a more western location of the line of demarcation was soon rewarded. In 1500, a Portuguese fleet under Cabral, carried out of its course around Africa to India, arrived at the coast of Brazil. The "papal" line so fell in South America as to include Brazil in the Portuguese sphere of influence, thus enabling Portugal to establish a colony there. In 1501, the Portuguese sent out an expedition which sailed hundreds of miles along the coast to South America. One member of this party was a Florentine merchant, Americus Vespucius, who later claimed that he had made four western voyages between 1497 and 1503. He wrote a letter in 1503 describing the land which he had seen and insisting that it was a new world. A German scholar, Martin Waldseemüller, included a second letter by Vespucius in a popular geography (1507), and suggested that the new land be called Amerige, or Americ's land, in honor of Americus. The name caught the fancy of Europe and stuck. Vespucius was not a navigator, and in all probability had not seen the mainland of America before Columbus. Chance, literary

<hr>

[13] Henry Harrisse, *The Diplomatic History of America* (London, 1897), should be supplemented by H. Vander Linden's "Alexander VI and the Demarcation of the . . . Domains of Spain and Portugal, 1493–1494," *American Historical Review*, XXII (Oct. 1916).

talent, and self-assertiveness brought an honor to his name which he did not deserve.[14]

In 1518 the Spaniards contended that the line of 1494 extended around the globe. How it divided the eastern hemisphere was not known. Were the valuable Spice Islands within the Portuguese or the Spanish sphere? Meanwhile, the exploration of America had demonstrated that the wealthy parts of Asia had not yet been reached by the western route. A Portuguese navigator, Ferdinand Magellan, convinced Charles I that a strait could be found through America that would lead to Asia, thus giving Spain a direct route to the oriental lands which might lie within the Spanish zone. Having secured a royal patent, Magellan sailed from Spain in September 1519 intent upon discovering a western passage to the Indies.

Proceeding by way of the coast of Brazil, Magellan finally entered the strait that now bears his name. For thirty-eight days his vessels threaded their way through this tortuous passage, often in the face of terrific winds. When at last he saw the western ocean, it seemed so calm that he named it the Pacific. Then followed the long, harassing voyage across its vast, dreary expanse. After intense suffering from hunger, when rats were sold on shipboard as food, Magellan's men and three of his vessels reached the Philippines. The resolute commander, who had withstood all manner of hardship and opposition, was killed by natives at the island of Matan. One of his vessels, however, visited Borneo and Moluccas, and returned to Spain by way of India and the Cape of Good Hope. It brought back a cargo of spices, which paid in full the cost of the expedition.[15]

The dispute between Spain and Portugal over the partition of the Indies now broke out afresh. In 1524 an attempt of the two states to locate the line of demarcation in the Orient failed. Finally, however, Charles I sold the Spanish claims to the Spice Islands to Portugal for three hundred and fifty ducats. It was agreed in 1529 to draw the line through a point seventeen degrees east of the Moluccas. This decision later confined the possessions of Spain in the Far East to the Philippine Islands, and left Portugal in undisputed control of the oriental trade.

[14] E. G. Bourne, "The Naming of America," *American Historical Review*, X (Oct. 1904).

[15] Edward F. Benson's *Ferdinand Magellan* (New York, 1930) presents its subject in an interesting manner. The best older study is F. H. H. Guillemard, *The Life of Ferdinand Magellan* (London, 1890).

## Spanish Exploration and Conquest

The first half of the sixteenth century witnessed a series of Spanish exploits unmatched in the annals of exploration. The fortune hunters who accompanied Columbus on his second voyage were outraged by the meager resources of the new Indies. His false accounts inspired hopes of gain which disillusionment speedily transformed into hatred of himself. His enemies returned to Spain and obtained from the queen special licenses for independent explorations in the region over which he had been made admiral and governor. His monopoly rights vanished into thin air. By 1502 his rivals had sailed along three thousand miles of the coast of South America. They searched for pearls, made raids to capture Indian slaves, and endeavored to find the desired strait to Asia, which was then thought to lie close beyond America. When such a strait was not found, the Spaniards turned their attention to the mainland. Lust for gold inspired imperial conquests. The natives who resisted were pursued with fire and sword, and the dread of Spanish arms spread far and wide. By 1550 the Spaniards had explored the eastern coast of America from Panama to Labrador and the western coast from Oregon to the Strait of Magellan.[16]

The conquests of the Spaniards were performed, not by the state through royal expeditions, but by small bands of adventurers whose leaders provided the necessary funds. First, however, such a leader had to secure a license from the king, without which an explorer was not permitted to sail in American seas. In order to obtain a royal license, the leader was obliged to show that he had financial backing sufficient to assure success; he then received the right to recruit soldiers and settlers and to fit out ships. He and his men (who were bound to him as if to the king) were entitled to the profits of the expedition. Royal agents went along to keep record of the treasure taken, one-fifth of which belonged to the leader and another fifth to the king. If the intended conquest promised to be especially important, it might receive financial assistance from the Crown. The leader was commonly required to take along a certain number of missionaries to convert the natives who submitted to Spanish rule.

When once a conquest had been made, the title to the land was vested in the king. The leader, however, received the right to hold a personal estate, the privilege of making land grants to his followers, and the power of putting the natives to forced labor on private lands.

[16] John Bartlet Brebner's *The Explorers of North America* (New York, 1933) is a superior introductory study. See chapters 1–9.

As an agent of the king, the conqueror might erect forts, serve as governor or captain-general of the colony, and appoint the local officers to govern it during its first year. The methods of Spanish conquest intensified individual leadership in America and established there the supreme power of the parent state.

During the early years of conquest the Spaniards used their settlements in the West Indies as bases for launching expeditions to the mainland. From Haiti in 1511 an adventurous planter, Vasco de Balboa, fled from his creditors to the Isthmus of Darien, where warfare with the natives brought him in touch with a leader who told of a region "flowing with gold where you may satisfy your ravening appetites," and reported that beyond the western mountains lay another sea. In the summer of 1513 Balboa, with a selected band of Spaniards and Indians, fought his way across the Isthmus of Panama, through forests and over cliffs, until on September 25 he reached a mountain summit, where—first among Europeans—he beheld the waters of the Pacific, "the great South Sea." His discovery was soon followed by Spanish exploration of the coasts of the new ocean.[17]

A few months before Balboa's exploit, another gold hunter, Ponce de Leon, had sailed from Puerto Rico and discovered Florida. A trader and first governor of Puerto Rico, he had heard from slave raiders of a strange land called Bimini, which in Indian legend was rich in gold and blessed with a fountain whose waters made men perpetually young. After his return from Florida to Puerto Rico in 1513, eight years elapsed before Ponce de Leon set out again to the desired land. This time he took settlers and livestock for a colony. Little is known of his attempted settlement in 1521 except that it was dispersed by hostile Indians. Severely wounded in the attack, Ponce de Leon returned to Havana to die.

An official at Santo Domingo, Lucas Vasquez de Ayllon, who was also interested in the North American coast, dispatched a vessel thither in 1521 under the command of one Francisco Gordillo. After falling in with some slave hunters, Gordilla sailed to the coast at 33° 30' north latitude. The Indian slaves whom he captured contrary to Ayllon's instructions were freed in Santo Domingo. Ayllon next secured a royal patent for colonization and exploration, and in 1526 headed an expedition which planted a settlement somewhere

---

[17] An outstanding figure in American historical writing is George Bancroft, whose *History of the United States* (6 vols., New York, 1885) was the most influential work of its time. Bancroft is noted for his democratic and patriotic bias. See Vol. I, chapters 1–2 on France and Spain.

between the Cape Fear River and the James. Engulfed by a sea of troubles and losing their leader, a victim of fever, the colonists abandoned the project in despair. Fewer than a fourth of their number finally returned to Santo Domingo.[18]

Shortly before Ayllon's failure, a Portuguese mariner, Estevan Gomez, sailing under Spanish auspices, had skirted the North American coast between Newfoundland and the fortieth parallel. Nowhere did he find evidence of gold or precious stones, while the trees, fruits, and fish which he beheld did not seem valuable. His unattractive picture of the coast, in conjunction with the failure of Ayllon's colony, led the Spaniards to concentrate upon Central and South America, thereby leaving the northern shore open to later occupation by the English, French, Dutch, and Swedes.

A turning point in Spanish enterprise occurred in 1519–22 when Hernando Cortés conquered the Aztecs of Mexico. While commanding an expedition under the governor of Cuba, Cortés violated his orders and became a conqueror in his own right. Posing as a deliverer of the oppressed Aztecs, he played one faction among them against another, and captured their emperor, Montezuma, and their capital, Mexico City. He then successfully defied the governor of Cuba and in 1522 gained recognition from the King of Spain as independent ruler of Mexico. His conquests brought to the Spaniards for the first time a large store of gold and silver and put them in command of an agricultural people who might be profitably exploited. Visions of inland wealth now dimmed the old lure of the East, and other Spanish conquerors strove to imitate Cortés—to subdue similar empires rich in silver and gold. Since the mines of America were widely distributed, the Spaniards undertook a series of extended explorations which finally carried them over the vast territory stretching between present-day Kansas and Peru.[19]

In 1520 the governor of Cuba sent an army to Mexico to arrest Cortés. Its leader was Panfilo Narvaez. Defeated and imprisoned for a time by Cortés, Narvaez conceived the design of conquering another empire on the northern shore of the Gulf of Mexico. Having returned to Spain, he obtained in 1526 a patent to Florida and the next year he set out with five vessels and six hundred followers. After two disasters in the West Indies, his expedition arrived at the coast of Florida in 1528. Lured inland by reports of an Indian city,

---

[18] Woodbury Lowery's *The Spanish Settlements* . . . (2 vols., New York, 1911) treats Spanish enterprise "within the present limits of the United States."

[19] F. A. Kirkpatrick's *The Spanish Conquistadores* (New York, 1934) is unsurpassed as a one-volume history (to 1550).

Apalache, supposed to abound with gold and pearls, he found only a miserable village. He pursued his explorations a few weeks until sickness and Indian hostilities obliged him to construct new boats and to embark for Mexico. A storm in the Gulf cast his shipwrecked followers upon the coast of Texas.

Four survivors finally reached Mexico in 1536. One of these was the treasurer of the expedition, Cabeza de Vaca, who had wandered far and wide between the Mississippi and the Gulf of California— "from the land of the cactus on the south to the ranges of the buffalo on the north." His fascinating account of his travels and the rumors he reported gave confirmation to Indian legends of populous and wealthy cities somewhere toward the north.[20]

In 1537, Cabeza de Vaca returned to Spain, where his narrative reached the ears of another adventurer, Hernando de Soto—lately returned from participation in the conquest of Peru. De Soto had brought back a share of the plunder of the Incas, and was already seeking new realms to conquer. After obtaining a royal license to colonize Florida, he set forth with a band of six hundred noblemen, officials, and servants, and arrived at Tampa Bay in 1539. Intent upon capturing Indian slaves, he brought along iron neck collars attached to chains and by cruelties inflicted upon the natives spread hatred and terror as the expedition advanced. Its route led to the Savannah River, across the piedmont of North Carolina, southward toward Mobile Bay, and thence to the Mississippi near the present site of Memphis.

The discovery of the "Father of Waters" did not delight de Soto; he regarded the river only as an obstacle in his search for wealth. After crossing the stream, he proceeded into the lands of present-day Arkansas and Oklahoma, and then floated down the Arkansas River to its mouth, where he died and was secretly buried in the Mississippi. Later, his followers constructed boats which carried them down the river, along the Texan coast, and finally to Panuco in Mexico (1543). For a half century afterward the Spaniards believed that the Mississippi had its source in a chain of mountains supposed to extend east and west between the highlands of Carolina and the Ozarks.[21]

---

[20] *The Chronicles of America* (ed. Allen Johnson, 50 vols., New Haven, 1918–21) is a series of short, entertaining volumes which combine readability and scholarship. Early Spanish enterprise is treated in this series in Herbert E. Bolton's *The Spanish Borderlands* (1921), chapters 1–4, and in Irving B. Richman's *The Spanish Conquerors* (1919).

[21] Theodore Maynard, *De Soto and the Conquistadores* (New York, 1930), is a delightfully written narrative.

At about the same time another romantic adventure was inspired in part by Cabeza de Vaca. In 1536 his narrative reached the viceroy of New Spain at Mexico City—Don Antonio de Mendoza. Indian legends then current told that north of Mexico lay great towns suggesting to the Spanish fancy the fabled land of Cibola, famed for its seven wealthy cities whose golden towers glistened in the sun. Such legends were seemingly confirmed by the tales of Cabeza de Vaca. Earlier Spanish expeditions to find the cities had failed for want of systematic preparations, but now, determined to extend the power of Spain over this mythical kingdom, Mendoza sent an advance party of Franciscan monks to chart the way. One of their number—Friar Marcos—penetrated far enough northward to see, at a distance, a promising Indian village. His description of its storied houses, built of stone, seemed to his uncritical hearers assurance that Cibola, in all the gorgeous splendor with which European tales time out of mind had invested it, was here at hand to be rediscovered.

Mendoza accordingly organized an ambitious expedition and chose as its commander the governor of the northwestern province of Mexico, Francisco de Coronado. So firm was the conviction of success and gain that Coronado had difficulty, not to enlist followers, but to persuade enough Spaniards to remain behind to protect their settlements. With three hundred and seventy soldiers, a large band of Indians, and a long train of cattle, horses, mules, and sheep, Coronado in 1540 ventured forth in search of the seven cities.

After traversing a mountainous wilderness and gaining the plains of southern Arizona, the Spaniards came upon the Indian village which Friar Marcos had descried in the distance. This they conquered, only to find an ordinary pueblo instead of a magnificent city rich in gold. Visits to other villages soon dispelled the illusion of the towered cities of Cibola, but the Indians told that farther north or east lay a land, Quivera, which was indeed a golden realm. Taking a band of twenty picked men, Coronado now pressed on to the plains of Texas where, first of Europeans, he beheld herds of buffalo, and then, turning sharply, he crossed wide, grassy wastes to central Kansas, where he again found only miserable tented villages destitute of gold. Bitterly disappointed, he returned to Mexico—an abject failure. Although he had penetrated to the heart of the northern continent, the Spaniards did not then care to conquer the disappointing lands which he had seen. But whatever their immediate value to statesmanship and commerce, the two explorations of de Soto and Coronado, reaching points but nine days' distance from each other, had made a striking contribution to the geographical knowledge of the New World.[22]

## THE SPANISH EMPIRE IN THE SIXTEENTH CENTURY

Long before England established successful colonies, the Spaniards had designed an elaborate system of colonial policy and administration. In 1600 the imperial area was twenty times larger than Spain. Theoretically, the colonies belonged to the king, who ruled them without interference from the Spanish parliament. They formed two distinct kingdoms, each of which in organization was somewhat similar to the kingdom of Spain, and united to it only through the king. In all its features the government of the colonies was monarchical in form.

The agency through which the Spanish king governed the colonies was the Council of the Indies. Formally organized in 1524, this body consisted of powerful officials appointed by and responsible to him alone. It selected colonial officials for his approval, superintended the imperial administration, shaped important policies, and also served as a supreme court to which the more serious cases arising in the colonies might be appealed. Its routine business was transacted in committees, but when it enacted laws (it was the source of colonial legislative power) at least three-fourths of its members had to attend.

Another governing body was the Casa de Contratacion—a sort of board of trade. Its officials gathered information about the commerce of the colonies, supervised all voyages to the New World, considered ways and means of promoting imperial trade, and operated at Seville a great trading house, or *casa*, used as a depot for all goods going to or coming from America. The primary object of this board was to strengthen the monopoly of colonial trade which Spain reserved to herself.

The two colonial kingdoms which existed in 1600 were known as New Spain and Peru. The former included the mainland north of the Isthmus of Panama, the West Indian islands, and the region that is now Venezuela. The kingdom of Peru comprised all territory south of New Spain except Brazil. Over each kingdom ruled a viceroy—a personal agent of the king, by whom he was appointed and removed —serving a three-year term, after which he was subject to a royal investigation or *residencia*. Such inquiries enabled the king's subjects to present complaints but did not offer any means of day-to-day con-

[22] A standard work is George P. Winship's *The Coronado Expedition, 1540-1542* (Washington, 1896).

trol of the viceroy's actions. Ordinarily the viceroy was reappointed at the end of his three-year term.

Even Spaniards in the colonies did not enjoy the privilege of self-government, for representative assemblies were never granted by the king. Only the towns (of which there were two hundred in 1575) had the right to elect councils, but such councils could act only with reference to matters such as sanitation and police regulations—not with respect to fundamental issues of taxation and economic policy. In the early days, the towns had sent delegates to general congresses, but this trend toward representative government was checked when Charles I ordered in 1530 that the townsmen should not assemble without his consent. All important officers, from viceroy to district magistrate, received their places from the king, and after 1557 offices were sold to the highest bidders. Officials were thus regarded as contractors with the king rather than as agents of the people.[23]

More important as an obstacle to self-government was the imperial policy respecting taxation. Generally speaking, popular control over taxes and appropriations is the final measure of self-government. The Spanish colonists, as has been observed, did not exercise such control; the king's revenues were collected without their consent. Every male native of working age had to pay a poll tax, excise duties were levied on goods sold within the colonies, and customs duties were collected on American exports and imports. The king regularly sold monopoly rights for the marketing of common products such as gunpowder, tobacco, and salt. Each vessel paid a convoy tax of 2 per cent of the value of its cargo, while contractors who purchased the monopoly of the slave trade paid a fee on every Negro slave imported into the colonies. The sale of offices also added to the income of the king. Finally, he received a fifth of the gold and silver from the American mines. All this revenue made it unnecessary for him to ask his subjects for money, and because they were not able to coerce him by withholding needed supplies they could not compel him to concede other political rights.

Agriculture supported the mass of the Spanish colonists. To favored leaders and the Church the king granted large feudal estates called *encomiendas*, grants which allowed the receiver to utilize the forced labor of the resident natives. Although such workers received wages, it was easy to keep them permanently in debt, and thus cause them to forfeit such liberties as they had theoretically retained, reducing

---

[23] Of major importance is Roger B. Merriman's *The Rise of the Spanish Empire in the Old World and the New* (4 vols., New York, 1918–34). See particularly Vols. II, III.

their status to one which was little better than that of serfs. The native population in 1575 numbered approximately five million souls, and about four thousand *encomiendas* existed then. American products raised in the colonies included cacao, vanilla, and Indian corn. The Spaniards introduced a great variety of European and other animals and plants: cattle, horses, sheep, mules, and hogs; wheat, barley, rye, and rice; sugar cane, alfalfa, beans, and peas; apples, quinces, pears, bananas, apricots, lemons, oranges, and cherries. On the other hand, the colonists were not allowed to raise certain products cultivated extensively in Spain, such as olives, grapes, flaxseed, and hemp. Wheat, Indian corn, and cattle supplied the common articles of food. The native workers merely eked out a bare existence, and even the overlords or *encomenderos* enjoyed only a life of rude plenty.[24]

Among the colonial industries, mining ranked second in importance. The silver mines of Mexico and Peru yielded the treasure which paid the administrative costs of the agricultural areas, and made it possible and profitable for Spain to retain her vast imperial possessions. The output of the mines increased nearly ninetyfold between 1500 and 1750. The extension of colonial mining was not entrusted to ordinary prospectors; instead, well-to-do promoters went forth with caravans of workers, mules, and supplies to locate new veins of ore. When the search was successful, buildings were erected around a courtyard into which the ore was brought for treatment. Mules were then used to tramp in quicksilver and salt which released the silver. After the quicksilver was removed by smelting, the silver was cast into bars and carried once a year by pack train to the colonial mints. The most common coins issued in the colonies were Mexican and Peruvian pieces of eight, ancestors of the American dollar.[25]

Not all the Spanish settlers in America, of whom there were 152,500 in 1574, were *encomenderos* or large-scale miners. Small farmers, attorneys, officials, traders, soldiers, and clergymen all played important parts in colonial life. Commercial manufacturing in the colonies, however, was successfully discouraged, and the use of manufactured goods—judged by European standards—was very slight.

Restrictions upon European emigration to Spanish America undoubtedly retarded its industrial progress. After 1555 only native Spaniards of Catholic faith were allowed to enter the colonies, a policy which aimed to exclude undesirable adventurers who might

[24] E. G. Bourne's comprehensive *Spain in America* (New York, 1904) is one of the best volumes of the *American Nation* series. A convenient survey is Charles E. Chapman, *Colonial Hispanic America* (New York, 1933).

[25] One of the most significant studies of recent times is Earl J. Hamilton's *American Treasure and the Price Revolution in Spain, 1501–1650* (Cambridge, 1934).

exploit the natives, to prevent the diffusion throughout Europe of knowledge of the wealth of the Spanish Indies, and to check the spread of heresy to the New World. In consequence, European culture and institutions transplanted to the colonies were exclusively Spanish, while the small number of Spanish settlers necessitated their intermarriage with the native Indians. The exclusion of non-Catholics from Spanish America accounts in part for their later migrations to the English colonies and for the latter's predominantly Protestant character.

One alien element admitted by the Spaniards was the Negro slave, first brought into the islands about 1503 and to the mainland in 1510. Slavery spread rapidly in Cuba, Haiti, and Puerto Rico, where the hard work on plantations rapidly decimated the Indians who were subjected to forced labor. Another region where slavery became prominent was the northern coast of South America. In Mexico the natives performed most of the work, while in the southern part of South America the altitude was unfavorable to the Negro.[26]

After 1510 Spain provided for the systematic importation of slaves. Not possessing slave trading stations in Africa, the Spaniards did not conduct this traffic as a government enterprise. Instead the king granted contracts which conferred monopoly rights upon private traders, such a contract being known as the assiento, and the contractors as assientists. Only a fixed number of slaves, usually between three and four thousand, could be imported legally into the colonies each year. The contractors paid a large bonus for the monopoly, which was commonly granted for a term varying from seven to ten years. Only Spanish vessels could be used for transporting the slaves, although Flemings, Genoese, Portuguese, Dutch, French, and English trading interests obtained the assiento at various times. Its effect was to limit the supply of slaves, to keep prices high, and thus to invite smuggling by interlopers. Prior to 1750 Spanish importations of Negroes averaged about three thousand a year.

Government control and monopoly extended to all branches of colonial commerce. Spanish exports to America consisted of wines, figs, olives, oil, quicksilver, iron, dry goods and other manufactures for which the colonists made payment with sugar, cacao, vanilla, cochineal, drugs, and gold and silver coin and bullion. Only Spanish vessels and merchants could engage in the trade. Even more striking was the commercial monopoly of the port of Seville. Between 1503

[26] Herbert I. Priestley, *The Coming of the White Man* (New York, 1929), an excellent study, begins the notable Schlesinger-Fox series, *A History of American Life*. See chapters 1–7.

and 1718 this city alone was allowed to sell to the colonies and to receive their products. Under the auspices of the government, two fleets were fitted out each year at Seville and provided with a naval convoy. The combined fleets sailed first to the island of Dominica, where they separated, one going to the mainland and the other to the islands. Only a few licensed ports in America—such as Porto Bello, Havana, Cartagena, and Vera Cruz—had the right to trade with the outside world. When the fleet arrived in harbor, a great fair was held for the exchange of products. The American traders would sell the native commodities which they had collected and buy European merchandise from agents of Spanish merchants who traveled with the fleet. The local traders then distributed their purchases throughout the settlements, while the two fleets proceeded to Havana and returned together to Seville under their naval escort.[27]

This scheme of commercial regulation imposed severe hardships upon the colonists. Let us consider how it affected a settler living on the banks of the Plata River in the Argentine. He was not allowed to ship his products to Buenos Aires to be conveyed directly to markets in Europe or in the eastern settlements of America, nor could he import directly from Europe. If he bought goods made in Holland, they had to be shipped first to Seville, whence they went to the Plata by way of Porto Bello, the Isthmus of Panama, and Peru. Over this roundabout route the settler also had to send his exports. In consequence, he paid exorbitant charges for European goods, while the lack of markets for his own products kept their prices at extremely low levels. Even after 1700, an ox could be bought at Buenos Aires for a dollar, a sheep for three or four cents, and a mare for ten cents. Only favored places along the established channels of trade—such as Mexico City and Lima—could afford to buy many European manufactured goods. Thus the mass of the people had to depend upon native handicrafts.

In spite of the protests of the colonial settlers, the monopoly of Seville remained intact until 1718, when Cadiz became the entrepôt of the American trade. This method of commercial control survived partly because it enabled the government to collect its import and export duties at a single place, while the fleet system justified itself also as a means of protection against European pirates who habitually plundered vessels carrying gold and silver to Spain. Moreover, the merchants of Seville formed one of the principal bulwarks of the monarchy. They exerted a lobbying influence at court somewhat com-

---

[27] Clarence H. Haring's *Trade and Navigation between Spain and the Indies* . . . (Cambridge, 1918) is the work of a leading authority on Spanish America.

parable to that of manufacturers upon tariff legislation in the United States since the Civil War.[28]

During the eighteenth century the Spanish government gradually relaxed its commercial restrictions. By 1778 the fleet system had been discontinued, and any port in the colonies was allowed to trade with any port either in Spain or in the other Spanish dominions. Before this time, however, the commercial policy of Spain had been much more rigid than that which England applied to her colonies. The Spanish system led eventually to a widespread contraband trade from which the English and the Dutch made the principal gains. Meanwhile, the colonies did not promote the industrial growth of Spain; they experienced too much difficulty in buying goods which were legally imported from Seville. In the end the stifling effects of regulation contributed a major cause of the successful revolt of the colonies during the Napoleonic wars.

Even so, the Spanish empire endured for a period nearly a hundred and fifty years longer than England's rule of her colonies in North America. In the Spanish empire religion bound the settlers closely to the king; in the English colonies it was mainly a dividing force. The King of Spain was virtually the head of the Catholic Church in the colonies, where it enjoyed an uncontested supremacy. From the papacy he had received the right to establish colonial churches and monasteries and to collect the tithes which all the people had to pay. He also possessed the exclusive right of appointment to ecclesiastical offices. The organization of the colonial Church resembled its European model. In 1600 there were four hundred monasteries directly under the king's supervision and four hundred local districts served by the secular clergy. The latter were grouped into bishoprics, which in turn formed the two archbishoprics of Mexico and Peru. The bishops, archbishops, and their cathedral chapters received half of the tithes collected; consequently, they possessed great wealth, prestige, and influence. Eventually the Church acquired about half of the property in the colonies."[29]

The king's privilege of collecting tithes carried with it the obligation to use the money in the service of the Church, a duty faithfully performed. Through the Church the government exerted a continuing influence against oppression, idolatry, and heresy. Royal funds were employed to send missionaries to the colonies, to erect monas-

[28] *The Establishment of Spanish Rule in America*, by Bernard Moses (New York, 1898), is brief, scholarly, and readable.

[29] For detailed studies see Bernard Moses, *The Spanish Dependencies in South America* (2 vols., New York, 1914)—particularly Vol. I, chapter 14; Vol. II, chapters 12–13, 20.

teries on the king's estates, and to assist also in establishing convents on private *encomiendas*. Priests and monks were not allowed to act as attorneys, to engage in business, or to work in the mines, lest such activity bring discredit upon the Church. The ecclesiastical courts could not impose fines upon the natives, condemn them to forced labor, or defraud them of their wages. Irresponsible soldiers and sailors who had committed offenses could not use the churches as sanctuaries. A law of 1619 called upon the clergy to learn the language of the natives, and another act (1634) required that the Indians should be taught Spanish—measures designed to bring instruction in the doctrines of Christianity to the people. In every town or district a time was set apart for religious worship when masters had to allow their Indian workers and Negro slaves to attend the services of the Church.

Religion thus relieved the harsher features of economic exploitation and at the same time buttressed the king's authority over the colonies. The bond of union between the colonial prelates and the Spanish court was especially intimate and strong. The clergy taught submission to the king's government, and through the Inquisition rooted out doctrines subversive to the blended authority of Church and state.[30]

## FRANCE IN THE NEW WORLD

The expansion of Portugal and Spain inspired France to follow their example. During the reign of Francis I (1515–47), the French government promoted four expeditions to America. Although the French monarchy was fairly well centralized in 1520, France had not yet become a first-rate power in Europe. Not until 1453 had she expelled the armies of England and overthrown the English claim to a large part of her territory; not until 1516 did the king obtain control over the Catholic Church in France when he received from the papacy the right to nominate bishops and abbots. In the days of Francis I, the French were surrounded by the lands of a powerful enemy—the Hapsburg emperor, Charles V, whose imperial dominions included Austria, Germany, northern Italy, the Netherlands, Spain, and the Spanish colonies. Moreover, Charles V aspired to annex the province of Burgundy which had been taken from his grandmother by an earlier French king. Encircled by the Hapsburg territories,

[30] H. C. Lea's *The Inquisition in the Spanish Dependencies* (New York, 1911) paints a dark picture.

France was in danger of being crushed and absorbed into the empire of her stronger rival.[31]

In a series of wars between 1521 and 1559 the French fought for their national existence. Other issues at stake were the mastery of Naples, Milan, the Netherlands, and Burgundy. Finally concluded by the Treaty of Cateau-Cambrésis (1559), these wars decided that France was to remain an independent state. Although she relinquished her claims to Italy, her acquisition of the three border bishoprics of Metz, Toul, and Verdun during the reign of Henry II (1547–59) began her historic advance toward the Rhine. Despite the fact that these wars absorbed the energies of the monarchy they nevertheless inspired the earliest French efforts to gain a foothold in America.

The cod fishery of Newfoundland first brought France into contact with the New World. It is probable that French fishermen were visiting Newfoundland as early as 1497, and after 1510 the markets of Normandy were supplied regularly with cod by fishing fleets from the Grand Banks. Shortly after Magellan's party returned to Spain in 1522, the chronicler of the expedition, Antonio Pigafetti, visited the French court, where he presented to the queen mother of Francis I a copy of the journal of the voyage. Soon afterward the king, who was one of the foremost patrons of the Renaissance in Europe, became interested in opening a French route to China. Doubtless he hoped to use the profits of the oriental trade to finance his wars with Charles V. Accordingly he engaged the services of a Florentine mariner, Giovanni Verrazano, a resident of Dieppe—then the base of French operations in the Newfoundland fishery.[32]

Summoned to court by Francis I, Verrazano displayed a matured interest in discovering a new route to Asia and revealed himself as a scholar and capable man of affairs. With a royal commission and four vessels provided by the king, he embarked in the early summer of 1523 and proceeded to the Madeira Islands, whence one of his vessels crossed the Atlantic and reached the coast of North America at about the thirty-fourth parallel. Later, he skirted the shore northward as far as Newfoundland and returned to France in July 1524. His success established the original claim of France to North America.

The exigencies of war did not allow Francis I to continue Ver-

---

[31] Due to its literary excellence, painstaking scholarship, and comparative freedom from personal bias, Francis Parkman's history of the French and English in America ranks as a masterpiece. On French explorations see his *Pioneers of France in the New World* (Boston, 1871), pp. 168–207.

[32] William B. Munro, *Crusaders of New France* (*Chronicles of America*, New Haven, 1918), chapters 1–2.

razano's work until after the Peace of Cambrai in 1529. Three voyages were then made to the Gulf of St. Lawrence by Jacques Cartier, a Breton pilot of the port of St. Malo. The first two voyages (in 1534 and 1535–36) were financed by Francis I, who continued to display a deep interest in exploration. The initial motive—to find a passage to the Orient—was supplemented after 1535 by the desire to obtain gold and silver, to plant a settlement on the St. Lawrence River, and to Christianize the Indians. The third expedition (in 1541–42) was promoted and commanded by a nobleman of Picardy, Jean François Roberval, to whom Francis I gave the title to the lands which Cartier discovered in 1535.

On his first voyage (1534) Cartier explored the Gulf of St. Lawrence and took possession of the region in the name of Francis I. He returned to France with two Indians whose tale of a great inland stream gave promise of the desired passage to Asia. The second voyage (1535–36) carried Cartier up the St. Lawrence River past the site of Quebec to an Indian village, Hochelaga, which lay at the foot of a mountain which the French named Mount Royal or Montreal. From its heights Cartier saw the Ottawa and St. Lawrence branches of the imperial stream. The Indians related that westward lay two or three great lakes beyond which stretched a fresh-water sea whose end was unknown, while the interior lands were thought to abound with silver and gold. After passing a difficult winter near Quebec, Cartier returned to France in July 1536.[33]

Employed as pilot for the third expedition, Cartier preceded Roberval in 1541 and planted a settlement twelve miles above Quebec, but his efforts to explore the St. Lawrence were halted by the rapids of the river and by fear of the Indians. The sufferings of another severe winter apparently bred despair; at any rate Cartier decided to return to France. He met Roberval in a Newfoundland harbor but managed to slip away, homeward bound. Roberval proceeded westward, and occupied the colony which Cartier had abandoned. He held on until the autumn of 1543, when he followed Cartier to France. Except that the colony disappeared, its fate is unknown.

These three expeditions designated the line of advance which France later followed in North America. For the time, however, the pressure of war in Europe made it impossible for the government to continue the work of Cartier, and France did not resume her activi-

[33] George M. Wrong and H. H. Langton have edited a series of short, popular volumes, *The Chronicles of Canada* (32 vols., Toronto, 1914–16). See the second volume, *The Mariner of St. Malo* (1914), by Stephen Leacock.

ties in the St. Lawrence region until after 1600. Efforts made between 1550 and 1565 by French Protestants to found colonies in Brazil and Florida also failed. Thus when the sixteenth century closed, Spain and Portugal alone among European pioneers had established colonial empires in the New World.[34]

The treasure which Spain received from her American empire enabled her to play a decisive role in European politics during the sixteenth century. As the outstanding champion of Catholicism in Europe, she drew upon her imperial wealth to oppose the progress of Protestantism, particularly in France, the Netherlands, and England. In the ensuing conflicts, the enemies of Spain quickly perceived the advantage which she derived from her colonies. In consequence, the English and the Dutch carried the war against Spain to the New World. First they endeavored to plunder Spanish settlements and ships. Such warfare gave birth to an ambition to acquire colonial sources of wealth comparable to Spain's, and to establish outposts in America which might be used as bases for attacks upon the Spanish empire. The conflict between Protestantism and Catholicism thus ushered in the second phase of European colonization in America.[35]

[34] The best recent general work on the French in North America is G. M. Wrong, *The Rise and Fall of New France* (2 vols., New York, 1928). See Vol. I, chapter 4.

[35] Philip A. Means, *The Spanish Main, Focus of Envy* (New York, 1935), is a vivid, interesting summary of research on international conflicts in Spanish America, 1492–1700.

## BIBLIOGRAPHICAL NOTE

Works Previously Cited: W. C. Abbott, *Expansion of Europe*, I, chs. 3, 5–6, 9–10; Lord Acton, *Lectures on Modern History*, ch. 2; E. P. Cheyney, *European Background of American History*, chs. 4, 5; J. Fiske, *Discovery of America*, I, chs 4–6; II, chs. 7, 12, C. J. H. Hayes, *Political and Cultural History of Modern Europe*, I, chs. 2, 5; A. P. Newton (ed.), *Travel and Travellers of the Middle Ages* (last essay, on the Portuguese), *Pageant of America*, I, chs. 3–7; E. J. Payne, *History of America*, I, 112–267 (discovery to 1525); J. Winsor (ed.), *Narrative and Critical History of America*, II (Spain); IV, chs. 1–2 (France).

Sources Newly Cited: Volume I of Frances G. Davenport (ed.), *European Treaties bearing on the History of the United States and its Dependencies* (3 vols., Washington, 1917) contains Spanish-French-Portuguese treaties, to 1600. *Narratives of the Career of Hernando De Soto* (ed. E. G. Bourne, 2 vols., New York, 1904) is a convenient collection. For de Vaca, de Soto, and Coronado see *Spanish Explorers in the United States, 1528–1543* (ed. F. W. Hodge and T. H. Lewis, New York, 1907—Jameson *Original Narratives* series). *The Journey of Coronado* (ed. G. P. Winship, New York, 1904) is a standard edition. H. P. Biggar's *The Voyages of Jacques Cartier* (Ottawa, 1924) is a scholarly edition for the special student. For Cartier documents see also James P. Baxter, *A Memoir of Jacques Cartier* (New York, 1906) and Henry S. Burrage (ed.),

*Early English and French Voyages* (New York, 1906—Jameson, *Original Narratives* series), pp. 3–110. The best recent general collection of source materials is Henry S. Commager (ed.), *Documents of American History* (New York, 1934). See Vol. I, nos. 1–3.

Sources Previously Cited: On Columbus, A. W. Lawrence and Jean Young (eds.), *Narratives of the Discovery of America*; and J. E. Olson and E. G. Bourne (eds.), *The Northmen, Columbus and Cabot*, pp. 87–418. See also A. B. Hart (ed.), *American History Told by Contemporaries*, I, pp. 35–68, 102–118; and *Old South Leaflets*, nos. 17, 33–36, 39, 71, 90.

Maps: D. R. Fox, *Harper's Atlas*, pp. 3–5; C. O. Paullin, *Atlas of the Historical Geography of the United States*, plates 1, 9–17, 38; W. R. Shepherd, *Historical Atlas*, pp. 105, 107–112.

# III

# THE REFORMATION AND THE NEW WORLD [1]

THE Protestant Reformation, inaugurated by Martin Luther in 1519, affected profoundly the colonization of America and the later history of the United States. The strife between Protestant and Catholic and internal conflicts among Protestants provided one of the mainsprings of European migration to America. Under the influence of religious beliefs the domestic institutions of the English colonies took shape, while the repeated colonial wars between England and France revolved in part around religious issues. The dominantly Protestant character of the United States, and the cultural traits which Protestantism has fostered—such as intellectual freedom, individualism, self-government, and independence—have determined largely the mold and spirit of American life.

## LUTHERANISM

The two leading movements of the Reformation were Lutheranism and Calvinism. In the history of colonial America, however, Calvinism far overshadowed Lutheranism. The early Lutherans did not migrate to the New World. At the outset the Lutheran movement appealed to a large number of German princes, who openly embraced the new faith. In 1530 they formed the League of Schmalkald to resist the efforts of the emperor of the Germanies, Charles V, to restore Catholicism. A religious war broke out in 1546 and continued intermittently until the Peace of Augsburg in 1555. This settlement established in Germany the principle that the prince might determine the religion of his subjects. It applied, however, only to Lutheran and Catholic princes. Thereafter, Lutherans living under a Lutheran prince enjoyed protection; those living under Catholic princes could move to near-by Lutheran states. A similar trend occurred in the Scandinavian countries. Lutheranism became the official state religion of Denmark and Norway in 1537 and of Sweden in 1593. Protected wherever they were numerous in Europe, the Lutherans did not need

[1] For the general student no book on its subject surpasses Preserved Smith's *The Age of the Reformation* (New York, 1920). See chapters 1–9, 14.

53

escape persecution, he lived at Basel, Switzerland, where he wrote his famous *Institutes of the Christian Religion*, aptly described as "the finest work of Reformation literature." By 1630, seventy-four editions, nine translations, and fourteen abridgments of this remarkable book had appeared in Europe. After 1536 Calvin lived at Geneva, where he fashioned and controlled the government of the city-republic. His untiring writing, preaching, correspondence, conferences, and educational activity made him so clearly the focus of Reformation thought that he became widely known as the Protestant pope.

Calvin's influence permeated four countries of Europe and affected vitally their internal history between 1560 and 1650. In France his followers were the Huguenots; in Holland, the members of the Dutch Reformed Church; in Scotland, the Presbyterians; in England, the Puritans. These four groups contributed the largest body of emigrants to English America. Calvinism thus became the strongest single religious force in the thirteen colonies. In consequence the ideas of Calvin and of his immediate successors have left enduring marks upon American thought.[4]

The theology of the Calvinists conditioned all their other beliefs. Man, in their sight, was an unworthy sinner; the world was a habitation of evil and temptation; life was a journey of sorrow and suffering leading the footsore pilgrim to his eternal home. Not earthly pleasure but the welfare of his immortal soul was man's imperative concern. His mission on earth was to glorify God, the omnipotent ruler of the universe, who decreed the destiny of His creatures and by means of His special providences warned, punished, and rewarded His saints on earth.

Calvin accepted the Bible as the inspired word of God, giving to man a divine rule of conduct and an approved form of worship. Every feature of the church should have the expressed authorization of the Scriptures; all traditions and ceremonies not thus sanctioned should be eliminated. In Calvinistic churches the laity exercised more influence than in the Catholic Church. The laity not only selected the pastors and the elders but also admitted new members and managed the finances of the congregation. Although the clergy were regarded as the authorized interpreters of the Bible, the final control over the church was vested in the whole body of true believers. Thus Calvin-

---

[4] *Calvin: a Modern Biography*, by Jean Moura and Paul Louvet (Garden City, N. Y., 1932), is a vigorous, readable account. See also James MacKinnon, *Calvin and the Reformation* (London, 1937).

ism was an expression of the religious thought of the individual members of the congregation rather than a creed imposed and interpreted by outside ecclesiastical authorities.

Fundamental in Calvinist theology was the doctrine of predestination. The sin of Adam had rent man from his Creator and implanted in the sons of man a corrupt love of self and material gain which caused them to struggle one against another. However, the Son of God, Christ, in His infinite compassion for man's suffering, had entered into a covenant with God for the salvation of a chosen few among the descendants of Adam. The vicarious sacrifice of Christ on earth had thus conferred the boon of eternal salvation upon the elect. The remainder of mankind were condemned to an afterlife of everlasting suffering. Wholly unworthy and insignificant in comparison with God, man could do nothing to achieve his own salvation. If he chanced to be among the elect his good fortune was due solely to the grace of God and the love of Christ. As a recipient of such a transcendent blessing, the sincere believer was naturally filled with an overpowering sense of gratitude and devotion to his divine benefactor.[5]

The theology of the Calvinists did not provide for compromise or a middle ground; it was compounded of two irreconcilable extremes. On the one hand were God, heaven, morality, and the elect; on the other, Satan, hell, evil, and the damned. Between these two forces there could be only warfare to the end. Thus the Calvinists rejected the idea of purgatory, and defined all actions as either godly or ungodly, condemning idle pastimes, merrymaking, card playing, dancing, and frivolity as sinful waste of God-given time and talent. In such a creed, toleration could have no sanction. Those who opposed the Calvinists were certainly not among the elect; and if God had condemned them to eternal suffering, it did not become His saints to countenance their false doctrines and evil ways. Toleration was thus regarded as defiance of God's will. Even those whom God had condemned were required to obey His laws in order that they might glorify Him on earth, for such was the duty of every man.

It might seem that this doctrine of predestination would fill men with a sense of futility and cover life with a shroud of gloom. But the true believers in Calvin's creed regarded themselves as the elect. Upon them God had set the seal of his special approval and thereby had exalted them—humble folk, as many of them were—above manmade nobles, priests, and even kings. In consequence the ardent Cal-

[5] An excellent introduction to European thought is Preserved Smith's *The History of Modern Culture* (2 vols., New York, 1930–34). See Vol. I.

vinists were confident and aggressive. Instead of becoming a prey to pessimism and despair, they plunged eagerly into the work of the world, determined to assert their divinely ordained right to rule. Trivial amusements seemed unnecessary to a people who attempted to reform church and society, took up arms against kings, waged righteous wars, and founded new commonwealths beyond the sea.[6]

The aggressive spirit of Calvinism and its idea of divinely appointed saints bred intense opposition among people of more moderate views. Particularly harsh appeared the Calvinists' view of predestination, because it condemned not only the mature man of evil ways but also the good heathen, the majority of children, and moral people of other creeds. This doctrine seemed to picture its author as heartless in the extreme—

> The monster dread who from the poison chalice
> Pours out the drug of hell in unctuous malice
> And makes the gracious God a very fiend.

The political philosophy of the Calvinists took form under the pressure of persecution which they endured at the hands of their Catholic enemies, particularly in France. Fundamentally, the Calvinists believed that the duty of government—both of ruler and subject—was to glorify God. Government had originated by means of a contract between the prince and his people by which the two parties were to labor together to realize the kingdom of God on earth. This contract implied a fundamental written law which was binding upon the ruler and his subjects alike. Such a law consisted of the moral code of the Scriptures—especially of the Mosaic law of the Old Testament—and of certain great charters and agreements entered into by the king and the people. The fundamental law therefore guaranteed to the subjects certain inherent rights—particularly the right of worshipping God in the manner approved by the Scriptures. If the sovereign usurped these rights, if he deserted the true faith, if he led the people away from God to false idols, then he violated the contract and forfeited his crown. Through their chosen representatives, the true believers might rise against such a prince and depose him. The Calvinists, however, did not approve of mob resistance; if the elected magistrates refused to oppose an unorthodox ruler, the only alternative open to the people was to select a new magistracy.[7]

These ideas implied a partnership of religion and government in

[6] James T. Adams's vigorous and well-written *The Founding of New England* (Boston, 1921) is hostile toward Calvinism. See chapter 4.

[7] H. D. Foster, "The Political Theories of the Calvinists," *American Historical Review*, XXI (Oct. 1915).

which the state served as a protecting arm of the church. To the church was entrusted the duty of education, while the state was obliged to maintain the purity of religious doctrine and to impose a moral and godly way of life upon the people. The state could never tolerate non-Calvinist doctrines. As Calvin's successor, Beza, said: "But obstinate heretics are worse than parricides and deserve death, even if they repent." "It is the duty of the state to punish them, for the whole ecclesiastical order is upheld by the political."

If the Calvinistic ideas are shorn of their religious aspects there remain the doctrines of contract, fundamental law, representative government, and the right of resistance. And if to these remaining ideas is grafted the principle of democracy, the result is the political philosophy which has prevailed in the United States.[8]

In their economic views the Calvinists stood midway between medieval and modern times. First of all they sanctified every form of productive labor. Calvin rejected the monastic ideal of withdrawal from the world; man at work was more Godlike than man in idle contemplation of the divine spirit. By the sweat of his brow should man earn his bread. *Navigation Spiritualized, Husbandry Spiritualized,* and *The Religious Weaver* were Calvinistic books which expressed the ideal that the production and enjoyment of wealth were wholly consistent with a godly life.[9]

It followed, therefore, that private property enjoyed a divine sanction; in fact, the Creator rewarded the pious man with material wealth; while an evil commonwealth could not prosper. "If God," wrote Richard Baxter, "show you a way in which you may lawfully get more than in another way . . ., if you refuse this, and choose the less gainful way, you cross one of the ways of your calling, and refuse to be God's steward." Social inequalities were a part of the divine order, because God had decreed that some men should be rich and some poor, "some high and eminent in power and dignity; others mean and in subjection." In general the Calvinists approved heartily of business, trade, and profit-making; even the taking of interest was legitimate in many circumstances.

But all these economic sanctions were subject to religious restraints. Continuous work insured against temptation. The man of large property was merely a steward of the Lord, a custodian who should use his surplus to advance the kingdom of God on earth. In times of

[8] H. L. Osgood, "The Political Ideas of the Puritans," *Political Science Quarterly*, VI (March, June 1891).
[9] R. H. Tawney's *Religion and the Rise of Capitalism* (New York, 1926), a profound, scholarly analysis, is especially recommended.

calamity the rich should share generously with the poor. Private wealth should not be used in any way detrimental to the public welfare. Merchants were entitled only to a fair profit; they should charge only just prices, and shun profiteering and monopoly as devices of Satan. The community should regulate prices and wages in the common good. Interest rates should not be extortionate; the charge to a poor man should be less than to the rich. Workmen ought not to ask for leisure and high wages, lest they spend their time and money upon tobacco, liquor, and idle amusements.

Thus the economic order was divinely arranged. The custodians of wealth had social duties to perform—to advance religion and education, to rule justly, and to enforce morality. If the servant must obey his master, so also the master should not exploit the servant, because "no man is made more honorable or more wealthy . . . out of any particular and singular respect to himself, but for the glory of his Creator, and the common good of the creature, man." [10]

This philosophy extolled the economic virtues of industry, thrift, frugality, prudence, temperance, and honesty—which all together imposed a godly discipline upon sinful man. In the English colonies Calvinism found a fertile soil. The trend of American development, however, weakened the religious restraints which the early Calvinists placed upon economic practices. But the other features of Calvinism remained and waxed strong. The sanctification of work, of private property, of the acquisitive spirit, of social inequality, of profit-making and interest-taking—these traits so characteristic of American life eventually came to be known as "rugged individualism." [11]

## THE FRENCH HUGUENOTS

The first Calvinists to attempt colonization in America were the French Huguenots. These Protestants, who probably represented 5 per cent of the population of France in 1550, belonged mainly to the upper middle class. On the whole they were industrious, earnest, thrifty, and prosperous—a group which exerted an influence greater than their numbers alone would have warranted. In 1559 the Huguenots formed a national church and adopted Calvin's confession of

[10] E. A. J. Johnson, "Economic Ideas of John Winthrop," *New England Quarterly*, III (April 1930). See also A. W. Griswold, "Three Puritans on Prosperity," *New England Quarterly*, VII (Sept. 1934).

[11] Max Weber's *The Protestant Ethic and the Spirit of Capitalism* (New York, 1930), a creative book, finds in Calvinism the germs of the capitalistic spirit. For a criticism of this view see H. M. Robertson, *Aspects of the Rise of Economic Individualism* (Cambridge, 1933).

faith as their creed. They were not content merely to be tolerated; they desired also to shape the religious policy of the state. Their compact organization added greatly to their strength.

Throughout the sixteenth century the Huguenots were subject to recurring persecutions. Francis I (1515–47) not only banished Calvin from France but consented to attacks upon his followers as the price of Catholic support of the monarchy. The successor of Francis I, Henry II (1547–59), was an intolerant foe of Protestantism. Having been educated in Spain, he desired to introduce the Inquisition into France; hence he created a special criminal court, *Chambre Ardente* (court of fire), which employed persecution to suppress heresy. Between 1562 and 1593 a series of religious wars threatened the Calvinists with destruction. Their political doctrines did not harmonize with the ideal of an absolute monarchy, since their desire for self-government in religion incited them to political agitation against enforced uniformity and subordination to the king's power and faith.[12] Courageous and self-righteous, they became involved in plots against the Catholic monarchy and by "image-breaking, assaults on processions, and general violence they made the part of tolerant Catholics difficult to play."

After 1550 Calvin's principal lieutenant in France was an influential nobleman, Gaspar de Coligny, who eventually became the Admiral of France, and a power in the government of Charles IX (1560–74). Earlier, Coligny had engaged in privateering enterprises directed against Spanish commerce. This business gave him an interest in establishing a base in America from which the Huguenot privateers might operate. He found an agent for this task in the person of Nicolas Durand de Villegagnon—a versatile but rather unstable adventurer. Converted to Calvinism, Villegagnon conceived the plan of establishing a Huguenot colony in Brazil. Both Calvin and Coligny approved, hoping to provide a refuge for persecuted Calvinists. Catholic leaders likewise consented, seeking to rid the land of obnoxious heretics. In July 1555, therefore, Villegagnon sailed from France with a band of Huguenot colonists and a sprinkling of seamen and bankrupt nobles and arrived at the harbor of Rio de Janeiro in November.

In 1557 a second party arrived. Unhappily, however, it included five disputatious Calvinist ministers. Villegagnon, who had a natural taste for theological argument, soon engaged in a sharp controversy with the ministers which resulted in his reconversion to Catholicism.

---

[12] Franklin C. Palm's *Calvinism and the Religious Wars* (New York, c. 1932) is an excellent brief introduction.

After sending three of the ministers back to France, he deserted the settlers and returned home. In 1558 Portuguese soldiers fell upon the weakened colony and destroyed it.

Undismayed by this failure, Coligny made new plans. While governor of the fortress of Le Havre in 1561, he summoned his followers and announced his intention of sending an expedition preparatory to the colonization of Florida. Again he aimed to provide a shelter for the Huguenots. In accordance with this plan, a Huguenot captain, Jean Ribaut, sailed in 1562 and explored the northern coast of Florida—"a country full of havens, rivers, and islands, of such fruitfulness as cannot with tongue be expressed." Proceeding northward, Ribaut planted a settlement (which he called Charlesfort), near the present site of Beaufort, South Carolina; then, leaving a band of thirty men to hold the garrison, he returned to France for reinforcements.[13]

After enduring innumerable sufferings, the settlers built a rude craft and embarked for France. Motionless calm was succeeded by violent winds; hungry and athirst on their water-soaked vessel the desperate survivors resorted to killing and eating one of their fellows. Finally they were rescued and taken as prisoners to England.

The promoters of the Huguenot colony, however, were not idle. In 1564 they sent forth another expedition under René de Laudonnière, which established a settlement, Fort Caroline, on the St. John's River in Florida. Nearly every ill which could beset an infant colony visited these pioneers: sickness, hunger, Indian hostilities, insubordination, and mutiny. Bent upon finding gold, the colonists neglected to till the soil. Laudonnière was on the verge of abandoning the project when Ribaut arrived in August 1565 with fresh supplies and a large party of soldiers, artisans, and fortune-hunting noblemen.

But the damage already done proved fatal. Several malcontents at Fort Caroline had seized two vessels from the colony and had taken to buccaneering in the West Indies at the expense of the Spaniards. Captured by their intended victims, they were carried to Havana, where they divulged the news of the Huguenot colony in Florida. The Spaniards believed that the French were colonizing with the intention of preying upon Spanish commerce from an American base. As Protestants the French were all the more odious, for they might corrupt the Indians of New Spain. A champion of militant Catholicism now stepped forward in Spain—Pedro Menéndez de Avilés. Fired with the ambition of extending the empire of Spain over Florida, Menéndez in 1565 secured a royal patent authorizing him to

[13] See again Francis Parkman, *Pioneers of France in the New World.*

explore, conquer, and colonize the region. Success was to confer upon him the powers of governor of Florida. Since he intended to attack the French he received assistance from the Spanish court—three vessels and six hundred troops. With this small army he sailed from Cadiz in June and founded St. Augustine in Florida, September 6, 1565.

Menéndez lost little time in marching overland and destroying Fort Caroline. More than two hundred of the French were put to the sword, and only a hundred were spared. Informed of Menéndez's conduct, Philip II remarked: "Say to him as to those he has killed he has done well: and as to those he has spared they shall be sent to the galleys." The death of Ribaut pleased Menéndez particularly, since "he was the most expert sailor and corsair known, and very skillful in the navigation of the Indies and the coast of Florida."

The story of Huguenot colonization was thus a tale of dismal failure. The Protestants did not have the ardent backing of the French government—a necessary requisite for new projects at the time. Moreover, France was distracted by factional warfare at home. Above all, these early ventures were falsely conceived. "The foundation was forgotten. There were no tillers of the soil. Such, indeed, were rare among the Huguenots; for the dull peasants . . . clung with blind tenacity to the ancient faith. Adventurous gentlemen, reckless soldiers, discontented tradesmen, all keen for novelty and heated with dreams of wealth—these were they who would build for their country and their religion an empire beyond the sea" (Parkman).

The Huguenot failures meant that later French Protestants did not enjoy a French retreat in America. In consequence many of their number, when afflicted with later persecutions, migrated to the English colonies in America.[14]

### THE CHURCH OF ENGLAND

While the French Huguenots were attempting to found colonies, England was in the throes of religious change. The Anglican Church, which took form during the reign of Queen Elizabeth (1558–1603), exerted a threefold influence upon English settlements in America. The policies of the Anglican leaders provided one of the potent causes of Puritan migration to New England. In the southern colonies, the

[14] *The Cambridge Modern History* (ed. A. W. Ward, G. W. Prothero, and S. Leathes, 13 vols., New York, 1907–11), a scholarly English work for advanced students, emphasizes ideas and politics. The second volume deals with the Reformation. See also Vol. I, chapter 19; Vol. III, chapters 1, 10, 17; and Vol. IV, chapters 8–12.

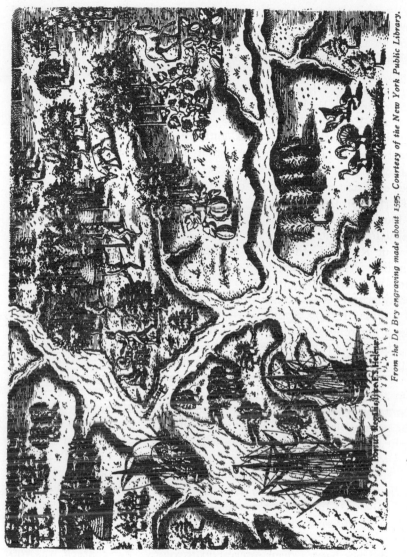

*From the De Bry engraving made about 1595. Courtesy of the New York Public Library.*

THE COAST OF FLORIDA

Anglican Church, although considerably modified, was established in law and served as the center of the social and religious life of the well-to-do planters. Finally, the fear that England might appoint American bishops—and tax the colonists for their support—contributed an active cause of the Revolutionary War.

The roots of the Reformation in England extend backward to the reign of Henry VIII (1509–47) and far beyond. His desire to secure a "divorce" from Catherine of Aragon—his Spanish queen—led him to induce Parliament to repudiate the authority of the papacy over the English Church (1534–35). Similarly the king effected the dissolution of the monasteries and the confiscation of their lands. But Henry VIII was not a Protestant. He sought to exercise supreme authority over the English Church; but aside from this he favored the ecclesiastical doctrines, ceremonies, and organization of pre-Reformation times.

During the reign of Edward VI (1547–53) England became radically Protestant. But his successor, Queen Mary (1553–58), was a devout Roman Catholic who obliterated nearly all official traces of English Protestantism. However, her reign was a period of hard times and national humiliation in foreign affairs, and the harsh persecution of Protestants which the queen instituted stirred up a wave of popular feeling against extreme Catholicism. At the time of her death her religious policy had been generally discredited.[15]

The problem which confronted Queen Elizabeth in 1558 was exceptionally delicate. She was the daughter of Henry VIII and Anne Boleyn, whose marriage had never been sanctioned by the papacy, and accordingly Pope Paul IV asserted that Elizabeth could not become queen without his consent, since her illegitimate birth nullified her natural claim. But Elizabeth resolutely refused to admit that her right to rule depended upon the will of an outside power. Hence she had to defy the papacy at the outset, and to look to the Protestants for support. She was not at heart a Protestant; all her preferences inclined her toward Roman Catholic beliefs and practices. Yet, since she depended upon the Protestants, she had to make concessions to them. At the same time she believed that it was the proper function of her government to determine the religious beliefs of her subjects. She did not have a deep interest in theology; her concern was with politics, and her aim was to promote the material welfare of the nation. Internal peace was necessary to this end, and religious uniform-

[15] Conyers Read's *The Tudors* (New York, 1936) consists of five stimulating essays on personalities and policies.

ity afforded the best assurance of peace. Elsewhere she saw that religious diversity led to destructive civil war. To avoid such a calamity in England she was determined to impose a common religion upon the country—one that would assert and uphold the supremacy of her own power.[16]

Two features of the religious settlement of her reign formed part of the background of English colonization. The first was the national character of the Anglican Church. The Reformation in England was "the last and greatest conquest of the State, the assertion of its authority over the Church, and of its absolute, undisputed supremacy within the national frontiers." The Act of Supremacy (1559) defined the sovereign as the Supreme Governor of the Church and required that all clergy take an oath affirming the royal authority. An Act of Uniformity (1559) prescribed that an English Book of Common Prayer should be used in the services of all the churches. Ministers who did not comply were to be punished, and any person who refused to attend the authorized ceremonies was obliged to pay a fine. The Bible was Anglicized by translation and an English litany and an English order of communion were introduced. Church and state formed a partnership in which the state was the dominating member. The sovereign became the custodian of the national faith, armed with far-reaching powers to compel submission among the people. Resolute opponents of the Established Church were therefore plunged into open conflict with the royal power.[17]

The second feature of the Elizabethan settlement was its compromise nature. The Anglican Church was neither Roman Catholic nor radically Protestant. The sovereign's title, "Supreme Governor," replaced the earlier title, "Supreme Head," in order to appease both Catholics and Calvinists. The former regarded the pope as Christ's vicar, and the latter considered Christ only and immediately, as the supreme head of the Church. While rejecting the authority of the papacy, the English Church retained the Catholic hierarchy of archbishops and bishops, and although the services of the prayer book were expressed in the English language, they were drawn largely from the old Church. But the Anglican creed (formulated in the Thirty-nine Articles in 1563) was dominantly Protestant. The Roman Catholic doctrine of transubstantiation was rejected, as well as the institution of an unmarried priesthood. Whereas the Roman Catholic

[16] C. Read, "Good Queen Bess," *American Historical Review*, XXXI (July 1926).
[17] A. F. Pollard, *Factors in Modern History* (New York, 1926) gives the penetrating conclusions of a leading English scholar. See chapters 4, 7–8.

faith embraced seven sacraments, the Anglican creed recognized only two—baptism and communion. Nor did Queen Elizabeth restore the monasteries.[18]

The English Reformation was not the work of a great reformer like Calvin or Luther; it was rather the product of political leaders. It has been likened to "the policy of a cabinet, full of compromise, not entirely satisfactory to any one, but tolerable to many" (Pollard). It had enough features of Roman Catholicism to satisfy the moderate Catholics, and enough of Protestantism to satisfy the moderate Protestants. It was accordingly accepted by the majority of the English people. However, neither extreme Protestants nor Roman Catholics were appeased. Their hostility produced a century of political agitation which had profound effects upon English colonization in America.

Soon after the Elizabethan settlement was effected, England became involved in a quasi-war with Spain. Under Philip II, the Spaniards, assuming the leadership of the Catholics in Europe, determined to suppress Protestantism and therefore assisted the English Catholics who desired to restore the authority of the papacy in England. In 1568 the Catholic queen of Scotland, Mary Stuart, fled to England from her Protestant foes. Her claim to the English crown and her religious faith made her the focus of anti-Protestant plots in England. In a general way these conspiracies anticipated a Spanish invasion of England and an uprising of English and Irish Catholics that would depose Elizabeth, restore the Roman Catholic Church, and place the exiled Scottish queen upon the English throne. Such plots, together with the commercial rivalry between England and Spain, brought the two countries to open war in 1587. One issue of the struggle was the right of England to maintain a national church free from foreign dictation. Accordingly, the extreme English Catholics found themselves in alliance with the alien enemies of the queen. Parliament in consequence enacted a series of anti-Catholic laws in order to strengthen the Established Church.[19]

One group of the English Catholics—the papists—sought to restore the papal supremacy; a second—the recusants—while not denying the queen's authority over the Church, desired to adhere to the Roman Catholic ritual and doctrines. The earliest laws against the

[18] Charles Sydney Carter's *The English Church and the Reformation* (London, 1925), a brief manual, emphasizes the period to 1565.

[19] Henry O. Wakeman's *An Introduction to the Church of England* (London, 1919) is the best short history from the point of view of conservative Anglicanism. See chapters 10–17.

Roman Catholics barred them from offices in Church and state, and required them to attend the services of the Established Church under pain of a fine of a shilling a week for non-compliance. After the pope had excommunicated Queen Elizabeth (1570) Parliament imposed the death penalty upon the partisans of Mary Stuart, as well as upon anyone who brought a papal decree into England. Two acts of 1581 made reconciliation with Rome a capital crime and raised the fine for non-attendance at the Anglican services to £20 a month. In 1585 all Catholic priests who had been trained in foreign colleges were expelled, and all English subjects studying in Jesuit schools abroad were ordered home. Two years later another law provided that the goods and two-thirds of the lands of recusants who did not pay the fines for non-attendance at Anglican services should be confiscated by the Crown. Finally, in 1593, Catholics who were too poor to pay fines were banished from the realm.

Most of these acts were intended not only to uphold the queen's authority in religion but also to augment the revenues of the state at the expense of the Roman Catholics. The laws against them became progressively more severe as the strife between England and Spain grew more acute. It was not intended, however, to expel the body of the Roman Catholics; the government preferred that they remain in England, subject to royal scrutiny, lest their migration to Europe should strengthen England's enemies there.[20]

In spite of these oppressive laws, the Elizabethan Catholics did not endeavor to establish colonies in the New World. First of all, the acts were not uniformly enforced. Queen Elizabeth preferred to ignore them, except in time of political crisis. Moreover, the Roman Catholics believed that better times would come. From the Spanish war, and later from James I and Charles I, they hoped for a Catholic restoration or at least for toleration. On the whole they were conservative, even reactionary, in their views: they yearned for the old ways—not for a new social order; consequently they did not wish to pull up their roots in England for the sake of establishing an experimental society in America. Belonging mainly to the landed class, they likewise did not respond to the lure of commercial profit with which the New World beckoned to merchants and capitalists. In addition, the Roman Catholic prelates discouraged emigration, lest the old Church should be completely uprooted in England. Proposals to establish Catholic colonies were therefore treated as Protestant plots. Eng-

[20] R. B. Merriman, "Some Notes on the Treatment of the English Catholics in the Reign of Elizabeth," *American Historical Review*, XIII (April 1908).

land was too important a country to be abandoned to Protestantism through the emigration of ardent Catholics, who—staying at home— would labor to restore the old faith.

For these reasons the English Catholics, harsh as the penal laws against them were, did not play an important part in the colonization of America. That was left to the other critics of the Anglican Church —the more extreme and uncompromising Protestants.[21]

## The English Puritans

When Henry VIII confiscated the lands of the monasteries he distributed them among his followers, thereby creating a new order of aristocrats who supported the Anglican Church with heart and soul, since a reversion to Catholicism would have stripped them of their titles and estates. This feudal basis of the Anglican Church found expression in its decorous ritual, which was in keeping with the ceremonials of aristocratic life, and which denied to the people an active part in divine service, thus carrying into religion the ideal of the supremacy of the aristocratic class. However, there were other groups in the community who were not long content with a passive role. Such were many of the clergy and the lesser landowners, as well as the rising artisans and merchants of the towns. Their growing sense of importance dictated that they should participate in the affairs of state and shape the policy of the church in response to their social and spiritual needs.[22]

Thus during the reign of Elizabeth there arose a body of radicals known as Puritans. Prior to about 1630 they desired merely to reform the Established Church from within. After 1630, however, the term Puritan came to have a broader meaning. In the intellectual sphere, the Puritans insisted upon the right of individual judgment as against the formulation of belief by nobles, priests, or kings. To achieve this end the Puritans fostered education in order that the individual might know the sources of religious truth. Other traits of the Puritans were a highly ingrained sense of the divine presence and an awareness of the sinful nature of man which must be repressed by rigid discipline and an austere moral life. Above all, a highly developed conscience was the mark of sincere Puritans. In practical affairs they were generally aggressive and self-reliant, somewhat in-

[21] Walter H. Frere, *The English Church in the Reigns of Elizabeth and James I* (London, 1904), is useful on the rise of Puritanism.
[22] A suggestive study is Oscar H. Marti's *Economic Causes of the Reformation in England* (New York, 1929).

tolerant of human weaknesses, hostile to compromise, inclined to impose their views on others, and actuated by a craving for self-expression and an eager desire to shape the course of human development toward spiritual ends.

Calvinism appeared in England around 1540, and rose to prominence during the Protestant reign of Edward VI. Expelled during the reign of Mary Tudor, many of the English Calvinists sought refuge at Geneva where their association with Calvin enhanced their ardor for the new faith. They returned to England after 1558, determined to realize their ideas at home. The first notice of a Puritan society in England refers to a London group which in 1566 was styled as "Puritans or unspotted lambs of the Lord." [23]

Several factors explain the growth of Puritanism after 1560. First was the feeling among many Protestants that the Elizabethan religious settlement was an insincere compromise, not truly Protestant or Christian. Many abuses disfigured the Established Church—pluralism in office-holding, ignorant and corrupt clergymen, and a yawning chasm between highly paid prelates and pauperized parish priests. Milton later spoke of the Anglican clergy as shepherds whose

> Hungry sheep look up and are not fed
> But swoln with wind and the rank mist they draw
> Rot inwardly and foul contagion spread.

Moreover, to the Puritans the society of their day seemed coarse, vicious, brutal, and corrupt, with crime rampant and idleness uncontrolled. Believing that the Church was the guardian of public morals, they held the clergy responsible for the evils of the time. In addition, many influential men who had the disposal of offices in the Anglican Church embraced the Puritan faith, with the result that some of the clergy assumed a Puritan pose in order to obtain appointments. Finally, the Puritans entered into an alliance with other opponents of the monarchy—those who resisted the sovereign's claims to absolute power. This alliance made each party much more powerful than if it had acted alone, and eventually (1642–49) enabled both to triumph over the Stuart monarchy and the Anglican Church.

The earliest manifestation of Puritanism was an attack upon the ceremonies of the Established Church, which exemplified the medieval view of the correct mode of worshipping God. The older theory was that man (whose mind was not attuned by nature to God) must apprehend Him through the senses—by means of beautiful services,

---

[23] Henry W. Clark's *History of English Nonconformity* (2 vols., London, 1911, 1913) is one of the best books on religion in England.

images, symbols, and music. The Puritans, on the other hand, believed that the elect who received Divine grace might know God directly through a spiritual medium; consequently ritual and elaborate ceremonies were unnecessary, and a sacrament was only a sign. As Milton said, faith needed not "the weak and fallible office of the senses to be . . . interpreters of heavenly mysteries." Catholics made "God earthy and fleshy because they could not make themselves heavenly and spiritual." [24]

In accordance with such views the Puritans objected to many features of the Anglican ceremony. Some targets of their criticism were the making of the sign of the cross on a child's head at baptism, the practice of kneeling in the communion service, the use of organ music, the observance of saints' days, and the wearing of the cap and surplice, and the changing of robes by the clergy. Failing to obtain reforms from the body of Anglican divines assembled in convocation (1563), the Puritan leaders began to hold private services, or conventicles, in which they replaced the Book of Common Prayer with their own observances. After Parliament in 1567 prohibited the holding of conventicles, the Puritans organized themselves into bodies of Protestant dissenters.

After 1570 the Puritan clergy became interested in modifying the government of the Established Church. A craving for self-expression led their leaders to hold meetings called prophesyings at which they exchanged ideas and practiced extemporaneous preaching. Queen Elizabeth objected to individual sermons, lest they destroy the uniformity of belief. She preferred that the clergy should merely read homilies prepared by the proper officials. The task of suppressing individual preaching was assigned to the bishops. In enforcing such policies the bishops naturally incurred the bitter enmity of the Puritan divines, and as a result the bishop's office became another target of Puritan discontent. In two "Admonitions to Parliament" (1572) the Puritans argued that the authority of a bishop over his diocese was no more justifiable than the authority of the pope over the Christian church. The court of the Archbishop of Canterbury was described as "the filthy quagmire and poisoned splash of all abominations that do infect the whole realm." Since the names of archbishops, archdeacons, lord bishops, and chancellors were "drawn out of the pope's shop, together with their offices, so the government which they use . . . is anti-Christian and devilish and contrary to the Scriptures."

In the 1570's most of the Puritans favored the Presbyterian scheme

[24] Edward Eggleston's *The Beginners of a Nation* (New York, 1897), a work both interesting and scholarly, emphasizes religious ideas. See Book II.

of Calvinistic church government which had been evolved in Scotland under the leadership of John Knox. The chief advocate of this system in England was Thomas Cartwright, a professor at Cambridge University, intellectual center of Puritan teaching.[25] The Presbyterian plan provided that each church should be governed by presbyters—its minister and lay elders—and that each church should be included in a district, the controlling agency of which was a presbytery or assembly of the local ministers and elders. Above the presbytery stood a larger regional conference—the synod—to which the presbyteries sent delegates. Crowning the structure there was to be a general assembly for the whole nation. In this arrangement the power of church government—shared jointly by the ministers and the lay elders—was concentrated chiefly in the presbytery and the local congregation. Authority ascended from the individual church to the larger conferences; under the Anglican rule, authority descended from the king and the archbishops through the bishops to the parish churches. The first presbytery was organized in England in 1572, and by 1590 there were probably five hundred ministers sustaining a Presbyterian organization within the Established Church.

Along with the Puritans arose a party of ultra-radical Protestants known as Separatists, who believed that each individual had the right to form his own religious creed. Such extreme individualism meant that, since different people would not reach identical conclusions, a single faith could not be imposed upon all. The only solution was to allow like-minded persons to form separate congregations and to worship free from all restraint. This attitude pointed directly toward religious toleration. Since the Established Church denied individual freedom of worship, the radicals felt that they must separate themselves from its errors.

The creed of the English Separatists was formulated by an Anglican clergyman, Robert Browne, who argued in the 1580's that the only church organization sanctioned by the Bible was that of a self-governing congregation. Hence the English Separatists became known as Brownists or Congregationalists. Because they rejected the authority of the state over religion they soon ran afoul of the national government. Two of their leaders, Barrow and Greenwood, were hanged at Tyburn in 1587; elsewhere their meetings were broken up, their property seized, and their leaders imprisoned. In 1597 a group of those imprisoned asked permission to migrate to America. This

[25] A. F. Scott Pearson, *Thomas Cartwright and Elizabethan Puritanism* (Cambridge, 1925), a careful, dignified study, treats religion without reference to other social forces.

was wholly natural, since the position of the Separatists in England was extremely weak. Their number in 1593 probably did not exceed six hundred; their primary ideas worked against an effective organization among themselves; their practices were contrary to the ingrained habits of the English people; and their defiance of the government required too much courage to be widely popular.[26]

The last years of the reign of Elizabeth brought a policy of increasingly severe anti-Puritanism. After the defeat of the Spanish Armada in 1588, the Spanish menace diminished and the persecution of English Catholics tapered off. The Puritans now emerged as the principal enemies of the monarchy, inasmuch as their ideas threatened to divide the people into hostile camps, and by destroying the unity of the queen's Church to undermine the royal authority within the state. Elizabeth accordingly appointed strict Anglicans to the highest ecclesiastical offices and proceeded to punish heretics and to dismiss a large number of Puritan clergy from their posts. For this purpose she utilized a special tribunal—the Court of High Commission—reorganized in 1583 with the object of imposing religious uniformity upon the land. This court was merely a mouthpiece of the sovereign, not an ordinary court of justice; it did not allow trial by jury or exempt the accused from testifying against himself. At this time, also, the queen's partisans advanced the theory that the office of bishop was divinely ordained.

A similar course was pursued by the successor of Elizabeth, James I, who ruled from 1603 to 1625. At the outset of his reign he refused to reform the Anglican Church along Presbyterian lines and warned the Puritans that he would make them conform or harry them out of the realm. A similar break with the Roman Catholics compelled the new sovereign to depend upon the Established Church —a natural alliance, since the Anglican principle of royal authority in religion harmonized with his view of the divine right of kings. But in spite of the animosity of the court, Puritanism continued to gain strength. Their ousted clergy gave unofficial lectures attended by their former parishioners, while the un-English foreign policies and the personal unpopularity of the king won allies and new recruits. Puritanism ceased to be a minor pest plaguing a popular queen who dominated a subservient Parliament; it became the central opposition to an unpopular king contending with a hostile Parliament. The movement reached its zenith during the reign of Charles I (1625-49), when some of England's greatest men—Sir John Eliot,

26 Winnifred Cockshott's The Pilgrim Fathers (New York, 1909) opens with two chapters on the Separatists.

John Pym, John Selden, John Milton, and Oliver Cromwell—were Puritans.[27]

As the strife between king and Parliament grew apace, Charles I gathered about him a party of high-church Anglican prelates extremely odious to the Puritans. This party became indoctrinated with the ideas of a Dutch theologian, Jacob Arminius, who criticized the theory of predestination because it seemed to make God the author of sin. The Arminian creed asserted that all who believed in Christ might be saved; divine grace was given freely to all who would seek it; salvation depended in part upon good works; and infants and virtuous heathens would not be eternally damned. Such beliefs were gall and wormwood to the Puritans—not only because they were an affront to Calvin, but also because they seemed to point backward to the creed of the Catholic Church. The first great victory of the Puritans occurred in 1628, when their leaders drafted and imposed upon Charles I the famous Petition of Right, which asserted the Calvinistic theory of fundamental law superior even to kings, and revealed that the Puritans had found powerful allies who resisted, on constitutional grounds, the claim of Charles I to tax his subjects without Parliament's consent.

The following year the Puritans struck at the religious policy of the king, when in March 1629 they attacked the Anglican clergy for discarding Calvinistic doctrines in favor of Arminianism. Resentful of what he considered impudent meddling, Charles I ordered parliament to adjourn. When the speaker of the Commons was about to read the royal order for adjournment, he was held down in his chair by two members, while Sir John Eliot read three resolutions to the House. One of these declared a public enemy any person who should "bring in innovation in religion, or by favor of countenance seem to introduce popery or Arminianism." The House became a scene of confusion as the doors were locked and the resolutions put to vote and carried. The speaker was then released, the doors were thrown open, and the members thronged out. Charles I immediately dissolved Parliament and thereby inaugurated a personal rule which was to have momentous consequences in both the Old World and the New.[28]

Unhampered by parliamentary restraints, the king now plunged

[27] A good brief account of the years 1628–60 by an outstanding authority is Samuel R. Gardiner's introduction to his edition of *The Constitutional Documents of the Puritan Revolution* (Oxford, 1880).

[28] George M. Trevelyan's *England under the Stuarts* (New York, 1930) contains a brilliant survey of the religious struggles, 1603–89. Another excellent treatment is Godfrey Davies, *The Early Stuarts, 1603–1660* (Oxford, 1937).

heedlessly along his own course. In 1633 he appointed William Laud Archbishop of Canterbury—a sincere and diligent but rigid and headstrong Anglican who had asserted the divine right of bishops and was suspected of Arminian sympathies. Laud tried to sweep away the evils of immorality, ignorance, sloth, and hypocrisy among the clergy, and to accomplish this he attempted to impose a hard-and-fast uniformity upon all the churches. He believed that the existence of a separate church outside the Anglican fold would create a state within the state. However, the reforms upon which he insisted were hateful to the Puritans, since they emphasized the externals of worship and showed a partiality to the Roman Catholic aspects of Anglican ritual. When the Puritans resisted what the archbishop regarded as his righteous aims, he attributed their opposition to irreligion, and classed them with wicked and dissolute persons—an intolerable insult to their spiritual pride. As head of the Court of High Commission Laud used it to enforce his decrees. The expelled Puritan clergy were hounded, their unofficial lectures were broken up, and their followers were arrested. A rigorous censorship of the press was enforced upon several vocal Puritans—Alexander Leighton, John Lilburne, and William Prynne—who were fined, whipped, shorn of their ears, imprisoned, or branded. The mass of the Puritans were not brutally persecuted, but they were threatened, harassed, and above all denied any influence in the affairs of Church and state—an unhappy circumstance for a party overstocked with strong leaders whose ardent spirits craved the right of translating their beliefs into official acts.[29]

Soon after Charles I began his personal rule one of the Puritan leaders—John Winthrop—wrote to his wife: "I am verily persuaded God will bring some heavy affliction upon this land, and that speedily; but if the Lord seeth it will be good for us, He will provide a shelter and a hiding place for us and others." God "is turning the cup toward us also, and because we are the last, our portion must be drunk to the very dregs which remain."

Gloomy indeed was the outlook for the Puritans in the 1630's. A wave of triumphant Catholicism seemed to be rolling over Europe. The Thirty Years' War was favoring the Catholic cause; the French Huguenots suffered a sorrowful defeat in 1628; the English queen, Henrietta Maria of France, was a devoted Catholic; the impecunious government of Charles I refused to aid the Protestants on the Continent; and the policies of Archbishop Laud seemed to the Puritans

[29] William H. Hutton's *The English Church* (London, 1903) is a standard work on the period 1625–1714.

to proclaim a forthcoming reunion between England and Rome. In 1633 the king issued the Declaration of Sports, which, in the old Catholic manner, allowed the people to play games on Sunday. Abhorrent as this was in itself to the Puritan believers in a joyless Sabbath, it was doubly obnoxious because it had to be read by the clergy from their pulpits on pain of losing their positions. Meanwhile, the parliamentary leaders of the Puritans had been cast into prison, where the purest soul among them—Sir John Eliot—contracted tuberculosis and died.

Such then was the religious background of the great Puritan migration to America. Ministers no longer allowed to preach in England gathered their flocks about them and departed for New England. The severity of Laud's rule over the church stimulated the movement westward until the collapse of the personal government of the king and the forward thrust of the Puritans in England in 1640 halted the exodus. By this time, however, a Puritan stamp had been placed upon a half dozen English colonies in the New World.[30]

## THE QUAKERS

The Civil War and the Puritan regime in England (1642–59) temporarily overthrew the Anglican Church and unloosed new forces of social unrest, but with the restoration of the Stuart dynasty in 1660 and the reëstablishment of the old religious order, a vigorous reaction set in. As a result there ensued another bitter conflict in which the government and the aristocracy were pitted against dissatisfied groups of the lower and middle classes that had become indoctrinated with radical ideas of freedom and individual right.

Foremost among such groups stood the English Quakers. The founder of this sect, George Fox, had displayed as a youth a precocious desire for religious truth which accepted creeds were unable to satisfy. "Not of high degree or elegant speech or learned after the way of this world," but by virtue of much solitude and long reflection this youthful seeker fashioned an individual faith consonant with his personal humility, gravity, and earnestness. Feeling himself divinely called to a public ministry, he preached and traveled with unwearied diligence, and drew about him a group of ardent evangelists who carried the tidings of the new salvation throughout England and to Germany and the Netherlands.

To George Fox and his followers the true religion had been prac-

[30] N. M. Crouse, "Causes of the Great Migration, 1630–1640," *New England Quarterly*, V (Jan. 1932).

ticed by the primitive Christians, but this had later been perverted
by kings and emperors to worldly uses. The Reformation had sought
to restore the pristine purity of the Church, but the triumph of re-
forming sects had corrupted them with a sense of power that induced
persecution—a negation of the Christian spirit. The object of the
Quakers was to restore religion to its primitive simplicity, charity,
and spirituality.[31]

The core of Quaker belief was the idea of the inner light or of
man's kinship with God. In every person there dwelt a spark of
divinity that might be enlarged by man's conscious effort until he
became wholly Godlike. The divine attributes of meekness, truthful-
ness, faith, love, charity, purity, and mercy should be cultivated as
opposed to the evil attributes of vanity, pride, envy, sloth, falsehood,
and anger. Divine grace and salvation were freely available to all on
condition that the sinner acknowledge his sins, repent, and mend his
ways. The ideal that salvation was to be achieved by man's works or
effort appealed with particular force to those classes in English society which were engaged in useful labor.

As members of the middle and non-privileged class in England the
Quakers readily embraced a faith which rejected ceremony, authority,
and inequality. Inasmuch as man might commune directly with God,
the office of priest was eliminated. Ministers need not be trained in
dogma or ritual, because they could speak truly only as the divine
spirit moved them. Church services became informal by virtue of the
right of each member to rise at will and utter words divinely inspired. Marriages were performed without the services of a minister,
since God sealed the union, not man. Taxes for the support of
churches were proscribed: "freely ye have received, freely give."
The Scriptures condemned oaths, even when legally administered,
since man was commanded to "swear not at all." Persecution was regarded as spiritual murder, out of harmony with the merciful spirit
of Christ. Since war and fighting issued from the sinful nature of
man, they were sternly outlawed. Such forms of social respect as the
tipping of hats and bowing to superiors were likewise rejected. The
words "thee" and "thou," then customarily addressed to servants and
children, were applied by the Quakers to the highborn and the lowly
alike.[32]

At the outset of the Quaker movement its popular appeal attracted

[31] Rufus M. Jones, *The Story of George Fox* (New York, 1919), is good reading—
the work of a leading American historian of Quakerism.
[32] On radical tendencies see George P. Gooch's able, concise *The History of English
Democratic Ideas in the Seventeenth Century* (Cambridge, 1898).

many of the more ignorant and superstitious poor, who marred the meetings with unseemly emotional demonstrations. Others asserted that the divine spirit directed their actions—evil ones included—and that they were thus above ordinary moral restraints. The Quaker leaders accordingly were obliged to develop a church organization and an effective discipline to check such excesses. The local congregation was made the central authority, acting through its monthly meeting. This body selected the minister, supervised the morals of members, investigated proposed marriages, kept records, and excommunicated the wayward who refused to reform. In addition to the monthly meetings there were quarterly meetings attended by representatives of the churches in a given county, and over all was the yearly meeting held at London. The quarterly and yearly meetings, composed of the most eminent and zealous Friends, afforded mutual counsel and aid—particularly in supporting missions and in defending Quakers persecuted in any part of the world.

In one respect the Quakers did not insist upon the ideals of primitive Christianity; they did not believe in poverty. In fact, they showed a marked capacity for acquiring and retaining wealth. They were generally intelligent and industrious people, conscious and resentful of social inequalities and privileges based upon force. Although they did not share the benefits of the ruling class, they were not of the servile or ignorant poor, but, rather, enterprising farmers, artisans, and merchants who felt the need of a larger place in the sun. Accordingly they disliked the aristocratic Anglican Church which denied to rising members of the community an active part in the conduct of divine service. Their doctrines which asserted the equality of man and the right of the individual to an active part in worship thus coincided with their growing economic importance and independence.[33]

In England the Quakers were regarded as upstarts who refused to pay homage to their privileged superiors. Their principles of equality were odious to a society based upon inflexible class distinctions. Their refusal to take oaths, to pay tithes, or to bear arms laid them open to the charge of refusing to support the state, and such refusal strongly suggested to the authorities a hidden impulse toward revolution.

One of the acts of Parliament known as the Clarendon Code (1661–65), which reëstablished the Church of England, provided that the Quakers, as dissenters, could not attend private religious meetings or conventicles. A fourth violation of this law was punisha-

[33] David Ogg's *England in the Reign of Charles II* (2 vols., Oxford, 1934), an important study, devotes most of Vol. II to religion and politics.

ble by a seven-year sentence to penal servitude in the West Indies. By another act the Quakers were fined £20 a month or two-thirds of their property if they refused to attend the Anglican services. Accordingly, they were sorely persecuted: their meetings were broken up; they were arrested, fined, imprisoned, and in extreme cases transported to the colonies; they suffered "mockings, contradictions, beatings, prisons, and many other jeopardies," so that "they seemed indeed to be as poor sheep appointed to the slaughter, and as a people killed all the day long." Like the Puritans before them, the Quakers looked to America as a land where they might live in peace and realize their peculiar aspirations, and accordingly they were active in colonizing schemes from 1675 until 1689—the year in which England finally adopted the general policy of religious toleration.[34]

## CONCLUSION

The religious contests after 1500 arose largely from the prevailing conception that church and state should be united. The sovereigns of Europe, and the privileged groups identified with them, felt that a single religion was necessary to unify the country and to maintain the authority and dignity of the ruling classes. In France, Spain, Germany, Holland, and England the Reformation established the principle that the secular power should preside over the national church. The adherents of state churches, protected at home, were not driven to seek shelter in other lands. Such protected groups were the Catholics in France and Spain, the Anglicans in England, the Calvinists in Holland, and the Lutherans in Germany and the Scandinavian kingdoms. Hence emigration inspired by religious motives was relatively slight among such protected groups. The opponents of state churches, however, were exposed to persecution, and consequently responded more readily to the lure of emigration. All these groups were prone to resist the absolute power of government. The mass of their members were drawn from the classes engaged in farming, industry, or trade. They could not settle in the colonies of France or Spain, which were closed to all but Roman Catholics. As a result they sought refuge in the American colonies of England and thus laid the foundations of a Protestant society prone to assert individual rights in defiance of external authority and to proclaim the freedom of farmers, artisans, and traders from the dominance of nobles,

[34] W. C. Dudley, "Nonconformity under the Clarendon Code," *American Historical Review*, XVIII (Oct. 1912). See also W. C. Abbott, "English Conspiracy and Dissent, 1660–1674," *American Historical Review*, XIV (April, July 1909).

priests, and kings. A further result was that English America soon made a strong appeal to the common folk of Europe and Britain who were not actuated by religious motives, but who desired to be free from the social and economic shackles which bound them in the Old World.[35]

[35] Ernst Troeltsch's *Protestantism and Progress* (New York, 1912) is a philosophical discussion of the influence of Protestantism in modern times.

## BIBLIOGRAPHICAL NOTE

WORKS PREVIOUSLY CITED: W. C. Abbott, *Expansion of Europe*, I, chs. 7–8, 11–15, 22; II, ch. 23; Lord Acton, *Lectures on Modern History*, chs. 4–8, 11; G. Bancroft, *History of the United States*, I, ch. 8; II, chs. 23, 27; H. E. Bolton, *Spanish Borderlands*, ch. 5; E. Channing, *History of the United States*, I, pp. 271–292; II, pp. 94–102; E. P. Cheyney, *European Background of American History*, chs. 9–12; C. J. H. Hayes, *Political and Cultural History of Modern Europe*, I, ch. 4; E. M. Hulme, *Renaissance and Reformation*, chs. 12–18, 21–24, 26; H. S. Lucas, *Renaissance and Reformation*, Book II; F. Schevill, *History of Europe*, pp. 91–190, 213–235; J. Winsor (ed.), *Narrative and Critical History of America*, III, ch. 7.

SOURCES NEWLY CITED: Henry Gee and William J. Hardy (eds.), *Documents Illustrative of English Church History* (London, 1896), devotes nos. 46–124 to the English Reformation. John Calvin, *Institutes of the Christian Religion* (2 vols., Philadelphia, 1921), is of primary importance. *The Journal of George Fox* is available in an Everyman's Library edition.

SOURCES PREVIOUSLY CITED: A. B. Hart (ed.), *American History Told by Contemporaries*, I, pp. 324–330 (Calvin); *Old South Leaflets*, nos. 20, 89, 100.

MAPS: W. R. Shepherd, *Historical Atlas*, pp. 114–116, 118–120.

## ☆ IV ☆

## THE ECONOMIC BACKGROUND OF
## ENGLISH COLONIZATION [1]

ENGLISH colonization was in the main an outgrowth of an economic revolution which marked the passing of the Middle Ages. Prior to about 1350, England occupied a minor place in the economy of Europe. But a series of profound changes occurred during the two centuries afterward—changes in agriculture, industry, and foreign trade that effected the transition in England from economic localism to importance in world commerce.

### MEDIEVAL ENGLISH ECONOMY

During the Middle Ages, agriculture supported the mass of the English people. The methods and organization of farming, however, were not conducive to economic progress. Spread over the country were a host of large estates in which the peasants carried on a semi-communal form of production. What gave their essential character to such estates or manors was the relation between the tillers of the soil and their lords, who held the land directly or indirectly from the king. The labor of the serfs provided the good things of life for the manorial lord, and consequently the serfs were bound to the soil—were not allowed to leave the manor even temporarily without the lord's consent. Since they had to work two or three days a week upon the land reserved to the lord (the demesne), it was imperative that they always be within his reach. During the remaining time they worked for themselves on little plots of ground, but they could eke out only a bare existence after the demands of the lord had been met.[2]

As long as this system remained, England could not become im-

---

[1] The best survey of the English background appears in E. Lipson's *The Economic History of England* (3 vols., London, 1920, 1931). Volume I is devoted to the medieval period and to early modern times; Vols. II and III to the age of mercantilism. A very valuable work.

[2] N. S. B. Gras, *An Introduction to Economic History* (New York, 1922) should be read by all students. It is original, scholarly and excellently written. See chapters 1—5. For more detailed studies by Professor Gras see *A History of Agriculture* (New York, 1925) and *Industrial Evolution* (Cambridge, 1930).

portant on the world stage of economic affairs. The country was too small to be a great producer of the commodities raised on the manor —grains and livestock—and obviously a people bound to the soil could not engage in seafaring, business, foreign trade, and colonization. Serfdom closed the avenues of economic progress; only when each person could go as he liked where opportunity beckoned could the maximum productive power of the nation be utilized. The manor itself cast a pall upon personal initiative—partly because so much of the fruits of the serf's toil went to the lord, and partly because the work of the serfs was regulated by custom and performed in common, so that the man of enterprise was held down to the speed of his more sluggish fellows. The methods of farming did not improve; the manor produced little surplus except for the overlord; the serfs, therefore, could not buy much of anything from the outside world. In the absence of money they paid their dues to the lord in labor and produce.

Such manufacturing as England carried on in the Middle Ages was performed chiefly in rising but struggling towns. Here the central feature was the craft gild. Since England did not as yet export manufactured products in quantity or conduct an extensive trade within the country, each town could exploit only a small market in its immediate vicinity, and consequently the gilds enforced a policy of restricting production within narrow limits. Each gild applied rigid rules to guarantee that every member should have his share of the available work. Only gild members were tolerated, and admission depended upon a long-term apprenticeship, while the number of apprentices was kept down in order to prevent overcrowding in any trade. Even the masters were closely regulated by the gild as to the quality and quantity of their work. Membership was a boon not to be surrendered lightly; hence the craftsmen were not disposed to leave their towns in search of better opportunities. Although such restrictions assured that apprentices would be properly chosen and well trained and that a high quality of work would be upheld, the gild ideal of monopoly and restricted production tended to keep industry within a narrow groove. Industrial expansion had to wait until wider markets appeared.[3]

The backwardness of England in agriculture and industry was reflected in foreign trade. In this sphere England depended largely upon foreign merchants. The area of external trade included only the Mediterranean, the Black Sea, the North Sea, the Baltic, and the

[3] L. F. Salzman's *English Industries of the Middle Ages* (Oxford, 1923) describes particular industries. Many illustrations. See chapters 9, 11, 13.

eastern border of the Atlantic Ocean. Moreover, the national state had not yet taken complete control over commerce; instead, merchants operated under the protection of their towns. Commercial treaties were negotiated and tariff duties imposed by the towns, to the infinite multiplication of restrictions upon trade. The exports of England consisted principally of raw materials—tin, copper, and raw wool. These were carried to distant markets by foreign merchants— by Italians who brought in the luxuries of the Orient, by German traders who imported forest products from the Baltic countries, and by Flemings who came with cloth from the Netherlands.

Such domination of foreign trade by alien merchants expressed the economic backwardness of medieval England, although in the long run it prepared the way for economic independence. In the days when the English monarchy was struggling for supremacy within the nation it was not opposed by a group of all-powerful commercial cities which frustrated political unification and the nationalization of commercial activity. England thus eventually became a compactly organized economic unit. But in the Middle Ages, the foreign merchants did not aggressively promote England's external trade. They were generally unpopular and consequently obliged to buy concessions and protection from the king, and were often exploited in a right royal manner. Frequently they were mobbed and despoiled of their property by an angry populace, as at the time of the Peasants' Revolt, when the German traders were a special target of the English mob. In the best of times trade could be carried on with only a few countries, and this the foreigners were prone to monopolize at the expense of their English customers. Moreover, the alien merchant regarded England as on the periphery, not as in a central area, of world trade. He did not seek to create a world market for English products, but only to export as many of them as could be sold through a single outlet—his own particular town and the commercial channels which it controlled. And since he did not engage in either industrial or agricultural production in England, he did not feel the powerful urge of a producer to widen the markets for his wares. All in all, then, the restrictions upon foreign trade harmonized with the restraints upon agriculture and industry which kept England in the background of European commercial progress during the early Middle Ages.[4]

[4] L. F. Salzman, *English Trade in the Middle Ages* (Oxford, 1931), is a satisfactory introduction, topically arranged.

## THE ECONOMIC REVOLUTION, 1350–1600

Such handicaps, however, were only relative, because a train of economic change was gradually undermining the old order. The basic revolution occurred in the breakdown of the medieval manor, an event which speedily transformed both industry and foreign trade. The essential change in agriculture was the alteration in the status of the worker from that of soil-bound serf to that of independent yeoman, rent-paying tenant, or hired laborer.

As industry and trade expanded in Europe—particularly in the towns of the Netherlands, Germany, northern France, and Italy—the standard of bourgeois well-being rose to new heights, accompanied by an increasing demand for good clothing. In those days woolen cloth was in well-nigh universal use, neither silk nor cotton having yet become widely practicable. England happened to be peculiarly suited to the raising of wool, and her farmers were soon supplying the looms of Europe with the finest grades available. The progress of sheep raising in turn revolutionized English agriculture. Small patches of land formerly cultivated by serfs were taken from them and enclosed as large sheep pastures. The evicted tenants could not all find new employment, since sheep tending required less labor per acre than the grain farming of manorial days. A large class of unemployed workers began to roam about as idlers and vagabonds. At the same time the population of England grew steadily—from about three million souls in 1485 to four million in 1603. The diversion of land from food growing to sheep raising meant that food supply did not keep pace with population growth, with the result that the growing army of unemployed struggled with a rising cost of living. Between 1461 and 1603 half the manors of England were enclosed. The rapidity of the revolution confronted the government with the specter of food shortage and the danger of internal strife due to high rents and prices and unemployment. Threats of class war induced the government to pass laws forbidding enclosures; nine such measures were enacted between 1485 and 1624. But because of the resistance of the landowners profiting by higher rents and of the merchants who reaped the profits of the wool trade, the enclosure movement could not be seriously checked.[5]

The exports of English wool to the Continent paid for the returning imports, part of which were gold and silver money. This came first into the towns, thereby enabling the bourgeoisie to buy more

[5] The best treatment of agricultural change is R. H. Tawney's *The Agrarian Problem in the Sixteenth Century* (New York, 1912).

farm products from neighboring manors. The unevicted peasants might sell a little surplus food to the towns for ready cash. The accelerating circulation of money not only raised the price of food but also gave the peasants a means whereby they could relieve themselves of payments to their lords in labor and produce. Instead of working two or three days a week upon the lord's demesne land, the peasants preferred to pay money rents which allowed them to work on their own plots of ground all the time. Having lost the customary workers for his demesne by this process of commutation, the lord could either put the land to sheep pasture or hire laborers to cultivate it for a money wage. The lord now ceased to care whether the peasants were bound to the soil or not, since he no longer expected them to be on hand for work upon his land. They in turn devoted themselves wholly to their own little farms, gained the freedom to come and go as they pleased, and discharged their former obligations of work and produce payments in a money rent.[6]

Hard upon the heels of the enclosure movement and the emancipation of the serfs followed a revolution within industry. Its essence was the progress of manufacturing, the decline of the gilds, and above all the emergence of woolen cloth working as England's foremost enterprise. In 1613 an English writer, John May, described the manufacture of woolen cloth as "the glory of our traffic and maintenance of our poor, many hundred thousands depending wholly on the same, chief pillar to our prince's revenue, the life of our merchant, the living of our clothier."

The plentiful supply of raw wool afforded by the enclosure movement gave the initial impetus to this all-important English industry. The universal demand for woolens furnished a large market, close at hand. Labor was plentiful, as the evicted peasants and runaway serfs sought the freedom of the manufacturing towns, and skilled artisans from abroad were welcomed into England to teach the secrets of cloth manufacture. About 1335, Flemings fled from the ravages of the Hundred Years' War, and Dutch craftsmen, whose finely made cloth was called in England the "new drapery," came in during the reign of Elizabeth, as did also a company of Huguenot weavers who sought relief from religious persecution in France. The protection and encouragement extended to such foreigners were but a part of a general policy of the English government to foster the woolen industry. Acts of Parliament, passed intermittently after 1337, aimed to restrain the exportation of raw wool and unfinished cloth and the im-

[6] E. P. Cheyney's *An Introduction to the Industrial and Social History of England* (New York, 1920) is compact, lucid, and well organized. See chapters 1–7.

portation of finished articles, in order that English producers might have prior access to raw materials and markets, foreign and domestic alike.[7]

One other factor necessary to manufacturing was present in England after 1400—ready capital. At that time capital was thought to consist of trading goods and money rather than of plants, machinery, and transportation facilities. The capitalist was one who circulated his trading stock rapidly with a profit to himself, not, as at present, one who deals primarily in long-term securities. Coined money was especially prized as capital, since it so readily effected the exchange of the country's stock of trading goods.

England's exportation of raw wool to the Continent accounted in part for her increasing supply of gold and silver, as did also the plundering of French towns and estates during the Hundred Years' War. During the reign of Henry VIII Parliament cut off money payments to the papacy, and thus put an end to one principal drain on the country's supply of coin. The working of silver mines in Bohemia and Germany between 1448 and 1492 augmented the European stock of money just before the Spanish colonies in America began to pour their treasure into Spain, whence it quickly seeped out, especially to the Netherlands, France, and England. The decline of feudalism and the dissolution of the monasteries released capital for industry and trade. As early as the close of the fifteenth century a Venetian observer wrote of London: "In a single street named the Strand leading to St. Paul's there are fifty-two goldsmiths' shops, so rich and full of silver vessels, great and small, that in all the shops in Milan, Rome, Venice and Florence put together I do not think there would be found so many of magnificence."[8]

The growing utilization of money as capital effected a change of attitude toward interest and moneylenders. Previously loans at interest had been made to kings and nobles, mainly for high living or war, and consequently were not regarded as productive of wealth. The Church condemned any person who lent at interest to humble folk, since money itself was unproductive. But as the rising capitalist class began to use money as a medium of exchange, thereby facilitating trade and extending production, the medieval attitude toward usury broke down. In England Parliament in 1545 legalized interest charges up to 10 per cent. This act acknowledged that a class of

---

[7] E. Lipson's *History of the Woollen and Worsted Industries* (London, 1921) is unexcelled.

[8] N. S. B. Gras exhibits a mastery of generalization in "The Economic Activity of the Towns," in *The Legacy of the Middle Ages* (ed. C. G. Crump, Oxford, 1926).

merchant-capitalists had arisen who were becoming increasingly important to the state.[9]

In the woolen industry the capitalist was both employer and merchant. He bought the raw wool, hired artisans to manufacture it into cloth, and sold the finished product. As the market for English cloth widened, the merchant-capitalists objected to the restrictions imposed upon production by the craft gilds and accordingly employed artisans in villages that were not under the rule of the gilds. There followed then a lively war between the older industrial towns and the new—a war which ended in the decay of the gilds and the established supremacy of the capitalist-employers within the woolen industry. Under the new domestic system the workers did not own the raw materials which they fabricated nor did they have any part in the marketing of the finished products. The wage system, subdivision of labor among carders, spinners, weavers, fullers, and dyers, improved tools and machines, the ideal of maximum production at minimum cost, and control of marketing by the employers—all these announced the coming of modern capitalistic economy.

In response to the advance of manufacturing, England's foreign trade assumed a new character as woven cloth replaced raw wool as the nation's primary export. About 1350 such exports consisted of thirty thousand sacks of raw wool and about five thousand pieces of cloth; in 1500 only five thousand sacks of wool were sold abroad as against sixty thousand pieces of cloth exported by one society of merchants alone. During these years another momentous change occurred. Foreign traders were gradually squeezed out of England's commerce and English merchants ventured throughout Europe in search of markets for their wares. In 1350 there were only 169 English merchants of consequence engaged in foreign trade; in 1500 there were at least three thousand.[10]

The change in exports from raw wool to manufactures was the principal factor making possible the commercial expansion of England. As long as the country exported only raw products, its available market was restricted, for they could be sent only to a relatively few Continental manufacturing towns. When, however, England had cloth to sell, her immediate markets widened immensely, for woolens could be carried directly to the consumer in every quarter of the

<hr />

[9] R. D. Richards, *The Early History of Banking* (London, 1929), is an outstanding study.

[10] *Studies in Economic History: The Collected Papers of George Unwin* (London, 1927) consists of penetrating accounts of medieval and early modern themes.

known world. Likewise, England became interested in colonies largely because she had manufactures to sell. Had she had only raw wool, hides, tin, and the like for export, she could have traded with advanced industrial regions, but hardly with the backward peoples of Africa and America.

From the merchant-employers came the driving impulse for commercial expansion. Here was a class of energetic, ambitious producers who pushed the sale of their goods throughout Europe with boldness and dispatch. With a potential market of unlimited extent and with seemingly boundless possibilities of production in England, the merchant-employers refused to depend upon foreign traders whose interest in selling English goods was not uppermost in their concerns. And so the English merchants went abroad, forcing their way into new markets, selling their goods with the ardor of an army bent upon conquering the world.[11]

AN ENGLISH MERCHANT OF THE SIXTEENTH CENTURY

Before the rise of the English woolen industry the principal traders of England—called the Merchants of the Staple—exported only raw products, which had to be shipped to a few designated ports. Sometimes these staple towns were located in England, sometimes on the Continent. The staplers declined as cloth replaced raw wool in England's export trade, being superseded by a new Company of Merchant Adventurers, whose main business was the exportation of cloth. Each merchant traded as an individual, owning the vessels he used and keeping private accounts. But the adventurers were banded together into a company which imposed common regulations upon all. Each merchant had to pass through a long apprenticeship, to pay a membership fee, and to abide by the decisions of the company's court in disputes with his fellows. A charter from the king (1407) had al-

[11] George Unwin's *Industrial Organization in the Sixteenth and Seventeenth Centuries* (Oxford, 1914) is an excellent, highly important survey of England's economy at the beginning of the colonizing era.

lowed the English traders abroad to act together through officers chosen by themselves, and eventually they established their own governing centers—one in London and one in the Netherlands, where most of their cloth was then sold. As a semi-political agency the company secured privileges for its members abroad and provided for their defense. During the fifteenth and sixteenth centuries the Merchant Adventurers controlled the bulk of England's foreign trade. Their very name indicates the aggressive and daring spirit that was then animating England's commercial expansion.

The gradual opening of new trading areas resulted in a need for commercial specialization; consequently, after 1550, the Merchant Adventurers were supplemented by new chartered companies, each with a monopoly of the commerce of a particular region. First came the Russia or Muscovy Company (1553 and 1555), then the Levant or Turkey Company (1581), next the Barbary or Morocco Company (1585), then the Guinea Company (1588), and finally the great East India Company, chartered in 1600. These companies, like the Merchant Adventurers, exported English manufactures, principally cloth, and they evinced the same all-powerful desire for extended markets.[12]

Two types of corporate organization were employed. The regulated company resembled the Merchant Adventurers—a society of private merchants conducting their trade on an individual basis, but submitting to a governor and court established by themselves, obeying common regulations, and by joint action securing privileges and providing for their own defense. Only merchants were admitted into these companies, and only after they had paid high membership fees. Such companies stood midway between the medieval gild merchant and the modern joint-stock corporation, which became increasingly popular after 1550. In the joint-stock company, membership was thrown open to investors in all walks of life who purchased shares. Each shareholder then had the right to attend the general court or stockholders' meeting, and to vote for the governor, treasurer, and board of assistants (or company directors) who managed the company's affairs. All assets were pooled and the business was carried on in a corporate capacity, profits being divided periodically among the shareholders. The first joint-stock companies were organized for single ventures, and endured only a few years, but by 1600 they were being established on a permanent basis. Widely utilized between 1560 and 1590 as a means of financing privateering and exploring

[12] Abbott P. Usher's *An Introduction to the Industrial History of England* (Boston, c. 1920) gives essential facts in well-organized form. See chapters 4–9.

ventures, the joint-stock companies earned enticing profits of 20 per cent or better, and thus exerted a tremendous popular appeal.[13]

Particularly suited to the promotion of foreign trade, the joint-stock company enabled England to seize the major commercial advantages of modern times. England's opportunity lay not in the mastery of the trade of Europe, which was already partitioned among a score of zealous and jealous states, but rather in the exploitation of areas which the age of discovery was revealing with bewildering rapidity—unappropriated areas that beckoned to a nation seeking fresh fields of endeavor. In the conduct of such trade, however, combined action was desirable. The great distances of the new areas from England and the necessity of winning the favor of native rulers as a condition to trade called for large capital outlays, while the hazard of uncharted enterprise clouded the prospect of success. In those days of small individual fortunes if one merchant were to venture his all upon the unknown his failure might spell his ruin. The joint-stock company, however, enabled a large number of investors to share the risk, each with but a fraction of his fortune, and thus to provide a large capital with little danger of ruining anyone.

As a condition to their hazardous ventures the promoters of new companies demanded and secured from the English government royal charters conferring monopolies of the trade with the areas which they proposed to open. Large initial expenditures might be necessary and profits slow; hence the exclusion of outsiders who might reap in the future where the promoters had sown. The conflicting claims of rival states made trading in new areas a thinly disguised maritime war, and if naval protection were provided by the original promoters, even their countrymen who did not bear the expense should not enjoy its benefits. Moreover, a single company was necessary in the trade with native peoples in order to exclude unscrupulous Englishmen who might, by plunder and fraud, give the whole English nation a bad name and turn the undiscriminating natives against English traders of more honorable intent.[14]

As exporters using their own vessels the English merchants were obliged to import return cargoes; hence their opposition to foreign merchants who had previously held the lion's share of the nation's import trade. After a century of conflict with their alien rivals the

---

[13] W. R. Scott's *The Constitution and Finance of English, Scottish and Irish Joint Stock Companies to 1720* (3 vols., Cambridge, 1910, 1912) is a monumental work.

[14] Alfred C. Wood, *A History of the Levant Company* (Oxford, 1935), explains trading organization and methods of this period. See chapters 1–5.

English merchants succeeded in dislodging them during the reign of Elizabeth. The Hansards at the Steelyard first lost their ancient privilege of paying duties lower than those exacted from English merchants and were excluded from the English cloth trade with the Netherlands (1560). Between 1588 and 1598 they were driven from the Steelyard, which was handed over to the City of London. The leader of this attack was Sir Thomas Gresham, prince of English merchants, founder of the Royal Exchange and friend and adviser of the queen. By 1532 the Flanders fleet had ceased to visit Southampton from Venice, and England's alliance with Portugal enabled her merchants to import oriental wares from Lisbon on advantageous terms.[15]

## MERCANTILISM

The transition from medieval to modern economy introduced a new economic philosophy which the eighteenth century designated as mercantilism—not a systematic program but a collection of regulations exhibiting a major trend. Politically mercantilism was an expression of the militant nationalism which arose upon the ruins of feudalism. Its objects were threefold: to achieve an economic self-sufficiency for the nation, to provide maximum profits to influential landowners, manufacturers, and merchants, and to yield an ample revenue to the Crown.

In the opinion of mercantilists the external trade of a country was similar to the business of a private merchant. Imports were analogous to the merchant's purchases, and exports to his sales; the nation's gain consisted in an excess of exports over imports, or in a favorable balance of trade, likened to the merchant's profit. Such excess value should, in part, assume the form of gold or silver money imported into the country.[16]

How was the desired excess of exports over imports to be achieved? Chiefly by fostering the exportation of manufactured goods. In English mercantilism the role of agriculture was to supply raw materials and foodstuffs for the country rather than for exportation; to this end the landowners received favors from the government through high duties on imports of foreign grain (the corn laws) and through acts which restricted the importation of foreign wool. Manufactured goods were preferred as exports because they bore higher prices than

---

[15] A standard work of great value is Sir William Ashley's *An Introduction to English Economic History and Theory* (2 vols., London, 1925). See Vol. II.

[16] A highly valuable recent work, *Mercantilism*, by Eli F. Heckscher (London, 2 vols., 1935), considers Europe as a whole, with special emphasis on England. Very important.

raw materials and hence tended to create a more favorable balance of trade. Consequently, parliament fostered home industries by enacting laws which placed high import duties on foreign manufactured articles (the protective tariff), which prohibited the exportation of needed raw products and semi-finished goods, and which encouraged the importation of raw materials not produced in England. The exportation of manufactured goods was more or less a necessity in the capitalistic scheme of production. Under the wage system and farm tenancy the workers did not receive enough buying power to enable them to purchase all the products of domestic agriculture and industry—for the simple reason that the total prices of all goods included profits to landowners and merchant-employers as well as the wages paid to the workers: the sum of wages did not equal the sum of prices. The profits of employers and landlords therefore represented a part of the product of industry that could not be sold to domestic workers; hence the need of foreign markets for such surplus goods. Similarly, it was undesirable to receive foreign goods of a value equal to that of manufactured goods exported; such imports would have curtailed the English market for English goods, a market that was inadequate to begin with. Hence the government assisted the merchant-employers to enlarge their outside markets by chartering companies which enabled the merchants to act in unison abroad.[17]

For similar reasons England fostered the development of an English-owned merchant marine. If goods were imported in vessels owned by foreigners, England had to pay the freight charges. But if English merchants carried their wares abroad in their own vessels, the foreigner had to purchase English labor and the use of English capital. Foreign owned shipping was thus regarded as an import, English-owned shipping as an export. Moreover, if merchandise were carried away from England by foreigners in their own ships they would make the profits of selling abroad, but if English vessels were employed they would generally go out laden with goods belonging to English merchants, who would thus reap the profit of selling directly to foreigners. One leading mercantilist wrote: "If the Italian merchants should come hither in their own vessels to fetch our corn, . . . in this case the kingdom should have but ordinarily 25s. for a quarter of wheat . . . , whereas if we carry these wares ourselves into Italy . . . , it is likely we shall obtain 50 shillings . . . , which is a great difference in the . . . vent of the kingdom's stock." As early as 1485 Parliament passed a navigation act requiring that certain articles in

[17] A leading French economic historian, Henri Sée, presents mature conclusions in his *Modern Capitalism* (New York, 1928). See chapters 2–5.

English trade should be carried only in English ships. The acquisition of a strong merchant marine also contributed toward the ideal of national independence in that age of small navies when commerce was the nursery of seamen—when England in time of war had to enlarge her fighting forces by pressing merchantmen into the naval service.[18]

A favorable balance of trade and the resulting influx of money were supposed to serve the nation well. As the sinews of war—*nervi bellorum*—money gave assurance of national security, particularly after the armed knights of feudal days had given way to the hired armies of modern times. Money was regarded as the motive power of industry and trade. Since paper currency and bank checks had not yet come into vogue, gold and silver coin had to serve as the common medium of exchange. It was the only convenient form of wealth that could be hoarded without deterioration. To the early capitalists it was peculiarly desirable because they periodically acquired surplus profits which they desired to convert into a form of non-perishable wealth that would be inexpensive to keep. Coined money was also in universal demand; hence the possessor of it could dispose of it at any time, either through loans at interest or through commercial purchases in any quarter of the world where an unusual opportunity for profits occurred. Neither of these benefits could be obtained if the capitalist had to keep his surplus wealth in perishable commodities for which there was not a continuous and general demand. Most important of all, money was indispensable to the new capitalistic mode of production. The hired artisans of the domestic system did not own the products upon which they worked. As specialists in industry they could not conveniently receive their wages in the finished product because they had neither the time nor the facilities for exchanging it for other things they needed. Hence the necessity of some measure of value that would express their share in the finished product; and coined money—or credit instruments based upon it—performed this function better than any other medium of exchange.[19]

Despite England's commercial advantages, there were, prior to 1600, many weak spots in her economy. First of all she did not possess either gold or silver mines, and thus was forced to rely upon trade as her source of specie. But certain branches of her commerce did not conform to the mercantilist creed. From the Baltic coun-

[18] Thomas Mun, *England's Treasure by Forraign Trade* (1664, reprinted Oxford, 1928), is a classic statement of mercantilism.
[19] Jacob Viner, *Studies in the Theory of International Trade* (New York, 1937), an erudite work by a leading authority, discusses the trade theories of mercantilism in chapters 1 and 2.

tries—Sweden, Russia, Poland, and Germany—she obtained naval stores and potash for her cloth industry; from southern Europe she purchased wine, silk, salt, sugar, and dried fruits; from Holland she imported fish; and oriental goods came through Portugal. Each of these trades had certain drawbacks. Each might be cut off unexpectedly by piracy or war, thus depriving the nation of essentials like naval stores, potash, and fish. Again, the commodities were subject to foreign duties and regulations manipulated in the interest of foreign princes or alien merchants at the expense of their English customers. It was also commonly believed that in these particular trades the balance of payments was against England, thereby inducing an outward flow of specie badly needed at home.[20]

In other words England's commerce did not provide sufficient markets in which the products of her own industry could profitably be exchanged for desired imports. Between 1530 and 1635 there was acute unemployment; the nascent industries of the country could not absorb all the workers who had been thrown off the land by the enclosure movement. The oversupply of labor was indicated by a heated contest between the older towns dominated by the gilds and the newly emerging towns patronized by the merchant-employers—a contest for manufacturing supremacy or control of markets not large enough to support all workers. In a futile effort to check the new trend in industry Parliament in 1557 prohibited the manufacture of cloth except in the older, gild-ridden towns. Severe social unrest had flared up in three major revolts between 1536 and 1552 and had threatened the existence of the monarchy itself. Most informed men thought England to be seriously overpopulated; in places a third of the people lived on poor relief. Vagabonds roved throughout the countryside—bands of "idle persons, which having no means of labor to relieve their misery, do likewise swarm in lewd and naughty practices, . . . pestering the land with pestilence and penury, and infecting one another with vice and villainy worse than the plague itself."[21]

## Economic Motives of Colonization

Such vagabonds and dissolute persons were regarded as the scum of English society. Above them in the social scale were servants, wage-earners, artisans, tenants, and farm hands. The latter suffered par-

---

[20] Gustav Schmoller, *The Mercantile System* (New York, 1931), an older brief introduction (1884), stresses the role of the state in mercantilism.

[21] E. Lipson, "England in the Age of Mercantilism," *Journal of Economic and Business History*, IV (Aug. 1932).

ticularly as a result of new economic trends, since the government had passed laws forbidding the farm worker to leave his parish in search of work and making it impossible for his sons to train themselves for the skilled trades. The new class of merchant-employers was separated from the wage-earners as by a gulf. Socially superior to the capitalists were the larger landowners—the gentry or squires; below them stood the yeomen who owned small farms. The landowners had stood to gain by the increased prices of agricultural produce but this boon was offset by the heavy burden of poor relief carried by each locality through taxes on the land. So crushing was this burden that the gentry found themselves sinking in the social scale, menaced by the rising capitalists who sought prestige by buying estates and living in a style of grandeur which the gentry could not afford. Despising the *nouveaux riches* as upstarts, many of the gentry thought that England was "going to the dogs." [22]

The crest of English society was graced by the aristocracy and nobility—owners of vast estates who were profiting by the enclosure movement—particularly the new magnates to whom Henry VIII gave the lands he confiscated from the monasteries. Politically the landed aristocracy was the most powerful group within the state. Comprising as it did the House of Lords, it was the bulwark of the Established Church and the Protestant monarchy—all three having profited by the seizure of the lands of the Roman Catholic Church.

To each of these classes colonies in the New World made an appeal. The paupers, vagabonds, and criminals, it was assumed, might find freedom, escape disgrace, and get a new start in life. Unemployed artisans and farm hands might secure work with a prospect of independence in the near future. The small landowners who sold out in England could secure larger estates in America and at the same time cast off the crushing burden of English taxes. Traders of small capital who were hard pressed in competition with the merchant princes and monopolistic corporations might earn larger profits in trades not yet preëmpted. The merchants as a class desired wider markets for their goods, and the gentry, as well-to-do emigrants, might keep from being overshadowed in society by their onetime inferiors. Many of the aristocracy in turn saw in colonies a chance of investing surplus funds at handsome profits.[23]

[22] A classic of major importance is William Cunningham's *Growth of English Industry and Commerce* (3 vols., Cambridge, 1921–27). Volume II, Part I, on mercantilism is especially recommended.

[23] A work of exceptional excellence is G. N. Clark's *The Seventeenth Century* (Oxford, 1929). See chapters 1–4, 10, 12.

One important group in England occupied a peculiar position. Contrary to the practice of European nobility, by which each son received a title and lands, English law provided that titles and estates should pass only to the eldest sons. This rule of primogeniture thus created a class of landless younger sons, bred with all advantages of social position and culture, men who shared the tastes of the aristocracy, yet educated with the idea that they must shift for themselves. If they desired to live as aristocrats—and they generally did—they had to achieve success in some field of endeavor. Thus while the eldest son remained upon the ancestral estate to raise a large family, the younger sons went afield—into the law or the Church, the army or navy, into business, colonization, and even piracy. The English aristocracy did not remain aloof from the work of the world; it not only preserved the principle of aristocracy in the eldest son but also created a class of ambitious, energetic leaders who carried the traditions of the English gentleman into other walks of life and into all corners of the world.[24]

These various motives for migration and colonization were intensified by a severe economic depression which swept over England between 1620 and 1635. Having its origin in the closing of England's markets on the Continent during the Thirty Years' War, it reached its height in 1629, paralyzing particularly the southeastern and central parts of England, chief seats of the cloth industry. "Overflowing multitudes" could not find work; even the best artisans could not earn more than a bare living; hard-pressed traders resorted to trickery and fraud, exposing the more honorable to unfair competition; and riots moved an observer to write that "it is not certain where this disturbance will end, but things certainly can not go on thus." Bad crops between 1629 and 1633 added to the distress. Food prices soared, causing merchants to refuse to export grain in fear of the people's wrath and forcing the government to prohibit the exportation of beer. Coinciding with the troubles of the Puritans, this protracted depression reinforced their purpose of emigration to America.

All the striving states of Europe embraced the ideas of mercantilism; consequently England could not find relief from her difficulties by compelling foreigners to trade with her on her own terms. Colonies, however, offered a better prospect of adjustment. The second promoter of English colonies, Sir Walter Raleigh, was preëminently a gold hunter who hoped that England might imitate Spain's success

---

[24] Volume I of *The Cambridge History of the British Empire* is the work of leading English and American scholars. It is excellent for imperial themes, but does not stress American conditions. See Vol. I, pp. 22–70, 93–135.

in exploiting American mines. The search for gold largely inspired
the settlement of Virginia: an early English play referred to the
colony as a place "where gold and silver is more plentiful than copper is with us." Colonies, moreover, would assist England in finding
and holding a new route to the Orient—first as exploring bases, later
as ports of call. As American resources became better known after
1600 these early interests abated, and colonies thereafter promised to
supply England with products she had formerly bought from foreigners—fish, naval stores, tobacco, iron, potash, lumber, furs, wines,
dyes, sugar, fruits, and silk.[25]

Such commodities would be produced by England's unemployed
turned colonists and paid for with English manufactures. "Now if
her Majesty take these western discoveries in hand, and plant there,"
wrote Richard Hakluyt in 1584, "it is likely that in short time we
shall vent as great a mass of cloth in those parts as ever we did in the
Netherlands, and in time much more." The colonial demand for
English wares would in turn employ the poor at home "who live
here idly to the annoy of the whole state," and taxes for poor relief
would be correspondingly reduced. England would no longer have
to buy her imports from foreigners who refused to take her own exports in payment. As dependencies of the king, colonies, moreover,
might be regulated to England's advantage. Their trade would not
be burdened by duties imposed by a hostile government or cut off at
the edict of a foreign prince in time of war, thereby endangering the
supply of needed commodities like naval stores. The long voyages
to America would employ a fine fleet of English vessels, and the
freights, insurance premiums, and profits would flow into the pockets
of the English merchant-shipowners. Every increase of trade would
swell the custom duties collected for the king. If the colonies produced commodities in excess of England's needs, the surplus could be
reëxported to Europe—another source of profit to the English merchants. In other words, the trade of colonies might be regulated so
that the balance of payments would favor England. Reduced purchases from foreigners would check the outflow of specie, while the
exports to the colonies would induce a returning stream of money and
commodities which would make England the financial center of the
world.[26]

[25] William Cunningham's *An Essay on Western Civilization in Its Economic Aspects*
(2 vols., Cambridge, 1923) presents the broad views of a great scholar. See chapter 2.
A briefer essay, equally stimulating, is Cunningham's *The Rise of Capitalism in England* (Cambridge, 1925).

[26] Sir Charles P. Lucas gives an excellent brief summary of commercial evolution in
his *Beginnings of English Overseas Enterprise* (Oxford, 1917).

## England and the Oriental Trade

Commerce between Europe and the newly opened areas of Asia, Africa, and America harmonized perfectly with the principle of mercantilism which stressed the profits of the merchant class. The products of those continents brought high prices in Europe, and because the native peoples did not have the same economic values as the Europeans they were willing to give liberally of their spices, precious stones, gold, ivory, furs, etc., in exchange for low-priced European wares. Hence the European trader could buy such foreign articles cheap and sell them dear, thereby operating on a wide margin of profit. For this reason the exploitation of new areas was woven into the central pattern of mercantilism.[27]

The first outpost in England of western seafaring was the port of Bristol, whence a trade with the Madeiras and the Azores had been developed late in the fifteenth century. Residing there in 1496 was John Cabot, a naturalized Venetian, Genoese by birth, who believed that Columbus had not discovered the wealthy parts of Asia, which presumably extended far enough toward the east to be reached by crossing the Atlantic. A patent was issued in March to Cabot by Henry VII, authorizing him to search in the east, west, or north for lands as yet unknown to Europeans. Cabot was to enjoy a monopoly of newly opened trade and the king was to receive a fifth of the profits of the voyage. Sailing in March 1497, the explorer gained the coast of America at Nova Scotia, Newfoundland, or Labrador, and returned to Bristol in August, convinced that he had visited Asia. During the following winter merchants of London and Bristol were busy fitting out a fleet of four or five vessels for a second voyage, with the object of erecting a trading post in the Orient. Should England divert the Far Eastern trade to her shores, Bristol would become a great commercial center. What happened to Cabot's second expedition is unknown, save that it failed. England at the time was too poor a state to spend freely upon exploration: Henry VII gave Cabot only £10 for the discovery which initiated England's claim to North America.[28] Yet Englishmen did not relinquish the hope of finding a trade route for themselves. The councillors of Henry VIII urged in 1511:

[27] On the English background, 1485–1558, no work excels James A. Williamson's *Maritime Enterprise* (Oxford, 1913). By the same author: *A Short History of British Expansion* (London, 1930).

[28] For the general reader the best introduction is C. R. Beazley's *John and Sebastian Cabot* (London, 1908). Henry Harrisse's *John and Sebastian Cabot* (London, 1896) is detailed and technical. A careful, precise study is J. A. Williamson, *Voyages of the Cabots* . . . (London, 1929).

". . . when we would enlarge ourselves, let it be that way we can, and to which . . . the eternal Providence has destined us, which is by the sea. The Indies are discovered and vast treasures brought from thence every day. Let us therefore bend our endeavors thitherward; and if the Spaniards and Portuguese suffer us not to join them, there will be yet region enough for all to enjoy."

Not until 1553, however, did England resume the search for a new route in earnest, when a joint-stock company with a capital of £6,000 was organized to open a passage around northern Europe. Three vessels then sailed forth under the command of Sir Hugh Willoughby and Richard Chancellor. Willoughby perished during the following winter, but Chancellor entered the White Sea and proceeded to Moscow, where he met the Russian czar, Ivan the Terrible, whose lands were then closed to European traders except the members of the Hanseatic League. When Chancellor returned to England he brought an agreement with the czar which opened Russia to English trade, via the White Sea, and thus furnished the impetus for the organization of the Russia or Muscovy Company on a permanent basis (1555). Although an active trade resulted, the voyage of Chancellor and Willoughby—together with the expedition of Anthony Jenkinson from Moscow down the Volga and across the Caspian Sea into the heart of Asia (1558–60)—convinced the English that a passage through the icebound Northeast was a frigid illusion.[29]

England's adventures into the frozen North had occurred during the reign of Queen Mary, a most pious Catholic and ally of Spain, who respected the claims of Portugal and Spain (derived in part from the papacy) to the routes which they had opened. After Elizabeth's quarrel with the pope, however, such inhibitions were speedily dispelled, and England no longer hesitated to encroach upon the preserves of her Catholic rivals. In the meantime English fishermen had kept the scene of John Cabot's discovery in view, as they visited the Banks of Newfoundland and returned with codfish to western England. The fishermen of France, Portugal, and Spain were similarly engaged, and many a lively contest among them and the English accompanied the quarrels of their respective states.

When the animosity between England and Spain was deepening, a faithful courtier and friend of the Virgin Queen, Sir Humphrey Gilbert, published in 1576 his *Discourse of a Discovery of a New Passage to Cataia*. Sir Humphrey argued that America was an island,

[29] This theme is treated attractively in Sir William Foster's *England's Quest of Eastern Trade* (London, 1933).

around whose northern coasts a water passage might be found which would lead to the Pacific Ocean and the populous parts of Asia.[30] First to act upon this idea was one of England's most intrepid seamen, Martin Frobisher. On his first voyage in 1576 he explored Frobisher's Bay, discovered Baffin's Land, encountered the Esquimaux, and brought home some ore which assayers pronounced rich in gold. This news, along with Frobisher's belief that he had found an open course to India, gave good cause for the second expedition of 1577, in which the queen invested £500. Great was the expectation of gold, now the principle lure. "Considering the greedy desire our country hath to a present savor and return of gain," Frobisher "bent his whole endeavor only to find a mine, to freight his ships, and to leave the rest (by God's help) hereafter to be well accomplished." Not until his third expedition of 1578 had brought back eight hundred tons of ore which proved to be worthless did the golden bubble burst and the original interest in the Northwest passage resume its sway.[31]

The first project of an English colony in America had its origin in the determination of Sir Humphrey Gilbert to realize his dream of a Northwest passage. A settlement at Newfoundland would not only strengthen the English fishery there and provide Sir Humphrey with a vast personal estate; it would also afford a station on the anticipated route to India. Accordingly, he obtained in 1578 a patent from Queen Elizabeth and made two preparatory voyages to America in 1578 and 1583, but without advancing the discovery of the desired route. And yet the belief in the Northwest passage would not die. Between 1585 and 1587 John Davis led three expeditions in the path of Frobisher, penetrating to Davis Straits and Baffin's Bay in the fruitless endeavor to find a track through the intricate network of seas, inlets, and bays. So also the pioneers of the Virginia Colony (1607–10) continued the search, hoping that the rivers emptying into Chesapeake Bay would disclose a continuous passage to the great South Sea.

The recession of English interest in a new route after 1610 followed a memorable event—the launching of the East India Company during the Anglo-Spanish war. Spain had annexed Portugal in 1581, thereby taking charge of the Portuguese monopoly of the oriental

[30] Nellis M. Crouse, *In Quest of the Western Ocean* (New York, 1928), scholarly and well written, discusses the search for a North American passage to the Orient. See chapters 1–4. See also George B. Manhart, *The Search for a Northwest Passage in the Time of Queen Elizabeth* (Philadelphia, 1924).

[31] William McFee's *The Life of Sir Martin Frobisher* (New York, 1928) is the work of a skilled writer who knows the sea.

trade. No longer were the English constrained to respect the claims of Portugal, and the India Company hustled to usurp as much of the established traffic as England's power would allow.

## THE ANGLO-SPANISH CONFLICT IN AMERICA

England and Spain adopted conflicting theories of the title to unappropriated lands in the New World. The Spaniards affirmed that prior discovery established the full right of possession, while the English insisted that occupation or utilization was the final test of ownership. Having taken little part in the feats of discovery, England did not propose to be excluded forever from idle lands merely because a Spanish explorer had happened first to sail along their coasts. Similarly the English, after their break with Rome, denied that the pope had authority to grant lands on the basis of discovery alone. The Spaniards, on the other hand, desiring to monopolize the commerce of their colonies, not only excluded English merchants from them on pain of death, but also withheld from England the right to make near-by settlements which might serve as bases for illegal trade.[32]

As the military power of Spain threatened to deprive Elizabeth of her throne, to overthrow the newly established national church, and to impose upon England the rule of pope and Spaniard, the loyal subjects of the queen readily struck at the principal source of that power, the wealth which Spain derived from her colonies. Hatred of Spain thus became a ruling passion among English seamen—that "nation of ravenous strangers which more greedily thirst after the English blood than after the lives of any other people of Europe." The Spaniards in turn perceived that England's strength lay in her foreign trade, and, when war came, did all in their power to ruin it. "The Spaniard," wrote an Englishman in 1588, "knowing the welfare of our country to depend upon the vent of our native commodities, not only forbade the use and bringing [of them] into any part of his dominions, but also then practised with the emperor and his Hanse towns and no less with the Easterly countries to the like effect," seeking to force the English merchant "to surcease his trade" and thereby to reduce a "great number of . . . unemployed to hard extremities."[33]

Through their trade with the Canaries and the Madeiras the sea-

---

[32] William Wood, *Elizabethan Sea-Dogs* (*Chronicles of America*, New Haven, 1918).

[33] An attractive, readable survey is Arthur P. Innes, *The Maritime and Colonial Expansion of England* (London, 1931).

men of western England became familiar with the traffic of the Atlantic which linked Spain and Portugal with Africa and America. Thus in the 1530's William Hawkins visited and traded with Brazil by way of Guinea. Shortly afterward, the English began to prey upon Spanish vessels engaged in American commerce, since Spain did not then protect them with naval convoys, and international law did not restrain the subjects of two nations at peace from acts of violence in distant waters. Such piracy became more pronounced after 1560 and provided the setting for the exploits of the first notorious English sea dog, Sir John Hawkins (son of William Hawkins), who as a boy had voyaged along the African coast in slave-trading vessels. The Spanish assiento then in force limited the number of slaves imported into the Spanish colonies and by raising the prices charged to the settlers offered ideal conditions for smuggling. The younger Hawkins rationalized slavery as a means of Christianizing the natives and justified smuggling as a means of enriching England and impoverishing Spain; his Protestant piety was equaled only by his intense hatred of the Spaniard. Accordingly, in 1562 he went to Sierra Leone in Africa whence he took three hundred Negroes to Haiti and returned to England with ginger, sugar, and pearls, which netted a profit of 60 per cent. He repeated the feat in 1564–65 but on his third voyage of 1567–68 he fell in with a Spanish fleet sent out by Philip II to stop his depredations. Hawkins allowed the Spaniards to enter the port of Vera Cruz, which he then commanded, but their pledges of friendship served merely as a cloak for a surprise attack which cost the lives of scores of Englishmen and sent Hawkins and two of his vessels scurrying away in a narrow escape.[34]

One fellow adventurer with Hawkins was his kinsman, Francis Drake. After the "treachery" of the Spaniards at Vera Cruz, Drake was animated by a consuming hatred of his "perfidious" foes. He now devised a scheme more profitable than smuggling slaves; he would plunder Spanish towns and treasure ships in the Caribbean. To this end he spent over a year (1572–73) in the vicinity of the West Indies and Panama, but found the Spaniards there too well protected to be an easy prey. His imagination then conceived one of the boldest adventures in history. He knew that the Pacific Ocean was a Spanish lake to which no foreigner had penetrated since Magellan's heroic voyage, and that the Spanish settlements and treasure vessels there were quite defenseless. Intent upon reaping "some of the Spaniards' harvest which they got out of the earth and sent to Spain to trouble all the earth," Drake in December 1577 sailed from England with the

[34] J. A. Williamson's *Sir John Hawkins* (Oxford, 1927) is especially recommended.

connivance of the queen and a faction among her statesmen who favored war with Spain, and with the backing of a joint-stock company in which she was a secret investor.

The consummate seamanship of Drake effected a safe passage of the Strait of Magellan in August 1578. As he proceeded northward along the western coast of America he looted unprotected ports and treasure vessels, almost at will, until his ship was ballasted with silver. Fearing to return as he had come lest the Spaniards waylay him, he sailed along the western coast of North America in search of a Northwest passage that would carry him eastward to the Atlantic, but, discouraged by the arctic conditions he encountered, he crossed the Pacific and took the route of the Spice Islands and the Cape of Good Hope to England, arriving in September 1580. The treasure he brought home amounted to £600,000, which netted £263,000 to the queen and profits of 4,600 per cent to his other sponsors.[35]

The Spanish ambassador forthwith demanded that Elizabeth censure Drake and return the plunder to Spain. The wily queen, however, intimated that the Spaniards had brought their troubles on themselves by attempting to exclude her subjects from America, and went aboard Drake's vessel, the *Golden Hind,* at Deptford and knighted him—"the most important knighthood ever conferred by an English sovereign, for it was a direct challenge to Spain and an appeal to the people of England to look to the sea for their strength." [36]

In view of Spain's priority of colonial power and her pretensions to dominion over America, England could realize her dreams of empire only through her prowess on the sea. The Spaniards, who were enchanted with the vision of ruling Europe, regarded their colonies as tributary to that end. They conceived themselves primarily as a military people, destined for glory and conquest through the deeds of their soldiers, whom they exalted above ordinary men. As the most progressive military leaders of the time, they applied their ideas of land combat to warfare at sea. A naval encounter should be a contest of armies on floating battlefields. Thus they filled transports with soldiers drawn up in proud array and sought to destroy the enemy by ramming his vessels, boarding them, and dispatching his soldiers in hand-to-hand fighting. To the Spaniards a sailor was but a menial servant of the soldier. For convoys to their transports they depended

[35] A careful, intensive study is Henry R. Wagner, *Sir Francis Drake's Voyage Around the World* (San Francisco, 1926).

[36] Edward F. Benson, *Sir Francis Drake* (New York, 1927), is a briefer, more popular account, as also is John D. Upcott, *Sir Francis Drake and the Beginnings of English Sea Power* (London, 1927).

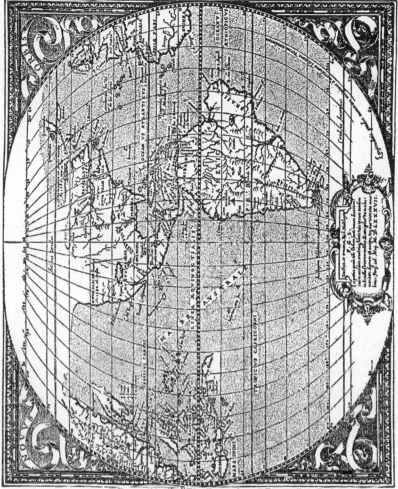

From Abbott's "The Expansion of Europe." © F. S. Crofts & Co.

## THE NEW WORLD IN 1587

This map, dedicated to Richard Hakluyt, represents the English knowledge of the American continents and of the Atlantic and Pacific oceans after Drake's voyage. It will be noted that there is no hint of the existence of Australia.

upon oar-driven galleys manned mostly by slaves. Such warships were
not suited for the long voyages to America because of the strain
placed upon the oarsmen and because the reliance upon man power
for navigation necessitated the carrying of larger supplies than could
be conveniently managed. Above all, a galley could fire only straight
ahead—not broadside—and thus could not fight in line formation and
attack the enemy from the side or rear.[37]

The art of warfare developed in another direction in England.
After she relinquished her ambitions of military conquests in Europe,
England had little need of a strong army, since her shores could be
invaded only by sea, and consequently the soldier was less esteemed
than the sailor. As an old song put it—

> We care not for your martial men
> That do the state disdain.
> But we care for your sailor lads
> That do the state maintain.

During the reign of Henry VIII the basis of English sea power was
laid when the sailing vessel was adapted to open fighting. The English "wasps" learned how to fire broadside and were thus able to dart
in and out around their enemies, inflicting telling blows and keeping
out of the range of floating armies that sought to board them. Moreover, the sailing warship could make the long voyages to the New
World with comparative ease, since wind and sails, unlike the galley
oarsmen, did not have to be fed en route. The official English
navy contained only a score of vessels, but overnight it could be
augmented by hundreds of private vessels manned by the hardiest,
boldest, most accomplished seamen of the age. The day had dawned
when England honored such men:

> As full of peril and adventurous spirit,
> As to o'erwalk a torrent roaring loud,
> On the unsteadfast footing of a spear,

—when Drake decreed that gentlemen at sea should "hale and draw
with the mariner" and when Raleigh proclaimed that he "who rules
the sea, rules the commerce of the world and to him that rules the
commerce of the world belongs the treasure of the world and indeed
the world itself."

In 1588 the destruction of Spain's "Invincible Armada," bound to
the Netherlands preparatory to an invasion of England, attested the

---

[37] Julian S. Corbett, *Drake and the Tudor Navy* (2 vols., London, 1898)—a vigorous, interesting narrative (important).

superiority of the new naval tactics adopted by the island state. From that day England's mastery of the seas was never long in doubt. With it came her golden opportunity in the West: across the Atlantic the rich prize of colonies beckoned to her, and Spain was no longer able to delay her advance.[38]

[38] Sir John R. Seeley's *The Expansion of England* (London, 1883) was a pioneer work in stimulating the study of English imperialism.

## BIBLIOGRAPHICAL NOTE

WORKS PREVIOUSLY CITED: W. C. Abbott, *Expansion of Europe*, I, ch. 6; G. Bancroft, *History of the United States*, I, ch. 3; *The Cambridge Modern History*, I, ch. 15 (economic change); III, ch. 9; E. Channing, *History of the United States*, I, pp. 115–142; E. P. Cheyney, *European Background of American History*, chs. 7–8; C. Day, *History of Commerce*, chs. 15–18; C. J. H. Hayes, *Political and Cultural History of Europe*, I, ch. 9; H. Heaton, *Economic History of Europe*, chs. 14–16; *Pageant of America*, I, ch. 8; A. F. Pollard, *Factors in Modern History*, chs. 2, 4; P. Smith, *Age of the Reformation*, chs. 10–11; J. Winsor (ed.), *Narrative and Critical History of America*, III, chs. 1–3; G. M. Wrong, *Rise and Fall of New France*, II, chs. 3, 5.

SOURCES NEWLY CITED: On English economy the best collection is R. H. Tawney and Eileen Power (eds.), *Tudor Economic Documents* (3 vols., London, 1924). A smaller collection, A. E. Bland, P. A. Brown, and R. H. Tawney (eds.), *English Economic History, Select Documents* (London, 1914), devotes Parts I–II to the period before 1650. The Everyman's Library edition of Hakluyt's *The Principal Navigations, Voyages, Traffiques and Discoveries of the English Nation* (8 vols., London, n. d.) is readily accessible. A more convenient selection from Hakluyt is E. J. Payne and C. R. Beazley (eds.), *Voyages of Elizabethan Seamen* (Oxford, 1907).

SOURCES PREVIOUSLY CITED: H. S. Burrage (ed.), *Early English and French Voyages*, pp. 111–419; J. E. Olson and E. G. Bourne (eds.), *The Northmen, Columbus and Cabot*, pp. 421–430 (Cabot); H. S. Commager (ed.), *Documents of American History*, I, nos. 4 5; A. B. Hart (ed.), *American History Told by Contemporaries*, I, pp. 69–101, 145–162; *Old South Leaflets*, nos. 37, 115–117, 124 (English Explorers).

MAPS: W. R. Shepherd, *Historical Atlas*, p. 185.

## THE ENGLISH PROMOTERS OF COLONIES

As IN the other states of Europe, so in England the course of internal political development determined the nature of colonization. The English government did not itself perform the task of planting colonies abroad but rather left it to private initiative. Prior to the reign of Henry VII (1485–1509) the monarchy had been weakened by the destructive War of the Roses, so that the work of restoring the royal authority and of pacifying the country occupied the first Tudor sovereign. Then followed the English Reformation and the protracted religious strife, absorbing the energies of Henry VIII (1509–47), Edward VI (1547–53), Mary Tudor (1553–58), and Elizabeth. More important, perhaps, as a deterrent to the participation of the government in colonization was the financial status of the monarchy. The English sovereigns did not attain absolute power of taxation but were obliged to act with the consent of Parliament, and the funds voted by it barely met the most pressing needs of domestic pacification and defense. Henry VII, who favored English expansion overseas, spent less than £300 on exploration during his whole reign.

When England's economic progress, sea power, and domestic tranquillity warranted expansion, the government fell under the control of the Scottish kings, James I and Charles I. Their reigns proved to be a time of rising prices when they could barely make the royal ends meet, and consequently they were forever seeking new sources of revenue. The intense struggle over taxes between king and Parliament after 1603 indicates that the English king was not free to spend money upon every project which caught his fancy. The checks which Parliament placed upon the royal income therefore necessitated that private persons supply the funds if exploration and colonization were to be carried forward in the New World.[1]

Such individuals, however, would not embark upon an untried

---

[1] Every student should become familiar with the extremely important work of Charles M. Andrews, *The Colonial Period of American History* (3 vols., New Haven, 1934–37), which affords the best account of promotional activities of English colonizers. See particularly Vol. I, chapters 1–4, 13, 15–18, Vol. II, chapters 6, 8, and Vol. III, chapters 4–5, 7.

venture without the backing of the government. The theory of English exploration was that the title to newly discovered land and political jurisdiction over it were vested in the sovereign. Thus the promoters of colonies had to seek a royal grant of land and the right of governing it in a manner conducive to their own profit. They also needed commercial privileges in or monopolies of the trade of the region upon which they spent their money. Moreover, they desired exemption from certain laws—those, for instance, which forbade an Englishman to leave the country or prohibited the exportation of various commodities required in a new colony. Such rights and privileges were conferred by the sovereign in a royal patent or charter. The preferred method was to obtain letters of patent under the Great Seal, in which case the Secretary of State directed the Attorney-General to prepare the document in coöperation with the agent of the promoters, whereupon it was engrossed upon the patent roll. Inasmuch as this was a costly business, involving much red tape and fees or bribes to officials and clerks, the men who obtained charters had to possess wealth, social position, and influence at court. By means of such grants a marriage was effected between private enterprise and government patronage.

### PIONEERS OF ENGLISH COLONIZATION

The Englishmen of the age of Elizabeth lived in spacious days when the national spirit of daring and adventure attained its greatest heights. Intense patriotism, self-confidence, and faith in their destiny inspired their leaders to unprecedented achievements. The vitality and originality of Elizabethan England found their fullest expression in Shakespeare, whose uniquely imaginative mind encompassed the world of his own day and ranged the epic heights of past times. From the vantage of

> This sceptered isle
> This earth of majesty, this seat of Mars,
> This other Eden, demi-paradise,

he and his contemporaries viewed the panorama of life. They perceived, as if suddenly revealed, the splendors of the earth—its strange peoples, remote kingdoms, and infinitely varied resources—and strove to conquer for honor, wealth, and fame.[2]

The peculiar English trait of blended insularity and cosmopolitan-

[2] Walter Raleigh's *The English Voyages of the Sixteenth Century* (Glasgow, 1906) is a brief discussion from the literary point of view.

ism characterized the work of a humble clergyman, Richard Hakluyt of Oxford. Like so many other Elizabethans, Hakluyt would make the whole world tributary to England. When nearly every breeze brought home a vessel with tales of new lands and wonders beyond sea, Hakluyt conceived the idea of systematically publishing this record, and in 1582 printed his first work, *Divers Voyages Touching the Discovery of America*. As the English "press-agent of adventure," he continued to issue the narratives of "the principal voyages of the English nation," which disclosed the tremendous sweep of English enterprise and familiarized his countrymen with every quarter of the globe. The poet Drummond celebrates his labors in verse:

> Thy voyages attend
> Industrious Hakluyt,
>     Whose reading shall inflame
>     Men to seek fame,
> And much commend
> To aftertimes thy wit.

Hakluyt also wrote a discourse in favor of planting colonies in North America, stressing their value as markets, as producers of commodities needed by England, as a boon to English navigation, and as sources of private profit. Above all, they might serve as bases for plundering the Spaniards in America, on the theory that as the "Spanish empire falls to the ground," the Spanish king "shall be left as bare as Aesop's proud crow," for "if you touch him in the Indies, you touch the apple of his eye." [3]

Closely associated with Hakluyt was a group of Devonshire men, whose leader, Sir Humphrey Gilbert, is rightly called the father of English colonization. In 1578 Queen Elizabeth issued a patent to Gilbert, conferring upon him the exclusive right "to inhabit and possess at his choice all remote and heathen lands not in the actual possession of any Christian prince." Thus equipped Sir Humphrey sailed in September 1578, for America, but was carried out of his course by a gale to the West Indies, where an unhappy encounter with the Spaniards forced him to return. Again, in June 1583, he ventured forth, to Newfoundland, with five vessels and two hundred and fifty men. After taking possession of the island in the name of the queen, he left a small band of servants on its bleak shore and set forth to discover a better site. The dismal setting dismayed the colonists, who

---

[3] George B. Parks, *Richard Hakluyt and the English Voyages* (New York, 1928) is excellent. E. G. R. Taylor has a splendid introductory sketch in his edition of *The Writings and Correspondence of the Two Richard Hakluyts* (printed for the Hakluyt Society, 2 vols., London, 1935).

soon dispersed to parts unknown.[4] Gilbert himself was lost at sea, in September 1583.

> He sat upon the deck,
> The Book was in his hand;
> "Do not fear! Heaven is as near,"
> He said, "by water as by land."

After the death of Gilbert his rights to America passed to his half-brother, Sir Walter Raleigh, politician, courtier, adventurer, and favorite of the queen. In 1584 Raleigh received a royal patent almost identical with that granted to Gilbert in 1578. Hakluyt's narratives had already awakened in Sir Walter an ardent interest in the New World, and he consequently commissioned the Oxford compiler to prepare his discourse of 1584 on "western planting." Raleigh's love of the sea, which had been kindled when he was a boy by tales of the mariners of southwestern England, was reinforced by his hatred of Spain, his devotion to the queen, and his passion for gold. The Newfoundland misadventure of Gilbert turned Raleigh's gaze toward more hospitable shores—toward the warmer climate and verdant slopes to which the Spaniards had naturally gravitated. Convinced that England was the best of all possible worlds, he believed that an English colony should be a miniature England, duplicating the class distinctions and aristocratic tone of society which, as a landed gentleman, he dearly cherished.[5]

Raleigh sponsored three expeditions to the island of Roanoke, off the coast of present-day North Carolina. The first party, in 1584, explored the country and returned with such favorable reports that Sir Walter rose to new heights in the favor of Queen Elizabeth, who honored Raleigh, herself, and the new land by naming it Virginia. The second venture of 1585–86, under the command of Sir Richard Grenville and Ralph Lane, and which had aspired to plant a colony, taught Raleigh that a settlement composed of gold hunters, sword polishers, and seekers for a Northwest passage, all dependent upon England for supplies, could not survive. His interest in permanent colonization, however, was already attested by the presence in the expedition of a chronicler, Thomas Hariot, and a painter, John White, who prepared sketches of the Indians, animals, and plants of the new

---

[4] A standard, scholarly biography is William G. Gosling's *The Life of Sir Humphrey Gilbert* (London, 1911). For a modern, journalistic account see Donald B. Chidsey, *Sir Humphrey Gilbert* (New York, 1932).

[5] Of the older biographies that of William Stebbing, *Sir Walter Ralegh* (Oxford, 1891), is the best. Hugh de Selincourt's *Great Ralegh* (London, 1908) devotes chapter 6 to Virginia.

country. The failure of his first colony convinced Raleigh that a better site should be selected northward in the Chesapeake Bay, inasmuch as Roanoke Island was exposed to severe storms, although Lane had described it "as the goodliest and most pleasing territory of the world," whose natives were "most courteous and very desirous to have clothes." In his modified plans—indicative of the capacity of the English to adapt themselves readily to new situations which was to assure their later success as colonizers and to transform emigrants from Englishmen into Americans—Raleigh prepared to make the colony self-sustaining, a normal community of families engaged in diversified economic pursuits. Accordingly the third expedition of 1587 brought the first English women and children to America. The colony was to be ruled on the aristocratic principle by a governor and a council of twelve gentlemen and to be held together by the cement of military discipline.[6]

With John White in command, the third expedition arrived at Roanoke in July 1587, where the colonists remained, contrary to Raleigh's wise instructions. White lacked the force of will necessary for the government of a band of people suddenly released from traditional restraints, and made the mistake of returning to England for supplies after only a month's stay in the colony. He found England astir with preparations for warding off the Spanish invasion; Raleigh, the court, and all the great English seamen were preoccupied with that paramount task and the colony could not be reinforced. White did set out with two vessels in 1588 but Spanish pirates at Madeira drove them back to England. It was not until 1591 that he again set foot on Roanoke Island, where he had left as pledges of his return his daughter and his granddaughter, Virginia Dare, the first English child born in America. But the colonists had vanished and no authentic trace of them has ever been found.[7]

## THE FOUNDERS OF VIRGINIA

The early experiences of Raleigh taught him that the expense of planting a colony was too great to be borne by one man. Hence in 1589 he enlisted the aid of a group of London merchants and investors, selling to them the privileges of trading with his projected colony. However, this group was not active until Raleigh in 1603 was

[6] The best modern biography is Milton Waldman's *Sir Walter Raleigh* (New York, 1928).

[7] Recent popular biographies written in a journalistic style for the general reader are Irvin Anthony, *Ralegh and His World* (New York, 1934), and Donald B. Chidsey, *Sir Walter Raleigh* (New York, 1931).

convicted of treason and stripped of his colonizing rights. Then in 1604 England made peace with Spain, but failed to secure from the Spaniards a recognition of England's right to take part in the exploitation of the New World. Many of the ardent anti-Spanish Protestants in England now sought a peaceful means of penetration into the Spanish sphere of influence in America. Accordingly the men to whom Raleigh had granted concessions organized a new colonizing venture and in 1606 obtained a charter from James I.

This charter authorized two groups of English promoters to plant settlements in America. One group was domiciled chiefly in Plymouth, the other in London. Each obtained a grant of 10,000 square miles of land. The Plymouth group received the exclusive right to colonize between the forty-fifth and forty-first parallels; the London group alone could operate between the thirty-eighth and thirty-fourth parallels. The intervening space, between the forty-first and thirty-eighth parallels, was open to occupancy by either group, provided however that the two colonies should be at least a hundred miles apart.[8]

In 1607 the London promoters established at Jamestown what became the first permanent English settlement in the area of the United States. Before 1609, however, this colony accomplished but meager results, due to a variety of causes later to be explained. The promoters in London felt that the colony needed additional resources, and accordingly they obtained a new royal charter in 1609. This enlarged vastly the territory of the colony. Its eastern boundary was to extend two hundred miles north and two hundred miles south of Old Point Comfort. Rather vaguely the grant said that the colony was to extend "west and northwest" to the Pacific Ocean. Moreover, the patent of 1609 incorporated the promoters into a joint-stock company. Fifty-six London companies and 659 persons were listed as charter members. The Virginia Company of London immediately took over the Jamestown colony and developed it until the company's dissolution in 1624.

Men of wealth and power dominated the Virginia Company and colony during this formative stage. There was, for instance, Sir Thomas Smith, perhaps the greatest merchant prince of the day, chief of English expansionists, a veritable embodiment of the commercial motives of colonization. Sir Thomas began his career with a large capital inherited from his grandfather, a founder of the Muscovy Company, and from his father, who had amassed a fortune while serving as collector of the queen's revenue. The younger Smith in turn

[8] E. P. Cheyney, "Some English Conditions surrounding the Settlement of Virginia," *American Historical Review*, XII (Nov. 1907).

was an organizer of the Levant Company in 1581, a principal figure and onetime governor of the Muscovy Company, a founder and first governor of the East India Company, and treasurer and a moving spirit in the Virginia Company. His career thus indicated the growing solidarity of merchant capitalism, anticipating the modern age of inter-locking directorates. Politically he belonged to the anti-Spanish party led by the Earl of Essex, and when Essex was executed in 1601 Sir Thomas was sent to the Tower where he remained a prisoner until the accession of the ally of Essex, James I. The interests of Smith in the Levant and East India Companies focused his attention upon the search for an American passage to the Orient: as a merchant he strove to enlarge the whole domain of English commerce. Thus the motives of personal profit and hatred of Spain found expression in the work of this prominent builder of the Virginia colony.[9]

A much greater figure, socially, than Smith was Robert Rich, sec-ond Earl of Warwick, nephew of the Earl of Essex and head of a powerful clan of relatives and Puritan merchants of London. Forsak-ing the pleasures of the court, Warwick embraced the strenuous life, "for his spirit aimed at the more public adventures, planting colonies in the western world." His early interests centered in privateering dep-redations upon the Spaniards, and perhaps he was mainly interested in Virginia as a base for such attacks. His fleet of vessels resembled a private navy, ever ready to strike at Spain. His speculative ventures also included the Council for New England, the Bermuda Company, the East India Company, and the Guinea Company of 1618. His ship the *Treasurer* carried the first cargo of Negro servants sold in Vir-ginia. The details of Warwick's vast interests were in the hands of his kinsman, Sir Nathaniel Rich, the business agent of the family. After 1619 Warwick and Rich, with Sir Thomas Smith, headed a faction in the Virginia Company which regarded colonization as a form of profitable exploitation. As insiders at court these leaders had benefited by and therefore favored the commercial monopolies granted by the sovereign to various trading companies and their capitalistic promot-ers.

Of somewhat different stamp was a fourth leader of the Virginia Company, Sir Edwin Sandys—"a religious gentleman," son of a Puri-tan Archbishop of Canterbury, high in the social order, educated at Oxford where he had studied under Richard Hooker, author of the famous *Ecclesiastical Polity*. As a young man Sandys had observed at

---

[9] Edward Keble Chatterton's *Seed of Liberty* (Indianapolis, 1929), published also as *English Seamen and the Colonization of America* (London, 1930), is a splendid study of early relations between England and America.

Geneva the Calvinistic institutions of government (somewhat republican in form) and considered them as almost divinely ordained. He became an ardent foe of James I, opposing divine right of kings with the Puritan doctrines of covenant between prince and people and of a fundamental law limiting the powers of government. The vigorous opposition of Sandys to private commercial monopolies was also in keeping with his Puritan faith. From the time he drafted the Virginia charter of 1609 until the end of the Virginia Company, Sandys played a prominent role in its affairs, leading a faction which came to blows with the Smith-Warwick party—a strife which eventually destroyed the company itself.[10]

Sir Edwin Sandys found an ally in a nobleman of vast wealth, the Earl of Southampton, a Catholic born but converted to Protestantism, probably by Sandys. Southampton, as a friend and ally of Essex, had been imprisoned in the Tower. Following his release by James I he had failed to realize his ambition for great political influence, due to his impetuosity and rashness; hence he busied himself with colonizing schemes and with patronizing the drama, particularly the work of Shakespeare. Bitterly hostile to Spain, he regarded the Virginia colony as a weapon of warfare against the ancient enemy. As treasurer of the Virginia Company, 1620-24, he fought the battle with Sandys against Smith and Warwick.

## The Council for New England

Through the fisheries of Newfoundland, certain adventurers and merchants in western England—at Bristol and Plymouth especially—kept in touch with the region of Sir Humphrey Gilbert's ill-fated colony. Three notable voyages were made after 1600 to what is now New England. Expeditions commanded by Bartholomew Gosnold in 1602, by Martin Pring in 1603, and by George Weymouth in 1604 were financed by Bristol merchants or the Earl of Southampton. They disclosed good prospects in New England of a lucrative fishery, a trade in furs with friendly natives, and fine resources of virgin timber. Such favorable accounts appealed particularly to two West country leaders of means and influence.

Sir John Popham, a Somerset lawyer and chief justice of England, believed that England's paupers might profitably be sent to build settlements in northern America. The other leader, Sir Ferdinando Gorges, governor of the port of Plymouth and onetime friend

---

[10] A. P. Newton, *The Colonising Activities of the English Puritans* (New Haven, 1914), emphasizes the interest of Puritans in regions other than New England.

of the Earl of Essex, had heard of Weymouth's voyage to the coast of Maine, which news, he said, "must be acknowledged the means under God of putting on foot and giving life to all our plantations." Gorges and Popham acted as a link connecting the government and interested promoters in western England. Largely through the influence of Popham the charter of 1606 was issued. This authorized a group of Plymouth patentees to colonize in the northern part of "Virginia." In 1607 they sent out an expedition commanded by George Popham, brother of Sir John, and by Raleigh Gilbert, son of Sir Humphrey, who made a settlement at the mouth of the Kennebec River. However, the sufferings of a terrible winter, 1607–08, coinciding with the death of Chief Justice Popham, caused the abandonment of this first attempt to colonize New England.[11]

During the next thirteen years Gorges sent trading and fishing vessels to the coast of Maine, advertised the region, and persuaded other West countrymen to join in the work of exploitation. Captain John Smith, of earlier Virginia fame, voyaged along the northern coast in 1614 and named the country New England. Then he entered the service of the Plymouth promoters, made a trading voyage for them, and in 1616 published his *Description of New England*—a glowing tribute to the region and its fishery. Soon afterward came news that a plague had nearly wiped out the Indians residing along the New England coast between the Penobscot River and Narragansett Bay. This calamity promised to open the northern area to peaceable settlement by the English.

In 1620 the Plymouth promoters reorganized and secured a royal charter which established the Council for New England—a limited body of forty members, representing the nobility rather than the merchants and more in the nature of a land company than a trading corporation. Chief among its leaders were Warwick, Southampton, Rich, and Gorges. The Council received title to all land between the fortieth and the forty-eighth parallels, from sea to sea, together with a monopoly of the trade and fishery of the territory and seas adjacent, as well as the right of selling licenses to traders and fishermen operating in this imperial domain.[12]

So dominant in the Council for New England was Sir Ferdinando Gorges that the Council has been called a "gorgeous affair." Its signifi-

---

[11] An excellent, scholarly history of these events is H. S. Burrage, *The Beginnings of Colonial Maine* (Portland, 1914). See chapters 1–8.

[12] On enterprise before 1628 see Charles K. Bolton, *The Real Founders of New England* (Boston, 1929).

cance lies in the fact that it possessed the title to all New England and that directly or indirectly it created the initial land grants of five colonies—Plymouth, Massachusetts, New Hampshire, Maine, and Connecticut. The original policy of Gorges, to sell licenses to English fishermen who fished in the waters of the company's grant and to use the money for promoting settlement, provoked a bitter contest between the Council and the West country fishermen, who not only objected to the monopoly, but also feared that rival fishing settlements in New England would destroy the industry as carried on from English ports.

Foremost among the associates of Gorges was John Mason, Anglican, ardent royalist, naval officer, adventurer, colonizer, businessman, and friend of the Duke of Buckingham, that shining favorite of Charles I who was eventually assassinated at Mason's house in Portsmouth. Between 1611 and 1621 Mason had been active in exploring and colonizing Newfoundland, where he served as governor after 1615. Upon Mason and Gorges the Council for New England in August 1622 conferred an extensive domain extending sixty miles inland between the Merrimack and the Kennebec Rivers. After making, in 1623, a futile effort to develop and govern its territory, the Council lapsed into inactivity. It was unable to obtain sufficient capital or settlers; between 1624 and 1629 the energies of Gorges were absorbed by wars involving England with France and Spain; and the Council thereafter could not enforce its rights or control the fishermen and settlers who were then pouring into New England. During the early 1630's occurred a heated rivalry between Gorges and the Puritan settlers of Massachusetts over land and fishing rights. Since the Council for New England was unable to cope with the Puritans, Gorges enlisted the aid of Charles I, seeking to substitute his potent authority for that of the moribund Council. In order to facilitate action by the king against the Puritans, the Council in 1635 surrendered its charter and ceased to function.[13]

In 1629 the Mason-Gorges grant of August 1622 was divided. Mason received the land between the Merrimack and the Piscataqua Rivers, which he now called New Hampshire, and Sir Ferdinando retained the area between the Piscataqua and the Kennebec, thereafter called Maine. Mason, who became a member of the Council for New England in 1632, received from it a final confirmation of his title in

[13] James P. Baxter's *Sir Ferdinando Gorges and His Province of Maine* (3 vols., Boston, 1890) is the standard authority. Volume I is a biography; Volumes II and III are documents.

1635, and Gorges obtained in 1639 a royal patent which made him the proprietor and governor of Maine.[14]

## THE PILGRIM FATHERS

While the great men of London, Plymouth, and Bristol were busy with projects of promotion, a little band of humble country folk were meeting at the village of Scrooby in Nottinghamshire to worship in defiance of the Established Church. Their leader, William Brewster, village postmaster and bailiff of Scrooby Manor—an estate belonging to the archbishopric of York—had been educated at Cambridge University, and afterward pursued a lively interest in theology, history, and religious poetry. He was described as "of a very cheerful spirit, very sociable and pleasant among his friends." The pastor of the Scrooby Separatists, John Robinson, was a mild, spiritual man who exemplified the Christian virtues of modesty, charity, and love of truth. A young farmer, William Bradford, devout reader of the Bible and later a student of many languages, shared the tolerant spirit of the group. "It is too great arrogance," he said, "for any man or church to think that he or they have . . . sounded the word of God to the bottom." Bradford later told the trials of the Pilgrims in his *History of Plymouth Plantation*, written in a straightforward, dignified manner that reveals the honesty and sincerity of his nature and his familiarity with the Geneva version of the Bible.[15]

Not long had the Scrooby group been active before they were molested by their neighbors, who regarded them as "freaks." Jeered at and insulted at home, and investigated by the church authorities of the province of York, the Pilgrims felt so exposed to attack that they decided to move to Holland, "where they had heard was freedom for all men." During the years 1607–09 they left in small bands, by stealth, for the law of England forbade a subject to leave the country without the king's consent. Arriving at Amsterdam they found so much religious strife among the Dutch that they moved to Leyden. Here they lived peaceably, working as laborers and "enjoying much sweet and delightful society and spiritual comfort together in the ways of God." But despite such felicity the exiles were not satisfied. They preferred to live under their "natural prince" and

[14] Charles W. Tuttle, *Life of Captain John Mason* (Boston, 1887) includes important documents.

[15] Of the many accounts of the Pilgrims see Ronald G. Usher, *The Pilgrims and Their History* (New York, 1918), Daniel Plooij, *The Pilgrim Fathers from a Dutch Point of View* (New York, 1932), and Arthur Lord, *Plymouth and the Pilgrims* (Boston, 1920).

feared that their children would be assimilated by the Dutch. So hard was their lot that their children had to work at a tender age and "their bodies bowed under the weight of the same, and became decrepit in their early youth." Others of their children were corrupted by the Dutch, "getting the reins from their neck, and departing from their parents. Some became soldiers, others took upon them far voyages by sea, and others some worse courses, tending to dissoluteness and the destruction of their souls." [16]

And thus a part of the Leyden congregation decided to migrate to Virginia. Through the influence of Sir Edwin Sandys they obtained permission to settle on the Virginia Company's lands and to enjoy the status of an independent community. James I promised that they would not be molested if they lived peaceably, although he did not guarantee protection or toleration. But his decision nevertheless opened the way to the settlement of English America by dissenters and is therefore one of the great landmarks in American history. By means of an agreement with London promoters the Pilgrims obtained capital for the emigration, and in 1620 they made the historic voyage from Delft Haven via Southampton and Plymouth, England, to the New England coast, where they began their settlement of Plymouth at Christmas time. Only a minority of the Leyden group voted to leave Holland. Since it had been agreed that the pastor, John Robinson, should serve the majority, he had to remain behind, while Brewster and Bradford led the Pilgrims who came to America in the *Mayflower*.

Landing, apparently by accident of weather, within the territory of the Council for New England rather than within that of the Virginia Company, the Pilgrims were obliged to obtain a land grant from the Council. This was done by the London promoters in 1621, when a patent was issued to John Pierce acting in their behalf. The leaders in Plymouth purchased this title in 1629 30, but never received a royal charter from the king. The little colony retained its separate identity until it was merged with its powerful neighbor, Massachusetts, in 1691. Life at Plymouth flowed along smoothly and uneventfully in the short and simple annals of a rural community. The Pilgrims' sojourn in Holland had left few marks upon their ways of life; only their custom of marriage by a civil magistrate can be traced to the Dutch. [17]

[16] Raymond P. Stearns, "The New England Way in Holland," *New England Quarterly*, VI (Dec. 1933).

[17] C. M. Andrews, *The Fathers of New England* (*Chronicles of America*, New Haven, 1919), chapters 1-3.

## The Genesis of Massachusetts

About the year 1622 a group of businessmen in Dorchester, England, decided to transform the English fishery as carried on in American waters. Previously annual fishing fleets had gone out from England in the late winter, returning at the close of autumn. The Dorchester men proposed to erect a fishing settlement in New England where the fishermen would reside throughout the year, selling their catches to trading vessels from England. This plan was designed to cut the labor cost by eliminating the idleness of the fishermen on the outward and inward voyages. Accordingly the Dorchester men formed a company, secured, perhaps, a land grant from the Council for New England, and in 1623 established a fishing settlement at the present site of Gloucester, Massachusetts. But profits were not forthcoming and in 1626 the Dorchester promoters withdrew. The settlers, under the leadership of one Roger Conant, removed from Gloucester and founded the town of Salem, "the peaceful."

High in the confidence of the businessmen of Dorchester was their pastor, Master John White, a moderate Puritan, philanthropist, organizer of poor relief—a true patriarch who presided over his parish as a father over his family. In close touch with the Dorchester Company, the good pastor believed that its settlement might become a retreat for the worthy poor and a base of missionary work among the Indians.[18] Hence when the company expired he appealed to many influential Puritan gentry and merchants of London, and in 1628 a group of them formed the New England Company to take over the defunct Dorchester concern. The new company obtained through the Earl of Warwick a huge land grant from the Council for New England. This was made while Sir Ferdinando Gorges was away at war, and he soon denounced the grant as improperly obtained and as conflicting with previous grants to his son Robert and to John Mason. The Puritan leaders of the New England Company needed a stronger sanction for their claim, and so they appealed to Charles I, who granted them a royal charter in March 1629, incorporating them into the Massachusetts Bay Company. Their land grant, reaching from three miles north of the Merrimack River to three miles south of the Charles River, and extending from the Atlantic to the Pacific, cut the heart out of the territory of the Council for New England. By what means this unusual encroachment upon the Council's land was effected is unknown.

The Massachusetts Bay Company, like its two immediate predeces-

[18] *John White*, by Frances Rose-Troup (New York, 1930), is a definitive biography.

sors, concerned itself at first with maintaining the Salem settlement as a commercially profitable venture. However, during the year 1629 two parties developed within the company. One, composed of moderate Puritans content to stay in England, preferred to operate the company for profit. The other party, headed by John Winthrop and consisting of dissatisfied Puritans who wished to escape the repression of Charles I, conceived that the company might be used as a Puritan shelter and as an instrument for building a godly kingdom or "a garden of the Lord" in the New England wilderness.[19]

John Winthrop, father of Massachusetts, leading Puritan of early America, well-educated country squire of the Manor of Groton, Suffolk County, was an exceptional leader of rare stability, judgment, power of decision, and force of character. Early in life he had made a covenant with the Lord whereby he pledged himself to shun the sins of vanity, sloth, pride, and worldliness. Sorely distressed by events in England in 1629, and dismayed by the harsh conditions which decreed that "children, servants, and neighbors, especially if they be poor, are counted the greatest burdens, which if things were right, would be the chiefest earthly blessing," he conceived that a Puritan colony might contribute to "the comfort and increase of the body of Christ, whereof we are all members." Aristocratic in temper and scornful of the *nouveaux riches* who were overreaching their social superiors, he felt in his commanding soul that if he remained in England "that talent which God hath bestowed upon him for public service is like to be buried." If life should be hard in New England, man must "learn with Paul to want as well as to abound"; the Lord had once "carried the Israelites into the wilderness and made them forget the flesh-pots of Egypt." [20]

A second leader of the Winthrop party was Thomas Dudley, steward of the Earl of Lincoln, a great Puritan noble. Although Dudley's English career had been undistinguished, he had demonstrated good business ability and had acquired a modest fortune. Austere, domineering, cold, intolerant, and imperious, he was the strictest of the strict, a strong believer in the right of government to coerce men in religion, and withal something of a scholar and poet. His last poem urged:

> Let men of God in courts and churches watch
> O'er such as do a toleration hatch.

[19] S. E. Morison's excellently written *Builders of the Bay Colony* (Boston, 1930) re-creates the Puritans as human beings. See chapters 1–3.

[20] The best formal biography is Robert C. Winthrop, *Life and Letters of John Winthrop* (2 vols., Boston, 1864, 1867). Volume I to 1630.

In August 1629 twelve members of the Winthrop party signed the Cambridge agreement, in which they pledged to migrate to New England provided that the government and charter of the Massachusetts Bay Company might be transferred with them to the colony. Immediately afterward the company at London voted that this should be done. The charter did not prescribe that the governing body of the company should be domiciled in England—an omission so unusual for the time as to create suspicion that the framers of the charter intended originally to transfer the government of the company to New England. The insistence of the Winthrop group that the transfer be made is more easily explained. The Puritans who agreed to migrate hoped to create a new religious commonwealth, and hence they demanded independence and self-rule. The Massachusetts Bay Company was an open corporation; any person could join simply by purchasing a share of stock. This meant that the company in England might easily fall into the hands of non-Puritans. Thus if the power over the Massachusetts colony remained with the company in England, the enemies of the Puritans might gain control and destroy the godly commonwealth which Winthrop envisaged in the New World. But such a calamity could not befall if the charter and governing body were in possession of Winthrop and his friends.[21]

With the charter transfer authorized, Winthrop was elected governor of the company and Dudley deputy-governor. In 1630 they led the first large migration to Massachusetts and founded Boston and several adjacent towns. The good tidings of success soon induced many ministers and devout Puritans to follow. Foremost among these was Master John Cotton, sometime fellow of Emmanuel College in Cambridge University and vicar of St. Botolph's church in Boston, Lincolnshire—which latter post he is said to have obtained when the mayor of Boston broke a deadlock in town council by unwittingly voting twice. The fame of Cotton as a persuasive preacher and his Puritan proclivities set the ecclesiastical authorities after him and in 1633 he fled from old Boston to new Boston. At once he achieved a commanding position and it was soon observed that whatever he preached in the pulpit became the law of the colony.[22]

High-minded, devout, and sincere as these Puritans certainly were, they can hardly be considered pioneers in the narrow sense. They

[21] Augustine Jones, *The Life and Work of Thomas Dudley* (Boston, 1900), is sympathetic toward its subject.

[22] Cotton Mather's *Magnalia Christi Americana* (2 vols., Hartford, 1820) contains many laudatory sketches of early New England worthies. For John Cotton, see Book III, chapter 1.

did not act until the technique of colonization was well developed. They studied their task in the light of much accumulated knowledge and they brought to bear upon it ample means and remarkable caution, foresight, and mastery of practical detail. None of the leaders had held important offices in England or had exercised much influence there. If it was heroic to face the wilderness so also it required courage for Puritans to remain in England and fight the battle against Charles I and Laud. James Truslow Adams suggestively points out that the migration of the Puritans is in keeping with the later American tendency to escape the complex problems of an old society by resorting to a simple and primitive frontier environment. But such a resort to the primitive is evidence of man's faith in his ability to create from new materials a better world.

## Promoters of the 1630's

High in the councils of the English Puritans was an impecunious nobleman of great personal ambition—Lord Saye and Sele. In the 1620's he had been the parliamentary strategist or "oracle" of the Puritans in opposition to the Stuart kings. Finding this theater of achievement closed by the personal rule of Charles I, Lord Saye turned to colonization, primarily to enhance his waning fortune. His chief ally, Lord Brooke, was a less active Puritan but nevertheless highly valued for his immense wealth. These two noble lords, with other prominent Puritans including Warwick, established in 1630 the Providence Company, intending to colonize three islands in the Caribbean, thus reflecting the anti-Spanish bias that had long found vent in privateering exploits against Spain. The Massachusetts Puritans were urged to settle under the Providence Company, but they decided that the get-rich-quick environment of the West Indies would be destructive to moral character. Both Saye and Brooke in turn offered to settle in Massachusetts, provided a titled ruling aristocracy could be created there with themselves at the head. This proposal was rejected, "with thanks."

In 1632 Saye and Brooke, with nine other leading Puritans, obtained from Warwick or the Council for New England a large tract of land about the mouth of the Connecticut River. Here in 1635 they established a small settlement called Saybrook which was intended as a retreat for the settlers of the Providence Company, should that venture fail, and as a means of preëmpting more New England soil for the Puritan cause. Under the command of John Winthrop, Jr.,

Saybrook survived as an independent settlement until it was purchased by the colony of Connecticut in 1644.[23]

The success of Massachusetts inspired two other Puritan worthies to found in 1638 the little colony of New Haven, which became in 1664 the western part of Connecticut. Theophilus Eaton, London merchant, and John Davenport, London divine, had been boyhood friends at grammar school in Coventry, England. Both were of well-to-do and established families. In early life their paths diverged, Eaton going to London as a merchant's apprentice to become an independent trader to the Baltic, member of the Eastland Company, and perhaps onetime agent of Charles I at the Danish court. Like other good Puritans Eaton did not believe in drinking toasts, and, as tradition relates, was once rescued from this offense by divine interference when, just as he was called upon to drink to the Danish king, the latter had a fit. Davenport had gone to Oxford and then to London, where he affiliated with Puritans and fell in again with Eaton, now the wealthiest parishioner in Davenport's church, St. Stephen's.

Davenport came to grips with Laud, took part in organizing the Massachusetts Bay Company, then left his church and went to Holland, where he became so deeply embroiled in theological disputes that he was not allowed to preach. Returning to England in 1637 he found Eaton ready to establish a colony in New England which would enable him to share the profits of American trade. To Davenport the plan opened an outlet for his suppressed energies. Outspoken, hearty, commanding, vigorous, and aggressive, he felt the need of the free air of America and the opportunity of creating a new commonwealth over whose destinies he could preside.

These two strong leaders gathered about them a band of colonists and embarked for Boston in 1637. Spending the winter there in spiritual concert with the Bay Puritans, but spurning entreaties that they remain in Massachusetts, they sailed in the following spring and formed their independent settlement, New Haven.[24]

Illustrative of the diversity of factors making for English expansion is the genesis of Maryland. Its chief founder, Sir George Calvert, owed his rise in life largely to a warm friendship with James I, by whom he was knighted and made Secretary of State. A cultivated gentleman, holder of two Oxford degrees, and an accomplished courtier, Calvert shared the prevailing enthusiasm for colonial ex-

[23] C. M. Andrews, *Our Earliest Colonial Settlements* (New York, 1933), contains six admirable essays. See chapters 1–3, 6.

[24] Isabel M. Calder's *The New Haven Colony* (New Haven, 1934) is the best account of its subject. See chapters 1–3.

ploitation. Between 1620 and 1627 he endeavored to develop a colony at Newfoundland, which he named Avalon, but when he visited it in 1627 he was disheartened by the illness of his settlers and by the long winter "from October to May." Meanwhile, he had become an ardent and avowed Roman Catholic and as a result had to vacate his office of Secretary of State—a loss for which James I compensated him by raising him to the Irish peerage as Baron Baltimore. When secretary he had appeared "as an honorable, well-intentioned man, courteous to strangers, full of respect toward ambassadors, zealously intent upon the welfare of England, but by reason of these good qualities, entirely without consideration or influence." [25]

Seeking a better site than Newfoundland for a province, Baltimore visited Virginia in 1629. The unoccupied land of the colony then belonged to the king, but Charles I had promised the Virginians that they should retain their territory as defined in the charter of 1609. The authorities at Jamestown, aware that Baltimore had designs upon their land, asked him to take the oath renouncing the pope's authority over the English Church. As a conscientious Catholic he refused and had to leave, which was precisely what the Virginians had intended. But this stratagem accomplished little, because in 1632 a royal charter to Baltimore carved out of the lands of Virginia a new colony named Maryland in honor of Queen Henrietta Maria. Its bounds were: at the north, the fortieth parallel; at the west, the meridian running through the western fountain of the Potomac; at the south, the southern bank of the Potomac; and at the east, the Atlantic Ocean.

Before the charter of 1632 was issued, Baltimore died, and the province was granted to his son Cecilius Calvert, second Baron Baltimore. Thus to the father belongs the credit of conceiving and initiating the enterprise, while to the son fell the task of actual colonization. Both had in mind the creation of a refuge for English Catholics and the extension of their faith in America. They also anticipated that a vast new estate would enhance materially the fortunes, dignity, and prestige of the house of Calvert.[26]

## PROMOTERS OF THE AGE OF CHARLES II

The Civil War and the rule of Cromwell put a halt to the founding of new colonies in North America, but with the restoration of

[25] William H. Browne's *George Calvert and Cecilius Calvert* (New York, 1890) is brief, informed, sympathetic toward the Calverts.

[26] Clayton C. Hall in *The Lords Baltimore and the Maryland Palatinate* (Baltimore, 1904) gives a good brief résumé in chapter 1.

the Stuarts occurred another wave of colonizing activity. In 1660 Charles II returned to the throne of his fathers, and immediately drew about him a host of devoted royalists, aristocrats, and believers in hereditary right—most of them outraged by the Puritan upheaval and now hastening as to a feast after long years of privation.

During the ensuing twenty-five years were laid the English foundations of six of the thirteen colonies—the two Carolinas, New Jersey, New York, Pennsylvania, and Delaware. It was an age of robust growth of English industry, shipping, and trade. Charles II himself did all in his power to extend the territorial and commercial dominion of his subjects. A divine-right Catholic at heart who might play fast and loose with his subjects' wishes in religion, court politics, and morals, he never betrayed the material interests of the country. His marriage to Catherine of Braganza, sister of the King of Portugal, added Bombay in India and Tangier in Africa to the English empire. He chartered two new commercial companies of primary importance— the Royal African Company and the Hudson's Bay Company, and in these he took a deep personal interest. His brother, James, Duke of York, a Roman Catholic of autocratic temperament, was equally active in these practical affairs. The two royal brothers appreciated fully the value to England of her rising colonies, and labored diligently to make them profitable to the Crown.

Surrounding the king was a small ring of favorites and statesmen who imposed upon England an aristocratic rule. They served as members of the Privy Council and on royal committees for colonies and trade, belonged to and shared the profits of the great monopolistic companies, presided over their own large estates, and received gladly the numerous titles and honors conferred upon them by the king. Under their guidance the House of Lords was restored; the Church of England, with bishops, prayer book, and ritual, was reëstablished; the Puritans were fully suppressed; other dissenters were persecuted; a subservient Parliament was retained by dispensing with elections; the Acts of Trade and Navigation were passed with the purpose of giving English merchants a monopoly of the commerce of the empire; and huge territories in the New World were bestowed by the king as an earnest of his gratitude to men who had served him during the dark years of exile.

The first new colony created by Charles II was the province of Carolina. Among the devoted followers of the king in England in 1660 was Sir John Colleton, recently a planter in the English sugar island, Barbados. That colony had originally been settled by small farmers but the introduction and spread of sugar culture had led, about 1650, to the growth of large plantations manned by Negro slaves. The small farmers, finding themselves relentlessly squeezed by the large producers, were acutely discontented. Colleton knew that on the American mainland between Virginia and Spanish Florida lay an immense country occupied only by Indians, where there was room for every hard-pressed planter of Barbados. Even though the region was claimed by Spain and though it had failed to attract English settlers by reason of its inaccessibility and reputed unwholesomeness, Sir John believed that it could be used for both the relief of Barbados and the profit of enterprising promoters. Moreover, by 1660 independent emigrants from Virginia had gone south to what is now Albemarle Sound and were making a success of an infant settlement there.[27]

One of Colleton's associates was Anthony Ashley Cooper, a landed gentleman, once an owner of a plantation in Barbados and now in 1660 an expert on colonies and trade. In 1671 he became Lord Ashley; later, as the Earl of Shaftesbury (after 1672), he achieved fame as the founder of the Whig party in England. Another man associated with Colleton in 1660 was Sir William Berkeley, governor of Virginia, who contributed much information about the Carolina country and his confidence in the success of a colony there. Since none of these men had large influence at court and since Cooper was actually mistrusted by the royalists (he had sided with the Puritans in the Civil War), they were obliged to secure the aid of more powerful men. In this they succeeded admirably. The most powerful ally they obtained was Arthur Hyde, Earl of Clarendon, Lord High Chancellor, father-in-law of James, Duke of York, and grandfather of the later queens, Mary and Anne. Clarendon had opposed Cromwell, had gone into exile, and returning with Charles II had become a titan of the new regime, chief author of the Clarendon Code, and an ardent patron of colonization. Equally prominent was General George Monck, Duke of Albemarle, who more than any one man effected the return of Charles II. Something of a popular idol, Albemarle was also a closefisted businessman who was not averse to profiting by his influence at court. A lesser figure, the Earl of Craven, companion of the aunt of the king, had plenty of money to invest in new projects which caught his fancy. John, Lord Berkeley, brother of Sir William, had served the Duke of York as governor of his exiled

[27] See again C. M. Andrews, *The Colonial Period of American History*, Vol. III, chapter 5. For sketches of English leaders who did not migrate see the *Dictionary of National Biography* (ed. Leslie Stephen and Sidney Lee, 63 vols. and index. London, 1885–     ).

household, raising funds in the hour of Stuart adversity. So also, Sir George Carteret, "the richest man in England," as governor of the Island of Jersey, had sheltered Charles II in 1649 and had defended the island against the Puritans in 1653. Both Lord Berkeley and Carteret were rewarded with offices, lands, titles, and charter membership in the Royal African Company, organized in 1660 with the Duke of York as its head.

To these eight men—Albemarle, Carteret, Ashley, Colleton, Craven, Clarendon, and the two Berkeleys—Charles II granted on March 24, 1663, the regal domain of Carolina, extending from sea to sea between the thirty-sixth and the thirty-first parallels. A second charter, of June 30, 1665, moved the southern boundary to the twenty-ninth parallel and the northern boundary to the now famous line, 36° 30′—a change which brought the existing settlement at Albemarle Sound within the limits of Carolina. As in the case of Maryland, the Carolina charter sliced a large strip of land from the territory given to Virginia in 1609.

Uppermost in the minds of the Carolina proprietors was the purpose of making money from their huge province; their interest was that of landlord or real-estate promoter rather than that of merchant. Like Lord Baltimore they intended to sell part of their lands, to keep and develop large estates for themselves, and to collect quit-rents from all purchasers or receivers of individual tracts. In developing the province they endeavored to produce commodities not yet raised in England or her dominions—products such as silk, wine, olives, raisins, currants, almonds, and naval stores, for which there was a ready demand and for which England had to resort to foreigners, paying for them presumably with specie in violation of the current principles of a favorable balance of trade. Socially, the proprietors hoped to duplicate the English order of nobles, yeoman farmers, tenants, and dependents, instituting in the American wilderness the class distinctions and feudal allegiance to superiors so strongly entrenched at home. The chosen model was the large English estate owned by a titled magnate who governed his dependents in a patriarchal fashion. All tendencies toward the growth of a "numerous democracy" such as the proprietors identified with Puritan New England and the turmoils of the Puritan Revolution in England were to be vigorously suppressed.[28]

For these various reasons the proprietors concentrated upon the southern part of their province, where they founded in 1670 a settle-

[28] A scholarly, thorough, detailed biography is Louise F. Brown, *The First Earl of Shaftesbury* (New York, c. 1933).

ment at old Charles Town, relocated at Charleston in 1680, nucleus
of the colony of South Carolina. The northern settlement at Albemarle Sound, though taken under the proprietors' control, was allowed to develop much in its own way. Prior to 1668 all the proprietors took an active part in Carolina affairs, with Colleton perhaps
the most influential, but afterward Lord Ashley was the dominating
member of the group, and he impressed his ideal of a landed aristocracy strongly upon the early history of Carolina. With the imagination of an empire builder he visualized a chain of supplementary
settlements—at Charles Town, at Albemarle Sound, on the Edisto
River, and in the Bahama Islands. Fearful that the latter might be
used by the Spaniards as a base for attacking Charles Town, he obtained from Charles II on November 1, 1670, a grant of the Bahamas
to himself and to the five remaining Carolina proprietors. Upon these
islands also he endeavored to impose a landed aristocracy of the English pattern.

Of equal importance with the creation of Carolina was the grant
on March 12, 1664, to the Duke of York of the region between the
Connecticut and Delaware Rivers, occupied at the time by weak,
scattered Dutch settlements which were conquered by the English
in the following August. This grant severed at the Connecticut River
the territory of Massachusetts, supposed by the charter of 1629 to extend to the Pacific Ocean. From his newly created domain the Duke
of York on June 24, 1664, separated the land lying between the Delaware and the Hudson Rivers and between the fortieth parallel at the
north and Cape May at the south, and conferred it upon his faithful
friends and servants, Sir George Carteret and John, Lord Berkeley,
naming it New Jersey in honor of Carteret's loyal services as governor of the Island of Jersey. Berkeley and Carteret valued this province for its potential profits, which they expected to realize through a
large-scale real-estate business. The Duke of York retained the remainder of his grant of March 12 as his personal principality or
estate, and accordingly its name was changed from New Netherland
to New York. The duke's territory also included Long Island, but he
did not make good his claim to the Connecticut River as the eastern
boundary of his province.

Berkeley retained his share of New Jersey only ten years—until
1674, when he sold it for £1,000 to John Fenwick, acting for a fellow Quaker, Edward Byllinge. This sale marks the entrance of the
Quakers upon the stage of colonial promotion. In 1673 George Fox
had returned from a tour of America full of zeal for building there a
Quaker commonwealth. It is possible that Byllinge was acting for the

Quakers as a whole, now intent upon realizing Fox's ideal. At any rate, in 1676 Carteret consented to the division of New Jersey into East New Jersey, which he retained, and West New Jersey, which he recognized as the property of the Byllinge Quaker interest. Then in 1692 Byllinge's rights (having been acquired in 1687 by Dr. Daniel Coxe) were purchased by a body of proprietors called the West New Jersey Society. East New Jersey, on the other hand, was purchased in 1680 from Carteret's estate, and soon passed into the hands of a numerous group of proprietors and business partners, a number of whom were Friends. Although after 1682 the Quaker interest in both parts of New Jersey was strong, they were not reunited into a single province until 1702.

The intent and spirit of the Quakers as colonizers found fullest expression in the work of William Penn, liberal, mystic, philosopher, and man of practical affairs.[29] Educated at Oxford, at a Huguenot academy in France, and in the law at Lincoln's Inn, London, he was exposed to the main intellectual currents of his time. His precocity and yearning for an independent spiritual life resulted in his expulsion from Oxford for worshipping with a group of nonconforming seekers for new truth. Through his father, Sir William Penn, admiral of the royal navy and friend of the Duke of York, the younger Penn occupied a high station in society. Fearful that his son's youthful radicalism would block his advancement in the world, the father had sent him to France to acquire the manners and tastes of a gentleman who would adorn the court. Then the young William went to Ireland to manage his father's estates but while there came in touch with a Quaker preacher, Thomas Loe, and was converted to the faith of the Friends. Numerous quarrels between father and son ensued, but the breach was always closed, due largely to their mutual respect and honorable conduct. After 1667 the younger Penn, in close touch with George Fox, sought by direct political action in England and by missionary tours in Holland and Germany to extend and to realize his Quaker ideals of peace, toleration, and liberty. As a result of his outspoken condemnation of injustice and oppression he was several times arrested and imprisoned in England. On the whole he remained steadfast in his faith, demonstrating in his voluminous writings and personal conduct a commendable purpose of integrating thought and conviction with the practical concerns of life.

Penn inherited in 1670 his father's estates and a claim to £16,000

[29] The best of the earlier accounts is Sydney G. Fisher, *The True William Penn* (Philadelphia, c. 1899).

owed to the admiral by the king. His wealth thereupon enhanced his
influence among the Quakers and he was soon able to grapple with
the material difficulties of colonization. In 1675 he entered the West
New Jersey enterprise and became one of its proprietors and probably
prepared the plans for the principal Quaker settlement at Burlington
in 1677. On March 4, 1681, he received from Charles II the province
of Pennsylvania, named at the insistence of the king to honor Penn's
father, and granted in consideration of the debt which the Crown had
never paid to the Penns. Bounded on the east by the Delaware River,
on the north by the forty-third parallel, on the west by a line five
degrees west of the Delaware, and on the south by the fortieth parallel, Penn's imperial domain was the largest, most valuable estate in
America ever granted to an individual by the Crown.

After the founding of Pennsylvania by settlers sent out in 1681
under Penn's deputy, William Markham, Philadelphia soon became
one of the four principal towns in English America. Penn visited his
colony in 1682, at which time he also received from his friend, the
Duke of York, the territory of present-day Delaware. This he immediately united with Pennsylvania proper, and so it remained for
twenty years until it was created into a separate colony in 1704. Penn,
however, retained his rights as proprietor and governor of the little
province.[30]

Like the Carolina proprietors and the Duke of York, Penn hoped
to obtain a revenue from land sales, rents, and his personal estates in
his colony. But perhaps he was more interested in his "Holy Experiment"—his design for a commonwealth in which men should live in
peace, brotherly love, toleration, sobriety, and charity, under an orderly, mild, and equitable government that would confer the twin
blessings of liberty and property. "Colonies," he wrote, "are the seeds
of nations, begun and nourished by the care of wise and populous
countries; as conceiving them best for the increase of human stock,
and beneficial for commerce." His ideas, particularly those on religious freedom, entered the main stream of American thought. "No
man, nor number of men upon earth," he wrote, "hath power or authority to rule over men's consciences in religious matters." He may
not have been a brilliant or original thinker, but his sincerity, benevolent nature, and courage cannot be questioned. "He was a man of

---

[30] There are three excellent recent biographies: Bonamy Dobrée, *William Penn,
Quaker and Pioneer* (Boston, 1932); Arthur Pound, *The Penns of Pennsylvania and
England* (New York, 1932); and Mabel R. Brailsford, *The Making of William
Penn* (London, 1930). The last is devoted to Penn's struggles before 1680.

great abilities, of an excellent sweetness of disposition, quick of thought, and ready utterance. . . . He may without straining his character be ranked among the learned good and great."

With the exception of the Pilgrim fathers, all the promoters who launched colonies from an English base were men of means, position, and political influence—aristocrats, landed gentry, or well-to-do merchants who shared the English philosophy of aristocracy and class distinctions. Their expectations of private profit from colonies induced them to extend to America the social and economic inequalities which they took for granted in England. By virtue of commercial monopolies and personal estates they intended to utilize the services of dependent classes to augment their own wealth. One result was the planting of the seeds of aristocracy in the American wilderness. Another was the extension from England to the colonies of the conflict between privileged and non-privileged groups—a prolonged strife which forms the central theme of colonial history. The genesis of class distinctions and group conflicts in America will become apparent as we survey the methods employed in founding colonies.[31]

[31] For biographical sketches of leaders who came to America see the immensely valuable *Dictionary of American Biography* (ed. Allen Johnson and Dumas Malone, 20 vols., New York, 1928–36). An indispensable work.

## BIBLIOGRAPHICAL NOTE

SOURCES: George P. Winship has edited *Sailors' Narratives of Voyages along the New England Coast, 1524–1624* (Boston, 1905). The most accessible edition of *Bradford's History of Plymouth Plantation* is that of William T. Davis in the Jameson *Original Narratives* series (New York, 1908). An attractive collection of important documents is Stewart Mitchell (ed.), *The Founding of Massachusetts . . . 1628–1631, Proceedings*, Massachusetts Historical Society, LXII (Boston, 1930). Some of Penn's writings are reprinted in an Everyman's Library edition under the title *The Peace of Europe*. For material pertaining to New England leaders see *Old South Leaflets*, nos. 48–50, 75, 77, 92, 118–122, 154, 207.

WORKS PREVIOUSLY CITED: See bibliographical note at the end of chapter 6.

## ☆ VI ☆

## THE FOUNDING OF COLONIES

THE English colonies did not just happen; they were products of careful business planning and management and of considerable expenditures of money. Settlers had to be transported three thousand miles across the sea and equipped with utensils, clothing, seed, tools, building materials, livestock, arms, and ammunition. Moreover, food had to be provided until a settlement could become self-sustaining. The cost of transporting and establishing a colonial family certainly amounted to several hundred dollars, as calculated today.

From the point of view of colonization three classes of people in England may be distinguished. First, there were moderately well-to-do members of the middle class who were willing to migrate to America and able to pay their own expenses. Secondly, there was a group of nobles and prosperous merchants and lesser people who had surplus funds to invest in colonies, but did not choose to leave England. The third group consisted of the mass of the workers, tenants, paupers, and unemployed who might be compelled to emigrate or be persuaded that they could improve their lot in America, but who lacked the means of paying their passage thither. The ordinary English laborer did not earn in a year enough to meet the cost of emigration; in fact his earnings barely sufficed for a mere subsistence, so that savings for this class were impossible. Since the members of the group first mentioned were not sufficiently numerous to people a colony, one problem of settlement reduced itself to this: how might the poor who were willing but unable to go, be financed by the well-to-do who were willing to invest but unwilling to go? [1]

This problem was solved in various ways. Two English colonies, Virginia and Massachusetts, were founded by chartered companies whose funds were provided by investors and used in the first instance to equip, transport, and maintain the colonists. By a second method, employed in the settlement of New Haven and of Massachusetts after 1629, well-to-do emigrants brought over their families and their

[1] Attention is again called to C. M. Andrews, *The Colonial Period of American History*, Vol. I, chapters 3–4, 13, 15–18; Vol. II, chapters 6, 8; and Vol. III, chapters 5, 7.

property and in addition paid for the transportation of personal servants. The method of founding Plymouth resembled that used for
Virginia, with this exception—that the investors in England who paid
the costs of the migration were not incorporated by a royal charter.
The other colonies—New Hampshire, Maine, Maryland, the Carolinas, New Jersey, and Pennsylvania—belonged to proprietors who
as landlords advanced or endeavored to advance out of their own resources the funds for settling tenants and servants upon their feudal
estates. This method was also employed earlier by Gilbert and Raleigh.[2]

Inasmuch as the promoters of colonies depended upon the exploitation of the land as a principal source of profit, their relations
with their servants and tenant colonists were shaped by the tenure
upon which land was held from the king. Theoretically all land in
England and her dominions belonged to the king, who granted individual estates to his subjects, exacting feudal dues and services from
the recipients, who were called his tenants-in-chief or vassals. Prior to
the year 1290 the tenant-in-chief had the right to "subinfeudate,"
that is, to grant his estate to a third person, exacting from him services
and payments similar to those which were owed to the king by the
tenant-in-chief. However, the statute *quia emptores* (1290) prohibited further subinfeudation by providing that if a tenant-in-chief
granted his land to a third person he lost all his rights and the new
holder paid his services and dues directly to the king. But in spite of
the fact that prior to 1600 subinfeudation had long been illegal in
England, it was revived and extended to the colonies by the charters
issued after 1630.

Technically both the proprietors and the chartered companies with
colonial grants were tenants-in-chief of the king. However, they paid
next to nothing for their lands. The charters did reserve to the king
a tenth or a fifth of all gold and silver discovered in the colonies, but
none being found, none was paid. Otherwise the payments were
trifling. Lord Baltimore, for instance, had to give the king each year
two Indian arrowheads and William Penn had to contribute yearly
two beaver skins. Regular payments of value were not required of the
proprietors because the land was practically worthless when given to
them by the king and because the prospects of profit from the colonies

[2] *The South in the Building of the Nation* (12 vols., Richmond, c. 1909–13)
comprises a series of articles, some by leading Southern historians. Volume I, *History
of the Southern States*, contains a good article on Virginia's beginnings by J. A. C.
Chandler; on Maryland by B. C. Steiner; on North Carolina by R. D. W. Connor.

were so uncertain that the promoters would not have acted if they had been obliged to make large yearly contributions to the crown.[3]

The early charters created two types of land tenure. The Virginia Company, the Massachusetts Bay Company, and the Council for New England did not receive the right to subinfeudate or to establish manors. These three companies might grant to individuals the lands they had received from the king, but when that was done the company was not overlord of the landholder and could not exact feudal services and dues. The grantee thus became a tenant, not of the company, but of the king. On the other hand the charters of Maryland, Maine, Carolina, and Pennsylvania conferred upon the proprietors the right to subinfeudate and to create manors and new forms of land tenure. In the proprietary colonies, therefore, the proprietor (as tenant-in-chief of the king) might grant lands, exacting from the recipients various feudal services and payments and also conferring upon them the power to govern the tenants on their estates. Hence a principle of feudal land law which had been abandoned in England since 1290 was applied to five of the American colonies.

## THE PROCURING OF CAPITAL

Inasmuch as prospective settlers could not emigrate without money, the prerequisite of colonization was the procuring of capital. Both Gilbert and Raleigh met the problem by using their own funds and by soliciting aid from friends to whom they promised American estates and from merchants to whom they offered commercial concessions. Raleigh, who derived a large income from monopolies, licenses, and offices bestowed upon him by Queen Elizabeth, claimed that he spent £40,000 on Virginia without earning a penny on the investment. The conflict with Spain then diverted much capital to war and privateering, but with the advent of peace in 1604, surplus funds rapidly sought more normal sources of profit. Moreover, the East India Company had turned out to be a financial success. Not only did its example stimulate new colonial-commercial enterprises, but the profit-makers of the company acquired excess funds which needed additional channels of investment.

The Virginia patentees of 1606 intended to duplicate the activities of the East India Company, and therefore conceived of their James-

[3] Viola F. Barnes, "Land Tenure in English Colonial Charters of the Seventeenth Century," in *Essays in Colonial History Presented to Charles M. Andrews* . . . (New Haven, 1921).

town settlement more as a trading post than as an agricultural colony. They advanced the capital for the support of their gold-hunting, Indian-trading settlers, expecting to derive profits, not from land sales, but from trade. The early failure at Jamestown arose in part from the fact that the backers in England, a small number of patentees, did not have enough capital. Accordingly the charter of 1609, by creating a joint-stock company, invited all English investors to participate in the enterprise. Every purchaser of a share of stock (the par value of which was £12 10s., or the cost of equipping and transporting one settler) became an adventurer in the company, entitled to dividends and to a land grant in Virginia. The company used its capital to send over settlers to labor as its employees for seven years. Any surplus they produced went to the company, which also carried on all trade with the colony. At the end of the seven years, the improved lands were to be divided among the company members, each receiving a hundred acres for every share of stock which he owned.[4]

The Virginia Company of 1609 was launched amidst an active campaign in which letters, pamphlets, and handbills were widely distributed, and the result of which was a large number of initial members. But afterward the company, due to its inability to make profits, met a stubborn sales resistance from the investors it solicited. Accordingly, a third charter issued by James I in 1612 authorized the company to raise money by lotteries, which were spoken of thereafter "as the real and substantial food" by which Virginia was nourished.

In 1618 the Virginia Company sank to its lowest ebb, financially. The peculations of Samuel Argall, its governor in the colony, had dissipated most of its property there. Lacking funds in its treasury in England, the company adopted a new policy. The initial seven-year period having expired, the members of the company were entitled to their hundred-acre tracts. Some of the leading members had invested sums ranging from £200 to £500, and hence were entitled to estates varying from fifteen hundred to four thousand acres. Moreover, each member was promised a second tract equal to the first, provided he settled colonists upon the first within a given time. This situation induced the company to authorize its members to form sub-companies or associations to which it granted large plantations, and these associations of wealthy "insiders" thereupon assumed the burden of financing new settlements. Between 1619 and 1624, seventy-eight patents were granted to such associations. The largest estate thus

[4] For a detailed chronicle of the founding of Virginia see Alexander Brown's *The First Republic of America* (Boston, 1898).

created, called Smyth's Hundred, contained 200,000 acres. Its proprietors sent out 310 settlers in May 1620. To a similar estate, Martin's Hundred, came 250 colonists in 1619. However, such plantations were only well begun when in 1622 a destructive Indian
massacre wiped out most of their servants and tenants and spread havoc
and ruin. The associations in England later sold their plantations to
individuals, who thereafter supplied the capital for further development.[5]

The Virginia Company attracted capital to the colony by another
method—that of granting lands to well-to-do families and individuals
who would colonize at their own expense. The famous "head-right"
system, introduced in 1618, gave fifty acres to any person who transported to the colony a settler who remained three years. Such head-
rights became the chief means of acquiring land in Virginia during
the seventeenth century. The system was later extended so that each
family head received fifty acres for every member of his family who
emigrated and for every servant he brought into the colony. As a result, merchants and shipmasters who imported settlers, as well as
families who came at their own expense, were compensated with land
for their capital outlays toward peopling the colony.

The Pilgrims, in founding Plymouth, resorted to methods of
financing similar to those employed by the Virginia Company. They
formed an agreement with seventy English "adventurers" who contributed £7,000 toward the cost of the migration. An unincorporated
joint-stock company was formed with shares of a par value of £10.
The Pilgrims and other settlers who were sent over agreed to work
for the company as its servants or employees, although the emigrants
were also members of the company. After seven years of such corporate labor, the goods and lands of the company were to be divided
among the members according to the shares of stock held by each.
Plymouth, like Virginia, failed to produce money profits for the English investors, and accordingly in 1624 they refused to contribute further and soon afterward withdrew from the enterprise.[6]

The first precursors of the Massachusetts Bay Company consisted
of 120 investors of the Dorchester Company who advanced a total
capital of £3,000, which was used to found the fishing settlement at

---

[5] Herbert L. Osgood's *The American Colonies in the Seventeenth Century* (3 vols.,
New York, 1904, 1907) is one of the great works of American history—the best
older study of the origins of political institutions. See Vol. I, pp. 3–135; Vol. II,
chapters 1–8, 10.

[6] Lyon G. Tyler's *England in America, 1580–1652* (New York, 1904—*American
Nation* series) is a useful compilation, though not outstanding. See chapters 1–4,
7, 9–12.

Cape Ann. When the Dorchester group failed to make a profit and was replaced by the New England Company in 1628, some of the Dorchester men received stock in the new company and were designated as the "Old Planters." The New England Company operated the settlement, now at Salem, selling new stock and sending out colonists who as servants or employees were supposed to produce profits for the investors. Then in 1629 the New England Company became the Massachusetts Bay Company. The decision of the latter in August 1629 to transfer its charter and governing body to Massachusetts created an unusual situation. The great majority of the members of the company did not intend to migrate. Those who did intend to go did not care to be employees of the company and work to produce profits for the stockholders in England. Winthrop therefore suggested that the company contribute most of its existing assets to the emigrants and exempt them from future payments to the members who proposed to remain in England. But the latter felt that they were entitled to some return on their investments. Finally a compromise was arranged. The stockholders agreed to write off two-thirds of the value of their shares and receive four hundred acres of land in Massachusetts for each £50 of their adjusted claims. Moreover, the investors received four concessions: (1) a monopoly of the business of transporting settlers to the colony, (2) one-half of the beaver trade, (3) a monopoly of the manufacture of salt, and (4) the privilege of trading with the colony through a "magazine." However, these concessions were to endure but seven years and were so hedged about that they could not be used to exploit the colonists. By virtue of this arrangement the members of the company who remained in England relinquished their claims to money dividends from the colonists, and consequently the company, when moved to Massachusetts in 1630, did not function there as a profit-making body.[7]

After the decision to transfer the charter was made in 1629, investors in England did not contribute additional capital except for the purchase of new "common stock," the proceeds of which were to be put to public uses, such as building churches in the colony, providing for its defense, and transporting poor families thither. The subscribers to this stock were promised a two hundred-acre tract of land in Massachusetts for each £50 contributed. Such contributions were made in part for philanthropic reasons and in part by London merchants who hoped to trade with the colony.

From these arrangements it appears that the Massachusetts Bay

[7] A good study of the business angle of colonization is Frances Rose-Troup, *The Massachusetts-Bay Company and Its Predecessors* (New York, 1930).

Company after 1629 did not have any funds to spend except the proceeds from the common stock; consequently it could not promote much additional settlement. The great migration of the 1630's was therefore financed by individual Puritans who bore the expense of transporting their own families. They sold their English estates and transferred the proceeds to New England. Thus the sale of Winthrop's estate netted £4,200. Another leader, John Haynes, brought some £7,000 into the colony. A later estimate revealed that the early emigrants invested £400,000, besides initial expenditures of £192,000 for the transportation of settlers, for the purchase and shipment of livestock, and for supplies of food, glass, iron goods, and arms and ammunition. These financial arrangements, which freed the Massachusetts settlers from debts to English promoters, indicate that the colony was developed after 1630 by men of considerable wealth.

The founders of New Haven Colony did not organize a chartered company, nor did they contract debts or other financial obligations as a means of procuring capital for the migration. Instead, the well-to-do parishioners of John Davenport utilized their own fortunes and thus established their colony on an independent economic basis. Theophilus Eaton, who was worth £4,000 in England, is said to have transferred £3,000 to the colony. Although the New Haven settlers were not numerous, they were relatively the wealthiest group which went to America during the seventeenth century.[8]

The methods of financing adopted by the proprietors of New Hampshire, Maryland, Carolina, and Pennsylvania bear a striking resemblance. In the first place, the proprietors made personal investments with the object of providing a nucleus of settlement that would attract future colonists and thus increase the value of the lands which the proprietors offered for general sale. All lands given away or sold were subject to a quit-rent or yearly payment which would provide the proprietors with a permanent income. The proprietors also retained for themselves American estates to be worked for their profit by servants or tenants whom they transported to their colonies. Lord Baltimore spent about £30,000 on the development of Maryland. The Calvert wealth is indicated by the family's possession of valuable Irish estates and by the fact that Sir George Calvert received £6,000 when he sold his claim to the office of Secretary of State. Similarly Captain John Mason spent large sums upon his New Hampshire colony on the Piscataqua, but never received any profit from it.

In 1663 the eight wealthy proprietors of Carolina reserved for themselves estates of twenty thousand acres each, and a new arrange-

[8] See again J. T. Adams, *The Founding of New England*, chapters 1–3, 5–6.

ment in 1669 set aside a fifth of all the lands of the province for their benefit. They financed in part the expedition which settled Old Charles Town in 1670; a decade later they wrote: "We have been at great expense, some 17 or £18,000 sterling, and have brought the colony to so prosperous a condition that men of estates have for years gone there on their own accounts." Each proprietor agreed in 1674 to spend £100 a year on the colony for five years—indicating not only the need for more capital but also their reluctance to become more deeply involved. Lord Shaftesbury at this time endeavored to establish a personal manor of twelve thousand acres to which he sent a shipload of servants and supplies. In 1679 the proprietors were unwilling to make further outlays, asserting that their previous investments had put the colony on its feet.

Like Lord Baltimore, William Penn derived an income from family estates in Ireland. His initial plans for Pennsylvania reserved to himself a tenth of all surveyed lands of his province, upon which he intended to establish personal estates. He said about 1698 that he had invested £30,000 in Pennsylvania, and complained that he had not received a sixpence profit during the preceding twelve years. His expenditures strained his credit, with the result that he was later thrown into a debtors' prison and eventually forced to mortgage the province and assign to his creditors the revenues he derived from quit-rents, land sales, and other Pennsylvania sources.[9]

As in earlier days, the proprietors active after 1630 found the cost of colonization too great to be borne singlehanded, and therefore enlisted the aid of wealthy men who may be called "proprietary associates." Thus Captain Mason joined with six London merchants in 1631 for the financing of New Hampshire settlement but two years without profit sufficed for the merchants and they retired. Lord Baltimore originally obtained associates by giving them a thousand acres of land for every five men they transported to Maryland. The size of such grants was increased to two thousand acres in 1636 and reduced to five hundred acres in 1649. These associates spent about £20,000 toward peopling their estates. Three of them—Thomas Cornwallis and two Jesuit fathers, White and Copley—transported 130 settlers to the colony.

The Carolina proprietors in particular relied upon wealthy associates. In the South Carolina expedition of 1669 were many adventurers, each transporting at his own expense a small group of servants.

[9] C. M. Andrews, *Colonial Self-Government, 1652–1689* (New York, 1904— *American Nation* series), gives essential facts, emphasizing legal foundations. See chapters 7–9, 11.

Proposals made for the colony in 1669 anticipated that a fifth of all its land should be assigned to such associates, who were also to form an order of nobles—landgraves and caciques. Lord Ashley said in 1671 that nothing would so foster "the growth and prosperity of the plantation as that men of estate should come to settle amongst you." Accordingly, during the 1670's generous grants were made to individuals and partners who transported groups of between ten and twenty servants. Each servant imported secured for the associate a tract of 100 or 150 acres of land. Thus Seth Sothell in 1675 received a manor of twelve thousand acres on condition that within five years he build thirty houses and "seat" 120 colonists. Between 1675 and 1684, nine grants bestowed estates ranging from one thousand to three thousand acres, while Sir Peter Colleton, then one of the proprietors, obtained title to 35,800 acres.

William Penn once said that the success of his province was due partly to the fact that it was "begun by men of estates." He enlisted many wealthy Quaker associates, each of whom bought for £100 a tract of five thousand acres which included a lot of one hundred acres in Philadelphia. Nearly half of the land sold by Penn in 1681–82 was purchased by about forty of these wealthy associates who probably intended to people their colonial estates with tenants.[10]

Besides investing their own funds and enlisting wealthy associates, the proprietors encouraged moderately well-to-do families to settle in their colonies. They did this by giving away land or by selling it at bargain prices. Lord Baltimore in 1636 offered land gratis to self-paying families: one hundred acres for each adult, including servants, and fifty acres for each child under sixteen. In 1658 the allotments were reduced to fifty acres for each person; in 1683 they were discontinued. The Carolina proprietors, prior to 1670, gave 150 acres for each man servant and one hundred acres for each woman servant and for each male servant under sixteen. In 1672 such grants were reduced to seventy acres and sixty acres respectively. The majority of farms established in South Carolina before 1685 did not contain more than three hundred acres. William Penn sold land at the rate of about 1s. an acre or one hundred acres for £5. To a company of German emigrants headed by Daniel Francis Pastorius he disposed of fifteen thousand acres for £300. The list of original purchasers who bought land from Penn before 1683 shows that 307 procured tracts ranging from 250 to one thousand acres—representing about three-fourths of the purchasers and half of all the land then sold. Penn at

[10] John Fiske's *The Dutch and Quaker Colonies* (2 vols., Boston, 1899) is a readable narrative. On Pennsylvania see Vol. II, chapter 12.

this time advised the self-paying settler to bring over two-thirds of his property in goods and the other third in money.

## THE PROCURING OF SETTLERS

The resources of English America required a large supply of labor for their exploitation—a demand far in excess of the supply afforded by the settlers who paid their own way. The promoters therefore had to recruit workers among the dependent classes in England. Accordingly, the colonies were pictured attractively to the poor as "places where food shall drop into their mouths." In 1630 Thomas Dudley, then in New England, observed that "honest men out of a desire to draw over others to them, wrote somewhat hyperbolically of many things here." America seemingly spread a table heaped up with fruits, berries, vegetables, and nuts; the rivers teemed with fish; and the forests abounded with game which had no keepers.

The most common method of procuring workers—adopted alike by companies, proprietors, and independent families—was the labor contract. Such a contract or indenture stipulated that the contractor should transport and maintain a servant for a given term during which the latter was bound to labor for his master. This system had its roots deep in the soil of England's aristocratic past. Earlier statutes had provided that laborers must work at fixed wages and that minors between the ages of twelve and twenty-one might be apprenticed by their parents or guardians and thus be obliged to work for a master until they became adults. Another act allowed magistrates to bind vagabonds to property owners who would put them to work and maintain them.[11]

However, the procuring of indentured servants for colonization raised new problems. If a worker were to remain forever a servant or tenant it was better for him to stay in England rather than to add the hardships and dangers of a wilderness frontier life to his dependent lot. As early as 1612 it was reported that escaped servants had returned from Virginia to England where they "endeavored by most vile and slanderous reports . . . of the country of Virginia . . . to bring the said voyage and plantation into disgrace and contempt." Such reports, added to the native repugnance of less enterprising groups in England for novelty and change, had to be counteracted by the promoters. Accordingly, many servants were obtained by force.

[11] Volume II of E. P. Cheyney's *A History of England from the Defeat of the Armada to the Death of Elizabeth* (2 vols., New York, 1914, 1926) gives a vivid picture of social conditions.

Kidnaping was resorted to by "spirits" who carried off drunkards from the taverns, seized poor people by "strong-arm" methods, and enticed others on board ships where they were held as prisoners. Moreover, judges sentenced criminals to servitude in the colonies where their services were sold to promoters or prosperous settlers. As early as 1612 we hear of servants in Virginia "sent thither as misdoers and offenders." [12]

The right sort of servants, however, could not be obtained by such methods, and accordingly the promoters (except in New England) were obliged to make attractive concessions which would induce the more industrious and responsible members of the dependent classes to enter into voluntary service. First, the promoters promised the servant his freedom after a term generally between four and seven years; secondly, the servant when free should receive a small tract of land, usually fifty acres in the back country; then thus emancipated he would be entitled to vote, and, if a Protestant, to enjoy religious toleration. By such concessions the promoters met the criticism of Lord Bacon that "it is a shameful and unblessed thing to take the scum of people and wicked, condemned men to be the people with whom you plant."

Under the Virginia charter of 1606 the promoters sent over three hundred settlers—a miscellaneous group of adventurers, gentlemen of decayed fortunes, and some of the "scum" of whom Bacon complained. Their utter incompetence as colonists induced the Virginia Company, after 1609, to seek hard-working farmers and artisans. The company's efforts to people Virginia were supplemented after 1618 by the associations formed within the company and by private planters who purchased servants for personal use. In each case the importers of poor immigrants offered land as the principal inducement. Under the charter of 1609 a servant over ten years of age who went to Virginia became a member of the company, entitled to one hundred acres at the end of seven years in its service. Similarly the associations formed within the company after 1617 offered their servants twenty-five acres each after a labor term of from three to eight years. It also became the custom for private planters to give to their servants the fifty-acre head-rights which the planters received as a bonus for importing the servants in the first instance. Thus most of the servants eventually emerged as landowning farmers. As such, if Protestants, they enjoyed religious toleration, because the promoters of Virginia did not impose any religious restraints except the oath of supremacy.

[12] A. E. Smith, "The Transportation of Convicts to the American Colonies in the Seventeenth Century," *American Historical Review*, XXXIX (Jan. 1934).

The charter of 1606, moreover, guaranteed to the colonists and their descendants all the "liberties, franchises, and immunities . . . to all intents and purposes as if they had been abiding and born within this our realm of England. . . ." This extension to the colonies of the liberties enjoyed by citizens of England laid the foundations of colonial self-government. Such liberties which were of most consequence, however, were enjoyed by English property owners, and thus the colonial servants had to become landholders before they attained the substantial benefits promised in the charter of 1606.[13]

The Pilgrims came to Plymouth Colony as both servants and members of the joint-stock company which they had formed with their English backers. Each emigrant received one share in the company, and for every £10 of property which he brought to the colony he received an additional share. Besides the Pilgrims, the English promoters dispatched a company of other settlers in the *Mayflower:* only thirty-five of its 102 passengers were Pilgrims. Until 1624 the company reinforced the colony with additional colonists from England. Among the non-Pilgrim group were several of the now historic figures of Plymouth—John Alden, Miles Standish, and Richard Warren.

Indentured servants occupied a minor place in the great Puritan migration of the 1630's. After 1629 the Massachusetts Bay Company did not transport settlers except certain poor families for whom a special fund was created. Some of the well-to-do ministers charitably financed the removal of deserving but needy families. Otherwise emigrants unable to pay their way were brought as servants of the wealthier Puritans. However, the leaders of both Massachusetts and New Haven did not seek servants merely as a labor force. They sought, rather, fit "instruments" for a religious commonwealth, feeling that the troubles of other colonies arose from the character of the settlers —"a multitude of rude and misgoverned persons, the very scum of the land." Hence the Puritans did not offer tempting concessions which would appeal to people whose "main end was carnal and not religious"—not even such concessions as freedom of worship and political rights. Individual Puritans and towns may have given land to worthy and devout servants at the end of their terms, but neither the Massachusetts Bay Company nor the New Haven leaders promised land wholesale to every servant who might arrive. By virtue of such

[13] The best one-volume political history of Virginia in the seventeenth century is Thomas J. Wertenbaker's *Virginia under the Stuarts* (Princeton, 1914). See chapter 1 and pp. 45–54.

precautions the Puritans could feel with complacency that all England had been sifted for the choicest grain for their New England planting.[14]

In early Maryland the indentured servants were entitled to land grants—at first from the individuals who transported them. There developed a traffic whereby shipmasters imported servants and secured the head-rights, which were sold to planters along with the servants. Until 1646 the servant could claim fifty acres from his employer or master; between 1646 and 1683, the proprietor gave the land. Lord Baltimore also recruited settlers by assuring religious freedom to Christians.

After 1665 the theory that England was overpopulated gave way before a contrary view that the nation was in danger of losing its man power. The effects of the emigration of thousands of able-bodied workers prior to 1640 were now severely felt. The Civil War had taken a heavy toll, while a destructive plague, originating in London in 1665, swept throughout the country—the greatest calamity of its kind since the Black Death of the fourteenth century. Wagons went through the London streets at night to the doleful cry of the drivers: "Bring out your dead." In spite of these population losses England was forging ahead rapidly as an industrial and commercial power, but this very growth augmented the demand for workers. Whereas the colonies had formerly been prized as an outlet for the unemployed, they now became a source of alarm. "Ireland and our plantations," said a publicist of the time, "rob us of all the growing youth and industry of the nation, whereby it becomes weak and feeble, and the strength, as well as trade, becomes decayed and diminished."

This new theory of population affected the policies of both the English government and the promoters of colonies. The establishment of the Royal African Company in the 1660's proclaimed the intention of supplying colonial employers with Negro slaves rather than with English servants. Between 1664 and 1684 measures were adopted to prevent kidnaping, which business supposedly was then draining the country of ten thousand workers annually. At the same time English judges with increasing frequency ordered criminals transported to the colonies, so that in 1670 Virginia, in view of "the great numbers of felons and other desperate villains sent hither from

[14] Charles Edward Banks has made valuable studies of the process of colonization in Massachusetts. His writings include *The Winthrop Fleet of 1630* (Boston, 1930) and *The Planters of the Commonwealth* (Boston, 1930). Banks stresses economic forces in emigration.

the several prisons of England," passed an act prohibiting such importations. The English convict policy obviously aimed to supply the colonies with workers whom England did not want.

With the shrinkage of English emigration the promoters of colonies began to solicit settlers in Europe. The Carolina proprietors and the English government coöperated in 1679 in locating French Huguenots near Charles Town. A short time later Penn began to seek settlers, not only in Ireland and Wales, but also in Germany and the Netherlands. He prepared two tracts, *A Brief Account of the Province of Pennsylvania* and *Some Account*, while in 1686 appeared a third, *A Further Account*. In the Netherlands his friend, agent, and fellow Quaker, Benjamin Furly, translated *Some Account* into Dutch, while one Jan Claus prepared a translation for circulation in Germany. In these pamphlets Penn gave a pleasant picture of his province, described his liberal purposes, and advised prospective settlers as to the practical details of pioneering. The sort of people he desired were "industrious husbandmen, carpenters, masons, weavers, shoemakers, and other mechanics, industrious spirits that are oppressed about a livelihood, younger brothers, and men of universal spirits who understand the promotion of a just government among a plain and well intending people." By means of such writings Pennsylvania became, perhaps, the best advertised and certainly the most cosmopolitan of the English colonies, notable for the presence of Dutch, Germans, Swedes, Irish, Finns, Welsh, and English in its early population.[15]

The proprietors of Carolina, New Jersey, and Pennsylvania also bid for settlers who were dissatisfied in the older colonies, particularly in Barbados, Virginia, and New England. Unable to attract enough wealthy associates the proprietors again had to fall back upon self-paying families. The competition for settlers tended to liberalize the concessions offered. The Carolina charters granted freedom of worship to law-abiding Christians, and the proprietors issued a list of concessions in 1665 and 1667 which promised a representative legislature with power to assent to laws and taxes. Prior to 1670 a servant in Carolina received one hundred acres of land at the end of service; after 1670 his "freedom dues" included a grant of seventy acres. From pamphlets advertising Carolina in 1682 we learn that servants there enjoyed a Saturday afternoon vacation, that work was not done

[15] This theme is treated at length in William I. Hull, *William Penn and the Dutch Quaker Migration* (Swarthmore, 1935). See also Sydney G. Fisher, *The Quaker Colonies* (*Chronicles of America*, New Haven, 1919).

on the Sabbath, that "juries were chosen by lot," and that "lawyers could not charge fees."

When Carteret and Berkeley were proprietors of New Jersey in 1665 they offered concessions identical with those granted to Carolina settlers—land grants, religious freedom, a representative assembly, and free elections. The Quakers who took possession of West New Jersey issued in 1677 a more generous charter of popular liberties than any drawn up before that time. It guaranteed the rights of jury trial and religious freedom, protected the settlers from arbitrary imprisonment for debt, and did not provide for capital punishment. The colony was promised a legislature, to be elected yearly by the settlers, which should enjoy free speech, hold meetings open to the public, and legislate freely without a governor's veto.

William Penn, who probably drafted the West New Jersey concessions, extended similar privileges to Pennsylvania. In addition Penn bestowed upon indentured servants (whose term in Pennsylvania was commonly four years) farms of fifty acres. Such privileges as those granted by Penn were more than a competitive bid for labor; they embodied the Quaker ideals of human freedom.

About 1830 an English observer noted the democratic spirit in the United States, which he explained by the character of the early settlers. "We sent them forth," he wrote, "poor and struggling only for the means of subsistence. . . . We severed the humble from the nobles of our land and formed the embryo of a plebeian nation. Is it we that should find fault with their extravagant abhorrence of rank, or their want of high breeding and gentle blood which we so sparingly bestowed upon them?"

## THE AMERICAN SCENE

Let us take passage with a shipload of emigrants bound from England to the colonies. The vessels engaged were small craft, mostly of not more than two hundred tons. The voyage commonly lasted between six and twelve weeks, during which time the passengers subsisted on bread, salted meats, and fish, beer and stronger drinks—and these in meager rations too. Vessels were unmercifully overcrowded, and the horses and cattle on board did not improve sanitary conditions. Storms and diseases, particularly scurvy, carried away perhaps a fourth of the emigrants, while infants rarely survived. On the *Arbella*—flagship of the Winthrop fleet—when the seasick "lay groaning in the cabins" a line was stretched on deck and they were brought out and made "to sway it up and down till they were warm, and by this means they soon grew well and merry." Ever on the lookout for pirates and enemy privateers, the passengers kept their swords sharp for the threatening encounter. No wonder that the Puritans punctuated the voyage with morning and evening prayers, relished two sermons on the Sabbath, and changed watches to the singing of psalms and prayers that were "*not* read out of a book." A tempest might blow the vessel out of its course or a total calm might seem to threaten the fate of the Ancient Mariner. And what relief when the American shore was sighted! And even before! "The air at twelve leagues distance smelt as sweet as a new-blown garden."

Coming in view of the new land the immigrant received his first glimpse of the dense forest that spread backward from the water's edge and extended from Maine to Carolina. The effect of the American scene upon the European newcomer was to invite him to remain and to enable him to obtain a foothold.[16] The climate generally appealed. "Heaven and earth," wrote John Smith in praise of Virginia, "never agreed better to frame a place for man's habitation," while Penn said of his colony: "The air is sweet and clear, the heavens serene, like the south parts of France, rarely overcast." And from a New Englander, Mr. Higginson, came this tribute: "Experience doth manifest itself that there is hardly a more healthful place to be found in the world that agreeth better with our English bodies. Many that have been weak and sickly in old England, by coming hither have been thoroughly healed and grown healthful strong. For here is a most extraordinary clear and dry air that is of a most healing nature to all such as are of a cold, melancholy, phlegmatic, or rheumatic temper of body." A later observer noted the keenness and brilliance of the air. "The fog of an English town is wanting; you are in a new world, and a world which knows the sun." Such a climate contributed to make the early settlers, when adapted to it, energetic, industrious, and optimistic.

The "forest primeval," with its profusion of white pines (from Maine to Massachusetts), its maples, poplars, beeches, hickories, oaks, and walnut trees offered the settler an abundance of cheap fuel and lumber for his houses, barns, furniture, and tools.

> And the ambitious vine
> Crowns with its purple mass
> The cedar reaching high
> To kiss the sky

[16] Ellen C. Semple, *American History and Its Geographic Conditions* (Boston, 1903; new ed., 1933) is the best short treatment.

> The cypress, pine
> And useful sassafras.

To England the virgin forest seemed a veritable treasure-house, for wood occupied a place in her economy comparable to that of coal and iron today. It was the raw material for ships, potash, and dyes, the source of the pitch, tar, and resin which made vessels seaworthy and watertight, and the fuel for iron, glass, and copper manufactures. Thus the virgin forest promised to the early settlers a prosperous export trade with the Old World.[17]

Equally inviting were the native food products of America. Of fish and seafood there were oysters, crabs, sturgeon, bass, cod, lobsters, eels, herring, shad, catfish, trout, and salmon. Turkeys, "fat and incredible of weight," ducks ("when they flew up there was a rushing and vibration of the air like a great storm coming through the trees"), rabbits, squirrels, partridges, quail, pheasants, elk, geese, and deer "bigger than ours" in England and "in places so many that venison is accounted a tiresom meat"—all these created a hunter's paradise. The woods displayed a wealth of raspberries, blackberries, strawberries, gooseberries, cranberries, grapes red and black, whortleberries, plums, crab apples, hickory nuts, black walnuts, chestnuts, butternuts, hazelnuts, and pecans. For a more substantial fare the settlers, like the Indians, could easily cultivate peas, beans, Indian corn, pumpkins, squashes, cucumbers, and melons, as well as sweet potatoes, tomatoes, and onions.

The land and climate were also suited to the common English grains—wheat, oats, barley, and rye. Imported swine fattened cheaply, if not copiously, upon acorns and ground nuts in the woods. When protected from wolves, sheep and goats did well, and cattle grew "to a far greater bulk of body" than in England. Transplanted fruit trees—apple, cherry, apricot, pear, quince, and peach—soon found their way into colonial orchards and afforded the settlers a varied bill of fare.[18]

Despite the richness of American resources, the settlers had to keep in touch with Europe in order to import a multitude of articles they could not produce. In this connection the coast-line served them well, providing as it did innumerable inlets and harbors which became the cradles of colonies. Only North Carolina and southern New Jersey

---

[17] T. J. Wertenbaker, *The First Americans* (New York, 1929). Chapter 1 discusses American resources in relation to English interests.

[18] Philip A. Bruce's *Economic History of Virginia in the Seventeenth Century* (2 vols., New York, 1896) presents a mass of detailed information, conveniently classified. See Vol. I, chapters 2-3 on aboriginal Virginia.

lacked harbors for ocean vessels, but even their shores could be readily visited by smaller boats from adjacent settlements. Majestic rivers such as the Kennebec, the Piscataqua, the Connecticut, the Delaware, the Susquehanna, the Potomac, the James, the York, the Rappahannock, the Santee, and the Savannah linked the coastal plain with the seaports and through them with Europe. Since the seaboard area was not tributary to one river system alone, many independent colonies could develop, each with its own outlets to the sea. The shore line and the rivers, therefore, at first spread population north and south along a narrow band of the coast so traversed by arteries of travel, especially at Chesapeake Bay, as to resemble a "sylvan Venice." [19]

On the other hand, the American environment prevented a rapid extension into the interior. The forests retarded a westward march—not only as an obstacle to travel and trade but also by virtue of the hard task of clearing the heavily wooded lands for farming. Of the rivers of North America, only two gave easy access to the interior—the St. Lawrence, held by the French, and the Hudson, dominated by the Dutch. The Appalachian Mountains, from which the rivers of the English colonies flowed to the sea, long arrested westward traffic for all save trappers and traders with pack trains carrying light and precious furs. The coastal plain, which below Delaware Bay reaches inland between a hundred and two hundred miles and widens as it extends to the south, meets the piedmont region at the fall line, where the falls impose a serious obstacle to navigation. The piedmont rises between a thousand and two thousand feet above sea level, until it merges into the mountains proper, whose lofty ridges and peaks include the White Mountains in New Hampshire and the Green Mountains in Vermont, separated by the Connecticut River, the Adirondacks and the Catskills, divided by the Hudson, and the Blue Ridge, rearing its massive wall before the Shenandoah valley. Within the Appalachian system as it extends to the southwest from Pennsylvania lies that great valley which is in reality a broad plateau at points two hundred miles wide and which, with its numerous hills and ridges running parallel to bordering mountains on the east, imposed a formidable barrier to westward travel and for a hundred years forced the English colonists to build compact settlements on the coastal plain and in the piedmont region.

In the long run, geography and resources shaped the industries of English America. Abundant rainfall and good soil fostered agriculture. New England, a glaciated area, was strewn with boulders, but

[19] Livingston Farrand's *Basis of American History* (New York, 1904—*American Nation* series) deals with the Indians and physiographic features of North America.

Based on Charles O. Paullin's "Atlas of the Historical Geography of the United States."
© Carnegie Institution of Washington. Reprinted by courtesy of the American Geographical
Society of New York.

INDIANS OF THE EASTERN UNITED STATES

once cleared the land did not quickly lose its fertility. However, the small area of level land and the short summers and long winters of New England made it an inferior farming country. The soil of eastern Pennsylvania and eastern New Jersey was good, but less fertile than the alluvial lands about the rivers of the coastal plain to the south where, in Maryland, Virginia, and North Carolina, a soil ideally suited to tobacco raising was found. However, as the coastal plain was originally a part of the ocean bed, the southern lands between the alluvial deposits in the river valleys were sandy and unproductive.

The slender farming resources of New England soon forced its people to develop a thriving lumber industry in the northeastern woods and to transform oak and pine into sturdy vessels. The cod fishery rapidly became the basis of prosperity in Massachusetts. And to all the infant colonies the forest beckoned with alluring profits from the trade in the furs and skins of beaver, deer, raccoon, panther, wolf, squirrel, fox, mink, muskrat, opossum, bear, elk, bison, and otter.[20]

> Instead of foxes, wolves and hungry bear
> That oft the Massachusetts herd do tear,
> Pequot has beaver, otter and the wary hare.

It was inevitable that the Indians of North America should come in conflict with the white intruders from England. Considering the vast extent of the continent, the Indians did not form a large population; they averaged scarcely more than two inhabitants to a square mile. Yet they probably felt the pressure of overcrowding, because their way of life required much land to support a few people. Although they did a little farming they relied chiefly on hunting and fishing. They lived in permanent villages to which the adjacent territory was attached; the idea of land ownership was well developed amongst them, and the various tribes had appropriated most of the lands suited to Indian economy. If a tribe moved from its traditional locality it was certain to encroach upon the lands of neighbors and enemies, thus precipitating war. The advance of the English therefore threatened a more intense pressure upon the Indians' means of subsistence.

This situation arose from the means of production employed by the red men. Before the arrival of the whites, the Indians utilized stone and wooden tools of a very primitive nature. They knew nothing of plows, wheels, axles, gunpowder, and firearms; they were ignorant

[20] Albert P. Brigham, *Geographic Influences in American History* (New York, 1903), is a satisfactory summary.

of horses, cattle, swine, and sheep. "Their houses," wrote Penn, "are mats or barks of trees set on poles . . . , but out of the power of the winds, for they are hardly higher than a man; they lie on reeds or grass. In travel they lodge in the woods about a great fire, with the mantle of duffels they wear by day wrapt about them, and a few boughs stuck round them." For clothing they depended chiefly upon skins. Their spoken language seemed abrupt, being confined to the use of major words without the shading supplied by tenses, moods, adverbs, and participles; and they were familiar with neither calendar nor writing. Their customs denoted a hunters' society quite at odds with the farmers' civilization brought to America by the early European settlers.[21]

From the English the Indians might readily have acquired advanced industrial methods which would have enabled them to support a larger population on a smaller area. Yet this did not happen, largely because the Indian differed so materially in outlook from the white. To the red man physical labor was repulsive and degrading, and consequently the bearing of burdens and work in the fields were assigned to women, who were primarily servants of the men. Hunting, fishing, war, and feats of prowess were the honorable pursuits which occupied the "braves." The adoption of European civilization required either that the warriors degrade themselves with labor in the fields or that the women perform all such work, with the onetime warrior-hunters degenerating in idleness. The Indians preferred to fight. The resulting wars, both with the English and among themselves, adjusted the native population to its contracting means of support. Moreover, the Indian's ignorance of medicine and his susceptibility to distempers spread by the whites—such as alcoholism, smallpox, tuberculosis, measles, and social diseases—kept the population within bounds and thus enabled the natives to adhere to their hunting, roving, predatory ways of life.

Temperamentally the practical, acquisitive, businesslike English settler was the antithesis of the easygoing, easily contented Indian. "The most merry creatures that live" who "feast and dance perpetually," the Indians were respectful of private property and yet exceedingly generous toward friends. "They are not disquieted with bills of lading and exchange, nor perplexed with chancery suits or exchequer reckonings. We sweat and toil to live"; said Penn, "their pleasure

[21] William C. MacLeod, *The American Indian Frontier* (New York, 1928), factual but controversial, states the case of the Indians against the settlers. A modern, readable study is Paul Radin, *The Story of the American Indian* (New York, 1934). The best survey is Clark Wissler, *The American Indian* (New York, 1922).

feeds them: I mean their hunting, fishing and fowling." "Give them a fine gun, coat, or other thing, it may pass twenty hands before it sticks. . . . Wealth circulateth like the blood, all parts partake, and . . . none shall want what another hath." [22]

The superiority of European weapons, together with the relative sparseness of the native population, enabled the English settlers to secure a foothold and to benefit by early contacts with the tribes. To the white strangers the Indians sold food in times of distress, taught the secret of cultivating important crops like tobacco and maize, revealed the trails of wilderness travel, and furnished fields already cleared. The fruits of immemorial experience with forest life became available to the settlers, almost overnight.

Contact with the Indian kept the colonists in close touch with his government—the channel through which all agreements between the two were made. The unit of Indian society was the tribe, and the tribes have been grouped, according to their language forms, into fifty-nine families. The Algonquin family—the most numerous of the eastern Indians—occupied both the seaboard area above North Carolina and vast stretches of the interior adjacent to the Great Lakes. Among its tribes were the Abenaki and Penobscot in Maine, the Pennacook in New Hampshire, the Massachuset and Wampanoag in Massachusetts, the Narraganset in Rhode Island, the Pequot and the Mohegan in Connecticut, the Delaware in eastern Pennsylvania and New Jersey, the Nanticoke in Maryland and Delaware, the Powhatan in eastern Virginia, and the Pamlico in North Carolina. Superior to the Algonquins in energy, prowess, and organization were the Iroquois, whose leading tribes, the Seneca, the Onondaga, the Cayuga, the Mohawk, and the Oneida (known as the Five Nations), occupied the Mohawk valley between the Hudson River and Lake Erie. The Tuscarora in North Carolina also belonged to the Iroquoian family. The third principal family of the East, the Muskhogean, held sway in the lower South and included the Creek, Chickasaw, Choctaw, and Seminole. The various tribes were grouped into confederacies, some of which, such as the Five Nations, were alliances of equals; others, like the kingdom of Powhatan, resembled an empire of conquered provinces.[23]

Within the tribe or village each person belonged to a clan—the

[22] Ellsworth Huntington, *The Red Man's Continent* (*Chronicles of America*, New Haven, 1919).

[23] A modern coöperative work consisting of scholarly essays is the *History of the State of New York* (ed. A. C. Flick, 10 vols., New York, 1933–37). Chapters 1–4 of the first volume, *Wigwam and Bouwerie*, discuss the land and the Indians.

PLAN OF A COLONIAL TOWN

This view, made at the end of the seventeenth century, shows fort, pinks, ocean ships and smaller craft, Indians, carts, settlers; well, guns, and houses.

unit which regulated daily life, protected its members, educated the young in the ancient customs, entertained visiting kinsmen, and exacted revenge for injuries on the principle of "an eye for an eye." Children belonged to the clan of their mothers; and inheritance was so devised that the property of a man would not pass to his own children but to his brothers or to his sister's children. Each clan had its symbol or "totem," such as the "bear," "beaver," or "wolf," and each elected its sachem or wise man who presided over his people as a supreme judge and custodian of morals and also represented them in the village council of the whole tribe. Smaller groups within the clan elected chiefs who led the warriors to battle. Such bands often made plundering forays against enemies, acting independently of the rest of the clan.

The ruling body of the tribal village consisted of a council attended by the chiefs and sachems. Here were decided issues of war, peace, and disposal of land which affected the whole tribe. In general the Indian government suggests an oligarchy in which old, experienced, forceful leaders—elected from hereditary ruling families, and mighty as the guardians of customs which did not change—held the reins of power. Among such leaders one might become a king, ruling his subordinate chiefs and sachems with cunning, energy, and tact, and bringing to conferences with the whites no little shrewdness, caution, and address.[24]

## THE PROCESS OF SETTLEMENT

The initial task of first settlers was to choose a site for their colony. Immediately afterward arose a fourfold problem of defense, shelter, food supply, and health. The pioneers of Virginia in May 1607 selected as the site of Jamestown a peninsula extending into the James River. There they could readily observe the approach of Spanish enemies by water and defend themselves against the attacks of natives by guarding a small strip of land. Located near the entrance to Chesapeake Bay and close to the great rivers of Virginia, Jamestown was also well placed for trade. But due to a near-by malaria-breeding swamp, the site proved to be fatally unhealthful.

Immediately the Virginians set to work constructing a fort, log huts, a storehouse, and a church. Then they planted wheat, pump-

[24] Francis Parkman's *History of the Conspiracy of Pontiac* (2 vols., Boston, 1885) opens with a brilliant chapter on the Indians.

kins, potatoes, and melons, but their agriculture did not sustain them for a long time to come. They were not farmers and they dissipated their energies in hunting gold, seeking a Northwest passage, and endeavoring to manufacture pitch, tar, soap ashes, and glass. Nor could they depend upon food sent from England. Such supplies were often damaged, destroyed, lost, or consumed en route, and other colonists who arrived before 1610 did not bring enough food for their own support, thus increasing rather than relieving the strain upon the slender rations of the colony. Only trade with the Indians enabled the settlers to survive.[25]

On the banks of the York River lay the capital of the emperor Powhatan, who ruled in lordly fashion some thirty-four tribes of his confederacy, which extended from the Roanoke River to the head of Chesapeake Bay. "He had such a grave, majestical countenance," said Captain John Smith, "as drove me into admiration to see such a state in a naked savage." Although frequently receiving the English with a show of friendship, and giving them Indian corn, turkeys, venison, bread, and vegetables in exchange for beads, knives, kettles, copper, and fishhooks, Powhatan suspected them from the start and planned to destroy them. "You have come here," he said, "not to trade but to invade my people and possess my country."

But among the English there arose a leader more than a match for the aged Powhatan. Captain John Smith was an adventurer whose exploits and hairbreadth escapes in the Netherlands, Austria, France, Transylvania, Russia, and Morocco read like tales from the Arabian Nights, and may have somewhat the same authenticity. An emblem of three Turks' heads on his coat of arms celebrated a hand-to-hand encounter in which he had dispatched three Turkish warriors. In command of expeditions which explored the Virginia rivers, Smith visited various Indian villages, where he proved to be a master trader, exciting the natives with dramatically displayed beads and other trifles or striking fear into their hearts by attacking them before they could attack him—always warily retaining his weapons when in the presence of Powhatan and his chiefs. The dauntless, resolute spirit of Smith is embodied in his phrase: "It is less perilous to go forward than to go backward." In 1608 he visited Powhatan with instructions to crown him as a king under English protection. Gifts of regal splendor were tendered and the emperor was asked to kneel to receive his copper crown. Fearing foul play, he refused, but the English "by leaning

[25] John Fiske, *Old Virginia and Her Neighbors* (2 vols., Boston, 1897). See Vol. I, chapters 8–9; Vol. II, chapter 15.

hard on his shoulders" forced him to stoop a bit, while a salvo from their boats proclaimed the coronation and startled him, with "a horrible fear." "Then remembering himself, to congratulate their kindness, he gave his old shoes and mantle to Captain Newport." [26]

Prior to 1610 the colonists were generally on the verge of starvation. They had settled on wooded land which could be cleared only with great effort, and they feared the Indians too much to risk a seizure of their open fields. In the resulting crisis John Smith assumed the powers of dictator, imposed military discipline, and forced all to work. But after his departure in 1609 a terrible winter—"the starving time"—ensued, and when relief came in the spring of 1610 only sixty of the five hundred left by Smith had survived, "subsisting on roots, herbs, acorns, walnuts, wild fruits, and snakes, with occasionally a little fish." [27]

The Virginia Company in London now breathed new life into the colony. Three expeditions arrived in 1610 and 1611 bearing fresh supplies and colonists who had been instructed to concentrate on farming. The Virginians obtained cleared lands from the Indians and thereafter kept large tracts under cultivation. They continued to secure food from the natives, developed a fishery, and imported livestock which increased rapidly. In 1612 occurred the memorable marriage of John Rolfe and the Princess Pocahontas, favorite daughter of Powhatan and, by tradition, savior of John Smith. Rolfe, who was interested in raising tobacco, saw the value of a peaceful alliance with the Indians which would provide the security and assistance needed for the new industry. Pocahontas, long a friend and protégée of the English, later visited the court of James I as the Lady Rebecca Rolfe and there enjoyed the attentions paid to her as a princess and social lioness of the season.[28]

During the decade after 1610 conditions steadily improved until 1619, when a new period of hard times set in with the arrival of a host of unseasoned settlers. An epidemic swept over the colony, taking a toll of nearly four thousand lives between 1619 and 1624. This pestilential fever seems to have been brought into the colony by the newly arrived immigrants. And while the plague was in progress occurred a terrible Indian massacre in 1622. Powhatan had been succeeded by his brother, Opechancanough, who witnessed with dismay

[26] John Gould Fletcher's *John Smith—also Pocahontas* (New York, c. 1928) is a brilliantly written personal narrative.

[27] Edward Keble Chatterton's *Captain John Smith* (New York, 1927) is the most interesting brief biography.

[28] P. A. Bruce's *The Virginia Plutarch* (2 vols., Chapel Hill, 1929) contains readable essays on early leaders. See Vol. I, chapters 1–5.

the encroachments of the English plantations upon his peoples' lands. The Indians had thus far proved ineffectual in battle with the soldier because their arrows could not penetrate his coat of mail, while their war paint did not stop his bullets. Only by a surprise attack could the Indians defeat the English. Feigning good will and friendship, Opechancanough and his men caught the settlers off guard and massacred 357 of them. Unable to engage the Indians in open fighting, the Virginians burned their cornfields. For a dozen years a guerilla warfare raged about the outskirts of the settlement with the result that the Indians were gradually pushed back. By 1630 the Virginians had demonstrated that an American colony could survive.[29]

The Pilgrims of the *Mayflower* selected, in December 1620, as the site of their colony a small clearing in the woods which fronted a good harbor—a scene somewhat suggestive of Plymouth in England. A recent plague had all but destroyed the Indians of the vicinity. The Pilgrims at first began to erect houses for communal dwellings, but soon decided "that every man should build his own house, thinking by that course men would make more haste." Disease immediately visited the little company; by March 1621 nearly half of the settlers were dead from scurvy and exposure. But the spring restored health and spirits, and none of the survivors deserted the colony.

The Pilgrims' fears of the natives were largely dissipated by visits late in March from two friendly Indians, Samoset and Squanto, who told of the recent plague among the near-by tribes. Squanto, who had previously been in England and had learned to speak English, remained at Plymouth, where he proved invaluable to the Pilgrims as guide, interpreter, and instructor in the arts of wilderness life. The chief of the nearest tribe, Massasoit of the Wampanoags, also paid his respects in person, and entered into a treaty of peace with Plymouth which was faithfully kept by both sides until his death in 1662. From a more remote tribe, the Narragansets, came the famous challenge of arrows in a snakeskin which the Pilgrims met by returning the skin filled with powder and shot. The Narragansets were apparently overawed by this display of courage or magic and did not attack. Beyond such threats and the petty thievery of an occasional prowler, the Pilgrims were not molested.

Meanwhile they were busily engaged in farming, fishing, trading, and receiving settlers sent by their London partners. The health of the colony steadily improved, although minor pests moved Bradford to write that "they are too delicate and unfit to begin new plantations

---

[29] Mary N. Stanard's *The Story of Virginia's First Century* (Philadelphia, 1928) is a trustworthy narrative of the familiar events.

that cannot endure the biting of a mosquito." By the end of 1624 the problem of food supply had been permanently solved.[30]

Nearly a thousand settlers came to Massachusetts in the Winthrop migration of 1630. The leaders selected Boston Bay instead of Salem as the center of the colony, and moved the capital first to Charlestown, where a lack of fresh water forced a removal to Boston. Winthrop had hoped to build one compact settlement protected by a fort at Newtown, now Cambridge, but the many agreeable sites about Boston intrigued his companions and they divided and founded the towns of Roxbury, Dorchester, Watertown, Medford, and Lynn.[31]

Arriving too late for planting crops, the Puritans had to eke out a bare existence during the winter of 1630–31, living on salt pork, hard-tack, shellfish, and a few supplies obtained from Indians. Against the blasts of winter the bark wigwams and sail-cloth tents of the settlers offered only a precarious shelter. Scurvy and some dread disease (probably typhus from the water at Charlestown) caused two hundred deaths and much illness, "so that in every family, lamentation, mourning and woe was heard, and no fresh food to be had to cherish them." The colony had reached its lowest depths in February 1631, when at last a vessel sent by Winthrop to Bristol returned with grain, peas, beef, and lemon juice, a cure for scurvy. Other supply ships soon arrived from Virginia or Ireland, boats were built for fishing, and farming was soon under way. In less than a year the crisis at Boston had been passed.[32]

Since the strength of the Indians depended largely upon their agriculture, the tribes in contact with the rocky New England soil were neither numerous nor powerful. Accordingly they did not menace the Puritan pioneers about Boston. In April 1631 the sachem of the neighboring tribe came to the English as a supplicant for aid in intertribal wars, and the Puritans gladly established relations of friendship.

The band of colonists who founded Maryland in 1634 settled upon the St. Charles River, a small tributary of the lower Potomac. Finding the resident Indians on the point of leaving to escape an enemy tribe, the newcomers secured the use of the Indians' houses and purchased their cleared lands. The site of the settlement (named St. Mary's) proved to be more healthful than that of Jamestown and the

[30] Although an older book, William B. Weeden's *Economic and Social History of New England* (2 vols., Boston, 1890) is still useful for its mass of well selected but poorly classified information. See Vol. I, chapters 1–3.

[31] Charles F. Adams discusses the settlement of Boston Bay in Volume I of his incisive essays, *Three Episodes of Massachusetts History* (2 vols., Boston, 1892).

[32] John Fiske, *The Beginnings of New England* (Boston, 1889), chapters 2–3.

winter climate was not so rigorous as in New England. The settlers—
the great majority of whom were farmers and artisans braced for hard
work—arrived in March 1634 and were able to raise a good crop of
maize during the year. In Virginia the Marylanders had an adequate
base of provisions; in fact the first expedition had reached the Potomac
after a sojourn in Virginia where fresh supplies were procured. Because of these initial supplies, Maryland was able to export Indian
corn after the first harvest. All in all, the colonists at St. Mary's accomplished the first tasks of settlement with a minimum of privation.[33]

After their failure in 1666–67 to establish a colony on the Cape
Fear River to the south of Virginia the proprietors of Carolina dispatched a second expedition in 1669 which proceeded by way of Barbados and Bermuda to the Kiawha River, where in 1670 a settlement
was begun at Albemarle Point. The country appeared "so delicious,
pleasant and fruitful that were it cultivated it would prove a second
paradise." A comparison of the early experiences of Virginia and New
England had convinced the Carolina proprietors of the superiority
of compact over scattered settlement, and accordingly they directed
their colonists to settle in towns. The nucleus of the colony at Albemarle Point was called Charles Town and the Kiahwa River was re-
named the Ashley.

At the outset the Charles Town settlers had to pay particular attention to defense. Not only did they fear hostile Indians, but they
also realized that the Spaniards, who claimed the South Carolina
country as part of Florida, had a strong garrison at St. Augustine
from which they could readily smite their ancient English foes. The
settlers, therefore, turned to the construction of a fort and of a palisade across Albemarle Point but the time consumed in this prevented
them from clearing land and raising sufficient food during the first
year, although they did plant corn and potatoes. By August 1670,
provisions were exhausted, but a supply ship from Virginia saved the
day. Meanwhile, the Indians had not offered resistance; in fact, a
near-by tribe, the Kiawhas, welcomed the English as allies against
their ferocious enemies, the Westoes. Among the colonists was Dr.
Henry Woodward, versed in the Indian language, who won the
friendship of the neighboring tribes and thus procured food from
them in times of extremity. The climate at Charles Town was good;
sickness was not acute; and only a few of the pioneers died.

By 1671 some of the Indians had become hostile and had turned
to the Spaniards as allies in a war for the extermination of Charles

[33] Bernard C. Steiner's *Beginnings of Maryland, 1631–1639* (Baltimore, 1903) is
a carefully written narrative.

Town. The scarcity of food persisted; so that in 1672 all but carpenters and smiths were ordered to farm and idlers were placed at forced labor. The proprietors sent provisions and cattle from Virginia, Bermuda, and New York, but in 1673 Sir Peter Colleton wrote: "our friends in Carolina sing the same song they did in the beginning —great want of vituals, clothes and tools." However, conditions gradually improved, and by 1675 the colonists had gained a secure foothold.[34]

The technique of pioneering learned by the English since 1607 enabled William Penn to establish his colony with a minimum of hardship and suffering. He instructed his colonists who sailed in 1681 to select on the western side of the Delaware River a spot "most navigable, high, dry and healthy, . . . where most ships may best ride, of deepest draught of water, if possible to load and unload at the bank . . . without boating." His plan for compact settlement in a "great town"—where the houses should be set in lawns "that it may be a green country town"—aimed to assure the benefits of society in "help, trade, education and government, also roads, travel, entertainment, etc." Arriving in 1682 Penn helped to lay out the city of Philadelphia on a neck of land two miles wide between the Delaware and Schuylkill Rivers. Ships could "ride in good anchorage in both rivers in six or eight fathoms of water," and the land was "level, dry and wholesome"—"a situation scarcely to be paralleled." The town plan of wide, straight streets and regular squares introduced the design of the later typical American city.

Penn's colony prospered from the beginning, by reason of the wealth of many of the Quaker settlers, the abundance of provisions in near-by colonies, the presence of Swedish and Dutch farmers in the lower Delaware valley, the friendly attitude of the Pennsylvania Indians, and the pains Penn had taken in planning the initial settlement. In 1684 there were nearly four hundred houses in Philadelphia, "divers of them large and well built with good cellars, three stories, and some with balconies." [35]

Believing that the Indians were the rightful owners of the soil, Penn joined them at the council fire and purchased from them the southeastern part of his province. His benevolent, peaceful spirit, his refusal to debauch them with rum or other "fire-water," his steadfastness in keeping agreements, and his avoidance of fraud, treachery,

[34] Mary Johnston, *Pioneers of the Old South* (*Chronicles of America*, New Haven, 1918), chapters 1–7, 9, 14.
[35] *Political Leaders of Provincial Pennsylvania*, by Isaac Sharpless (New York, 1919), contains interesting sketches of well-to-do emigrants.

and violence endeared him to his red brethren, who affectionately called him Onas (a pen) and revered him as a paragon of virtue among the English leaders. The peace and friendship thus established were major factors in the rapid growth of Pennsylvania.

### BIBLIOGRAPHICAL NOTE

WORKS PREVIOUSLY CITED: G. Bancroft, *History of the United States*, I, chs. 4, 7–9, 17–18; II, chs. 24, 36–38 (Indians); *Cambridge History of the British Empire*, I, pp. 53–93, 136–167; E. Channing, *History of the United States*, I, pp. 143–225, 241–268, 293–340; II, pp. 15–30, 102–126; W. Cockshott, *The Pilgrim Fathers*, chs. 3–13; E. Eggleston, *Beginners of a Nation*, Book I; J. Fiske, *Discovery of America*, I, ch. 1 (aboriginal America); *Pageant of America*, I, pp. 1–69 (Indians) and chs. 9–10, 12–14; J. Winsor (ed.), *Narrative and Critical History of America*, I, ch. 5, 6 (Indians); III, chs. 5–6, 8–9, 11–13; V, ch. 5.

SOURCES NEWLY CITED: A widely used collection is William MacDonald's *Documentary Source Book of American History* (3d ed., New York, 1926). For colonial charters see nos. 1–3, 6, 8, 11, 16–18, 21, 23. The Jameson *Original Narratives* series contains four useful collections: Clayton C. Hall (ed.), *Narratives of Early Maryland, 1633–1684* (1910); Lyon G. Tyler (ed.), *Narratives of Early Virginia, 1606–1625* (1907); Alexander S. Salley (ed.), *Narratives of Early Carolina, 1650–1708* (1911); and Albert C. Myers (ed.), *Narratives of Early Pennsylvania, West New Jersey and Delaware, 1630–1707* (1912). See also John Smith, *The Generall Historie of Virginia* in *The Travels of Captaine John Smith* (2 vols., Glasgow, 1907). On the southern Indians [James] *Adair's History of the American Indians* (ed. S. C. Williams, Johnson City, Tenn., 1930) is a classic eighteenth-century account.

SOURCES PREVIOUSLY CITED: H. S. Commager (ed.), *Documents of American History*, I, nos. 6–10 12–13, 15, 25; A. B. Hart (ed.), *American History Told by Contemporaries*, I, pp. 164–182, 187–218, 275–284, 291–301, 313–371, 563–576; *Old South Leaflets*, nos. 7, 87, 95, 153, 167, 170, 171, 176.

MAPS: D. R. Fox, *Harper's Atlas*, pp. 6–9, C. O. Paullin, *Atlas of the Historical Geography of the United States*, plates 2–7, 18–19, 33, 42–43; W. R. Shepherd, *Historical Atlas*, p. 186.

## ☆ VII ☆

## GOVERNMENT AND RELIGION

THE basic institutions of American government and the prevailing political philosophies of today were shaped in large measure during the colonial period. The office of governor, an elected, representative assembly, a two-house legislature, written constitutions, the order of local government with counties and townships, sheriffs and justices of the peace, the common law and the system of interior and superior courts—all these have their roots in the colonial past. The English origin of the colonies has placed an indelible stamp upon the political habits of the United States.[1]

And yet American political development has not slavishly duplicated that of England. New forces emerged from the American environment which gave to transplanted English institutions an American twist. When the colonies were founded, England adhered to the principle of a close union between religion and government as expressed in the Established Church, which survives today. That principle was planted in the colonies, but the American climate proved unsuited to it; instead, the American trend was toward separation of church and state—a goal attained soon after 1776 as the result of colonial experience. In England after 1600 the central government became increasingly important; in the colonies and the United States the vast extent of the country and a resulting social diversity strengthened local government at the expense of a central sovereign authority. Whoever would understand the United States must think of it not as a centralized nation but as a confederation of communities in which the habit of local government remains a powerful force.

Four pervasive factors affected the political growth of the colonies. First, the leaders—as men of large property—favored a government that would lodge power in the hands of the few. The American frontier, however, created economic opportunities for the lesser folk, enabled them to achieve a measure of independence, and caused them to champion the democratic principle of the rule of the many. Both groups received the English heritage of political liberty—the rights of jury

[1] Attention is again called to H. L. Osgood, *The American Colonies in the Seventeenth Century,* Vol. I (Virginia, New England); Vol. II (proprietary provinces).

trial, representative government, and protection of one's home, family, person, and property from arbitrary action on the part of governing bodies. Finally, the colonial charters conferred definite powers upon political agencies and implied that the king's government must respect certain rights reserved to freemen or property owners. The charters therefore accustomed the colonists to the idea of a written, fundamental law, superior to the officers of government.[2]

American history exhibits a profound, continuing conflict between two opposing tendencies. One is the trend toward the concentration of wealth and power in the hands of the few; the other, a movement for the dispersion of wealth and power among the mass of the people. In colonial days the first or aristocratic tendency was introduced by promoters of colonies who sought to establish a rule by landlords, capitalists, and clergy. However, in order to obtain settlers, the promoters were obliged to grant land to the rank and file of the immigrants. There arose accordingly a mass of small landowners, who by virtue of property owning became entitled to the guarantees of English liberty. In England the class of property owners who enjoyed political rights was small, so that English political liberty was then quite consistent with aristocracy. When large numbers of American settlers acquired property, the result was a democratizing of English liberty. Thousands of transplanted Englishmen became entitled in America to political rights which they had not enjoyed in England—the right, for instance, to vote and to hold office. They escaped the dependent status of servant or tenant and became independent farmers or artisans. The American frontier conferred economic freedom and property, and these entitled the settler to the benefits of English liberty. However, the large property owners, endeavoring to protect their interests by controlling government, came into conflict with the lesser folk who were impelled by a similar motive. The ensuing strife has been a central theme of American history. Both the aristocratic and democratic groups endeavored to interpret or use the charters to their special advantage. Inasmuch as the New England charters diffused political power rather widely among the settlers, they tended to advance the democratic principle. The charters of Maryland and Carolina, on the other hand, concentrated power in a few hands, thus fostering the aristocratic principle and sharpening the conflict between the many and the few.[3]

[2] Vernon L. Parrington's *The Colonial Mind* (New York, 1927) is a brilliant analysis of colonial thought. Very important. See Book I, Part I.

[3] Thomas F. Moran, *The Rise and Development of the Bicameral System in America* (Baltimore, 1895), is a formal study for the specialist.

## The Genesis of Representative Government

The royal charters affirmed the sovereignty of the king over the colonies, conferred upon promoters the powers of government, and invested the settlers, if freemen, with the liberties of English subjects. The Virginia charter of 1606 created a royal council of thirteen members appointed by the king, who were to reside in England and exercise the king's sovereign power over the colony. A second council of thirteen members, appointed by the royal council and empowered to elect its president and fill vacancies in its membership, was given the task of applying in Virginia the regulations of the royal council. This scheme of dual control proved ineffectual. The councillors in Virginia were of equal rank; their president was their own creature; authority was not sufficiently centralized. The first president, Edward M. Wingfield, a mild, unaggressive man, failed to rule with a firm hand and was deposed by his fellow councillors, as was also the second president. When John Smith became president and dictator in 1608 he demonstrated the value of a strong, centralized authority as against "the equality of governors" and "some outrages and follies committed by them," which had "shaken so tender a body."

The charters of 1609 and 1612 shifted the control over the colony into the hands of the Virginia Company. Its general court of stockholders received the right to elect the officers of the company, including its treasurer, to make laws for the colony, and to dispose of its lands. The company ruled Virginia through its governor and council residing there. Between 1610 and 1618 the governors enforced an iron discipline, imposed harsh laws, and meted out severe punishments. The councillors assumed military titles, the settlers were essentially soldiers, and the colony resembled a military outpost of the company.[4]

But such government by dictatorship did not make the colony pay, and the company in 1618 adopted a new policy. Previously all the land had belonged to the company and all the settlers labored as its servants. When, however, the company decided to grant land to individuals, it created a class of property owners, who—in English practice—became entitled to a voice in government. Moreover, the members of the company resident in Virginia were entitled equally with the English members to a part in the management of the colony. Accordingly, in 1618, the company appointed Sir George Yeardley governor and sent him to Virginia with instructions to set up a representative

---

[4] P. A. Bruce, *The Institutional History of Virginia* . . . (2 vols., New York, 1910), is a thorough, technical study of religion and government in the seventeenth century. See Vol. I, Parts I, III; Vol. II, Parts IV–V.

assembly. In 1619, Yeardley arranged for a division of the company's lands, assigning a hundred acres to each settler who had come to the colony before 1616 and fifty acres to those who had arrived afterward. A call was also issued for an election of representatives to a House of Burgesses, which first met at Jamestown, August 9, 1619. Sitting with the governor and council it passed laws on a variety of subjects. The elected body was by no means independent because its acts could be vetoed by the governor or set aside by the company in England, and the latter could impose its decrees upon the colony. But nevertheless the germ of self-government had been introduced into the political order of English America.

With the dissolution of the Virginia Company in 1624 its rights and powers reverted to the king. The political framework of the colony, however, remained unchanged. The king now appointed the governor and his council, but the House of Burgesses continued as before. The royal governor, who was always an Englishman and generally a man of high rank, was supposed to guard England's stake in the colony. He received from Westminster royal instructions which he was required to put into effect. He enforced the laws of the colony, commanded the militia, and issued land patents in the name of the king. His office combined the duties of head of the Anglican Church in Virginia and of foreign secretary in charge of the colony's external affairs. He had a vote in the council, of which he was a member; he summoned the legislature into session; he could veto its acts, adjourn its meetings, or dissolve it and order a new election. He appointed the local officials such as the justices of the peace, who dispensed justice in the localities, and the sheriffs, who collected taxes and enforced the law. This power of appointment enabled him to build up a party of followers and thus at times to control the House of Burgesses. An act of 1680 made him independent of the legislature by granting his salary from a permanent tax of 2s. on each hogshead of tobacco exported, so that he did not have to curry the favor of the burgesses in order to obtain his yearly means of support.[5]

Like the governor, the council after 1624 was appointed by the king, and its members held office at his pleasure, although ordinarily they served for life. They composed a small group of the wealthiest and most influential Virginians. Their familiarity with local affairs gave them an advantage over the governor, who as a stranger and an out-sider had frequently to depend upon them for information and advice. Moreover, the governor could not act without their consent. Should

[5] L. G. Tyler, "Virginia as a Royal Province," in *The South in Making of the Nation*, Vol. I, chapter 2.

he seek personal profit from his office, he could distribute favors to the wealthiest men of the colony, who generally approached him through the council. As the upper house of the legislature the council could propose bills and vote down measures offered by the elected assembly; as the highest court of the colony it could dominate the local courts and magistrates. The strategic position of the council made it the political center of gravity in Virginia during most of the seventeenth century—an oligarchy that could frustrate the elected house, thwart a hostile governor, dominate one who was weak, and bargain with one who was disposed to sell favors at a price.

Because of the checks which the governor and councillors could impose upon House of Burgesses, it occupied before 1689 a position of secondary importance. However, since its consent was necessary to the enactment of laws and the levying of taxes, it could restrain the governor and council, although it could not control them. It appears that before 1670 all freemen of Virginia (i. e., all men not slaves or indentured servants) had the right to vote in the election of burgesses, but acts of 1670 and 1684 limited the suffrage franchise to freeholders or landowners. In early times most of the freemen, except tenants, had been landowners; and as voting was by voice, the tenants had to declare their votes publicly and were therefore somewhat constrained to vote as their landlords dictated. But by 1670 a class of freemen who had neither property nor masters had arisen and were making "tumults" at elections and choosing "improper" persons as burgesses. From this class the suffrage was taken by the acts of 1670 and 1684, which thus strengthened the hold of the oligarchy of wealth upon the government of the colony.[6]

The aristocratic temper of the Virginia leaders found expression in the establishment of the Anglican faith as the official religion of Virginia. The first assembly of 1619 met in the Anglican church at Jamestown, the session was opened with Anglican prayers, and the members took the oath of supremacy. As the only colony in which the majority of the people were Anglicans, Virginia established the parish as the unit of local government, imported its ministers from England, and required all property owners to pay taxes for the support of their parish clergymen.

As the wealthy Virginians shaped the colonial government and generally controlled the governor, so also they dominated the Anglican

[6] J. A. C. Chandler, *Representation in Virginia* (Baltimore, 1896), and *History of Suffrage in Virginia* (Baltimore, 1901). These are detailed monographs for the special student.

Church and modified it to suit American needs. Due to the dispersion of settlements in Virginia, the parishes combined a large territory with a small population. One result was inadequate financial support for the churches; another was extremely irregular attendance at divine worship; a third was a marked deviation from English forms of service; and a fourth was the domination of the Church by the Virginians themselves rather than by English officials. Although Virginia formed a part of the diocese of the Bishop of London, his control over the planters was only nominal. The wealthy men of each parish, serving as vestrymen, selected the ministers and managed the finances of the church. The meager salaries and perquisites offered to the clergy did not attract men of the best caliber. The difficulties of travel made heavy inroads upon church attendance, so that the more conscientious ministers complained of a general neglect of religion, became discouraged, and departed. Those who remained enjoyed little influence in public affairs, were continually reminded of their dependence upon the planters, and bitterly complained of their want of income.[7]

Although one function of the Anglican Church in Virginia was to express, through its decorous services, the aristocratic aspirations of the planters, even in this sphere it departed from its English model. Unable to maintain an adequate ministry, the Virginians had to admit lay readers to the pulpit and allow laymen to read funeral services. Burial in a distant churchyard gave way to burial on the planters' private grounds. Marriages were commonly performed in private houses, the sacraments were administered without the proper ornaments and vessels, the holy days of the church were not observed, and communion was partaken by people who had not been confirmed. Thus even the Anglican Church—solace of kings and nobles—became somewhat popularized under the impact of the American wilderness.[8]

The decision of the Pilgrims in November 1620 to settle outside the territory of the Virginia Company nullified the privilege of self-government which had been given them. Since they had never received a royal charter, and because some of their companions talked of mutiny and anarchy, the leaders signed the Mayflower Compact, in which they agreed to erect a civil society and to enact laws to which they pledged obedience—the first American example of government of the people and by the people. Afterward the settlers met together

[7] See again T. J. Wertenbaker, *The First Americans*, chapters 4–5.

[8] A detailed and scholarly work, H. J. Eckenrode's *Separation of Church and State in Virginia* (Richmond, 1910), devotes chapter 1 to the Anglican Church.

in an assembly or General Court, where they framed laws and elected a governor and a council of assistants. When the Plymouth colony gained independence from its English backers in 1627, the settlers divided all property among themselves and formed a quasi-corporation known as the "old comers," who thereafter composed the General Court of the colony. As freemen they possessed the right to vote and to hold office. Newcomers were given political rights when the General Court voted to include them as freemen. For eighteen years the General Court was a primary assembly of all freemen who could attend the yearly meetings, but in 1638 and afterward each of the towns (of which there were ten in 1643) elected deputies to a representative assembly, which now became the General Court.

The right to vote for deputies was liberally bestowed, in that non-freemen, called inhabitants, were so privileged, although only the freemen could serve as deputies and participate in electing the governor and assistants. The legislature of Plymouth always consisted of a single house. Since the governor and his council were elected by the freemen and were not allowed to veto measures passed by the deputies, Plymouth approximated a democracy. Its foundations were Congregationalism in religion and a fairly even distribution of wealth among the people.

True to their Separatist principles, the Pilgrim Fathers did not at first create a state church, impose religious qualifications for voting, or require that churches be supported by taxes. Each congregation was a self-governing unit, unrestrained by superior church authorities. And yet the Pilgrim conception of liberty did not mean license. All freemen had to take an oath of allegiance to the king and an oath of fidelity to the colony, to possess "competent estates" (£20 value in 1669), and to qualify as men of good character and conversation. By an act of 1659, Quakers were denied the ballot; so also were opponents of "the true worship of God," as well as "liars, drunkards, swearers." After 1640 probably only a third of the adult males of Plymouth were freemen.[9]

Intent upon transforming Massachusetts into a "Bible commonwealth," John Winthrop, Thomas Dudley, and their Puritan associates felt that they must retain to themselves the powers of governing the Bay Colony; otherwise their opponents might seize control and overthrow the Puritan state. The rule of the many therefore must give way to the rule of the enlightened few. Neither Winthrop nor Cotton believed in democracy; both considered it the meanest, most contempti-

[9] A standard work is Albert E. McKinley, *The Suffrage Franchise in the Thirteen English Colonies* . . . (Philadelphia, 1905).

ble form of government. For his chosen people, the Israelites, God had ordained monarchy and aristocracy as the proper trustees of political power.[10]

The situation in Massachusetts in 1630 seemed propitious for the realization of Winthrop's ideals. The charter of Massachusetts lodged all power over the colony in the general court of the company, which in turn was composed of its shareholders, called freemen. Now only a very few freemen came to Massachusetts with Winthrop, less than one per cent of the inhabitants, and yet they possessed all the political power. However perfectly this situation suited Winthrop, it did not suit the men who were denied a part in government. Accordingly a group of 108 settlers demanded in 1630 that they be admitted as free-men of the Massachusetts Bay Company. Winthrop found himself in a quandary: if all who demanded admittance were accepted, the con-trol of the General Court would pass to the multitude; if the petitioners were denied, they would probably leave with a large following, thus weakening the colony at its very inception. In deciding the issue, the leaders admitted the 108 petitioners but about the same time devised a means of withholding political rights from men who were not of their mind.

An act of 1631 ordered that only members of an approved Puritan church might be made freemen of the company. A second act in 1636 provided that new churches could be created only with the consent of the Puritan authorities. These laws laid the foundation of the Puritan state as it endured until 1664 — a state dominated by upper-class leaders acting as magistrates (also called assistants). The clergy, as advisers of the magistrates on all sorts of subjects, exerted a great political in-fluence which was enhanced by their right to exclude new applicants from church membership. Only freemen could vote and hold office; only church members could become freemen; only men approved by the clergy could become church members. Admission to a church en-tailed a threefold scrutiny of the applicant's religious experience: first by the pastor (who might reject the applicant), then by the church officers, and finally by the congregation. From this ordeal timid persons shrank, but that was held to be their fault. In the seventeenth century only a minority of the people were church members, and all church members were not necessarily freemen; only by a special vote of the General Court could one be made a freeman.[11]

Although the body of freemen was enlarged in 1630, Winthrop

[10] Stanley Gray, "The Political Thought of John Winthrop," *New England Quarterly*, III (Oct. 1930).

[11] See again C. M. Andrews, *Colonial Period of American History*, Vol. I, chapter 20.

and the magistrates were not willing to allow them to exercise the rights conferred upon them by the charter, which stated explicitly that the freemen assembled in General Court should pass laws, grant lands, elect officers, and levy assessments. The leaders kept the charter out of sight and—between 1630 and 1634—limited the power of the freemen to the election of the governor and the council of assistants. Once a year the freemen assembled, usually at Boston, and cast their votes in the General Court. Then the governor and assistants exercised the real powers of government. However, the spirit that had moved the 108 petitioners to demand that they be admitted as freemen also moved them, when admitted, to insist that they have a larger part in managing the colony's affairs.

The first complaint came in 1632 from the people of Watertown, who objected to paying taxes that had been imposed by the governor and assistants, declaring that "it was not safe to pay moneys after that sort, for fear of bringing themselves and posterity into bondage." Winthrop rebuked the Watertown remonstrants and they apologized. But the Watertown spirit seems to have spread throughout the colony. It appears that in 1634 each of the towns selected two representatives who met at Boston and demanded to see the charter. There in black and white they read that the powers of enacting laws and of levying assessments were vested in the General Court of the freemen. Winthrop explained that the governor and the assistants had usurped these powers because the body of freemen had been so enlarged that the General Court could not function efficiently as a legislature. This explanation did not appease the representatives, however, and they declared emphatically that only the General Court had the power to raise taxes, dispose of lands, make laws, and admit freemen—in short that it was "the chief civil power of this commonwealth." [12]

To meet Winthrop's criticism about the size of the General Court and to obviate the expense and trouble incident to a yearly meeting of all the freemen, the General Court in October 1634 adopted a representative plan. The freemen of each town thereafter selected two or three deputies to represent them in the General Court, which now became a chamber composed of the deputies and assistants. The two arms of the court, however, did not always move in harmony. The assistants expressed the ideals of the few wealthy aristocratic leaders; the deputies reflected the more democratic spirit of the laboring settlers. The division widened until in 1644 it split the General Court into two

[12] George H. Haynes, *Representation and Suffrage in Massachusetts, 1620–1691* (Baltimore, 1894), is concise and clear. See again S. E. Morison, *Builders of the Bay Colony*, chapter 3 and pp. 339–346.

houses—the court of deputies and the court of assistants. A poor widow, Mrs. Sherman, had become embroiled in a lawsuit with a rich merchant, Captain Keayne. Early in the case, the issue of which was the owner-ship of a stray pig, the decision had favored merchant Keayne. Then when the widow accused him of theft, he sued her for defaming his character and obtained a verdict of £20 damages. Knowing that he was widely unpopular as an oppressor of the poor, the embattled widow appealed to the General Court. The majority of the assistants favored Keayne, but the widow had a majority of the votes of the deputies and assistants combined. The case exposed the danger that the assist-ants might be subordinated to the more numerous deputies, and thus led the next year to the division of the court into two houses, with each chamber receiving a power of veto over the other—a distinct triumph for the assistants.[13]

Through these developments the Massachusetts Bay Company, originally a trading corporation, was transformed into the governing body of a commonwealth. Membership in a Puritan church replaced the purchasing of stock as the means of becoming a freeman. The General Court ceased to be a primary assembly of the freemen, due to the adoption of representation, and the division into the two houses conformed to English parliamentary tradition rather than to the prac-tice of English trading companies. The charter of 1629 remained un-changed, but by a course of "broad construction" it had been adapted to practical needs.[14]

### THE FOUNDING OF CONNECTICUT AND RHODE ISLAND

The unrest in Massachusetts which led to the uprising of the free-men in 1634 also embroiled the colony in serious internal strife and eventually induced an exodus of malcontents who founded the new commonwealths of Connecticut and Rhode Island.

The conservative spirit of the Winthrop party which dictated the withholding of political rights from the settlers also cropped out in the granting of lands. The early settlements at Dorchester, Roxbury, Newtown, and Watertown had been planted close together, so that by 1634 many of their inhabitants felt that their lands were inadequate. What they heard of the rich soil of the Connecticut River valley made their dissatisfaction with the rule of the Massachusetts oligarchy in-

[13] E. E. Brennan, "The Massachusetts Council of the Magistrates," *New England Quarterly*, IV (Jan. 1931).

[14] A concise, well-written, modern treatment is John F. Sly, *Town Government in Massachusetts* (Cambridge, 1930), which summarizes various theories of the origins of New England towns.

creasingly acute. The Winthrop regime did not afford sufficient scope for the political talents of all the Puritans, and the stony land of Massachusetts offered but a feeble compensation.

In 1633 the Reverend Thomas Hooker arrived at Boston and forthwith took up residence as pastor at Newtown. Before long Hooker found many things of which to complain. He had been a very eminent divine in England, but he soon felt himself somewhat overshadowed by John Cotton, now the spiritual father of the Bay Colony. Apparently Hooker disliked the Massachusetts policy of admitting only a minority of the people as members of the approved churches, and he certainly disapproved of the oligarchy which Cotton sponsored. Cotton urged that the assistants should have a vested interest in their offices—that they should be reëlected annually and not be ousted except for grave cause—just as they could not "turn a private man out of his freehold, etc., without a public trial." Practice adhered to this theory because the same leaders were repeatedly elected assistants. To Hooker such a ruling caste savored of tyranny. He preferred a government in which power was more widely dispersed among the proper people, to whom the assistants should be, not superior, but subordinate.[15]

On one other point Hooker criticized the Massachusetts oligarchy. The assistants performed the functions of judges or magistrates in hearing and deciding cases at law. Cotton believed that in framing sentences the assistants should consult with the clergy who would advise what laws and punishments to apply. The colony did not yet have a codified body of law, so that the assistants were free to enforce the Mosaic law of the Scriptures, the law of England, or the code of Hammurabi. To Hooker such a procedure seemed a government not of laws but of men. In his opinion all offenses and penalties should be clearly defined: "Let the judge do according to the sentence of the law."

In 1634 some of Hooker's parishioners in Newtown petitioned the General Court for permission to migrate to the Connecticut valley. The deputies were willing to comply but Cotton and the assistants opposed, so that a decision was postponed, while the Newtowners were offered additional land in Massachusetts. But having already expressed "the strong bent of their spirits to remove thither," they persisted and gained, in May 1635, permission for themselves and for residents of Watertown, Roxbury, and Dorchester to move where they would, provided that they remain under the government of Massachusetts.

[15] George L. Walker's *Thomas Hooker* (New York, c. 1891) is the best biography available.

In 1635 the exodus began and continued during the following year. Driving their cattle and hacking their laborious way through the New England forest, little bands of pioneers journeyed to the promised land where they settled in the three river towns of Hartford, Windsor, and Wethersfield. Hooker arrived with his Newtown congregation in 1636, locating at Hartford, which became the capital of the newborn colony.

Although Massachusetts had created, in March 1636, a special commission to govern the Connecticut towns, the emigrés held steadfastly to their ideal of independence. When threatened by an Indian war early in 1637 the three settlements each elected three deputies who met at Hartford as a General Court and assumed the powers of a sovereign government. Success in the Pequot war entitled the Connecticut people to a permanent government of their own. Accordingly on May 31, 1638, Hooker expounded in his famous election day sermon the political creed of the colony. "The foundation of authority," he said, "is laid . . . in the free consent of the people, to whom belongs the choice of public magistrates, by God's own allowance." "They who have the power to appoint officers and magistrates, it is in their power also to set the bounds and limitations of the power and place unto which they call them." On these lofty principles the residents of Hartford, Windsor, and Wethersfield erected their frame of government when they adopted in January 1639 the "Fundamental Orders of Connecticut." [16]

This charter of the "people" declared their purpose of forming a confederation to preserve the purity of the Gospel and the discipline of the churches, and to provide laws for a civil government. Once a year all the freemen were to assemble in a court of election and there to choose a governor and court of assistants. Hartford, Windsor, and Wethersfield were each to select four deputies who were to meet with the governor and the assistants, thus forming a General Court. Its powers included the granting of lands, the levying of taxes, the framing of laws, and the admitting of freemen, who alone were entitled to hold office and to vote for governor, assistants, and deputies. The General Court outranked the governor in importance: it could be adjourned and dissolved only by a vote of the majority of its members; it could be called into session without his approval. The governor lacked the power to veto its measures and he could vote only in case of a tie. He could not serve two consecutive years or become eligible for the office until he had been an assistant. Similarly the assistants were

[16] H. L. Osgood, "Connecticut as a Corporate Colony," *Political Science Quarterly*, XIV (June 1899).

restricted to one-year terms. The assistants and the deputies sat together as a single house until 1698, although the assistants in 1645 received the right to reject measures passed by the deputies.[17]

The "Fundamental Orders" were not a constitution in the modern sense, inasmuch as they could be discarded or modified by a majority vote of the General Court. Although they did not create a democracy, they registered the gains that the freemen of Massachusetts had wrung from the Puritan leaders prior to 1635. Particularly significant were the safeguards imposed to prevent the assistants from becoming a permanent, self-perpetuating ruling caste. And yet the aristocratic spirit asserted itself in the action of 1645 giving the assistants a negative voice in the General Court.

Otherwise the social order in Connecticut resembled that in Massachusetts. True, there was no religious qualification for voting as in the Bay Colony, but the suffrage was restricted to freemen; and the General Court in admitting freemen accepted only men of orthodox belief. Only a member of an approved congregation could serve as governor. All the Connecticut leaders scornfully rejected the ideal of toleration; they believed with Winthrop and Cotton that the state should labor with the church to maintain uniformity of religious creed. The colony's laws of 1642 provided that if "any man after legal conviction shall have or worship any other God but the Lord God, he shall be put to death." Two years later the General Court enacted that residents who refused to contribute voluntarily to the Puritan church should be taxed for its support. Other acts fined both the negligent who failed to attend divine service and troublemakers who spoke contemptuously of the doctrines preached by the clergy. Neither Massachusetts nor Connecticut welcomed the dissenter. The chief difference between the leaders of the two colonies was that Hooker would base the government on the consent of the orthodox church members whereas Winthrop and Cotton preferred an oligarchy of ministers and assistants.[18]

Connecticut expanded both by planting new settlements about the three river towns and by absorbing the colonies of Saybrook and New Haven. In 1635 John Winthrop, Jr., arrived in Massachusetts commissioned to govern the territory near the Connecticut River to which Lord Saye and Sele, Lord Brooke, and others laid claim by virtue of a patent issued to them in 1632 by the Earl of Warwick. The younger

[17] Perry G. Miller, "Hooker and Connecticut Democracy," *New England Quarterly*, IV (Oct. 1931).

[18] M. Louise Greene's *The Development of Religious Liberty in Connecticut* (Boston, 1905) is admirable. See chapters 1-3.

Winthrop in November 1635 founded the town of Saybrook at the mouth of the river. By a doubtful purchase Connecticut annexed it in 1644.[19]

The Puritanism of John Davenport and Theophilus Eaton, founders of New Haven, was the purest of the pure. They and their associates, called free planters, met at New Haven in June 1639 and declared that the Scriptures offered perfect guidance for a commonwealth, and expressed their willingness to submit to a government which would enforce the laws of God. Then they selected twelve men who in turn chose seven of their number "to begin the church." Only the settlers admitted as church members by the committee of seven could become free burgesses or voters privileged to choose the governor and a court of magistrates and "to have the power of transacting all the public civil affairs of this plantation, of making and repealing laws, dividing inheritances, deciding differences that may arise, and doing all things . . . of like nature."

Rapidly a cluster of towns sprang up around New Haven—Fairfield, Medford, Guilford, Stamford, Greenwich, and Branford—and in 1643 they united to form the colony of New Haven. Their representatives provided for a general government of the now familiar New England type. The fundamental law of the colony, like the earlier law of New Haven town, limited the privileges of voting and office-holding to members of an approved Puritan church. The freemen or free burgesses, either personally or by proxies, elected the governor and a court of magistrates who met with deputies (elected by the free burgesses of each town) to form a one-house General Court which levied taxes, enacted laws, scrutinized and restrained the magistrates, and served as a supreme court to which all cases might be appealed. So strongly entrenched was the power of the inner ruling group that Theophilus Eaton occupied the governor's chair during the first seventeen years of the colony's existence. Otherwise the similarity of the political order in New Haven to that in Connecticut facilitated the unification of the two colonies in 1664-65.[20]

The stern, inflexible Puritanism of Massachusetts drove into exile four courageous leaders of independent spirit who founded the colony of Rhode Island. Roger Williams, the foremost liberal of seventeenth-

[19] The Tercentenary Commission of Connecticut has published sixty brief essays on Connecticut history (New Haven, 1933–36). Of particular value are: Dorothy Deming, *The Settlement of the Connecticut Towns*, no. 6 (1933), Warren S. Archibald, *Thomas Hooker*, no. 4 (1933), and Charles M. Andrews, *The Beginnings of Connecticut*, no. 32 (1934).

[20] C. M. Andrews, *The Rise and Fall of the New Haven Colony* (New Haven, 1936 —Connecticut Tercentenary Commission, no. 48).

century America, came to New England in 1631 where he preached both at Plymouth and at Salem. He was essentially a humanitarian—a man who could see the good in all sorts of people and who was prone to resist oppression of the weak and lowly by the powerful. Combining the traits of martyr and prophet, he judged issues by the test of justice and equity rather than by expediency or legality, and threw petty considerations of personal advantage and comfort to the winds. Insight and intuition moved him to eloquent, passionate utterance of truth as he felt it, irrespective of logic and authority. Although a man of fine presence, charming personality, and deep moral earnestness, he was not of the dictatorial, commanding type of leader before whom followers prostrate themselves in blind obedience.

In championing the cause of religious toleration Roger Williams declared war upon the most powerful forces of his time. Persecution was an instrument which all the entrenched churches employed to uphold their supremacy. In Massachusetts the Puritan leaders conceived of themselves as agents of God to whom He had entrusted a monopoly of divine truth. Toleration of contrary views would propagate errors which would corrupt the commonwealth and so anger the Lord that He would punish or destroy it. The persecution of His enemies was therefore necessary to propitiate a jealous God.

Roger Williams questioned all these assumptions. First, he denied that any church had a full understanding of the divine mysteries. "The experiences of our fathers' errors," he wrote, "our own mistakes, . . . and the great profession of light to come . . . may abate the edge, yea sheath up the sword of persecution." He also denied that only a Puritan state could enjoy divine favor; many great cities had prospered without adhering to the Puritan creed. Persecution tended to defeat its own ends because it inspired and strengthened the persecuted and gained sympathy and converts for their cause. Above all, the state should not persecute, because political power was often held by irreligious leaders who would use it to oppress the truly devout.[21]

Roger Williams also differed with the Massachusetts leaders over the treatment of the Indians, whom he visited, studied, and befriended. He reminded the Bay Puritans that the conversion of the Indian had been presented to the English public as the main purpose of the Massachusetts colony, and chided them for failing to carry on the good work with the funds contributed. And to whom did the land of America belong? Williams insisted that the Indians were the real

[21] James E. Ernst, *Roger Williams* (New York, 1932), is the most complete modern biography—a study in ideas rather than in personality.

owners. The Massachusetts authorities were willing to recognize and purchase the right of the natives to land they occupied and cultivated. But even though the Indians' hunting lands were as necessary to them as were their cleared fields, the Puritans insisted that all land not actually occupied belonged to the colony by virtue of its charter. The contrary views of Williams on this point were particularly obnoxious in Boston because they questioned the validity of the charter—the sacred shield of the colony's independence.

While preaching at Salem, Williams charged that the Massachusetts churches were not Christian because they upheld the right of the state to coerce and punish dissenters. He also complained that the Puritans had never formally separated from the Church of England. The Massachusetts leaders insisted that they had separated only from the *errors* of the mother church. In fact, however, they adopted the congregational system which had been first introduced by the Pilgrims at Plymouth and later accepted by John Endicott when governor at Salem before the arrival of Winthrop. Thus there were neither bishops, hierarchy, nor Anglican ritual in the New England towns. In this case the substance did not satisfy Roger Williams and he called upon his fellow Puritans to complete the separation from the Anglican Church by an open declaration.[22]

At another point Williams took issue with the Boston authorities. They believed it proper for the magistrates on occasion to administer to all inhabitants an oath required by law, whereas he insisted that the administering of an oath was an act of worship which should be performed only by truly religious people. If an oath were administered indiscriminately it would be taken by irreligious persons, and the magistrate would be guilty of having communion with wicked men in the worship of God, and thus of taking the name of the Lord in vain.

Once admonished by the Boston leaders, Williams continued to assert his unorthodox views and in 1635 was summoned to trial before the General Court. In the crisis the majority of his congregation at Salem failed to support him. His opinions respecting land titles, oaths, and the relation of the Massachusetts churches to the Church of England, together with his view that the power of magistrates extended only to the "bodies, goods and outward estate of men"—not to their consciences—provided the charges against him. The court found him guilty of unsound belief and banished him from the colony. Although

[22] Emily Easton, *Roger Williams* (Boston, 1930), is a straightforward narrative, with many excerpts from Williams's writings. Edmund J. Carpenter's *Roger Williams* (New York, c. 1909) is a brief, sympathetic study.

permitted to remain until spring because of illness, he returned to Salem and resumed his "offensive" preaching. Warned by Winthrop of the intention to arrest him, he fled in January 1636 to Plymouth and then in the spring repaired with a few friends to Narragansett Bay where he founded Providence, the nucleus of Rhode Island colony.[23]

Perhaps the most painful thorn to the Massachusetts Puritans was Mrs. Anne Hutchinson, disciple of John Cotton, who landed in Boston in 1634. Winthrop described her as "of a haughty and fierce carriage, of nimble wit and active spirit and a very voluble tongue"—"more bold than a man, though in understanding . . . inferior to many women." Consumed with a passion for theology and self-expression, she began to hold Thursday meetings in her commodious house where she repeated the gist of the Sunday sermons for the benefit of hard-working wives unable to attend church. Before long she was expounding her own views and passing judgment upon the ministers.

The chief pastor of the Boston church, the Reverend John Wilson, was a rather dour, uninspired gentleman for whom Mrs. Hutchinson conceived a violent dislike. On the other hand, she considered that the second pastor (or "teacher"), John Cotton, was blessed with rare spiritual gifts and that her brother-in-law, John Wheelwright, another minister, also enjoyed the divine favor in uncommon measure. In her discourses on religion, Mrs. Hutchinson intimated that Wilson lacked spiritual insight, or that he was under "a covenant of works"—meaning, presumably, that he was deficient in divine grace and could only repeat at second-hand the revelations to earlier men of God as recorded in the Scriptures. But it was not thus with Cotton and Wheelwright. They were under "a covenant of grace"; in them dwelt the Holy Spirit; they received fresh inspiration from on high and thus were able to interpret correctly the divine mysteries.[24]

Out of these vague concepts arose a veritable tempest. Mrs. Hutchinson and her followers, who controlled the Boston church, were called Antinomians and accused of an heretical belief that a truly spiritual person was above the written moral law. To the defense of Wilson rallied Winthrop, Dudley, and most of the ministers. In their

[23] H. B. Parkes, "Cotton and Williams Debate Religious Toleration," *New England Quarterly*, IV (Oct. 1931). G. A. Stead, "Roger Williams and the Massachusetts-Bay," *New England Quarterly*, VII (June 1934).

[24] Mrs. Hutchinson receives friendly treatment in three popular biographies, none definitive: Helen Augur, *An American Jezebel* (New York, c. 1930), Winnifred K. Rugg, *Unafraid* (Boston, 1930), and Edith Curtis, *Anne Hutchinson* (Cambridge, 1930).

sight Mrs. Hutchinson's conduct was unbecoming to women, whose place was in the home. She had bred a faction in the Boston church, humiliated its pastor, Wilson, and had therefore besmirched the prestige and authority of the clergy upon whom the integrity of the colony rested.

In January 1637 Wheelwright preached a fast-day sermon to the Boston church in which he urged his partisans to wage spiritual warfare against their enemies. When nearly all the clergy testified that their beliefs classified them as Wheelwright's enemies, the General Court found him guilty of sedition and contempt of the constituted authorities. Then in the summer of 1637 the clergy held a synod with the object of winning Cotton away from the Antinomians. In the end he said that he saw the light as the other clergy saw it, and Mrs. Hutchinson was thus isolated. In November the General Court (the colonial government now strongly opposing the Antinomians) banished Wheelwright, found Mrs. Hutchinson guilty of "slandering the ministers," and ordered her to depart. In the proceedings against her she was not allowed counsel or a jury trial and was not even informed of the reasons for her expulsion. Wheelwright went north at the beginning of winter in 1637 and founded Exeter, New Hampshire, while Mrs. Hutchinson's Boston friends established the town of Portsmouth in Rhode Island in 1638.[25]

The defeat of the Antinomian party tightened the control of the clergy in Massachusetts. The issue at stake had been: were the clergy as interpreters of the Scriptures the final source of religious truth, or did religious persons, including laymen (and laywomen), receive revelations and inspiration directly from God? The decision in 1637 favored the clergy and thereafter their inflexible rule was supreme.

While the Antinomian controversy was raging in Boston there arrived one Samuel Gorton, a London clothier and self-appointed "professor of the mysteries of Christ." Perceiving that his unorthodox views and his extreme distaste for authority would never appeal to the Bay Puritans, he departed for Plymouth, where he soon was at swords' points with the minister at whose house he lived, and was ordered out of the colony. Thence he proceeded to Portsmouth, the new stronghold of the Antinomians, ruled in patriarchal fashion by William Coddington, formerly champion of Anne Hutchinson in Boston. Gorton was soon leading a faction against Coddington, whereupon the latter again sought the wilderness and in 1639 founded the town of Newport

[25] Brooks Adams traces the growth of religious liberty in *The Emancipation of Massachusetts* (Boston, 1886). See chapters 1–2, 4.

on Rhode Island. But Coddington continued to claim the land at
Portsmouth, and eventually his followers and Gorton's engaged in
a hand-to-hand fight in which Gorton was beaten and expelled.[26]

Gorton now journeyed to Providence, where new troubles over
land titles caused his enemies to seek aid from Massachusetts. Threats
from the Bay Colony forced him to move once more, and this time he
founded in 1643 his own settlement, Shawomet, twelve miles from
Providence. But at the behest of Indians who claimed the land at
Shawomet, Massachusetts sent an armed band thither which brought
Gorton to Boston. After a stay in prison he and his followers were
ordered to leave the colony. In 1645 he went to England, where a
parliamentary commission (headed by the Earl of Warwick) granted
him the right to live at Shawomet. After his return in 1648 he renamed
his town Warwick, and thereafter he was not molested by the Massachusetts authorities.

In 1643 the settlements about Rhode Island found themselves in
a precarious position. None of them had obtained a royal charter
from the king or an official title to its lands. Massachusetts asserted a
hostile attitude (fearful lest neighbors so unorthodox might spread
their heretical opinions) and repeatedly attempted to bring them under
her own authority. But the people whom she had expelled had no intention of submitting again to her yoke, and accordingly they united to
ward off her encroachments. In 1640 Portsmouth and Newport combined under a common government. Then in 1643 Roger Williams
went to England, where in March 1644 he procured from a parliamentary commission on colonial affairs a charter which organized the people
of Providence, Newport, and Portsmouth into the corporation of
Providence Plantations in Narragansett Bay. The inhabitants received
permission to form a government of their own choice (by majority
vote), to enact and enforce laws, and to appoint and dismiss judicial
officers. The charter also defined rather vaguely an area thus to be
governed.[27]

Inasmuch as in securing the parliamentary charter of 1644 the
Rhode Islanders had ignored the king's authority, they waited until
he had been decisively defeated in the Civil War (1647) before they
united the four towns of Providence, Newport, Portsmouth, and
Shawomet under a common government. The landowners of each
town after 1650 elected deputies who met with a governor and a
council of assistants (also elected by the freeholders) to form a general

[26] K. W. Porter, "Samuel Gorton," *New England Quarterly*, VII (March 1934).
[27] J. E. Ernst, *The Political Thought of Roger Williams* (Seattle, 1929), stresses
Williams's opposition to the power of the state.

assembly. The spirit of localism found expression in the rules that the voters of the towns might either propose measures to the general assembly, or refuse to accept for their localities any of its enacted laws— rules that continued in force until 1663. The Rhode Islanders insisted upon complete separation of church and state; religious liberty meant to them the right to worship without coercion from the civil authorities, although it did not exempt one from paying taxes or sanction revolution or even resistance to established government. The institutions which developed under the charter of 1644 were approved and continued when Charles II issued a royal patent to the colony in 1663 (July 8).

Although not a democracy in the strict sense, Rhode Island made a notable advance in the direction of popular or local government. The voluntary union of the four towns exemplified the idea of federalism which later created the United States. And the little colony was the first to proclaim what has become the traditional American policy of religious freedom. Of the felicities of its settlers Roger Williams wrote in 1654: "We have long drunk of the cup of as great liberties as any people we can hear of under the whole heaven. We have not only been long free . . . from the iron yoke of wolfish bishops, and their popish ceremonies. . . . We have not felt the new chains of Presbyterian tyrants, nor in this colony have we been consumed with the over-zealous fire of the (so-called) godly Christian magistrates. Sir, we have not known what an excise means; we have almost forgotten what tithes are, yea, or taxes either, to church or commonwealth." [28]

### GOVERNMENT IN THE PROPRIETARY COLONIES

The governments of the proprietary provinces exhibit a fundamental similarity, whether the province belonged to an individual (Maryland, Maine, Pennsylvania) or to a group of men (as in the case of Carolina). The charters of all these colonies (except Pennsylvania) conferred upon the proprietors the powers of the Bishop of Durham in England —an office which had arisen in the days of incessant warfare between England and Scotland when a powerful ruler was needed to defend the northern border against the Scots. The Bishop of Durham was virtually a king over his domain, subject to the English kings chiefly in that decisions might be appealed from his courts to Westminster.

[28] The best full-length work is I. B. Richman's philosophical history, *Rhode Island, Its Making and Its Meaning* (2 vols., New York, 1902). The same author's *Rhode Island, A Study in Separatism* (Boston, 1905) gives a compressed account in chapters 1–2.

The proprietors who received the powers of the Bishop of Durham therefore became virtually sovereign in their territory, and the governments they established were monarchical in form.

The proprietors of Maryland, Maine, and Carolina were the owners and grantors of all lands within their provinces. As the source of honor they might confer titles of nobility and appoint all provincial officers, and such appointments did not need to be confirmed by the king. As the fountain of justice, the proprietors could erect courts, hear appeals, and punish or pardon offenders; their powers included the right to create, equip, and command armies and to defend their colonies; they could establish churches and make ecclesiastical appointments. Not only did they receive all revenues arising in their provinces; the king promised not to subject them to royal taxes. They could make laws, issue ordinances, enforce decrees, administer oaths, and establish towns, ports, markets, and fairs. Their laws, however, must conform to the laws of England, and judgments might be appealed from their courts to the king.

The charter of Pennsylvania did not confer upon Penn the right to create titles of nobility or grant to him the powers of the Bishop of Durham. Laws passed in the colony had to be submitted within five years to the king, who might nullify them within six months after they were received. Penn was also required to keep an agent in England to answer charges brought against him there. The king and Parliament together might tax the colony. Otherwise, the rights of Penn duplicated those bestowed upon Baltimore, Gorges, and the Carolina magnates.[29]

All the proprietary charters for those colonies begun by Englishmen contained one clause of momentous importance: laws should be enacted and taxes levied with the advice and consent of the freemen of the respective colonies. This guaranteed some sort of a legislature through which influential colonists might resist the proprietary interest. However much the proprietors might resemble the king in theory, actually they were but a shadow of royalty. They commonly lived in England, not in their provinces, and thus had to rule through deputies. In their persons they reflected none of the splendor of the divinity that doth hedge a king. Nor did they possess financial resources equal to their rights and pretensions. The colonists therefore were not inhibited from encroaching upon their privileges. As the House of Commons in England strove to limit even the king's power, so also the colonists en-

[29] H. L. Osgood, "The Proprietary Province as a Form of Colonial Government," *American Historical Review*, II (July 1897) and III (Oct. 1897, Jan. 1898). See also Osgood's "The Corporation as a Form of Colonial Government," *Political Science Quarterly*, XI (June, Sept., Dec. 1896).

deavored to frustrate the proprietors. The ensuing conflict endured until the Revolutionary War finally overthrew the monarchical principle as embedded in the then remaining proprietary governments of Maryland and Pennsylvania.

In all the proprietary colonies the proprietors appointed the governors, removed them at will, invested them with their powers, and advised them what acts to perform. The governor was both the political agent of the proprietor and the overseer of his landed estates. "Wherever the governor was, there also was the proprietor." The vast powers conferred upon the proprietors by the charters—executive, legislative, judicial, appointive, ecclesiastical, and military—were exercised in their behalf by the governors, whose primary business was to protect the proprietary interest.

With respect to other features of the proprietary governments—the governor's council, the legislature, and religious policy—variations occurred in the early development of Maryland, South Carolina, and Pennsylvania which gave each colony an individual character.

In Maryland the members of the governor's council were appointed by Lord Baltimore (usually upon recommendation of the governor) and served at the pleasure of the proprietor. As his personal representatives they were supposed to supervise the governors and to compel them to act as he directed. The council during the seventeenth century was a small body varying from three to ten members, who, once appointed, generally held office for life.

Since the Maryland charter did not specify the nature of the legislature to be created, and since it came into being after the governor and council were appointed, its development depended largely upon concessions made to the freemen or landowners by the proprietor. Before 1650 the governor consulted with the freemen in the enactment of law. Sometimes they were all summoned to a general assembly; at other times they elected representatives the method employed being determined by the governor, who called the legislature into session. The plan of a direct primary assembly of all the landowners obliged those unable to attend to assign their proxies to others present at the meeting. This practice tended to concentrate too many votes or proxies in a few hands; hence in 1650 the freemen petitioned that the scheme of elected delegates be adopted permanently. With this request Lord Baltimore complied, and thereafter the Maryland legislature adhered to the representative plan.[30]

[30] Newton D. Mereness, *Maryland as a Proprietary Province* (New York, 1901), is one of the best monographs on colonial government but is too detailed for the general reader.

In the early days the freemen or their delegates had met in joint session with the governor and the council. However, the freemen felt somewhat overawed and constrained by the power and dignity of these officials, and accordingly requested that they might meet together in a separate chamber where they would enjoy greater freedom of action—a proposal that was granted, also in 1650. The resulting division of the legislature into two houses gave the council a veto over the delegates and *vice versa*. Although the impetus for the change came from the freemen, in the long run this division strengthened the council by giving it power to thwart the delegates. Otherwise, had a single chamber existed, the delegates would have gained control as their number and independence increased.

Lord Baltimore attempted to limit the right of the freemen in the legislature to the mere privilege of ratifying measures proposed by himself. But the freemen insisted that they too should propose or initiate bills. A heated contest broke out over this issue and a deadlock ensued when the freemen refused to assent to the proprietor's measures and he refused to recognize their demands. Finally, in 1650 he gave way and conceded to the delegates the right of proposing measures on their own initiative.

Another major dispute arose between the freemen and the proprietor over his exercise of the veto power. They pointed out that his governor could veto acts of the legislature and contended that one such veto was enough. Lord Baltimore, however, insisted upon his right to veto laws that had been signed by the governor. A survey made in 1674 showed that, of all the acts of the previous forty years, only thirty had been approved by the proprietor. His right to veto at will all the others created a sense of insecurity as to the legal foundations of the colony. On this issue, however, the Calverts would not surrender; all the delegates could obtain was the promise that if the laws were not vetoed by the proprietor within eighteen months after their passage, they were to stand as approved.[31]

Despite the gains made by the freemen, the government of Maryland in the seventeenth century was essentially a Calvert oligarchy. The governor could adjourn or dissolve the legislature and veto its acts. By virtue of his exercise of the appointing power, he built up a family party which controlled the public administration. The council, which could thwart the House of Delegates, consisted generally of picked men: in 1669 it included three Calverts, a Calvert brother-in-law, and two intimate friends of the family. Only landowners could

[31] See again C. C. Hall, *The Lords Baltimore*, chapters 2–4.

vote for the delegates, and they in turn might be overridden by the council, by the governor, and by the proprietary veto. The people had no control over appointments, land grants, or executive action. However, some steps toward popular government had been taken. The House of Delegates had established the representative principle, won the right to initiate bills, and wrung from the proprietor his promise to exercise his veto power within eighteen months. Above all, taxes could not be imposed or laws enacted without the consent of the elected house. The freemen therefore could resist, even if they could not dominate, the proprietor.

The interest of Lord Baltimore largely determined the religious policy of Maryland. As a Roman Catholic he desired to provide a shelter for his co-religionists, but he could not establish a state church contrary to the laws of England; consequently he could neither make Catholicism an official religion nor in any way discriminate against Anglicans. Neither Catholics nor Anglicans came to Maryland in large numbers, so that in order to obtain settlers he had to offer religious toleration to other Protestants. Catholics, Protestants, and Anglicans therefore all found a welcome.

Realizing the dangers of religious strife, Baltimore warned the Catholic leaders in charge of the colony not to persecute or give offense to Protestants, who composed a majority of the laboring settlers. Eventually he had to suppress a small but ardent group of Jesuit priests who attempted to shape the destinies of the colony. They arrived with the first expedition in 1634 and procured large tracts of land from the proprietor. Then through their Indian missions they acquired other great grants from the natives. Soon they were asserting their virtual independence of the proprietor, implying for instance that they were exempt from taxes and the jurisdiction of his courts. Determined to be master in his own household, and fearing that the Jesuits would turn the English government against his colony, Lord Baltimore asserted the supremacy of his laws over the priests, and in 1641 he extended to Maryland the English statute of mortmain, which provided that religious orders could not acquire additional lands. Meanwhile, the papacy had decreed that the Jesuits should surrender the lands obtained from Indians and refrain from sending other priests to the colony. The existing Jesuit missions remained, but in strict subordination to the proprietor.[32]

In the 1640's the relative importance of the Catholics in Maryland

[32] The special student may consult George Petrie, *Church and State in Maryland* (Baltimore, 1892).

declined as the Protestants—especially Puritans from Virginia—increased in numbers. The triumph of the Puritans in the English Civil War further exposed the proprietor to attack. Accordingly in 1648 Lord Baltimore appointed a Protestant governor and sent over to the colony a bill which became the famous Toleration Act of 1649. It guaranteed freedom of conscience to all Christians who respected the rights of the proprietor. Any person who disturbed a Christian in his chosen worship should pay treble damages and a fine of twenty shillings. Should any troublemaker call a fellow colonist an offensive name—such as heretic, schismatic, idolator, popish priest, or roundhead—he was to be punished by fine or whipping and imprisonment. The act asserted openly its underlying principle of political expediency: "the enforcing of conscience in matters of religion hath frequently fallen out to be of dangerous consequences in those commonwealths where it hath been practised."

Except for a brief period, 1654–58, the Toleration Act of 1649 guided the religious policy of the proprietors, and as a result the radical Protestants multiplied until they accounted for three-fourths of the population, as against a sixth who were Anglicans and a twelfth who were Roman Catholics. Later, when the king had taken charge of the government of Maryland, the Anglican Church was officially established in 1692, but it did not attain the supremacy which it enjoyed in Virginia.

The proprietors of Carolina never achieved an effective control over their two colonies. The division of the proprietary rights among eight men, most of whom were preoccupied with other affairs in England, deprived their councils of a strong, guiding hand. By the time Old Charles Town was founded in 1670, two of the proprietors (Colleton and Albemarle) had died, Clarendon was in exile, and John, Lord Berkeley had lost interest. Within twenty years after 1663 the entire personnel of the proprietary board had changed, and the new proprietors were generally incompetent or indifferent. Although two or three men usually dominated the proprietary board, the necessity of considering the rights of the others restricted their power to act. That there were two colonies to be managed instead of one also complicated matters. By and large the proprietors devoted their efforts to the Charles Town settlement, and left the northern colony about Albemarle Sound to shift for itself. They provided a separate government for each colony until 1691, when North Carolina was placed under a deputy of the governor at Charles Town. In effect, however, each colony retained a separate government, and in 1712 an independent governor was appointed for North Carolina. About 1700 the names North Carolina and South Carolina came into vogue.[33]

When Lord Ashley was the moving force in Carolina affairs in 1669 he had prepared a scheme of government known as the Fundamental Constitutions of Carolina. Despite the failure of the proprietors to impose it upon the colonies, it had an important effect on their political development. It designated the most important proprietor as the "palatine," and anticipated that each proprietor should exert an individual influence in provincial affairs. Instead of the single authority of the proprietary board there was to be a division of powers among the individual proprietors, with provision for their coöperation in matters of joint interest. This division of power contributed materially toward the weakness of the proprietary rule.

The peculiar feature of government in the Carolinas was the position of the governor and the council. The chief proprietor, or palatine, appointed the governor for each colony, while each of the other proprietors appointed a deputy councillor. The deputy councillors formed the proprietary council in each province, with the result that the governor, as deputy of one proprietor, was only a leader among equals. Powers exercised by the governor alone in Maryland were exercised in each of the Carolinas by the governor and deputy councillors jointly—powers such as the calling, proroguing, and dissolving of the legislature, the appointing of officials, the spending of proprietary funds, and the ratifying or vetoing of colonial legislation. The governor and the deputy councillors also sat with elected delegates as a part of the legislature or local parliament.

The proprietors allowed the landowners in each colony to elect another set of councillors, who often met with the deputy councillors to form a sort of grand council. The elected councillors served for indefinite terms, save that they might be removed at the pleasure of the proprietors. Acting together, the two sets of councillors prepared bills for the legislature to consider, expended money appropriated by it, raised military forces, declared war and negotiated treaties. The elected councillors did not share the other functions of the deputy councillors, nor were they members of the legislature. The joint council survived until 1691; afterward, all the councillors were appointed by the proprietors.

The legislature in each of the two colonies consisted of the governor, the deputy councillors, and delegates elected by the resident

[33] John S. Bassett, *The Constitutional Beginnings of North Carolina, 1663–1729* (Baltimore, 1894), is a good brief statement.

freeholders. Since measures of the delegates could be vetoed by the deputy councillors, or set aside by the proprietors, and because the delegates could consider only bills presented to them by the grand council, their legal position was secondary. However, in 1693 the proprietors conceded to the delegates the right to prepare and submit bills of their own. Originally, the legislature of each colony had been unicameral, but in each case the representatives separated from the governor and the council to form a two-house parliament (about 1700).[34]

During the formative period, 1670–90, conditions in South Carolina were favorable to the growth of a small ruling class of the wealthiest colonists. Only freeholders could vote for delegates to the legislature, and the powers of the delegates were narrowly circumscribed; consequently the most influential men were the councillors, whom the remote and indifferent proprietors could not keep in check. On the most vital issues—such as the enforcement of the Fundamental Constitutions—the deputy councillors defied the proprietors and united with the elected councillors to defeat them. The refusal of the proprietors to continue the elected councillors after 1691 is evidence that a colonial oligarchy was developing which acted in defiance of the proprietary interests.

With reference to religious policy, the Carolina proprietors intended that the colonial legislatures should provide for the erection and maintenance of Anglican churches. Other law-abiding sects which professed a belief in God should enjoy freedom of worship, although their ministers should not be supported by public taxes. By 1700 the Anglicans, who then composed half of the population of South Carolina, had erected two churches there. Baptists and Quakers had each an organized congregation, and there were three French Huguenot societies, as well as a church supported jointly by Presbyterians and Congregationalists. A South Carolina act of 1697 granted religious toleration to all Christians except papists. Not until 1672 did North Carolina receive the benefit of public worship, when Quaker preachers came into the colony, and not until 1702 was a meeting-house erected. Quakerism was the dominant faith among the North Carolinians during those early years.[35]

The government of Pennsylvania evolved in experimental fashion. Penn was not a doctrinaire; he believed that governments "like clocks go from the motion men give them, and as governments are made

[34] Edson L. Whitney, *Government of the Colony of South Carolina* (Baltimore, 1895)—a technical study, for the advanced student.
[35] Stephen B. Weeks, *The Religious Development of North Carolina* (Baltimore, 1892), is a monograph of the detailed type.

and moved by men, so by them they are ruined, too . . . Let men be good and the government cannot be bad; if it be ill, they will cure it." Once he urged the Pennsylvanians "not to give away anything of liberty and property that they do at present enjoy," and again he wrote: "Any government is free to the people under it . . . where the laws rule and the people are a party to those laws. . . ."

In April 1682 Penn issued his "first frame of government" as a constitution for the colony. It provided for a council of seventy-two members who were to be elected by the resident landowners. As a part of the legislature, the council alone could propose measures; as an executive body it was to function through four committees. The first frame also created an assembly of two hundred members, likewise selected by the landowners, which had the privilege of accepting or rejecting the bills submitted by the council. The governor, appointed by Penn, had a triple vote in the council, but was not authorized to veto the acts approved by the council and assembly. Both of these bodies proved to be too large for the infant colony; consequently in 1683 Penn issued a "second frame," which reduced the number of assemblymen and councillors to thirty-six and eighteen respectively. It also gave to the assembly the right to amend the bills proposed by the council and conferred the suffrage franchise upon owners of fifty acres of land or of other property worth £50.[36]

Penn's governor, William Markham, issued in 1696 a "third frame," which provided that the council should consist of twelve members and the assembly of twenty-four. The assembly now gained the right to propose legislation. By the "fourth frame" in 1701 Penn vested all legislative power in the assembly, thus creating a one-house legislature and confining the council to executive and judicial functions. Thereafter Penn appointed the councillors and endowed the governor with the veto power. He issued the fourth frame because the elected council and the elected assembly had quarreled incessantly, each claiming to represent the voting property owners. The change to a one-house legislature was urged by the most wealthy men of the colony, and since they generally controlled it afterward, the innovation did not spell a triumph for democracy.

In accordance with their religious convictions, Penn and his fellow Quakers did not give legal preference or support to any church in the colony. All believers in God enjoyed the blessing of free worship,

[36] Two attractive, readable sketches are Isaac Sharpless, *Two Centuries of Pennsylvania History* (Philadelphia, 1900) and *A History of the Quaker Government in Pennsylvania* (2 vols., Philadelphia, 1898, 1899). See again C. M. Andrews, *The Colonial Period of American History*, Vol. III, chapter 7.

while all Christians were eligible for the right to vote and to hold office. Pennsylvania thus became a secure retreat for Protestants of every persuasion.

The seventeenth century witnessed the rapid emergence of a colonial ruling class. In the major colonies the council became the most powerful political force. Its members, who represented the families of superior wealth, held office year after year and thus mastered the technique of politics and the details of local administration. As the social elite in each colony, they were the natural associates of governors or officials sent from England by proprietors or the king. In constant touch with such officials, they had every opportunity to influence their views and conduct and thus to frustrate in large measure the efforts to shape American development from England. Similarly the councillors had an advantage over the lesser colonists represented in the elected house—not only by means of their negative voice in the legislature but also by virtue of their long tenure, intimate association together, and compact organization. Even the elected house was not a democratic body, inasmuch as the suffrage was generally limited to property holders, thus excluding indentured servants, tenants, and wage-earners from participation in politics.[37]

On the other hand the establishment of the elected house and its success in winning the right to initiate legislation, together with its right to share the powers of legislation and taxation, afforded an agency through which the smaller property owners could resist the aristocratic council. As the body of small landowners increased they found ready at hand in the elected house an instrument for democratic action. The aristocracy of large landowners and the democracy of small or expectant landowners readily came into conflict, because—among many other interests—both strove to possess available lands which at any given time were limited in extent.

[37] W. N. Franklin, "Some Aspects of Representation in the American Colonies," *North Carolina Historical Review*, VI (Jan. 1929).

### BIBLIOGRAPHICAL NOTE

WORKS PREVIOUSLY CITED: C. F. Adams, "The Antinomian Controversy," in *Three Episodes of Massachusetts History*—a vigorous indictment of the orthodox Puritans; J. T. Adams, *Founding of New England*, pp. 160–174, 189–205; C. M. Andrews, *Colonial Period of American History*, I, ch. 9, chs. 22–23; II, chs. 1–3, pp. 100–124, 299–324; C. M. Andrews, *Colonial Self-Government*, chs. 10, 12; C. M. Andrews, *Our Earliest Colonial Settlements*, chs. 4–5; G. Bancroft, *History of the United States*, I, ch. 9; I. Calder, *New Haven Colony*, chs. 5–7; *Cambridge History of the British Empire*, I, pp. 167–182; E. Channing, *History of the United States*, I, pp. 340–413, 511–524; E. P. Cheyney, *European Background of American History*, chs. 13–16; W. Cockshott, *The Pil-*

*grim Fathers*, ch. 14; E. Eggleston, *Beginners of a Nation*, Book III, chs. 2–3; S. E. Morison, *Builders of the Bay Colony*, ch. 3; L. G. Tyler, *England in America*, chs. 8, 13–15; T. J. Wertenbaker, *Virginia under the Stuarts*, pp. 29–42, ch. 3; R. C. Winthrop, *Life and Letters of John Winthrop*, II (for 1630–1649).

SPECIAL STUDIES FOR ADVANCED STUDENTS: Two leading American scholars, Herbert B. Adams and Herbert L. Osgood, gave a strong impetus to the study of colonial political institutions. Adams between 1876 and 1901 directed many researches at Johns Hopkins University which were published at Baltimore in the *Johns Hopkins University Studies in Historical and Political Science*. The works cited in the footnotes to this chapter by Moran, Chandler, Haynes, Petrie, Bassett, Whitney, and Weeks appear in this series. It also includes the following: H. B. Adams, *The Germanic Origin of New England Towns* (1882); William E. Foster, *Town Government in Rhode Island* (1886); Edward Ingle, *Local Institutions of Virginia* (1885); Percy L. Kaye, *The Colonial Executive Prior to the Restoration* (1900); Paul E. Lauer, *Church and State in New England* (1892); and Lewis W. Wilhelm, *Local Institutions of Maryland* (1885). Edward Channing contributed two studies to the series: *Town and County Government in the English Colonies . . .* (1884) and *The Narragansett Planters* (1886).

Among the studies made under Osgood at Columbia (1890–1918) and published at New York in the *Columbia University Studies in History, Economics and Public Law* are: Cortlandt F. Bishop, *History of Elections in the American Colonies* (1893); Percy S. Flippin, *The Royal Government in Virginia, 1624–1775* (1919); Charles J. Hilkey, *Legal Development in Colonial Massachusetts, 1630–1686* (1910); Elmer I. Miller, *The Legislature of the Province of Virginia* (1907); William R. Shepherd, *History of Proprietary Government in Pennsylvania* (1896); Edwin P. Tanner, *The Province of New Jersey, 1664–1738* (1908).

Other special studies are: Nelson P. Mead, *Connecticut as a Corporate Colony* (Lancaster, 1906), and Cyrus H. Karraker, *The Seventeenth-Century Sheriff* (Philadelphia, 1930).

SOURCES NEWLY CITED: Two standard collections contain the colonial charters. They are: Francis N. Thorpe, *The Federal and State Constitutions, Colonial Charters and Other Organic Laws . . .* (7 vols., Washington, 1909), and Benjamin P. Poore, *The Federal and State Constitutions, Colonial Charters, and Other Organic Laws of the United States* (2 vols., Washington, 1877). The Jameson *Original Narratives* series includes the following important sources: J. Franklin Jameson (ed.), *Johnson's Wonder-Working Providence* (New York, 1910), and James K. Hosmer (ed.), *Winthrop's Journal*, "History of New England, 1630–1649" (2 vols., New York, 1908). *The Fundamental Orders of Connecticut* are reprinted as no. 20 of the Connecticut Tercentenary Commission publications (New Haven, 1934). An attractive collection of important records is the *Documentary History of Rhode Island* (ed. Howard M. Chapin, 2 vols., Providence, 1916).

SOURCES PREVIOUSLY CITED: H. S. Commager (ed.), *Documents of American History*, I, nos. 11, 16–17, 22, 25, 29; A. B. Hart (ed.), *American History Told by Contemporaries*, I, pp. 218–225, 247–261, 373–423; W. MacDonald, *Documentary Source Book of American History*, nos. 4, 5, 9, 10, 14; *Old South Leaflets*, nos. 7–8, 53–55, 66, 164.

# VIII

## COLONIAL NEIGHBORS

DURING the seventeenth century three European powers besides Spain challenged England's growing ascendancy in North America. The most immediate threat came from the Dutch Republic, which in 1624 planted on the Hudson River a colony which later menaced the unity of England's colonial possessions. Rivalry and warfare between these two aspiring powers continued for fifty years until the Dutch were defeated and forced to surrender their North American territories. By what means and for what reasons were the Dutch able to get a foothold in the Hudson and Delaware valleys, and why did they ultimately fail as colonizers there?

### DUTCH AND SWEDISH COLONIZATION

The birth of the Dutch Republic unfolds some striking parallels to the formation of the United States. Seven provinces of the northern Netherlands—Holland, Utrecht, Friesland, Gröningen, Overyssel, Gelderland, and Zealand—united in 1579 to form a loose confederation. Inhabited by people of Teutonic stock, these provinces—once a part of the Holy Roman Empire—had passed under the control of the Duke of Burgundy, from whose grandson they were inherited by Charles I, King of Spain. The Dutch nobles and burghers had long enjoyed extensive rights. Each province had its own assembly which made voluntary grants of money to the reigning duke or king. About 1550 Protestantism, especially Calvinism, spread rapidly among the Dutch, indoctrinating the landed nobles and the townsmen alike.[1] Holland, with its busy industrial and commercial towns—Amsterdam, Rotterdam, Haarlem, and Leyden—towered above its sister provinces. Economically, the Dutch occupied at the mouth of the Rhine a tremendously valuable region which united the rich hinterland of Germany with the outside world. Due to the small extent of their land and their strategic location for trade the Dutch had concentrated upon industrial and maritime pursuits. Their manufactures of woolen and linen cloth, especially after 1550, were

[1] Petrus J. Blok, *A History of the People of the Netherlands* (5 vols., New York, 1908–12) is the outstanding modern authority. See Vol. III.

unexcelled. Amsterdam, it has been said, was founded upon the herring fishery. The supremacy of the Dutch in commerce arose from a
variety of factors: "Their cheap freights due to building ships which
cost less, sailed with fewer hands, and were adapted to particular
trades . . .; the light customs which made their ports the center of
the world's traffic; their low rates of interest which facilitated the conduct of business on the most advantageous terms; their banking system which served 'to make a small sum equivalent in trade to a
greater' . . .; their education of children, daughters as well as sons;
their practice of equal inheritance; their thrift; their toleration in
religion; their encouragement of immigration and inventions; their
swift determination of suits in which mercantile interests were involved; and, lastly, the presence of experienced merchants in their
councils of state." [2]

Under the Emperor Charles V (King Charles I of Spain), who
ruled the Netherlands from 1519 till 1555, the Dutch were on the
whole well satisfied. The emperor, himself born and bred in the
Netherlands, elicited warm personal support from his Dutch subjects. However, his successor, Philip II, was spiritually an alien who
hated the spirit of independence abroad in the Netherlands and used
the Inquisition in a merciless campaign to eradicate Protestantism.
When the Dutch resisted his invasion of their traditional rights, he
imposed upon them a ruthless military despotism which provoked one
of the most savage wars in history. Seemingly impotent in the face of
the mighty King of Spain, the Dutch found a leader of inflexible purpose and courage in Prince William of Orange, a large landowner in
Holland, and a convert from Catholicism to Calvinism, whose refusal
to compromise led his followers to call him William the Silent. In 1579
the seven provinces formed the Union of Utrecht and in 1581 declared their independence of Philip II, thereby creating the United
Netherlands. They erected a loose federal government ruled by a weak
Council of State and an Estates-General composed of delegates from
the provincial assemblies, which, by retaining to themselves the power
of taxation, asserted their individual sovereignty. The weakness of the
central government greatly militated against unified resistance, but
William the Silent and his son, Maurice of Nassau, by personal leadership provided the necessary cement of union.

In 1609 Spain agreed to a twelve-year truce which contained a
veiled recognition of the independence of the Dutch. One great asset
in their favor had been their superior prowess on the sea which had

[2] Quoted from E. Lipson, *Economic History of England*, by permission of the publishers, A. & C. Black, London.

enabled them to plunder Spanish trading and treasure ships. England in 1585 entered a military alliance with the Dutch which eventually led to the defeat of the great Spanish Armada in 1588. Spain then became involved in war with the French Protestants; in 1592 her greatest agent in the Netherlands, Alexander Farnese, Duke of Parma, died; and Philip II passed away in 1598. These events sealed the doom of the power of Spain in the northern Netherlands. Although she resumed the war in 1621, the futility of her efforts forced her in 1648 to recognize at Westphalia the unconditional independence of the Dutch Republic.

As the pressure from Spain abated, the Dutch people divided into two bitterly hostile parties. Maurice of Nassau commanded one faction, the Orange party, which stood for a strong central government (even a monarchy) and for a vigorous continuation of the war with Spain. In opposition were the Republicans, led by John of Oldenbarneveldt, advocate of peace and champion of the sovereignty and independence of the provinces. Religion finally brought the two factions into open conflict. The Republicans favored toleration and inclined toward the Arminian creed which questioned the Calvinist doctrine of predestination in its harshest form. Like other strict Calvinists, the leaders of the Orange party believed in persecution and the regulation of religion, morals, and popular amusements by law. Nor would they modify their conviction that God had irrevocably predetermined the salvation or damnation of all individual souls.

The war with Spain inevitably drew the Netherlands into the race for colonial empire. After Spain had annexed the Portuguese colonies in the Far East in 1581 it was only natural for the Dutch to encroach upon her new preserves. In 1602 John of Oldenbarneveldt organized the Dutch merchants who had become concerned in the oriental trade into the Dutch East India Company—a move to forestall a similar action by the Orange party. However, the peaceful inclinations of the Republican leaders who controlled the company dictated a Spanish policy of appeasement and hence they avoided giving unnecessary offense to Spain. It is probable that, at the approach of peace, they sought a non-Spanish, non-Portuguese route to the Orient, and thus commissioned an English navigator, Henry Hudson, to discover an all-Dutch passage around northern Europe. Hudson sailed from Amsterdam in April 1609, but soon despaired of penetrating the frozen North, abandoned his original plan, and crossed the Atlantic to North America in search of the elusive Northwest passage.[3]

---

[3] Henry C. Murphy, *Henry Hudson in Holland* (The Hague, 1909), is the best study of the object of Hudson's voyage.

From the coast of Maine Hudson sailed to Chesapeake Bay, then discovered Delaware Bay and finally reached the mouth of the great river which now bears his name. His little vessel, the *Half-Moon*, proceeded up the river, perhaps to the present site of Albany, where he entertained a band of Mohawk Indians and made them merry with brandy. His return to England ended his service with the Dutch, but the sailors of the *Half-Moon* brought to Holland the story of the discovery, the lure of a rich trade in furs, and the promise of a country "pleasant with grass and flowers and as goodly trees as ever they had seen." [4]

During the first years of the truce the influence of the Republicans prevented a grand offensive against the Spanish power in America. However, individual merchants of Holland and Friesland obtained from their provincial governments the privilege of exploring the country visited by Hudson and of trafficking with the Indians for beaver, mink, and otter skins. A few trading houses were erected on Manhattan Island and Dutch voyagers in 1614 explored the Delaware region and pushed eastward through Long Island Sound, ascended the Connecticut River, visited Narragansett Bay, rounded Cape Cod, and sailed northward to Massachusetts Bay. Shortly afterward a group of Amsterdam merchants who had promoted this exploration formed the New Netherland Company and procured from the Estates-General a three-year monopoly of trade with the country between Cape Cod and Delaware Bay.

This monopoly expired just before a political revolution occurred in the Netherlands. In 1618–19 Maurice of Nassau and the Orange party overthrew the Republicans, executed John of Oldenbarneveldt, seized control of the Dutch governments, imposed their stern Calvinism upon the country by promulgating the Dordrecht Creed, and expelled two hundred of the Republican preachers from their pulpits. Closely allied with the Orange leaders was an exiled Fleming, William Usselinx, a restless promoter who had fled to Amsterdam from Antwerp to escape the Spaniards. Usselinx since 1606 had been urging upon the Dutch a grand project for colonization in America—partly as a means of crushing Spain, partly to obtain gold and silver, partly to increase the sale of Dutch manufactures, and above all to gain a rich trade in American products which could be procured cheap and sold dear. Since Usselinx had proposed to colonize in Spanish America he had been an ardent advocate of the war. The triumph of the war

---

[4] The best biography, Llewelyn Powys, *Henry Hudson* (New York, 1928), presents new material with literary skill. A slight biography is Thomas A. Janvier's *Henry Hudson* (New York, 1909).

party in 1618 and the end of the truce in 1621 finally gave the signal for a determined attack upon Spain in the New World.[5]

On June 3, 1621, the Estates-General incorporated the Dutch West India Company and bestowed upon it a twenty-four-year monopoly of the trade of western Africa, of the eastern coasts of North and South America, and of all the islands in between. Conceived very largely as a weapon against Spain, the company was empowered to build forts, maintain troops, make alliances with natives, and wage war; and toward these ends it received from the Estates-General a promise of a million florins and the use of "sixteen well-appointed ships and four yachts." Although the inside promoters of the company regarded it primarily as a means of plundering the Portuguese in Brazil and the Spaniards in the Caribbean, its charter authorized it to "advance the peopling of fruitful and unsettled parts." A governor and a board of nineteen directors managed the company's affairs and appointed and discharged its subordinate officers. The union of public and private interests was further effected by allowing the civil officers of the provinces to choose the company's directors from among the largest stockholders.

The first settlers sent to North America by the Dutch West India Company arrived at Manhattan Island in 1624—about thirty families of French-speaking Walloons—Protestant exiles from the southern Netherlands, which had remained Spanish and Catholic. Since these settlers were under strict orders from the company as to where they should go and what they should do, and because the company's interest in North America centered in the fur trade, they divided into small bands and located in four or five scattered trading posts. The largest group proceeded up the Hudson and founded Fort Orange at the present site of Albany. The next largest group went to the Delaware River and founded Fort Nassau, opposite the site of present-day Philadelphia. A few men proceeded to the mouth of the Connecticut River, while another band remained at Manhattan to hold the island and to build Fort Amsterdam—the seat of government for these widely dispersed forts. The company then sent over an engineer instructed to lay out ten farms on Manhattan Island along the waterfront. Behind these was to be erected a pentagonal fort, surrounded by a wide moat, with gates on two sides connecting a main street traversing the fort and leading to a central market place. Within the fort were located the residences and offices of the officials, a school, hospital, church, warehouse, magazine, and quarters for the com-

---

[5] The outstanding study is J. Franklin Jameson, *Willem Usselinx* (New York, 1887).

*From Abbott's "The Expansion of Europe." © F. S. Crofts & Co.*

NEW AMSTERDAM ABOUT 1630

From Hartgers's *Beschrijvingh van Virginia.* Interesting not only in itself, but also as an example of the many descriptions of the world produced in Holland during the seventeenth century.

pany's employees. By 1626 the fort had been constructed and farmers had arrived with tools and livestock; New Netherland was well under way.[6]

Although Usselinx had taken a leading part in launching the Dutch West India Company, it did not assume the form which he intended. It was so organized as to aggrandize a few great capitalists, whereas he had advocated a large measure of state control. When in 1623 he was refused adequate compensation for his services to the company, he left Holland and later visited Sweden. Under the leadership of their brilliant king, Gustavus Adolphus, the Swedes were then rapidly forging ahead in all lines of endeavor. Sweden (which in 1624 controlled Norway and a part of Denmark) was commercially backward and deficient in capital, but Gustavus Adolphus, an advocate of mercantilism, was striving by state action to force a rapid growth of national industry and commerce. Usselinx in 1624 laid before the great king a plan for a vast Swedish trading company designed to operate throughout the world. Much as the king approved of the scheme, he was prevented from carrying it out by his participation in the Thirty Years' War. His death occurred in 1632, just after he had attained the leadership of the forces which were fighting to save Protestantism in Germany and northern Europe against the onslaughts of the ardent Catholic emperors of the Holy Roman Empire.

After the death of Gustavus Adolphus, the project of a Swedish trading company was revived by the regent and chancellor, Oxenstiern. The South Company, as chartered in 1637, received a rather indefinite land grant on the shores of Delaware Bay—a region which the Dutch had not yet fully occupied. The company might establish a colony and appoint its governor, while its trade with Europe was confined to Swedish ports. An expedition sent by the company established Fort Christina in 1638, located at the present site of Wilmington, Delaware, and some twenty-seven miles below the then Dutch post, Fort Nassau. In 1643 the Swedes erected a second settlement, New Gottenberg, about fifteen miles above Fort Christina. A few farmers took up land in the vicinity, but the settlements under the Swedish company, called New Sweden, did not ever include more than four hundred souls or extend more than thirty-five miles along the Delaware. The company focused its main interest upon the fur trade, so that farming was encouraged mainly as a means of support

[6] Thomas A. Janvier, *The Dutch Founding of New York* (New York, 1903), a collection of readable magazine articles, is concerned chiefly with the Dutch West India Company.

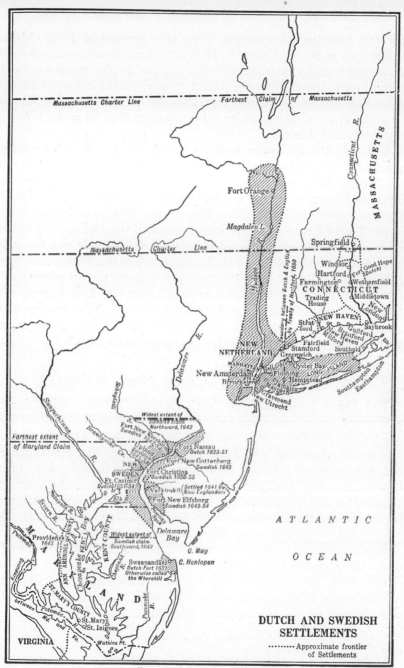

Massachusetts Charter Line    Farthest  Claim  of  Massachusetts

MASSACHUSETTS

Connecticut R.

Fort Orange

Magdalen L.

Springfield

Massachusetts    Charter    Line

Windsor
Hartford
Farmington    Wethersfield
Fort Good Hope (Dutch)

CONNECTICUT
Trading
House
Middletown
New London

Hudson

Boundary between Dutch & English by Treaty of Hartford, 1650

Stratford    NEW HAVEN    Saybrook
Guilford
New Milford    Branford
Fairfield    New Haven
Stamford    Southold
Greenwich

NEW
NETHERLAND

Delaware R.

Susquehanna R.

Brandywine Cr.

MANHATTA    Hell Gate
New Amsterdam    Flushing    Oyster Bay
Breuckelen    Jamaica    Hempstead
Masspeth    LONG    ISLAND
Gravesend    Southampton    Easthampton
New Utrecht

Widest extent of
Swedish claim
Northward, 1642
Fort New
Korsholm
Swedes
Tinicum
Island

Fort Nassau
Dutch 1623-51

Fort New Gottenberg
Swedish 1643

NEW
SWEDEN

Fort Christina
Swedish 1638-55
Ft. Casimir
Dutch 1651-54
Elk R.
Verkinskill
(Settled 1641 by
New Englanders)
Fort New Elfsborg
Swedish 1643-54

Farthest extent
of Maryland Claim

ATLANTIC

OCEAN

Widest extent of
Swedish claim
Southward, 1642
Delaware
Bay
C. May
C. Henlopen

Swaanandael
Dutch Fort 1631
Otherwise called
the Whorekill

M
A
R
Y
L
A
N
D

Providence
1643
ANN ARUNDEL COUNTY
KENT COUNTY
Chesapeake  Kent  Bay
Severn R.
Patapsco R.

Potomac R.

boundary between Md. and Va.
ST. MARY'S COUNTY
St. Marys
St. Inigoes
Patuxent R.
Potomac R.
Watkins Pt.

VIRGINIA

Pocomoke R.

DUTCH AND SWEDISH
SETTLEMENTS
·········· Approximate frontier
of Settlements

Based on "Atlas of American History."  © Harper & Brothers.

for the company's employees. Two able governors, Peter Minuit (1638–40) and John Printz [7] (1643–53) maintained good order and preserved friendly relations with the Indians. Lutheranism was designated by the company as the official religion of the colony, although toleration was extended to the Calvinists of the Dutch Reformed Church. In the villages, divine service was marked by an Old World regularity and decorum.

Claiming the Delaware region as they did, the Dutch protested against the Swedish occupation, although they did not seriously molest the Swedes for many years. The Swedish forts on the Delaware cut off Fort Nassau from the sea and made it worthless to the Dutch. Inasmuch as the Swedes and the Dutch were fighting on the same side in the Thirty Years' War, the latter tolerated the little colony on the Delaware as long as they needed Swedish aid in their war for independence from Spain. In 1655, however, when the Dutch no longer needed such aid, they sent an expedition of seven vessels which easily forced the surrender of Fort Christina, since the Dutch army was larger than the whole body of Swedish settlers. New Sweden now became a part of New Netherland, although the Swedes were permitted either to retain their lands or to return to Sweden. [8]

## WHY THE DUTCH FAILED IN NORTH AMERICA

The Dutch possessed New Netherland only forty years, during which time its progress was relatively slight. Why was this so? For one reason, the Dutch were not a migrating people. Their homeland was not overcrowded, and New Netherland offered no advantages, either religious or political, which they did not already enjoy. Their fishery, carrying trade, commerce, agriculture, and manufactures afforded economic opportunities for all classes. Only a few Dutch people became permanent settlers in New Netherland; consequently the colony had to depend upon alien groups. In 1644 it was said that eighteen different languages were spoken at and near Fort Amsterdam. Although the Dutch composed the largest racial group, English settlers were dominant on Long Island and Swedes along the Delaware. French, Walloons, Germans, Norwegians, Danes, Irish, Scots, and Negroes were less numerous. The population of the colony was

[7] Amandus Johnson, *The Instruction for John Printz* (Philadelphia, 1930), contains the best biographical sketch.

[8] The authoritative, definitive history is Amandus Johnson, *The Swedish Settlements on the Delaware, 1638–1664* (2 vols., New York, 1911). Johnson's material is presented in more attractive form in Christopher Ward, *The Dutch and Swedes on the Delaware, 1609–64* (Philadelphia, 1930).

declining in 1638, and in 1650 the governor, Peter Stuyvesant, welcomed refugees from New Haven Colony, whether "noble or ignoble, freeman or slave, debtor or creditor, yea, to the lowest prisoner included." As late as 1667 the inhabitants numbered only about eight thousand souls.[9]

The colony, moreover, made but a feeble appeal to farmers. Local leaders complained in 1649 of "petty traders who swarm hither with great industry, reap immense profits and exhaust the country without adding anything to its population or security," while "agriculture and many necessary matters remain neglected." The diversity of racial stocks magnified the problem of government and the dispersion of the settlers among widely scattered posts multiplied contacts with hostile neighbors and imposed a heavy burden of defense. The conquest of New Sweden, financed by a loan from the city of Amsterdam, saddled the colony with a huge debt, the repayment of which dictated a policy of commercial exploitation of the settlers.

A further weakness is traceable to the attitude of the Dutch West India Company. Its magnates saw little profit in New Netherland comparable to the gains from plundering Spaniards in the Caribbean. The capture of the Spanish silver fleet in 1627 netted the company a tremendous sum, but instead of devoting it to the development of New Amsterdam, the magnates declared a dividend for themselves. So profitable was the war at this time that the Dutch rejected a peace overture from Spain in 1629. Moreover, the company had a monopoly of Dutch trade with Africa, whose gold, ivory, pepper, and Negro slaves made even the furs of New Netherland seem insignificant. The capital subscriptions of the company were not large to begin with, and no stock was issued after 1623. Due to ill-advised expenditures in Brazil, the company became bankrupt about 1645, and was thereafter forced to neglect New Netherland—even its most necessary defenses. The profit-makers of the company did not cherish an unprofitable colony.[10]

In the 1620's, however, a faction within the company favored the development of an agricultural colony near Manhattan Island, but, since the company as a whole refused to act, the promotion of farming was entrusted to private enterprise. A charter of privileges issued in 1629 provided that a member of the company might secure a large

[9] S. G. Fisher, *Men, Women and Manners in Colonial Times* (2 vols., Philadelphia, 1898), a group of discursive essays, has a readable account of the Dutch in Vol. II, chapter 8. See again C. M. Andrews, *The Colonial Period of American History*, Vol. III, chapter 3.

[10] J. H. Innes, *New Amsterdam and Its People* (New York, 1902), is a scholarly essay in local history, too specialized for the general reader.

estate in the colony on condition that he people it with fifty adults within four years. The landlord, or patroon, should supply his tenants with cattle, tools, buildings, and mills; they in turn paid him rent, had their grain ground in his mill, gave him the first opportunity to buy their surplus produce, and submitted to the jurisdiction of his manorial court. The tenant was free to leave the estate after his lease expired, but livestock could not be removed from the colony. The company promised the patroons an eight-year exemption from duties on trade and gave their settlers a ten-year exemption from taxes.

Only five men took up patroonships, and only one succeeded—a certain Kiliaen Van Rensselaer, Amsterdam diamond merchant, who obtained the land of present-day Albany County, to which he sent settlers in 1630. By 1635 the other patroonships had reverted to the company. A primary cause of failure was the difficulty of securing settlers who would accept the dependent status of long-term tenancy. The patroonships thus indicate another weakness of New Netherland —the refusal of the company to offer attractive conditions to settlers. Tenancy was no lure to colonial farmers who could own land outright in Virginia or New England. The company liberalized the patroon system somewhat in 1638 and 1640, but this gesture was soon canceled by the effects of a devastating Indian war.[11]

The interests of the Dutch and the Iroquois tribes of the Mohawk valley proved to be supplementary. The Iroquois held one of the keys to the fur trade of the Great Lakes region and were thus able to supply the Dutch traders at Fort Orange with pelts on very profitable terms. The Dutch in turn furnished the Iroquois with firearms, which not only increased their efficiency as hunters but also gave them a tremendous advantage in war over enemy tribes. Among the enemies of the Iroquois were the Algonquin tribes which occupied the territory about the mouth of the Hudson—tribes which had already been conquered and rendered tributary to the Iroquois. The Dutch, however, refused to sell firearms to the Indians in the vicinity of Fort Amsterdam, and thus made them more than ever a prey to the Iroquois. Moreover, as farms began to extend on Manhattan Island, Staten Island, Long Island, and the mainland, the Algonquins began to fear for their own fields and hunting grounds. Occasionally disputes and fights occurred over such prosaic things as stray cattle or stolen pigs. Apparently the Indians were becoming restive when the company's agent, William Kieft, levied a tax upon the river Indians for repairs at Fort Amsterdam. Hostilities broke out in 1641 which inspired

[11] Attention is again called to A. C. Flick (ed.), *History of the State of New York*, Vol. I, chapters 6–9, and Vol. II, chapters 2–4 (important).

Kieft with hatred of the tribes and a desire to crush them. In February 1643 a band of Algonquins fled down the river and sought protection near Fort Amsterdam from a war party of Mohawks, armed with rifles. Kieft seized the occasion to launch a treacherous attack upon two camps of the unsuspecting Algonquins—a massacre that cost 120 Indian lives. Eleven Algonquin tribes immediately took up the tomahawk against the Dutch and attacked the farms and settlers between the Raritan River and the New Haven Colony. The colonists who escaped deserted their homes and crowded about Fort Amsterdam, while the Indians plundered and burned with a free hand. The tide turned early in 1644 when the Dutch sent a force of 130 men against an Indian rendezvous in the eastern part of present-day Westchester County. The soldiers advanced in stealth upon the village. "It was a full moon, . . . and the white snow made it like day, when at midnight they rushed upon the stronghold. . . . Before daybreak all was over. The village was in ashes, eight Indians had escaped and seven hundred corpses lay reddening the snow." Fifteen soldiers were wounded, but none killed.[12]

By the time peace was restored in August 1645, New Netherland was exhausted. Perhaps two thousand settlers had been slain during the war. "Our fields lie fallow, our dwellings and other buildings are burnt . . . the crops which God permitted to come forth during the past summer remain in the fields standing and rotting"—such was the colony's lament in October 1644. Kieft's Indian war dealt New Netherland a blow from which the Dutch never fully recovered.

Perhaps the most fatal weakness of New Netherland was its government. The Dutch West India Company appointed the local officials and allowed the settlers no semblance of home rule. Its chief representative at New Amsterdam, the director, received his orders from the company and held office at its pleasure. He was assisted by a council, also selected by the company, which issued local regulations and served as a court in both civil and criminal cases. The company imposed laws upon the colony from Amsterdam and sent over subordinate officials such as the schout fiscal (or sheriff and prosecuting officer), the koopman (or bookkeeper of wages), the clergymen, and the schoolmasters. Local government was exceedingly undemocratic. The town officials of New Amsterdam, appointed originally by the director, formed a close corporation which filled vacancies in its membership. There were neither town meetings in the localities nor elected assemblies for the whole colony.

[12] Maud W. Goodwin, *Dutch and English on the Hudson* (*Chronicles of America*, New Haven, 1919).

In view of the great influence of the director, it was unfortunate that the company thrice appointed men who were not properly qualified. Director Wouter Van Twiller (1633–38) embroiled the colony in heated quarrels in which he was accused of profligacy and drunkenness, while his indecisiveness earned him the sobriquet, "Wouter the doubter." The treachery, blundering, and cowardice of his successor, William Kieft (1638–46), prompted the settlers to demand his removal. Then came Peter Stuyvesant (1647–64), a harsh, irascible, overbearing soldier to whom the company once remonstrated: "You have now learned by experience how too much vehemence may draw upon you the hatred of the people." He announced that he intended to rule as a father over children, proclaimed contemptuously that popular elections would place thieves, rogues, and drunkards in office, and with dire threats commanded the settlers not to appeal to the Estates-General in Holland. He packed the council with his own henchmen, appropriated the company's property to his own use, and ruled more autocratically than any other governor of the colony.[13]

The directors of New Netherland made a gesture toward representative government when they selected leading citizens to act as an unofficial advisory council. Thus there were the "twelve men" and the "eight men" under Kieft and the "nine men" of Stuyvesant. The latter allowed the property owners to nominate eighteen men, from whom he chose nine—three merchants, three burghers (artisans and tradesmen), and three landowners. Although these special bodies had only advisory powers, they often opposed the director. For such resistance Kieft dismissed his "eight men" in 1645 and Stuyvesant successfully defied his "nine," so that this institution was significant chiefly as a mouthpiece of discontent.

Stuyvesant's difficulties arose because the company expected that he make the colony profitable but did not provide him with the necessary resources. His rule therefore assumed the character of exploitation of the settlers, and on many occasions they protested. In 1649 the "nine men" petitioned that the Estates-General take over the government of the colony from the company and presented a long remonstrance which attributed their ills to "1. Unsuitable government; 2. Scanty privileges and exemptions; 3. Onerous imposts, duties, exactions and such like." This remonstrance breathes an American spirit; it expressed the view of men who regarded New Netherland as their home and who desired a government that would promote education, religion, and peace and guarantee property rights. Complaining of the power of the director to confiscate private property, the remonstrance

---

[13] Bayard Tuckerman, *Peter Stuyvesant* (New York, 1893), is a brief sketch.

observed that "a covetous chief makes poor subjects." Although the
Estates-General recommended concessions, the company stood pat and
replied by confirming the autocratic powers of the director.

Again, in 1653, the leading men of the colony, assembled in a
"landtag," demanded that they be given a part in the enactment of
ordinances and the selection of officials. This action, however, was
immediately declared illegal and the assembly was ordered to disperse. The English settlers in New Netherland who were familiar
with New England's representative scheme may have intensified the
popular discontent, particularly after 1650. At any rate, the widespread dissatisfaction with the rule of the Dutch West India Company
caused New Netherland to become an easy prey to English conquest
in 1664. In the meantime arbitrary government had given the colony
a bad name and had deterred people "from going thither to settle."
After 1664 the English discarded the institutions of New Netherland,
so that the Dutch made but a slight impression upon the thirteen
colonies, their chief contribution being that of a good racial stock.[14]

### NEW FRANCE AND NEW ENGLAND

While the Dutch were fighting for their independence from Spain,
France was emerging as a great power in Europe. In 1589 the strife
between French Catholics and Protestants placed upon the throne the
Protestant leader, Henry of Navarre. His religion was offensive to
the mass of his subjects, yet his claim to the crown was incontestable,
and the only alternative to his rule was the subjection of France to
the power of Spain—a condition as humiliating to French patriotism
as a heretic king was offensive to French Catholicism. From this
dilemma Henry IV rescued the nation in 1593 when he embraced
the Catholic faith. By 1598 he had freed France from Spanish domination and had granted a large measure of toleration to the Huguenots. He proved to be an immensely popular king whose guiding purpose was the material progress of the country. His "new deal" for
France included domestic pacification, the fostering of agriculture, a
public works program of roads and bridges, and the introduction of
new industries, particularly silk manufacturing. His vision of national
wealth and grandeur also encompassed projects of empire in America.[15]

From Verrazano and Cartier France had acquired a title to North

---

[14] A. E. McKinley, "The English and Dutch Towns of New Netherland," *American Historical Review*, VI (Oct. 1900).

[15] Justin Winsor, *Cartier to Frontenac* (Boston, 1894), is an excellent general
account. See chapters 4–8.

America and knowledge of the St. Lawrence region. Moreover, fishermen of Normandy and Brittany for a century had visited the area between Nova Scotia and the St. Lawrence and had engaged in the fur trade with the resident natives, from whom they heard rumors of inland seas (the Great Lakes) which supposedly connected the Atlantic and Asia. The early English efforts to colonize Newfoundland having failed, the great northern region lay open to French enterprise in fur trading, fishing, seeking a new route to the Orient, and missionary work among the Indians.

Such enterprise had to be entrusted at first to individuals, due to the poverty of the government; and in order to attract investors Henry IV granted monopolies of the northern fur trade, the only ready source of profit. The colonizing efforts of two such monopolists failed before a successful promoter, the Sieur de Monts, acquired the rights in 1603. Having visited the St. Lawrence, de Monts favored a more southern site for a settlement; and accordingly he obtained a grant to the region between the fortieth and forty-sixth parallels—a land supposed to be so pleasant that it was called Arcadia or Acadia. In 1605 de Monts established a colony at Port Royal harbor. Although the "Acadians" who settled there were dispersed in 1613 by an expedition from Virginia, they returned to hold Acadia or Nova Scotia as a province of France.[16]

The colonization of Canada was largely the work of a French navigator, map maker, and friend of Henry IV—Samuel de Champlain. After taking part in expeditions under de Monts to Acadia in 1604–07, when he explored and mapped the region as far south as New England, Champlain became convinced that this area was unsuited to the fur trade and persuaded de Monts to concentrate upon the St. Lawrence. Thus it came to pass that Champlain led the expedition which founded Quebec, July 3, 1608. Despite a first winter of hardship and sickness the little colony survived—partly because the resident Indians (the Montagnais) were too weak and degraded to resist.[17]

Fascinated by the American scene and eager to promote the fur trade, to find a passage to the Orient, and to Christianize the natives, whose savagery appalled him, Champlain was immediately drawn into the vortex of Indian warfare and politics. To gain his ends he supported the tribes near Quebec against their dreaded enemies, the

[16] H. P. Biggar's *The Early Trading Companies of New France* (Toronto, 1901) is a valuable, standard work. See chapters 1–9.

[17] Charles W. Colby, *The Founder of New France* (*Chronicles of Canada* series, Toronto, 1915).

Iroquois, who were bent upon mastering the country between the St. Lawrence and the Mississippi. In 1609 Champlain proceeded along the Richelieu River to Lake Champlain, where he encountered a party of Iroquois. The firearms of the French threw the latter into a panic-stricken flight. Thus began a century of warfare between the two.

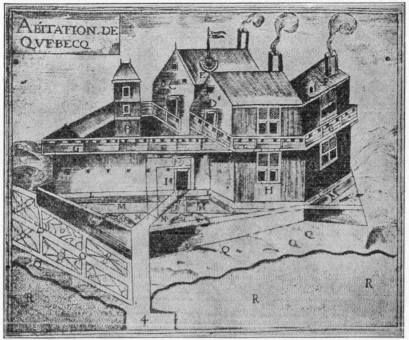

*From Champlain's "Voyages," published in 1613. Courtesy of the New York Public Library.*

CHAMPLAIN'S "HABITATION" AT QUEBEC

The enemies of the Iroquois, particularly the Hurons, adhered to the arms of France and brought their furs to Quebec, where they obtained the kettles, axes, knives, and firearms which were soon indispensable to the red man, while the Iroquois turned to the Dutch at Fort Orange as their source of supply.[18]

Later Champlain pursued westward exploration. He lived among the Hurons and learned their customs; then in 1615 he traveled by the Ottawa River to Lake Huron and thence to Lake Ontario. One of his lieutenants, Jean Nicolet, in 1634 pushed on to the Straits of Mackinac, Lake Michigan, Green Bay, and the Fox River in present-

[18] Louise P. Kellogg's *The French Regime in Wisconsin and the Northwest* (Madison, Wis., 1925) is a book of great merit. See chapters 1–8.

day Wisconsin. Sent by Champlain to make an alliance with western Indians in order to open the interior to trade and exploration, Nicolet visited the Winnebago tribe, from whose chiefs he heard of a great river (the Mississippi) leading to a "great water," presumably the Pacific. Thus Champlain's work not only revealed the Great Lakes but also kept alive the dream of a Northwest passage through Canada.[19]

Beyond such achievements New France made but slight progress, largely because of inadequate backing in France. The death of Henry IV in 1610 resulted in canceling the monopoly of de Monts, although Champlain remained in command at Quebec. The control over New France was now given to great nobles interested only in a personal income from the colony. This they obtained by selling trading monopolies to French merchants who opposed settlement as injurious to the fur trade, which netted profits as high as 40 per cent. However, by 1624 France had fallen under the sway of Cardinal Richelieu, apostle of absolutism, defender of Catholicism, and champion of colonization. He revoked all previous concessions in Canada, and in 1628 formed the Company of New France, composed of a hundred associates who contributed a total capital of £13,000. The company received a perpetual monopoly of the fur trade and absolute title to the lands of New France. Richelieu insisted upon colonization; hence the company was required to transport four thousand settlers within fifteen years, to support each settler for three years after arrival, and to maintain three priests in each settlement.[20]

The plans of Richelieu for a populous, agricultural colony were not realized and the fur trade remained the economic basis of New France. The profits of the trade were not sufficient to enable the company to establish the required quota of settlers. Moreover, a war between England and France weakened the company by virtue of English seizures of several of the company's ships and a conquest of Quebec in 1629, although France recovered Canada by the treaty of St. Germain in 1632. Only Frenchmen who were Roman Catholics were admitted as settlers, and the French were not a migrating people, believing that "next to heaven, France is the most beautiful of all lands." As late as 1637 only two agricultural settlers had arrived. The population consisted of traders, officials, soldiers, employees, and priests.[21]

[19] Reuben G. Thwaites, *France in America* (New York, c. 1905), a brief survey by a great editor, is available in the *American Nation* series.

[20] *Canada and Its Provinces* (ed. Adam Shortt and Arthur G. Doughty, 23 vols., Toronto, 1914–17) is a coöperative work consisting of reliable articles by qualified writers. See Vols. I and II entitled *New France* (1914).

[21] A group of attractive biographical essays is C. W. Colby, *Canadian Types of the Old Regime* (New York, 1908). See chapters 1–4.

New France was without benefit of clergy until 1615, when four fathers of the Recollect order arrived—followers of St. Francis of Assisi who served the poor in a spirit of love and self-sacrifice. However, the Recollects, who were pledged to poverty, lacked funds for missions, and because the fur traders did not choose to bear the expense, the work was entrusted after 1625 to the Society of Jesus—a rich, powerful order, whose members displayed an almost superhuman courage in facing danger and privation for the salvation of souls and the glorification of the Roman Catholic Church. Since the Jesuits labored chiefly with the Indians their efforts contributed to the success of France in extending her sway in the northern fur trade. The willingness of the French to treat the Indians as human beings, to associate with them on friendly terms, to adapt themselves to the natives' way of life, and to aid them in war also explains the secret of France's early ascendancy in Canada.[22]

The country south of Acadia, now Maine and New Hampshire, was destined to become a theater of strife between New England and France. Massachusetts coveted this territory, partly that she might so control it as to protect her Puritan churches from undesirable neighbors, partly that she might share the wealth of its rich timber resources, its fur trade, and its fishery, and partly that she might defend herself against the French. Since 1622 this region had been subject to the claims of Captain John Mason, whose title applied to the land between the Piscataqua and the Merrimack Rivers, and of Sir Ferdinando Gorges, who held the area between the Piscataqua and the Kennebec.

The principal towns of New Hampshire were founded between 1623 and 1640: Dover and Portsmouth by Anglicans; Exeter by the unorthodox Puritan followers of Wheelwright; and Hampton by orthodox Puritans acting under the authority of Massachusetts. All were annexed by Massachusetts, 1641–43, an act explained in part by the death of Mason in 1635 and by the Puritan uprising in England against his party, the royalists. In justification, Massachusetts interpreted her charter in such a way as to include New Hampshire within her territory. Although the charter of 1629 indicated that the northern boundary of Massachusetts was to be located three miles north of the *mouth* of the Merrimack, the Bay leaders insisted that the boundary should extend three miles north of the source of the Merrimack. Moreover, Massachusetts had received from Lords Saye and

---

[22] Francis Parkman, *The Jesuits in America* (Boston, 1870), is a masterpiece. See also Thomas G. Marquis, *The Jesuit Missions* (*Chronicles of Canada* series, Toronto, 1916).

Brooke and other English Puritans a title to Portsmouth and Dover which they had previously purchased.

Due to the religious diversity of the New Hampshire towns and to their former privileges of self-government, Massachusetts granted them a liberal measure of home rule. They managed their local affairs in their town meetings, elected deputies to the General Court at Boston, and were exempted from the church membership requirement for voting then in force in Massachusetts. They remained a part of Massachusetts until 1677, when English judges decided that New Hampshire was not a part of the Bay Colony. In 1679 England converted New Hampshire into a royal province whose governor and council thereafter were appointed by the king, while the elected representatives formed a separate assembly.

The hold of Massachusetts on Maine proved to be more enduring. Four groups took part in founding settlements there. Sir Ferdinando Gorges was responsible for establishing the towns of York, Kittery, Wells, and Saco—all on the southern coast of Maine; the Pilgrims of Plymouth erected a fur trading post on the Kennebec at the modern site of Augusta; English merchants set up similar posts at Pemaquid and on Monhegan Island; and rivals of Gorges developed settlements at Casco Bay, where Portland and Scarborough now stand. Between 1652 and 1658 Massachusetts annexed the four Gorges settlements and those at Casco Bay. After the death of Gorges in 1647 had left his colonists without a guiding hand, the towns of York, Kittery, and Wells endeavored to form an independent union akin to that of Rhode Island. In this they were frustrated by Massachusetts, whose leaders justified the annexation by their interpretation of the northern boundary, which gave Massachusetts a claim to more than half of Maine. Massachusetts had also purchased the claims of one of Gorges' rivals. Moreover, the annexation occurred after the Puritans in England had lessened the influence of the Gorges family, adherents of the royalist cause.[23]

After the restoration of Charles II, Ferdinando Gorges, grandson of Sir Ferdinando, carried on a long struggle with Massachusetts for the possession of southern Maine. In 1677 the Privy Council decided against the Bay Colony, and the latter then secretly purchased the Gorges rights for £1,250. Previously Massachusetts had regarded Maine as an integral part of her territory and had granted the northern towns privileges similar to those enjoyed by New Hampshire when a part of Massachusetts. Between 1677 and 1684 Massachusetts

[23] See again H. S. Burrage, *Beginnings of Colonial Maine*, chapters 10–23, and J. P. Baxter, *Sir Ferdinando Gorges*, Vol. I.

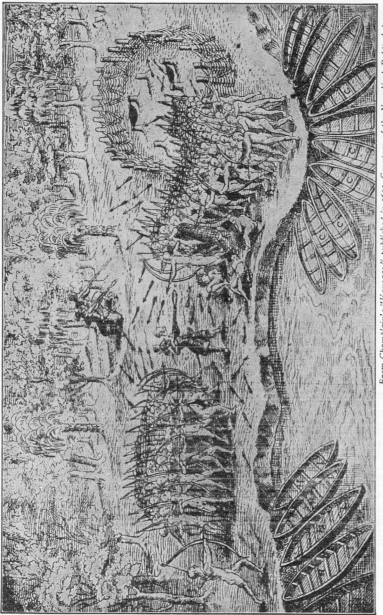

From Champlain's "Voyages," published in 1613. Courtesy of the New York Public Library.

CHAMPLAIN'S FIRST FIGHT WITH THE IROQUOIS

held Maine as proprietor in place of Gorges and endeavored to collect quit-rents from the northern settlers.

### THE CONFEDERATION OF NEW ENGLAND

The presence of the Dutch, French, and Indians, coupled with a
series of boundary disputes among the New England colonies, induced them in 1643 to form the first voluntary American union. The
original impetus for this came from hostilities with the Pequot Indians on the Connecticut frontier. The extension of Puritan settlement into the Connecticut valley brought into bold relief the irreconcilable conflict between two economic orders. The Indian's dependence
upon hunting and trapping necessitated a large area to support a small
population, whereas the New Englanders required additional lands to
support a rapidly growing farming population. Accordingly, the Puritans refused to recognize the title of the Indians to lands they did not
occupy and cultivate, advancing the theory that cultivation conferred
the right of ownership and thus denying to the red man his hunting
lands which were as indispensable to him as was farming land to the
English settler.

The penetration of the Puritans into the Connecticut valley gave
rise to numerous quarrels with the resident Pequots which resulted
in the murder of several settlers at Saybrook and Wethersfield in
1635–36. Prior to this, Massachusetts, in order to avenge the death of
an English trader, John Oldham, had sent into the Pequot country
an expedition which plundered the Indians and infuriated them. A
leader at Saybrook remarked to John Endicott, in charge of the expedition, "You come hither to raise these wasps about my ears, and
then you will take wings and flee away." And so it happened. When
the resulting Indian outrages had become general, Massachusetts appealed to Plymouth for aid and succeeded, through the influence of
Roger Williams, in detaching the Narragansets from an alliance with
the Pequots. But the settlers on the Connecticut could not wait for
aid from Boston, and in May 1637 they raised a force of ninety men
which was placed under the command of John Mason and John
Underhill, two accomplished Indian fighters. The Pequot stronghold was on the Pequot River, between Saybrook and Narragansett
Bay. At the suggestion of Mason, the Connecticut force sailed from
Saybrook to Narragansett Bay, thus suggesting to the Pequots that
the force was returning to Massachusetts and throwing them off their
guard. Then the settlers landed and made an all-day march to the
Pequot fort, to which they set fire at night. Five hundred Pequots

were burned alive or killed as they tried to escape over the palisade, while the New Englanders lost but two men. Reinforcements now arrived from Massachusetts, and the surviving Pequots were ruthlessly tracked down, captured, and turned over to other tribes, enslaved by the Puritans, or sold to the West Indies. The Pequots were virtually exterminated, while the prowess and diplomacy of the Connecticut Puritans enabled them to make a treaty with the Narragansets, and peace prevailed on the New England frontier for nearly forty years after the Pequot War.[24]

The New Englanders also came into conflict with the Dutch, who claimed that New Netherland extended to the Connecticut River, and who in 1633 built a trading post, the House of Good Hope, at the site of Hartford. Plymouth established a similar outpost at Windsor about the same time. The Dutch in 1634 and 1635 sent expeditions against the Pilgrims' fort and Saybrook, but the New Englanders refused to move and appeared to be too strong to be dislodged by force. By 1640 the founding of New Haven and the westward expansion of Connecticut brought the English within forty miles of Manhattan Island. The two parties also struggled for possession of Long Island as the New Englanders occupied its eastern end and expanded westward toward the Dutch settlements there. Neither Connecticut nor New Haven had a legal claim to the territory in dispute but they enjoyed the backing of the English government, which persistently refused to recognize the Dutch claim to the land between the Connecticut and the Delaware. The English position was expressed by an English representative at The Hague, who advised his countrymen to "crowd on, crowding the Dutch out of those places they have, but without hostility or any act of violence." The English had the better title by virtue of discovery; the Dutch defended their right by prior occupation; while in the disputed area east of the Hudson the English outnumbered the Dutch at least three to one.[25]

The relations among the New England colonies furnished another source of trouble. Massachusetts, the most populous and powerful colony, felt a mission to dominate her weaker neighbors and to control the whole of New England. Since the smaller colonies did not possess land patents issued by the king, and because of conflicting grants and the uncertainty of geographical locations, Massachusetts was in a position to extend her claims in all directions. Thus, when

[24] Howard Bradstreet, *The Story of the War with the Pequots, Re-Told*, (New Haven, 1933—Connecticut Tercentenary Commission, no. 5).

[25] John G. Palfrey's *A Compendious History of New England* (4 vols., Boston, 1884), a learned, well-written political narrative, devotes much space to intercolonial relations.

Plymouth established a trading post on the Connecticut in 1633, Massachusetts refused to coöperate and then in 1635 laid claim to the Pilgrims' land when it was desired by emigrants from Massachusetts. The dispute was finally settled by allowing the Massachusetts settlers to occupy fifteen-sixteenths of the land, although the Bay Colony had no legal title. Governor Bradford spoke of the incident as an "unkindness not so soon forgotten."

Again, Massachusetts interfered in a dispute that had arisen in 1634 at the trading post established by the Pilgrims on the Kennebec. In this case also Massachusetts had no title to the land in question, yet she took upon herself the settlement of the quarrel, arrested one of the Plymouth magistrates, and obliged other Plymouth leaders to go to Boston to adjust the matter. After the establishment of Connecticut, that colony contended with Massachusetts over their common boundary, while the Bay leaders refused to consent to a scientific survey. Likewise, Massachusetts laid claim to a large part of the territory of Plymouth. Such frontier disputes revealed the need of some scheme of united action by which the smaller colonies might protect themselves from the aggrandizement of Massachusetts.[26]

At the same time, however, the Puritan colonies had many things in common. New England was a geographical and economic unit, with Boston its commercial center; a few settlements excepted, there was a fundamental unity in government, religion, and ideals; the people were exclusively of English stock: all these factors favored coöperation. Moreover, after 1642, the New Englanders could not refer their disputes to a common umpire in England or look thither for protection—torn as England was by civil war. Nor could England coerce or punish the colonies for usurping sovereign rights when they united to form a miniature league of nations with the object of exercising powers which properly belonged to England.

In 1637 Massachusetts proposed a union of the colonies with the suggestion that she be given some preëminence in its deliberations. Connecticut declined the offer, fearful that she would thus fall under the domination of her more powerful neighbor. But when Connecticut was having Indian troubles in 1642, she advanced a similar proposal, with the result that in May 1643 representatives of four colonies met in Boston and adopted articles creating "The Confederation of the United Colonies of New England." Its members were Massachusetts, Connecticut, Plymouth, and New Haven. The towns of Rhode Island, Maine, and New Hampshire were not admitted, partly

[26] See again J. T. Adams, *Founding of New England*, pp. 175–188, chapters 9–10, 14.

because their people did not see eye to eye with the orthodox Puritans of the four member colonies, and partly because Massachusetts desired to annex those towns—and therefore could not recognize them as independent colonies by admitting them to a confederation of equals. When Rhode Island applied for membership in 1648 the condition was imposed that she become incorporated into Massachusetts—and to this she would not consent.[27]

The articles declared the purpose of the united colonies to be "a firm and perpetual league of friendship, for offense and defense, mutual advice and succor upon all just occasions, both for preserving and propagating the truths of the Gospel and for their mutual safety and welfare." Each colony received a guarantee of its independence and territory. New members could not be admitted or a member colony merged with another member except by vote of the Confederation. The general court of each colony elected two commissioners to meet regularly once a year and on special occasions with similar commissioners from the other three colonies. The eight commissioners had the power to declare war, make peace, and apportion military expenses among the colonies in proportion to their adult male population, although the general court of each colony actually levied the taxes. Six of the eight commissioners had to vote for such measures before they became effective. The commissioners were also authorized to settle boundary disputes, to provide for the capture and return of fugitives from justice, and to make recommendations to the respective colonies. The only executive provided was the president of the commissioners (chosen yearly), who was merely a moderator presiding over equals.

The Confederation was fairly active until 1665; afterward its influence was negligible. Its functioning exposed two fundamental weaknesses. First, its work necessarily involved foreign powers—the Dutch and the French—yet in this sphere England refused to recognize, and thus negatived, its actions. For instance: in 1650 the commissioners negotiated with Peter Stuyvesant the Treaty of Hartford, which aimed to dispose of pending conflicts between New England and New Netherland and to locate a definite boundary between the two. Although this treaty was ratified by Holland, England refused to acknowledge it, insisting that the Dutch had no rights in North America.[28]

The second weakness arose from the fact that Massachusetts would

[27] Richard Hildreth's *The History of the United States* (6 vols., New York, 1854–55) is a vigorous, realistic work. Writing from the Federalist point of view, Hildreth, a New England journalist, stressed the historical background of the American Union.

[28] John Fiske, *New France and New England* (Boston, 1902), chapters 2–4.

not treat the smaller colonies as equals and that the latter would not recognize her as superior. Massachusetts therefore felt free to ignore the Confederation and to act alone when her interests so dictated. A bitter conflict broke out over the town of Springfield, located within Massachusetts in the Connecticut valley. In 1644 Connecticut purchased Saybrook and proceeded to collect the purchase price by levying duties on goods shipped down the river. Springfield, claiming that she was outside of Connecticut's jurisdiction, refused to pay the duties; Connecticut insisted that she should, since the fort at Saybrook protected her commerce. When the matter was referred to the Confederation, Plymouth and New Haven supported Connecticut, while Massachusetts supported Springfield. Unable to obtain exemption for Springfield from the duties, Massachusetts in 1649 retaliated by taxing the products of Plymouth, New Haven, and Connecticut which entered Boston—the port from which most of such exports were shipped to Europe. Massachusetts would not yield, and this led the commissioners to ask whether her opposition agreed "with the law of love and with the tenure and import of the articles of confederation," adding that they desired "to be spared in all farther agitations concerning Springfield."

A second defiance on the part of Massachusetts occurred during the first war between England and Holland (1652–54). Connecticut and New Haven, asserting that the Dutch at New Netherland were plotting to attack western New England with Indian allies, induced seven of the eight commissioners to vote for a war against the Dutch. However, Massachusetts, having little interest in the issue at stake, refused to participate, affirming that the commissioners could declare only a defensive, not an offensive, war, although the articles clearly sanctioned warfare of both kinds. A European peace ended the war without a New England campaign against the Dutch, and hence Massachusetts was credited with another victory over the Confederation.

The leaders of Massachusetts also ignored the Confederation in their dealings with the French. Soon after France recovered Acadia from England in 1632 that region became the object of rivalry between two French magnates, each of whom aspired to dominate it as governor. Charles d'Aulnay, who held the land to the north and east of the Bay of Fundy and was an uncompromising Catholic and enemy of the English, insisted that France possessed all North America to Florida. His rival, Claude de La Tour, who claimed the territory on the western side of the Bay of Fundy, was a lax Catholic with leanings toward Protestantism and friendship with New England, whose merchants he allowed to trade with Nova Scotia. After a series of con-

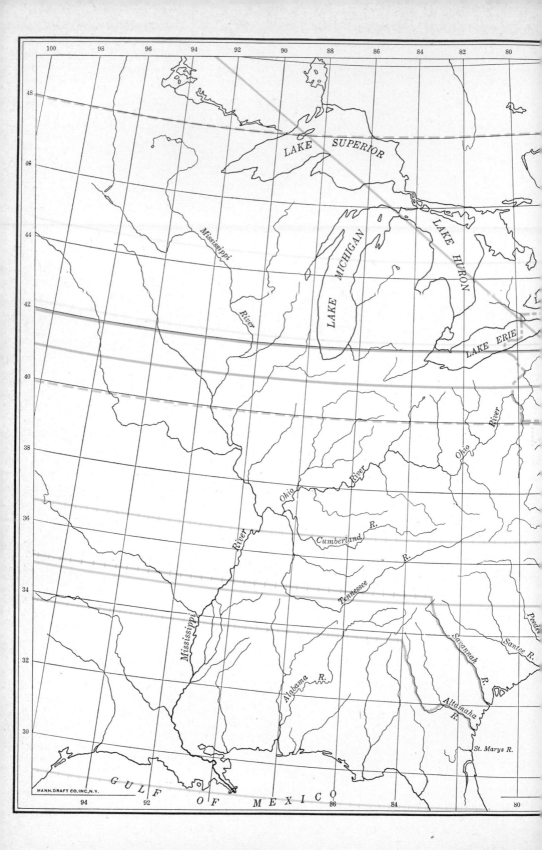

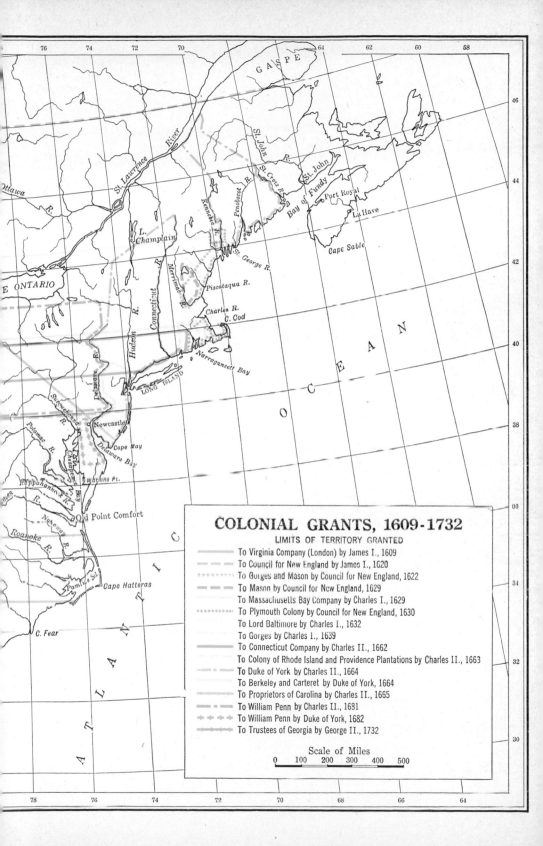

### COLONIAL GRANTS, 1609-1732

#### LIMITS OF TERRITORY GRANTED

To Virginia Company (London) by James I., 1609
To Council for New England by James I., 1620
To Gorges and Mason by Council for New England, 1622
To Mason by Council for New England, 1629
To Massachusetts Bay Company by Charles I., 1629
To Plymouth Colony by Council for New England, 1630
To Lord Baltimore by Charles I., 1632
To Gorges by Charles I., 1639
To Connecticut Company by Charles II., 1662
To Colony of Rhode Island and Providence Plantations by Charles II., 1663
To Duke of York by Charles II., 1664
To Berkeley and Carteret by Duke of York, 1664
To Proprietors of Carolina by Charles II., 1665
To William Penn by Charles II., 1681
To William Penn by Duke of York, 1682
To Trustees of Georgia by George II., 1732

Scale of Miles
0    100    200    300    400    500

flicts, La Tour appealed to Boston for aid against Aulnay. It was decided by Governor Winthrop and an inner group of leaders that Massachusetts could not act officially, but they permitted La Tour to raise volunteers who went forth and plundered Aulnay's settlement. In the end, however, Aulnay secured the backing of the French court, crushed La Tour's plantation, and became governor of Acadia. Massachusetts then had to recognize Aulnay and recompense him for its part in La Tour's attack. The Winthrop group had acted without submitting the matter to the General Court, because, as Winthrop explained, "We knew they would not have given him [La Tour] aid without consent of the commissioners of the other colonies, and for a bare permission, we might do it without the court." The commissioners, on the other hand, resolved against any future acts of war such as the Massachusetts leaders had permitted. The episode showed that the men in control of the strongest colony were not willing to be bound by the Confederation when coöperative action entailed a sacrifice of their particular interests.[29]

Some of the most effective work of the Confederation was performed in the shaping of a general New England policy. The commissioners made numerous recommendations, many of which were adopted by the several colonies, thus contributing to their social solidarity. For instance, the Confederation suggested that well-to-do Puritans should make gifts to its president for the support of the Puritan center of learning, Harvard College. Each colony was advised to tax its inhabitants who did not contribute voluntarily toward the maintenance of the Puritan ministers and to banish all Quakers under pain of death for returning. Each church was called upon to keep a careful watch over its membership, so that only those persons might be admitted who had "had an effectual calling and had entered by an express covenant," while all errors contrary to the Scriptures, to Sabbath observance, and to the authority of the clergy were to be rigorously suppressed. Thus in the religious sphere the spirit of the Confederation was one of intolerant orthodoxy. Moreover, the Confederation served as an agency for missionary work among the Indians. It coöperated with an English Society for Propagating the Gospel in New England, from which the commissioners received funds for disbursement. One branch of this work was a program for educating young Indians at Harvard College.

Several factors finally put an end to the Confederation. The conquest of New Netherland by England in 1664 removed one of the

[29] Richard Frothingham, *The Rise of the Republic* . . . (Boston, 1873), presents a political interpretation of American history. See chapter 2.

hostile neighbors who had made the union necessary, while in 1665 Connecticut, contrary to the terms of the articles, absorbed New Haven, thus leaving only three member colonies. Moreover, after the reëstablishment of the English monarchy in 1660, the home government resumed its authority over America in matters of diplomacy and defense, and since the New Englanders had never had a legal warrant for their union, they could no longer act together as semi-independent states without incurring the displeasure of the king. Finally, the charter of Massachusetts was annulled in 1684 and England then imposed upon the New England colonies an imperial union which deprived them of their powers of independent action. The Confederation, however, had enabled the New Englanders to coöperate during the time when England was paralyzed by civil upheaval, and thus it fostered among them a spirit of self-reliance and independence which could not be eradicated afterward.

The weakness of the Confederation became apparent again in 1675–78, when New England faced a grave domestic crisis, King Philip's War, which was essentially a struggle for land.[30] During the thirty-five years after 1640, the settlements of New England had been expanding until they extended fifty miles or more along the eastern and southern coasts and reached up the Connecticut valley to the northern boundary of Massachusetts, while the white population had increased from 22,500 in 1640 to 52,000 in 1675. This steady advance threatened eventual disaster to the Indians as they felt a growing pressure upon their scanty means of subsistence and saw that the land hunger of the whites could not be appeased. Two weeks after the outbreak of the war a letter from Boston said that Indian lands worth £10,000 had already been gained from the struggle, and the land factor was further indicated by an act of Massachusetts promising land bounties to soldiers who expelled the natives from the Narraganset country.[31]

Meanwhile, the attitude of the settlers toward the red man had become increasingly hostile and contemptuous. Although many Puritans had sincerely desired and labored to Christianize the Indians, their efforts could not prevent the inevitable conflict between two antagonistic ways of life. The New Englanders did not establish isolated forest missions, but rather endeavored to bring the Indians at the fringe of settlement into the English villages for the services at the

[30] The best narrative is George W. Ellis and John E. Morris, *King Philip's War* (New York, c. 1906).

[31] J. A. Doyle's *English Colonies in America* (5 vols., New York, 1882–1907), a formal and conventional English treatment, emphasizes political institutions and events. Valuable as a reference work.

community churches. In consequence, the natives who were Christianized lived close to the whites—at Nantucket, Martha's Vineyard, and
along the Massachusetts frontier, while their remoter brethren retained their savage customs and beliefs. Foremost among the New
England missionaries was the Reverend John Eliot, a saintly Christian and man of humane spirit who translated the Bible into the Indian language and who protested against Indian slavery, saying that
"to sell souls for money seemeth to me a dangerous merchandise."
Nearly four thousand Indians who had been Christianized remained
loyal to the English. Had they too taken up arms the war might have
been far more costly to New England.

As the Puritans gained knowledge of the Indians and became the
more powerful they adopted an overbearing attitude. Cotton Mather
once referred to the natives as those "pernicious creatures," while another Puritan leader called their foremost warrior a "great naked
dirty beast." The colonial governments forced the red man to acknowledge the English as overlords, to pay tribute, to submit his disputes to English arbiters, to secure the consent of the colonial authorities to his land sales, and to surrender his firearms upon demand.
English laws and customs were forced upon him, and his misde-
meanors were punished by fines, whipping, or confiscation of lands.

Many of these indignities were inflicted by Plymouth Colony upon
Philip, son of the Wampanoag chieftain, Massasoit. A humiliating
treaty imposed upon him in 1671 spurred him to opposition which
in 1675 set the frontiers ablaze. Philip's forces were not organized,
but his sporadic raids on isolated settlements caught them off guard
before a general alarm could be sounded. Other tribes, the Narragansets and the Nipmucks, joined King Philip and the Wampanoags
and gained repeated victories during 1675. The turning point came in
December, when the New Englanders surrounded an Indian stronghold and killed between four hundred and a thousand of the foe, after
the manner of the earlier Pequot massacre. In 1676 peace was made
with the southern New England tribes, but meantime the war had
spread to New Hampshire and Maine, where it continued in unorganized fashion until 1678.

The New Englanders demonstrated that they were good fighters,
although unused to military discipline and disinclined to coöperate
with forces from other colonies. Every male inhabitant between the
ages of sixteen and sixty was liable to military service; hence the
war reached into every quarter, regardless of personal disinclina-
tions to military service. Massachusetts provided the death penalty for
those who refused to serve, while Connecticut forbade the emigration

of able-bodied men. The colonies at the start had no system of war supply, so that some expeditions had to be abandoned because provisions failed to arrive in time. On the other hand, the Indians were outnumbered four to one and they received no assistance from the French, except on the Maine frontier, where they were supplied with ammunition and arms. The principal weakness of the tribes was due to their hand-to-mouth way of living. They had no food reserves, and were unable to fight and support themselves at the same time; hence in 1676 they stood face to face with starvation, the primary cause of their failure.[32]

The war cast a pall of gloom over New England; the Puritans felt that Providence was punishing them for their sins—because they had been lenient toward Quakers and because men had been wearing periwigs and women were guilty of "cutting, curling and immodest laying out of their hair." Twenty towns in Rhode Island and Massachusetts were destroyed or abandoned, while the war took a toll of a sixteenth of the male population of New England and cost Plymouth, Massachusetts, and Connecticut upward of £90,000. Hatreds deepened on both sides as the colonists exacted vengeance by executing the native leaders and forced captives into servitude or sold them as slaves to the West Indies. The participating tribes were not utterly prostrated as the Pequots had been, and thereafter they turned to the French for assistance against their New England foes.

[32] Elroy M. Avery, *A History of the United States* (7 vols., Cleveland, 1904–10), is an accurate, profusely illustrated narrative, written for the general reader but now useful as a reference work.

## BIBLIOGRAPHICAL NOTE

WORKS PREVIOUSLY CITED: W. C. Abbott, *Expansion of Europe*, I, chs. 17–19; C. M. Andrews, *Fathers of New England*, chs. 5, 8; G. Bancroft, *History of the United States*, I, chs. 10. 15; II, chs. 22, 32; J. B. Brebner, *Explorers of North America*, chs. 10–14 (French); I. Calder, *New Haven Colony*, chs. 9–11; *Cambridge Modern History*, IV, chs. 4, 21 (France); E. Channing, *History of the United States*, I, pp. 100–111, 414–484; J. Fiske, *Beginnings of New England*, chs. 4–5; J. Fiske, *Dutch and Quaker Colonies*, I (New Netherland); E. M. Hulme, *Renaissance and Reformation*, ch. 25 (Dutch Republic); A. G. Keller, *Colonization*, ch. 10 (Dutch); W. B. Munro, *Crusaders of New France*, ch. 3; H. L. Osgood, *American Colonies in the Seventeenth Century*, I, pp. 371–422, 527–576; II, chs. 5–7, 16; *Pageant of America*, I, ch. 9, pp. 285–308; F. Parkman, *Pioneers of France in the New World* (Champlain); H. I. Priestley, *Coming of the White Man*, chs. 8–12 (French, Dutch); F. Schevill, *History of Europe*, pp. 191–211 (Dutch); L. G. Tyler, *England in America*, chs. 16–18; J. Winsor (ed.), *Narrative and Critical History of America*, IV, chs. 3–6, 8–9; G. M. Wrong, *Rise and Fall of New France*, I, chs. 6–11 (important).
SOURCES NEWLY CITED: The Jameson *Original Narratives* series contain a

volume on the Dutch, *Narratives of New Netherland, 1609–1664* (ed. J. F. Jameson, New York, 1909). W. L. Grant has edited the *Voyages of Samuel de Champlain, 1604–1618* (New York, 1907—Jameson *Original Narratives* series). For another selection see E. G. Bourne (ed.), *The Voyages and Explorations of Samuel de Champlain* (2 vols., Toronto, 1911); R. G. Thwaites (ed.), *The Jesuit Relations* (73 vols., Cleveland, c. 1895–1901), gives original French texts and English translations of reports of Jesuit missionaries. *The Indians in North America* (ed. Edna Kenton, 2 vols., New York, c. 1927) contains excerpts from *The Jesuit Relations* pertaining to the Indians of New France. See Vol. I. On French colonial economy see H. A. Innes (ed.), *Select Documents in Canadian Economic History, 1478–1783* (Toronto, 1929). For King Philip's War see Charles H. Lincoln (ed.), *Narratives of the Indian Wars* (New York, 1913—Jameson *Original Narratives* series).

SOURCES PREVIOUSLY CITED: H. S. Commager (ed.), *Documents of American History*, I, nos. 14, 18; F. G. Davenport (ed.), *European Treaties bearing on the History of the United States*, II, nos. 41–42; A. B. Hart (ed.), *American History Told by Contemporaries*, I, pp. 121–132, 426–467, 517–554; W. MacDonald, *Documentary Source Book of American History*, nos. 7, 12, 20; *Old South Leaflets*, nos. 21, 52, 69, 72, 88, 91, 94, 96, 143, 168–169.

MAPS: D. R. Fox, *Harper's Atlas*, pp. 8–9, 11; C. O. Paullin, *Atlas of the Historical Geography of the United States*, plates 18, 19, 21, 39; W. R. Shepherd, *Historical Atlas*, p. 117.

# IX

## ECONOMIC FOUNDATIONS

### The Genesis of Individual Enterprise

THE mainspring of American economic development has been private enterprise—the ownership and conduct of businesses by individuals, rather than by the community. The founders of the colonies did not seek to create an economic order different from the one with which they were familiar in Europe; instead they hoped to make money in accustomed ways. The New World did inspire one famous plan for an ideal society—that set forth in Sir Thomas More's *Utopia* (1516). To Sir Thomas the ills of mankind—crime, poverty, and war—issued from the lust and strife for the possession of land. In the New World he saw an extent of land so vast that all inhabitants might share it in common, and accordingly he conceived of Utopia as a place where the land would be owned jointly by the people and would be rotated among them, free from rents to overlords. Even houses were to be exchanged every ten years by lot. Under a planned community life each person would have to work only six hours a day, dividing his time equally between city and rural pursuits. "Shun the precious metals," urged Sir Thomas, "till the land, let all share alike and so build up a new community founded on peace, good will and equity." However, colonial promoters did not follow this idealistic advice. Instead they searched diligently for the precious metals and introduced private ownership of land, economic inequality, and the profit motive.[1]

In the first colonies, Virginia and Plymouth, individual enterprise did not take root until after experiments with corporate production and trade had failed. The promoters of each colony devised a scheme whereby the settlers labored as servants of the company, which was domiciled in England. The produce of their labor went into a company storehouse, from which they were fed and clothed. Any surplus they produced belonged to the company, to be sold in England to provide profits for the company's investors. If the settlers' produce

[1] An attractive and able study is E. A. J. Johnson, *American Economic Thought in the Seventeenth Century* (London, 1932).

proved inadequate for their maintenance, they were supported by supplies sent by the company from England. This scheme meant that all land in each colony temporarily belonged to the company, and that the company had to carry on all trade, since all the produce raised in the colony belonged to it. However, both the Virginia and Plymouth promoters had provided that after a seven-year term all the improved lands and other property were to be divided among the company investors in proportion to the shares of stock owned by each.

This plan did not yield good results. In Virginia the settlers "loafed on the job," since they got a living, irrespective of their personal efforts. They could receive but little, if any, benefit from the colony's surplus; hence a surplus was not produced. The Plymouth colonists became acutely dissatisfied for a number of reasons. The labor of unmarried men benefited other men's families; married men did not like to have their wives work for other settlers; the older men objected to being placed on a par with the younger; and the industrious workers thought it unjust that they received no more than the idlers. Since the plan provided only a niggardly subsistence for the settlers and because it failed to provide profits for the English investors, it was soon abandoned: in Virginia in 1614–18, in Plymouth in 1623–24.[2]

The first step toward a new economy was the transfer of land from the companies to individual settlers in order that they might enjoy in full the fruits of their labor and thus feel a stronger incentive to work. The Virginia Company accomplished this change in four ways: by renting small plots to farmers; by giving hundred-acre tracts to settlers who had labored for the company seven years; by issuing patents for large tracts to societies composed of wealthy English investors with the understanding that they would develop extensive plantations; and by offering head rights to emigrants who would establish themselves in the colony at their own expense. By 1624 the improved lands of Virginia had passed into private hands, and thereafter the English government, as the owner of ungranted lands, continued the policy of selling or giving farms to individual settlers.

Similarly, the Pilgrims at Plymouth became owners of their lands after 1627. In 1623 a food shortage in the colony caused a temporary abandonment of the corporate method of farming, and in 1624 the English investors wrote that they did not intend to spend any more money on the colony and offered to sell their claims to the Pilgrims

---

[2] Henry J. Carman's *Social and Economic History of the United States* (Boston, 1930) contains a store of well selected information, presented in an interesting manner. See Vol. I, pp. 62–83.

if the latter would pay certain debts due in England. After negotiations, 1627–30, the Pilgrim leaders acquired title to the land of Plymouth Colony and agreed to pay (in nine annual £200 installments) debts due in England amounting to £1,800. The leaders then divided the lands and other property of the colony among the settlers, who thereby became known as the "purchasers" or "old comers" and who made themselves responsible for paying the £1,800 debt. The "purchasers" also acquired a monopoly of the fur trade and fishery of the colony, which they assigned to a group of "undertakers," who managed it for the benefit of the settlers and thereby procured the money to discharge the English debt. Some of the "undertakers" operated in the colony and some in England. Due to misappropriation of funds by the latter, the debt was not fully paid until 1648.

The introduction of private landowning is a major landmark in American history because it determined the course of later economic development. Essentially it came about because the English people had a deep-seated desire for title to land, which had become the basis of social position to which they were accustomed. When the early settlers saw such great stretches of idle land about them they were not satisfied to work as employees or tenants of English companies. Only with individual ownership did the colonist feel the spur to industry necessary in subduing a hostile wilderness.[3]

As soon as settlers of Virginia and Plymouth became owners of their farms, they also owned the produce they raised and therefore demanded the right to sell it to the highest bidder. No longer could a company in England insist upon a monopoly of trade, as it had done when it owned all lands and produce. Obviously a monopolistic company might set prices on both the farmer's produce and the wares sold to him, and thus appropriate his surplus and destroy the advantages of ownership. Hence the introduction of private ownership was soon followed by the abandonment of corporate trading monopolies. After 1624 the trade of Virginia and Plymouth was carried on by private traders, either as individuals or in partnerships, who usually operated with a small capital and at first competed among themselves for the business both of supplying the farmer with the wares he needed and of marketing his crops.

The unhappy experience of Virginia and Plymouth with the corporate scheme of ownership, production, and trade demonstrated its weakness to later colonial promoters. All the English colonies founded

[3] A work of great value is the *Encyclopaedia of the Social Sciences* (ed. E. R. A. Seligman and Alvin Johnson, 15 vols., New York, 1930–35). Excellent articles on economic topics are arranged alphabetically.

after 1629—Massachusetts, Maryland, Connecticut, Rhode Island, New Hampshire, New Haven, New Jersey, the Carolinas, and Pennsylvania—immediately introduced private landowning and with it a competitive trade in farm produce, carried on by individual merchants.

Another business enterprise in the colonies, the fur trade, also resisted monopolization or corporate control. This traffic, by virtue of the large profits it afforded, appeared to promoters and traders as a certain road to riches.[4] The wealthy nobles and bourgeoisie of Europe were willing to pay high prices for luxurious furs which proclaimed the superior affluence and social status of their possessors. Such furs could be obtained at low cost in America in exchange for cheap articles like hoes, axes, knives, beads, trinkets, bright colored cloth, guns, ammunition, and strong drink, particularly rum. Transportation charges were not excessive; all the goods could be carried overland by pack horse or along the rivers in small boats or canoes. When the natives became better acquainted with the value of their furs, unscrupulous traders resorted to various frauds such as using false weights and measures or supplying the Indians with rum, then driving hard bargains while they were intoxicated. William Penn reported that profits in the fur trade ran as high as 100 per cent. "For a sixpence worth of rum," he wrote, "one may buy the fur from them [the Indians] that five shillings in any other commodity shall not purchase."

Five regions in English America yielded furs during the seventeenth century. In New England, Plymouth Colony established trading posts on the Connecticut, Kennebec, and Penobscot Rivers, while Connecticut and Massachusetts, prior to 1650, operated in the Connecticut valley, where Springfield was a trafficking center. New Netherland had its posts at Fort Orange, Fort Nassau, and the House of Good Hope. Pennsylvania soon developed a trade with the Susquehanna region, and traders from Virginia and South Carolina ranged throughout the back country of those colonies. The principal furs of the middle and New England colonies were beaver, otter, mink, bear, raccoon, and fox; south of Maryland, the importance of deerskins made the traffic primarily a leather trade, although raccoon, fox, beaver, and mink furs were also obtained. By 1650 the fur trade of western New England had practically disappeared, but that carried on by New Netherland with the Iroquois was still the mainstay of that colony. In 1656 Fort Orange exported about 35,000 beaver and

---

[4] Clarence A. Vandiveer, *The Fur-Trade and Early Western Exploration* (Cleveland, 1929), is a clear, concise, brief introduction. See chapters 1–7.

DISTRIBUTION OF POPULATION
1650

LEGEND

EACH DOT (·) REPRESENTS
APPROXIMATELY 200 RURAL IN-
HABITANTS LOCALIZED BY
CIVIL TOWNSHIPS, PARISHES
AND COUNTIES

SCALE

otter furs. Exports from South Carolina in 1687 did not exceed £2,000, but by 1705 the fur trade was the chief branch of the colony's commerce.[5]

North of Maryland the English and Dutch fur traders conducted their business through posts, "trucking houses," or "mansion houses" to which the Indians brought their furs, whereas the traders of Virginia and South Carolina traveled long distances to bargain with the

[5] Francis X. Maloney's *The Fur Trade in New England, 1620–1676* (Cambridge, 1931) shows what an undergraduate can do with a bachelor's thesis.

natives in their villages. The French also sought out the Indians in their forest haunts, even accompanying them on the hunt. The advantage to the French of their intimate contacts was offset by the high price of their trading goods. The English at Albany often charged less than half of French prices at Montreal. Low production costs in English industry accounted in part for this difference.

The profits of the fur trade led colonial promoters to attempt to monopolize it. Thus the Dutch West India Company reserved the New Netherland traffic to itself, even excluding the patroons, except in communities where the company had no trading posts. So also Plymouth managed its trade as a colony enterprise, and an agreement made by the Massachusetts Bay Company in 1629 provided that one-half of the beaver trade was to be reserved to investors in England while the other half was to be free to the settlers. In 1632 Massachusetts granted a year's monopoly of the settlers' share of the trade to a Mr. Pynchon. The Carolina proprietors sought to control the South Carolina traffic, by having it managed by the governor for their profit. William Penn also proposed that he receive a long-term monopoly of the trade in his colony.[6]

But such efforts generally failed largely because officials and merchants in the colonies "traded on their own"; and by virtue of the difficulty of excluding such "interlopers" from the vast American wilderness, the monopolists could not enforce their claims. Thus in New Netherland both the employees of the company and the patroons traded privately in defiance of its monopoly, while in Massachusetts, Virginia, South Carolina, and Pennsylvania local merchants and officials successfully resisted corporate or proprietary control.

In consequence, the dominance of private merchants became the distinguishing feature of the fur trade. Such merchants imported trucking goods from Europe and sold them on credit to Indian traders or hired the latter to make inland trading expeditions. The business rapidly centered in a few places—Albany, Charleston, and Philadelphia—where the furs were brought to the merchants, who then exported them to Europe. Similarly the trade soon fell under the sway of a small group of rich merchants, largely because it required a considerable capital. A year's shipment of trucking goods might cost £1,000, and because the goods had to be carried inland long distances the returns to the merchant were slow. Again, there were strategic points like the Mohawk valley which might be controlled by merchants who had established friendly contacts with the resident tribes. For these reasons only a few men could engage in the trade on a profitable basis—a fact which tended to reduce competition among the merchants, since they could agree among themselves upon prices at which their goods were bartered. However, competition was not eliminated, as indicated by the rivalry after 1680 between New York merchants and Pennsylvania merchants for the trade of the Susquehanna region, and by the struggle between South Carolina and Virginia for control of the southwestern trade (1695–1710). In the lat-

[6] Sydney Greenbie, *Frontiers and the Fur Trade* (New York, 1929), is a popular, discursive account.

ter contest the Charleston merchants emerged victorious and tightened their grip upon the great southern traffic in deerskins.[7]

The westward advance of the fur trade further entrenched the wealthy merchants, by virtue of the larger capital outlays required for distant operations. The extension of the trade proceeded more rapidly than the growth of settlement. The demand created by the white trader led the Indians to destroy furbearing animals to an extent greatly in excess of the red man's primitive needs, and thus compelled trappers and traders to go farther and farther inland. By 1700 the New England fur trade centered in Maine; New York traders were then visiting Lakes Erie and Ontario; Pennsylvanians had penetrated, via the Susquehanna, Allegheny, and Ohio Rivers, to the mouth of the Wabash; Virginians had explored the upper waters and southern tributaries of the Ohio; and South Carolinians had journeyed a thousand miles inland from Charleston.[8]

## COLONIAL AGRICULTURE

During the seventeenth century between 90 and 95 per cent of the settlers were engaged in agriculture, although the colonial farmer was also generally a hunter, builder, artisan, and in places a lumberman and a fisherman. The New England and middle colonies developed a diversified, nearly self-sufficient economy centering in grains, live stock and household manufactures. The surplus and therefore the exports of the middle colonies consisted chiefly of wheat, flour, beef, and pork, while New England—less adapted to farming—produced little or no surplus of foodstuffs and depended more upon household manufacturing and specialized trades such as lumbering, shipbuilding, shipping, and fisheries. Thus New England's exports which matched the grains, cattle, and meat of the middle colonies were fish, lumber, ships, shipping services, earthenware, woodenware, leather goods, woolen cloth, and even ironware. Virginia and Maryland produced more pork, Indian corn, vegetables, and fruits than did New England but less than the middle colonies. Tobacco, the great staple of Virginia and Maryland, taking the place occupied by manufactures and the fishery in New England and by wheat in the middle colonies,

[7] For the best description of the southern fur trade see Verner W. Crane, *The Southern Frontier* (Durham, 1929), chapter 5.

[8] A. H. Buffinton, "New England and the Western Fur-Trade, 1629–1675," in *Publications,* Colonial Society of Massachusetts, XVIII (Boston, 1917); H. Broshar, "The First Push Westward of the Albany Traders," *Mississippi Valley Historical Review,* VII (Dec. 1920).

enabled the Southerners to purchase such provisions and merchandise as they needed. By 1700 New England did not produce all its own foodstuffs, and hence exported its manufactures, shipping services, and fish to pay for the balance it imported. The middle colonies produced a surplus of foodstuffs which they sold abroad in order to buy manufactures, since their industries were less developed than New England's. Virginia and Maryland supplied themselves with most of their food but, lacking manufactures, they were obliged to exchange their tobacco for finished articles and some provisions. North Carolina resembled Virginia and Maryland save that tobacco was less important and food production and household manufactures relatively more important. The agriculture of South Carolina was of the diversified type until the growth of rice production in the 1690's.[9]

The colonial farmer labored in the shadow of the American forest. His first great task, and an arduous one too, was to clear a planting field. From the Indians he learned how to "girdle" trees—to cut a ring around them and thus to kill them by preventing the sap from rising. Then, after clearing away the underbrush, he could plant his crop in the spaces between the tree stumps. Energetic pioneers cut down the trees and rooted out the stumps. One method used was to cut part way through the trunks of several trees and then to fell a "monarch" at the head of the line thus bringing them all crashing to earth like ninepins. Fallen branches and tree trunks were burned and the ashes left as fertilizer. So laborious was this work that a family could clear only an acre a month. In New England the removal of stones doubled the pioneer's burden. The early clearings looked ragged, gaunt, and rather dismal.[10]

In cultivating these irregular patches the pioneer could use only spades, hoes, and rakes, a limitation which prevented his raising wheat at first, since it could be grown only after wilderness land had been thoroughly plowed. Indian corn proved to be the ideal initial crop. Not only could it be cultivated in hills by hand labor but its seed yielded a seventyfold increase, and it provided a variety of dishes for the settler and feed for his livestock. Beans planted in the hills entwined themselves about the cornstalks, while pumpkins could be grown in between. Indian corn gave American agriculture its start, from Carolina to Maine.

[9] Albert H. Sanford's *The Story of Agriculture in the United States* (Boston, c. 1916) is a satisfactory elementary sketch. See chapters 1–8.

[10] Joseph Schafer, *The Social History of American Agriculture* (New York, 1936), contains two able lectures on the colonial period. See chapters 1 and 2.

The absorbing interest of the Virginia Company in profit led to early efforts to develop products for sale in Europe rather than to create a self-sustaining economy for the settlers. However, experiments with the production of wine, hemp, flax, naval stores, iron, silk, potash, and glassware came to little, save that they emphasized the desirability of commodities which might be exported at a profit. Such a commodity was soon found in tobacco, first successfully raised by John Rolfe in 1612. Thereafter tobacco growing spread with phenomenal rapidity. Here was a product which satisfied the demands of mercantilism. Whereas in 1615 England was exporting £200,000 in specie to buy foreign tobacco, principally from Spain, Virginian tobacco could now be paid for with English goods and handled by English traders, thus preserving England's stock of specie, enlarging the markets for her wares, and affording profits to her merchants. The rich alluvial lands of Virginia were perfectly suited to tobacco production, and because of high prices prevailing in England the settlers could make five or six times more from tobacco than from any other crop. By 1627 Virginia's exports amounted to 500,000 pounds and tobacco was so basic in her economy that one writer said the colony was in danger of being founded upon smoke. In the 1630's Maryland became a producer and North Carolina followed in the 1660's, so that "king tobacco" thereafter guided the social, political, and economic destinies of his subjects in three of the English colonies.[11]

Tobacco paved the way for large units of production and for the employment of servile or slave labor. The demand in Europe seemed unlimited since by 1620 smoking had become something of a social craze; accordingly it was possible for the planters to concentrate upon tobacco, exchanging it for other things they desired. Such specialization in turn meant that large farms could be operated profitably, provided that enough laborers could be found, but at this point the tobacco grower encountered his greatest problem. The abundance of open land in America constantly drew workers from employers to the frontier with its promise of land ownership and independence. A relatively large number of landowners, all bidding against each other for a limited supply of laborers, sent wages to levels much higher than in Europe and thus created among employers a prejudice against the free, independent wage-earner. They found a way out by obtaining indentured servants and Negro slaves. The indentured servant labored for four years or more without pay in return for his transportation to

[11] Meyer Jacobstein, *The Tobacco Industry in the United States* (New York, 1907), is a standard work. See chapter 1.

America, his maintenance, and possibly a tract of land at the end of his term. The Negro slave, of course, was condemned to a lifetime of labor, without pay other than a bare subsistence.[12]

In Virginia and Maryland indentured servants formed the bulk of the non-free laboring population until about 1680. Although Negroes had been imported into Virginia as early as 1619, they did not become of primary importance until more than sixty years later. Negro slavery spread after 1680 partly because of a rapid development at that time of the English and Dutch slave traffic, partly because the increasing competition among tobacco planters necessitated lower production costs and therefore cheaper labor, and partly because the opening of Pennsylvania in 1681 diverted thither thousands of indentured servants from Europe when the supply of English servants was diminishing. In addition the system of indentured servants had inherent defects. The worker received his freedom just as he became most valuable to his employer, who thereupon had to train new hands, while the freed servant might set up as a planter, thereby competing with his former master.[13]

Since neither the indentured servant nor the Negro slave received direct payment, his labor was generally given reluctantly and therefore tended to be unskillful and inefficient. Furthermore the Negroes of the seventeenth century, recently arrived from Africa, were ignorant of the white man's ways. Both servants and slaves therefore could be used to most advantage in an employment which called for little skill and enabled the employer to supervise their activities within a restricted area. Tobacco cultivation met this requirement perfectly, consisting as it did of a series of simple operations that extended throughout the year. First the seed was sown in winter in a forest soil. The tobacco plant had to be cultivated separately and the seeds were so small (about ten thousand to a teaspoonful) that this could not be done without transplanting. Hence when the seedbeds had been prepared the growing field was made ready by ridging it into hills about three feet apart. When the spring rains had moistened the hills the shoots were transplanted. Later care consisted of hoeing, removing hornworms, and cutting off the top and lower leaves of the plant so that it would produce a suitable number of large, heavy leaves. At the close of summer the plants were cut as they turned yellow and the stalks were fastened to laths and hung to dry on the rafters of

---

[12] An outstanding work is Lewis C. Gray's *History of Agriculture in the Southern United States* (2 vols., Washington, 1933)—one of the foremost products of American scholarship. See Vol. I, chapters 1–3, 5–10, 14–15, 17. Very important.

[13] Ulrich B. Phillips, *American Negro Slavery* (New York, 1918), is the best one-volume work in its subject. See chapters 1–4, 6.

barns. In the following spring the dried leaves were stripped from the stalk, then sorted and packed into hogsheads, which were rolled to the planter's wharf where vessels took them for exportation. All these operations were simple and easily learned; hence they could be performed by ignorant slaves, while large-scale production made possible the working of several hands under the direction of an overseer.[14]

Although practically all the planters of Virginia and Maryland were tobacco growers, they also produced food for their families, servants, and slaves. They raised Indian corn, a little wheat, beans, peas, hogs, cattle, poultry, and fruits, while the woods afforded venison, partridges, turkeys, and other game. Virginia's stock of cows, oxen, bulls, and calves increased fivefold in sixteen years—from 20,000 in 1649 to 100,000 in 1665. Sheep raising, however, was impracticable, due to the scarcity of pasture land. Without tobacco, the native products of the southern colonies would have afforded only a rude living, but tobacco exports enabled the planters to supply themselves with hardware and tools, as well as wine, sugar, household goods, clothing, and other amenities of life.[15]

Small farms usually varying in size from ten to two hundred acres dotted the landscape in New York, Long Island, western New Jersey, and Pennsylvania. The people did not live together in villages but more or less isolated on their individual holdings. Economic pursuits were highly diversified, most of the labor being performed by the farmer, his family, and his indentured servants. The variety of tasks involved and the impossibility of working several hands in one series of large-scale operations precluded the widespread use of ignorant and indifferent slaves who labored most efficiently under close supervision. The worker on the farms of the middle colonies had to be a "Jack-of-all-trades"—farmer, woodsman, and artisan.[16]

Once the pioneering stage had passed wheat became a principal crop. After the land was prepared by three plowings, the seed was sown broadcast by hand, most commonly in September, and harvested with sickles in July. Then the sheaves were stored in barns, where the threshing took place in fall or winter when the weather prevented outdoor work. The colonial "threshing machine" was a wooden hand flail consisting of a handle about four feet in length to which a "striker" about two feet long was attached by a leather thong. After

[14] U. B. Phillips, *Life and Labor in the Old South* (Boston, 1929), gives mature conclusions in an entertaining manner. See chapters 1–3.

[15] P. A. Bruce, "Economic and Social Life of Virginia in the Seventeenth Century," in *The South in the Making of the Nation*, Vol. I, chapter 3.

[16] Lyman Carrier's *The Beginnings of American Agriculture* (New York, 1923) affords the best introduction to farming techniques.

the kernels had been separated the grain was thrown against the wind to remove the chaff. In raising Indian corn, the farmer plowed his fields in March and planted the seed by hoe and hand in April or May. When, after much "backbreaking" hoeing, the plants were full grown in September, the blades were stripped from the stalks and fed to the cattle as fodder. The ripened ears were harvested and stored in October and then the farm children did the shelling during their spare time, scraping the ears over shovel edges or the handles of frying pans.

Flax also became an important crop in the middle colonies. Late in March the seed was sown broadcast on newly plowed ground. Then when the plants were three or four inches high, barefoot women and children weeded the fields. The plants, having ripened by July, were pulled up by the roots, tied in bundles, and dried in the sun. Next the heads of the stalks were pulled through a comb, thus removing the seed "bob," and the bundles were then stacked in a pool of water and left to rot. When the pith between fibers had rotted, the stalks were dried in a flax kiln—an E-shaped stone wall within which a fire was built while the stalks were placed on poles laid across the top. Thus were the fibers made ready for linen manufacture.[17]

Other crops grown in the middle colonies included barley, oats, rye, buckwheat, and tobacco—the latter for family consumption. Gardens yielded beets, parsnips, onions, parsley, radishes, beans, peas, red peppers, lettuce, and sage. Cabbage was often planted two or three times a year, the heads being cut down for sauerkraut or stored in the cellar to be used as greens. Orchards, fence-enclosed, consisted mainly of apple, cherry, and peach trees. Surplus peaches (the clingstone was a colonial favorite) were fed to hogs, and apples to the cows and horses.[18]

The middle colony farm raised its own poultry and livestock. The best cows (generally small, tough, and weather-beaten) yielded about four quarts of milk daily in times of good pasturage but little or none during the winter months. The colonial horse, small and rarely shod, resembled a pony more than a modern work horse. From the meadow came the supply of hay, which was cut in May and August, dried, and placed in cone-shaped stacks raised on poles a few feet from the ground. Although the farmer's sheep were of the English variety, they produced a staple only a third as long as that of their English

[17] Percy W. Bidwell and John I. Falconer, *History of Agriculture in the Northern United States, 1620–1860* (Washington, 1925), is the standard work on its subject. Important.

[18] An ably written, comprehensive text is Edward C. Kirkland, *A History of American Economic Life* (New York, 1932). See chapter 2.

rivals. The colonial hog—a fierce, tough, fleet, long-legged fellow of the "racer" or "razorback" sort—had to hold his own among the wild animals of the woods, where he picked up his scanty livelihood from plants and acorns.[19]

Seventeenth-century New England wore an aspect altogether different from that of the southern and middle colonies. The New Englanders lived in villages which resembled medieval English farming communities. On the outskirts of the village lay a community grazing field for horses and cattle; near the center were located the "home lots"—tracts varying from three to five acres where the farmers had their houses, barns, orchards, gardens, and cattle yards. Behind the home lots lay the arable fields devoted to grain. In most villages there was uncleared and ungranted land held in common by the town proprietors where they could obtain timber, firewood, and stone. Low, marshy land served as the meadows which produced an inferior sort of hay.[20]

The early New England farmer did not own one large arable field; instead he possessed small tracts scattered throughout the township— a fact explained by the slow process of clearing land. The founders or proprietors of a new village would first allot only a part of its arable land, each receiving a small parcel; later clearings would be similarly divided, so that in the end the farmer's fields would be scattered throughout the village, and these he reached by paths or roads. In many cases, however, the tracts were enclosed by a single fence forming a large "common field" and the farmers in their town meeting would decide what crop should be grown there, although each cultivated his own tract. After harvest, the common fields became pasture as the cattle were turned in to graze on the stubble, each landowner having the right to pasture a certain number of animals, depending upon the amount of land he owned. Such a right might entitle the landowner to pasture one ox, horse, or cow for every four acres he held in the common field.[21]

In New England Indian corn took the place occupied by wheat in the middle colonies. About 1660 the black-stem rust attacked the northern wheat and although the Connecticut valley remained a good wheat-growing country, Sir Edmund Andros, referring to Massachusetts in 1690, spoke of "no wheat having grown but blasted there

---

[19] Louis B. Schmidt and Earl D. Ross (eds.), *Readings in the Economic History of American Agriculture* (New York, 1925), is a valuable collection.

[20] Anne B. MacLear's *Early New England Towns* (New York, 1908) is a competent monograph.

[21] Melville Eggleston, *The Land System of the New England Colonies* (Baltimore, 1886), is a good short essay.

for about thirty years past, nor have they cattle or other grain beyond their own consumption." Sheep raising depended upon protection from wolves; hence it first took root on islands where they could be exterminated—on Martha's Vineyard, Nantucket, and the islands in Narragansett Bay. Only when the frontier had been pushed well inland could sheep growing thrive on the mainland. New England raised rye and barley in small quantities, as well as all sorts of garden produce and fruits, particularly apples, which in the form of cider, pies, dumplings, and apple butter figured largely in New England's diet.[22]

The village system of scattered tracts and common field cultivation did not result in efficient production. The farmer spent too much time going to and coming from his small holdings. When the village cattle mingled promiscuously on the common pasture selective stock breeding was impossible. Moreover, regulated cultivation in the common fields prevented crop experimentation and confined the more enterprising farmers within a routine geared to suit the slower workers.

All in all, it was a hard, primitive, meager life which the ordinary farmer endured. His tools would have been familiar in ancient Babylonia. His plow, awkward and cumbersome, operated something like a shovel pulled through the earth, was so prone to pull out of the soil that it took two men to hold it down and two or three horses or four or five oxen to draw it along. Since the farmer could raise only as large a crop as he could harvest, his dependence upon the sickle set the limits of his productivity, and one man could harvest only five acres a season. The cheapness and abundance of land bred a type of farming which quickly "mined" the fertility of the soil. The seventeenth-century farmer used neither fertilizer nor crop rotation, preferring to let exhausted land stand idle and become overgrown with weeds, a practice which failed to restore its productivity.[23] Pasturage was generally very poor. Speaking of New England cattle in 1723 a writer said: "Our flesh [are] like carrion for want of feeding, there being no provender or pasture but rancid sour stuff, never renewed since the days of Adam, nor any hay but what spontaneously arrives, etc., no straw to litter our cattle, so that most of them die for hunger and cold." An exaggerated picture, perhaps, and yet colonial cattle generally had "a lean and hungry look." Horses and pigs, always tempted by the growing grain fields, orchards, and gardens, were prone to

[22] Albert L. Olson, *Agricultural Economy and the Population in . . . Connecticut* (New Haven, 1935, Connecticut Tercentenary Commission, no. 40).

[23] R. R. Walcott, "Husbandry in Colonial New England," *New England Quarterly,* IX (July 1936).

jump over the crude wooden fences in order to partake of a self-invited feast. Such encroachments were the source of many a rural argument, in spite of the practice of fastening wooden yokes about the necks of the stock to restrain their leaping propensities. Fruit trees grew without benefit of pruning and grafting, attacked by a variety of parasites which the farmer did not understand. Clouds of mosquitoes and flies harassed both man and beast; chickens fell a prey to raccoons, weasels, and minks; rabbits helped themselves to turnips and cabbage; and squirrels and crows made merry in the cornfields. Is it surprising that a pious traveler found the colonial farmer a profane man? [24]

## HOUSEHOLD MANUFACTURING

The colonial settler was determined not only to retain his European way of life but also to improve his economic condition as much as possible. Because a rising standard of living entailed an increasing utilization of manufactured products, the procuring of such goods was a paramount interest. These the settler purchased partly in England, but due to his limited buying power he had to produce many commodities with his own labor. Two types of industrial production developed during the seventeenth century. The more prominent was household manufacturing—the making of articles by members of the family, primarily for their own use. The second—commercialized industry which produced goods to be sold at a profit in a general market —made but slow progress before 1700. The open frontier drew laborers away from the older settlements, thereby creating a labor shortage that kept wages two or three times as high as in Europe and hence retarded industries dependent upon hired workers. Moreover, the colonists lacked capital, not only machines and large workshops, but also a surplus of specie or cash which employers need in order to support their operations while advancing goods to their customers on credit. Above all, the market of the colonies was too small to nourish large-scale enterprises. As late as 1700 the population of the mainland settlements did not exceed 300,000 souls; hence the American demand for manufactured goods was not great enough to support large plants that could cut production costs by utilizing machinery and a subdivision of labor. England, on the other hand, manufactured for a world market and accordingly benefited by increasing production economies due to the division of labor, specialized skills, and improved tools.

[24] Percy W. Bidwell, *Rural Economy in New England at the Beginning of the Nineteenth Century* (New Haven, 1916) gives an intimate view of rural New England.

The colonial industries which developed before 1700 had two things in common. First, they took advantage of the resources which America afforded so abundantly and so cheaply, and secondly, the manufacturing processes employed were so simple as to require but little capital. By and large, colonial industries merely converted raw materials into crude products.

First of all the colonial household supplied itself with articles of food now prepared in bakeries, creameries, cheese factories, packing houses, canning factories, sugar refineries, and breweries. The busy housewife, using the wheat, rye, or Indian corn that had been raised on the farm and ground at the neighborhood mill, baked the family's supply of bread, as well as hardtack biscuits which were made in copious quantities and served with bowls of milk. The women and children labored at the hand churn to produce a potent, salty kind of butter. After the farmer had slaughtered his hogs the hams and shoulders were kept for six or eight weeks in brine and then smoked in the smokehouse. A large part of the family meat supply went into head cheeses and sausage. Since the housewife did not have sealed jars, preserves had to be made so rich that they would keep uncovered. Apples, melons, and gourds were cut into pieces and strung up to dry in the kitchen, while peaches were cut in quarters, dried in the oven, and packed away in bags. Applesauce boiled in cider made apple butter. Unable to obtain much white sugar, the household used honey, molasses, and maple sugar for sweetening. In the early spring the sugar maple trees were tapped; when the sap began to run in the trunks it was drained into wooden troughs and then boiled in kettles over a woodland fire. The light work involved and a holiday spirit made maple sugar time a sort of picnic when the family camped out in the forest.[25]

The colonial farmer was not a prohibitionist. He manufactured his own beer, using not hops but malt from barley, rye, or wheat. His "table beer" was made from persimmons, his "small beer" from molasses. Honey and water thoroughly boiled gave him mead, an ancient and very potent drink; brandy he made from peaches, persimmons, and apples; while cherry, blackberry, wild grape, raspberry, or currant wine might grace his table. Not content with these beverages he concocted many others: "grog," a mixture of rum, water, and sweetening; "cider royal," made of cider and brandy; "milk punch," consisting of rum, milk, and sweetening; and "cherry bounce," a combination of cherry wine and rum.

[25] Rollo M. Tryon's *Household Manufactures in the United States, 1640–1860* (Chicago, 1917), the standard authority, is a careful analysis. See chapters 1–3.

The farmer in the middle colonies and New England acquired no little skill with axe, saw, and hammer. He felled the timber for his house and barn, shaped planks, rafters, shingles, clapboards, and flooring, and did much of the actual construction, although his neighbors helped him to put the heavy framework into place. He also quarried and dressed stone but he generally employed a stonemason to build the chimneys and foundation of his house. Using twisted tree limbs or branches he fashioned sled runners, scythe handles, ox yokes, harness hames, and hay forks. In place of a wagon he depended upon a cart, the wheels of which he made from ends of large tree trunks cut crosswise, while the feed troughs for his stock were probably hollowed-out logs. Spade and shovel handles, flails, plows, harrows, axe-helves, rakes with wooden teeth, brooms made from hickory saplings or hemlock branches, baskets fashioned from birch bark—all these testified to his skill as a woodworker. His house contained homemade chairs, benches, tables, bedsteads, stools, cradles, chests, spoons, and plates or trenchers (blocks of wood hollowed out on top). As a cooper he manufactured boxes, casks, and barrels. In the tobacco colonies indentured servants who were coopers or carpenters specialized in their trades, thus leaving the planter free to farm or manage his estate.[26]

The rural household north of Maryland habitually manufactured its own supply of linen and woolen cloth. By 1710 it had been said that in New Hampshire from the governor's family "to the meanest peasant" homespun was worn, that the Long Islanders made serge "that any man may wear," and that the people of New York produced two-thirds of their linens and woolens. The tobacco colonies, on the other hand, turned to the manufacture of cloth only in times of trade depression when tobacco exports would not pay for imported goods— and then the planters found themselves unskilled in the textile crafts.

The manufacture of woolens occupied the farmer's whole family. After the sheep had been shorn, the wool was mixed with hog's lard to make it soft and pliable. Next came the carding process which straightened the fibers of the fleece. Then the farmer combed the fibers, using T-shaped combs with iron teeth, the wool being placed upon one comb and carefully stroked with the other so as to make the long hairs smooth for spinning. The farm women operated the spinning wheel, the wool being fastened to the spindle, and as the wheel spun around the yarn was drawn and twisted into an even thread. If

[26] L. H. Bailey (ed.), *Cyclopedia of American Agriculture* (4 vols., New York, 1907–09) contains in Volume IV "Aboriginal Agriculture—The American Indian," by G. K. Holmes, and "Historical Sketch of American Agriculture," by Thomas N. Carver: both significant articles.

a strong thread were desired, the yarn was spun twice, such thread making a stiff, wiry cloth, while a single spinning sufficed to produce knitting yarn for softer garments. Weaving, a laborious task, was performed by the men at a hand loom operated by a hand shuttle. A single weaver could make a piece of cloth only as wide as the reach of his arm. After the grease had been washed from the cloth the material was scraped several times to even the threads. Finally, homemade dyes were applied, the colors being obtained from bark, leaves, flowers, and berries, or from imported products such as indigo, logwood, or cochineal. The colonial housewife used a large part of the yarn for knitting bags, stockings, shawls, and mittens.[27]

The manufacture of linen was also a complicated process. When the flax had been rotted, washed, and dried in the flax kiln, the stalks were opened, thus exposing the fibers. The latter were combed in order to remove the pith, then pulled through finer combs to separate the tow, and finally sorted as to fineness. Coarse tow was used to make bags, the finer tow for trousers, shirts, and bed ticking, the finest tow for suiting, towels, and fine linen goods. After the fibers had been spun into thread the skeins were washed and bleached in a solution of ashes and hot water. Since the cloth—which was woven on a semi-homemade frame—had a light brown color, it was washed and bleached in the sun. Pure white fabrics could be obtained by soaking bleached linen in buttermilk.

So great was the labor of making cloth and clothing that textiles had to be carefully conserved. Servants had to wear the cast-off garments of master and mistress, and children ordinarily "inherited" the clothes of their older brothers and sisters. When cloth was finally discarded it was completely worn out.

As leather workers the northern farmers made their coonskin caps and deerskin leggings and breeches and lined their overcoats with fur. Calfskins from the farm were generally taken to a near-by tanner, who kept part of the leather as his pay. The men of the household might work the leather into shoes, but because the farmer was ordinarily not a skilled leather worker he commonly hired a traveling shoemaker. This work was so crudely done that a shoe fitted either foot equally well (or poorly). The northern farm also produced its own harness, utilizing raw leather, wood, and hemp, while collars for horses were made of straw. A series of acts passed in Maryland, Connecticut, Massachusetts, New Jersey, Pennsylvania, and New York between 1662 and 1717 prohibited the exportation of raw hides

[27] One of the most outstanding studies of an industry is Arthur H. Cole's *The American Wool Manufacture* (2 vols., Cambridge, 1926). See Vol. I, chapters 1–3.

and tanned calfskins, thus denoting the growing importance of the colonial leather industry. Homemade shoes were mentioned at this time as a principal manufacture in Maryland, although they were "not to be had but at far dearer rates than from Great Britain." In Virginia, however, a writer noted in 1705 that hides were either wasted or used only "for covering dry goods in a leaky house." [28]

The commercial industries which nowadays provide fuel and light for the home were carried on by the seventeenth-century household. The settler's axe and brawn supplied him with firewood from the forest, used alike for heating and cooking. At night his house was lighted by the glow of the open fire and by homemade candles, the manufacture of which was a special art. During the autumn months the farmer boiled tallow, deer suet, moose fat, or bear's grease in great iron kettles. Then the melted tallow was twice skimmed and poured into another kettle containing boiling water. If candles were made by "dipping" the farmer used candle rods—short sticks to which were attached six or eight strings or candle wicks. The wicks were dipped into the molten tallow and the candle rod then hung in a cool room in order that the tallow might harden. With each dipping the wicks acquired more tallow until the candle attained the desired size. A good candlemaker worked slowly, taking particular pains to allow the tallow to cool and harden thoroughly before the wicks were again dipped; otherwise the candles became brittle and broke easily. Two hundred candles were a good day's output for an accomplished worker. The colonial household also made candles by a molding process. Candle molds consisted of several metal cylinders in each of which a wick was fastened before the melted tallow was carefully poured in. The largest molds had as many as twenty-four cylinders. Since candle-making with molds required some little skill and special equipment it was often done by traveling chandlers who brought their own molds, though the farm supplied the tallow.

The colonial household was also a soap factory and a laundry. Refuse fats from cooking and slaughtering were preserved during the winter and then boiled with lye to produce a soft "jelly" soap. The farmer obtained lye by filtering water through a barrel containing wood ashes from the fireplace. A better grade of soap, hard and sweet-scented, was made of oil pressed from bayberries. About once a month the women of the household did the family laundry at the washhouse, located on a near-by stream. Here the clothes were boiled in a large iron kettle which contained a generous quantity of jelly soap. A crude

[28] Frederick J. Allen's *The Shoe Industry* (New York, 1922) is *the* book on its subject.

washing machine consisting of a wooden barrel and a wooden pounder sufficed for the coarser clothes while the finer fabrics were rubbed, rinsed, and wrung by hand. The housewife had neither washtub, washboard, nor wringer to lessen the drudgery of her work. The rural folk also had to do their own dry cleaning. When powdered soap-stone spread over spots on clothes had absorbed some of the grease the powder was rubbed off, thus cleaning the garment. Crude as such methods were, laundering did not impose an intolerable hardship for the simple reason that the ordinary colonial household possessed only a small quantity of fabrics and clothing, and most textiles were dyed in dark blues, grays, and browns.

## COMMERCIAL INDUSTRIES

Commercialized industry differed from the household crafts in that it produced goods to be sold at a profit, not for the immediate use of the manufacturer. It required a fairly substantial capital in the form of tools, ships, or mills owned by a capitalist and operated for his profit by workers to whom he paid wages. The principal commercial indus-tries which developed during the seventeenth century were the fishery, lumbering, shipbuilding, flour milling, and the manufacture of iron.

Throughout colonial times Massachusetts dominated the fishing in-dustry. The reports of mariners who explored New England between 1600 and 1615 had called attention to the fishery as the most likely source of wealth, Captain John Smith, for instance, having taken forty thousand fish in 1614 from the waters off the Maine coast. He ob-served that "the main staple from hence to be extracted for the pres-ent, to produce the rest, is fish; which however it may seem a base commodity, yet who will but truly take the pains and consider the sequel, I think will allow it well worth the labor." By this time mer-chants in western England were turning from dreams of fabulous golden riches to more solid prospects of profit from timber, tobacco, and codfish and had already developed a lucrative fishery at New-foundland, which they carried on by means of vessels sent out yearly from their home ports. New England promised an even better op-portunity. Not only did its waters teem with a variety of fish—hake, haddock, halibut, mackerel, and pollock—but, more important, the chief profit-maker, the codfish, was larger, more numerous and earlier in its arrival in the fishing season than at Newfoundland. The New England fishery could be operated from the shore throughout the year; in consequence New England fish sold at higher prices in Europe than Newfoundland fish "because 'tis taken all winter and in cold weather is better cured."

Massachusetts did not achieve her mastery of the fishing industry without a struggle. When the Council for New England obtained its patent in 1620 it received the right to sell licenses giving to fishermen the privilege of operating from the shore. By charging 3s. 4d. a ton for every vessel entering New England harbors, the Council aroused the wrath of the fishermen of western England and the leaders of the Virginia Company—both of whom cast covetous eyes upon the New England fishery. Under the leadership of Sir Edwin Sandys the opponents of the Council sought through Parliament to cancel the monopoly but in this they were defeated by the king. Several vessels fishing without licenses were seized in 1623 when the royal navy undertook to enforce the monopoly. Legitimate promoters, therefore, had to operate with the consent of the Council, and this was done, prior to 1630, by the colonists at Plymouth, by the Dorchester Company, and by its two successors, the New England Company and the Massachusetts Bay Company.[29]

The capital for the initial development of the New England fishery was contributed by English merchants, some of whom operated by sending vessels from England and others by financing fishing settlements on the American coast. The number of vessels engaged rose from eight in 1616 to thirty-five in 1622 and fifty in 1624. However, after the arrival of the Massachusetts Puritans in 1630 the financial control of the fishery rapidly passed into the hands of the resident settlers. They fished at the start simply to supply themselves with food, but when they produced a surplus they soon felt that the profits earned by English capitalists might as well enrich themselves. In the 1620's English merchants furnished the settlements with fishing supplies (salt, hooks, lines, knives, and boats) at a 40 per cent price increase and reaped 30 per cent profit on the sale of the fish they purchased. As early as 1633 the New Englanders were building their own fishing shallops—and more cheaply than they could be made in England. Meanwhile the efforts of the Council for New England to enforce its monopoly had forced most of the English fishermen to withdraw from New England and to concentrate upon Newfoundland. Then when the Council ceased to function in 1635 the path was cleared for New England enterprise, while the disruption of England's trade and fishing during the Civil War gave relief from English competition for nearly a decade. Massachusetts fostered the fishery

[29] Raymond McFarland, *A History of the New England Fisheries* (New York, 1911), covers this subject most completely. See chapters 1–4.

by excusing seamen from military service during the fishing seasons and by granting a seven-year tax exemption to owners of property used in taking, curing, and transporting fish. In 1642 the Bay Colony sent 300,000 dried fish to market; by 1660 she had established her supremacy in the New England waters.

Gloucester, Marblehead, and Salem became the principal bases of operations, which were conducted by small capitalists who owned the boats, fishing supplies, and stages. They obtained the utmost labor from their workers by giving them between a sixth and a tenth of the season's catch. By 1720 complaints were made that the fishery had fallen under the sway of a few wealthy capitalists. The fish were sold to Boston or Salem merchants (some of whom were also operators in the industry) and exported to distant markets. The better grades, called merchantable, went to Spain, Portugal, France, the Madeiras, the Canaries, and Ireland, while the inferior fish, called refuse, were sent to the West Indies for the use of Negro slaves. Wholesale prices for the refuse were only about half as high as those for the merchantable grades.

As in the fisheries so in lumbering the abundance of raw material, the utilization of concentrated capital, and an extensive foreign market provided conditions suited to capitalistic enterprise. The forest products prepared for commercial sale included ship timber, for which pine, cedar, spruce, and oak were utilized as masts, spars, yards, bowsprits, and planks. Shingles, clapboards, and building frames, preferably of cedar, were in great demand, while red and white oak served admirably in the manufacture of staves for pipes, barrels, and casks in which meat, fish, flour, sugar, molasses, and rum were carried to market. The lumber-timber industry first took root on the New England coast between Boston and the Kennebec River, and this region remained the chief producing center during the seventeenth century. Lumbering also developed to a considerable extent in the Hudson valley and after 1680 in Pennsylvania and North Carolina. England and the shipbuilding towns of New England bought the northern masts and ship timbers, while the West Indies and the mainland settlements along the coast purchased most of the building lumber and cooperage stock.[30]

A fair degree of specialization marked the progress of lumbering in New Hampshire and Maine. The farmer-lumbermen lived in forest villages; many of the northern settlements were primarily logging

[30] Victor S. Clark, *History of Manufactures in the United States, 1607–1860* (Washington, 1916), the most comprehensive and authoritative work on American industry, gives a pragmatic view. See chapters 1–9. Very important.

camps. The woodsman felled the trees with his axe, whereupon they were hauled overland to a near-by sawmill or harbor, forty oxen being needed to drag the largest mast trees; in winter the logs could be pulled over the snow or loaded onto sleds. The small, crude sawmills which dotted the northern region stood at the falls of the rivers, which fortu nately in northern New England were but a few miles from the sea. The water wheel of the mill operated a saw in crosswise motion, the ro tary saw not having yet been invented. The first mill erected in Maine was probably built near York in 1623 and the first in New Hampshire in 1635.

Whatever the deficiency of the early sawmills they offered a vast improvement over the strenuous work of sawing logs by hand, since the labor of one mill operator was about twenty times more effective than that of a hand sawyer. This fact gave to the mill owner a strategic position in the industry. The first mills carried only one saw and could be operated by the owner assisted by his son or a hired worker. A mill that cost between $500 and $1,000 would produce a thousand feet of lumber a day and net its owner a daily return of between five and ten dollars. Such profits were commonly invested in additional mill equipment. In the development of the industry it became cheaper for owners of the established mills to add additional saws rather than to erect new plants; consequently the control of the industry tended to center in a few hands. By 1700, when the New Hampshire mills were generally operating four saws or more, it was reported that the lumber-timber trade was dominated by a dozen men; and although there were then forty mills in New York, the erection of a new mill operating twelve saws indicated the trend toward the concentration of capital. The enlargement of the mills in turn increased the number of wage-earners employed by the owners. The sawmills of New England had done their work so well by 1720 that a stretch of the coast six miles wide between Boston and the Kennebec had been denuded of trees, and there was keen rivalry among the northern lumbermen to obtain title to the remaining timber lands.

The initial impetus to shipbuilding in New England arose from the fishery; as early as 1614 Captain John Smith constructed seven small fishing boats on the coast of Maine and after 1630 the growth of co-lonial commerce added to the demand. From the northern forests came the best of white oak planks for the construction of the lower parts of ships and the best of white pine timbers for the decks and superstructures; needed materials which the colonies did not produce, such as anchors, sailcloth, and cordage, could readily be imported from England, while skilled shipwrights migrated to the colonies at an early date. One arrived at Plymouth in 1624; others came with Winthrop in 1630; and artisans emigrating to Pennsylvania had orders for vessels before the town of Philadelphia was laid out.[31]

Economic conditions in England favored the growth of colonial shipbuilding and gave the industry its larger significance. The opening of new world trades—with India, Africa, America, and the West Indies—created an almost insatiable demand for new vessels as shipping became one of the most fruitful sources of profit to seventeenth-century capitalists. On the other hand, due to the scarcity of ship timber in England, the expense of constructing vessels there was excessively high in comparison with the costs paid by the Dutch, England's chief rival on the sea. Early in the seventeenth century England had permitted the Dutch to carry much of her commerce, but after 1651 she excluded their vessels from most of her foreign and all her colonial trade—a policy adopted at a time when she did not have enough ships to meet her rapidly growing needs. By virtue of the abundance of timber in New England shipbuilding costs there were from 20 to 50 per cent lower than in England. So great was the competition in shipping that English merchants sought the cheapest vessels afloat; hence they fostered American production by purchasing ships in New England, and the government permitted skilled shipwrights to migrate thither. England found it more profitable to build in the colonies the vessels needed in her world-wide trade than to import the timbers for home construction. By loading the colonial built vessels with cargoes bound for England, the timber of which the vessels were made not only paid its own way across the Atlantic but also earned the freights on the cargoes carried.[32]

The launching at Boston in 1631 of a thirty-ton vessel, the *Blessing of the Bay*, built for Governor Winthrop, may be regarded as the inauguration of the colonial industry. A New England built vessel of fifty tons put to sea in 1641 and a three hundred ton ship in 1650. By 1670 Massachusetts had turned out 730 vessels and between 1696 and 1713 the colony's production amounted to at least 1,118 vessels of 69,500 tons—over half of which were built at Boston. All the New England shipwrights in 1721 produced about 160 vessels of which 40 per cent were sold to England and the West Indies and the other 60 per cent to colonial investors, principally the merchants of Boston. The average burden of these vessels was sixty-two tons.

[31] James L. Bishop, *History of American Manufactures, 1608–1860* (3 vols., Philadelphia, 1866–68) is a useful compilation for the advanced student. See Vol. I.
[32] Malcolm Keir, *The Epic of Industry* (*Pageant of America*, V, New Haven, 1926), chapters 1–2.

During the seventeenth century Boston and Charlestown built more than half of the vessels made in New England. Salem ranked second and Scituate third. A number of other Massachusetts towns engaged in the industry to a lesser extent, as did also Maine, Connecticut, and Rhode Island. Much of the capital employed was contributed by English merchants who placed orders for vessels in advance of construction and forwarded the necessary ship iron, canvas, and cordage. Thirty vessels were thus ordered in 1670 and more than fifty in 1709. Despite the dispersion of the industry it was affected by the trend toward concentrated operations. A master shipwright performed the work on contract with merchants, such contracts being very carefully drawn as to the size and cost of the vessel. He owned his own tools and shipyard, purchased the necessary timber, and employed apprentices and skilled artisans to whom he paid wages. As early as 1641 Massachusetts provided for the careful inspection of the shipwrights and the work they performed, so that the trade was restricted to artisans of proper training. As the industry expanded the best shipwrights received more orders than they could execute by themselves; consequently they devoted themselves to supervising the work of their artisans and to the business side of the industry. That the average burden of the vessels constructed was about sixty-two tons is explained, not by the inability of the shipwrights to build larger ships, but by the hazards of seventeenth-century trade. The toll of shipping taken by storms, wrecks, pirates, privateers, and accidents was so high that shipowners preferred to invest in a number of small vessels rather than in a few large ones. Fishing boats and vessels built for the New England coasting trade ranged from ten to thirty tons; the ketches used in the West Indian trade averaged about sixty-eight tons; and the ships sold to English merchants averaged about 102 tons.[33]

From American resources early colonial promoters had hoped to develop an iron industry beneficial to England. Before 1700, when iron ore was smelted with charcoal, England's position as an iron producer was precarious due to the depletion of her forests by virtue of the clearing of land for sheep and wheat raising. Since the colonies possessed bog iron deposits in swamps and ponds and a superabundance of wood, they might furnish England with smelted iron at low cost, thus preserving England's timber resources and taking off England's manufactured goods in payment. Experiments made in Virginia resulted in sending several tons of iron ore to England in 1608 and in the erection of a colonial ironworks in 1620, which, however, was de-

[33] R. H. Gabriel, *Toilers of Land and Sea* (*Pageant of America*, III, New Haven, 1926), chapters 1–4.

stroyed in 1622. The industry was not resumed during the next hundred years; tobacco crowded out iron production in the Old Dominion.

New England made a little progress during the seventeenth century—not, however, in producing iron for exportation but in supplying some of its own needs. Two types of crude iron were prepared: pig or cast iron, hard and brittle, used for making pots, kettles, pans, etc., and wrought iron, tough and malleable, manufactured into edged tools. In its simplest form the equipment of an ironworks consisted of a bloomery which produced "blooms" or pig iron, and an anvil where the carbon impurities in pig iron were removed by hammering, thus yielding wrought iron. More advanced equipment included a furnace in which iron ore, charcoal, and limestone were melted and the ore refined (the furnace draft being furnished by bellows operated by water power). Then the pig iron was hammered into wrought iron at a forge where the hammers were also operated by water power.

The first successful ironworks in New England were established at Lynn and Braintree, Massachusetts, about 1644. Despite many efforts to develop the industry in Connecticut, Rhode Island, Plymouth, and Massachusetts only five plants existed in 1673. The sponsors of the industry secured capital by organizing partnerships or companies of "undertakers," securing subscriptions both in England and the colonies. Then they engaged skilled managers for their works and employed hired helpers. One drawback to progress was the hostility of the Indians, since the works were often located on the frontier where timber was plentiful. The Indians destroyed the Virginia ironworks in 1622 and a plant at Pawtucket in 1675, when they also crippled the well-established Raynham works on the Plymouth frontier. The foremost promoter of the New England industry was John Winthrop, Jr., who visited England in 1641 to secure capital for the enterprise and succeeded in 1643 in organizing a "company of undertakers for the iron works." Massachusetts granted the company a twenty-one-year monopoly with the right to obtain three square miles of land in six different places and exempted its property from taxation and its workers from military service. Although the company erected plants at Lynn and Braintree it became involved in so many quarrels "that instead of drawing out bars for the country's use, there was hammered out nothing but contention and lawsuits, which was but a bad return for the undertakers." [34]

In all the colonies flour milling overshadowed the iron manufacture.

[34] John R. Commons and Associates, *History of Labor in the United States* (2 vols., New York, 1918) discusses in Vol. I the relation of the laborer to industrial organization.

Gristmills commonly made their appearance as soon as a community was settled. Operated in the main by water power and located on small streams (due to the cost of damming the larger rivers), the ordinary gristmills ground the farmers' grain into meal preparatory to the bolting process of sifting the refuse from the meal so as to produce a high-grade flour. Most seventeenth-century gristmills were small local affairs which produced only ten or twenty barrels of flour or meal a week.

The owner of a gristmill operated it himself with the aid of his family or an assistant or two. Since the work was of a seasonal nature it did not provide employment throughout the year; hence the mill owner had to find supplementary work. In slack times the mill was used to grind malt for beer or rags for paper manufacture or its water wheel was attached to saws and converted into a sawmill. Frequently the owner engaged in farming on the side and more commonly in trade. The farmers who brought in grain paid the miller by giving him a share of their meal or flour. In New England he received a twelfth of the Indian corn and a sixteenth of the other grains; in Virginia and Maryland, where mills were less numerous, the charge was commonly a sixth. Gristmills were regarded as vested with a public interest and their charges were accordingly regulated by law. Since the miller received payment in grain he had to find a buyer for it; thus he became a trader. He could also act as an agent or buyer in the marketing of the surplus grain which the farmers had to sell. His trading contacts led him to import foreign merchandise as a stock for a general store and then to advance goods to the farmers on credit in anticipation of their future grain deliveries. In the middle colonies the milling establishments gradually increased in size and capital equipment as the owner supplemented his gristmill with a bolting mill, erected a cooper's shop and a flour packing house, and even operated a bakery where hardtack biscuits were prepared for the export trade. The milling business thus offered the mill owner an opportunity to acquire considerable wealth and local influence.[35]

Between the commercialized industries and the household crafts there was an intermediate form of industrial organization represented by skilled artisans. In a new, sparsely settled community such specially trained craftsmen traveled from farm to farm where they labored in the household on materials furnished by the farmer, receiving their pay in board, lodging, and produce or money. Chief among such traveling artisans were shoemakers, chandlers, carpenters, weavers,

[35] Charles B. Kuhlmann, *The Development of the Flour-Milling Industry in the United States* (Boston, 1929), devotes chapter 1 to the colonial period.

blacksmiths, and masons. As a community became more compactly settled the traveling artisan established a permanent workshop. In the earliest stage of this development, the settled artisan received orders from his neighbors who furnished the raw materials and paid him with produce or money. He then devoted his spare time to producing goods for general sale—goods which he might display at his shop, sell to near-by storekeepers, or dispose of to peddlers or town merchants. Should his business expand he would take apprentices and hired journeymen into his home and shop. He commonly owned a plot of ground sufficient to supply him with fruits, vegetables, meat, and dairy products. The crafts represented by the settled artisan in New England and the middle colonies during the seventeenth century included brick-making, leather tanning, weaving, fulling and dyeing, shoemaking, candlemaking, blacksmithing, and the manufacture of pottery, paper, and hats. Some of these trades could not be carried on by traveling artisans and consequently did not appear until communities were developed sufficiently to support a settled craftsman.[36]

[36] N. S. B. Gras, "Stages in Economic History," *Journal of Economic and Business History*, II (May 1930).

## BIBLIOGRAPHICAL NOTE

WORKS PREVIOUSLY CITED: C. M. Andrews, *Colonial Self-Government*, ch. 19; P. A. Bruce, *Economic History of Virginia in Seventeenth Century*, I, chs. 4–7 (agriculture), 17–18 (manufactures); G. Bancroft, *History of the United States*, I, ch. 5 (slavery); H. S. Burrage, *Beginnings of Colonial Maine*, ch. 9 (fishery); I. Calder, *New Haven Colony*, ch. 8; A. C. Flick (ed.), *History of the State of New York*, I, ch. 10; W. Cockshott, *The Pilgrim Fathers*, ch. 11; A. Johnson, *Swedish Settlements on the Delaware*, I, chs. 31–32; H. L. Osgood, *American Colonies in the Seventeenth Century*, I, pp. 56–79, 424–466; II, pp. 16–55; W. B. Weeden, *Economic and Social History of New England*, I, chs. 3–4, 6, pp. 244–267; T. J. Wertenbaker, *The First Americans*, pp. 49–86 (New England economy).

SOURCES NEWLY CITED: A useful compilation is Ernest L. Bogart and Charles M. Thompson, *Readings in the Economic History of the United States* (New York, 1929). See chapters 1–3.

# X

# COMMERCE, BUSINESS, AND FINANCE

DESPITE the diversity and extent of their manufactures the colonies were unable to produce all the articles they needed in order to uphold a European standard of living and to sustain a growing system of production. Necessity dictated that they buy from the older industrial communities of Europe a wide range of capital goods (commodities used to produce or acquire wealth). Such imports included mill machinery, ship iron, canvas, cordage, Indian trading goods, hardware, bricks, nails, bellows, paint, and instruments of navigation. The colonial farmers and artisans generally worked with tools of European manufacture—spades, shovels, axes, saws, knives, chisels, grindstones, planes, hammers, cant hooks, trowels, and the iron parts of plows and other implements. Throughout the seventeenth century colonial soldiers waged war with imported cannon, powder, shot, and firearms. To the colonial housewife came a variety of kitchen utensils—kettles, measuring cans, milk trays, bowls, ladles, sieves, pans, graters, funnels, pepperboxes, flour boxes, punch strainers, and woodenware, while her table might display imported spoons, platters, porridge dishes, saucers, salts, tankards, and other pewter ware. As a seamstress she probably used English buttons, thread, needles, thimbles, pins, tape, ribbons, and filleting. Miscellaneous household aids from abroad included mousetraps, beer taps, lanterns, tinderboxes, calendars, combs, basins, and inkhorns. Wealthier families imported textiles—woolens, crepe, damask, flannel, lace, calico, gauze, cambric, gingham, cottons, and linsey-woolsey. Such families also purchased various foreign luxuries like wine, brandy, spices, sugar, books, and paper as well as some of their furniture—looking glasses, candlesticks and snuffers, curtain rings, chests, chairs, and cradles. From the beginnings of settlement the importation of such commodities increased in volume and variety until by 1700 most of them were coming into the colonies in three or four sizes, grades, or colors. To determine the wealth of a colonial family one needed only to observe how large a proportion of its possessions were of European manufacture. No family was so poor as to be without at least a few imported articles. After the coming of the white man to America even the Indians could not get along without the goods which he brought from the Old World.[1]

This import trade was the fundamental fact around which revolved the economic development of the colonies. From it sprang in large measure their value to England. The central feature of colonial trade was the exchange of American products for European wares; the central economic problem facing the colonies was that of finding the means of paying for their imported supplies.

## THE TOBACCO TRADE

The foreign commerce of Virginia, Maryland, and Carolina during the seventeenth century consisted of a direct exchange of tobacco and furs for European goods. For the most part this trade was carried on with England, although the Dutch managed to obtain a large share of it in the years 1630–60. So great was its importance to Virginia and Maryland that their economic position depended almost exclusively upon it. What was that position? Was the balance of trade so adjusted as to place them in a situation of independence and affluence or in a plight of dependence and uncertainty? Did the planters or European merchants reap the chief advantages of the trade, how did it affect the prosperity of England, and what part did it play in shaping the relations between colonies and mother country? The answers to these questions are keys to major issues of colonial history.

The essential features of the tobacco trade remained constant throughout the seventeenth and eighteenth centuries, although we do not have adequate statistics of its volume until after the year 1696.[2] The English customs records show that in eighteen years after 1698 Virginia, Maryland, and South Carolina bought goods from England which had an average value of £154,200 a year. In return the three colonies shipped to England commodities of a yearly average value of £245,900. Thus it appears at first glance that these colonies had an annual balance of trade in their favor amounting to £91,700. However, these figures give a false impression of the real balance of payments. The estimates of colonial imports represent the value of the goods before they were shipped from England and the estimates of colonial exports represent the value of the products before they were shipped from the colonies. Consequently the customs records do not

[1] C. M. Andrews, "Colonial Commerce," *American Historical Review*, XX (Oct. 1914).

[2] George L. Beer's *The Origins of the British Colonial System* (New York, 1908), one of the foremost studies of the colonial period, discusses commerce in relation to British policy. See chapter 9.

reveal several invisible charges which the southern planters had to pay. Chief among such invisible charges were freight payments to English shipowners, the profits and commissions earned by English merchants, the outlays made by the planters to purchase indentured servants and slaves, the insurance premiums on cargoes carried, and the interest charges assessed against the planters on loans extended to them by English capitalists.

All these invisible earnings were made by the merchant capitalists of England who conducted a highly diversified business. They bought and sold colonial produce, purchased English and foreign wares for resale to the planters, owned ships and thus provided shipping, carried on the servant and slave trade, supplied the capital for the insurance business, and from their surplus earnings lent money to the planters at interest. In their employ was a host of attorneys who protected their interests in the courts and constantly sought and obtained support from the English government. The stake of the merchant class in the southern colonies was all-important—so paramount in fact that the regulations imposed on colonial trade by England were dictated by the necessity of preserving the profit opportunities and investments of this dominant class.[3]

Not, however, that the merchants formed a harmoniously unified group; rather they were divided into two competing factions. The merchants of London composed one bloc which struggled incessantly against the merchants of the "outports"—Bristol, Liverpool, Southampton, Plymouth, and many lesser seacoast towns. Each party fought for the lion's share of the colonial trade but year by year the London merchants strengthened their position of dominance until by 1700 London was the great entrepôt of English commerce. The two groups used different methods in the conduct of colonial trade, the analysis of which will reveal the manner in which each derived profit from the colonies and explain why the planters were confronted with an adverse balance of payments.

The merchants of the outports commonly purchased in England the various commodities needed in America, carried them abroad in their own vessels, sold them to the planters or colonial traders, and used the proceeds to purchase colonial tobacco and furs. In this process the outport merchants supplied the capital and assumed the risks of trade. Obviously they added to the English price of their wares the cost of bringing them from England to the southern colonies. Such costs included the freights and insurance on the voyage across and the

[3] For the advanced student: Violet Barbour, "Marine Risks and Insurance in the Seventeenth Century," *Journal of Economic and Business History*, I (Aug. 1929).

profits earned by the merchants as exporters. Moreover the outport merchants sold goods to colonial planters and merchants on credit, thus adding interest charges to their earnings. We know but little about the total gains made by the outport traders save that they carried on only a minor part of the southern trade. We do know, however, that the prices of English goods in the colonies were two or three times as high as English prices, so that the English customs records which value colonial imports at their English prices do not indicate the bill which the planters had to pay to the outport merchants in the form of freights, insurance, profit, and interest.[4]

Far more important were the earnings of the London merchants. Ordinarily they did not engage in the trade independently, nor did they invest their capital in trading goods or assume the risks involved. Instead they acted as commission agents for the planters. To Virginia and Maryland they dispatched each year their vessels which sailed along the coast from plantation to plantation where they loaded the planters' tobacco for shipment to England. The London merchants did not buy the tobacco outright; instead the planter consigned the shipment to the merchant with instructions to sell it on the London market. At the same time the planter would place with the merchant an order for various European goods to be purchased with the proceeds from the sale of the tobacco, with the understanding that such goods would be delivered to the planter in the ships that came the following year. The payments which the planters made to the London merchants included commissions for buying the merchandise sent to the colonies—a charge of $2\frac{1}{2}$ per cent of the English price of the goods. Next the merchant was entitled to the freight and insurance on shipments to America. The London merchants must have earned, in the period 1690–1718, at least £18,000 a year from such freights, insurance, and commissions. Above all, the planters purchased their servants and slaves from English merchants and paid for them, year by year throughout the seventeenth century, considerably in excess of £30,000.

When the tobacco of the planters was sold in London not all the proceeds belonged to the planter. From the English wholesale price several charges had to be deducted. First, the merchant was entitled to the freight charges on the voyage to England, since he owned the ships employed. Freight charges (including insurance) on tobacco and furs to London varied between £6 and £9 a ton in time of peace, rising to £12, £14, or £16 a ton in time of war. In the years 1703–18

---

[4] Attention is again called to L. C. Gray's *History of Agriculture in the Southern United States*, Vol. I, chapters 11–12, 18.

### THE OLD EAST INDIA WHARF, LONDON
*From a painting by Peter Monany in the Victoria and Albert Museum*

The eighteenth-century terminus of Britain's oriental trade, monopolized (via the Cape of Good Hope and Cape Horn) by the British East India Company.

the average freight earnings from tobacco carried to England amounted to at least £82,000 a year. Secondly, the planters were obliged to pay various charges connected with the handling of tobacco in London—for unloading, trucking, inspection, and storage; and moreover the planters had to stand any loss due to shrinkage or damage. Thirdly, the English import duties had to be deducted from the wholesale price. During the seventeenth century such duties were steadily increased until by 1703 they amounted to 6⅓d. a pound although the price of tobacco in the colonies was then only 1d. a pound. When tobacco was reëxported from England to the Continent (and about two-thirds of the colonial tobacco was so reëxported) the government remitted all the import duty except ½d. a pound, but considering the low price of tobacco in the colonies this was still a high charge, and meanwhile the planters had to provide bond for the payment of the full import duties on tobacco in storage in England before it was reëxported. Finally, the merchant deducted from the wholesale price a commission to pay him for the trouble of handling it and of finding a buyer. The most common commission charge was 2½ per cent. This was based, not upon the colonial price of the product, but upon English wholesale prices, which included freight and customs. Such charges increased the English price, which for this reason was five or six times above the colonial price. An estimate of the commissions earned in London in 1720 gives a figure between £12,500 and £15,000.[5]

Theoretically all these charges deducted from the planter's proceeds should have represented items in excess of his cost of production and his profit. In actual practice, however, this did not always occur. On several occasions, especially in time of war when the European market for colonial tobacco was curtailed, English wholesale prices fell to such a low level that they barely covered, or failed to cover, customs, freights, insurance, commissions, and handling charges. In such situations neither the government nor the London merchants abated their claims against the tobacco and accordingly the planters found that all the proceeds went to pay the English charges. A leading planter of Virginia, William Byrd I, complained that "When there's any hopes of profit, then we may have a little after the owners [of vessels], masters and sailors are served"; a colonial governor wrote in 1713 that "though the merchant takes care to secure his freight and commission, the owners [planters] are often brought in debt over and above the loss of their principal venture"; and London merchants admitted in

[5] M. S. Morriss, *Colonial Trade of Maryland, 1685–1715* (Baltimore, 1914), is a superior study.

1714, "that of late years plantation tobacco hath been often sold for less than custom, freight and charges, [and] that the exports of our woolen and all other manufactures to Virginia and Maryland are diminished at least one-half."

When tobacco prices fell so low that they would provide only for customs, freight, and commissions the planters obviously had no proceeds with which to pay for English goods. But the merchants were willing to provide them with supplies on credit; otherwise the whole trade would soon have been ruined. The planters generally seem to have been hopeful of getting high prices for their tobacco and were accordingly prone to place large advance orders for goods. Frequently when the proceeds from tobacco were not sufficient to pay for the English goods ordered, the merchant would supply the planter on credit, for thereby the merchant was assured that he would handle the next year's crop through which the planter would have to pay the debt. Moreover, the planters borrowed funds outright from the merchants, pledging future tobacco deliveries as security. As a result of these business methods the planters became increasingly indebted to the merchants as short-term loans secured by crop liens were gradually converted into long-term loans secured by mortgages on the planters' lands and slaves. Indebtedness in turn created an additional invisible item in the balance of payments against the planters in that they were obliged to pay an interest charge of 6 per cent or more to their merchant creditors.[6]

That the balance of payments favored England as against the southern colonies is attested by several facts. The southern planters repeatedly complained of a scarcity of European goods in their colonies and lamented that such wares were commonly sold at two or three times above their English prices. Moreover, the coined money which came into the tobacco colonies was quickly exported as a partial means of redressing the unfavorable trade balance. An acute shortage of specie resulted which forced the planters to utilize tobacco as their common medium of exchange. Finally, the planters became seriously involved in debt. In 1706 Governor Seymour of Maryland observed "how much the country is indebted" to London merchants, "very many plantations being mortgaged to them, of which there seems little probability of redemption, considering the growing interest." Similarly the London merchants in 1709 described how loans were advanced to the planters on their future crops—"the very foundation

[6] J. S. Bassett, "The Relation between the Virginia Planter and the London Merchant," *Report*, American Historical Association, 1901, I, pp. 551–575.

on which the credit was solely given, and by which those plantations have been supported and peopled, and the trade itself sustained and without which it had been altogether unable to have been carried on." Again in 1714 a Maryland act recited how the planters "are become vastly indebted, and no prospect as yet appearing of any means whereby they may extricate themselves out of their miserable and deplorable circumstances."

From the standpoint of mercantilism the colonial tobacco trade suited England perfectly. It brought a huge yearly revenue to the government in import duties and relieved the country from dependence on foreign tobacco supplies which presumably had been purchased with English specie. The southern colonies afforded a market for English merchandise, thus providing profit to manufacturers and employment to artisans which in turn reduced the English tax burden for the support of unemployed workers on poor relief. To the merchant class the tobacco trade offered handsome incomes from profit, commissions, freights, and insurance, and provided a field for the investment of surplus funds. One vital feature of the rising capitalistic system of England was the accumulation of capital surpluses which the merchants desired to invest in profitable channels. Investments made in the tobacco colonies by extending loans to the planters were not only productive of interest and protected by mortgages which were safeguarded by the English government but also had the effect of strengthening the merchant's control of the trade by forcing the planter to market his future crops through his creditor in order to pay his past debts. These benefits to England explain why her merchants and her government were united in a firm alliance to control the colonial trade in tobacco.

On the other hand the conditions of the trade were less satisfactory to the planters. The employment of seagoing vessels to carry European goods in small lots directly to their private wharves and to collect their individual crops was certainly not an economical practice. Moreover, the planter was at a disadvantage in that he could not supervise the sale of his produce or the purchase of his supplies in England. His merchant could have at best only a vicarious interest in his welfare; the freedom of the merchant from the planter's scrutiny must have been conducive to carelessness or fraud—perhaps both. At any rate the correspondence of the planters bristles with charges that the merchants sold tobacco at excessively low prices and sent over inferior English goods at excessive prices—the very refuse of the shops of London. Indebted planters often felt themselves "in the clutches" of their creditors. Thus William Byrd II once sold lands and slaves to clear his debt to his merchant, asserting that "I had rather incommode myself a little than continue in the grip of that usurer." [7]

Why did the organization of the tobacco trade persist in face of its obvious disadvantage to the planters? Had they supplied their own shipping and marketing facilities they might have retained more of the profit of the trade for themselves, but this, they were unable to do. When the tobacco industry first took root in the colonies it was the most profitable means of employing capital and labor; hence the planters invested their surplus in additional lands, servants, and slaves. In an expanding economy the rise in land values increased the planter's credit, while an enlarged output seemed to justify borrowing for the purchase of new workers and productive equipment. Since the planters' capital thus went into agriculture and since their produce had to be sold in Europe there was no alternative to the employment of European capital in the marketing of their crops. Then when the productive system of the tobacco colonies declined after 1700 the planters found themselves with heavy fixed investments in land, labor, and equipment that could not readily be transferred to other pursuits. Moreover, they could borrow new capital only from England—and to obtain this they were obliged to continue the tobacco industry in order to provide the means of paying their debts. Finally, the English government excluded foreign merchants and vessels from the tobacco trade, thus increasing the dependence of the planters on England for ships, marketing services, credit facilities, and manufactured products.

## The Trade of New England and the Middle Colonies

The mechanism of the trade of Virginia and Maryland differed materially from that of the commerce of the middle colonies and New England—a fact explained by the lack of staples in the northern settlements which could be exchanged directly for English goods. In order to protect English agriculture Parliament after 1660 prohibited the importation into England of colonial fish, flour, wheat, and meat. Since such commodities were the staples of the northern colonies, the sale of their native products to England was limited to small quantities of ship timber, furs, whale oil, and whalebone. On the other hand the desire for European goods was as insistent in the North as in the South. In eighteen years, 1698–1717, New England and New York purchased each year from England goods of an average value of

---

[7] G. L. Beer's *The Old Colonial System* (2 vols., New York, 1912), a work of major importance, gives in Vol. II much information on trade.

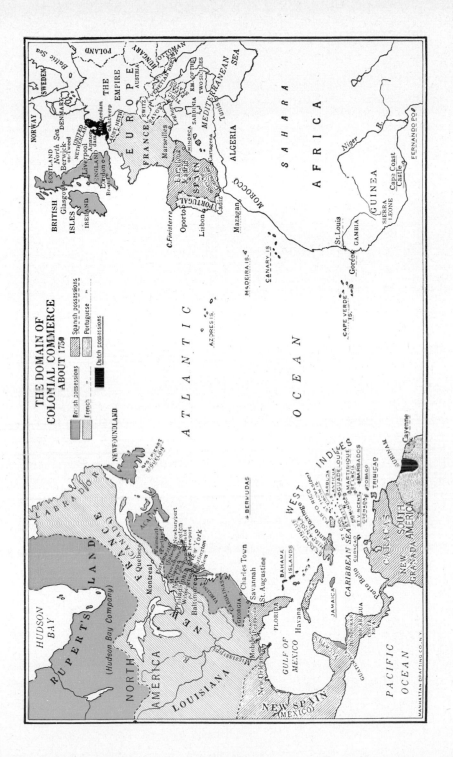

THE DOMAIN OF
COLONIAL COMMERCE
ABOUT 1750

British possessions
French  "  "
Spanish possessions
Portuguese  "
Dutch possessions

EUROPE

NORWAY
SWEDEN
Baltic Sea
POLAND
DENMARK
North Sea
BRITISH
ISLES
SCOTLAND
Glasgow
Berwick-on-Tweed
Liverpool
England
London
Bristol
IRELAND
NETHER-
Amsterdam
Antwerp
AUS. NETH.
THE
EMPIRE
HUNGARY
AUSTRIA
OTTOMAN
EMP.
FRANCE
SWITZ.
SAVOY
VENETIAN REP.
Marseilles
SARDINIA
KM. OF THE
TWO SICILIES
SPAIN
PORTUGAL
Minorca
MEDITERRANEAN SEA
C. Finisterre
Oporto
Lisbon
Madrid
Cartagena
Cadiz
Mazagan
MOROCCO
ALGERIA
Tunis
TRIPOLI
SAHARA
AFRICA

AZORES IS.
MADEIRA IS.
CANARY IS.
CAPE VERDE IS.

St. Louis
Gorée
GAMBIA
GUINEA
SIERRA LEONE
Cape Coast Castle
FERNANDO PO
Niger R.

ATLANTIC OCEAN

NEWFOUNDLAND
ST. PIERRE
MIQUELON

LABRADOR

HUDSON BAY

RUPERT'S LAND
(Hudson Bay Company)

NORTH AMERICA

NEW FRANCE
ACADIA
Quebec
Montreal

NEW ENGLAND
Portland
Portsmouth
Boston
Newport
New York
Philadelphia
Baltimore
VIRGINIA
CAROLINAS
GEORGIA
Charles Town
Savannah
St. Augustine
FLORIDA

Mobile
New Orleans
LOUISIANA
Mississippi

GULF OF MEXICO

NEW SPAIN
(MEXICO)

Havana
BAHAMA ISLANDS
JAMAICA
CARIBBEAN SEA

HONDURAS
NICARAGUA
COSTA RICA
GUATEMALA

Porto Rico
STO. DOMINGO
ST. DOMINGO

WEST INDIES
BERMUDAS
ST. CHRISTOPHER
ANTIGUA
BARBUDA
GUADELOUPE
MARTINIQUE
ST. LUCIA
ST. VINCENT
GRENADA
BARBADOS
TOBAGO
TRINIDAD
CURAÇAO

CARACAS
NEW GRANADA
SOUTH AMERICA
SURINAM
Cayenne

PACIFIC OCEAN

MANHATTAN DRAFTING CO. N.Y.

£103,500 and sent in return products having a yearly average value of only £37,400, thus incurring an unfavorable balance of trade of £66,100 a year. And not all the exports of those colonies consisted of their native products; the latter paid for about only one-sixth of the goods imported. The central problem which faced the northerners was that of converting their fish, lumber, wheat, flour, livestock, and meat products into some means of paying for European wares.[8]

In solving this problem the northern colonies attained a much stronger commercial position than did their southern neighbors. For one reason invisible items did not figure largely in the balance of payments between England and the northern mainland. Boston, Philadelphia, and New York each contained merchants who traded in their own vessels. The freights, profits, and commissions earned by English merchants as exporters to the northern colonies were nearly balanced by similar earnings of the northern merchants in carrying their products to England and selling them in the English market. Moreover, the northern towns did not consume all the European goods they imported; their function was that of distributor to surrounding communities. Besides, the Northerners engaged in a variety of outside trades which enabled them to get remittances to England on terms highly favorable to themselves. Such trading activities are explained largely by three things: shipbuilding, shipowning, and the methods of marketing goods—all intimately related.[9]

Boston, Philadelphia, and New York each served as an entrepôt to which foreign goods were brought in ocean going ships and then carried in small vessels to the surrounding mainland settlements. Similarly, to the three northern towns were transported the products of the colonial fishery, farms, and forests preparatory to exportation abroad. Thus the three commercial towns acted as exchange centers, receiving all sorts of commodities from all parts of America, the West Indies, and Europe and making up cargoes suitable to every market of the time. Although Boston, Philadelphia, and New York all traded with every region on the mainland, each town had a special trading area which it dominated. Thus Boston was supreme in New England and eastern Long Island; New York (New Amsterdam before 1664) served western Long Island, eastern New Jersey, and the province of New York; and Philadelphia after 1682 dominated western New Jersey, Delaware, northern Maryland, and Pennsylvania. During the

---

[8] Roland M. Hooker, *The Colonial Trade of Connecticut* (New Haven, 1936—Connecticut Tercentenary Commission, no. 50).

[9] N. S B. Gras, "The Rise of Big Business," *Journal of Economic and Business History*, IV (May 1932).

seventeenth century Boston ranked first in importance, New York second, and Philadelphia third. Boston's supremacy arose from the fact that she had the most populous hinterland, that she was well situated with reference to all centers of colonial commerce (particularly the fishing and lumbering regions), and that her merchants had arrived early on the scene and had always pushed aggressively into every available trade. Prior to 1700 New York and Philadelphia were commercial satellites of Boston, and Philadelphia was a lesser satellite of New York.

The relations of these three towns with the mainland communities resembled in miniature the relations between London and the tobacco colonies. Each town supplied the American settlements with European goods, rum and molasses from the West Indies, and needed products from the other colonies. Moreover, the northern merchants owned most of the vessels engaged in the trade and therefore earned the freights on shipments to the adjacent settlements. Similarly the merchants provided the marketing services and thereby reaped profits on their sales. Such freights and profits, added to the first cost of the goods, meant that the settlers had to pay high prices. On the other hand they received only the first cost of the articles they produced. Moreover, the need of foreign goods among the settlers was so great that they were prone to buy more than their own produce would pay for; in consequence the balance of trade between country and town generally favored the latter. One result of this was that the hard money which came into the rural settlements quickly flowed away to the towns. Boston drew money from all parts of America—even from New York and Philadelphia—and thus became the financial center of the colonies.[10]

The rural communities, particularly Virginia and Maryland, also made additional payments to the towns by sending bills of exchange drawn on England. Bills of exchange, which always played a vital part in colonial commerce, were somewhat similar to modern bank checks. When a colonial merchant or planter shipped a cargo of produce from America to England with instructions to an English merchant that it be sold on arrival, the colonist was due to have funds at his disposal there. Accordingly he could write an order (or draw a bill of exchange) upon his English correspondent directing that a certain sum be paid to the receiver of the bill. Such a bill could then be used like a modern check; endorsed from person to person it would circulate until sent to England and paid from the proceeds of the sale

[10] An elementary manual is Clive Day's *History of Commerce of the United States* (New York, 1925). See chapters 1–6.

of the produce which the drawer of the bill had previously shipped. Since the tobacco planters were constantly anticipating credits from the sale of their tobacco in England they could buy foreign merchandise from the northern towns by giving bills drawn on English merchants.[11]

Remittances from the rural settlements to the towns by money and bills did not generally redress the unfavorable balance of trade; hence the town merchants were obliged to extend credit to their country customers. In their trade with the southern colonies the northern merchants consigned their goods to agents who sold to the planters on credit and as attorneys protected the merchants' interests. In the northern colonies the merchants advanced goods to local traders or storekeepers and the latter sold to the settlers on credit. The settlers would pay their existing debts by delivering their surplus produce to the country traders and they in turn would consign it to the town merchant in payment of their debts. This arrangement placed the settlers in a somewhat exposed position due to the fact that the charges imposed by the merchant—freights, profit, and interest—tended to remain fixed whereas the price of what the farmer produced might fall abruptly, and thus in time of depression all his surplus might be needed to pay existing debts.

As previously noted the produce shipped from the colonial towns to England did not begin to pay for their importations. In order to secure additional remittances the northern merchants carried on external trades with Newfoundland, southern Europe, the Wine Islands, and the West Indies whereby they obtained coin, bills of exchange, and commodities which could be marketed in England. Prior to 1700 Boston practically monopolized the trade with the fishing settlements of Newfoundland. The Bostonians exported provisions, lumber, and rum which were exchanged for the settlers' fish and this in turn was sold for coin, bills of exchange, or European goods to vessels that came to Newfoundland from Britain or Europe. It was said that the Bostonians never loaded fish when they could get money or bills, that their vessels returned to Boston in ballast and in departing left not a shilling of coin behind. One English official observed that the Newfoundland trade enabled New England to make remittances to England which equaled in value the native products which she shipped directly to the mother country.[12]

[11] Emory R. Johnson *et al, History of Domestic and Foreign Commerce of the United States* (2 vols., Washington, 1915, 1922), is a useful compilation for the special student. See Vol. I, chapters 1–2, 4–5, 10–11.

[12] Ralph G. Lounsbury's *The British Fishery at Newfoundland* (New Haven, 1934) is a careful monograph, very detailed. See chapter 6. For a good résumé see R. G.

Boston also carried on an extensive trade with Portugal, Spain, and France, sending thither the best grades of fish, which were sold for coin, bills of exchange, or southern European produce. Such proceeds were then carried to England and there used to pay for part of New England's imports of English goods. After 1690 ship timber was also exported from New England to southern Europe and in similar fashion converted into buying power in the English market. A large part of New England's fish was taken to southern Europe by English vessels which procured the fish at Boston in exchange for English goods imported. After 1700 Salem rapidly superseded Boston as the exporting center in the southern European trade.

To the Spanish and Portuguese Wine Islands (the Canaries, Madeira, and Fayal) the northern colonies sent fish, lumber, and provisions—all used to purchase wine. Part of the wine procured was carried back to the colonies and part of it was shipped to England, where its sale enabled the northern merchants to obtain additional purchasing power for English goods.

Far overshadowing all these trades was that carried on between the northern towns and the Caribbean.[13] The northern exports consisted of fish, horses, lumber, wheat, flour, biscuit, beef, pork, bacon, peas, and Indian corn. The Northerners sold such products to the sugar planters of the British islands of Jamaica, Barbados, Antigua, Montserrat, Nevis, and St. Christopher's or St. Kitt's, to the Danish sugar island St. Thomas, and to the Dutch sugar colony Surinam (Guiana). Similar northern commodities reached the Spanish colonies in America by way of Jamaica and the Dutch island Curaçao; other shipments went to Yucatan or Campeche Bay. This diversified trade enabled the Northerners to procure various commodities for exportation to England. First of all they obtained Spanish money—chiefly pieces of eight —which flowed into Jamaica, Curaçao, and Barbados in payment for European goods, Negroes, and northern colonial products sold by English and Dutch traders to the Spaniards at Havana, Vera Cruz, Porto Bello, and Cartagena. From the sugar colonies the northern towns also secured sugar, molasses, rum, indigo, fustic, dyewoods, cotton-wool, and minor commodities including lime juice, lignum vitae, and ginger. The sugar islands also paid for northern products with bills of exchange drawn on English merchants. At Campeche

Lounsbury, "Yankee Trade at Newfoundland," *New England Quarterly*, III (Oct. 1930).
   [13] A splendid introductory study is A. P. Newton, *The European Nations in the West Indies, 1493-1688* (London, 1933).

Bay the Northerners procured logwood, highly valued as a dyestuff for the woolen industry. Most of the commodities thus obtained by the northern traders—coin, bills of exchange, sugar, logwood, ginger, fustic, cotton-wool, and indigo—were shipped to England and there exchanged for English goods or taken to the mainland towns and later reëxported to England. Rum and molasses (the raw material of rum) were carried to the mainland colonies where they were used in the fur trade, the New England fishery, and the Newfoundland trade—in each instance enabling the Northerners to obtain additional remittances to England. Another important commodity returned to the mainland was salt, procured chiefly at the island of Tortuda. Indispensable to the fishery and to cattle raising, it contributed its part to all the trades in which colonial fish and cattle were important items. The northern merchants further increased their buying power in England by earning the freight charges and profits on the cargoes they carried in their vessels directly to England from the Wine Islands, the West Indies, and southern Europe.[14]

In all these external trades the balance of payments favored the northern towns. Their merchants owned most of the shipping employed and thus earned the freight charges on voyages to and from the various markets. Similarly, the Northerners sold their cargoes through their agents or stores abroad, thereby obtaining the profits of both importer and exporter. Their gains are indicated by the fact that prices of northern products in the West Indies were fully 50 per cent higher than in the northern towns. By selling their exports on credit the Northerners added interest charges to their earnings and attained a position of dominance over their customers (particularly at Newfoundland) comparable to the position of London in the tobacco trade. These varied external contacts not only made it possible for the northern towns to complete their payments for English imports; they also provided handsome profits which accumulated in the hands of the merchants and thus fostered a rising capitalistic class.[15]

New England possessed one other form of remittance to England— the ships that were built in her seacoast towns on order of English merchants. During the latter part of the seventeenth century such vessels must have netted New England between £20,000 and £40,000

---

[14] Three excellent books on the West Indies are Vincent T. Harlow, *A History of Barbados* (Oxford, 1926); J. A. Williamson, *The Caribbee Islands under the Proprietary Patents* (Oxford, 1926); and Charles S. S. Higham, *The Development of the Leeward Islands under the Restoration, 1660–1688* (Cambridge, 1921).

[15] Malcolm Keir, *The March of Commerce* (*Pageant of America*, IV, New Haven, 1927), chapter 1.

a year. Certainly their value exceeded that of all the other New England commodities—fur, ship timber, and whale products—which were exported from Boston to England.

While the external trades of the northern colonies remained open and adequate they supplied the resident merchants with attractive opportunities for profit making. England also benefited in that the northern settlements provided an expanding market for her own wares, while external trade afforded the colonists the necessary means of payment. Moreover England prized her sugar colonies in the West Indies as extremely lucrative sources of revenue to the Crown and of profit to her merchants. Hence the northern colonies had an added value in that they furnished the sugar planters with indispensable work animals, foodstuffs for their slaves, and lumber for hogsheads, sugar works, and houses. In other respects, however, the activities of the northern merchants seemed injurious to English merchants and in consequence there occurred an intense conflict between the two—a conflict which will be discussed in the succeeding chapter.[16]

## CURRENCY AND FINANCE

The course of American commerce determined the currency problems with which the colonists had to contend. Their principal monetary troubles issued from an acute and persistent shortage of specie or coin. The very process of founding colonies created a scarcity of money by virtue of the necessity which impelled the first emigrants to take with them things that were essential for life in their new homes. What money they may have had at the start they were obliged to exchange in England for goods with which they could stock the detached farms on which they were to settle. However, a few years after a settlement had been planted coined money began to filter in—brought by newly arriving settlers wherewith to purchase provisions, or returned in the course of external trade. But such money never remained long in the colonies; it speedily accumulated in the commercial towns whence it was remitted to England to redress the unfavorable balance of trade. In other words the colonists found it more profitable to use coined money for purchases abroad than to retain it as a domestic medium of exchange.[17]

Meanwhile the English government did not desire to supply the colonies with a large stock of coined money. English officials insisted

[16] J. W. McElroy, "Seafaring in Seventeenth-Century New England," *New England Quarterly*, VIII (Sept. 1935).

[17] Curtis P. Nettels, *The Money Supply of the American Colonies before 1720* (Madison, Wis., 1934), chapters 2–5 (commerce), 6–7, 9 (finance).

that the colonies should provide England with specie—not England the colonies. The ideal colony exchanged its produce in England for manufactured goods, and the transactions involving money should preferably be performed in England rather than America. The creed of mercantilism placed great emphasis upon a country's supply of coin. As the most permanent and flexible form of wealth, specie enabled the merchant class to convert their surplus profits into a stable type of property that could be utilized in any additional profit-making enter- prise, due to the universal demand for silver and gold. Coined money was also highly esteemed as the lifeblood of manufacturing indus- tries, providing as it did a ready means of purchasing raw materials and a wage fund for specialized artisans who could not be paid con- veniently in the products of their labor. England objected to the growth in the colonies of industries that would compete with her own; consequently she did not desire them to obtain a large stock of specie which would provide a currency in which the wages of specialized artisans might be paid. Furthermore, English officials believed that England's own stock of precious metals was inadequate to her three- fold needs of currency, trade, and war. Particularly important in this connection was England's commerce with the Orient. During the seventeenth century silver was regarded as the metal best suited to currency purposes, but it so happened that silver had a higher intrinsic value in India than it had when minted into English coins. The great demand for silver in the India trade led to the melting and clipping of English coins, since the metal could be more profitably employed in the Orient than in England. The English silver coinage became seriously deranged; incessant complaints bewailed the scarcity of money at home; and the East India Company was roundly berated as a thief of the nation's treasure. So great were the profits of the In- dia trade, however, that in 1663 Parliament legalized the exportation of foreign coins and bullion, although it refused to lift the ban against the exportation of English coin. In the face of these conditions it seemed out of the question for England to supply her American col- onies with hard money. Prior to 1663 she did not permit the exporta- tion of any coin or bullion to the colonies and after 1663 did not allow the exportation of English coin. She did not erect special mints in America to provide an American coinage and when the New Eng- landers independently erected their own mint she speedily dismantled it. Nor would she allow the colonies to prohibit the exportation of coin and bullion from America to England.[18]

[18] See again W. B. Weeden, *Economic and Social History of New England*, Vol. I, chapters 5, 7; pp. 314–336, 379–387.

Although the colonists possessed practically no English coins they continued to make their financial reckonings in English monetary terms (or to use pounds, shillings, and pence as their money of account). Out of the scarcity of English coin issued a series of currency makeshifts which never adequately solved the financial problems of the colonies. During the seventeenth century all the colonies resorted to the use of commodity money. The colonial legislatures enacted that certain important local products should be designated as money— lumber in New Hampshire; wheat, pork, beef, cattle, peas, Indian corn, barley, and rye in New England, the middle colonies, and North Carolina; and tobacco in Virginia and Maryland. Before 1660 beaver and wampum (shells or beads much sought after by the Indians) figured largely in the currency system of New England and New Netherland. The laws of the colonies uniformly provided that commodity money should be legal tender in all public payments and legal tender in private payments unless contracts called for another kind of currency. Ordinarily the receiver of commodities used as money did not want them for personal use; sooner or later they had to be sold in commercial markets and thus converted into some more durable form.[19]

One of the persistent defects of commodity money was the difficulty of determining its real value. The legislatures generally decreed that the money commodities should pass at fixed legal prices in public payments. Thus Connecticut at one time valued wheat at 4s. a bushel. In private transactions, however, the legal prices did not apply; the parties concerned agreed between themselves as to the value of the commodity tendered; failing in this they referred the issue to impartial judges who decided it for them. Due to the wide variations in the quality of different units of a given commodity the task of determining value was a most baffling one. The products used as currency in a locality were its staples; nearly every farmer raised them and hence operated a mint. Great was the temptation to debase the currency by using inferior products for local payments. In the respectable town of New Haven the deacons of the church once complained "that the wampum that is put into the church treasury is generally so bad, that the elders to whom they pay it cannot pay it away but it is returned to them again." The tendering of such inferior products evoked much protective legislation. Connecticut ordered that no wampum should pass unless it was "in some measure strung suitably, not small . . . and disorderly mingled as formerly," and the New England and

[19] William Z. Ripley, *The Financial History of Virginia, 1609–1776* (New York, 1893), is a precise, discriminating study.

middle colonies appointed inspectors of products to guarantee that corn "be sweet and clean and every way well conditioned" and that prepared meats be properly packed. Despite such precautions the settlers commonly paid their taxes in their inferior products and even private creditors were often at the mercy of local judges who favored debtors by overvaluing the commodities tendered in payment of debts that were recorded in pounds, shillings, and pence.[20]

The transportation of commodity money proved to be another serious disadvantage. Frequently the colonial prices of products were so low that commodity currency worth 5s. weighed fifty or sixty pounds. The costs of carrying tax money from the localities to the seat of government usually consumed between 5 and 10 per cent of the produce. In Massachusetts, when cattle were driven to Boston as a means of remitting tax money, the General Court provided that "if they be weary, or hungry, or fall sick or lame, it shall be lawful to rest and refresh them for a competent time in any open place that is not corn, meadow, or inclosed for some particular use." Once commodity money had been delivered there arose the added problem of storing it. Ordinary barns had to serve as banks where produce deposits were exposed to fire, theft, shrinkage, or deterioration. Instead of earning interest on his deposits the owner had to pay a high storage fee. In one case the cost of storing Indian corn eleven months amounted to 18 per cent of the quantity stored.

Merchants and creditors had other objections to commodity money. In times of high prices their debtors endeavored to pay their worst products; in times of low prices the commodities received became a drug on the market and could not be sold abroad. North of Maryland there was another difficulty—the money commodities could not be sent to England and exchanged for European goods. "The ordinary estates which we have in plantations," wrote John Winthrop, Jr., "cannot be converted into such as may suit correspondence with Europe, or carrying on such works as require the labor and help of such artificers who expect pay in the commodities of England, or such as will presently procure them." Only when the northern staples had been sent to the West Indies or other intermediate markets could they be exchanged for English goods. The costs of such roundabout shipments added to the colonial price of English goods imported and correspondingly depressed the price of the northern staples. The northern legislatures then placed a legal value on their products higher than their prices when sold for exportation—hoping thus to correct the price

[20] On wampum see W. B. Weeden, *Indian Money as a Factor in New England Civilization* (Baltimore, 1884).

disparity between European imports and their own produce. This resulted only in creating two price levels: commodity money or "country pay" prices which governed strictly local transactions, and foreign exchange or sterling prices which governed foreign trade. The merchants commonly reckoned in the lower foreign exchange price scale and hence it was also called the "merchant's price." These different price levels contained the seeds of protracted conflicts in which colonial debtors strove to pay their debts in commodities valued at the higher colonial level rather than at the lower figure of sterling or foreign exchange prices.[21]

Another remedy for the low price of northern staples when exchanged for European goods was widely advocated during the seventeenth century—that of producing commodities in the north which might be exchanged directly for English goods. John Winthrop, Jr., and William Penn were the leading advocates of this solution. They secured laws in their colonies encouraging the production of hemp, tobacco, and cotton, the opening of mines, and the building of ships. Such products might be exported to England at low cost, thereby purchasing English goods for the northern colonies on more favorable terms or at lower prices.

Despite the drawbacks of commodity money it served the colonists reasonably well during the seventeenth century. Its use was most common in the rural districts where the need for money was not so acute as in the towns. The colonial family produced so many of its own foodstuffs and manufactures that exchange was reduced to a minimum. Moreover, a large part of local trade was carried on by simple barter; each settler became an expert in bargaining his surplus products for other articles possessed by his neighbors. This rural trait, vividly described in Mark Twain's *Tom Sawyer*, had its origins in the remote colonial past. Credit likewise loomed large in colonial economy. The settlers ordinarily purchased goods from the local stores on credit, paying with later deliveries of farm produce. The stores also bartered products; a housewife, for instance, might buy a dozen eggs' worth of butter or cloth. Credit instruments provided another substitute for money. A man of means and reputation would give his promissory notes payable after several months and these would pass from hand to hand on endorsement until they became due and were paid. Bills of exchange circulated in the same manner. So also the colonial treasurers issued notes in advance of tax collections—notes which served as a crude form of paper money until the taxes were collected and the

[21] See again P. A. Bruce, *Economic History of Virginia in the Seventeenth Century*, Vol. II, chapters 17–20.

notes redeemed. Similarly coined money played a very small part in the colonial labor system, since apprentices, indentured servants, and slaves received payment, not in money, but in food, lodging, clothing, medical care, and vocational instruction. Such currency substitutes, common to all the colonies, helped to fill the void occasioned by the scarcity of coin.[22]

The New England colonies eliminated money payments in many other ways. The general courts and the towns granted lands without cash payments and did not exact quit-rents from the freeholders. They also paid salaries or wages to soldiers, officers, ministers, and public officials with land bounties; and compensation was given to public servants and encouragement to new undertakings like an ironworks by exempting the individuals concerned from paying taxes. Every able-bodied man between the ages of sixteen and sixty had to serve in the militia and the town police; thus these vital services were secured without money payments. Similarly the settlers were required to work without wages on certain public works such as highways, dams, harbors, bridges, and meeting-houses. Voluntary coöperation among the people further enabled them to carry on without using money, as at house-raisings, huskings, quilting parties, and funerals, or when misfortune disabled a farmer from caring for his fields.

The defects of commodity money prompted the colonists at an early date to seek a metallic currency. The establishment of colonial mints seemingly offered a way out of the difficulty. Massachusetts erected a mint in 1652 and at one time or another most of the other colonies desired to follow her example. The coining of money, however, was a prerogative of the king; his subjects could not operate mints without his permission and the charters issued to the colonies generally did not confer this privilege. Only when the king was in exile did Massachusetts venture to erect the Boston mint and although it continued to function until 1684, the coins it issued were all stamped with the date 1652.[23]

In the opinion of the colonists local mints were required by two major conditions. The foreign coins of Spain, France, Holland, and Portugal which came into the colonies after 1640 varied so widely in weight and alloy that the ordinary settler knew little of their real value in terms of English money. Due to the clipping, shaving, or "sweating" of coins even those of the same denomination differed considerably in metallic content. This made the use of coin so confusing

[22] See again E. L. Bogart and C. M. Thompson (eds.), *Readings in the Economic History of the United States*, chapters 2–3.

[23] See again S. E. Morison, *Builders of the Bay Colony*, chapters 5, 9.

that frauds could readily be practiced on the unwary. The colonists therefore assumed that if local mints were erected the confusing foreign coins could be melted down and the bullion converted into uniform pieces. Furthermore, English and European coins had the habit of speedily departing from the colonies. Seeing their specie leave, the colonists concluded that they needed a special kind of money—a coin so designed that it would always remain in America and provide all the advantages of a metallic currency.

The various proponents of colonial mints suggested that if coins issued in the colonies contained less silver than corresponding English coins they would have a higher value in the colonies than in England and would thus remain at home. Massachusetts acted upon this assumption in operating her mint. The famous pinetree shilling minted at Boston contained only seventy-two grains of silver as against ninety-three grains in the standard English shilling; consequently the province debased its coin, in comparison with sterling, to the extent of 22½ per cent. If seventy-two grains of silver were worth a shilling in Boston (so the argument ran) and worth only three-fourths of a shilling in England, then the pinetree coins would always remain in the colony. But this assumption proved to be false. The importers of goods raised the price of their wares so that they would get for a given article a certain amount of silver regardless of how it was coined. Prices of imported goods were therefore higher in pinetree shillings than in English shillings. On the other hand the prices of Massachusetts produce in pinetree shillings did not rise so rapidly as the pinetree prices of imported goods. This outcome, declared the deputies of the General Court, brought "an undervalue upon all commodities raised among ourselves" and so utterly frustrated "the end and use of money amongst us." So rapidly were the pinetree shillings exported as bullion that in 1654 the General Court prohibited such exportations under heavy penalties. The experiment of Massachusetts exposed two monetary theories common to the colonies: first, that a specially designed colonial currency would remain in America, and second, that by declaring a given amount of silver to be worth more shillings in the colonies than it was worth in England in English shillings, the colonial supply of money would be increased, the prices of colonial produce would rise, and the colonists would therefore be able to buy more foreign goods. What actually happened was that the price of foreign goods (as measured in pinetree shillings) rose more rapidly than the price of colonial produce (also measured in pinetree shillings), that importers obtained as much silver for their wares as formerly, and that in consequence the pinetree shillings were exported as bullion in order to pay for European goods.[24]

The Boston mint brought upon Massachusetts the accusation that she had usurped the king's prerogative—one of the charges which led to the annulment of her royal charter in 1684. Immediately afterward the authorities of the province petitioned that the mint be allowed to continue, asserting that an ample supply of coined money was necessary in order to uphold the value of colonial produce and property. English officials, however, rejected the plea on the ground that separate colonial mints would create a dozen or more coinage or price systems in America, to the infinite annoyance of merchants. English officialdom preferred that all the colonies use a common standard of value, that of sterling coin issued at the royal mint in the Tower of London. An earlier opinion delivered by English treasury officials in 1662 was now reasserted: "the preserving one certain standard of weight and fineness of . . . gold and silver coins in all your Majesty's kingdoms and dominions is very much for the security and advantage of your Majesty, and the altering or debasing of the . . . standard . . . cannot be practised or allowed in any one of your Majesty's dominions without eminent prejudice to all the rest." Inasmuch as the chief purpose behind projected colonial mints was that of issuing a debased coinage, this opinion sealed the fate of the Boston mint and it was not allowed to resume operations.

Underneath the English ban on colonial mints lay the fear that they would draw to the colonial towns a fund of specie which would provide them with a money economy and thereby stimulate colonial commerce and manufacturing industries in competition with English enterprises and investments in America. In the philosophy of mercantilism the power over the currency was an attribute of sovereignty and independence; consequently the English government refused to allow its colonial dependencies to influence debts, prices, and the movement of commodities in trade by managing coinage systems of their own.[25]

Another element in the money supply of the colonies consisted of the foreign coins previously mentioned. Since the colonists kept accounts in pounds, shillings, and pence, the various foreign coins which they used had to be evaluated in terms of sterling. The colonial legis-

---

[24] For the economic background see M. H. Gottfried, "The First Depression in Massachusetts," *New England Quarterly*, IX (Dec. 1936).

[25] E. A. J. Johnson, "Some Evidence of Mercantilism in Massachusetts-Bay," *New England Quarterly*, I (July 1928).

latures accordingly enacted laws declaring that various foreign coins should pass in the colony concerned as worth a certain number of shillings. In this case also the colonies declared that the silver in a foreign coin should be worth more shillings in America than it would have been worth if minted into English shillings. A Spanish piece of eight, for instance, which had a bullion content equal to 4s. 6d. in English coin was declared to be worth 5s. or more in the colonies. After 1680 occurred a currency war among the colonies in which the various legislatures progressively raised the legal value of foreign coin until the piece of eight in places was rated as high as seven or eight shillings. A similar policy at the present time would provide that a dollar of today should pass at a dollar and a half tomorrow.[26]

Two underlying reasons dictated this practice of raising the shilling value of foreign coins. In Massachusetts, Pennsylvania, and New York it was assumed that higher rates there would draw in money from the outside. If a foreign coin was declared to be worth 5s. in the West Indies and 6s. in Pennsylvania, then presumably the owners of money would send it to Philadelphia in order to make purchases there, thus giving a great stimulus to local trade. For a short time high money rates did draw in coin because the price of colonial produce did not rise so rapidly as the change in currency values was effected, and accordingly the possessors of money would have more shillings and thus be able to buy more produce at former price levels. Before long, however, local prices would rise high enough to reduce the purchasing power of the overvalued coins to their old figure. When such a point was reached the inflow of money would decline and merchants were then tempted to repeat the process by placing a still higher value on foreign coins. An act of one colony tended to draw money from its neighbors, so that in self-defense each felt it necessary to boost its own money rates. With a dozen colonies involved it seemed that the contest might never end.[27]

This competitive bidding for foreign coin coincided with a wave of piracy and privateering which washed a considerable amount of treasure upon the colonial shores. Rumor surmised that the pirate crews brought in £50,000 of treasure or more at a time, although records of seizures by officials indicate more modest sums—between £1,300 and £12,000 to a vessel. At any rate the supply of coin in the

[26] W. G. Sumner, "The Spanish Dollar and the Colonial Shilling," *American Historical Review*, III (July 1898).

[27] An outstanding though brief study is Charles J. Bullock, *Essays on the Monetary History of the United States* (New York, 1900). See Part I, chapters 1–3.

colonies was particularly abundant in the 1680's and 1690's when piracy was at its height. It also happened that the colonies which saw the most of the outlaws—South Carolina, New York, Pennsylvania, and Massachusetts—placed the highest shilling value on the foreign coins which were taken from vessels in the Caribbean and the Red Sea.[28]

A second reason which motivated the raising of the shilling value of foreign coins applied to Virginia and Maryland and the sugar islands, Barbados and Jamaica. In those colonies a large proportion of the planters staggered under the debts they owed to English merchants and the Royal African Company—debts which might be reduced by a revaluation of the currency. When a piece of eight was valued at 5s. the payment of a debt of 60s. would require twelve pieces of eight; if the piece of eight were then revalued at 6s., the debtor might pay with only ten pieces. But inasmuch as England's trade and investments centered in these four colonies the home government kept a sharp watch over their currency measures in order to protect English merchants and creditors. Moreover, these colonies paid substantial revenues to the Crown or (in the case of Maryland) to a proprietor resident in England—payments which also might be reduced by currency revaluation. For these reasons England forbade the sugar and tobacco colonies to raise the legal value of foreign coins. On the other hand, because the Crown did not derive any revenues from New England, Pennsylvania, and South Carolina and because the English merchants had only slight investments in those colonies, their currency measures were not called into question until they had all succeeded in establishing much higher foreign coin rates than those prevailing in the tobacco and sugar colonies. The latter then complained that their coin was rapidly drawn away to the commercial towns. English merchants had no particular desire to provide the southern planters with a large stock of money, but they did object to the drainage of coin from the sugar and tobacco colonies to Boston, Philadelphia, and New York. Such a trend in the movement of money meant that the southern planters bought their supplies from colonial merchants instead of from English merchants. The profits and specie thus accumulated by the northern merchants increased their capital and strengthened their position as competitors of their English rivals. But should all money pass at a single rate in America, the advantage of the mainland towns would be taken from them and the

---

[28] Shirley C. Hughson, *The Carolina Pirates and Colonial Commerce* (Baltimore, 1894), a pioneer study, is of interest to the specialist.

coin of the southern colonies might go directly to England, to the profit of English merchants and shipowners.[29]

In order to effect the desired uniformity of coin values the English government in 1704 issued a royal proclamation which prescribed that a piece of eight of 17½ pennyweight should not pass in any colony at more than 6s. All other foreign coins were rated proportionately, depending upon their bullion content. In this manner England created the fiction of "proclamation money." Since the piece of eight rated at 6s. was intrinsically worth 4s. 6d., the proclamation meant that coin worth £100 sterling might pass in the colonies at £133⅓ proclamation money. This measure aimed to lower the rates of foreign coin money in South Carolina, Pennsylvania, New England, and New York—the colonies which had previously valued foreign money at a higher level—while Virginia and Maryland were permitted, although not required, to raise their lower values to the new maximum level. But the proclamation contained no provision for its own enforcement, and accordingly the northern colonies and South Carolina ignored it completely and with perfect immunity. At the same time the governors of Virginia and Maryland prevented its violation there. Foreign coin rates in the tobacco colonies remained disproportionately low with resulting complaints that specie continued to flow away to neighbors who retained the higher rates.[30]

With the object of giving legal force to the proclamation, Parliament in 1708 enacted it into law and provided that any person who paid or received foreign coin when valued in excess of the proclamation rate should be imprisoned six months or pay a fine of £10. Even Parliament, however, could not bring the colonists to terms. The assemblies resorted to a new device; they now valued silver as worth a certain number of shillings an ounce instead of defining the value in shillings of each foreign coin. When England protested that excessive evaluation of bullion violated the proclamation Massachusetts and New York refused to make appropriations for the support of government unless the money appropriated bore the former (and higher) values. After a long contest with the Assembly of New York Governor Hunter surrendered. " 'Tis not in the power of men or angels," he wrote, "to beat the people of this continent out of a silly notion of their being gainers by the augmentation of the value of plate [bullion]." Only Maryland adopted the official standard; Virginia put

[29] Clarence P. Gould, *Money and Transportation in Maryland* (Baltimore, 1915), is one of the best discussions of colonial currency.

[30] Viola F. Barnes, *The Dominion of New England* (New Haven, 1923), a standard work, has a good technical chapter (7) on currency and trade.

into effect a new rate slightly below the proclamation level, while New York, Pennsylvania, South Carolina, and the New England colonies all retained values at a higher figure. Whereas by the proclamation foreign coins were not to be valued in excess of 33⅓ per cent above English values, most of the colonies rated silver bullion at 8s. an ounce, which amounted to 55 per cent more than its value in English shillings. The Northerners objected to the lowering of their foreign money values, fearful that such a measure would make it difficult if not impossible for them to draw in foreign money from the outside. Meanwhile, England prevented the violation of the proclamation in Maryland, Virginia, Barbados, and Jamaica, so that uniform money rates throughout the colonies were not established. After 1710 the interest of the colonists in altering the value of foreign coins declined as paper money became the center of the currency question.[31]

The legislation of the colonies pertaining to currency exhibits one common tendency and two resulting causes of strife between them and England. When they evaluated either the silver which was minted into coin or the commodities they used as money the colonies set the monetary values at higher figures than the commercial price of such commodities and silver. Two reasons for this policy are evident. First, the indebted farmers and planters desired to increase the supply of shillings, to raise the price of their produce, and thus more readily to obtain the money with which to pay their debts. Secondly, the merchant class desired high rates on coin in order to attract it from the outside, thereby enabling them to pay cash in Europe for the imports around which all colonial trade revolved. Coined money also afforded a durable form of wealth in which surplus profits could be safely conserved pending future investments, and provided a reliable and convenient medium of exchange highly essential to the merchant class. For contrary reasons England did not favor the currency policies of the colonies. Money rates which benefited colonial debtors injured English creditors, while measures to attract coin to the colonial towns strengthened their merchants in competition with English merchants for the profits of American trade. Moreover, a money economy in the colonies might stimulate the growth of colonial manufactures, cut down American imports from abroad, and in the end make the colonies economically independent of their parent state.[32]

[31] A brief outline of colonial problems appears in chapter 1 of Davis R. Dewey, *Financial History of the United States* (New York, 1922).

[32] For the advanced student: A. H. Cole, "Evolution of the Foreign Exchange Market in the United States," *Journal of Economic and Business History*, I (May 1929).

# XI

# ENGLAND AND THE COLONIES

UPPERMOST in the political history of the United States has been the federal problem—the relationship between the states and the federal government. The origins of this problem are to be found in the contacts between England and the thirteen colonies; British imperialism was the parent of American federalism. The distinct individuality and interests of the colonies, together with the vast extent of the territory occupied by the settlers, made it impossible for England to impose upon them a centralized and unified government. Each colony instead was treated as a separate unit and permitted to exercise particular privileges which fostered a feeling of independence, localism, or "state rights."

And yet, since all the colonies fell within the circle of England's rule, they were subject to common regulations framed by Parliament and the king. The problems of English imperial government, like those of American federalism, embraced first of all a series of economic contacts among the various communities of the empire. Commerce, navigation, manufacturing, currency, and property rights cut across colonial boundaries and necessitated some common regulations for the protection of England's interests in America. Relations with foreign states required a uniform system of diplomacy and a single navy. Such common agencies and regulations in turn called for a central or imperial government which could exercise both legislative and administrative powers. But since each colony had its separate legislature there arose at once a delicate problem of dividing powers between the imperial government and the colonial governments. Economic policy, diplomacy, and war gave birth to an imperial government and with it to the problem of dividing powers between the Crown and Parliament of England and the colonial legislatures in America.[1]

[1] A. C. McLaughlin, "The Background of American Federalism," *American Political Science Review*, XII (May 1918).

## The Conflict between England and the Dutch

Of the various influences which shaped England's colonial policy prior to 1675 the most profound was her prolonged struggle with the Dutch for the mastery of the world's commerce—and of this the colonial trade formed no inconsiderable part. After 1616 England's interest in American commerce revolved primarily around the tobacco exports of Virginia and Maryland. Here were sources of wealth which might readily enrich the English merchant class. In the direct trade with Virginia the English merchants desired first of all to supply the colony with English goods and to reap the profits on the sales. Secondly, the merchants desired to market the tobacco in England, thereby earning commissions or profits on such transactions. The transportation of the tobacco would employ the vessels owned by the merchants and bring them an income from freight and insurance charges. Any tobacco exported from Virginia to Europe should similarly be handled by the English merchants, involving as it did added freight earnings and commissions, while such sales would augment England's favorable trade balance and bring home an increased stock of the precious metals, so vital to the merchant class. Before 1615 England had purchased most of her tobacco from Spain—a trade to which the merchants objected because it did not afford employment for their vessels or payments for their marketing services. They said in 1620 that England's importation of Spanish tobacco drained the kingdom yearly of £120,000 of specie and was the chief cause of a scarcity of hard money in England. Could England obtain tobacco only from her own colonies, her merchants might pay for it with English manufactures instead of money, earn the freights, profits, and insurance premiums involved, and export to Europe the surplus tobacco which England did not need, thereby gaining additional profits and procuring in payment an increased fund of specie.[2]

In their efforts to realize this aim the English merchants encountered sharp competition from Dutch merchants, whose trading activities and whose shipping surpassed England's at this time. The Dutch used Fort Amsterdam on the Hudson as a base from which their vessels carried European goods to Virginia and obtained tobacco for the European markets, thus threatening to crowd the English merchants out of the trade. The latter took their case to the English government and secured a series of protecting regulations—a natural outcome, because both King James I and Charles I desired to obtain

[2] See again *The Cambridge History of the British Empire*, Vol. I, chapters 6–7, 9 (important).

a large revenue from the importation into England of Virginia tobacco, and that in turn depended upon driving Dutch merchants out of the English colonies.

In furthering these interests the English government required that tobacco exported from Virginia should be shipped directly to England. This policy was adopted in 1620–23, when James I endeavored to limit the amount of tobacco which the Virginia Company could legally ship to England and the company in retaliation threatened to send its entire supply to the Netherlands. A compromise in 1622 provided that the company could import into England unlimited quantities on condition that none of the tobacco be carried from the colony directly to a foreign port. Later orders and proclamations of the king in 1623, 1624, and 1631 continued this policy of requiring that all Virginia tobacco be first exported to England, in order that English merchants might reap the full profit of marketing it.[3]

A second regulation in 1624 prescribed that all Virginia tobacco should be exported from the colony in English ships—a rule which guaranteed that English merchants would earn the freights involved and that the tobacco would be carried directly to England, as previously ordered. In 1633–34 the king further directed that all foreign traders be excluded from Virginia, thus tightening the monopoly of the English merchants. Inasmuch as the levying of English import duties on Virginia tobacco hampered the reëxportation of that part of the crop not consumed in England, the crown in 1628 granted a "drawback" or remission of half the import duty for all such reëxports. The position of the merchants was further strengthened by royal orders (1620–36) which forbade the growing of tobacco in England, authorized constables to destroy home-grown plants, and imposed fines upon violators of the orders. Finally, the Crown favored the English merchants by prohibiting the importation of all foreign tobacco except a small yearly quantity of the Spanish variety, and upon this the import duty was greatly in excess of that levied on tobacco from the English colonies. By giving the colonial planters a virtual monopoly of the English tobacco market these regulations appeared to benefit them as well as the English merchants.

Soon after these regulations for the protection of the English merchants had been proclaimed the Civil War broke out in England, affording the Dutch an opportunity to usurp a large share of England's colonial trade as English merchants found themselves at a

[3] G. L. Beer's *The Commercial Policy of England toward the American Colonies* (New York, 1893) is a general, preliminary survey.

competitive disadvantage.[4] In the first place the Civil War greatly disrupted English industry, due to the military service of a large part of the working people and a widespread destruction of property. The costs of production in England soared, thus forcing upward the price of English manufactures and enabling Dutch merchants to undersell their English rivals in outside markets. Secondly, the war drastically curtailed English shipping. The country was roughly divided into two military sections, the king and his forces controlling the northwestern part and the Puritan-Parliamentary party controlling the southeast. Each faction pressed as many commercial vessels as possible into service as privateers to prey upon the commerce of the ports in the hands of its enemies. Vessels bound for Puritan ports were seized by the king's privateers, while Puritan privateers captured vessels trading with the king's ports, so that England waged a destructive warfare on her own commerce. Due to the high prices of English goods and the danger that cargoes bound for England might be seized by privateers, Dutch vessels met a welcome reception in the English colonies. They brought cheap products—"all sorts of domestic manufactures," particularly dry goods, beer, liquors, and hardware. At least fifty Dutch merchants were trading to Virginia and England's West Indian colonies in 1651. They procured and marketed the two colonial staples, sugar and tobacco, carrying them directly to European ports and thus depriving England of the profits of her former colonial trade. So extensive was the commerce of the Dutch with New England that Dutch money became there a common medium of exchange. Virginia in 1643 and Maryland in 1649 formally opened their ports to Dutch traders and vessels in defiance of orders from England. In the English sugar colonies, Barbados and the Leeward Islands, Dutch capitalists supplied goods to the planters on credit, equipped them with machinery for their sugar works, and sold them Negro slaves from African trading posts which the Dutch had seized from the Portuguese. As a result it was reported in 1652 that the Dutch had engrossed the whole commerce of Barbados. The French statesman, Colbert, indicated the power of the Dutch at this time when he estimated that they owned sixteen thousand of the twenty thousand vessels engaged in Europe's trade.[5]

The execution of Charles I in 1649 and the establishment of the

[4] The best introduction to its subject is George Edmundson's *Anglo-Dutch Rivalry during the First Half of the Seventeenth Century* (Oxford, 1931).

[5] Violet Barbour, "Dutch and English Merchant Shipping in the Seventeenth Century," *Economic History Review*, II (Jan. 1930).

Puritan regime under Oliver Cromwell inaugurated a new era in colonial policy. The Puritan merchants of London had formed the backbone of the opposition to the king, and London carried on three-quarters of England's external commerce. When installed in power the Puritans were determined to recapture the trade of the English colonies and to deprive the Dutch of the gains they had made during the Civil War. Accordingly, in 1650 the Puritan Parliament, now a mouthpiece of the London merchants, passed a Navigation Act which prohibited the vessels of any foreign nation from trading with England's American colonies—an act which anticipated that all colonial commerce would be carried on with England, to the enrichment of the merchants of London.

On issues of colonial and foreign policy the Puritan leaders divided into two parties. One group, headed by Cromwell, looking backward to Elizabethan times, stressed religious issues, regarded Spain as England's great rival in the New World, and desired to conquer Spain's colonies, thereby diverting their wealth to the Protestant cause in Europe. A second party believed that the Spanish power had passed its zenith and that the energetic and aggressive Dutch held out the greatest threat to England's commerce and prosperity. The programs of these two parties, however, were antagonistic. If England went to war against Spain she needed Protestant allies, and since the Dutch were the strongest Protestant power in Europe, England should join them in a Protestant league against Spain. Cromwell approved of a plan whereby England and the Dutch should divide and monopolize all colonial trade—the Dutch to enjoy the commerce of India, the English to possess all America except Brazil, and the two to divide the slave trading stations of Africa. Behind this scheme was Cromwell's theory that the Caribbean islands and the Spanish lands in lower America offered the most lucrative sources of colonial profit. An advocate of "tropical colonization," he hoped to acquire the Spanish colonies and to transfer English settlers from North America to the Caribbean region.[6]

In order to establish a Protestant league against Spain Cromwell carried on negotiations with the Dutch in 1650–51, but to no avail. The Dutch demanded as their price the privilege of a free trade with England's American and West Indian colonies—a concession to which the Puritan merchants of London would not consent. After the failure of the negotiations in 1651 the anti-Spanish plans of Cromwell were shelved, the commercial rivalry with the Dutch flared up anew, and

[6] For this period an excellent brief account is Charles H. Firth, *Oliver Cromwell and the Rule of the Puritans* . . . (New York, 1900). See chapters 18–19.

in October 1651 parliament passed a sweeping Navigation Act which precipitated the First Anglo-Dutch War of 1652–54.

This act aimed to eliminate the Dutch not only from the commerce of the English colonies (which exclusion had already been decreed by the act of 1650) but also from the carrying trade between England and other countries. Goods from America, Asia, and Africa could enter England, Ireland, and the English colonies only if carried in English, Irish, or colonial ships; and goods from Europe could enter England, Ireland, and the colonies only if brought in English ships or foreign ships of the country "of which the said goods are the growth, production or manufacture." Fish, oil, and whalebone could be imported into and exported from England only in English ships, and the coasting trade between English ports was confined to English vessels. Under the terms of the acts of 1650 and 1651 the only important shipping business with England open to the Dutch was that of importing Dutch goods into England directly from Holland and of exporting English goods (except fish) to Europe. And since Amsterdam was an entrepôt to which the Dutch brought products from all parts of the world, the act of 1651 forbade even English vessels to bring from the Netherlands any articles except those produced by the Dutch.[7]

This measure to exclude the Dutch from most of England's trade, together with numerous commercial disputes between the two powers and the fact that the Dutch were sheltering the exiled heir to the English throne, culminated in the First Dutch War—a naval conflict in which England made the larger gains. The Dutch had neglected their navy, and having far more vessels afloat than England, suffered disproportionate losses as English privateers captured fifteen hundred prizes. The peace concluded in 1654 provided for a defensive alliance between the two powers, for the exclusion of the Stuarts from the Netherlands, for the continuation of England's Navigation Acts, and for the settlement of other English grievances. Cromwell was now free to push his earlier designs against Spain.

The Spaniards still adhered to their policy of excluding English subjects from the trade of Spanish America and even denied to England the right to hold her possessions in the Caribbean. In 1635 they had seized from the English the island of Tortuga and in 1641 they conquered the Puritan colony of Providence in the Caribbean. Cromwell, having pacified England, Scotland, and Ireland, decided in 1654 to retaliate against the Spaniards by seizing one of their important

[7] G. L. Beer, "Cromwell's Policy in Its Economic Aspects," *Political Science Quarterly*, XVI (Dec. 1901) and XVII (March 1902).

colonies which might serve as a base for the eventual conquest of Spanish America. He therefore dispatched a fleet under Robert Venables and William Penn, the elder, with instructions to occupy Puerto Rico, Hispaniola, or Cartagena on the mainland. "The design in general," he wrote, "is to gain an interest in that part of the West Indies in possession of the Spaniard, for the effecting whereof we shall not tie you up to a method by any particular instructions." The force sent out from England, about twenty-five hundred civilians of poor fighting quality, failed to conquer Hispaniola, but did succeed in taking Jamaica in 1655—an island of slight value then but destined to loom large in the British empire as a profitable sugar colony and a center of English trade with Spanish America.[8]

The return of Charles II to England represented a compromise between contending parties. The restoration of the Stuart monarchy and the reëstablishment of both the Church of England and the House of Lords appeased the royalist and aristocratic forces, while Charles II consented to a commercial policy which gratified the London merchants. This policy was embodied in the famous Acts of Trade and Navigation, the foundation stones of England's colonial system until after the American Revolution. Of the first importance was the Navigation Act of 1660, reënacted in 1661, sometimes called the English Magna Carta of the sea. With respect to the colonies it contained three momentous provisions. All trade of the colonies had to be carried in English ships—vessels that were English built and owned, commanded by an English captain, and manned by a crew three-fourths of whom were English sailors. The word "English" was defined in 1662 as meaning "only his Majesty's subjects of England, Ireland, and the plantations." Second, the act of 1661 excluded all foreign merchants from the commerce of the English colonies, and, third, it required that certain enumerated articles produced in the colonies be exported only to England, Ireland, Wales, Berwick-on-Tweed, or to other English colonies. Sugar, tobacco, cotton-wool, indigo, ginger, and such dyewoods as fustic, logwood, and braziletto composed the original list of commodities thus enumerated.

The second act of major importance, the Staple Act of 1663, provided that goods en route from Europe to America should first be shipped to England, Ireland, Wales, or Berwick-on-Tweed and there landed before reshipment to the colonies. Direct exportations to the colonies were permitted in only three instances: servants, horses, and

---

[8] F. Strong, "The Causes of Cromwell's West Indian Expedition," *American Historical Review*, IV (Jan. 1899).

provisions from Scotland, wine from Madeira and the Azores, and salt for the North American fisheries.[9]

These acts intended to give England a monopoly of the trade of her colonies—not a monopoly to particular persons, but a national monopoly in which all English merchants should share. The Staple Act meant not only that English merchants would get the business of selling to the colonies but also that English manufacturers might dispose of their wares at an advantage in that the foreign goods which had to pass through England en route to the colonies might be taxed, thereby raising their prices and enabling English goods to undersell them. Similarly, the enumerated article principle assured that most of the colonial staples important to England would be exported by English merchants, who were also guaranteed employment for their vessels through the exclusion of foreign vessels from the English colonies. Since the colonists had to do most of their buying and selling in England, the London merchants could safely sell their wares on credit, thus adding interest charges to the freights, profits, and commissions which they reaped from their American trade.

The acts of 1660–63 threatened to exclude the Dutch completely from the English colonies and consequently new fuel was added to the old rivalry. In 1664 occurred the Second Anglo-Dutch War, notable for England's conquest of New Netherland—a move for the stricter enforcement of English colonial policy. Since the Dutch had long used New Amsterdam as a center from which they conducted their trade with Virginia, Maryland, and New England, the English desired to hold Manhattan as a means of enforcing their Navigation Acts by depriving the Dutch of their American trading base. The English also desired New Netherland in order to complete the chain of English territory along the coast, to acquire the Hudson River fur trade, and to obtain land for additional settlement. The treaty of 1667 which closed the Second Dutch War ceded New Netherland to England while England withdrew from the Spice Islands, limiting her oriental trade to the mainland of India. England also obtained the Dutch slave trading stations in Africa, and her Navigation Acts remained in force.[10]

Despite these material gains England again went to war against the Dutch in 1672—largely through personal intrigues of King Charles

---

[9] For a British view see Hugh E. Egerton, *A Short History of British Colonial Policy* (London, 1897), Book I, and Book II, chapters 1–3.

[10] Gerald B. Hertz, *The Old Colonial System* (Manchester, 1905), an English study, contains a chapter (3) on colonial policy.

II, in secret alliance with France. Although a Dutch fleet recaptured New Amsterdam in August 1673 the treaty of peace in 1674 once more restored it to England—an act which marked the passing of the Dutch menace to England's North American trade. Never a successful colonizing nation, the Dutch afterward confined themselves to the commerce of Europe, Africa, the Far East, and the Caribbean.[11]

## The Conflict between the Merchants

### England versus New England

The Navigation Acts and the exclusion of the Dutch from the English colonies presented to the merchants of Puritan New England a commercial opportunity of which they quickly took advantage. Ever since 1645 the trade of Massachusetts had been growing by leaps and bounds. The initial impulse to its development was a severe economic depression which struck New England in 1640 by virtue of the cessation of Puritan emigration from England. In the 1630's New England's economy had been in a fair state of balance. The two basic needs of the settlements—an adequate supply of foreign goods and a market for the surplus products of the New England farms—had been met by the arrival of thousands of immigrants who brought their property to the colonies chiefly in the form of English goods, which they exchanged there for livestock, seed, foodstuffs, other New England products, and land. When the immigration ceased in 1640 the settlers lost this steady market for their surplus produce and were unable to obtain sufficient supplies of foreign goods. Prices of New England commodities dropped drastically as the farmers could not find buyers and prices of foreign goods soared in face of an extreme and sudden shortage.

From this impasse New England extricated herself through the development of external trade. The merchants of Boston collected the surplus farm products, lumber, and fish of the surrounding settlements and carried them to the West Indies, southern Europe, the tobacco colonies, and Newfoundland, where they exchanged them for European goods or the means of buying such imports. The disruption of England's external trade in the 1640's aided the New Englanders much in the same manner as it had aided the Dutch. By 1660 the merchants of Boston and Salem, closely identified with the fishery,

---

[11] John Beresford, *The Godfather of Downing Street* (London, 1925), is primarily a study of Anglo-Dutch relations. See chapters 9–11.

shipbuilding, and New Hampshire lumbering, formed the dominant economic interest in the New England colonies.[12]

The Navigation Acts further strengthened the position of New England, in that they decreed the exclusion from the colonies of Dutch merchants and vessels—then the chief competitors of the Boston merchants. Moreover, England excluded foreign vessels before she had enough vessels to carry on all her colonial trade, and New England merchants and shipbuilders (to whom the Navigation Acts gave the same privileges which were conferred upon English shippers) rushed forward to fill the gap. During the Civil War and the Puritan regime England had been too busy at home and in Europe to supervise the colonies closely; hence the New England traders had been free to trade wherever they could make a profit, and they came to feel that they were independent of English restrictions such as were imposed upon them by the acts of 1660 and 1663. Accordingly, they proceeded to ship the enumerated articles directly from the colonies to European ports and to import European wares on the return voyage without bringing them first to England as the Staple Act required. Such illegal trade caused the utmost concern among the English merchants because the New England trader could undersell them in America, exempt as he was from paying the customs duties on goods that passed through England. Moreover, direct shipments between Europe and the colonies were less expensive than the roundabout trade which the English merchants carried on through English ports.

In other words, the Boston merchants were rapidly succeeding the Dutch as the competitors of English merchants in the contest for the American trade. By supplying the colonies with European instead of English manufactures, the Bostonians threatened to deprive the English manufacturer of the colonial market. Their marketing of colonial produce in Europe similarly robbed the English merchants of the profits of such business, as well as the profit of supplying the colonies with needed imports, while the employment of New England vessels in colonial trade reduced the freight earnings of English merchant-shipowners. Above all, New England's direct trade with Europe diminished the king's revenues, since the products involved did not pass through English ports and accordingly did not yield custom duties to the Crown. Once more the allied interests of the king and the English merchants were threatened and once more they prepared vigorous measures to protect their stake in the colonies.

[12] The third volume of H. L. Osgood's *American Colonies in the 17th Century* deals with imperial relations (important).

Massachusetts in the meantime had taken the stand that she was not subject to acts of Parliament, arguing that "our allegiance binds us not to the laws of England any longer than we live in England." Not only did the Massachusetts Puritans fear that Parliament might overthrow their religious system but the Boston merchants were loath to admit that parliamentary statutes could regulate American trade so as to restrict colonial profits. For these reasons Massachusetts between 1630 and 1680 stubbornly resisted every effort toward imperial control. Her government refused to recognize Charles II as king in 1660 and consistently supported the Boston merchants in their defiance of the Acts of Trade and Navigation.[13]

The headstrong attitude of Massachusetts brought a royal commission to Boston in 1664 to investigate charges that the colony had rejected England's authority. The four commissioners met only obstruction and hostility from the Boston government and accomplished nothing—an outcome which encouraged the Bay merchants in their violation of both the Staple Act and the clause in the Navigation Act of 1661 pertaining to the enumerated articles. A common method of evading the latter act was that of shipping sugar and tobacco from the southern colonies to Boston and then reëxporting the products to foreign ports. By an oversight this act permitted the exportation of the enumerated articles from one English colony to another without requiring the payment of any duties. Boston merchants could obtain such articles tax free, whereas English merchants had to pay English import duties, a difference which enabled the Bostonians to undersell their competitors in foreign markets. To relieve this situation, Parliament in 1673 passed another trade act which placed a "plantation duty" on enumerated articles exported from one English colony to another—a tax equivalent to the duty on such articles when imported into England, so that the colonial merchant lost his former advantage of tax exemption. Furthermore, English officials construed the act of 1660 so as to prohibit the reëxportation of enumerated articles from intermediate colonial ports to foreign countries.[14]

The act of 1673 necessitated a staff of officials in the colonies to collect the export duties on the enumerated articles shipped to the other English colonies. Foremost among such custom officials was one Edward Randolph, who was sent to New England in 1676 to investigate colonial trade. Two years later he was appointed collector of

[13] A. H. Buffinton, "The Isolationist Policy of New England," *New England Quarterly*, I (Jan. 1928).
[14] Lemuel A. Welles, *The History of the Regicides in New England* (New York, 1927), gives the American careers of three of the judges who condemned Charles I.

*From a contemporary engraving (1663) in the collection of J. H. Innes, Nyack, N.Y.*

## THE LONDON CUSTOMS HOUSE

During the great days of Elizabeth, especially after the fall of Spanish sea power, English commerce spread apace. East, south, and west, farther and farther from the Thames, went the adventurous traders of England. The old customs house in London received the cargoes of a swiftly growing merchant fleet. England was taking a new place in the world.

the king's revenue in Massachusetts. A staunch Anglican and royalist, Randolph despised nearly everything cherished by the Massachusetts Puritans. As a "watchdog" of the English merchants it was his duty to expose and stamp out all illegal trade in New England and in so doing to safeguard the king's revenue. Related to the Mason family in England which claimed New Hampshire, he vigorously combated the pretensions of Massachusetts to that region, and was largely instrumental in having it separated from Massachusetts and set apart as a royal province in 1679. When he returned from a visit to New Hampshire in 1679 he was greeted with this welcoming verse:

> Welcome, Sir, welcome from the eastern shore
> With a commission stronger than before
>    To play the horse-leech, rob us of our fleeces,
>    To rend our land, and tear it all to pieces
> Welcome now back again.

Determined, tactless, and overbearing, Randolph persistently harassed the Massachusetts Puritans over a half-dozen years, relentlessly prying into all their affairs with the sole object of making out as strong a case against them as possible. In 1680 he drew up twenty-nine charges against the colony, twenty-three of which related to violations of the Navigation Acts. He accused the Puritans of operating their mint at Boston—a manifest usurpation of the king's prerogative—and of fitting out pirates who preyed upon the commerce of the Caribbean. The authorities of Massachusetts, he said, worked hand in glove with the lawbreaking merchants and put every sort of obstacle in his path. Such was an act in 1681 creating a colonial naval station whereby the colony was to receive all fines arising from judgments against violators of the Navigation Acts, whereas the king's instructions directed that such fines should go half to the king and half to the informer— and Randolph was the principal informer. Local juries, he charged, refused to convict merchants accused of illegal trade. He concluded as early as 1679 that the king's revenues and the English merchants could be protected only if the charter of Massachusetts were revoked and the locally elected officers of the colony were replaced by agents appointed by the king. In season and out he urged this policy upon the English government.[15]

During the years 1660–80 many other charges were leveled against Massachusetts. Her religious policies, which discriminated against Anglicans by denying them the right to vote and by forcing them to

[15] H. L. Osgood, "England and the Colonies in the Seventeenth Century," *Political Science Quarterly*, XVII (June 1902).

pay taxes for the support of the Puritan churches, manifestly violated the colony's charter, requiring as it did that colonial laws should be consistent with the laws of England. In her boundary quarrels with Connecticut, Rhode Island, and New Hampshire, Massachusetts brought upon herself the accusation of unfair and illegal treatment of her smaller neighbors. In the 1650's the Boston Puritans assumed the attributes of sovereignty when, for purely religious causes, they executed four Quakers—an act clearly outside the province of a corporation such as the Massachusetts Bay Company. Above all, the Puritan leaders claimed virtual independence when they refused to take the oath of allegiance to the king or to recognize the authority of Parliament, insisted that judgments of the local courts could not be appealed to the Privy Council, asserted that the king possessed no powers over the colony except those mentioned in the charter, and claimed the sole right to judge whether the colony's laws were consistent with the laws of England. Orders and requests from the king were consistently ignored or evaded. And when this spirit of independence expressed itself in violations of the Navigation Acts and threatened to deprive England of the economic value of her colonies, an intolerable situation called for drastic action. After long negotiations in which the Puritan authorities refused to yield an inch, the Privy Council brought suit in the court of chancery against the Massachusetts Bay Company. Finding its charter privileges had been abused, the court on October 23, 1684, declared the charter forfeited.

## Imperial Administration

After the revocation of the Massachusetts charter the English government imposed upon New England a highly centralized administration—a scheme of control toward which English officials had been striving (rather fitfully, to be sure) since 1620. In order to induce promoters and investors to establish colonies it had been necessary to grant them liberal powers of governing their territories, but as the economic value of the colonies increased, such powers were often used to deprive English merchants and the Crown of the profits from colonial resources and trade. It therefore seemed desirable to curtail colonial privileges and so to regulate the colonies that they might be of maximum value to English interests. The Dominion of New England, 1686–89, exhibited this tendency at its height, but behind it lay a long trend toward imperial control.[16]

[16] An excellent discussion of English backgrounds appears in George N. Clark's *The Later Stuarts, 1660–1714* (Oxford, 1934), chapters 1–5, 12.

The initial step was taken by the Crown in 1624 when it assumed the power of governing Virginia. Under the charters of 1609 and 1612 the Virginia Company had acquired and exercised that power— not, however, with very satisfactory results. Between 1620 and 1624 the company was split into two bitterly hostile factions, headed respectively by Sir Edwin Sandys, leader of the party in control, and Sir Thomas Smith, spearhead of the opposition. In 1622–23 the Smith faction leveled a series of charges against the administration by the Sandys group. It was asserted that Sandys and his friends had only slight investments in the company, that they kept control by manipulating votes, that they suppressed free discussion and criticism, and that they spent the company's money recklessly and unprofitably. Settlers had been sent to Virginia faster than the colony could absorb them; adequate provision was not made for their support, health, or protection; the company's agents in the colony had embezzled the company's funds there; and even the Indian massacre of 1622 was attributed to the mismanagement of Sandys. So appallingly high was the death rate in the colony that it was likened to a slaughterhouse. Moreover, with reference to plans for granting the company a monopoly of importing tobacco into England, it was charged in 1623 that the Sandys group was preparing to give its partisans some needless "soft jobs" at excessively high pay.[17]

The strife within the company and distress in the colony moved the king's Privy Council to appoint in April 1623 an investigating commission which soon brought in a report that strongly condemned the policies of Sandys. When he had taken charge in 1618 there were one thousand settlers in Virginia; four thousand emigrants had been sent afterward, and yet in 1623 there were only twelve hundred alive. The tactics of Sandys had disgusted many important members of the company, causing them to lose interest, while the intense factional strife was imperiling the colony. The Privy Council accordingly recommended that the company surrender its charter and place the government of Virginia in the king's hands. When the company refused to do this the Privy Council brought against it a suit of *quo warranto* which terminated in 1624 in a decision annulling the charter. Although the powers of governing the colony were now transferred to the king, the company was allowed to operate as a trading body. Its failure, however, to earn profits ended its commercial activities in

---

[17] Alexander C. Brown's *English Politics in Early Virginia History* (Boston, 1901) contains much information but has been superseded by Wesley F. Craven's *Dissolution of the Virginia Company* (New York, 1932)—a first-rate monograph. See also W. F. Craven, "The Dissolution of the London Company for Virginia," *American Historical Review*, XXXVII (Oct. 1931).

1632, when bankruptcy revealed that it had lost more than £200,000 in the Virginia enterprise.

Having taken over the government of Virginia the king now was confronted by the task of evolving a colonial administration. Should the province be managed by Parliament or the king? Both James I and Charles I insisted that colonial administration fell solely within the prerogative of the sovereign, who had originally asserted his power by issuing the charters which conferred land titles and the right to govern the colonies. During the contest between the Sandys and Smith factions James I had directed Parliament not to interfere on the ground that his Privy Council had charge of the matter, and immediately after 1624 the king continued to supervise the colonies, Parliament not even being in session between 1629 and 1640. The royal authority was made effective during these years through the agency of the Privy Council, but since it was too large a body to consider details, small temporary committees of its members—usually experts on trade—performed the task of drafting and enforcing regulations for the colonies. After 1624 the general administration of Virginia was assigned to such a special commission. Due, however, to the preoccupation of Charles I and his court with issues foreign and domestic, this commission was inactive and the real government was entrusted to the king's governor and his council in Virginia.[18]

The economic relations between the tobacco planters and the English merchants illustrate the part played by the king's government in colonial administration. It was customary after 1620 for the merchants to sell goods to the planters on credit and to receive payment in tobacco. The initial profits of tobacco growing forced a rapid increase in production so that Virginia's exports multiplied seventy-fivefold between 1617 and 1640. In consequence, the price of tobacco, which was as high as five shillings a pound in 1617, had dropped below the cost of production by 1630, and between 1627 and 1638 its average was only about twopence a pound. The drastically reduced incomes of the planters were not sufficient both for the payment of debts incurred when tobacco prices were high and for the purchase of new supplies of English goods, whose prices did not fall at a corresponding rate. As a remedy the planters, through their local legislature, experimented with statutory price-fixing. An act of 1619 required that the better grades of tobacco should be sold in the colony at 3s. a pound, and the inferior grades at 1s. 6d. a pound. A second act

[18] C. M. Andrews, *British Committees, Commissions, and Councils of Trade and Plantations, 1622–1675* (Baltimore, 1908), the standard work, is detailed and technical.

(1631–32) imposed heavy penalties on planters who sold their tobacco at less than 6*d*. a pound, while a similar measure of 1640 provided for the inspection of all tobacco and the destruction of all the
bad and half of the good, the remainder being valued for payments
of debts at the rate of forty pounds of the selected product for one
hundred pounds of ordinary tobacco.

Such acts did not appeal to the English merchants, who argued
that the actual price of tobacco was determined by general European
market conditions and that if they paid a higher legal price to the
planters they would be ruined. In self-protection the merchants priced
the goods they sold to the planters so as to correspond with the inflated tobacco prices. The planters then complained to the king that
the merchants were guilty of profiteering. In this contest the king
and his advisers sought to protect the merchants by ordering the governors of Virginia in 1626 and 1634 not to enforce any colonial
statutes which arbitrarily fixed the price of tobacco. In the meantime
the Crown had framed its regulations granting in substance a monopoly of the colonial tobacco trade to English merchants. Thus the
planters could neither trade with foreign merchants nor dictate prices
to the English monopolists.[19]

New England also engaged the attention of the king's advisers during the reign of Charles I. Several non-Puritans whom Massachusetts
had expelled charged in a petition to the Privy Council in 1632 that
the New Englanders had withdrawn from the Anglican Church and
were striving for complete independence from England. After 1633,
Archbishop Laud extended his ecclesiastical investigations to the Puritan migration, and Charles I, convinced that the exodus to New England was weakening England and strengthening the stiff-necked Puritan colony, created in 1634 a special commission known as the
Lords Commissioners for Plantations in General. Composed of England's leading churchmen and statesmen, though actually functioning
through a sub-commission of lesser men who made recommendations
to guide the decisions of the great men, this commission had a general
jurisdiction over the colonies, with special instructions to regulate
emigration and to examine the colonial charters in order to ascertain
whether any "privileges hurtful to us or our Crown . . . have been
prejudicially suffered or granted."

The commission immediately brought suit against Massachusetts

---

[19] G. L. Beer's *Origins of the British Colonial System* is very important here. Beer
emphasizes England's concern with the colonies as sources of supply. For a criticism,
see C. P. Nettels, "The Place of Markets in the Old Colonial System," *New England
Quarterly*, VI (Sept. 1933).

and called upon the company to produce its charter and to answer the charges that the local authorities had violated its terms. But the Bay Puritans refused to send the charter to England, and since the governing body of the company was in New England, the legal proceedings could not be completed and the charter was not officially annulled. Charles I nevertheless assumed control of the colonies and appointed as governor-general of New England the most bitter and active foe of the Bay Puritans—Sir Ferdinando Gorges—then quarreling with Massachusetts about land titles and the control of the New England fishery. It was at this time that the Council for New England surrendered its patent in order to expedite the proceedings against the Massachusetts charter. The year 1635–36 witnessed preparations on the part of Gorges to raise a force to subdue Massachusetts, impose his authority on the colony, and compel the surrender of the charter. Determined to resist by force of arms such an "invasion," the Bay Puritans were equally busy with preparations for defense. However, Charles I failed to back Gorges with financial aid and his plans had not been carried out when the rumblings of civil war in England forced the king to ignore the remote colony. Massachusetts escaped unscathed—its first successful resistance to English authority. The colonial leaders had not desired nominal independence but they did crave the right to manage their affairs in their own way.[20]

When Parliament functioned without the king during the Civil War it asserted that it possessed supreme authority over the colonies and thereupon created a special commission upon which it conferred almost unlimited powers to govern them. The high priest of Puritan colonial promoters, the Earl of Warwick, headed this commission with the title of Governor-in-Chief and Lord High Admiral of all the English colonies. Having escaped from the regulations which Charles I was seeking to impose upon them, the colonies had no intention of submitting to the potentially stronger authority of Parliament. Particularly was this the case in Virginia, where the planters realized that the London merchants who desired to monopolize the tobacco trade at the expense of the planters formed the backbone of the parliamentary party. The Virginians therefore proclaimed their loyalty to Charles I but this amounted to little more than a declaration that they opposed the regulation of their trade by the London merchants. Massachusetts also rejected the authority of Parliament, even refusing to accept legislation friendly to the colony "lest in after times . . . hostile forces might be in control, and meantime a prece-

[20] Attention is again called to G. L. Beer's *The Old Colonial System*, Vols. I and II (important).

dent would have been established." So occupied was Parliament with the war that it could not interfere with the colonies and they hastened to shake off all imperial authority and to carry on a free trade with foreign countries.

After the parliamentary forces had disposed of the king and established their uncontested supremacy in England they proceeded to bring the refractory colonies to terms. New England had not openly defied the English Puritans but Virginia, along with the island colonies, had proclaimed their loyalty to Charles II when their legislatures declared anyone guilty of treason who denied his right to the throne. In 1652 Cromwell sent to the colonies an expedition which forced the islands, Virginia, and Maryland to recognize the newly won authority of Parliament. Terms of surrender in 1652 provided that Virginia and Maryland should not be taxed except through their own legislatures and that they should enjoy a free trade with "friendly" nations. The latter concession occasioned a dispute as English officials interpreted it as subject to the Navigation Acts of 1650 and 1651 which excluded foreign vessels and merchants from colonial trade, while the planters construed it to mean free trade in a literal sense. Some effort was made to enforce those acts, naval vessels being employed to seize foreign ships trading with the colonies. On the whole, however, Cromwell and his fellow Puritans were too much preoccupied with European affairs to impose a firm rule upon the colonies. The Virginia House of Burgesses was allowed to elect its own governor and to function as a miniature republic, while the New England colonies managed their own affairs and operated their independent league of nations, the Confederation of New England.

The compromise between the London merchants and the English aristocracy which placed Charles II upon the throne in 1660 meant a continuance of the commercial policies of the Puritan regime. As far as the new king had a consistent policy it was that of promoting England's industrial, commercial, and imperial growth—a policy which was bound to lead to a strict control of colonial trade. He conceded to Parliament a share in the regulation of the colonies by assenting to the Acts of Trade and Navigation; he favored the merchants by appointing select councils of trade and plantations whose primary duty was to make the colonies profitable to the merchants and the Crown.[21] These councils had a checkered career until 1675 when they were superseded by a committee of the Privy Council known as the Lords of Trade—a body of men of high station, influence, and wealth.

[21] R. Bieber, "British Plantation Councils of 1670–1672," *English Historical Review*, XL (Jan. 1925).

Both the Lords of Trade and the earlier councils acted upon royal instructions which embodied the views of the London merchants. Such instructions directed the councils to supervise the colonies with an eye to making them valuable to England as markets, as sources of raw materials, merchants' profits, freights, and Crown revenues, and as fields for the investment of English capital. To this end the councils were ordered to obtain all possible information about the colonies, to prepare instructions for the colonial governors, to scrutinize colonial acts and court proceedings, and to investigate and expose all violations of English orders and statutes. The councils did not possess actual authority; they merely gave advice to the king and his Privy Councillors, who in turn appointed colonial officials, framed regulations, and ordered their enforcement in the colonies.

During the first decade of his reign Charles II pursued a fairly conciliatory policy toward the colonies. With the memory of the Civil War only too fresh in mind he refrained from oppressive measures that would antagonize his subjects before he was securely established on the throne.[22] Responding to the declarations of loyalty issued by the leaders of Connecticut and Rhode Island he granted those colonies their liberal charters of 1662 and 1663 which recognized them legally as virtual republics, empowered through their assemblies to pass laws and elect their own governors. He appointed Sir William Berkeley governor of Virginia after he had been chosen by the House of Burgesses. When Massachusetts refused to submit to the royal commissioners in 1664 the king did not press the charges against the colony, allowing it to go its own way unmolested. Liberal powers of government were conferred upon the proprietors of New York and Carolina, while after the conquest of New Netherland the Dutch settlers were granted religious freedom and permitted to retain their property and customs. However, this policy of leniency toward the colonies proved to be merely a prelude to measures which aimed to reduce them to a state of abject subordination to England's authority.[23]

## THE DOMINION OF NEW ENGLAND

The close of the Third Dutch War in 1674 definitely removed the Dutch menace to England's colonial trade. Charles II, now fourteen years upon the throne, had acquired a sense of security that dis-

[22] Percy L. Kaye, *English Colonial Administration under Lord Clarendon* (Baltimore, 1905), treats adequately the years 1660-67.

[23] Ralph P. Bieber, *The Lords of Trade and Plantations, 1675-1696* (Allentown, Pa., 1919), is a formal study of administration. See also W. T. Root, "The Lords of Trade and Plantations, 1675-1696," *American Historical Review*, XXIII (Oct. 1917).

posed him to assert, however secretly, his father's theory of absolute rule. Year by year the colonies were becoming more valuable to England, although the evasion of the Navigation Acts by New England merchants remained a disturbing challenge to England's supremacy. After Dutch competition in North America had been crushed, the king was at last in a position to discipline New England. In this policy he could count upon the aid of the English merchants, who were firmly resolved to make their New England competitors respect the Navigation Acts.

The trend toward a closer control of the colonies by England appeared in the Revenue Act of 1673. Two years later Charles II created the Lords of Trade, thus dignifying colonial administration by entrusting it to the most powerful men in the kingdom. Another step was taken in 1679 when the right of the Mason family to govern New Hampshire was restored to the king and a royal governor was placed over the province. The charter of Pennsylvania of 1681 made the colony subject to taxes levied by Parliament and required the proprietor to enforce the Navigation Acts, to submit the laws of the province for the king's approval or disapproval, and to maintain an agent in England to answer charges brought against the province. Refusing to approve of a proposal to erect a new proprietary province in Florida the Lords of Trade in 1682 declared it inexpedient "to constitute any new proprieties in America or to grant any further powers that may render the plantations less dependent on the Crown." Then followed the annulment of the Massachusetts charter in 1684. The trend was reinforced in 1685 when Charles II was succeeded by his brother, James II. Determined to rule as an absolute monarch over England, the new king naturally did not intend to allow the dependent colonies to defy his royal will.[24]

Two obstacles to a firmer control over the colonies had come to light prior to 1675. First, the charters had conferred extensive rights behind which the colonists had been able to resist England's authority. Hence it seemed urgent that the charters, particularly those of the New England colonies, be revoked and their privileges returned to the king. Secondly, the existence of many separate colonial governments greatly complicated the task of imperial administration. If, on the other hand, all New England, New York, and New Jersey could be brought into direct dependence upon England, the king could appoint one set of officials who would act as a unit in enforcing the

[24] An admirable study of colonial administration is Louise P. Kellogg's *The American Colonial Charter*, *Report*, American Historical Association, 1903, Vol. I, chapter 1.

Acts of Trade and Navigation. A single government, moreover, would be far less expensive to England than the maintenance of six or eight separate colonies. Should the whole northern and middle area be converted into one large royal province its economic resources might be so developed, and its commercial activities so directed, as to yield maximum returns to English interests. Although the northern area was already immensely valuable to England, it presented an acute problem in that its people were not producing staples that could be marketed directly in England. The lack of such staples had forced the Northerners to engage in external trade (in which they had rapidly become effective competitors of English merchants) and to develop home manufactures that threatened to deprive England of the northern colonial market for textiles, leather goods, earthenware, woodenware, and ironware. But if England established a uniform, all-powerful government over the whole northern area, its resources might be developed so as to divert the people from manufacturing and foreign trade. They might develop lead and copper mines and produce hemp and naval stores, thus obtaining staple raw materials that could be exchanged directly for English manufactures. Such a direct trade would halt the growth of colonial manufactures and at the same time lessen the dependence of the northern area on outside trades, which, while they provided it with purchasing power for English goods, also fostered a class of merchants who competed with English merchants for the profits of the commerce of the New World.[25]

A new factor in British policy came into play after 1675. As the Anglo-Spanish rivalry had been succeeded by the Anglo-Dutch rivalry, so also the Dutch menace was followed by a menace from France. At Newfoundland and Nova Scotia and on the New England and New York frontiers the expansion of the English and French was drawing the two people into a new contest for colonial supremacy. It therefore happened that the French menace focused attention upon the northern area just when it was so notorious for its violation of the Navigation Acts. And in the impending contest France was likely to derive an advantage from her scheme of imperial government. All Canada was included in one dominion, administered by a single body of officials who were appointed by the king and unrestrained by colonial legislatures. Since both Charles II and James II felt a spiritual partiality for French absolutism it is quite understandable that they used the Dominion of Canada as their model for the Dominion of New England.

[25] See again Viola F. Barnes's important *The Dominion of New England*.

This experiment in colonial absolutism endured but three years. In May 1686 James II appointed Sir Edmund Andros as governor of New England with autocratic powers over all the northern colonies except Connecticut and Rhode Island. The colonial legislatures were abolished and their powers transferred to Andros and a local council whose members were appointed by the king. Andros and his council were authorized to levy taxes, enact laws, erect courts, and grant lands in the name of the king. All such acts might be set aside by the king, while judgments of the colonial courts involving £300 or more might be appealed to the Privy Council. Land grants made in the future were subject to a quit-rent of 2s. 6d. a hundred acres. So drastic were these provisions that they constituted a complete overthrow of the Puritan social and political order, and it is not surprising that the Puritans afterwards referred to the years 1686–89 as the period of usurpation.

Andros did not arrive in Massachusetts until December 1686; in the meantime a temporary government had been erected, consisting of a council of which the secretary was Edward Randolph and the president was Joseph Dudley, son of Thomas Dudley the founder.[26] On the whole the people of Massachusetts submitted tamely to the new regime. The strict Puritans accepted it as a divine judgment upon the people for their sins; the non-Puritans even welcomed it as an escape from the harsh, discriminating features of the old order. Dudley, however, soon found himself between two fires. He was regarded by the Puritans as a traitor to the colony—as an agent of tyranny— while Randolph felt that, because the institutions of the colony were left intact, Dudley was indifferent toward England's interests. After the arrival of Andros both Connecticut and Rhode Island were brought into the Dominion and organized into counties, although Andros admitted important men from both colonies into his council and neither had its charter legally annulled. A new commission issued to Andros in 1688 by James II made him governor of all New England, New Jersey, and New York. Accordingly, he formally annexed those middle colonies to the Dominion—an act, however, of little significance, for a few months later the whole new system toppled to the ground.

The Dominion expired in 1689, primarily because it had engendered intense opposition among the New Englanders. It introduced the Anglican Church into Massachusetts, imposed an Anglican governor upon the Puritans, brought an Anglican rector to Boston,

[26] Everett Kimball's *The Public Life of Joseph Dudley* (New York, 1911) devotes chapters 1–3 to the imperial problem in Massachusetts.

and destroyed the legal foundations of the Puritan church. These grievances were aggravated when the Puritans were forced to allow Anglicans to worship in their own South Meeting House in Boston. All the religious ideals for which they had struggled seemed doomed.

As Andros strove to enforce the Navigation Acts he was accused of stifling New England's trade, while his powers over land grants resembled a sword suspended over property rights. Acting with his council he might investigate, confirm, or annul all existing land titles. And it so happened that most of such titles were of doubtful legality, derived from sub-corporations of town proprietors which had been created by the general courts. The New England charters, however, did not authorize the general courts to incorporate towns, and hence the town grants and the individual titles derived from them might be declared illegal. Most of the land had been granted in this manner; consequently the whole body of landowners felt that their most cherished property might be taken from them. Furthermore, in order to obtain money for the support of the Dominion government, Andros was authorized to require that all lands to be newly granted should be subject to a quit-rent. Thus existing titles might be set aside and the landowner forced to pay a permanent quit-rent as the price of a new title. The money thus paid would support a "tyrannical" government and also, perhaps, an odious church.

Andros, however, did not seriously disturb existing land titles; nor was he able to obtain sufficient revenue from quit-rents to support his government and to provide for colonial defense. His council therefore was forced to impose taxes upon the property owners in defiance of the New England tradition that taxes should be levied only by the General Court. Protests soon filled the air, particularly in the towns of Topsfield and Ipswich—chief hotbeds of resistance—where one of the foremost colonial liberals, the Reverend John Wise, vehemently denounced Andros's levies as illegal and proclaimed that only the elected representatives of the property owners could levy taxes. That the Andros regime was no shadowy threat to Puritan liberties soon became evident when thirty "rebels" were arrested, of whom six were clapped into jail and fined.[27]

In the face of these issues the most bitter enmity was bound to separate the New England Puritans and Andros. Although he was an able and honest man, his foes accused him of the harshest tyranny and ill will. His failure to conciliate the Puritans did not arise from his personality; his task was inherently too odious. Nearly all the important groups were outraged by the policies which he was instructed

[27] See again J. T. Adams, *The Founding of New England*, chapters 12–17.

to carry out. The devout Puritans could not stomach the preference shown to the Anglican Church, the merchants feared a stricter enforcement of the Acts of Trade, the landowners were outraged by the unsettling of land titles and the menace of quit-rents, and the voters in all the colonies deplored the loss of their local liberties and elected assemblies. No governor who was ordered to tear up a country's institutions by the roots could be popular, whatever his personality. Perhaps the best work of Andros was done in improving the defenses of New England, yet such was the animosity toward him that his absence from Boston on defense and Indian affairs gave birth to the baseless rumor that he was in league with the French, plotting an Indian war against the Puritans which was to deliver New England to France and the pope. As long as Andros endeavored to obey his instructions from England (and this he conscientiously tried to do) there was not the remotest likelihood of a friendly adjustment—unless the New England Puritans submissively abandoned everything which they had previously cherished. They regarded him as a usurper and awaited an opportunity to renounce him and all his works.

On the 18th of December 1688, King James II, the sponsor of Andros, fled from England to France. In less than three years of his reign he had so antagonized the most influential groups in England that they united to invite William of Orange, Stadtholder of Holland, to invade England in order to preserve her ancient liberties. Bishops, archbishops, and landed aristocrats had been outraged by the apparent determination of the king to foster his own religious faith, Catholicism, even to the point of undermining the Anglican Church. Landowners and townsmen bitterly resented his claim that he was privileged to suspend the enforcement of acts of Parliament. In foreign affairs he had defied the English merchants by courting France, now their chief rival in colonization and overseas trade. The opposition crystallized in June 1688 when the birth of a royal son threatened to perpetuate indefinitely a Catholic monarchy in a Protestant country. On February 13, 1689, William of Orange was proclaimed King of England.[28]

When the news of the "Glorious Revolution" reached Massachusetts in March 1689 it fanned the embers of Puritan discontent into the flame of revolution. In April a mob in Boston, probably instigated by the Puritan leaders, seized and jailed Randolph and other Dominion officials. Andros later surrendered and was imprisoned at

[28] The political struggle in England, 1603–89, is ably presented in George B. Adams, *Constitutional History of England* (New York, c. 1921), chapters 11–14.

Castle William on an island in Boston harbor, where the "usurpers" remained until they were sent to England the following February. The dominion immediately fell apart as Connecticut, Rhode Island, and Plymouth resumed their separate identities and reinstated their elected governors and assemblies. A council of safety ruled Massachusetts during the revolutionary interim; then, hoping that the colony might return to the good old days of the charter, the Puritans placed in office the officials who had been serving when the charter was annulled.

But such good fortune was not in store for Massachusetts. The attack upon her liberties represented more than the whims of two tyrannical kings; it represented the fixed purpose of the English merchants and the Crown to force the New England merchants to conform to the English colonial system. To William III and his advisers, therefore, a return to the old course of independence was inadmissible. As early as 1688 "the foremost American Puritan," Increase Mather, had gone to England to seek a modification of the Dominion government, and after its complete overthrow he strove to restore to Massachusetts her charter of 1629. When the Lords of Trade rejected this plan, Mather—a practical man not averse to compromise—agreed to a new charter, issued in 1691, which restored many of the essential features of the earlier government.[29] New Hampshire remained a separate province but Plymouth and Maine were joined to Massachusetts. Several important changes were intended to subordinate the colony to England's authority. No longer was the governor to be elected by the Puritan freemen; now he was to be appointed and removed by the king and to act as the king directed. No longer was the legislature to be a law unto itself; its acts might now be vetoed by the royal governor and, even when signed by him, reviewed and disallowed by the Privy Council. Nor did the freemen continue to elect the governor's council. The first councillors to serve under the new charter were appointed by the king; afterward vacancies were filled by vote of the house of representatives and the council in joint session, while the governor might reject the nominees thus designated. The charter forbade religious tests for voting, requiring property ownership instead. Judgments of the colonial courts which involved £300 or more might be appealed to the Privy Council. On the other hand, the property owners retained many of their former privileges by virtue of the continuation of the town meet-

---

[29] Kenneth B. Murdock discusses this subject in his definitive biography, *Increase Mather* (Cambridge, 1925).

ings and the restoration of the elected house of the legislature. Thus was effected a compromise between imperial authority and home rule by property owners in the colony.[30]

The Revolution of 1688 in England enabled New England to defend its liberties very much in the manner that the Puritan uprising after 1640 had warded off the encroachments of Charles I. The English revolutions emphasized the political and economic rights of English property owners, and to such rights the propertied groups in the colonies also laid claim (and successfully, thanks largely to English examples). But there was a difference between 1640 and 1689. When the Puritan Revolution broke out the colonies were of minor importance to English merchants and moreover the merchants were not strong enough to overthrow a hostile king until after nearly a decade of warfare. In 1689 the colonial empire was of major value to the merchants and they were strong enough to dispose of a hostile king without bloodshed, thus preventing another decade of neglect of the colonies such as had occurred after 1640. Instead, the Massachusetts charter of 1691 proclaimed that they were to be kept in close dependence upon England. Both revolutions had augmented the powers of Parliament, the agency through which the rising merchant class now strove to monopolize colonial trade. As the interests of the English merchants and the colonists diverged, so also the colonists and Parliament were to draw farther apart. Thus the revolutions of the 1640's and of 1688 sowed the seeds of a third and—to America—more significant revolt.[31]

[30] For additional material on colonial administration see Gertrude A. Jacobsen's scholarly, technical *William Blathwayt* (New Haven, 1932).

[31] H. L. Osgood, "England and the Colonies," *Political Science Quarterly*, II (Sept. 1887).

## BIBLIOGRAPHICAL NOTE

Works Previously Cited: W. C. Abbott, *Expansion of Europe*, I, ch. 20; II, ch. 26; Lord Acton, *Lectures on Modern History*, chs. 12–13; B. Adams, *Emancipation of Massachusetts*, ch. 6; C. M. Andrews, *Colonial Period of American History*, I, chs. 7–8, 14; C. M. Andrews, *Colonial Self-Government*, chs. 1–4, 16; C. M. Andrews, *Fathers of New England*, chs. 6–7, 10–13; G. Bancroft, *History of the United States*, I, chs. 6, 11–14, 16; II, chs. 25–26; *Cambridge Modern History*, IV, chs. 16, 25; V, chs. 5, 7–10; E. Channing, *History of the United States*, I, pp. 485–509; II, pp. 155–203; V. S. Clark, *History of Manufactures in the United States*, I, chs. 2, 5–9; E. Lipson, *Economic History of England*, III, ch. 4 (important); David Ogg, *England in the Reign of Charles II*, I, and II, ch. 8; A. F. Pollard, *Factors in Modern History*, chs. 7, 9 (English politics); F. Schevill, *History of Europe*, pp. 279–313 (English background); W. B. Weeden, *Economic and Social History of England*, I, ch. 7; T. J. Wertenbaker, *Virginia under the Stuarts*, ch. 4.

SOURCES NEWLY CITED: Two important seventeenth-century essays on trade and policy are Sir Dudley North, *Discourses upon Trade* [1691] (ed. J. H. Hollander, Baltimore, 1907), and Sir Josiah Child, *A New Discourse of Trade* (London, 1804). On the revolution in New England (1689) see C. M. Andrews (ed.), *Narratives of the Insurrections* (New York, 1915—Jameson *Original Narratives* series), pp. 167–297.

SOURCES PREVIOUSLY CITED: E. L. Bogart and C. M. Thompson (eds.), *Readings in the Economic History of the United States*, ch. 4; H. S. Commager (ed.), *Documents of American History*, I, nos. 23–24, 27; W. MacDonald, *Documentary Source Book of American History*, nos. 15, 19, 22 (Navigation Acts); no. 24 (Massachusetts charter, 1691).

# XII

## THE SOCIAL STRUCTURE

THE transition from medieval to modern society effected a change in the social structure of Europe. The three estates of the Middle Ages —the clergy, the nobles, and the peasants—were replaced by the new groupings of the upper class, the middle class, and the propertyless working class. This change was brought about by the growth of industry and commerce which produced a society more complex than that which prevailed in early medieval times, when agriculture was supreme. Inasmuch as the colonists were steeped in the social traditions of Europe and because the economic forces active there also operated in America, the settlers tended to duplicate the social structure of the Old World, with certain important exceptions to be noted later.

During the seventeenth century a colonial upper class took form, although this incipient aristocracy was numerically weak. Its members consisted of the largest landowners, the most wealthy merchants, and the royal and proprietary governors. The latter may be regarded rather as representatives of English upper-class groups than as aristocrats in their own right. Economically, the basis of the colonial aristocracy was the ownership of wealth so extensive that the owner could support an ostentatious way of living without engaging in manual labor. The upper class, therefore, occupied itself with leisure interests, military affairs, government, business management, and intellectual pursuits. Its activities were self-directed and its members never served in a dependent capacity. All their social arrangements and usages— such as dress, manners, and etiquette—proclaimed their exemption from toil and their possession of leisure and means sufficient to enable them to acquire the decorative graces of a refined way of living. Judged by English standards the social techniques of the colonial aristocracy may have been somewhat crude, but nevertheless they were sufficiently advanced to differentiate its members sharply from the laboring farmers and artisans.[1]

Due to the widespread ownership of land in the colonies the middle

[1] An original, penetrating study which all students should know is Thorstein Veblen, *The Theory of the Leisure Class* (The Modern Library, New York).

class occupied a particularly important place. Its members included professional men (principally clergymen and teachers), lesser merchants who conducted their own small businesses, landowning farmers, artisans who employed servants or hired workers, officials of the proprietors and the king, shopkeepers, clerks of the great merchants, overseers of plantations, and ship captains. Such people were set apart from the upper class either because they did not possess enough wealth to exempt them from laborious work or because they depended upon employment by the upper class or upon the custom of their fellow settlers, as in the case of shopkeepers, who, however, preferred the patronage of the well-to-do. Socially, the middle class copied the manners and dress of the aristocracy. But having neither the wealth nor leisure to warrant an intensive cultivation of refined manners they failed to attain the aristocratic standards. As a whole they aspired to enter the upper class, strove to acquire property, felt themselves superior to the propertyless laboring groups, and endeavored to eliminate all evidence of degrading toil from the appearance they presented to the world.

## THE UPPER CLASS

The aristocracy or planter class which emerged in Virginia, Maryland, and South Carolina during the seventeenth century had its basis in extensive private landowning and in a labor system which exempted the wealthy planter from physical toil. Prior to 1680 the labor force consisted chiefly of indentured servants, afterward increasingly of Negro slaves. How deep was the social gulf between owner and worker appeared in the layout of the plantation, where the owner's house stood apart amidst shrubs, while the workers occupied cabins at a distance, not far from the pens and barns which housed the livestock. By 1700 there were fifty planters in Virginia whose wealth amounted to $50,000 as calculated in values of today. The estates of two men, Robert Beverley and William Byrd I, were probably worth a quarter of a million dollars each. Beverley owned at least 37,000 acres of land and Byrd over 15,000 acres. Other large estates were those of John Carter (18,570 acres), Richard Lee (12,000 acres), and Samuel Mathews (9,000 acres), although the average large holding included only about 5,000 acres.[2] As early as 1624–25 there were fifteen planters who owned ten or more servants and one who owned forty. An observer writing in 1649 told of a planter who "hath a fine house and all things answerable to it; he sows yearly [a] store of

[2] J. T. Adams's *Provincial Society, 1690–1763* (New York, 1928) contains a mass of well-classified facts. See chapters 3 and 4.

hemp and flax, and causes it to be spun; he keeps weavers, and hath a tan-house, causes leather to be dressed, hath eight shoemakers employed in their trade, hath forty Negro servants, brings them up to trades in his house. He yearly sows abundance of wheat, barley, etc. The wheat he selleth at four shillings the bushel, kills store of beeves, and sells them to victual the ships when they come hither; hath abundance of kine, a brave dairy, swine great store and poultry."

In founding Maryland Lord Baltimore endeavored to introduce manors on the European model and to people them with tenants subject to the political and judicial authority of the owner. However, workers could not be obtained who would place themselves permanently in the dependent status of tenants, and the early manors were forced to rely upon indentured servants and Negro slaves; in consequence the manor was converted into a plantation of the Virginia type, although the name survived.[3] Similarly, the proprietors of Carolina failed in their efforts to graft a landed nobility and a manorial regime of tenants or serfs on the Charles Town colony. However, the plantation readily developed in South Carolina. Between 1675 and 1684 nine planters received land grants varying from 1,000 to 3,000 acres, one received 12,000 acres, and another 35,800 acres. In 1670 the ownership of one Negro slave and three indentured servants justified the employment of an overseer; in 1677 the estate of Sir John Yeamans possessed fourteen slaves; in 1694 the largest plantations were rated as worth about £5,000. After the development of rice culture in South Carolina in the 1690's, the plantation multiplied rapidly; as early as 1700 Negro slaves outnumbered the white residents of the colony.

Since many of the planters were descended from well-to-do members of the English middle class they were able to establish themselves in the colonies by virtue of inheritance and family assistance. William Fitzhugh, for instance, a son of an English barrister, migrated to Virginia about 1670, purchased an estate on the Potomac, and settled at once into the leisurely life of a planter. As estates grew in size the owners entrusted the supervision of the daily work to overseers and devoted themselves to sports (hunting and horse racing were prime favorites), business management, land speculation, politics, social affairs, and military pursuits. They drank heartily, gambled freely, relished vigorous physical exertion out of doors, cultivated the refined manners of drawing-room society, and attended, none too punctually, the religious observances of the Anglican Church. The need of defending their property and of upholding the social struc-

[3] John Johnson, *Old Maryland Manors* (Baltimore, 1883), is a brief sketch.

ture, coupled with the desire to maintain individual physical prowess, induced them to an active military life, serving as they almost invariably did as captains and colonels in the county militia. They readily developed a political philosophy of isolation, self-rule, or "estate rights," whereby each man should order his economic affairs without external restraint. Through their influence on the governor's council they could defeat proposed laws hostile to their interests; as local magistrates they dispensed justice among their lesser neighbors; as plantation owners they governed their servants and slaves. Living in isolation with numerous dependents they deemed it imperative to maintain their authority and prestige at a high pitch; consequently they could not tolerate insubordination from inferiors. In personal intercourse among their equals they were governed by a code of honor, the chief purpose of which was to preserve their dignity and good repute.[4]

During the seventeenth century a progressive improvement in the planter's way of living was evident, although it still remained somewhat rough and crude, judged by modern standards. His dwelling, its furnishings, and his personal apparel all proclaimed his affluence and his superior social status. He lived in the "great house" or "manor house," usually a simple, plain building, square or rectangular, with chimneys at each end, lacking architectural graces and not as yet set off by beautiful lawns and flower gardens, although bushes and shrubs softened its harsher aspects. As his wealth increased the planter added rooms to the main structure; by 1700 the largest mansions, as that of William Fitzhugh, contained a dozen rooms—a great hall or dining room, a parlor, bedchambers, kitchens, a dairy, an overseer's room, and closets. The great hall, where the planter dispensed a generous hospitality, was furnished with a long center table flanked with benches. Side tables and cupboards resplendent with pewter plates, knives and spoons and various silver dishes gave an impression of wealth while perhaps a few original portraits adorned the paneled walls of cedar or walnut. Lighted by narrow windows or at night by candles and the glow of the open hearth, the room presented a rather somber aspect; in winter it was cold and draughty. Linen, even damask, napkins and tablecloths graced the dining table on special occasions. Colored and decorative fabrics gave a warmer tone to the bedchambers—curtains, woven rugs, tapestry on the walls, and figured coverlets and quilts. The large bed, not yet canopied, stood high above the floor, so that a child's trundle bed could be rolled underneath

[4] See again P. A. Bruce, *Economic History of Virginia in the Seventeenth Century*, Vol. I, chapter 9; Vol. II, chapters 10–14.

during the day, where it was screened by valances. Canvas mattresses, feather-stuffed, sheets, pillows, and blankets all bore evidence of gentility. In a chest or trunk, usually of leather, highly ornamented, were stored the most highly prized possessions of the household, while a chest of drawers, with mirror above, served for everyday articles of apparel. Chairs with leather, rush, or embroidered seats, screens, escritoires, and brass andirons also suggested means and refinement. All such furnishings, imported from England, resembled those in vogue among the upper classes there.[5]

The class feeling of the planters expressed itself likewise in dress. In their wardrobes were to be found such articles as linen shirts with pewter or silver buttons, silk and woolen stockings, leather shoes with brass, steel, or silver buckles, periwigs, felt and beaver hats, linen neckcloths, broadcloth, camlet, or serge coats with decorative buttons and cuffs or ruffles on the sleeves, waistcoats of many colors, plush or broadcloth breeches, and scarfs edged with lace. The attire of the women of the planter's family included silk and flowered gowns, laced shoes, decorated fans, colored scarfs, white, scarlet, and black hose, calico hoods, palmetto hats, lace-trimmed bonnets, and black tippets. And when adorned with pearl necklace, gold pendant, silver earrings, and gold rings a lady was not to be mistaken for a woman who worked at menial tasks, nor could her husband or father be ranked as other than a member of the upper class.

Somewhat similar to the southern plantations were the large estates which took form in New York during the seventeenth century, vast holdings of certain wealthy Dutch, Scottish, or English families—the Van Rensselaers, Schuylers, Beekmans, Morrises, Livingstons, Van Cortlandts, Heathcotes, Philipses, and Lloyds. The founders of the colonial branches of these families had come to New Netherland, for the most part, during the years between 1634 and 1664, bringing with them considerable wealth which was invested in land and the Indian trade. Located chiefly in the Hudson valley their estates were gradually enlarged by various devices until in the eighteenth century they covered immense areas. Rensselaerswyck, which extended on both sides of the Hudson, with its geographical center at Albany, included 700,-000 acres, while the Van Cortlandt, Livingston, and Beekman estates consisted of 140,000, 160,000, and 240,000 acres respectively. The early grants made by the Dutch West India Company were confirmed by the Duke of York as a means of winning the support of the most influential men in the province, and after 1664 new patents were is-

---

[5] P. A. Bruce, "Economic and Social Life of Virginia in the Seventeenth Century," in *The South in the Making of the Nation*, Vol. I, chapter 3.

sued in order to build up a party loyal to the proprietor.[6] Boundaries were but vaguely described and surveys long delayed; the resulting uncertainty enabled the magnates to enlarge their holdings, often by sheer force. Politics, favoritism, and bribery, rather than *bona fide* purchase, seem to have been the legal means of obtaining the estates. Governor Benjamin Fletcher particularly offended by receiving bribes for excessive grants during the 1690's.

Such vast holdings, of course, included much waste land, with only a small part under cultivation. The requirement that the landlord pay the proprietor or the king a yearly quit-rent of a bushel of wheat per hundred acres was more honored in the breach than in the observance. Due to the difficulty of obtaining tenants the magnates could not develop their estates rapidly; consequently they did not appear so affluent as the southern planters, although their social ideals, pastimes, manor houses, and living standards were of the same pattern. The cleared land was cultivated by tenants who were generally supplied by the owner with tools and farm animals and were therefore forced to give him a share of the increase of the livestock, as well as to pay regular rents in grain, most commonly wheat. Not until the late seventeenth century were these estates legally converted into manors. Politically the magnates dominated local government through the sheriffs, their allies; they dispensed justice among their tenants, and in the provincial legislature they acted after 1693 chiefly through the elected house—entitled in some instances to representatives for their estates, and always dominating elections in their districts. Religious fellowship in the Anglican and Dutch Reformed churches, together with multiple ties of marriage and blood relationship, sealed the bonds of union among these wealthy, aristocratic families.[7]

In the northern towns the growth of merchant capitalism had produced, by 1700, the nucleus of an upper class. Here also wealth distinguished the leading merchants from their lesser competitors. When a merchant acquired extensive property and devoted his time to its general supervision rather than to routine business, and when his income was derived primarily from his investments, he had attained a distinctly upper-class standing. The secret of his economic progress was his accumulation of profits beyond his needs for current expenditure and the investment of his surplus in income-producing enterprises.

---

[6] Clarence W. Rife, "Land Tenure in New Netherland," in *Essays in Colonial History Presented to Charles M. Andrews.*

[7] Ernest Wilder Spaulding's *New York in the Critical Period, 1783–1789* (New York, 1932) has an excellent chapter (3) on the landed aristocracy. S. G. Nissenson, *The Patroon's Domain* (New York, 1937), is thorough and legalistic.

At the close of the seventeenth century such wealthy. merchants were to be found in the northern towns. At Boston the most prominent were Samuel Lillie, Andrew Faneuil, Andrew Belcher, John Foster, Samuel Phillips, William Clarke, and Benjamin Gallop; at Philadelphia, Samuel Carpenter, Robert Turner, James Claypoole, Isaac Norris, and Edward Shippen; at New York, Stephen De Lancey, John, Abraham, and Cornelius Van Horn, Caleb Heathcote, Andrew Fresneau, Benjamin Faneuil, Abraham De Peyster, and Rip Van Dam. A very large majority of these merchants came to the colonies with trading capital they had inherited or acquired as merchants in Europe, and to which many of them added by marriage into wealthy families. As early as 1670 there were thirty merchants in Massachusetts with estates ranging between £10,000 and £30,000. The rate of profit in the seventeenth century was exceptionally high: an observer said of Pennsylvania in 1686 that "merchants find themselves encouraged by the profit, which is seldom less than 50 per cent, the which is a great advance." [8]

Such profits went into many channels of investment. The wealthy merchant owned his own private wharves and his warehouses, where his counting-room or business office was located and where he often operated a retail shop. Equally important was his investment in ships. Most commonly he preferred to purchase shares in several vessels rather than to own a few outright; thus he spread the risk of loss at sea. In 1700 seventeen Boston merchants owned shares in ten or more vessels, and in 1715 eight New York merchants owned shares in five or more. The advance of goods on credit to fur traders or the erection of trading posts afforded another source of profit to the merchants. They also dealt in real estate. Thus the first outstanding merchant of Boston, Robert Keayne, as a large investor in the Massachusetts Bay Company, received four hundred acres of land in the colony in 1639. The leading merchants of Philadelphia bought five or ten thousand acres apiece in the province in 1681–82—a good investment, since lands that sold for £2 a hundred acres in 1682 brought between £8 and £25 in 1701. A New England merchant, Philip English, owned fourteen houses at Salem in 1692. John Hull of Boston, goldsmith, merchant, and mintmaster, similarly owned several farms in Massachusetts and an estate on Block Island, the products of which he carried to market in his own vessels. Likewise Hull and his fellow mer-

[8] Carl L. Becker, *The History of Political Parties in the Province of New York* (Madison, Wis., 1909), a work of major importance, discusses New York society in chapter 1.

chants invested in sawmills or gristmills; at Philadelphia Samuel Carpenter anticipated that such investments would yield 8 per cent.

An especially fruitful source of income to the merchants was the loan business. An interest charge always accompanied the advance of goods on credit to farmers or country traders—a charge compounded semi-annually. As the bankers of the time the merchants also made long-term loans on real estate or short-term loans on personal security. In most cases they insisted upon ample security, the merchants of Philadelphia once refusing to lend to William Penn because he could not provide sufficient guarantees. So also they insisted upon prompt payment and the precise fulfillment of contracts; John Hull, though lenient, even threatened to sue a Puritan minister for a debt long over-due. Interest charges in the northern colonies during most of the seventeenth century were nominally 8 per cent. Massachusetts in 1693 reduced the charge to 6 per cent, excepting maritime contracts, and New York followed in 1717. Such phrases in colonial laws as "the great and excessive usury now commonly taken in this province" indicate that moneylending was a very profitable business.[9]

With mounting incomes derived from commercial profits, land sales, rents, freights, warehouse charges, and interest the merchants were able to extend their investments and at the same time to support an increasingly opulent manner of living. Their houses, furniture, dress, and social standards all resembled those of the southern planters, copied as they were after a common model, that of the landed aristocracy of England, to whose social eminence the English bourgeoisie had always aspired. As a colonial merchant prospered he moved his residence from the business quarter of the town to the "suburbs," where he could enjoy a semi-country estate surrounded by lawns and gardens and travel to and fro in his own carriage. The northern merchants also matched the southern planter class in political influence. They generally controlled the governor's council and the local governments of their towns. A host of colonial acts reveal their influence—New York acts which, until 1695, gave the town of New York a monopoly of flour making; a Pennsylvania act of 1711 providing that in the settlement of estates, debts due to residents of the province be paid before debts due to outsiders; and a Massachusetts act of 1682 which prohibited sales to seamen on credit lest the imprisonment of seafaring debtors delay the departure of vessels. Whenever the in-

[9] On social classes see chapters 8 and 10 in *Under Duke and King* (1933), the second volume of A. C. Flick (ed.), *History of the State of New York*. On the aristocracy see chapter 5 of the third volume, *Whig and Tory* (1933).

terests of the merchants were concerned they acted in unison, chiefly by presenting petitions to the local authorities. It is not misleading to regard the governor's councils of New York, Massachusetts, and Pennsylvania as committees acting in behalf of this powerful class.

In many respects the psychology of the northern merchants distinguished them from the southern planters. In religion they inclined toward the Calvinistic churches—the Congregational, Presbyterian, French Huguenot, and Dutch Reformed—while the Quakers were well represented in Philadelphia. As their wealth increased they exerted a conservative influence within the churches, favoring refined, decorous, formal, and conventional services. Samuel Sewall, a Salem merchant, indicated this social trend in his spiritual reflections: "I had a sweet and very affectionate meditation concerning the Lord Jesus, nothing was to be objected against his person, parentage, relations, estate, house, home." Living as they did in towns—not isolated amidst a host of dependents—employing workers rather than owning slaves, obliged to maintain a multitude of contacts with business associates of all degrees, the merchants were not prone to vigorous physical sports, preferred calculation to gambling, eschewed dueling and the ideals of a code of honor in favor of amicable settlement of disputes, avoided military pursuits and did not covet the title of captain or colonel. Instead of depending upon personal force and mastery they relied upon the sanctity of contracts, the give-and-take of bargaining, and the letter of the law, over which they kept a watchful eye.[10]

The demands of business required that the merchant possess a diversified knowledge and a cosmopolitan point of view. As an employer and creditor he had to be a good judge of human character; as a buyer he must know the humble details of farming and industry in order to determine accurately the quality of all sorts of products; as a shipper he had to be familiar with the art of navigation and the geography of remote places; as a trader he needed to keep posted on prices, market conditions, rates of exchange, currencies, tariffs and treaties pertaining to all parts of the world, and to be advised about politics, foreign and domestic, and wars and rumors of wars. Fresh news of this sort he sought with avidity. Such practical concerns also directed his intellectual interests to mathematics, accounting, modern languages, law, politics, and the economics of business, while travel enlarged his outlook by giving him contact with the cultural life of other countries.

[10] D. R. Fox's *Caleb Heathcote* (New York, 1926) is a spirited portrait of a New York merchant.

## Farmers and Workers

The mass of the colonial population was composed of working farmers and artisans, who were roughly divisible into three groups. A minority of the farmers were moderately well-to-do, owners of land up to a thousand acres and regular employers of farm hands or indentured servants. Similarly, certain master artisans—shipwrights, millers, shoemakers, hat makers, fullers, blacksmiths, and weavers— owned their shops and tools and employed journeymen or apprentices. Economically, such artisans were less independent than the substantial farmers, depending as they did upon the custom of their neighbors, although employed by the community as a whole rather than by a single person. Both groups generally enjoyed the right to vote and their social station depended upon the amount of their property and the number of their employees. Most of them doubtless came to the colonies with a small amount of capital and established themselves as independent settlers, although many indentured servants, when free, rose into this class.[11]

Such farmers and artisans exhibited several common characteristics. Ambitious, energetic, highly skilled and efficient in their occupations, with a well-developed instinct of workmanship and a deep respect for work, they possessed more than a usual fund of initiative and managerial ability which qualified them as employers and directors of labor. Actuated by a competitive and emulative spirit, they steadily strove to improve their standing in society, and the social standards to which they aspired were those of the upper class. Their ownership of property, an upper-class attribute, and their desire to increase their wealth through the employment of dependent workers, also indicate their spiritual kinship with the privileged groups. However, their investments were not large enough to exempt them from work or to afford them leisure to cultivate the refined graces of aristocratic society; consequently they blended the traits and attitudes of the laboring workers and of the leisured upper class. They generally lived well and comfortably but did not consume their substance in ostentatiously extravagant living, preferring rather to save their surplus and invest it in additional land or equipment—a process by which they could gain the respect of their neighbors more effectually than by lavish personal expenditures. As the settlements expanded the farmers and artisans of this class were increasingly concentrated in the older, thickly settled

[11] Edward Eggleston's *The Transit of Civilization* (New York, 1933) is good reading. On classes see chapter 6.

parts of the colonies, which afforded the best opportunities for extended operations wherein several workers could profitably be employed.

Numerically the largest group in the colonies consisted of the less affluent farmers—men who owned a hundred and fifty or fewer acres, who worked their own land with the assistance of their families and the occasional aid of a hired hand, who possessed a little capital in the form of tools and livestock, and who commonly were entitled to vote. This class was sprung largely from immigrants who came to the colonies as employees or indentured servants.[12] Lack of initial capital compelled such farmers to borrow money in order to purchase land, or to equip their farms, and since their debts often became a permanent possession they developed a pronounced debtor psychology. Equally conspicuous was a spirit of independence—a dislike of being "bossed"—which induced them to prefer a free life in the wilderness to a dependent status in older settlements. Although they toiled at heavy, laborious work, they were generally easygoing, easily contented, not unusually gifted with foresight, inclined to live from day to day; many of them were actually shiftless. Living very largely in isolation they relished the companionship of strangers and neighbors, displayed a sociable, familiar, and inquisitive manner, had few if any intellectual interests beyond the Bible and the church, felt only a slight urge to neatness and orderliness, and concerned themselves with immediate, practical tasks which limited their conversation to crops, the weather, neighborhood news, and family happenings. Since they worked "from sun to sun" their dress and appearance openly proclaimed their occupation and place in society, even on holidays. Among them the emulative spirit was not strongly developed; instead of striving for social advancement they preferred an out-of-door life under the spell of nature and the privilege of working on their own terms. Simple-hearted, neighborly, coöperative, narrow in outlook, and firm in their convictions, they lived their uneventful and useful lives, obeying the scriptural command to replenish the earth, for they brought more children into the world than they could provide with a generous patrimony and many of their descendants were forced to move on and build new settlements in the West.

Even though these less wealthy farmers and their families were essentially working people, they too shared an attribute of the upper class—the ownership of land. They too coveted more acres, more ad-

[12] On the small farmer in the South the most important works are those of T. J. Wertenbaker: *Patrician and Plebeian in Virginia* (Charlottesville, 1910) and *The Planters of Colonial Virginia* (Princeton, 1922). See also his *The First Americans*, pp. 27–48, 283–301.

vantages, more of the good things of life. Their economic independence bred a sense of self-importance and self-respect. When a farmer's son went forth "to make his way in the world," his father might advise him: "Remember that you are as good as any man—and also that you are no better." Despite their property ownership, the farmers remained primarily workers, drawing their income from their labor rather than from investments, treating the occasional servant as one of the family, showing without concern the evidences of toil so odious to the upper class, and retaining their deep-seated respect for useful work and the man who could perform it well. Thus the American environment acted upon the European social heritage so as to produce a property-conscious democracy of farmers and workers who sought a share in social advantages previously confined to the upper classes in the Old World.[13]

Below the settled yeoman there existed a class of nomad farmers who made a business of pioneering. They went into the virgin forest, erected cabins and cattle pens, cleared a few acres of timberland, planted a little Indian corn, corralled some livestock—and later sold their improved property to permanent settlers who came after them. This class usually possessed few worldly goods beyond a cart, a pack horse, a gun, axe, hoe, the coarsest of clothing, and the crudest of household utensils; they merely "squatted" on the land, and sold, not the title to their clearings, but the improvements they had made. They lived partly by hunting and fishing, performed heavy, unskilled labor, presented an extremely unkempt and uncouth appearance; true denizens of the forest, they seemed to outsiders as half-civilized wretches, hardly distinguishable from the Indians among whom they consorted and with whom they fought.

Other groups inferior to the yeomen included tenant farmers, traveling artisans, and wage-earners such as dock hands, journeyman artisans, and farm hands. Possessing little or no property and not privileged to vote, such workers were doomed to a life of dependence unless they managed to save enough of their earnings to buy land or displayed force and ambition sufficient to gain them a place among the employing artisans. In the southern colonies skilled workers commonly gave up their trades and became farmers, due partly to the loss of time involved in traveling between remote plantations and partly to the absence of money, which compelled them to accept payment in heavy, bulky raw products which they could not conveniently transport, store, and exchange for consumer's articles. Another dependent group consisted of fur traders, sailors, and fishermen—all wage-earners without capital

[13] See again L. C. Gray, *History of Agriculture in the Southern United States*, Vol. I, chapters 16, 21–22.

who labored at dangerous and strenuous work which did not appeal to men of that cautious, prudential temperament which delights in saving, accumulation, and investment. The letdown after intense physical exertion in isolated and hazardous circumstances was often followed by periods of protracted idleness when such workers freely distributed their accumulated wages at taverns, over the gambling table, and in other dubious ways.[14]

The mode of living attained by the mass of the colonial farmers and workers gives a striking illustration of their place in society. In the first stage of settlement the colonists had to live in huts, caves, or tents. Soon they erected log houses or cabins—probably first constructed by the Swedes on the Delaware and afterward particularly characteristic of new settlements in the middle region and the South. Selecting a site near a stream or a fresh-water spring, the settler usually built upon high land a cabin which faced south. With the aid of his neighbors he erected a rectangular, one-story hut consisting of a kitchen and sleeping room, with a small attic above—a rude structure held together by joints and wooden pegs. A stone fireplace and chimney built within the cabin was the center of the household's activities; openings sawed in the log walls served as windows; a single door was swung on leather hinges; the ground sufficed at first as the cabin floor; and the roofing consisted of clapboards which resembled barrel staves. In the kitchen a ladder led to the attic, used as a storehouse, while an opening in the interior wall gave into the sleeping room, which, having neither windows nor fireplace, was ventilated by cracks in the wall. Two tiny windows in the kitchen were covered with paper made weatherproof with lard.

If a settler remained at his first clearing he worked several years at odd hours preparing materials for a permanent house—cutting, hewing, and squaring timbers, quarrying and dressing stone, splitting clapboards from logs, and making shingles by slicing chips from cedar blocks. Then in the spring, when the frost had left the ground, he dug the cellar, employed a local mason to lay the foundation, and put together the frames for the sides of the house. With all in readiness a call was sent to his neighbors and on an appointed day they gathered with their own tools, and, working under the direction of the mason, they lifted the frames into place on the foundation, made them fast with crossbeams, braces, floor joists, and rafters, and laid the flooring of oak plank. This completed the house-raising, which closed with a christening ceremony and a general celebration. Afterward the farmer laid the roof boards, pegged down the shingles, built the fireplace and nailed on

[14] Samuel McKee's *Labor in Colonial New York* (New York, 1935) contains the best short account of free labor.

the laths (dried split saplings) which he covered with plaster made of straw, clay, and lime. Whitewash applied to the plaster gave the only decorative effect; wainscoting, paint, varnish, and wallpaper were beyond the ordinary farmer's means.

The architectural designs of the houses varied, but like the interiors they were uniformly simple and plain. In the northern and middle colonies the most common type was a house two stories in front with a single pitched roof that sloped to one story in the rear. Downstairs a central hall separated five low-ceilinged rooms; the upstairs was divided lengthwise into two rooms. The principal room on the ground floor, the kitchen, was located on the the south side of the front; behind was a storeroom or workroom, while across the hall were three bedrooms. The room upstairs over the kitchen and workroom served as a bedchamber, the other room as an attic. A ladder in the kitchen gave access to the upper floor. Each room had at least one window (the kitchen usually had three); sliding shutters served as blinds.[15]

By far the most important as well as the largest room was the kitchen —parlor, living room, workshop, and dining room, scene of constant bustle and activity where the family toiled, ate, relaxed, and enjoyed life. Its furniture, chiefly homemade, was designed with two primary objects in mind—to be useful and to conserve space. Thus the table, consisting of boards laid on movable legs, could be lengthened into a dining table and then taken down when not in use, while a bed drawn up against the wall during the day could be lowered into the room at night. On one side of the table boards plates were formed by hollowed spaces so that dishwashing consisted of scrubbing the table top and the "dishes" could be put away by turning over the boards. Since the houses contained no closets clothes had to be stored in chests or hung on pegs in the rooms, and for chairs the family had to use blocks of wood, stools, benches, or remodeled barrels. A narrow cupboard housed such articles as wooden spoons and trenchers, iron forks, and leather, wood, or gourd cups, bowls, bottles, and dippers. About the fireplace stood the warming pan, flatirons, skillets, teapots, gridirons, and kettles. Some of the cooking utensils were fastened to legs so that they could be set into the fire; others were placed upon movable trivets. Above the fireplace was hung the trusty fowling piece, while the mantelpiece was graced with tinderbox, clock or hourglass, tobacco box, pipe tongs (to extract coals from the fire), and candlebox. Other objects within the kitchen included a flour bin, water barrel, candle molds, spinning wheel, mortars for

[15] The books of Alice M. Earle are popular, readable accounts. Among them see *Home Life in Colonial Days* (New York, 1913), and *Two Centuries of Costume in America* (2 vols., New York, 1903).

pounding mustard or corn, hanks of yarn or thread, and a Bible or Bible-box.

The bedrooms were exceptionally plain. Bedsteads (high enough that children's trundle beds could be rolled underneath and often made of cedar as a deterrent to pests) supported brown linen cases stuffed with straw and placed on a network of cords instead of springs. Furnished only with a chair or chest, generally devoid of curtains, rugs, dressers, mirrors, and wall ornaments, poorly lighted, unheated in winter, such bedrooms were dreary and cheerless in the extreme. On winter nights a warming pan was used to take the chill from the beds, but even so, the intense cold discouraged the retiring farmer from taking off more than his shoes and heavy outer garments.[16]

Three storerooms in the rural houses held the miscellaneous possessions of the family. In the downstairs workroom or tool shed the farmer kept his carpenter's tools, anvil, and loom, together with such articles as wool, seed, cordwood, feed, charcoal, and empty boxes and barrels. The attic contained the smokehouse and housed certain objects not in regular or current use—quilting frames, discarded furniture, old clothing and bedding. Entering the cellar by an outside sloping door, one found a single room with dirt floor, lighted only by narrow openings which were kept closed in the winter with dirt or manure, and pervaded by a dark, dank atmosphere. Here the farmer stored his reserve food supply. On shelves, away from rats and mice, were placed preserves, smoked hams, bacon, cheese, sausages, butter, and eggs, while the floor space was devoted to jars of pickles, boxes of apples, barrels of sauerkraut, heaps of potatoes, parsnips, and turnips, kegs or barrels of vinegar, cider, and ale, and jars of rum.

Few indeed were the conveniences of the rural household. Water had to be carried in from the outside unless the farmer was fortunate enough to live near a spring from which it could be conveyed by a trough to the kitchen water barrel, whence the overflow was taken off by a lower trough. The brackish water of creek and river was generally unfit to drink; hence the popularity of wine, cider, beer, rum, mead, and ale. "Early to bed" was sensible advice when houses were fitfully lighted by the glare of the fireplace, tallow candles, and ill-smelling, dismal lamps—shallow containers filled with tallow, lard, or grease into which a cotton rag wick was inserted through a projecting spout. In winter the kitchen was the only heated room and even there on cold days water froze a few yards from the fireplace. Since matches were unknown, great care was taken to preserve the fire, generally kindled by sparks

16 P. A. Bruce, *Social Life of Virginia in the Seventeenth Century* (Richmond, 1907), is a good brief survey of classes.

from stone on steel which ignited scorched linen used as tinder. Within the fireplace, about five feet from the floor, was placed a lug-pole from which hung kettles, spits, and other cooking utensils. A backlog of hickory (so huge that two men were needed to put it in place) and a smaller front log made a firebox that was filled with corn cobs or chips. At the side of the fireplace was placed the oven, in which, after a fire had been built and the coals removed, the accumulated heat did its baking work.

The sanitary arrangements of these rural homes left much to be desired. Floors were swept and then sanded. No screens protected the windows, so that the household was at the mercy of gnats, mosquitoes, and flies, while other pests disturbed the night's slumber. Lice in children's hair were treated with a solution of itch-weed and boiled water. Winter bathing was confined to the hands and face; in the summer the boys and men went swimming. Shaving was a luxury in which the men indulged only upon occasion. All in all, it was not an easy or effete way of life.[17]

In summer the clothing of the men consisted of long pantaloons, linen shirts, and cloth caps, sans shoes and stockings, while winter attire included home-knitted woolen stockings and mittens, coonskin caps, buckskin breeches and leggings, fur-lined overcoats, shirts of homespun tow cloth, and heavy work shoes. The women of the household had to be content with such garments as homespun dresses and petticoats of linen and wool, dyed in sober colors. Exposure to the weather and the kitchen fire gave a leathery, reddish complexion against which face powder would have been utterly ineffectual.

## Servants and Slaves

Indentured servants composed the largest dependent class during the seventeenth century. These were workers who served under a labor contract in return for their transportation to America. Some of these servants entered into agreements in England so that they knew in advance who their masters would be. Others—called redemptioners or free-willers—made bargains with ship captains or merchants which entitled the servant to find a master in the colonies who would pay the transportation costs; if the immigrant failed to do this, his services could be sold by the importer to the highest bidder. Ordinary indentured servants—the most numerous group—were auctioned to farmers or traders when the vessel arrived at a colonial port. Although thousands of immigrants came as voluntary servants, a considerable minority

[17] See again S. G. Fisher, *Men, Women, and Manners in Colonial Times*.

arrived through accident or force—convicts from prison who were sentenced to labor service in the colonies, vagrants or vagabonds who were seized by ship captains, and innocent people without social influence who were kidnaped by "spirits." After a stated term of employment the servant became a freedman privileged to go where he pleased. The common term of service in Maryland, Virginia, Pennsylvania, New Jersey, and Carolina was four years; in New England, about seven years. The prices paid by masters for such servants ranged between £10 and £20 sterling, depending upon the length of service. Of this about £5 represented the cost of transportation and the remainder went to the importer as profit. In case of voluntary agreements made in England either the servant, his family, or his creditors received the excess above the transportation charge.[18]

Employed chiefly as farm hands and domestic servants these workers composed the principal dependent labor force in English America prior to 1690. Between 1635 and 1705 the tobacco colonies imported between fifteen hundred and two thousand servants each year; in Virginia they composed 40 per cent of the population in 1625, while in 1683, when they numbered about twelve thousand, they represented 16 per cent of the whole. Of the people arriving in Maryland in the 1630's about 16 per cent came as indentured servants, whereas this class accounted for 36 per cent of the emigrants to Pennsylvania in the 1680's. Although the wealthier landowners of New England imported many servants, the niggardly soil of New England and the poverty of the mass of the farmers compelled them to depend upon the labor of their families and the assistance of their neighbors. "Our want of servants and help . . . in our harvest," wrote John Winthrop, Jr., of Connecticut in 1666, "is great, so that all hands are fully improved," while such an important man as Cotton Mather later made it "an article of special supplications before the Lord, that He would send a good servant." [19]

Each colony at a very early date devised a legal code to govern the indentured servants. Such acts required that masters should feed and clothe their servants and provide them with medical care, shelter, and certain "freedom dues" prescribed in their contracts. William Penn ordered in 1683 that "servants be not kept longer than their time, and [that] such as are careful be both justly and kindly used in their service, and put in fitting equipage at the expiration, according to custom." The

---

[18] Marcus W. Jernegan, *Laboring and Dependent Classes in Colonial America* (Chicago, n.d.), is a group of important, definitive essays. See pp. 45–56.
[19] A good brief discussion appears in chapter 3 of Lucy M. Salmon's *Domestic Service* (New York, 1901).

legal privileges of the servant included the right to sue his master for breach of contract, in which case a local magistrate might free the servant, reduce the time of servitude, or order that compensation be given to him by his master at the end of his term. Thus a Maryland act of 1715 imposed such penalties upon any master who failed to supply "sufficient meat, drink, lodging and clothing, or shall unreasonably burden servants beyond their strength, or debar them of their necessary rest or sleep, or excessively beat or abuse them, or shall give them more than ten lashes for any one offense." In Pennsylvania and the southern colonies the freedom dues included fifty acres of land granted either by the master or by the colony; in New England they consisted of tools, clothing, and livestock, or, in lieu of these, money payments varying from £2 to £5.[20]

In return for such benefits the servants were required to labor diligently and obediently at the behest of their masters and were forced to accept a legal status midway between that of minors and slaves. They could not buy liquor or frequent taverns, nor could they leave their master's premises without his consent, stay out late at night, or engage in buying and selling, lest they surreptitiously dispose of his property. Neither could they marry without his permission, and they might be transferred by sale or bequest from one master to another. New Haven Colony in 1656 imposed fines upon any persons who "shall harbor or entertain any such servants in the night, . . . or shall suffer them disorderly . . . or to play at shovel-board or other . . . games, to drink, spend money or provisions, or shall . . . suffer any sinful carriage, conference, counsel or songs." Since the servants did not possess property they could not be required to pay fines, and they could not be imprisoned without injuring the master. Accordingly they were punished in two ways: by whipping and by requiring that they serve additional time beyond the terms of their indentures. When a court fine was assessed against a servant it was paid by the master who compensated himself by exacting additional service.[21]

What treatment the servants received depended upon the disposition of their masters, although it is safe to assume that most of them endured a pretty hard lot. Not only was the work performed inherently strenuous and virtually without end; the master who could command the labor of the servant only a few years had no material interest in him save that of obtaining the maximum service within a short time. In this

[20] M. W. Jernegan, "Forgotten Slavery of Colonial Days," *Harper's Magazine*, CXXVII (Oct. 1913).

[21] James C. Ballagh, *White Servitude in the Colony of Virginia* (Baltimore, 1895), is a pioneer work, not superseded.

respect, servitude wore a harsher aspect than chattel slavery: the owner of a slave would at least conserve his personal property. The legal right of the master to whip the servant often placed excessive power in irresponsible hands; in extreme cases masters were accused of whipping servants to death. One observer said of Maryland servants that "they groan beneath a worse than Egyptian bondage," while a versifier attributed these sentiments to a servant in 1708:

> In better times, e'er to this land
> I was unhappily trapanned
> Perchance as well I did appear
> As any lord or lady here. . . .
> But things are changed, now at the hoe,
> I daily work and barefoot go,
> In weeding corn or feeding swine,
> I spend my melancholy time.
> Kidnaped and fooled, I thither fled . . .
> And to my cost already find
> Worse plagues than those I left behind.

Such dissatisfaction explains the ease with which the servants succumb to the temptation to run away—a practice so common that the legislatures provided stringent penalties. An apprehended fugitive was required to serve several additional days without pay for every day that he was absent without leave. Moreover, the colonies had their fugitive servant laws which enjoined the local officers to pursue the escaped servants and authorized them, at public expense, to requisition boats for the pursuit. Similarly, rewards were granted to captors and heavy fines assessed against persons who knowingly assisted a fugitive in any way.[22]

Undoubtedly the blame in the servant question was not always wholly attributable to the masters. The servant class included many convicts, idlers, and ne'er-do-wells whose aversion to work was prodigious, as well as many who were "stubborn, refractory and discontented" and those who "withdrew themselves from their master's service to improve their time to their own advantage." A particularly grave problem arose from the relations between white servants and the Negro slaves; nearly all the colonial legislatures had to prohibit the marriage of such workers. In this connection, however, some masters were culpable. A Maryland act of 1664 provided that, if a servant woman married a slave, the children should belong to the master, but this act had to be repealed because unscrupulous masters encouraged

[22] An able, compact study is Karl F. Geiser, *Redemptioners and Indentured Servants in . . . Pennsylvania* (New Haven, c. 1901).

such marriages. Expenditures which the parishes in Virginia made for the care of illegitimate mulatto children give further light on the character of one element in the servant class.[23]

In spite of such undesirables a large majority of the servants were industrious and reliable workers who, when free, became independent artisans and farmers. During the seventeenth century a hundred thousand persons passed through the servant class of the tobacco colonies into the ranks of freemen. An observer in New England, about 1650, noted that "there are many hundreds of laboring men who had not enough to bring them over, yet are now worth scores, and some hundreds of pounds." Of Maryland servants a writer said in 1666 that they are no sooner free "but they are ready to set up for themselves, and when once entered live surprisingly well." Probably a majority of the small farmers of the middle and southern colonies rose from the servant class. Entitled to vote and to hold office, such emancipated yeomen formed the main current of the democratic movement in the colonies. In 1663, the Virginia House of Burgesses included thirteen members (43 per cent of the total) who had come to the colony as indentured servants.[24]

An important group in the servant class consisted of boys and girls who were bound to work for a master until they became of age. A large number of such minors were sent under contract from England and sold for sums varying from £5 to £10. Likewise many poor children or orphans in the colonies were assigned to masters—only, however, with the consent of parents, guardians, or magistrates. When a master took charge of a poor child he ordinarily did not make a payment; he merely promised to provide a home for the child in return for such labor as the child could perform. In one case, however, a New Haven master offered to give a cow to a poor widow in exchange for her son. Legally indentured children occupied the same position as an adult servant; their masters might transfer them to other employers and they were subject to strict discipline. A refractory servant boy was told by the New Haven town magistrates in 1661 that since he "stood bound to do faithful service" he was "not upon every dislike to run away" and was reminded "how he had carried stubbornly, stoutly and rebelliously,"—"which were carriages not to be borne." "After which he was committed to prison." On the other hand, fines were imposed upon masters who failed to give proper care to their servants of tender

[23] E. I. McCormac, *White Servitude in Maryland* (Baltimore, 1904), is an outstanding study of colonial labor.

[24] Cheesman A. Herrick, *White Servitude in Pennsylvania* (Philadelphia, 1926), is thorough, comprehensive, reliable. See also J. S. Bassett, *Slavery and Servitude in North Carolina* (Baltimore, 1896).

years. At the age of twenty-one the servant gained his freedom and received two suits of clothing and often a small sum of money. If he had inherited any estate he received that also from his guardian-master.[25]

Distinct from the children serving as indentured servants (who worked at all sorts of tasks about the household and the farm) were apprentices bound to an artisan on condition that he support them and give instruction in reading, writing, accounting, and the secrets of his trade. As a rule such indentures required that the parents of the boy pay to the master an advance sum of between £2 and £6; hence the apprentices were socially a step higher than ordinary servants—children of artisans or farmers of some means. Quite commonly an artisan trained one of his sons in his own trade and apprenticed the others to workers in other lines. The terms of service varied usually from one to eight years in New England and the middle colonies, where apprenticeship was more common than in the South. If the master died or failed to give the intended instruction the apprentice would be transferred to another artisan in the same trade. Freedom dues consisted of apparel and money. In one case a master was to pay £4 if he had taught the apprentice a trade and £10 if he had not. Coopers, carpenters, merchants, ship captains, tailors, blacksmiths, and shipwrights were the chief employers of apprentices. When free the latter customarily served at first as traveling artisans or journeyman employees of settled craftsmen.

By accustoming employers to the complete though temporary control of their workers, bonded servitude prepared the way for the introduction and spread of actual slavery.[26] Perhaps the first Negroes brought to Virginia in 1619 were sold as servants; at any rate, slavery took root soon afterward. The institution, however, was not an invention of the colonists; from time out of mind natives in Africa had been held as slaves—captives taken in war or evildoers punished for their crimes. It was not unnatural, therefore, that when European traders appeared in Africa the native chiefs should have exchanged their slaves and other property for European goods. With the growth of the traffic the Portuguese and later the Dutch and English established trading posts or garrisons along the slave coast to which traders periodically brought hordes of slaves who were bound together by leather thongs and marched overland, single-file, to be exchanged for cloth, ironware, rum, and trinkets. At the garrisons the European traders refused to buy

[25] Alice M. Earle's *Child Life in Colonial Days* (New York, 1909) is brief and interesting.
[26] See again U. B. Phillips, *American Negro Slavery*, chapters 1–4, 6.

any Negroes who were old or sick; such were left on the coast to die as the vessel departed with its strange cargo. After the slaves had been branded and placed in chains they were packed in a space between the decks so low that they were unable to stand. Overcrowding on shipboard and exposure to tropical heat and disease took a heavy toll of these unwilling passengers, for it was cheaper to let many of them die than to provide decent accommodations for all.[27]

During the seventeenth century the slaves were first landed at the West Indies and there seasoned before they were sold to mainland colonies. This required about three years, during which the novices were placed in the company of experienced hands and cared for by an old slave skilled in the art of nursing. So severe was the change from native to European ways that about half of the Negroes died within three or four years after their removal from Africa. On the other hand, the psychological adjustment to plantation life was not difficult: the Negroes had been accustomed to a tribal system in which the authority of the chief resembled that of the plantation owner. Generally, they were healthier on the North American continent than in the islands, due largely to better food and fewer disease-breeding insects. Adjustment was further facilitated by the selection of young Negroes who evinced a pliant disposition. Since they came from different tribes and spoke different dialects they were obliged to learn English in order to converse among themselves. By and large they proved to be highly cheerful and adaptable people who readily adjusted themselves to a new life. One writer remarked that "their juvenile minds entertain no regrets for the loss of their connections. They acquire the English language with great ease, and improve daily in size, understanding and capacity for labor."

In 1700, when the Negroes in the mainland settlements numbered between twenty and twenty-five thousand, they accounted for less than a tenth of the inhabitants, although they were to be found in nearly all the colonies. They were brought into New Netherland by the Dutch West India Company—one of the leading slave trafficking agencies of its time. Virginia's slave population rose from 2,000 in 1671 to 4,000 in 1690, while South Carolina's in 1708 was 4,100. Although the New England Puritans had few moral scruples against slavery they found it unsuited to their region. Their small diversified farms called for a servant who could perform a variety of operations and who would work effectively without close supervision, whereas the Negroes were profitable only in regions where they could labor in gangs at a common

[27] See the introduction to Vol. I of the monumental *Documents Illustrative of the History of the Slave Trade* (ed. Elizabeth Donnan, 4 vols., Washington, 1930–35).

task, and in climates that did not require expensive winter clothing and housing. Nor did the industries of New England suit the Negro. Navigation and shipbuilding were trades too specialized for his skills, while fishing exposed him to rigors of winter too severe for his constitution. In 1680 there were only about two hundred slaves in New England, of whom twenty were owned in Connecticut and 120 in Massachusetts—most of them being employed in domestic service.[28]

Even among the slaves in the plantation area a tendency toward social differentiation soon appeared. Those who worked about the household partook somewhat of the honor and dignity of the master, to whom they had especially commended themselves and with whom they were in close contact. Attendance upon the planter's family required that such domestics should conform to its standards of decorum and appear in decent attire. On the larger plantations some of the most intelligent slaves were trained as artisans, and their special skills made them more highly esteemed than the ordinary field hands, the group at the very bottom of the social scale. The crude huts in which the field hands lived, their diet of corn and salt pork, and their cheap clothing —linsey-woolsey pantaloons and shirts—all proclaimed the inferior status of their class.[29]

As a species of private property the slaves of course enjoyed no legal or political rights. In New England they were not allowed to buy liquor or to sell any property; if they struck a white person or stayed out-of-doors at night they were severely whipped. Their unhappy position is well indicated by an act passed by the humanitarian Quakers of Pennsylvania in 1693 which authorized any persons "to take up Negroes, male or female, whom they shall find gadding abroad on the first days of the week without a ticket from their master or mistress . . . [and] to take them to jail, there to remain that night, and that without meat or drink, and to cause them to be publicly whipped next morning with 39 lashes, well laid on their bare backs, at which their said master or mistress shall pay 15d. to the whipper." [30]

In three notable respects the social order of the colonies differed from that of Europe—a divergence explained largely by the influence of the American environment. First, the colonies did not produce a class of serfs bound to the soil or a titled, hereditary nobility dependent

---

[28] Carter G. Woodson's *The Negro in Our History* (Washington, c. 1922) is a reliable factual survey. See chapters 1–2.

[29] Jeffrey D. Brackett, *The Negro in Maryland* (Baltimore, 1889)—for advanced students.

[30] Edward Raymond Turner, *The Negro in Pennsylvania* (Washington, 1911), is an exceptionally good study. See chapters 1–4.

upon such a class. Secondly, Negro slavery, especially in the plantation area, became a peculiarly American institution. And finally, while social classes existed in the colonies, each individual was not permanently placed at one level. It was relatively easy for a servant to become a small landowner or independent artisan, although very difficult for the latter to enter the ranks of the upper class. Excepting the fixed status of slaves, the flexibility of colonial society was its distinguishing feature.[31] And yet the notion of class distinctions was firmly imbedded in the colonial mind. An act of Massachusetts in 1650 states: "We declare our utter detestation and dislike that men and women of mean condition should take upon themselves the garb of gentlemen, by wearing gold or silver lace or buttons, or points at their knees, or to walk in boots, or women of the same rank to wear silk or tiffany . . . scarfs, which though allowable to persons of greater estates, or more liberal education, yet we cannot but judge it intolerable in persons in such like condition."

This act epitomizes social trends in the colonies. It reveals the class consciousness of the leaders in control and manifests their desire to keep their inferiors in their places. Class lines in New England were also indicated by the forms of address in vogue. Some of the titles denoting good repute were: "esquire" or "gentleman" for wealthy landowners and merchants who had belonged to the English upper middle class; "master" for clergymen who possessed the degree of master of arts; "mister" for professional people and substantial landowners and merchants (about one man in fourteen was addressed as Mr.); and "goodman" for ordinary yeoman farmers. Such military titles as captain and ensign also signified an honorable station. Indentured servants, tenants, and wage-earners were unceremoniously called by their family or given names. Church pews were assigned on the basis of social status, while the names on the student register at Harvard College were listed, not alphabetically, but according to family rank.

The Massachusetts act of 1650 further reveals that the standards of social decorum of the colonial upper class stemmed from the aristocracy of England. It also exposes the social aspirations of many of the lesser folk—their desire to emulate the upper class—and it indicates that the American environment was enabling them to improve their external condition and appearance. That the act of 1650 was powerless to check the determination of the people to attain a higher standard of living appears in a comment on Boston in 1720: "The tradesmen or

[31] Two specialized studies for the advanced student are Edward McCrady, "Slavery in . . . South Carolina, 1670-1770," *Report*, American Historical Association, 1895; and Henry S. Cooley, *A Study of Slavery in New Jersey* (Baltimore, 1896).

mechanical part, they are very ambitious of appearing above themselves, and will not be seen in anything beneath the merchant or more substantial, which is the produce of Europe." The tendency of the times was not to abolish class distinctions but for the individual to strive to rise in the social scale.

## BIBLIOGRAPHICAL NOTE

WORKS PREVIOUSLY CITED: C. M. Andrews, *Colonial Self-Government*, ch. 18; H. J. Carman, *Social and Economic History of the United States*, I, pp. 83–103; E. Channing, *History of the United States*, I, pp. 367–400; J. Fiske, *Dutch and Quaker Colonies*, II, ch. 15 (New York); J. Fiske, *Old Virginia and Her Neighbors*, II, ch. 14; A. Johnson, *Swedish Settlements on the Delaware*, I, ch. 33; M. Stanard, *Virginia's First Century*, ch. 14.

SOURCES: Bartlett B. James and J. F. Jameson (eds.), *Journal of Jasper Danckaerts* (Jameson *Original Narratives* series, New York, 1913), is replete with observations on social life in 1679–80.

# XIII

## SOCIAL CONFLICTS

DESPITE the diversity and fluidity of early colonial society two dominant classes emerged during the seventeenth century—the aristocracy of wealthy landowners and merchants and the democracy of the small yeoman farmers. And in spite of the ideals of individual improvement entertained by members of the latter class they were not averse to united action in their struggle for social betterment. At many points, however, the democracy found the way to advancement blocked by the influence of the upper class. In consequence there ensued a series of social conflicts between the hostile forces—conflicts common to all the colonies because the underlying causes were present throughout the whole settled area. Assuming various forms of expression and flaring up intermittently in different localities, these conflicts exhibited one major issue: who should control the land and the products it yielded to the labor of the settlers?

With the growth of settlement along most of the seacoast there appeared a uniform tendency for a small group of wealthy men to acquire large landholdings worked by servants, tenants, or slaves. The temporary efficiency of larger producing units gradually forced the smaller farmers in the oldest areas to fall behind in the competitive struggle. If they sold their farms to the landed magnates or lost them through foreclosure proceedings, the trend toward larger holdings was accelerated. In the interior, however, lay vast stretches of virgin land to which the dispossessed farmers or the propertyless freedmen might repair for a new start. But even here they did not escape the influence of the magnates. The property and enterprise of men of wealth in the seaboard areas yielded increasing profits which demanded fresh fields of investment—and one such outlet was found in the financing of settlers in new areas.

Due to the cheapness of land it was usually easy for the poor freedman to acquire fifty acres of back country, but he generally lacked tools, seed, and livestock, and these he was obliged to purchase on credit. Two kinds of loans were available. The wealthy planters engaged in lending money on fairly long terms, while the merchants of the seacoast supplied imported goods on short-term credit. Now, one peculiar characteristic of the early land system in the colonies was the freedom with which land might be transferred—sold, bequeathed, divided, or taken in payment of every species of debt. Hence the colonial creditors, both merchants and planters, could safely give credit on land security, knowing that the improvements made by the farmer would augment its value and thus provide an increasingly ample guarantee to creditors, should it be necessary for them to foreclose in order to collect existing debts.

In this situation the farmer often found himself at a disadvantage. His debts, which were registered at a fixed sum in pounds, shillings, and pence, had to be paid in farm produce, which was valued at its current market price whenever payments were made. Thus if the price of such produce declined abruptly the farmer might have to deliver all his surplus to his creditor in order to discharge his debts. When this occurred in his dealings with a merchant, the farmer would be obliged to seek a new loan for the purchase of the year's supply of store goods and depend upon the next crop to pay the obligation. This meant that he again had to deliver his surplus produce to his creditor—a circumstance which placed him at a further disadvantage in that he had only one marketing outlet: his creditor was not forced to bid against competitive buyers; hence the complaint of low prices of farm products that were delivered to creditors. And when the farmer became hopelessly involved in debt he might lose his land by foreclosure, thus adding to the holdings of the wealthy class and extending into new areas the trend toward concentrated ownership. In this manner the farmer came to feel that the wealthy merchants and planters were his enemies in a contest for land titles and in a struggle over the prices of farm produce and laws affecting currency and debts.

A second series of social conflicts involved the colonial aristocracy in controversies with groups in England. Just as the colonial merchants became competitors of English merchants, so also the landed aristocracy opposed both the English laws which regulated trade and the claims of the proprietors of Maryland, Pennsylvania, and the Carolinas who held the immediate title to lands desired by the colonial magnates. Since the English merchants and the great proprietors generally had the support of the English government, the colonial aristocracy was impelled to resist imperial control. In the ensuing strife the planters could count upon the aid of the small farmers, who also opposed England's trade regulations, who also disliked to pay quit-rents to the proprietors, and who also desired to acquire proprietary lands. On the other hand, in their conflicts with the small farmers as debtors, the planters and merchants received the support of the English government, always a staunch defender of creditor rights. The strategy of the colonial aristocracy, therefore, was to use the yeoman farmers in opposition to English merchants and proprietors and to depend upon the English government for protection against measures demanded by the yeomen for their relief as a debtor class.

## CLEAVAGE IN VIRGINIA

Of all the early conflicts between the small farmers and the upper class the most critical contest occurred in Virginia in 1675–76, by which time the social stratification of the colony had become well marked. The planter class had evolved in response to many circumstances. During the Civil War and the Puritan regime in England many moderately well-to-do partisans of Charles I had migrated to Virginia. Although they were called Cavaliers they were not aristocrats but, rather, substantial members of the English middle class. They invested their money chiefly in tobacco lands and in the fur trade—and at an auspicious time. During the years 1640–60 Virginia enjoyed the benefit of free trade with foreign countries and prospered through relatively high prices of tobacco and furs. Such prosperity prompted the Dutch merchants to extend credit to the planters whereby they might purchase additional lands and servants. Two results followed. The most successful planters enlarged their landholdings in the tidewater area while at the same time a large host of workers completed their terms of servitude and became freedmen. From the profits of tobacco and the fur trade the planters were able to make loans to such freedmen when they acquired small farms on the frontiers.[1]

As a result of the Navigation Acts of 1660 and 1663 and the forcible exclusion of Dutch merchants from the tobacco trade an acute depression fell upon Virginia after 1660, when the planters were required to ship their products directly to England and to depend solely upon English shipping, which was not yet sufficient for their needs. One critic of England's policy wrote: "If the Hollanders must not trade to Virginia how shall the planters dispose of their tobacco? The English will not buy it, for what the Hollander carried thence was a sort of tobacco, not desired by any other people. . . . The tobacco will not vend in England, the Hollanders will not fetch it from England; what must become thereof?" Moreover, the Second Anglo-Dutch War dealt a severe blow to Virginia's trade: in 1667 Dutch warships in Chesapeake Bay captured twenty vessels of the English tobacco fleet. Reduced

[1] T. J. Wertenbaker, *Virginia under the Stuarts*, chapters 5–8, is the best discussion of Bacon's Rebellion.

shipping and wartime risks boosted freight rates from the normal figure of £7 a ton of tobacco to charges ranging from £12 to £17 a ton—and this added cost had to be paid indirectly from the planters' profits. As markets contracted, the price of tobacco in the colony fell to a half-penny a pound—a return that did not yield the cost of production to the interior farmers. The secretary of the province in 1667 estimated the yearly income from the crop of the average settler as only fifty shillings—"which, when the taxes . . . shall be deducted, is very little to a poor man who hath perhaps a wife and children to clothe and other necessities to buy." Everywhere the shortage of imported goods was so extreme that observers spoke hyperbolically of "the nakedness of the country."

A brief respite followed the Second Dutch War, only to be suc-ceeded by another spell of hard times during the Third Dutch War of 1672–74. In the winter of 1672–73 an epidemic carried off half the cattle of Virginia—a loss of fifty thousand head before the spring brought relief. Once more the Dutch attacked the English tobacco fleet in the Chesapeake and in 1673 captured nine ships at the mouth of the James River. Vessels coming from England were so few that they brought goods and tools sufficient for only one planter in five; tobacco prices fell to a quarter of what they had been in "normal" times; and the colony seemed filled with "indigent persons who could barely sup-port themselves with their utmost exertions." [2]

This protracted depression further strengthened the wealthy plant-ers at the expense of the poor farmers. As it became necessary to cut the cost of production the planter who had large landholdings and ample credit in England could buy additional servants or slaves, en-large the scale of his business and reduce the unit cost of production. Menaced by the competition of the larger plantations (which enjoyed another advantage in their superior location for trade), the poor farmer found himself relentlessly squeezed by the necessity of paying fixed debts from sadly depleted income. "The poverty of the country," said Nathaniel Bacon in 1675, "is such that all the power and sway is got into the hands of the rich, who by extortious advantages, having the common people in their debt, have always curbed and oppressed them in all manner of ways."

The desperation of the small farmers led them to demand relief. But the peaceable channels of political action were closed, since the government of Virginia was completely in control of the upper class. The governor, Sir William Berkeley—an inflexible aristocrat, irascible, imperious, and arbitrary—was determined to rule the "rabble" with a

[2] See again P. A. Bruce, *The Virginia Plutarch*, Vol. I, chapters 6–7.

firm hand, convinced that toil, ignorance, and subservience were the proper attributes of the common people. The large planters and merchants, allied with Berkeley, held all the offices in his executive council, which they used to secure personal land grants and to exempt themselves from taxes. Even the House of Burgesses, supposed to represent all the freemen, had become a satellite of the aristocracy. It is probable that between 1661 and 1676 no election of members of the lower house had been held, and it is certain that there was not more than one election, so that the burgesses serving in 1676 were ten or fifteen years removed from a popular mandate. A majority of them had become mere henchmen of the governor, who had secured their compliance by virtue of his power to grant land and to appoint revenue collectors, sheriffs, and officers of the county militia. Accordingly, all agencies of local government, both executive and judicial, were completely dominated by the governor's party. In 1670 the aristocracy enacted a law which denied the ballot to every resident who was not a freeholder.[3]

Similarly the financial system of the colony was honeycombed with favoritism and privilege. Since 1619 the principal revenues for the support of government had been derived from poll taxes levied upon freemen, servants, and slaves. Although the large planters had to pay the taxes for their servants and slaves, the small farmers considered the poll levy unjust and preferred instead a land tax, since the inequalities in land ownership were much more marked than differences in tax payments determined on the poll basis. Moreover, land taxes would have prevented the engrossing of large estates by the planters for speculative purposes and would therefore have opened such holdings to the poorer settlers—a consideration which induced the aristocracy to support the poll tax at all costs. Another grievance of the small farmers grew out of the power of the justices of the peace (representatives of the aristocracy) to impose direct levies without any semblance of the consent of the taxpayers. Moreover, the justices, meeting every second month, composed the county courts, which decided all cases involving less than £10 sterling; hence the poor farmers felt that in disputes with the aristocracy the county courts were merely its champions. Finally, the yeomen charged that the governor's party used public funds to line the pockets of its members and sycophants, so that the colony derived little benefit from taxes levied for fortifications, the construction of buildings at Jamestown, and the encouragement of domestic manufactures.[4]

[3] See again J. Fiske, *Old Virginia and Her Neighbors*, Vol. II, chapters 11–13.
[4] See again Mary Johnston, *Pioneers of the Old South*, chapters 12–13.

When to the other woes of the interior farmers was added the distress of a destructive Indian war their plight became unbearable. In 1675 a raid of the Senecas from the north drove into western Virginia a band of Susquehannocks, who upset the existing balance between settler and Indian on the frontier. Preliminary quarrels and skirmishes in the summer of 1675 finally evoked a general massacre which cost the lives of more settlers than any Indian outbreak of the preceding fifty years. When the farmers appealed to the governor for aid they met a disappointing response. Berkeley and his friends at the time had a virtual monopoly of the western fur trade which they were loath to endanger by harsh measures against the Indians, while their practice of equipping the red men with powder, guns, and shot had been responsible for much of the bloodshed of the frontier war. In January 1676 Berkeley did assemble a military force, only to disband it when he feared that disaffected farmers, once armed, might turn upon the government. Thereafter he favored defensive measures, particularly the building of forts at the falls of the main rivers. This policy did not appease the harassed frontiersmen, who favored vigorous offensive raids into the Indian country and charged that the forts "were a design of the grandees to engross all their [the settlers'] tobacco in their own hands." Meanwhile the governor even refused to issue to frontier officers commissions authorizing them to wage, independently, an offensive war.[5]

Such was the setting when Nathaniel Bacon, a young Englishman who had lived in the colony less than two years, assumed the leadership of the disaffected farmers. As a member of the governor's council Bacon had become contemptuous of Berkeley's defense policy, particularly after the Indians had attacked Bacon's own frontier plantation in Henrico County and killed its overseer. His independent spirit prompted him to organize a force of volunteer frontiersmen and to lead them in vigorous attacks upon the Indians. Berkeley declined to grant him a military commission and proclaimed him a rebel when he refused to disband his men. His followers were described by one of the Virginia aristocrats as "a rabble of the basest sort of people, whose condition was such as by a change could not admit of worse."

Bacon's successful exploits on the frontier made him such a power among the small farmers that Berkeley was obliged to yield concessions, and at last he ordered a new election of burgesses. The free-

---

[5] William E. Dodd has published the first volume of his projected four-volume work, *The Old South*, under the title *Struggles for Democracy* (New York, 1937). This book, written in a liberal spirit and in a leisurely, familiar manner, is the fruit of a long and penetrating inquiry into Southern history.

holders of Bacon's county sent him to Jamestown as their representative. There, however, he failed to obtain his desired commission, nor could he persuade the governor to reverse his frontier policy. Thor-

oughly exasperated, he finally used force to terrorize the council and to extract a commission from Berkeley. Then, when the insurrectionists had been called away to the frontier by new Indian raids, the governor raised a counter-revolutionary army, whereupon Bacon returned posthaste to Jamestown. Berkeley fled to the eastern shore as Bacon took charge of the government (styling himself "general by the consent of the people") and prepared to resist some royal troops which were presumably on the way to Virginia from England in response to Berkeley's hurried call for aid.[6]

While in control of Jamestown the insurrectionists burned the town, Bacon himself setting fire to the Anglican church. Then in October he died, a victim of fever, and his leaderless following (which now included many runaway servants and slaves) became a disorganized, plundering mob. Berkeley returned from Accomac, rallied the eastern planters, suppressed the revolt, and exacted a terrible vengeance by hanging a score of insurrectionists and decreeing the confiscation of many estates. While this liquidation of the rebels was in progress three commissioners arrived from England with eleven hundred troops. Sent by Charles II to suppress the revolt and to examine into its causes these commissioners were soon at odds with Berkeley, who treated them with the utmost contempt and opposed them in every possible way. Their condemnation of his proceedings finally compelled him to return to England, where he encountered icy reproaches from the Lords of Trade and the displeasure of the king. He died in July 1677, a discredited and broken man. Of his tyranny Charles II is supposed to have said: "That old fool has hanged more men in that naked country than I have for the murder of my father."

Two gains for the yeomanry issued from the rebellion—the dismissal of Berkeley and the negotiation of a treaty with the Indians which restored peace to the frontiers. Otherwise the fundamental institutions of the colony remained intact. There was no change in the personnel and power of the council nor in the privileged status of the aristocracy with respect to landholdings, taxation, credit relations, and local government. The bitter experience of the planters may have antagonized them toward indentured servants and freedmen, may have caused them to depend increasingly upon Negro slaves; at any rate the progress of slavery after 1680 deepened the gulf between rich and poor. Meanwhile the English government did not champion the cause of the "underdog"; instead it insisted that the right to vote be limited to freeholders and attempted, unsuccessfully, to deny to the House of Burgesses the privilege of initiating legislative measures. Nor did England relax the trade and navigation laws which had contributed so materially to the colony's distress.

Continued dissatisfaction and agitation among the small farmers during the 1680's plainly indicated that the causes of popular dis-

---

[6] *The Story of Bacon's Rebellion*, by Mary N. Stanard (New York, 1907), is a brief account.

content had not been removed. Three unsatisfactory governors served after Berkeley—Sir Henry Chicheley, old, infirm, and "superannuated"; Lord Culpeper, a spoilsman who used his office to enhance his private fortune; and Lord Howard of Effingham, a petty autocrat who mirrored the conceptions of absolute power held by his royal master, James II. The attempt of England to assert her authority over the colony resulted in a government not much more satisfactory than that of Berkeley and his clique. Disaffected groups, however, had been so thoroughly defeated in Bacon's Rebellion that no uprising in Virginia accompanied the Revolution of 1688 in England, although the news of the accession of William and Mary was received with "unfeigned joy and exaltation." [7]

## Conflicts in the Proprietary Colonies

In seventeenth-century Maryland the upper class consisted of the friends, relatives, and agents of the proprietor, Lord Baltimore, who regarded and administered the colony as his personal estate. As the owner of all ungranted land, as the possessor of several private plantations, and as the receiver of quit-rents paid by all the settlers, the proprietor occupied a commanding position. Upon his relatives and friends he bestowed landed estates, offices, and revenues, thereby dominating the executive, judicial, and military branches of the government. Opposed to the Calvert party were the independent landowners, both large and small, who tended to act in unison against the proprietor. As the owner of ungranted lands desired by the settlers and as the recipient of their quit-rent payments he was more or less their natural enemy. Since they acted through the elected House of Delegates it became imperative for him to hold it in check—a purpose which he accomplished by bribing its members, by limiting each county to two representatives, by vetoing its laws, and by restricting the suffrage (in 1670) to freeholders or owners of personal property worth £40. The staunch Catholicism of the proprietor also set him apart from the majority of his Protestant and Puritan settlers. Among the landowners who did not belong to the proprietary party the cleavage between rich and poor was not so marked as in Virginia— chiefly because of the greater difficulty in securing extensive land grants in Maryland. Not only was the colony much smaller than Virginia; more important was the fact that the land belonged to one man who made grants sparingly, with an eye to his future income, whereas in Virginia the unoccupied land, owned by the king, was

[7] See again Mary Stanard, *Virginia's First Century*, chapters 22–23.

granted by governors who derived no personal advantage by conserving the royal domain but rather profited through generous grants to individuals who could contribute something to the governor's personal fortune. On the whole the royal governors were much more liberal dispensers of the king's acres than were the proprietors in disposing of their lands. Similarly the quit-rents exacted by Lord Baltimore were nominally high: 4s. a hundred acres as against 2s. in Virginia.[8]

Between 1660 and 1689 five revolts against the proprietor occurred in Maryland. The first (which dominated the colony's history between 1652 and 1657) was engineered by Puritan settlers who had come from Virginia after 1644 to escape religious persecution at the hands of Governor Berkeley. In Maryland, however, these Puritans had little cause of complaint since they enjoyed religious toleration, and since Lord Baltimore submissively acknowledged the Puritan rule of Cromwell in England. But the Puritan colonists, familiar with New England land tenure of fee simple ownership, looked askance upon quit-rents exacted by a proprietary overlord—especially one who was a Roman Catholic. In 1654–55 the Puritans deposed Lord Baltimore's governor, seized control of the colony, defeated a proprietary force sent to subdue them, and erected an independent government. The revolt ended with an agreement in November 1657 which restored Baltimore's authority, guaranteed religious toleration to the Puritans and promised that their land titles would be respected. In the crisis Baltimore had been able to secure the support of the London merchants who desired to terminate all strife in the colonies which was destructive of trade.[9]

A second outbreak in 1660 led by one Josias Fendall, then acting governor for Baltimore, threatened to destroy the proprietary government and to establish a republic to be ruled by the elected house. But when Charles II came to the throne Baltimore recognized him as eagerly as he had submitted to Cromwell and in consequence obtained royal orders which denounced Fendall's revolt and directed the Marylanders to acknowledge the proprietor's rights. Again the revolt collapsed, and during the next fifteen years Lord Baltimore reëstablished a firm grip on his province.

The third revolt, in 1676, which was inspired by Bacon's Rebellion, involved only a handful of malcontents and was speedily suppressed

[8] See again C. M. Andrews, *The Colonial Period of American History*, Vol. II, chapters 8–9.

[9] On these conflicts see John H. Latané, *The Early Relations between Maryland and Virginia* (Baltimore, 1895), and B. C. Steiner, *Maryland under the Commonwealth* (Baltimore, 1911).

by an energetic governor who arrested and executed the leaders. Next occurred an outbreak in 1681, engineered by Fendall and another conspirator, John Coode. Once more the proprietary party acted with decision and quelled the revolt by arresting the leaders. Fendall was now fined forty thousand pounds of tobacco and expelled from the province.

Such revolts were significant because they indicated widespread discontent with the proprietary regime. For several reasons the out breaks had been suppressed with comparative ease: because the proprietor had the backing of the English government, because the division of the colony by Chesapeake Bay into two parts made united action difficult, and because the distress of the farmers was not sufficiently acute to drive them to extremes. The colony had not suffered from an Indian war as had Virginia before Bacon's Rebellion, nor had Lord Baltimore favored the fur traders at the expense of the farmers. Although the quit-rents remained in force, they were payable, after 1671, in tobacco, which was arbitrarily valued for this purpose at 2d. a pound, irrespective of its market price, so that tobacco worth only ½d. a pound would pay a quit-rent of 2d. But in spite of these advantages the Maryland farmers suffered acute distress during the depression of 1664–76, and their poverty made them restless under an overlord who benefited at their expense. Their early revolts demonstrated that they would seize the first opportunity given by events in England to repudiate Lord Baltimore's rule.[10]

Thus when the Marylanders learned of the expulsion of James II from England and when Baltimore (through accidental circumstances) failed to proclaim William III as the new sovereign, they organized a Protestant association with John Coode in command, and in July 1689 seized possession of St. Mary's, the provincial capital. The revolutionary party, now including both the wealthier planters and the small farmers, erected a temporary government in place of the proprietary regime. Then in 1691 England took the colony under her wing and appointed a royal governor. Baltimore retained his position as landlord but not until 1716 did he recover his right to govern the colony, so that Maryland functioned during twenty-five years as a royal province.[11]

The early history of South Carolina also exhibits a bitter conflict between the proprietors and the settlers—a conflict which grew out

[10] Francis E. Sparks, *Causes of the Maryland Revolution of 1689* (Baltimore, 1896), is the most complete account.

[11] B. C. Steiner, "The Protestant Revolution in Maryland," *Report*, American Historical Association, 1898, is excellent.

of the efforts of the former to dominate the government and the economic life of the colony to the detriment of the latter. In 1669 John Locke prepared for the proprietors his famous "Fundamental Constitutions of Carolina," which embodied in particular Lord Ashley's ideas of an aristocratic society. This design for a planned economy proposed to fasten upon the American wilderness a nobility consisting of landgraves and caciques—German and Indian titles respectively, since the charter prohibited the use of English titles in Carolina. The colony was to be divided into counties, each of which was to consist of eight seignories (one for each of the eight proprietors), eight baronies (to be granted to one landgrave and two caciques) and twenty-four colonies to be apportioned among the freemen. Since each seignory, barony, and colony was to contain twelve thousand acres, this scheme meant that two-fifths of the land would belong to the proprietors and the nobles and three-fifths to all the other settlers. Moreover, in the colonies reserved for the freemen, manors of between three thousand and twelve thousand acres might be erected and peopled with leet-men or serfs. Thus the social structure would consist of the proprietary overlords, nobles, owners of large estates, small freeholders, and serfs—a duplication of feudal society of medieval times.

The Fundamental Constitutions further provided for a highly aristocratic government. All executive and judicial power was to be concentrated in the hands of the proprietors and the nobles. Only a landgrave could serve as governor, and although a parliament was to be erected the plan of representation was extremely undemocratic. Each proprietor was entitled to appoint one member and each county was to be represented by its three nobles and four elected delegates, while only owners of five hundred acres or more could qualify as deputies of the freemen.

This elaborate and archaic constitution could not be applied while South Carolina was in its infancy. When the settlers numbered only a few hundred souls it was impossible to create and people counties consisting each of 480,000 acres. Accordingly, the proprietors at first provided for compact settlement in towns. Necessity dictated that the settlers engage in diversified farming and the fur trade, not in the production of staples suited to large estates. The order of nobles could not be created until the land had been surveyed and peopled, although the proprietors did confer the nominal title of landgrave in order to qualify governors. Land grants were also shaped by necessity. The proprietors created a few large holdings and sold or gave away many small tracts, so that in 1685 the majority of farms did not exceed three hundred acres. The widespread distribution of land in turn affected the colony's government, inasmuch as the freeholders dominated the elected assembly and used it as a means of defending their interests against the proprietors.[12]

Early in the 1680's, when the colony was successfully launched and population had increased to about twenty-five hundred, the proprietors at last endeavored to give real force to the Fundamental Constitutions —a move which antagonized the settlers and united the small landowners and the wealthier men in vigorous opposition, since enforcement meant the withdrawal of lands from the reach of the settlers, the imposition of serfdom, and the control of government in the interest of proprietors. The wealthier colonists, who were deeply involved in trade, objected to proprietary restraints. Their chief source of profit, the fur trade, was endangered when the proprietors attempted to monopolize it for their own benefit. Allied to the fur trade was a traffic in Indian slaves who were obtained from the interior—natives enslaved originally by enemy tribes and sold to the white traders. This traffic meant that the South Carolina traders had to ally themselves with one group of warring tribes, thereby tending to embroil the settlers in intertribal strife—a result distasteful to the proprietors who desired peace with the Indians as a condition for the prosperous development of the colony. And when the Charles Town traders evaded the English Navigation Acts (which they did with boldness and ingenuity) they placed the proprietors at a further disadvantage. The English government expected the proprietors to enforce the acts within their province and warned that repeated violations would lead to the annulment of their charter rights—no empty threat in view of the treatment of Massachusetts in 1684. Another issue between proprietors and settlers arose in the 1680's when the proprietors made land grants subject to a quit-rent payable in money. The strife over trade and land induced the settlers to struggle to control the government and to resist the philosophy of the proprietors as expressed in a rebuke to the governor: "Pray, are you to govern the people or the people you?"

The conflict became increasingly sharp until, in 1685, twelve members of the colonial parliament were expelled because they refused to assent to the Fundamental Constitutions. Then occurred a complete break in 1688 when the governor proclaimed martial law and dissolved the parliament. Two years later the settlers launched a counterattack and seized control—only to be dislodged again in 1691. At that time

[12] Edward McCrady's *The History of South Carolina under the Proprietary Government, 1670–1719* (New York, 1897) contains a mass of detailed information, chronologically arranged. See again C. M. Andrews, *The Colonial Period of American History*, Vol. III, chapter 6.

the proprietors appointed Philip Ludwell governor, and although the Fundamental Constitutions were not yet officially abandoned they were now in fact a dead letter. The South Carolinians had successfully resisted the proprietors and their aristocratic program.

In North Carolina the proprietors encountered similar opposition. This region did not seem very attractive to them and had been allowed (before 1673) to go its own way. Settled by poor frontiersmen from Virginia who managed to eke out a niggardly subsistence on isolated farms, the little colony seemed to outsiders the abode of an easygoing, indolent people who regarded self-government as no government and taxes as robbery. Their meager exports consisted of tobacco and furs, and since the settlements had no harbors that could accommodate ocean-going ships, their trade had fallen into the hands of New Englanders who came to the coast in small vessels. Before 1673 the New England traders had been shipping tobacco directly to Europe; hence the North Carolina settlers were indirectly implicated in violations of the enumerated article clause of the Navigation Act of 1660.

Two grievances arose to plague the North Carolinians after 1670. The original settlers had obtained their land titles from Governor Berkeley of Virginia; hence when the Carolina proprietors asserted their claim to the province, there was danger that earlier grants would be annulled. Moreover, the proprietors demanded quit-rents—a real burden to farmers who lived in poverty. Secondly, the Navigation Act of 1673 inflicted a painful blow by levying a duty of 1d. a pound on North Carolina tobacco exported to New England. A part of this tax apparently was shifted by the New England traders to the farmers, and since it equaled the sale price of their tobacco it practically wiped out their profits. The proprietors, however, in order to keep the good will of English colonial officials, insisted upon the enforcement of the hateful tax. A series of riots and outbreaks ensued which culminated in a revolt in 1677–79, when the disgruntled farmers, led by George Durant and John Culpeper, deposed the governor and took possession of the colony. Culpeper was eventually arrested and taken to England for trial, where he was exonerated on the ground that since there was no settled government in North Carolina he had not been guilty of treason. In a later uprising the farmers drove out another governor— Seth Sothell, one of the proprietors. Meanwhile the Fundamental Constitutions had been opposed and frustrated as effectively as in South Carolina. The first phase of the northern colony's tumultuous history ended in 1691 when Philip Ludwell was appointed governor of both the Carolinas and his deputy was placed over the turbulent farmers at Albemarle Sound.

## CLASS CONFLICT IN NEW YORK

Between the years 1664 and 1685, when the province of New York was the personal estate of James, Duke of York, there occurred a series of conflicts between proprietor and inhabitants somewhat comparable to those in Maryland and the Carolinas. More fundamental, however, in the early history of New York was a protracted internal strife between aristocratic and democratic forces. The Duke of York did not take a deep personal interest in his province—a fact attested by his gift of New Jersey to Berkeley and Carteret in 1664 and by his failure to insist upon the Connecticut River as the eastern boundary of New York as provided in the duke's grant from Charles II.[13] In the 1680's the Connecticut boundary was fixed at a line running north from a point twenty miles east of the mouth of the Hudson. Hence New York during the duke's rule was a small province—limited to Long Island, Manhattan, other islands along the coast, and a strip of the Hudson valley about fifty miles wide, extending up the river to Albany. The occupation of the Mohawk valley by the Iroquois blocked the extension of settlement into the west.

The economic life of the colonists revolved around four major pursuits. The town of New York domiciled the merchant class engaged in wholesale commerce; at Albany the fur trade was the principal interest; on the mainland and on Long Island small farms produced livestock and grains; and Long Island in addition carried on a whale fishery. Socially the small farmers and fishermen of Long Island and the farmers in the lower Hudson valley, together with the wage-earners, artisans, and small traders of the town of New York, formed a democratic party in opposition to an aristocracy composed of the Albany fur traders, the city merchants, and the owners of large estates. In the early days the lines were not closely drawn between these aristocratic groups. The Albany fur traders and the city merchants both acquired landed estates, while the owners of large landholdings worked by tenants had to engage in trade in order to dispose of the produce in which their tenants paid their rents. The economic pursuits of the province were described in 1684 by the officials of the town of New York: "The manufacture of flour and bread . . . hath been and is the chief support of the trade and traffic to and from this city and the maintenance of its inhabitants in all degrees. . . . All other parts of this province have some particular advantage and way of living, as Long Island by husbandry and whaling; Esopus being the fat of the land by tillage;

[13] A. E. McKinley, "The Transition from Dutch to English Rule in New York," *American Historical Review*, VI (July 1901).

Albany by Indian trade and husbandry; this city [has] no other advantage or way of living but by traffic and dependence one on another chiefly upheld by the manufacture of flour and bread."

Prior to 1691 the government of New York was more undemocratic than that of any other of the English colonies. The grant of 1664 from Charles II conferred upon the Duke of York the power to name the governor and council, to impose legislation and taxes, to appoint local officials, and to control the judiciary and militia of the province. He was not obliged to erect a representative legislature, and in the exercise of his almost despotic powers he was subject to only two restraints: his laws must conform to the laws of England and appeals might be made from his provincial courts to the Privy Council. A firm believer in autocratic rule, the duke at first refused to grant the settlers a representative assembly, fearing as he did "the aptness of such bodies to assume to themselves many privileges which prove destructive to or very oft disturb the peace of the government wherein they are allowed." [14]

In view of the concentration of political power in the hands of the proprietor it is not surprising that the aristocratic groups in the colony allied themselves with his appointed agents. In order to derive an income from the province the duke had to rely upon duties levied against its trade, and the collection of such duties was facilitated when commerce was centered in the port of New York. The principal upper-class group, the merchants, desired to monopolize the commerce of the province, so that their interests coincided with the proprietor's desire to have all imports and exports pass through the town which they controlled. The fur traders and the proprietor (who collected a duty on furs exported) united to extend England's sway among the Iroquois and to resist the encroachments of the French *voyageurs* from Canada. And as the owner and grantor of lands, the proprietor was courted by the great men who sought to obtain estates on easy terms. The small farmers and the fishermen, on the other hand, opposed the monopolization of trade by the town merchants and the exaction by the proprietor of duties on trade to which they did not give their consent. Due to the aristocratic temper of the proprietor and the prevailing social standards of the time it was natural for his agents in the province to associate with and heed the advice of the wealthy colonists. The small farmers, finding themselves excluded from a government which increasingly represented the interests of an absentee landlord and a hostile aristocracy, demanded that a representative assembly be erected through which they might defend their own particular interests.

[14] See again J. Fiske, *Dutch and Quaker Colonies*, Vol. II, chapters 10–11, 13.

CAPTAIN KIDD AT EXECUTION DOCK, MAY 23, 1701

Sentenced on May 9 to be hanged, Captain Kidd said: "My Lord, it is a very hard sentence. For my part, I am the innocentest person of them all."

During the term of Colonel Richard Nicholls, first governor of New York (1664–68), the government of the province assumed the form it retained until 1691. For the benefit of New Englanders who had settled on Long Island and at Westchester on the eastern bank of the lower Hudson, Nicholls prepared a code which he designated as the duke's laws. They guaranteed freedom of worship and existing property rights, provided for a property rather than a religious qualification for voting, and committed the government of the towns to a constable and eight overseers elected by resident freemen. The administration of justice was entrusted to justices of the peace, appointed by the governor, who met yearly as a court of assize where, with the consent of the governor, they might enact laws. Intended primarily for the settlers from New England, the duke's laws in many respects duplicated the codes of New Haven and Massachusetts, although they did not confer the boon of town meetings. A convention of deputies from Westchester and the Long Island towns ratified the laws in 1665, rather unwillingly, but the settlers themselves complained loudly that they were not permitted to assent to taxes, to elect the justices, or to control their local militias. Demanding an elected assembly so that their deputies might "be joined with the governor and council in making the laws," the emigrés from New England waged a continuous fight against the new regime. However, by virtue of the "gentleness, wisdom and intelligence" of Governor Nicholls the province escaped acute strife until 1668, and the duke's laws were extended to the other settlements. A fellow official said of Nicholls's political skill that "he kept persons of different judgments and divers nations in peace when a great part of the world was in wars." [15]

Although the Dutch reconquered New York in 1673 it was restored to England by the Treaty of Westminster, February 19, 1674, and surrendered in the following October to Major Edmund Andros, recently appointed governor by the Duke of York. Imbued with the military spirit, Andros was an honest and able man, a devoted servant of the duke whose interests he placed above those of local groups. Perceiving the weakness of the farmers in the government he recommended that the duke establish an elected assembly, intending possibly to provide a counterweight to the local aristocracy. At any rate Andros incurred the hostility of the merchants, who refused to pay the customs duties from which the duke derived his income from the province, and hence the faithful Andros was summoned to England for an accounting.

[15] See again A. C. Flick (ed.), *History of the State of New York*, Vol. II, chapter 3.

The next governor, Thomas Dongan, who ruled between 1683 and 1688, identified himself chiefly with the upper-class groups in the colony. In 1686 he granted a charter to the city of New York which gave to the merchant class a larger measure of home rule. An earlier charter of 1665, while it granted a monopoly of trade to the freemen of the town, provided that the mayor, aldermen, and sheriff should all be appointed by the governor. Dongan's charter now allowed the freemen of the town to elect the aldermen. Meanwhile the commercial policies in force in the province tended to aggrandize the merchant class. One regulation decreed that all flour exported from the province should be bolted or sifted in the town of New York—a rule which forced the farmers to market their flour through a single channel, gave the merchants control of the flour trade, and brought to their doors the whole provincial supply of wheat and flour, which they could buy after harvest when stocks were large and prices at the lowest level. That the bolting monopoly was used to depress the price of wheat and to uphold the price of flour appears in the establishment, after 1680, of independent mills in the country districts. When such mills threatened the merchants' monopoly Governor Dongan in 1683 instructed the sheriffs to seize all flour bolted and packed outside the town of New York.

Another conflict involved the towns of Southold, Southampton, and Easthampton on eastern Long Island. These settlements fell within the trade area of Boston; hence it was most profitable for them to send thither their grain and whale products to be exchanged for European goods. The New York merchants, desiring to monopolize the Long Island trade, secured an act which levied a duty of 10 per cent *ad valorem* on all European goods imported into Long Island from Boston. When Governor Dongan found that the Long Islanders ignored the act he ordered that all Boston ships should call at the port of New York before they delivered goods to Long Island and return to New York with the outgoing cargoes. To the Long Islanders this policy savored of tyranny. It aimed to force them to depend upon the New York vessels and merchants, thus enabling the latter to dictate prices and freight rates. When prices were higher at Boston than at New York the Long Islanders could not ship directly to their best market, and when the New Yorkers failed to send enough vessels they had no outlet at all for their surplus products.

Governor Dongan also indicated his sympathies by making several large land grants to wealthy men of the province, and in 1686 he favored the fur trading interests by granting Albany a new city charter which conferred upon that town a monopoly of the fur trade.[16]

Due to popular opposition and resistance to his oligarchical regime the Duke of York finally yielded and in 1683 instructed Dongan to call a representative assembly. The Long Island towns since 1665 had been in a state of near rebellion, frequently refusing to pay taxes and issuing protests which were ignored by the magnates in control of the governor's council. Dongan thereupon ordered an election of delegates who met as the first Assembly of New York in October 1683. Its members enjoyed the privileges of free discussion and of considering bills but the measures they approved were subject to vetoes by the governor and the proprietor. This first assembly enacted fifteen laws, the most important being a charter of liberties and privileges which lodged the legislative power with the governor, council, and assembly, extended the ballot to all freeholders and freemen, provided for elections by the "free choice and vote" of the majority, and set up a proportional scheme of representation by counties. Other sections of the charter outlined the principles of land tenure, inheritance, and judicial procedure and guaranteed freedom of worship and trial by jury. Unfortunately for the New York farmers the duke changed his policy after his accession to the throne in 1685 had transformed the province into a royal colony. The acts of the session of 1683 and of two other sessions in 1684 and 1685 were never fully confirmed by James either as proprietor or as king. Instead, new instructions to Dongan in 1685 ordered the abandonment of the representative assembly and once more vested all legislative power in the governor and council—an act in keeping with the autocratic program which the king and the Lords of Trade had in mind for the northern colonies. Then in 1688 New York was annexed to the Dominion of New England and placed under the arbitrary rule of Sir Edmund Andros.

Preoccupied as he was with New England affairs, Andros had to govern New York through a deputy, Captain Francis Nicholson, who, during a brief term until May 1689, continued the policies previously in force, thus allowing the magnates to retain their grip upon the province. Their power was now well-nigh supreme. In 1686 Dongan had given the aristocratic councillors the right to act as justices of the peace in all counties, and as members of the supreme court of the province they were empowered to hear appeals from all subordinate courts. In the towns of New York and Albany the magnates controlled the local governments and dominated the mayor's courts which pronounced

---

[16] See again C. M. Andrews, *Colonial Self-Government*, chapters 5–6 (New York); chapters 13–14 (Virginia); chapter 15 (Maryland).

final judgment in all cases involving less than £20. So absolute was the sway of the aristocracy in government and so unyielding was its rule that the unprivileged farmers, traders, and workers could not expect concessions through legal channels and accordingly were driven to open revolt.[17]

The news of the flight of James II from England and of the fall of Andros at Boston inspired the discontented groups of New York to revolutionary action. The farmers on Long Island and in Westchester County took up arms and threatened to march on New York City, where they could count upon the support of the unprivileged workers, called mechanics, and many of the small traders and shopkeepers who were restive under the rule of their creditors and competitors. But a march of the farmers became unnecessary when in May 1689 the city "rabble," as the aristocrats styled their opponents, seized the fort at New York. Their aggressive and energetic leader, Jacob Leisler, a German merchant of democratic sympathies who did not belong to the charmed circle of aristocratic families, proved to be more than a match for the indecisive, hot-tempered Nicholson and his council of magnates. On June 24 Nicholson deserted his post and stole away to England, realizing that the revolution in England had erased his authority in the colony. The democratic party then seized control of the customhouse and set up a de facto government or council of safety which proclaimed Leisler commander-in-chief. His rule, which endured until March 1691, rested upon the support of the small farmers and the city workers and upon his control of the provincial militia. In April 1690 he summoned a legislature which enacted only two laws, one of which destroyed the trade monopolies of the New York merchants. This significant act declared that "all towns and places shall have equal freedom to bolt and bake and to transport where they please directly to what place or country they think fit, anything their places afford, and that the one place shall have no more privileges than the other."

Leisler's Revolt was primarily an internal class struggle, although the charges which were bandied about at the time tended to confuse the issue. While many of the royal officers under Nicholson were Catholics, the insurrection was not a religious outbreak, since the magnates allied with Nicholson were as staunch in their Protestantism as were the followers of Leisler. The accusations that Nicholson intended to deliver the province to the French also fail to explain the revolt, since Albany, most exposed to French attack, remained hostile to Leisler

[17] See again H. L. Osgood, *American Colonies in the Seventeenth Century*, Vol. III, chapters 12, 15 (New York), 16 (Maryland).

until the spring of 1690. The chief magnate at Albany, Robert Livingston, was reinforced by the leading opponent of the insurrectionists, Nicholas Bayard, who escaped from New York City and fled north, where he exerted his influence to keep Albany under the control of the old guard. Only when Indian warfare threatened destruction did the Albany men surrender to Leisler in the spring of 1690 and welcome the protection of his troops.

Not until March 1691 did Colonel Henry Sloughter, first governor appointed by William and Mary, arrive at New York. He was preceded by Major Richard Ingoldsby in command of two companies of British soldiers. Leisler unfortunately disputed Ingoldsby's authority and refused to surrender the fort—an act which his opponents, without just cause, construed as treason. When Sloughter arrived soon afterward, Leisler submitted—only to find that the new governor had permanently allied himself with the aristocratic party. The magnates emerged from their storm cellars, assumed control of the government, and brought ten of the Leisler leaders to trial for treason. Two were acquitted, six were found guilty but pardoned, and Leisler and his son-in-law, Jacob Milborne, were condemned and hanged in May 1691— an act of unwarranted vengeance, since Leisler and Milborne were denied the right of appeal to the king and only casuistry could construe their actions as treason to William III, whose authority, when properly displayed, they had duly recognized. The pressure which the magnates exerted to induce Sloughter to sign the death warrants of the two popular leaders suggests that an appeal to England would have exonerated them. Some tardy justice was done to their memories in 1695 when Parliament reversed the attainder against them and restored their estates to their families.

The outcome of Leisler's Revolt is indicated by a comment of a later governor, Cadwallader Colden, who wrote in 1734 that great changes in society were effected only by the rich and powerful; "any other commotions generally produced only some short lived disorders and confusions." Certainly an era of reaction followed the execution of Leisler. Governor Sloughter died in 1691—a victim of intemperance, his character indicated by the tradition that he signed Leisler's death warrant while intoxicated. Ingoldsby then served as acting governor until he was succeeded by another anti-Leislerian, Colonel Benjamin Fletcher, who abetted the merchant magnates in their adventures in piracy and granted lands with a free hand. In the words of Colden, Fletcher was "a generous man" who "gave away the king's lands by parcels of one hundred thousand acres to a man, and to some particular favorites four or five times that quantity." His government was described by his successor, the Earl of Bellomont, as "corrupted and de-bauched." [18]

One gain for the democratic forces issued from the confusion of the time. Governor Sloughter was instructed to restore the elected Assembly, and this body held its first meeting in April 1691. Although only about 8 or 10 per cent of the inhabitants were entitled to vote, the elected house afforded the small farmers a means of defending their interests. Thus in 1695 they obtained an act which abolished the flour monopoly of the town of New York and allowed all farmers to engage in bolting, baking, and packing. At this time the Assembly refused to pass any other measures until its free flour act was accepted. The issue arose again in 1700 when the city officials adopted an ordinance placing heavy duties on flour and biscuit imported into the city from the outlying farms. The Assembly then refused to provide for the support of the government until this obnoxious order was repealed. Bellomont wrote that the "city merchants were as obstinate for maintaining their ordinance, so that the money bill was very near miscarrying." Finally, however, he persuaded them to revoke the offending order. Bellomont's successor, Lord Cornbury, in alliance with the merchants, suggested that the city be given as many representatives in the Assembly as all other parts of the province. But this was not done and the city did not recover its monopoly rights.

Leisler's Revolt, as an internal class struggle, was the counterpart of Bacon's Rebellion—not primarily a protest against England's authority as was the Revolution of 1689 in New England, whose leaders represented the upper class. English policy, however, contributed to the causes of the disorders in both Virginia and New York by virtue of the practice of appointing as councillors and advisers of governors the wealthiest men of the colonies. Then when outbreaks against the local aristocracy occurred, England dispatched troops to suppress rebellion and restore the authority of the governor and council. But in the treatment of "rebels" England showed far more leniency in New England than did the colonial magnates in Virginia and New York. Although the aristocratic spirit prevalent in England predisposed the king's advisers to favor the colonial aristocracy, yet when its rule became unduly harsh they insisted upon some concessions to the less influential groups. Bacon's Rebellion gained protection for the frontier settlements of Virginia and Leisler's Revolt brought an elected Assembly to New York.

[18] See again E. Channing, *History of the United States*, Vol. II, chapters 2 (New York), 3 (Virginia), 7 (revolutions, 1689).

## Social Conflicts in New Jersey

The struggles of the democracy in New Jersey exhibited the grievances of settlers against proprietors, as in Maryland and Carolina, and the complaints of farmers against merchants, as in New York. It will be remembered that in 1674 Lord John Berkeley sold the western part of New Jersey to Quakers; that in 1676 the colony was divided into two provinces; and that in 1680–82 was sold the Carteret claim to East New Jersey, also to Quakers. The center and capital of East New Jersey was established in 1665 by Philip Carteret, who led an expedition of thirty colonists and founded a settlement at Elizabethtown. During the preceding year many farmers from New England had migrated to East New Jersey and had obtained land grants from Colonel Nicholls, governor of New York. Other emigrants from New England later responded to the generous concessions offered by Carteret, so that by 1675 the New Englanders formed the strongest party in his half of the colony. West New Jersey, which in 1676 had a nucleus of Dutch and Swedish settlers, was peopled afterward principally by the English Quakers, who established their seat of government at Burlington in 1677. Both parts of New Jersey enjoyed elected assemblies.

The principal social conflicts in New Jersey occurred in the eastern province, where the small farmers were squeezed between the proprietors and the merchants of New York. The settlers from New England retained their preference for the land system of the Puritan colonies –grants by the legislature to town proprietors and by them to the individual farmer, so that the latter held his land in fee simple tenure, free from quit-rents or other payments to an overlord. The proprietors of East New Jersey, on the other hand, adopted the method of making grants directly to individuals and of exacting a yearly quit-rent. Those New Englanders who had obtained grants from Governor Nicholls of New York insisted that they were not tenants of the proprietors of New Jersey—a claim that would have made them independent landowners, since the Duke of York had surrendered his rights as overlord of New Jersey. The opposition among the New Englanders to quit-rents became so intense that two of the towns which derived their titles from Nicholls rejected the proprietary authority and established their own governor and assembly—an act of defiance, however, that they were unable to make good. The bitter antagonism between Puritans and Quakers intensified the opposition of the New Englanders to quit-rent payments after East New Jersey passed into the hands of Quaker proprietors in 1682.[19]

[19] H. L. Osgood's *The American Colonies in the Eighteenth Century* (4 vols., New

Commercially, East New Jersey belonged within the trade area of the town of New York, whose merchants were determined to retain their hold upon the trade in this area which they had developed before New Jersey was separated from New York. Both the proprietors of East New Jersey and the resident farmers desired the privilege of free trade with the outside world and accordingly they established a port at Perth Amboy, where trading vessels did not have to pay the heavy import and export duties then in force in New York. This act threatened the New York merchants with the loss of the trade of East New Jersey, since goods sent thither from New York had to pay the New York import duties whereas goods shipped from other places entered Perth Amboy duty free. Moreover, the New York merchants charged that imports could be brought into Perth Amboy and then carried into New York, there to undersell their own wares on which the New York duties had been paid. Similarly, New York produce could be exported via Perth Amboy in order to evade the payment of New York's export duties.

In order to equalize trading conditions the New York merchants insisted that goods entering and leaving East New Jersey should be subject to the duties in force at New York—a demand supported by the Duke of York and later by the king because the free trade of Perth Amboy lessened the proprietary and royal revenues of New York. At first the New Yorkers established an official at Perth Amboy to collect the same duties that were payable in New York and later required that all vessels trading to and from New Jersey should enter the port of New York in order to make the payments there. In this conflict the East New Jersey farmers received the support of the proprietors, who asserted that a free trade was indispensable to the prosperity of their province. New York could not rightfully collect such taxes because the people of New Jersey had never given their consent. And when the New Jersey farmers had to trade exclusively with New York its merchants held a monopoly that enabled them to fix prices as they pleased, free from the competition of other traders.

These contests led eventually to the establishment of a royal government over New Jersey. It had never been clear whether the proprietors of the Jerseys had received the right to govern their territories. The original grant from the Duke of York to Berkeley and Carteret did not openly confer such a right. During the term of Andros as governor of New York he had endeavored to extend the authority of the duke over New Jersey, but the proprietors had resisted and secured an opinion

York, 1924), a work of great scholarship, deals primarily with constitutional controversies. See Vol. I, pp. 382–397.

from an English arbiter which upheld their rights as governors of their provinces. In 1688 the Jerseys were temporarily annexed to the Dominion of New England after the proprietors had consented to surrender their political rights in return for a confirmation of their title to the land. Then, following the overthrow of the Dominion of New England, they resumed their powers of government. During the 1690's, however, East New Jersey was torn by strife over the quit-rents and by the commerical conflict with New York. The proprietors derived no profit from the colony apart from land sales and quit-rents; hence their interest became increasingly that of landlord. Moreover they incurred opposition in England by virtue of their inability to suppress piracy and to enforce the Navigation Acts in New Jersey. Confronted by attacks from the Crown, from their own settlers, and from New York, and realizing that an assertion of their dubious claim to political authority was not worth the cost, they surrendered to the Crown in 1702 the rights of governing their province. The proprietors of West New Jersey did likewise and accordingly New Jersey became a royal province.

The settlement of 1702 allowed the proprietors to retain their rights as landlords and guaranteed to East New Jersey the privilege of free trade through Perth Amboy. England reunited the two little provinces, appointed a royal governor and council and permitted the now consolidated elected assembly to continue. Until 1738 New Jersey was ruled by the governor of New York through a deputy; after 1738 it had its own governor. The commercial policy enforced by England required that the custom duties in force in New York should also be collected in New Jersey.

The internal conflicts of the seventeenth century issued from two main sources—from the antagonism of the workers and small farmers to the merchant-planter upper class, as in New York, Virginia, and New Jersey; and from the animosity of the landowners, both large and small, toward the colonial proprietors, as in Maryland, New Jersey, and the Carolinas. While these conflicts were in progress England had one primary concern—to protect her own stake in the colonies: an interest which made her critical of the proprietary governments, since popular unrest lessened their effectiveness as protectors of that stake. With respect to the internal conflicts in New York and Virginia, England acted to suppress the revolts, to defend her own interests, to restore the colonial aristocracies to power, and to moderate somewhat the harsher features of their rule. Of all the parties involved in these conflicts—the colonial aristocracy, the colonial democracy, the English merchants, the Crown, and the proprietors—the last were in the weakest position, a fact which explains the gradual elimination of the proprietary governments: from New Hampshire in 1679, from New York in 1685–88, from Maine in 1691, from Maryland between 1691 and 1716, from New Jersey in 1702, from the Carolinas in 1719–29, from Georgia in 1751, and from Maryland and Pennsylvania in 1776.

## BIBLIOGRAPHICAL NOTE

SOURCES: *The History of Bacon's . . . Rebellion* (Cambridge, 1867) is a contemporary narrative, edited by Charles Deane. See also C. M. Andrews (ed.), *Narratives of the Insurrections*, pp. 3–164, 301–401; and A. B. Hart (ed.), *American History Told by Contemporaries*, I, pp. 242–246, 262–267.

## ☆ XIV ☆

## ENGLAND, FRANCE, AND SPAIN

The success of England in establishing and strengthening her American colonies placed her in a position of potential conflict with any power of Europe bent upon westward expansion, for the fields of colonial exploitation were limited and England's claims to strategic areas denied imperial opportunities to ambitious rivals. Ever since the accession of Henry IV in 1594 France had been growing in stature as a powerful, centralized state. Two crafty and determined prime ministers, the Cardinals Richelieu and Mazarin, had guided the destinies of France between 1624 and 1661, striving relentlessly for an absolute monarchy. By crushing the feudal nobles as a political power, by imposing tax upon tax for the benefit of the king's treasury, by warring against the Protestants as a means of attaining internal religious unity, and by bringing the provinces under the dominance of Paris through royal agents or *intendants* vested with extreme powers in local government—by such methods these two worldly churchmen prepared the way for the triumph of absolutism in the person of the Sun King, Louis XIV.[1]

Animated by a love of power and cherishing illusions of grandeur, this Grand Monarch in 1661 became his own prime minister, taking into his own hands the reins of government, retaining the *intendants* as an agency of local control, reducing his ministers to the status of "yes-men," creating efficient bureaus of central administration, and in general making a reality of the famous phrase attributed to him: "I am the State." As a mirror of his personal splendor and glory he built the gorgeous palace of Versailles, whence emanated the canons of fashion and etiquette that guided aristocratic society throughout Europe. Under his foreign minister, Lionne, he developed the most highly trained and efficient corps of diplomats of the age; his war minister, Louvois, constructed a war machine amply supplied with royal revenues and unrivaled in size and modernization; his finance minister, Colbert, fashioned an integrated system of economics along the lines of mercantilism. All this concentrated force the Sun King aspired to use in

[1] L. B. Packard, *The Age of Louis XIV* (New York, c. 1929), is a readable survey, designed for undergraduates.

355

military conquest for the territorial aggrandizement of his royal house, and circumstances dictated that the arms of France should conquer in the north, toward the Rhine. Such an advance imperiled the Dutch Republic, then screened from French aggression by the Spanish Netherlands (modern Belgium). Meanwhile the colonial ambitions of France menaced England; accordingly after the English and the Dutch had resolved their mutual conflicts in 1674 they united in opposition to the perennial design of Louis XIV for colonial expansion and the conquest of the Spanish Netherlands.[2]

The trend toward absolutism in France prior to 1660 had retarded the growth of industry and trade. The merchant occupied an inferior status in French society, which conferred its honors and prestige upon courtiers, landed nobles, high churchmen, or officials of the king, and betrayed a contemptuous attitude toward men engaged in gainful pursuits. In consequence the wealthy merchants did not train their sons for business and equip them with capital for trade but rather educated them for careers of gentlemen in the service of the court. At the same time the heavy burden of taxes carried by the French people to maintain the monarchy and the army greatly diminished their ability to buy the products of home industry, with the result that —although France had developed certain industries to a high point (cloth, wine, lace, furniture, paper, glass, and thread)—a state of depression and unemployment clouded the early years of the reign of Louis XIV. Foreign commerce was languishing and, excepting her trade with the Levant, France depended upon the shipping of the Dutch, while her imports exceeded her exports, a striking manifestation of the decay of her domestic industries. From this plight Louis XIV and Colbert were determined to extricate the kingdom, and because so much of the national income found its way into the king's treasury it became imperative that the government supply a large part of the capital for economic rehabilitation. The poverty of the mass of the people—in contrast to the great wealth of nobles and courtiers— meant that an adequate domestic market for French products could not be created and consequently Colbert concluded that the way to salvation lay in the development of overseas trade.[3]

As the chief minister of Louis XIV between 1661 and 1683 Colbert adopted and applied the English policy of fostering colonies as pro-

[2] A. J. Grant, *The French Monarchy* (2 vols., Cambridge, 1925), is an admirable, brief survey. See Vol. II, chapters 10–15.

[3] An outstanding study of great value is Stewart L. Mims, *Colbert's West India Policy* (New Haven, 1912).

ducing areas rather than the Dutch policy of using overseas possessions primarily as trading posts. He envisaged an integrated empire of four supplementary parts. France, as the center and heart of the system, was to supply manufactured goods, capital, merchants' services, and shipping. Hence he first endeavored to foster home industries and for this purpose a high protective tariff wall was raised in 1665 to exclude competing foreign goods from the French market. In order to procure capital he organized great trading companies in which the king, his officials, and the merchants made large investments. One such firm, the West India Company, formed in 1668, received extensive privileges for trade and colonization in western Africa, North and South America, and the West Indies. The merchants were now elevated in society by favors and honors bestowed upon them at court as the wholehearted patronage of the king was given to their enterprises. Colbert, by insisting that all foreign traders and vessels be excluded from the commerce of the French colonies, reserved it as a monopoly for the native merchant-shipowners. Even the privileges of the West India Company did not exclude private French traders from the colonies, and when the company expired in 1674 all such traders were allowed to share in the national monopoly.[4]

The colonies of France in the West Indies—St. Christopher, Santo Domingo, Martinique, and Guadeloupe—composed the second element in Colbert's imperial scheme. As producers of sugar, tobacco, indigo, cotton, ginger, and dyewoods they fulfilled a threefold function: they supplied articles for consumption in France, thus cutting off payments to foreigners for such commodities of foreign origin; they provided raw materials for French industries; and they afforded articles that might be sold in export trade. The West Indies in turn were to buy French manufactures and employ French capital, shipping, and merchants' services. The denial to the colonies of free trade with foreigners meant that the planters had to pay high prices for their visible and invisible imports from France, and this in turn greatly retarded colonial development. However, Colbert preferred a slow growth in the colonies which would benefit France exclusively to a rapid progress from which foreigners would reap the principal profits.

As the third link in the imperial chain Colbert favored the erection of slave trading stations in Africa where slaves might be purchased with French manufactures and shipped to the planters of the West Indies. Finally, settlements in Canada had their part to play as buyers of

---

[4] See again G. M. Wrong, *The Rise and Fall of New France*, Vol. I, chapters 13–20; Vol. II, chapters 21–23.

French goods and as producers of foodstuffs, work animals, and lumber needed on the West Indian plantations.[5]

How would these colonial possessions benefit France? First, they would stimulate her industries, give employment to her idle workers and take off her surplus manufactures that could not be sold at home. By supplying her with West Indian products the colonies would relieve her from dependence upon foreign states for such commodities, thereby reducing imports for which payment had to be made to foreigners in specie. The earnings of French investors, shippers, and merchants in the form of interest, freights, and profits would give France a favorable balance in colonial trade; similarly, the reëxportation of West Indian staples from France would improve her trading relations with European states. A favorable trade balance in turn would yield an adequate supply of gold and silver, thus providing the sinews of war and a fund of surplus capital that might be devoted to commercial, industrial, and colonial expansion.

Before Colbert's death in 1683 France had driven the Dutch from the trade of the French West Indies, which they had virtually monopolized in 1660. French industries and shipping had been greatly strengthened and extended; the colonies had made substantial if slow progress; and modest success had been attained in the slave trade. At one point, however, Colbert's aims had not been realized: Canada had failed in its role of producer of provisions, lumber, and work animals for the West Indies. New England and New York proved to be better suited to that purpose and consequently they increasingly performed the function originally assigned to Canada. Since Colbert's system aimed to exclude all foreigners from the trade of the colonies, it became imperative that the French West Indies obtain these supplies from French sources. Canada having failed in this connection, the French aspired to acquire New England and New York.[6]

## The Anglo-French Conflict in America

Under the guidance of Colbert France embraced the very policies that had been adopted by England and chose to operate in the same colonial spheres—hence the bitter and prolonged struggle between the two. Besides the ambition of France to acquire England's northern colonies as a feeding ground for the French West Indies she was also determined to monopolize the American fur trade—that source of

[5] E. B. Greene, *Provincial America* (New York, 1905), is a notable volume in the *American Nation* series. See chapters 7–10.

[6] Francis Parkman, *The Old Régime in Canada* (Boston, 1880).

fabulous profits which realized so perfectly all the purposes of the mercantilist's creed. By 1660 the Indians of North America had become utterly dependent upon the traffic in furs. Now accustomed to the white man's tools, they were rapidly losing their primitive skill in the art of making and using stone implements. Their dependence on trade increased the importance of trapping and hunting, the source of their purchasing power for European goods; hence their contacts with the white man, instead of leading them to a settled way of life, intensified their roving, predatory characteristics. The fur trade in turn led to a rapid destruction of fur-bearing animals, since peltries and skins had to be obtained in quantities greatly in excess of the Indians' primitive needs. As furs became more scarce and valuable the tribes—now utterly enslaved by the traffic—were forced to struggle against each other for control of the available supply. In the resulting wars European fire-arms played the decisive role, and the procuring of firearms therefore became a primary concern. In short, the fur trade made the Indians increasingly dependent upon trapping and hunting; the ensuing competition for furs bred intertribal warfare; and such strife in turn intensified the trade which supplied the weapons of war. The Indians had become involved in a vicious circle of trade and strife that carried them toward destruction.[7]

The fur-producing area which the French and English sought to dominate was the vast region adjacent to the Great Lakes. One route which led France westward from Quebec and Montreal followed the St. Lawrence River, Lake Ontario, the Niagara River, and Lake Erie, thus giving access to the upper Ohio valley. Thither went the French *coureurs de bois* in their canoes bound for the hunting lands; along this route the interior tribes brought their furs to Montreal. The great English trading interests at Albany—commanded by the Livingstons and Schuylers—obtained their furs through the Iroquois who dominated the country which links the Hudson River and the Great Lakes. As middlemen between the English and the interior tribes the Iroquois were natural enemies of the French, since their trade diverted the flow of furs from Montreal to Albany. Repeated hostilities between the Iroquois and the French had not been quieted by a treaty between the two in 1666–67, and after 1680 the strife became more acute as the French began to penetrate into the Illinois country which the Iroquois considered their special domain. In peace the Five Nations could be counted upon to trade with Albany; in war they might cut France's communications with the West at the Niagara River. After 1667 both

---

[7] Harold A. Innes, *The Fur Trade in Canada* (New Haven, 1930), is a detailed, factual treatment. See pp. 1–84.

France and England claimed that the Iroquois were subjects of their respective kings. Not only did England desire to use the Iroquois as middlemen in the fur trade; they also formed a barrier against a French attack on New York via the only likely routes—from the Great Lakes by way of the Mohawk River and from Quebec by way of Lake Champlain and the Hudson.[8]

Representative of the vigor which Colbert infused into colonial affairs was the administration of his governor in Canada between 1672 and 1682—Louis de Buade, Count Frontenac. Instructed by Colbert to develop compact settlements about Quebec in order to foster agriculture, Frontenac instead succumbed to the lure of the great West and became a promoter of interior exploration second only to Champlain. A patron of fur traders rather than of missionaries, Frontenac exalted commercial profit above conversion of the Indians.[9] The French advance westward had halted after Nicolet's memorable expedition to Green Bay in 1634. Now, in 1673, Louis Joliet, a fur trader, and Father Marquette, a Jesuit missionary, resumed the old quest for an inland waterway to the South Sea. Proceeding from Green Bay by the Fox River they crossed the portage to the Wisconsin, whose waters they followed to the Mississippi and then floated down the imperial stream to the mouth of the Arkansas River. Convinced that the Mississippi did not flow into the western ocean they returned to New France, bringing reports of the unrivaled agricultural and timber resources of the great valley.[10] Among those whose imagination was fired by these reports was René Robert Cavelier, Sieur de La Salle—one of the boldest, most resolute figures in the annals of exploration. With the vision of an empire builder La Salle conceived a grand design for the colonization of the interior and the extension of French influence eastward until the English colonies might be conquered and all North America become a province of France. Accordingly, in 1674 he obtained from Louis XIV permission to explore the Mississippi to its mouth—an ambition which he finally accomplished in 1682 after two failures and indescribable hardships which he met with inflexible purpose and heroic courage.[11]

[8] Francis Parkman, *Frontenac and New France under Louis XIV* (Boston, 1880).
[9] Charles W. Colby, *The Fighting Governor* (*Chronicles of Canada* series, Toronto, 1915).
[10] Agnes Repplier's *Père Marquette* (Garden City, N. Y., 1929) is brilliantly written. For a more accurate and formal sketch see R. G. Thwaites, *Father Marquette* (New York, 1902). Francis B. Steck, *The Jolliet-Marquette Expedition, 1673* (Washington, 1927), is a detailed, scholarly study, for the special student.
[11] Francis Parkman, *La Salle and the Discovery of the Great West* (2d ed., Boston, 1892), presents La Salle in heroic outlines. The best modern biography of La Salle

The penetration of the French into the Illinois country south of
Lake Michigan sharpened their conflict with the Iroquois, who had
long regarded this region as their principal source of furs. Thither now

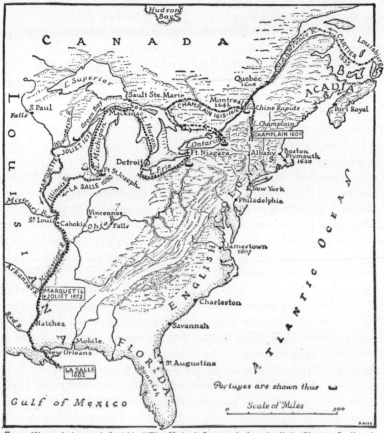

From Wertenbaker and Smith's "The United States of America." © Charles Scribner's
Sons.

### FRENCH EXPLORATIONS AND SETTLEMENTS

went the *coureur de bois*, the Jesuit missionary, and even the French
settler, for the Illinois country—with its rich farming land and its outlet down the Mississippi—promised to realize Colbert's dream of an
agricultural colony that would supply the French West Indies with
lumber, livestock, and food. The threatened domination of the Illinois
country by France aroused the fears of the Albany traders, vigorously

is Frances Gaither, *The Fatal River* (New York, 1931). A popular biography in the
romantic vein is Leo F. Jacks, *La Salle* (New York, 1931).

supported after 1683 by Governor Dongan, who aspired to wrest the fur trade from the French. By offering protection to the Iroquois and by sending English traders into the upper Lake country, Dongan incurred the wrath of the authorities in Canada, who accused him of inciting the Iroquois and who in 1687 sent a raiding party into the land of the Senecas, thus foreshadowing an open war between New France and New York.[12]

At another strategic point—the Newfoundland fishery—the impetus given by Colbert to French expansion led to conflict with England. In every respect the Newfoundland fishery conformed to the canons of mercantilism. During the winter season vessels were fitted out in the Atlantic ports of France and in the western ports of England for voyages to Newfoundland. Well stocked with provisions and fishing supplies and manned by French or English seamen, such vessels afforded an export market for capital, labor, and domestic products. The catches of the fishing fleets were carried in part to the home ports, thus curtailing foreign imports of fish, while the remainder were shipped to Portugal, Spain, or Italy—a trade that employed a large volume of shipping, earned freights and profits for the merchants concerned, and gave both states additional exports which contributed toward a favorable balance of trade and the importation of specie.

During the seventeenth century the English fishery at Newfoundland gave rise to a bitter strife between two competing groups—the merchants of the western ports and the merchants of London. The former operated by sending annual fishing fleets from their home ports which returned at the end of the fishing season; the latter endeavored to establish at the island a colony of fishermen who would reside there the year round and exchange their fish for supplies sent from London. Because the West Country merchants had pioneered in developing the industry and because their trade centered in England they generally enjoyed the backing of the English government and held the upper hand in the fishery. However, the London merchants by 1660 had established several fishermen colonists on the southwestern coast of the island and were seriously threatening the vested interest of the West Country ports, although the influence of the latter was still so strong that England did not assist the settlers by providing them with protection or a colonial government.[13]

In 1662 France strengthened her fishery by establishing a fort and

[12] Clarence W. Alvord's *The Illinois Country, 1673–1818* (Springfield, Ill., 1920), is excellent. See chapters 1–6.

[13] Charles B. Judah, *The North American Fisheries and British Policy to 1713* (Urbana, 1933), treats a weighty subject with a light touch. See also R. G. Lounsbury, *The British Fishery at Newfoundland*, chapters 4–7.

settlement at Placentia on the southern coast of Newfoundland, then the principal scene of French activity. Due to a climate more favorable than that of the English settlement, to the subsidizing of the fishermen by the French government, to the stationing of royal troops at the fort, and to protection given by warships, the Placentia colony made material progress as a supply center for the vessels that came from France. The English fishery steadily lost ground to its more efficient rival until by 1689 the French were far in the lead. Meanwhile the English West Country merchants, still bitterly hostile to the English colony, minimized the danger from the French and opposed any measures which would transfer the seat of the fishery from England to the island. In this course they had the support of Charles II and James II, whose pro-French sympathies dictated a policy of inaction. However, the underlying causes of friction remained and were accentuated when William III became king in 1689.

New England also felt the threat implicit in the advance of France. Laying claim to all North America the French had more or less open designs of conquering the Puritan colonies, while the growth of the French fishery at Newfoundland menaced the most important industry of New England. The French settlers of Acadia and the English in Maine struggled for control of the furs, fishery, and timber resources of that region. Here the French, exercising great influence over the Indians (the Abenaki), supplied them with firearms and incited them to resist the encroachments of New England. As long as France retained Acadia and Canada she could use her colonial ports as bases for dispatching vessels to prey upon the commerce and fishery of Massachusetts —perhaps the most menacing threat to New England's security. Should France succeed in conquering New York the Puritan colonies would be isolated and encircled by their foes; hence New England's interest in the defense of Albany equaled that of New York. And when Louis XIV after 1680 enforced a policy of severe persecution of the French Calvinists the determination of the Puritans to resist conquest by their Catholic foes was stirred to a fever heat.[14]

Due to the pro-French policies of Charles II and James II the colonial rivalry in North America was held in abeyance until the English Revolution of 1688. The accession of William III, however, plunged England into a European war that had broken out in 1688. Still intent upon conquering the Spanish Netherlands, Louis XIV had provoked William of Orange to form an alliance with Spain, Austria, and many German states to resist the aggression of France, and the

[14] J. T. Adams's vigorously written *Revolutionary New England, 1691–1776* (Boston, 1923) stresses social and economic forces. See chapters 4–5.

primary object of the Dutch Stadtholder in accepting the English crown was to bring England into the war. Thoroughly dissatisfied with the policy of James II which subordinated their commercial ambitions to France the English merchants rallied around William III and accordingly his accession gave the signal for an English offensive against France in those colonial spheres where conflict between the two powers was reaching a critical stage.[15]

King William's War in America was opened with a grand project of Louis XIV for the conquest of New York. In 1689 Count Frontenac was sent back to Canada as governor with instructions to invade New York in conjunction with a naval force that was to sail to Manhattan from France; after the conquest the non-Catholic English settlers in New York were to be expelled. Arriving at Quebec, Frontenac found Canada in a demoralized state due to Iroquois raids, and accordingly he abandoned the design of conquest in favor of counterattacks on the English frontiers. In the winter of 1689–90 he dispatched three expeditions—one of which fell upon a settlement, Salmon Falls, on the Maine-New Hampshire boundary. A second force took possession of the English post, Fort Loyal, where Portland now stands, while the third in February 1690 destroyed the town of Schenectady, thirteen miles west of Albany. In the meantime the English colonists had failed to carry out their plans for a conquest of New France. The collapse of the Dominion of New England destroyed the political unity of the Puritan colonies, while New York was torn by Leisler's Revolt. Frontenac's raids, however, prompted Massachusetts, Plymouth, and Connecticut to send commissioners to New York where, under the leadership of Leisler, plans were made in May 1690 for the conquest of Canada. An expedition of New York and New England troops, supported by a large band of Iroquois, was to advance from Albany by way of Lake Champlain and join at Quebec a naval force to be dispatched by Massachusetts to the St. Lawrence.[16]

In May 1690 the New Englanders won an encouraging victory when a force from Boston commanded by Sir William Phips occupied Port Royal in Acadia and then returned to Boston, amply rewarded with spoils of war. The larger plan of conquest, however, failed. The expedition which set out from Albany—weakened at the start by a disappointing response from the Iroquois—proceeded only to the foot of Lake Champlain and there abandoned the campaign. In the summer of

[15] G. N. Clark's *The Dutch Alliance and the War against French Trade* (Manchester, 1923) emphasizes the influence of William III in Anglo-French relations.

[16] See again H. L. Osgood, *American Colonies in the Eighteenth Century*, Vol. I, pp. 42–183, 399–522.

1690 Phips sailed from Boston with two thousand troops and arrived at Quebec, only to procrastinate, to launch a feeble attack, and then to retire when victory was within easy reach. These maneuvers decided the outcome of the war. Neither France nor England contributed much to the American campaigns and the hostile colonies were not yet strong enough for one to overcome the other. The treaty of peace concluded at Ryswick in 1697 provided for a return to the *status quo ante bellum*.[17]

### QUEEN ANNE'S WAR

A brief interval of peace after 1697 proved to be merely a prelude to the decisive War of the Spanish Succession, precipitated in 1701 by Louis XIV. In November 1700 the King of Spain, Charles II, died, leaving a will which named as heir to the Spanish throne and its vast possessions the grandson of Louis XIV, Philip of Anjou. Hastily accepting this inheritance for his grandson, Louis established him at Madrid as King Philip V of Spain—a move which meant the domination of the Spanish Netherlands and the Spanish colonies by France. What Louis XIV had failed to accomplish by arms seemed at last within his reach by diplomatic means. William III, still defender of Holland and guardian of England's commercial interests, again assumed command of the anti-French forces and organized another Grand Alliance whose armies took the field in 1702. Refusing to accept Philip V as King of Spain, England recognized the rival claims of an Austrian candidate, the Archduke Charles, and endeavored to place him upon the Spanish throne. Thus during the War of the Spanish Succession (Queen Anne's War in America) Spain was united with France, whereas during King William's War Spain had been a partner in the alliance against Louis XIV. This difference explains a great change that occurred on the colonial stage of the conflict—the extension of the war to the Carolina frontier and to the vast area of the Spanish colonies in America.[18]

Of all the causes of strife between England and France none had greater weight than their rivalry for the trade of the Spanish colonies. The commercial and industrial decline of Spain after 1650 gave to England, France, and Holland a tempting opportunity to divert the major part of the wealth of the Spanish Indies to their respective shores. In every respect the commerce of Spanish America realized the aims of mercantilism. First, it enabled the commercial states to increase their exports of domestic manufactures—either directly to the Spanish

[17] See again J. Winsor, *Cartier to Frontenac*, chapters 9–16.

[18] G. M. Wrong, *The Conquest of New France* (*Chronicles of America*, New Haven, 1918), chapters 1–3.

colonies or to Africa, where they were exchanged for slaves. These in turn were sold to the Spanish planters in the Americas and the West Indies—a trade which netted both silver and gold, thus supplying the European powers with the coveted precious metals. Silver played a vital part in the East India trade: an indispensable export from Europe, it enabled the European traders to purchase those oriental goods which yielded such remarkable profits when reëxported to foreign states and to America. Thus the African, Spanish American, and Far Eastern trades became inseparably united and together they afforded the finest profit opportunities of the age. They employed a vast amount of shipping, enriched the merchants with freights, profits, and interest, provided markets for surplus manufactures and afforded Europe her principal supply of silver—then esteemed more precious than gold. Here certainly was a prize worth fighting for to the end.[19]

England reasserted her ancient interest in this vital trade when Charles II in 1660 incorporated a group of merchants as the Royal African Company and by later charters of 1663 and 1672 gave it the exclusive right to carry slaves from Africa to the English colonies and the exclusive right to hold land in Africa from Morocco to the Cape of Good Hope. The company established forts and trading posts in the Gambia River region and on the Gold Coast, successfully waged war against a rival Dutch company, and profited immensely from the sale of slaves to English planters in the West Indies. Then, after 1680, the company devoted itself primarily to trade with the Spanish colonists. Spain did not engage in the slave traffic but rather sold to assientists or private contractors the exclusive right to supply her colonies with slaves (the assiento). Such contractors customarily purchased Negroes at the West Indies from the great slave trading interests of Europe. Due to war in Africa between France and the Dutch the English company gained a favored position with the assientists, who came to Jamaica to buy Negroes or arranged to have the company deliver slaves to Spanish colonial ports—Cartagena, Havana, and Porto Bello.[20]

The growth of this traffic benefited England in another way: it enabled her merchants to smuggle English merchandise into the Spanish colonies in the slave ships that sailed from Jamaica. Since Spain still required that European goods should go to her colonies by way of

[19] Alfred T. Mahan's *The Influence of Sea Power upon History, 1660–1788* (New York, 1890) discusses international conflicts, considering all important factors and assigning the decisive role to sea power. Mahan wrote so persuasively of this "lesson of history" as to stimulate international competition for naval supremacy. See chapters 1–5.

[20] G. F. Zook, "The Company of Adventurers Trading into Africa, 1660–1672," *Journal of Negro History*, IV (April 1919).

Seville, the English at Jamaica, by shipping directly to the colonists, could undersell the highly taxed goods that arrived over the roundabout route from Spain. Two governors of Jamaica in the 1680's, who were virtually agents of the Royal African Company, promoted the traffic so effectively that England secured the lion's share of the assiento business. Again, in 1694, when a Portuguese company obtained the assiento, the English arranged to supply it with slaves at Jamaica. In the meantime the Royal African Company had been neglecting to provide the English planters with slaves—a circumstance which encouraged private traders or interlopers to break in upon its monopoly. So great was the value to England of the traffic with Spanish America—now yielding large quantities of silver annually—and so urgent was the need of supplying the English colonists with slaves that Parliament in 1698 opened the trade to the interlopers on condition that they pay—toward the maintenance of the company's forts—a tax of 10 per cent of the value of the merchandise they imported into Africa.[21]

In 1701 France endeavored to break the grip of England on the Spanish American trade. Since the days of Colbert various French companies had been developing a slave traffic with the French West Indies but as yet France had not profited greatly from the Spanish trade—largely because she was periodically at war with Spain. The tactics of France in the Caribbean had been to plunder Spanish settlements and ships. However, the chief French agent in the West Indies, M. Du Casse, became convinced that France had more to gain from regular commerce with the Spanish colonies than from privateering depredations. Accordingly, he urged that Louis XIV secure the assiento for France. Undoubtedly the latter accepted the Spanish crown for his grandson largely because France might thereby dominate the trade of the Spanish Indies. One of the first acts of Philip V was to confer upon the French Guinea Company a ten-year monopoly of the slave traffic of Spanish America, as well as certain other privileges which promised France a large share of the trade in general merchandise. Perceiving that these concessions would deprive them of all the gains they had made in the Spanish empire the English merchants became vigorous supporters of the war.[22]

"Should the French settle at the disemboguing of the river Mississippi," wrote an English publicist about 1700, "they would not be long before they made themselves masters of that rich province, which would be an addition to their strength very terrible to Europe." The

---

[21] G. Scelle, "The Slave Trade in the Spanish Colonies of America: the Assiento," *American Journal of International Law*, IV.

[22] See again C. P. Nettels, *Money Supply of the American Colonies*, chapter 1.

idea thus expressed by Davenant was not merely a fantasy: as early as 1684 La Salle had given his life in a fruitless, tragic effort to establish a French colony at the mouth of the Mississippi. He had visualized an inland empire that would divert to France the great southern trade in furs and deerskins, then exploited by the merchants of Virginia and South Carolina, and would perhaps enable the French to descend upon the kingdom of New Spain and possess themselves of its silver mines. La Salle's hopes were realized in part when in 1699 one Pierre Le Moyne d'Iberville founded a settlement at Biloxi near the mouth of the Mississippi—a move which forestalled the English, at that very time on the point of sending thither a colonizing expedition. Although the new French province of Louisiana made only slow and painful progress, it served as a base from which French *voyageurs* penetrated into the southwestern area previously dominated by English fur traders. And Louisiana not only threatened the English trade on the southern frontier; it also strengthened the Spaniards in Florida in opposition to their neighbors in South Carolina. The union of France and Spain in Europe thus united their colonies in the remote American wilderness against the common English foe.[23]

The events of King William's War greatly altered the situation on the New York frontier. The raiding parties which Frontenac sent against the Iroquois had wrought widespread destruction and had given them, for the first time, a wholesome respect for France and a lively dread of French arms. Feeling that they had been let down by the English during the war, the Five Nations abandoned the strong pro-English stand they had previously maintained and turned a friendly ear toward Canada, realizing now that war carried a greater threat to their security than did French competition in trade. They divided into pro-French and pro-English factions, received French agents into their villages, began to trade with Montreal, and in 1701 made a peace with Canada that implied a recognition of their subjection to the French king. Thus they adopted what later writers interpreted as a policy of maintaining a balance of power between France and England on the northwestern frontier.

Meanwhile the French were not idle. With the increasing importance of the Mississippi valley, the route to which traversed the Iroquois country, the French perceived the advantage of placating the Five Nations and accordingly sought to secure their good will or at least their neutrality as a condition to the peaceful development of New France. Recognizing the right of the Iroquois to trade with

[23] J. H. Schlarman, *From Quebec to New Orleans* (Belleville, Ill., 1929), is a scholarly study of the French in America. See pp. 15–125.

Albany, although hoping to divert as much of their traffic to Montreal as possible, the French made the peace of 1701, and at the outbreak of Queen Anne's War Louis XIV instructed his officials in Canada not to attack the Iroquois. The latter—determined not to become solely dependent upon the French—agreed that they would remain neutral "on condition that Albany be spared from attack." The new Iroquoian policy of cultivating both sides was extended by an agreement of 1701 in which the Five Nations ceded to the King of England their hunting lands on either side of the Great Lakes.[24]

The lesson of King William's War had not been lost to the Albany traders; they too perceived that France and England were as yet so evenly matched in North America that warfare meant, not a decisive gain for either party, but a virtual destruction of the fur trade—which, during the years 1690–96, had shrunk to trifling proportions. Preferring an understanding with France to the former state of war, fear, and alarms, an important faction of the Albany traders strove to enforce a policy of neutrality and peace. The then governor of New York, Lord Bellomont, favored aggressive measures, chiefly the establishment of English forts and trading posts on the Lakes—a program which would have aroused the French and angered the Iroquois by threatening to deprive them of their status of middlemen between Albany and the West. For these reasons many Albany traders opposed and defeated Bellomont's plans. Meanwhile Albany was developing a traffic with Montreal whereby the French were supplied with cheap English goods for the Indian trade. A delegation of Albany traders visited Montreal in the spring of 1701 and returned with a project for neutrality which they submitted to the council of New York. By virtue of these factors New York and Canada remained at peace during the first half of Queen Anne's War. Between 1702 and 1706 New York spent only trifling sums for frontier defense. On the other hand, New England became at once involved in the renewed hostilities, since the causes of her antagonism toward New France had not been removed; and consequently she had to bear alone the brunt of the early war in the North.[25]

Despite much talk about the conquest of Boston, the French focused their military efforts upon the New England frontier, where their influence among the Indians was paramount—a legacy, in part, of King Philip's War. Raiding parties sent out by the governor of Canada, the

[24] Francis Parkman, *A Half-Century of Conflict* (2 vols., Boston, 1892), Vol. I, chapters 1–8.

[25] See again L. P. Kellogg, *The French Regime in Wisconsin and the Northwest*, chapters 9–13.

Marquis de Vaudreuil, harassed exposed settlements from Wells on the Maine coast to Northampton in Massachusetts. Particularly savage was the massacre at Deerfield, where in 1704 the French and Indians launched a surprise attack upon the sleeping villagers, killed fifty-three, and took a hundred and eleven captives, seventeen of whom perished on the subsequent march to Canada. Such raids provoked reproaches in New England against New York, for Albany was prospering by the sale of firearms to the Indians who spread havoc on the eastern frontier. Looking to the conquest of Canada as their only salvation, the New Englanders in 1708 asked Britain to take decisive steps to bring that to pass.[26]

Their chief spokesman was one Samuel Vetch, a Scottish merchant, soldier of fortune, and friend of Joseph Dudley, governor of Massachusetts. Interested in acquiring Canada or Acadia as a region for Scottish colonization, Vetch wrote a tract, *Canada Surveyed*, which convinced the British colonial officials of the necessity of the conquest. Lord Bellomont's earlier policy of aggression had reflected the views of the king's advisers, but England had been unable to act prior to 1708 because of the European war. Successes on the Continent, however, now enabled her to promise aid for a colonial assault upon Canada and accordingly it was arranged that a land expedition should proceed from Albany to the St. Lawrence and that a naval force should sail from Boston to Quebec. The land force was barely under way when news that Britain had not contributed her part to the naval force caused the expedition to disband. New York at this time was participating vigorously in the war, since Britain's offers of aid promised results which the province could not hope to accomplish alone.

After the fiasco of 1709 a congress of colonial governors resolved in favor of the conquest, and Peter Schuyler, now chief director of affairs at Albany, carried their petition to England, taking with him four Iroquois warriors as a means of attracting attention at court.[27] Then, in 1710, a British and colonial force commanded by Francis Nicholson sailed from Boston and conquered Port Royal, Acadia—not a particularly glorious victory, however, since the British outnumbered the Acadians eight to one. Port Royal being the only Acadian settlement of consequence, its seizure meant the conquest of the whole province, and this time Britain did not restore it to France.

[26] Samuel A. Drake, *The Border Wars of New England* (New York, 1897) is a thorough, compact, readable narrative, 1689–1711.

[27] W. T. Morgan, "The Five Nations and Queen Anne," *Mississippi Valley Historical Review*, XIII (Sept. 1926).

The climax or anticlimax of the war came in 1711, when another land force of Iroquois and colonials advanced to Lake Champlain and a grand fleet of seventy-one vessels and twelve thousand men left Boston for Quebec. Commanded by Sir Hovenden Walker, this fleet encountered fog and storms in the St. Lawrence, lost ten ships and nine hundred men, and returned to Boston without striking a blow—an unwarranted retreat, since even after the wreck Walker and his fellow commander, John Hill, an incompetent political appointee, still had enough men for the conquest of all Canada. New York and the Iroquois now sought refuge in their earlier policy of neutrality and the conflict in the North ended in 1713 without other noteworthy events.

In the South the war began in earnest when the Spaniards, early in 1702, launched a land attack from Florida on South Carolina. Warned by friendly Indians (the Creeks), the English managed to raise a defensive force and to drive back the Spaniards and their Indian allies. South Carolina now took the offensive in the autumn of 1702 by dispatching a band of militia and Indians in a small fleet to St. Augustine. Although successful in destroying that ancient Spanish town the English invaders failed to take the fort and were obliged to retreat when two enemy warships appeared. The French and Spaniards retaliated in 1706 by sending a fleet from Havana against Charleston, but the South Carolina farmers rallied to the defense of their port town, routed a part of the enemy force that had landed, and compelled the French commander to beat a hasty retreat. These expeditions demonstrated that the two contestants on the southern frontier were too evenly matched for either to win a campaign for conquest, although the inconclusive engagements indicated that the South Carolinians had a slight advantage over Spaniards and their French and Indian allies.

In the Caribbean, the principal theater of the war in America, the conflict resolved itself into attacks by the European powers upon the commerce and colonies of their foes. The trade between Europe and Spanish America fell largely into the hands of the French—a condition which England met by sending privateers and warships to seize French and Spanish merchantmen, by allowing English traders to carry on an open trade with friendly Spanish colonists, and by conducting a campaign of propaganda among the settlers with the aim of inducing them to reject the authority of Philip V and to recognize the Archduke Charles as King of Spain. While not successful in breaking the power of France and Spain in the Caribbean, England managed to protect her own island colonies, to capture a large number of French and Spanish ships, and to retain and strengthen her grip upon the trade by which her merchants at Jamaica obtained Spanish silver in payment for English goods and slaves—a trade which now supplied England annually with money and bullion worth £200,000.[28]

By the Peace of Utrecht (1713) France ceded to Britain the Hudson Bay region and Acadia, excepting Cape Breton Island, and acknowledged the suzerainty of Britain over the Iroquois. Britain also obtained complete title to Newfoundland and its adjacent islands, although the French received the privilege of drying fish on the western and northern shores between Cape Bonavista and Cape Riche. In return for recognizing Philip V as King of Spain Britain received a thirty-year monopoly of the slave trade of the Spanish Indies. This monopoly conferred the privilege of selling 4,800 slaves a year to the Spanish colonies and of importing directly into Britain (in British vessels) the money, bullion, and produce taken in payment for the slaves. The British assientists were permitted to send once a year a licensed vessel privileged to sell a large cargo of general merchandise to the Spanish colonists at Porto Bello. Britain granted the assiento to the famous South Sea Company, organized in 1711 as a means of establishing Britain in the trade of the Pacific. After 1713 the South Sea Company concentrated upon the trade in general merchandise and used the licensed vessel, permanently stationed off Porto Bello, as a floating warehouse from which British goods were constantly carried to the Spanish colonists. By and large the Peace of Utrecht favored Britain although in two places—Canada and Louisiana—the power of France was not seriously curtailed.

## IMPERIAL POLICIES, 1689–1713

As the political victory of the English merchant-capitalists in 1689 led to war against their most potent foreign enemy, France, so also it resulted in the tightening of the imperial system, with the object of restraining their other rivals, the merchants of Scotland and of the colonies. One phase of the colonial policy of William III was a campaign to render the colonial governments more dependent upon England, primarily in order to assure a more stringent enforcement of the Navigation Acts. Thus the Massachusetts charter issued in 1691 provided that the governor of that province be appointed by the king and empowered to reject the nominees to the council who were proposed by a joint assembly of deputies and the existing councillors. Massachusetts, Plymouth, and Maine were now united and since the governor of Massachusetts was also appointed governor of New Hampshire

[28] G. N. Clark, "War Trade and Trade War, 1701–1713," *Economic History Review*, I (Jan. 1928).

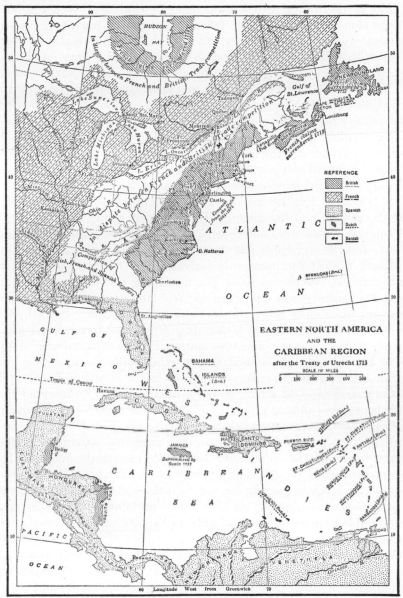

REFERENCE

| | |
|---|---|
| | British |
| | French |
| | Spanish |
| | Dutch |
| | Danish |

ATLANTIC

OCEAN

EASTERN NORTH AMERICA
AND THE
CARIBBEAN REGION
after the Treaty of Utrecht 1713

SCALE OF MILES
0    100    200    300    400    500

GULF OF

MEXICO

Tropic of Cancer

WEST

BAHAMA

ISLANDS
(Brit.)

Havana

CUBA

INDIES

CARIBBEAN

SEA

PACIFIC

OCEAN

80    Longitude  West  from  Greenwich    70

a large northern royal province was created including all New England except Connecticut and Rhode Island. So also the Crown took into its hands the government of Maryland in 1691, of Pennsylvania in 1693, and of New Jersey in 1702, in each case assuming control of the executive agencies of the province. Penn's political rights were restored to him in 1694, Lord Baltimore's in 1716; New Jersey remained a royal province. In the meantime, English officialdom labored to bring the other colonies (Connecticut, Rhode Island, and the Carolinas) under royal control, and opposed the establishment of new colonies in which governors and councillors were not appointed by the king. Additional rights of self-government were not to be granted, and those already conferred were to be curtailed as soon as possible.[29]

By 1695 the English merchants had become dissatisfied with England's regulation of the colonies The Lords of Trade, then in charge of colonial affairs, were nobles who represented the aristocracy or the court; and the merchants felt that the colonial administration was indifferent toward the mercantile interests, and careless and inert in enforcing the Navigation Acts. The merchants therefore prepared to have Parliament—now the organ of their interests—assume the management of colonies and trade through a parliamentary council. But William III, ever jealous of his kingly prerogatives, forestalled Parliament's action and at the same time appeased the merchants by creating, May 15, 1696, a new colonial agency—the Lords Commissioners of Trade and Plantations, commonly known as the Board of Trade.

Composed of eight active, working members who represented the merchant class (although high dignitaries of state were nominal members and occasionally attended its meetings) the Board of Trade immediately undertook to subordinate the economic activities and the governments of the colonies to England's mercantile interests. Its creation therefore recognized the power of the merchants in the councils of state. While not empowered to make and enforce decisions it was authorized to investigate all matters pertaining to colonies and trade and to prepare recommendations to Parliament and the executive departments of the Crown. Since the members of the Board served continuously and labored diligently they became the best informed officials in England on colonies and trade and consequently exerted a dominating influence on imperial policy. Always upholding and advocating the principles of mercantilism, the Board made recommendations which were generally given legal force through orders in council or acts of Parliament, and although many such orders were not strictly en-

[29] George H. Guttridge, *The Colonial Policy of William III* (Cambridge, 1922), is a good brief survey.

forced and although many of the policies urged by the Board were not adopted, even so, few actions were undertaken, few measures were approved in the commercial-colonial sphere unless they had first been sanctioned by the Board of Trade.[30]

The English merchants obtained further support in 1696 when Parliament passed a supplementary Navigation Act to strengthen the existing colonial system. In the future all colonial governors (whether elected as in Rhode Island or appointed by proprietors as in Carolina) were to serve only when approved by the king and were required to take an oath to enforce the Navigation Acts under pain of dismissal if they did not. Merchants who reëxported from a colonial port any of the enumerated articles which had been brought from another colony were now required to give bond to assure that such articles would not be carried to foreign ports. Should such bonds prove to be forged or fraudulent a fine of £500 awaited the offender. English customs agents in the colonies received the rights of search possessed by similar officials in England and owners of ocean-going and coastwise vessels engaged in colonial trade were required to register them at London.

The Navigation Act of 1696 did not extend the basic principles of the colonial system; it merely provided for a more efficient administration of existing laws. Of similar effect was the establishment of admiralty courts for the trial and punishment of violators of the acts. Prior to 1697 persons accused of such violations were generally tried in the regular courts of the colonies—a practice upon which English officialdom looked with disfavor: first, because the judges were colonists who tended to deal leniently with colonial merchants; secondly, because such courts granted jury trials, with the result that juries were partial to their accused neighbors. It is not surprising therefore that the colonial courts rarely gave judgments in favor of the English merchants at the expense of colonial merchants or that English agents like Edward Randolph found the judicial cards in the colonies stacked against England.[31]

In 1697 the Privy Council authorized the colonial governors to erect vice-admiralty courts and to appoint the necessary judges, advocates, registrars, and marshals. Eventually, twelve such courts were established in the colonies—all subject to a ruling of the king's Attorney-General in 1702 which forbade them to allow the accused a trial by jury. Presumably these measures should have given England complete

[30] One of the best studies of British policy and administration is W. T. Root, *The Relations of Pennsylvania with the British Government* (New York, 1912).

[31] Helen J. Crump, *Colonial Admiralty Jurisdiction* (London, 1931), is the best study (technical).

judicial power over violators of the Navigation Acts, but one question remained: how far did the jurisdiction of the admiralty courts extend? The English navy was too small to make numerous captures on the high seas of vessels engaged in illegal trade; consequently English agents commonly made such seizures in colonial ports and waters. The colonial courts claimed jurisdiction in the ensuing cases and fought stubbornly to remove them from the admiralty courts. To this end the colonial courts reversed decisions rendered by the admiralty judges and freed from prison the traders whom the latter had sentenced. This intensely bitter struggle for control of the means of enforcing the Navigation Acts continued until the Revolutionary War.

By 1690 illegal trade had assumed the virulent form of piracy. Since the time of Drake and the Elizabethan sea dogs pirates had been wont to prey upon the commerce of rival nations in distant waters, even in time of peace. When open war broke out such marauders were commissioned as privateers in the king's service, but after the end of formal hostilities they were prone to resume their old piratical ways.[32] A revival of English privateering and piracy swept over the Caribbean region after Cromwell's expedition against the Spanish Indies in 1654–55. Jamaica now became the center of operations and the treasure of the Spanish colonies the principal source of ill-gotten wealth. Since gold and silver could be disposed of at any place (and no questions asked) the pirates were always on the lookout for ships bearing treasure. Although the English government prior to 1665 had done little to suppress piracy in the Caribbean a new trend of policy appeared afterward as the result of two treaties with Spain in 1667 and 1670 which recognized England's claims to the colonies she actually possessed in the West Indies. Then occurred the growth of the legal slave trade between Jamaica and the Spanish colonies—a traffic which promised greater profits to English merchants than the old game of piracy. Because the outlaws preyed upon friendly Spanish vessels trading with Jamaica, and therefore retarded the growth of peaceful commerce, England undertook to suppress piracy in the Caribbean. Warships were provided to convoy vessels in the Jamaica trade, privateers were ordered not to molest friendly Spaniards, and pirates were offered pardons on condition that they surrender and forsake their evil ways. Due to these measures English piracy and privateering in the Caribbean declined rapidly after 1680.[33]

[32] Violet Barbour, "Privateers and Pirates of the West Indies," *American Historical Review*, XVI (April 1911).

[33] C. H. Haring, *The Buccaneers in the West Indies* (New York, 1910), is an authentic, well-written narrative.

But it soon broke out in a new quarter—in the Red Sea and Indian Ocean, where the pirates now fell upon English vessels carrying silver to the Orient or returning with valuable cargoes of East Indian goods. Many merchants of Massachusetts, New York, South Carolina, and Pennsylvania became involved in this traffic. Some of them actually financed the pirates and shared the plunder; some supplied them with provisions in return for money and East Indian goods; while others carried on a regular trade with Madagascar, which was the base of the pirates' operations for the Red Sea. Colonial officials—particularly Governor Benjamin Fletcher and Councillor Nicholas Bayard of New York and Governor William Markham of Pennsylvania—were accused of selling protection to pirates who sought refuge in American ports, while shopkeepers and the people generally were receptive to the ill-gotten wealth which was liberally spent in shops and taverns or used to refit marauding vessels for new exploits. Such gains of the colonists, however, were destructive of the coveted India trade and consequently England extended her campaign against piracy to the Red Sea.

The foremost enemy of the pirates in North America was the Earl of Bellomont, governor of New England and New York between 1697 and 1701, one of the most energetic, efficient, and industrious of England's colonial administrators—a governor who attempted to subordinate all groups in the colonies to England's mercantile interests. Bringing emphatic instructions for the suppression of piracy and illegal trade, Bellomont made New York the principal target of his attack. He endeavored to prevent pirate ships from landing, instituted searches for money and goods already brought in, insisted that departing vessels should give bond as an assurance against piracy, and removed from the council five of its members who were charged with illegal trade. So effective were his efforts that his enemies complained he had kept £100,000 out of the province in less than a year.[34]

Before leaving England Bellomont joined with other great men to finance an expedition for the suppression of piracy in the Red Sea—a venture that was expected to yield profits through the recovery of spoil. In command was one Captain William Kidd, who proceeded from New York to Madagascar, only to find that the pirates there had made themselves scarce. Apparently Kidd's crew grew restive when no pirates' plunder came their way and thereupon took to piracy on their own account. Whether they forced Kidd into submission or whether he joined willingly remains a mystery. At any rate they captured some

[34] John Masefield, *On the Spanish Main* (New York, 1906), relates pirate exploits with the art of a great writer. See chapters 8–15.

vessels in the India trade and eventually put into port at Boston, where Kidd was arrested on Bellomont's order and later sent to England for trial. Convicted of both murder and piracy Captain Kidd paid for his conduct on the gallows—an execution that may be regarded as the climax of England's war against piracy.

In 1700 Parliament provided legal machinery for the trial of pirates in the colonies by authorizing the king to erect special courts consisting of governors, councillors, admiralty judges, captains of naval vessels, and customs agents. Although distinct from the admiralty courts these special tribunals functioned in the same manner—without jury trial— and were empowered to sentence convicted pirates to death. After the outbreak of Queen Anne's War the pirates once more found a legal course open to them as privateers; their enlistment under one of the flags of the belligerent powers transformed them into allies or enemies at war, and measures taken by England against enemy privateers, together with the campaign against ordinary pirates, removed the old evil from the mainland colonies.[35]

In extenuation of piracy William Penn once said that all the money which they brought into Pennsylvania was remitted to England in the course of trade—a reference to the difficulty with which the northern colonies had long grappled in seeking to find means of payment for their imports of English goods. Without doubt the money derived from piracy had afforded the colonies a large fund of returns during the years 1680–1700; hence its suppression promised to curtail colonial buying power and thus to diminish the market value to England of New England, Pennsylvania, and New York. Due to the population growth of the northern colonies they had been rapidly extending their purchases of English goods and were becoming more and more valuable as markets—thus realizing one objective of English mercantilism. And yet the native products of the northern colonies could not, for the most part, be sold in England, with the result that the colonists had been forced to engage in various pursuits like piracy and illegal trade in order to obtain the necessary means of payment.

In the fields of general commerce the northern merchants had developed their trades with Newfoundland, southern Europe, the Wine Islands, and the West Indies in order to obtain remittances for English imports—coin, bills of exchange, and foreign commodities that could be traded in England for English goods. In many respects, however,

[35] C. N. Dalton seeks to rehabilitate Kidd in *The Real Captain Kidd* (New York, 1911). Harold T. Wilkins, *Captain Kidd* (London, 1935), is mainly a selection of source quotations.

these trades were detrimental to England. They built up a class of colonial merchants who competed effectively with the merchants of England for the freights and profits of American commerce and gave to the colonists a variety of trading contacts which enabled them easily to violate the Navigation Acts. To Portugal New Hampshire sold ship timber needed by the royal navy; to Newfoundland the Boston merchants sold rum which induced drunkenness among the resident fishermen and weakened the English fishery there; from the Dutch in the West Indies the Northerners bought European goods which were smuggled into the English colonies; and at Newfoundland colonial ship captains enticed sailors away from English vessels, thus building up the colonial merchant marine at the expense of English shipping.[36]

The suppression of piracy and the closer regulation of colonial trade promised to benefit English merchants but in the process the colonists might lose a large part of their remittances to England and that in turn would curtail their value as markets. Moreover, the colonial demand for manufactures was so great that if the colonists could not buy them in England they would be forced to produce them at home. The progress of manufacturing industries in the northern colonies would inevitably yield a surplus of articles above the needs of local consumption with the result that the Northerners, sooner or later, would export that surplus to the tobacco colonies and the West Indies. England therefore would lose not only the markets of the northern colonies but also those of the plantation area. Such a loss would mean that colonial merchants would gain control of the marketing of southern produce, since they would receive it in exchange for colonial manufactures. Hence the progress of manufacturing industry in the northern colonies threatened to break the grip of English merchant capitalism on American trade.

In 1699 the manufacture of woolens, still the mainstay of English industry and object of the tender solicitude of the government, was in a declining state, because—as Parliament asserted—"great quantities of . . . manufactures . . . have of late been made and are daily increasing in the kingdom of Ireland and in the English plantations in America which will inevitably sink the value of the lands and tend to the ruin of the trade and woolen manufactures of this realm." Undoubtedly the cloth industry had made great progress in New England and Long Island, where the people were fabricating their own woolen goods and rapidly improving the quality of their products. In order to

[36] C. P. Nettels, "The Menace of Colonial Manufacturing," *New England Quarterly*, IV (April 1931).

check this trend Parliament inserted a clause in the Woolen Act of 1699 which prohibited the exportation of wool or woolen cloth of American production from any colony, thus permitting household manufacturing but thwarting the growth of the woolen industry on a commercial scale.[37]

England's campaign against piracy and illegal trade, by diminishing colonial remittances for English goods, tended to foster colonial manufactures. These in turn were proscribed by the Woolen Act of 1699. Yet the crucial problem of the trade of the northern colonies remained unsolved, since they could not long be restrained both from obtaining buying power in England and from manufacturing for themselves; something had to be done to supply them with the means of paying for English goods. In this connection the Board of Trade—which strongly advocated the enforcement of the Navigation Acts and the suppression of colonial manufactures—undertook to develop in the northern area staple commodities, similar to tobacco and sugar, which could be exchanged in England for manufactured wares.

The timber resources of New England and New York, the needs of English shipping for naval stores, and the fact that England had been buying such stores from northern Europe, paying for them presumably with specie rather than with her manufactures, formed the basis of the plan proposed by the Board of Trade to solve the problem of colonial returns. After an extended survey made by the Board of the productive capacity of the New England forests, Parliament in 1705 passed an act to encourage the naval stores industry in the northern colonies. Three things about this act deserve notice. First, it granted substantial bounties for pitch, resin, tar, turpentine, ship timber, masts, and hemp which were produced in the colonies and imported into England. Secondly, it placed these products on the enumerated article list, thereby assuring that they would be sold exclusively in England as a means of paying for English exports to the northern colonies. Thirdly, the act provided that pine trees in the forests of New England, New Jersey, and New York should be reserved for the production of naval stores—not used for ordinary lumber. Behind this act lay the assumption that the northern colonies would produce all the stores required by English shipping, yield a surplus which could be reëxported to Europe, provide the colonies with purchasing power for English goods, divert them from competing manufacturing industries, and center their trade in Eng-

[37] Robert G. Albion's *Forests and Sea Power* (Cambridge, 1926), an admirable study, discusses the English background of the colonial naval stores industry. See chapters 3–6.

land, thereby lessening their dependence on piracy, illegal trade, and other branches of commerce which had proved detrimental to the English merchants.[38]

Immediately after the passage of the act of 1705 the Board of Trade sent one John Bridger to New England to instruct the inhabitants in the art of producing naval stores and to preserve the most suitable trees in the northern woods from destruction by the colonial lumbermen. Primarily an agent of the English merchants trading to the colonies, Bridger labored with all diligence at his task, only to encounter heated opposition from the lumbermen of New Hampshire, who, he said, threatened to shoot him "if they ketch me in the woods." As long as New Englanders served as colonial officials, he concluded, "the king must not expect any justice as to the woods, for all the people on the frontiers depend on the woods for their livelihood and say the king has no woods . . . and [that] they will cut what and where they please."

Another effort made by England in behalf of colonial naval stores centered in New York, whither the Board of Trade in 1710 sent a company of three thousand refugees from Germany to establish the industry. Parliament voted £10,000 for their support, and they were placed in charge of Governor Robert Hunter. For two years after their arrival he supported the project against numerous odds and then was forced to admit defeat and abandon the cause, just as the first products were nearing completion. Neither New York nor New England, therefore, developed naval stores as staple returns to England; instead the industry took root in the pine forests of the Carolinas where conditions of production were more favorable than in the North. The merchants of New England, however, were able to export the Carolina products by way of Boston to England, thus obtaining the bounty and adding to their purchasing power for English goods. This outcome increased the external commercial activity of New England instead of diminishing it, as the authors of the naval stores program had intended.[39]

Fundamentally the new industry did not take root in New England because it was antagonistic to the major interests already developed there—lumbering, manufacturing, and external commerce. The leading merchants of New England contributed little to this policy which was designed to center their trade in England and to render them

[38] Eleanor Lord, *Industrial Experiments in the British Colonies of North America* (Baltimore, 1898), emphasizes the Baltic trade in English policy.
[39] See again E. B. Greene, *Provincial America*, chapters 1–5 (British policy, 1690–1713).

tributary to their English rivals. During the last years of Queen Anne's War the problem of returns was solved when England transmitted large sums of money to New England and New York for the prosecution of the war—money that was immediately utilized to pay for English goods imported into the colonies. After 1713 the northern colonies found another means of obtaining purchasing power in England—trade with the foreign colonies in the West Indies. This trade, however, soon menaced the English sugar planters in the Caribbean and provoked a deadly conflict between them and the northern merchants which finally terminated in the Revolutionary War.

## BIBLIOGRAPHICAL NOTE

Works Previously Cited: W. C. Abbott, *Expansion of Europe*, I, chs. 25, 27, 29; Lord Acton, *Lectures on Modern History*, chs. 14, 15; G. Bancroft, *History of the United States*, II, ch. 35; J. B. Brebner, *Explorers of North America*, chs. 17–19 (French); C. W. Colby, *Canadian Types of the Old Regime*, chs. 5–10; *Cambridge History of the British Empire*, I, chs. 10, 18; *Cambridge Modern History*, V, chs. 1–2, 13–14; E. Channing, *History of the United States*, II, pp. 131–154, 217–281; G. N. Clark, *The Later Stuarts*, chs. 6–7, 12; V. W. Crane, *The Southern Frontier*, chs. 1–6; H. E. Egerton, *Short History of British Colonial Policy*, Book II, ch. 4; J. Fiske, *Dutch and Quaker Colonies*, II, pp. 209–244; A. C. Flick (ed.), *History of the State of New York*, I, ch. 6; C. J. H. Hayes, *Political and Cultural History of Europe*, I, ch. 6; H. Heaton, *Economic History of Europe*, pp. 285–301 (French economy); G. A. Jacobsen, *William Blathwayt*, chs. 9–14; L. P. Kellogg, *The American Colonial Charter*, chs. 2–4 (imperial rule); W. B. Munro, *Crusaders of New France*, chs. 4–10; A. Shortt and A. C. Doughty (eds.), *Canada and Its Provinces*, I, II; J. Winsor (ed.), *Narrative and Critical History of America*, IV, ch. 7.

Sources Newly Cited: On the French in the interior see Louise P. Kellogg (ed.), *Early Narratives of the Northwest* (New York, 1917—Jameson *Original Narratives series*). Isaac J. Cox (ed.), *The Journeys of René Robert Cavelier Sieur de La Salle* (2 vols., New York, 1905), is an attractive, well selected collection. J. F. Jameson (ed.), *Privateering and Piracy in the Colonial Period* (New York, 1923), will appeal to more advanced students. See pp. 145–289. For source materials on Captain Kidd see Graham Brooks (ed.), *The Trial of Captain Kidd* (Edinburgh, 1930), and Don C. Seitz (ed.), *The Tryale of Capt. William Kidd* (New York, 1936).

Sources Previously Cited: F. G. Davenport (ed.), *European Treaties bearing upon the History of the United States*, II, nos. 79, 84; III, nos. 89–90, 92, 96–107; A. B. Hart (ed.), *American History Told by Contemporaries*, I, pp. 133–144; W. MacDonald (ed.), *Documentary Source Book of American History*, no. 25.

Maps: D. R. Fox, *Harper's Atlas*, pp. 12–15; C. O. Paullin, *Atlas of the Historical Geography of the United States*, plates 20, 22–26, 37, 161; W. R. Shepherd, *Historical Atlas*, pp. 125–126, 128B.

## ☆ XV ☆

## IMMIGRATION AND EXPANSION

PRIOR to the year 1680 the American colonies had in the main realized the early ambition of Sir Walter Raleigh to create little Englands beyond the sea, for nine-tenths of the colonists were of English stock. Only the Dutch and Swedish colonists in the middle region broke the racial unity of the settlements, since the white inhabitants of New England and the southern colonies were almost exclusively of English descent. After 1680, however, England ceased to be the chief source of emigration to the colonies, being superseded in that role by six other regions—France, Germany, Ireland, Scotland, Switzerland, and Africa, which sent out hordes of emigrants who began the historic American process of racial amalgamation. In respect to America the eighteenth century was preëminently the century of the foreigner: in 1760 the foreign-born represented a third of the colonial population whereas in 1912 they accounted for only a sixth of the people of the United States.[1] Crèvecoeur, writing at the time of the Revolutionary War, described the fusion in the colonies of the diverse European national groups which was producing the American type, citing the case of a grandson of an Englishman who had married a Dutch woman and whose five sons had married wives of different nationalities. The formation of the American people from several European stocks introduced a new principle in nation-building: the voluntary union of many national groups hitherto hostile to one another in Europe—a fusion achieved through self-selection or intermarriage among free settlers, not, as previously in history, through conquest and the subjugation of the conquered by the conquerors. Of all the factors at work in eighteenth-century America none had greater influence than the immigration of the foreigners, for this made possible that vigorous expansion which is the dominant note of the age. The population of the colonies, which in 1690 amounted to about a quarter of a million, was to double every twenty-five years (thanks partly to the foreigners) until in 1775 it numbered more than two and a half million souls.[2]

[1] See four important articles by Max Farrand, "Immigration in the Light of History," *New Republic*, IX (Dec. 2, 9, 16, 23, 1916).

[2] E. B. Greene and Virginia D. Harrington have prepared statistical estimates of colonial population in *American Population before the Federal Census of 1790* (New York, 1932). Valuable as a reference work.

## THE CAUSES AND PROCESS OF IMMIGRATION

The social and economic system of Europe, which increasingly concentrated control over the means of production in the hands of a relatively few landowners and merchants, condemned large masses of the peasants and workers to such a low level of subsistence that serious disturbances in the economic order spread havoc and starvation. The mercantile theory that commerce was one nation's loss and another's gain bred destructive wars and repressive legislation, while European states still resorted to religious persecution as a means of bolstering up the ruling classes. To the poor peasants and workers of Europe, immersed in poverty, war, and religious persecution, the English colonies beckoned with an irresistible appeal. There at least one might enjoy peace and security, freedom of Protestant worship, and the economic opportunities of cheap land and high wages: there perhaps one might pass beyond the grasp of the tax-collector and the sound of marching armies.[3]

So great was the emigration from Germany to America that it has been likened to the Germanic migrations at the dawn of the Middle Ages. From the Rhine country—the Palatinate, Wurtenberg, and Baden—thousands of peasants fled from wars that had intermittently devastated their fertile land. First the Thirty Years' War; then the campaigns of Louis XIV against the Dutch; then the War of the League of Augsburg, and finally the War of the Spanish Succession: what horror, suffering, famine, and pestilence they spread throughout southern Germany. Fighting for their independence in alliance with the enemies of Louis XIV, the German princes periodically felt the scourge of armies which he sent into their lands to destroy the crops that otherwise would have fed the anti-French forces. The War of the League of Augsburg witnessed the burning of the cities of Heidelberg, Mannheim, Speyer, and Worms, and when in 1707 Louis XIV again dispatched an army into the Palatinate on a food-destroying mission, that unhappy country seemed indeed a land of doom. This last invasion gave the final impetus to the modern German *völkerwanderung* which transplanted thousands of peasants to the New World.

To wartime distress were added other causes of discontent. In the Palatinate the peasants who had become radical Protestants or Pietists (Mennonites, Moravians, Socinians, Schwenkfelders, Dunkers, Amish, Quakers) were ruled by Catholic princes bent upon enforcing religious uniformity. The confiscation of property, the seizure of churches and

---

[3] Albert B. Faust, *The German Element in the United States* (2 vols., Boston, 1909; New York, 1927), is preëminent in its field. See Vol. I, chapters 1–10.

the expulsion of the most refractory Protestants—such were the measures employed to subdue and impoverish the peasants. Moreover, the German princes, enamored of the court of Louis XIV and striving to imitate its splendors, drew from the substance of the peasantry the means to sustain their vicarious glory.[4]

The impoverishment of the German peasants meant that the great majority of them could not pay the costs of emigration to America. However, merchants and ship captains able to advance the necessary money employed agents called "newlanders" who visited the peasants and persuaded them to leave the fatherland. Posing as American settlers temporarily sojourning in Germany, wearing flashy clothes and displaying watches and jewelry, the newlanders told wondrous tales of the riches of the colonies. "They would convince one that there are in America, none but Elysian fields abounding in products which require no labor; that the mountains are full of gold and silver, and that the wells and springs gush forth milk and honey; that he who goes there as a servant becomes a lord; as a maid, a gracious lady; as a peasant, a nobleman. . . . Law and authority, they say, is created by the people and abrogated at their will." When the newlander had persuaded a group of peasants to migrate he took them down the Rhine to Amsterdam or Rotterdam, where they were packed in vessels bound for America. In return for their passage they agreed to allow the ship captain to sell their labor in the colonies for a term of years. This traffic in human hopes netted a large profit to the newlanders and their employers.[5]

Quite different were the forces which drove emigrants from France to English America. In order to consolidate his kingly power Louis XIV in 1685 revoked the Edict of Nantes, which had given the Huguenots something of the status of a state within the state. New royal decrees now forbade Protestants to leave the country, to worship in churches, or to hold services in private homes. Having successfully withstood earlier persecution the Huguenots were too strong and loyal to their faith to be subdued by mild measures, and Louis XIV did not shrink from crushing all who would not enter the Catholic fold. Royal troops, employed to break up Huguenot conventicles, perpetrated several massacres; soldiers were quartered in Huguenot homes and given every license; the faithful who tried to escape were thrust into underground prisons or consigned as slaves to the galleys; and other

---

[4] A good introductory study is Lucy F. Bittinger, *The Germans in Colonial Times* (Philadelphia, 1901).

[5] Frank R. Diffenderffer, *The German Immigration into Pennsylvania* (Lancaster, 1900), is a factual, topical treatment.

dissenters were sold as servants to Catholic planters in the French West Indies. Whippings, denial of burials, indignities inflicted upon bodies of the dead—such were added horrors of the persecution, the spirit of which was expressed by the Secretary of War in an official order: "If it happen again to be possible to fall upon such [Huguenot] gatherings, let orders be given to the dragoons to kill the greatest part of the Protestants that can be overtaken, without sparing the women, to the end that this may intimidate them and prevent others from falling into a similar fault." Confronted now by the absolute power of the state and unable to offer armed resistance, the Huguenots had to choose between submission and flight.[6]

On one occasion the French government withdrew its decree against the emigration of Huguenots, only to be greeted by such an outrush of the oppressed that the ban was immediately restored. Even so, a large number of the Huguenots managed to escape—by avowing Catholicism at the frontier, by bribing or evading guards, or by using false passports. Forced to depend upon such methods of stealth the Huguenots could not make preparations in France for a direct voyage to America; instead they were obliged to convert their property into money or foreign credits and then to steal away to near-by states, Holland, Germany, Denmark, or England. For this reason an emigration traffic could not be carried on within France by newlanders; moreover, the expense and difficulty of escape limited the body of emigrants to a group of relatively well-to-do exiles who could finance their removal to America.[7]

Comparable to the Germans in influence and numbers were the Scotch-Irish emigrants driven from Northern Ireland after 1700 by poverty induced by oppressive measures of the English government. Here was a people already accustomed to the status of colonists under the English crown. One phase of colonizing activity of the seventeenth century had been the establishment in 1607–09 of the Plantation of Ulster in Northern Ireland. At the time of the accession of James I the Irish Catholics, long restive under English rule, had launched an armed revolt against the new sovereign. This uprising, like its many predecessors, was suppressed by the English overlords, and this time the king determined to subdue Northern Ireland by establishing garrisons and Protestant settlers among the disaffected Irish. Lands of the

[6] A strongly pro-Huguenot view is presented in Henry M. Baird, *The Huguenots and the Revocation of the Edict of Nantes* (2 vols., New York, 1895).

[7] Charles W. Baird, *History of the Huguenot Emigration to America* (2 vols., New York, c. 1885), emphasizes Huguenot leaders and families. See Vol. II.

"rebels" were widely confiscated in the northern counties (Donegal, Londonderry, Tyrone, Fermanagh, Armagh, and Cavan) and entrusted to companies and "undertakers" on the condition that they be peopled with non-Catholic farmers. The promoters then brought in thrifty, hard-working Scottish tenants, whose industry soon converted Ulster from the most backward to the most prosperous part of Ireland. Presbyterianism now replaced Catholicism as the dominant religion of Ulster, while the Plantation created a new "racial" group, the so-called Scotch-Irish, although the phrase "the Scots settled in Ireland" gives a more accurate description.[8]

Unfortunately for the Scotch-Irish they became too efficient competitors of English landlords and manufacturers. First they developed such a thriving livestock industry that Irish cattle became famous for their excellence. But since the best export markets were in England and Scotland, the Scotch-Irish farmers soon ran afoul of the powerful landed interests in those countries. At the behest of the English landlords, Parliament between 1665 and 1680 prohibited the importation into England of Irish cattle, sheep, swine, beef, pork, bacon, mutton, butter, and cheese, while similar acts of the Scottish Parliament excluded such products from the Scottish markets. As these measures threatened to ruin their cattle industry the Scotch-Irish, with commendable enterprise and adaptability, shifted their production to wool growing and the manufacture of cloth. Now they were able to export light and non-perishable products to all countries, with the result that they encroached upon England's markets and menaced her woolen industry. Parliament struck again through the Woolen Act of 1699 which prohibited the exportation of raw wool and woolen cloth from Ireland to any country. Ruin now visited the farmers and artisans of Ulster, whose doleful plight was described in the 1720's by Dean Swift in his *Irish Tracts*. "Whoever travels through this country," he wrote, "and observes . . . the faces and habits and dwellings of the natives, would hardly think himself in a land where either law, religion or common humanity was professed." "The old and sick" are "every day dying and rotting by cold and famine and filth and vermin. The younger laborers cannot get work, and consequently pine away for want of nourishment to a degree that if at any time they are accidentally hired at common labor, they have not the strength to perform it."[9]

[8] William E. H. Lecky, *A History of England in the Eighteenth Century* (8 vols., 1878–1890), describes vividly the condition of Ireland and Scotland. See Vol. II, chapters 5–7.

[9] Henry J. Ford, *The Scotch-Irish in America* (Princeton, c. 1915), is an outstanding study of an immigrant group.

The loss of foreign markets might not have been disastrous had the Scotch-Irish farmers been allowed to retain all the produce of their farms, but that was impossible when they had to pay rent to absentee landlords. Shortly after 1685 many thousand families had migrated from Scotland to Ireland and had taken up land on long-term leases. When these leases expired in 1717, the landlords demanded double or treble rents for the future and evicted the Scot-Irish who would not pay, replacing them with Irish tenants whose standard of living was incredibly low. Meanwhile the Scotch-Irish had been denied any influence in government, for an act of the English Parliament in 1704 excluded Presbyterians from civil and military offices. Thus like the Germans the Scotch-Irish had to choose between poverty, hunger, and legal discrimination or escape to the New World.

The precursors of the great Scotch-Irish exodus migrated to New England in 1714. Belfast, the commercial center of Ulster and the chief port of embarkation, sent fifty-five shiploads of immigrants to America during the following six years. Due to the poverty of the Scotch-Irish the great majority of the emigrants came as indentured servants, aglow with hopes inspired by newlanders who plied their artful traffic from Belfast. In many instances congregations migrated *en masse* under the leadership of pastors who had made advance investigations and arrangements whereby the emigrants placed themselves under colonial employers in one locality and were thus able to maintain their group solidarity and Old World culture and religion.

Southern Ireland also sent forth a considerable stream of emigrants, among whom were doubtless a large number of Roman Catholics. Some were probably driven from Ireland by the exactions of landlords; others sought to escape the impoverishment that afflicted the artisan and laboring classes at home; still others responded to the lure of commercial opportunity in the colonies. Such emigrants appear to have migrated as individuals or in small groups, and to have settled in all the thirteen colonies—especially in Maryland and in Pennsylvania. Because they generally did not preserve their national identity, either through churches or by other means, they have been very hard to trace. As Roman Catholics they found sentiment in most of the colonies extremely hostile toward their faith. For the most part they seem to have been compelled to conform to Protestant ways, with the result that they were absorbed into their adopted communities. Among noteworthy men of Irish descent at the time of the Revolution were two American generals, John Sullivan and Richard Montgomery, the well-known naval officer, John Barry, two state governors, George Clinton of New York and Thomas Burke of North Carolina, and many other political leaders, including George Bryan of Pennsylvania and Charles Carroll of Maryland.[10]

Another body of emigrants came directly from Scotland—victims of a social revolution within their homeland which occurred after 1745. Previously the Scots of the Highlands had lived in clans which kept alive the spirit of independence so characteristic of that wild and picturesque country. Under the clan system the people owned their land in common and while they gave services and payments to their chieftains they regarded the latter only as leaders to whom they accorded voluntary allegiance. In 1745 the Highlanders participated in an uprising which aimed to place the Young Pretender, Bonnie Prince Charley (Charles Edward Stuart), upon the throne from which his grandfather, James II, had been driven in 1688. After decisively defeating the Highlanders at the battle of Culloden Moor in 1746 the English prepared to erase from Scotland that spirit of devotion to the ancient Scottish royal house which had periodically threatened the security of the Hanoverian dynasty, established in Britain as a result of the Revolution of 1688. Accordingly Parliament enacted a series of laws which forbade the clansmen to wear their peculiar national dress, deprived the chiefs of their hereditary jurisdiction, abolished the communal ownership of the soil, and parceled the land anew among renegade chieftains and commissioners representing the Crown. Then there followed a revolution in the mode of production as small farmers were evicted and their holdings united to form large sheep pastures. The exaction of rents was particularly hateful to the clansmen, reducing them as it did from the status of proud freemen to that of semi-servile tenants. Moreover, the chiefs were forced to disband their armed retainers, thus swelling the ranks of the landless unemployed. The earlier migrations from Scotland to Ulster had attested the fact that Scotland was a poor farming country, and now when eviction, tenantry, and dependence were added to the lot of the Highlanders their condition became indescribably miserable. George Buchanan, the foremost Scottish writer of the time, has left descriptions of terrible want and suffering which eloquently explain the emigration of the Highlanders to America.[11]

The fifth country that contributed to the peopling of the colonies was Switzerland, where in the eighteenth century unemployment was

[10] Michael J. O'Brien, in *A Hidden Phase of American History* . . . (New York, 1920), argues that the Irish composed 35.8 per cent of the American soldiers in the Revolution—a somewhat exaggerated claim refuted by J. F. Jameson in the *American Historical Review*, XXVI (July 1921), 797–799.

[11] J. P. MacLean, *An Historical Account of the Settlements of Scotch Highlanders in America* (Cleveland, 1900), is useful to the special student.

a common specter and poverty and pauperism the lot of a people oppressed by a landowning nobility composed of a few patrician families.
The poor and unprivileged, utterly without opportunity to improve
their living conditions or social status, were harassed by laws such as
that prohibiting artisans from carrying wares under the arcades of
Bern, "so that the patricians might walk through them in comfort," and
another which closed the vegetable market to the common people until
after the nobles had had opportunity to buy all the choice produce. In
1740 there were 69,000 Swiss mercenaries serving for low pay in the
armies of Europe—convincing proof of the lack of economic opportunity at home. Since such mercenaries were recruited by Swiss noblemen,
the poverty of the people became a source of profit to their masters.
Of the Swiss emigrants to America we learn that one Hans Märchen
had "one wife, four children and otherwise nothing," and that Martin
Gass had "one wife, eight children and nothing more." [12]

Early in the eighteenth century the governments of the Swiss cantons
encouraged the emigration of paupers, religious radicals, and com-
munists in an effort to be rid of such undesirables. But when emigration
became general and menaced the business of supplying mercenary
soldiers the official attitude changed. Decrees were issued which prohibited the sale of property by prospective emigrants and which defined
emigration as an act of desertion punishable by loss of property, citizenship, and inheritance rights. Moreover, the governments examined
mail from America in order both to suppress letters which presented
an attractive picture of conditions there and to distribute accounts which
described the hardships and disappointments of a settler's life. Other
acts made it an offense for any person to persuade or assist another to
migrate, so that the newlanders had to operate in secret and to use
many subterfuges to escape detection by watchful officials. Even then
they were often arrested, imprisoned, and in extreme cases executed.
As a result of these measures the Swiss emigrants had to steal out of
the country to Holland or France for embarkation to America. [13]

No form of profit-making enterprise—not even the slave trade or
slavery itself—exhibited the horrors which accompanied the immigrant
traffic in indentured servants. From the time the vessels sailed from
Rotterdam, Amsterdam, Belfast, etc., until they arrived in the colonies
the passengers endured a fate worse than that of most prisoners on
land. With between three hundred and six hundred immigrants packed
into the vessels each person was allotted quarters six feet by two feet

[12] A. B. Faust, "Swiss Emigration to the American Colonies in the Eighteenth Century," *American Historical Review*, XXII (Oct. 1916).
[13] See again J. T. Adams, *Provincial Society*, chapter 7.

between decks—forced to lie flat for days when the ship pitched about in terrifying storms. "Imagine the vile atmosphere in an unventilated space containing hundreds of people many ill with all manner of contagious diseases, living and dead side by side, without medical attendance, moaning and shrieking, praying and crying, and perhaps crazed by hunger and thirst" (Jernegan).

During the dreary voyage lasting from four weeks to four months or longer, scurvy, smallpox, and other afflictions took a toll of between a third and a half of the passengers; children under seven rarely survived: one passenger reported that on a single voyage thirty-two little children perished. In extremities food was doled out at the rate of three ounces daily—dirty, spoiled biscuit, repulsive with worms, and even rats and mice were eaten.[14]

What little property the servant immigrant possessed was frequently either lost, destroyed, or stolen en route. His contract with the ship captain contained loopholes which allowed the latter to extend the term of service in order to pay extra charges occasioned by a protracted voyage. Similarly, a husband or a wife might be sold for a longer term as a means of paying the passage of the mate who had died at sea. Should the immigrants refuse to consent to such modified terms they might be kept prisoners on shipboard after the arrival in port—a form of exquisite torture to sea-weary travelers who longed to leave the hateful vessel as soon as possible. When the servants were auctioned on the ship children were frequently separated from parents; husbands and wives were sold to different masters; and the old and sick, instead of being succored at once, were kept longest on board as buyers chose the most vigorous of the workers. Among the purchasers was a class of "soul drivers" who took their human merchandise for sale to employers in the towns and at the country fairs.[15]

## THE INFLUENCE OF IMMIGRATION

The coming of the foreigners made possible in large measure the growth of settlement and the vigorous expansion of productive forces which characterized the colonies during the eighteenth century. By providing an enlarged labor force immigration supported the development of enterprises conducted on an increasingly large scale: farming, the fishery, shipbuilding, shipping, plantation production, and the fur trade; and by virtue of the employment of such labor the colonial

[14] See again K. F. Geiser, *Redemptioners and Indentured Servants in Pennsylvania,* chapter 1.

[15] See again C. A. Herrick, *White Servitude in Pennsylvania.*

merchants and planters were able to increase their capital accumulations and thereby to strengthen their position in colonial society. Thus the rise of Philadelphia between 1700 and 1770 from a minor status among colonial towns to the rank of the largest and most prosperous commercial center in North America is traceable to the growth of adjacent settlements which afforded wonderful profit opportunities to the city merchants. The main stream of immigration flowed into Philadelphia and from there fed the settlements of interior Pennsylvania and the piedmont and mountainous regions of Maryland, Virginia, and Carolina—a population trend which raised Pennsylvania and the back country of the South to a position of influence equal to that previously held by New England and the southern tidewater area. The reasons why the immigrants settled in this area are obviously of primary importance.[16]

Due to a variety of causes New England did not attract the foreigners. The poor farming land of the region, the occupation of the most accessible areas during the seventeenth century, the presence of hostile Indians on the frontiers, the need of outlets for the growth of native population, and the unfriendly attitude of the Puritans toward foreigners—all these had a deterring influence upon immigration. Moreover, lands were granted in the New England towns by the town itself, with the result that (in view of the small size of the original townships) the inhabitants struggled to obtain any ungranted lands for themselves. Indentured servants were not promised farms at the end of their service, and care was taken to prevent undesirable settlers from obtaining land in the Puritan towns. The early experience of the Scotch-Irish in New England after 1715 illustrates many of these factors. Drawn thither by the bond of common Calvinistic religion the Scotch-Irish immediately found themselves discriminated against wherever they settled. They were not permitted to establish their own Presbyterian churches; instead they were required to attend the existing Puritan churches and contribute toward their support. When they learned of more favorable conditions in Pennsylvania many of them repaired thither and drew after them the great body of their kinsmen who later migrated from Ulster. Some of the Scotch-Irish pioneers in New England moved northward to the frontiers where they were welcomed and tolerated for their unexcelled prowess as Indian fighters. Illustrative of this group was John Stark, a settler on the New Hampshire frontier and a leader in the French and Indian War. New England as a whole, however, remained overwhelmingly English in its

---

[16] See again H. L. Osgood, *American Colonies in the Eighteenth Century*, Vol. II, pp. 483–525 (important).

racial composition: only 5 per cent of its population in 1775 was of non-English descent.[17]

For somewhat different reasons New York did not draw a large body of immigrants. There the preëmption of vast estates by the local magnates, the system of tenantry in vogue, the presence of the Iroquois in the Mohawk valley, and the barriers of the Catskills and the Adirondacks made settlement unattractive. Moreover, the unhappy experience of the Palatine Germans who arrived in New York in 1710 advertised the drawbacks of the province. Sent over by the English government to produce naval stores, the Palatines endured a terrible voyage during which a fourth of their number died. Their children were apprenticed in other colonies, the land which was promised to them in return for seven years of labor devoted to naval stores production proved to be pine barrens unsuited to farming, and when they became rebellious they were worked in gangs under military discipline. Finally in 1712 Governor Hunter's funds for the project ran out and it was abandoned. Thereupon the Palatines moved to the Schoharie valley only to find soon afterward that the land upon which they settled had been granted by Hunter to seven Albany partners who demanded rents. Hopeful of securing aid from England the harassed Palatines sent thither three agents who were clapped into a debtors' prison when they finally arrived after many misfortunes. The upshot of the episode was that some of the Palatines remained on the Schoharie as tenants, some removed to other parts of New York, and the remainder, at the invitation of Governor Keith, migrated to Pennsylvania, where at last they received friendly treatment. Their sufferings in New York were vividly reported to their countrymen abroad and thereafter the Germans shunned that province and regarded Pennsylvania as the promised land.[18]

Apart from a sizable migration of the Swiss and French to South Carolina, the southern colonies as a whole did not serve as ports of entry for many of the newcomers from Europe. In Virginia and Maryland the available lands of the tidewater area had been occupied by 1700 and the planters there were depending chiefly upon the slave trade for their labor supply. North Carolina lacked ports suitable for ocean vessels, while direct immigration into both Carolinas was retarded by the pine barrens—a strip of land about a hundred miles wide,

[17] C. K. Shipton, "Immigration to New England, 1680–1740," *Journal of Political Economy*, XLIV (April 1936).

[18] Sanford H. Cobb, *The Story of the Palatines* (New York, 1897), a readable, unpretentious narrative, has now been superseded by Walter A. Knittle, *Early Eighteenth Century Palatine Emigration* (Philadelphia, 1937), the most thorough study of one phase of colonial immigration.

lying between tidewater and the piedmont, where the soil was too light
for cultivation in the days before fertilizers came into use. Immense
landholdings—like that of Lord Granville, which included the north-

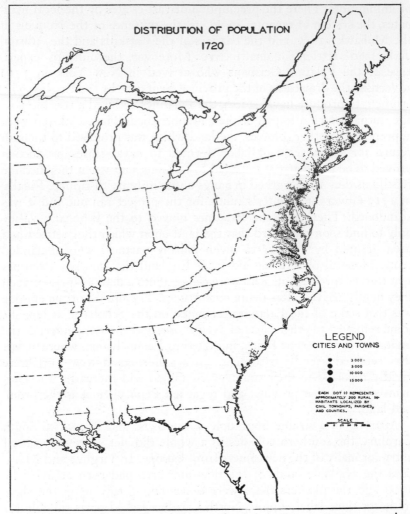

ern third of North Carolina—also made the southern area unattractive
to settlers. Among the Germans North Carolina received a bad reputation by virtue of the sufferings of a group of Palatine fugitives who had
migrated thither in 1710. A Swiss nobleman, Baron de Graffenried,
together with other associates, purchased a large tract of land from the
Carolina proprietors and arranged for the transportation of six hundred
and fifty Germans and a hundred Swiss—only half of whom survived

the voyage. Their experiences upon arrival at the Neuse River included acute suffering from disease and hunger before they established their settlement, New Bern, and then within two years they were attacked

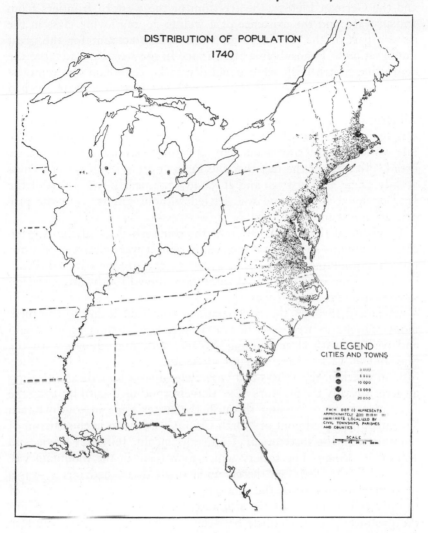

DISTRIBUTION OF POPULATION
1740

LEGEND
CITIES AND TOWNS

by Indians and forced to disperse throughout the southern part of the province. This tragic outcome, coinciding with the sufferings of the Palatines in New York, helped to divert the later German migration to Pennsylvania.[19]

[19] C. M. Andrews, "Immigration and Population of the South to 1783," in *The South in the Making of the Nation*, Vol. V.

The excellent port of Philadelphia, the large area of fertile farm lands in the Delaware, Schuylkill, and Susquehanna valleys, the absence of a tax-supported state church, the affinity between the Quakers and the German Pietists, the freedom of the western frontiers from Indian wars, and the existence of a well-to-do employing class in the eastern part of the province—all these factors account for the great immigration to Pennsylvania after 1710. In the westward advance the aggressive Scotch-Irish were generally to be found on the remotest frontiers, one stage beyond the peace-loving Germans. Scarcely had the Scotch-Irish servant become a freeman before he plunged into the wilderness, occupying land by squatter's right and asserting that "it was against the laws of God and nature that so much land should be idle while so many Christians wanted it to work on and to raise their bread." In spite of the fact that the Penns were selling western lands at only 2s. an acre in 1719 and at 3s. in 1732 nearly two-thirds of the land occupied at this time was settled without grants from the proprietary government.[20]

By virtue of the low elevation of the southern ridge of the Appalachian mountains and the water gaps therein, it was relatively easy for the immigrant pioneers to gain access to the great valley of Pennsylvania. Thence, the course of migration moved southward, carrying settlers after 1726 into western Maryland and the great valley of Virginia and through the water gaps of the Blue Ridge to the piedmont region—an area described as a "rare combination of woodland and pasture, with clear running streams and mild climate." In the Shenandoah valley, Virginia land speculators had obtained large tracts of land which in the 1720's and '30's they offered for sale at a shilling an acre. Steadily the pressure of settlement continued until by 1750 the frontiersmen were passing through the water gaps in southwestern Virginia to the piedmont of North Carolina. Moving in this stream of pioneers were the ancestors of Abraham Lincoln, Jefferson Davis, and John C. Calhoun. The society which took form in the mountain valleys and in the piedmont, based upon small diversified farms, was a projection southward of the economy of Pennsylvania rather than of the plantation system of the tidewater South—a fact which explains the protracted social conflicts between east and west in the southern colonies.[21]

In the economic sphere the eighteenth century immigration tended

[20] S. G. Fisher's *The Making of Pennsylvania* (Philadelphia, 1906) describes the colony's racial elements.

[21] A readable, compact, popular account is Oscar Kuhns, *The German and Swiss Settlements of Colonial Pennsylvania* (New York, 1901).

to weaken the survivals of feudalism in America and to strengthen the position of the colonial merchant capitalists. The Germans, the Swiss, the Scotch-Irish, and the Scots had all been sorely oppressed by Euro-

pean landlords and the state churches, military establishments, and burdensome taxes associated therewith. Quite naturally these immigrant groups brought to the colonies a deep-seated hatred of the institutions which had exploited them—an antagonism which inspired them to fight against such semi-feudal survivals in America as huge speculative estates, quit-rents, and tax-supported religions. By 1775 the Scotch-

Irish and Germans formed a powerful group in four colonies still dominated largely by landlords. In Pennsylvania, where they composed two-thirds of the population, they struggled against the Penn family for the control of the proprietary lands; in North Carolina, where they numbered a half of the inhabitants, they were in conflict with the land claims of Lord Granville; in western Virginia, where they composed a third of the settlers, they encountered the great estate of Lord Fairfax; in Maryland, where they accounted for a fourth of the population, they ran afoul of Lord Baltimore's rights as overlord. By occupying lands without title and by refusing to pay quit-rents they steadily undermined existing landlordism until the American Revolution finally destroyed the Penn, Baltimore, Granville, and Fairfax estates.

The French Huguenots, on the other hand, took up residence principally in the plantation area and in the commercial towns. A well-to-do middle-class group to begin with, they soon produced some of the leading commercial families of colonial times—the Faneuils of New England, the Bayards and De Lanceys of New York, and the Laurenses and Manigaults of South Carolina.[22] In a larger sense, however, the whole eighteenth-century immigration fostered the growth of the commercial class. The poor servant immigrants, once they had completed their terms of service, had to begin an independent life without capital assets. Obviously their labor as servants had produced a surplus to the employing capitalist groups; otherwise the system of indentured servitude would have been unprofitable. Such surplus was used in part to finance the freed servant at the expiration of his term—either by means of long-term loans which enabled him to acquire and equip a farm or through short-term credits extended by merchants for the purchase of store goods. The indebted farmers were thereupon obliged to deliver their produce to their creditors immediately after harvest, with the result that the price of farm produce fell to low levels when deliveries were made. On the other hand the prices paid by the farmers for store goods and credit remained practically constant; consequently the merchant creditors were able to extract handsome profits from their dealings with their farmer debtors. This, in fact, was the chief source of the capital accumulations of the merchant class.

The growth of the body of small farmers strengthened the democratic movement in the colonies, since when the freed servant acquired land he became entitled to vote for representatives in his colonial assembly. Against absentee landlords he fought for title to land; against

[22] Arthur H. Hirsh's *The Huguenots of South Carolina* (Durham, N. C., 1928) is one of the best studies of immigration.

his merchant creditors he struggled for relief from debt. In this manner the progress of settlement intensified the conflict between the democratic and aristocratic forces in colonial society.

The growth of population in the middle colonies and the back country of the South also sharpened the antagonism between the colonial merchants and their English rivals. The surplus products of these settlements—grains and livestock—required market outlets which the colonial merchants sought increasingly in the French West Indies. This trade, however, tended to undermine the British sugar plantations and thus to imperil the shipping interests and investments of the British merchants in the Caribbean. The latter could protect themselves only by injuring the trade of the northern merchants and that in turn menaced the economy of the middle region which was expanding so rapidly under the impact of immigration. The policies which England eventually adopted to protect her stake in the West Indies bore a strong resemblance to the measures by which Parliament had destroyed the cattle and woolen industries in Ireland after 1665. When the revolutionary crisis occurred in the colonies the Scotch Irish rose almost as a man in opposition to Parliament's authority, their attitude eloquently expressed by their foremost orator, Patrick Henry.[23]

A third major conflict of the eighteenth century—that between England and France—was also accentuated as the immigrants rapidly extended England's settled area toward the western outposts of the French.

Although immigration tended to diversify social life in the colonies it did not materially modify the basic political institutions which the English settlers had established during the seventeenth century. In most colonies the foreigners at any given time were a minority; hence in their external relations they had little choice except to conform to the customs of the country. Political thought in the colonies remained essentially English; the immigrants were compelled to become an English-speaking people; and political leadership resided chiefly in the English group—a fact attested by the names of Franklin, Washington, Jefferson, Adams, Madison, Marshall, and Lee.[24]

Similarly, by virtue of naturalization, the foreigners became English subjects. Ordinarily in eighteenth-century Europe emigration meant loss of civil rights such as the privileges of voting, holding office, acquiring land, and inheriting property. The colonies, however, in order to attract settlers, liberally bestowed upon foreigners the benefits of

---

[23] Maude Glasgow, *The Scotch-Irish in Northern Ireland and in the American Colonies* (New York, 1936).

[24] See again E. B. Greene, *Provincial America*, chapter 14.

citizenship and even extended unusual privileges: Virginia and Mary-land, for instance, gave to foreigners a five-year exemption from suits for the recovery of debts contracted before emigration. Prior to 1740 the rights of colonial citizenship were conferred by act of an individual colony, with the result that a naturalized immigrant, as a citizen of Massachusetts or Virginia, lost his civil rights if he moved to another colony. Parliament in 1740 enacted that a foreigner who became a citizen of one colony automatically became a citizen in all the English colonies. First he must have resided in one colony for seven years, have taken the oath of supremacy, and have received the sacrament accord-ing to the rites of the Anglican Church. Such religious tests, however, were modified to permit the naturalization of Jews and Quakers. After these conditions had been met the foreigner was entitled to civil rights in all the colonies, although he could neither become a privy councillor of the king, serve as a member of Parliament, or hold offices under the Crown in Great Britain and Ireland. The parliamentary statute of 1740, slightly modified, endured throughout the remainder of the colonial period and later formed the pattern of the first naturalization law of the United States.[25]

In the sphere of private family life and religion the immigrants were able to retain their Old World traditions and thus to contribute to the diversity of colonial society. Since most of the non-English groups were Protestant in faith they strengthened the Protestant character of the existing settlements, while the Scots and Scotch-Irish, as sturdy Cal-vinists, reinforced the Puritanism of New England. Sectarianism re-ceived a fresh impetus by virtue of the numerous sects among the Ger-mans, the tendency of the French Huguenots to become Anglicans, and the growth of the Baptist and Methodist churches on the frontiers. The non-Anglican immigrants who settled in the back country of the south-ern colonies became bitter opponents of the Anglican church which they were called upon to support by taxes, and by resisting its domi-nance they helped to effect the separation of church and state in the plantation colonies.

## ENGLISH MIGRATION AND THE GENESIS OF GEORGIA

The triumph of the English middle class in the Revolution of 1688, which installed the Whig party in power, altered the course of English emigration to America. As representatives of the commercial and manu-

[25] A brief introduction is Emberson E. Proper, *Colonial Immigration Laws* (New York, 1900). See also A. H. Carpenter, "Naturalization in England and the Amer-ican Colonies," *American Historical Review*, IX (Jan. 1904).

facturing groups the Whigs rejected the earlier policies of the Crown and the landed aristocracy which had oppressed the religious dissenters of the middle class. The Toleration Act of 1689, by granting freedom of public worship to Protestants who believed in the divinity of Christ, terminated the persecution which had previously driven Quakers and other dissenters to the colonies. Thereafter political and religious oppression ceased to operate in England as a cause of emigration.[26]

Deeply interested in the development of the colonies the Whigs endeavored to people them with foreign Protestants, in view of the decline of emigration from England. Thus a Whig Parliament financed the transportation of Palatines to New York in 1710, and in the 1720's Whig colonial officials worked out a scheme for the systematic colonization of South Carolina by foreign Protestants. Townships of twenty thousand acres were laid out along the main rivers east of the fall line and divided into farms of fifty acres. Because of an unfavorable climate and the poor soil of the pine barren region this project failed: only one settlement of German redemptioners, at Orangeburg on the North Edisto River, survived. Nevertheless, the Whig policy of encouraging Protestant exiles to settle in America made possible the great eighteenth-century immigration and is therefore a memorable feature of English colonization, sharply differentiated from the French and Spanish practice of excluding all but Catholic subjects from New France and New Spain.

The rising middle-class groups in England profited immensely by colonial immigration, for it converted aliens into buyers of English manufactures and producers of surplus produce from which English merchants made their profits. The increase of colonial population provided a major stimulus to the growth of English commerce: thus in 1662–69 the American and West Indian colonies supported about a tenth of England's external trade; in 1770 about a third. Between 1700 and 1770 England's commerce with America and the West Indies increased about fourfold, whereas her total trade, foreign and colonial, increased only twofold.

This commercial expansion in large measure sustained the English Industrial Revolution of the eighteenth century. The American demand for manufactures kept the workshops of England busy and provided employment for her artisans and sailors. No longer did England seem overpopulated; in fact the relative shortage of workers now inspired inventors to develop labor-saving machines and to unleash new sources of industrial power. In response to this trend English officials increasingly discouraged the emigration of efficient workers and sea-

[26] See again E. Channing, *History of the United States*, Vol. II, chapter 14.

men and encouraged the emigration of certain "undesirables"—criminals, paupers, and debtors.[27]

In pursuance of these aims several measures were taken. For one thing the government maintained agents at port towns to scrutinize the contracts of servants embarking to the colonies, seeking by this means to stop the business of kidnaping able-bodied workers and of spiriting them to America. In 1765 Parliament forbade the emigration of skilled industrial operatives—a measure which also intended to prevent the dissemination of England's industrial secrets abroad. In like manner the Board of Trade tried to check the desertion of seamen and fishermen from English vessels at Newfoundland and their subsequent employment in New England, where—lured by higher wages and better working conditions—they strengthened the colonial fisheries and merchant marine to the detriment of their English competitors. As early as 1691 it was reported that in this way England was losing more than a hundred seamen and fishermen annually. Prior to 1729 England did not establish a settled government at Newfoundland; instead the commodores in command of the annual fishing fleets from England were empowered to regulate the fishery. They were instructed by the Crown to curtail the exodus to New England, and toward this end they required that masters of vessels from Boston give bond not to take English seamen to the mainland colonies. For many years after 1715 the Board of Trade urged that the settlers at Newfoundland be removed in order to destroy their trade with New England which occasioned the drain of seamen, and when in 1729 England established a civil government in the island one of its objectives was to suppress this long-standing "abuse."

On the other hand England continued to use the colonies as a dumping ground for her criminal population. Parliamentary statutes of 1662 and 1717 authorized judges to sentence convicts to servitude in America: for seven-year terms in case of lesser crimes and for fourteen-year terms in case of offenses punishable by death. Primarily a means of decreasing prison costs in England and of converting convicts into productive workers, this policy was rationalized as a method of enabling them to start life anew, free from the stigma of a criminal past. All told, about fifty thousand convicts were shipped to America—to nine colonies at least: in Maryland, which alone received twenty thousand, they formed the mass of indentured servants during the eighteenth

[27] Notable among recent works is Lawrence H. Gipson's *The British Empire before the American Revolution* (3 vols., Caldwell, Idaho, 1936)—a work planned to give a bird's-eye view of the whole empire about 1750. Volume I describes British and Irish backgrounds.

century. Particularly unsavory was the trade in convict servants carried on by contractors with the English government. Undoubtedly the presence of the convict element depressed the condition of all the indentured servants and aggravated the harsh and oppressive features of the entire immigrant traffic. To the colonists the whole business seemed outrageous. Franklin objected that "these thieves and villains introduced among us spoil the morals of the youth and the neighborhoods that entertain them." It would be as reasonable, he said, for America to send its rattlesnakes to England as for the English to send their jailbirds to America. "Their emptying their jails into our settlements is an insult and a contempt, the cruelest that ever one people offered to another." From 1670 onward the southern and middle colonies passed laws to exclude these undesirables: acts which placed prohibitive duties on imported convicts or which required ship captains to give bond for the good behavior of such immigrants. All such acts, however, were declared null and void by the English government, with the result that the English policy of convict dumping became a serious cause of estrangement between the colonies and the mother country.[28]

Writing in 1729 an English mercantilist, Joshua Gee, suggested that criminals and the unemployed be transported to the frontiers of the southern colonies, "by which means those vast tracts of land now waste will be planted, and secured from the danger we apprehend of the French over-running them." For thirty years after 1700 the unoccupied region between South Carolina, Florida, and Louisiana had evoked proposals in England for the establishment of a buffer colony against the French and Spaniards. Here was a land, presumably, which—in conformity with the mercantilist creed—might produce such commodities as silk, wine, rice, dyes, naval stores, and even gold. More immediately, the control of this region (present-day Georgia and Alabama) meant the control of the lucrative fur trade of the southwest. Before 1729 the English title to the area was vested in the Carolina proprietors, but they had neglected both to colonize and to defend it. The South Carolina Assembly, responding to the interests of the local fur traders, had been more active and after 1715 had established forts on the Savannah and Altamaha Rivers. Only a little aid had come from Britain so that the South Carolinians had had to stagger alone under this burden of frontier defense.

Among the members of Parliament after 1722 was James Edward Oglethorpe, "a young gentleman of very public spirit"—once an English officer in the war with Spain and now a vigorous defender of Eng-

[28] James D. Butler, "British Convicts Shipped to American Colonies," *American Historical Review*, II (Oct. 1896).

land's interests against the Spaniards in America. A man of liberal and humane sympathies, he served as chairman of a parliamentary prison board which exposed the degrading conditions of prison life and the brutal treatment of the inmates, many of whom were decent people, victims of debt, injustice, and poverty. Oglethorpe's interest in these outcasts reflects a humanitarian spirit that was growing among the Anglican clergy and a few enlightened members of the upper class. To such men it appeared that imprisoned debtors might be rescued from the horrors of English jails and be sent to establish the much-needed buffer colony north of Florida. Accordingly in 1732 they obtained from George II a charter which authorized them to colonize the land extending between the Savannah and Altamaha Rivers, from the Atlantic Coast to the South Sea.[29]

The charter of Georgia differed sharply from all other grants to English colonial promoters. It placed control over the province in a board of trustees empowered to raise money, grant lands, enact laws, and levy taxes. The trustees could not derive any personal profit from the enterprise; their actions were subject to close supervision by the king; and their powers were to endure but twenty-one years, after which Georgia was to become a royal province. In addition the charter provided for a common council of trustees, resident in England, authorized to appoint the governor, judges, and other officers of the colony. In a larger sense the enterprise was not strictly philanthropic because it aimed to reduce the cost of maintaining the poor in England, to protect the profitable South Carolina plantations against Spanish incursions, and to strengthen England's grip on the southern fur trade. Earlier experience with profit-making corporations as colonizing agencies had proved, as in the case of Virginia, that such ventures were not profitable; hence the ordinary corporate form of colonization could not be employed. Similarly, English merchants and officials were now unalterably opposed to the creation of new proprietary colonies which transferred too much power to proprietors and local interests and thereby tended to weaken that imperial control which was deemed necessary to assure to England the profits of colonial development. Since neither the corporate nor proprietary type of colony could be established, the charter of Georgia created a new method of control—the trust—which guaranteed that the powers of colonial government and

---

[29] The best recent biographies are Leslie F. Church, *Oglethorpe: A Study in Philanthropy in England and America* (London, 1932), and Amos A. Ettinger, *James Edward Oglethorpe, Imperial Idealist* (New York, 1936). For an older narrative see Henry Bruce, *Life of General Oglethorpe* (New York, c. 1890).

the ownership of ungranted lands should revert to the Crown as soon as the colony had become firmly established on a profitable basis.

Given the principal object of the colony—to raise a bulwark against the Spaniards—the trustees decided that Negroes, both slave and free, should be excluded, lest they join the enemy in time of war. The ban on slavery in turn outlawed large plantations in accordance with the aim of trustees to foster an economy of small farms in order to create the most numerous body of soldier-settlers—a policy which determined the course of Georgia's history before 1750.

The money spent in founding the colony came from two principal sources. First, the trustees solicited contributions from philanthropic persons and in this manner obtained about £20,000; secondly, Parliament made yearly grants ranging from £8,000 to £26,000—the larger part of which was devoted to defense. Most of these funds were spent by the trustees in England and transmitted to Georgia in the form of provisions and equipment, although the governor in the colony was permitted to draw bills on the trust for the purchase of supplies from English merchants. Indicative of the work of the trust were the separate funds into which the money was divided—a fund for establishing the colony, one for religion, one for agriculture, one for schools, and one for the transportation of Swiss and German settlers. Besides money grants the trustees also received other gifts for the settlers—principally Bibles, catechisms, prayer books, and furniture. Financial transactions were handled in London through the Bank of England.[30]

Shortly before the colony was founded Parliament passed an act which released a large number of prisoners from jail but such was the stigma of their past that Oglethorpe soon found that these "miserable wretches" were "starving for want of employment." To such unfortunates the trustees appealed in a well-conducted advertising campaign which portrayed the attractions of a free and independent status in a new country. Before accepting applicants as settlers the trustees required that their good character be certified by their parish officials; by this means it was hoped to exclude criminals, idlers, and drunkards, and because the colonists were prospective soldiers against Catholic Spain, no papists were accepted. Otherwise, the trustees guaranteed religious freedom to Protestants, foreign as well as English, and offered to each settler a farm of fifty acres, while the charter conferred the liberties and privilege of English subjects. Particular efforts were made to secure ambitious, industrious young men and heads of large families, and when they enlisted they were given instructions in farming and

[30] See again V. W. Crane, *The Southern Frontier*, chapter 13.

trained in the art of war by sergeants of the royal guard. The trust provided free transportation to the colony, supplied each settler with adequate food, clothing, tools, and utensils and provided for community production during the first year until individual self-supporting farms could be established by each family.

Other victims of misfortune and oppression—particularly persecuted Protestants of Germany and Switzerland—were welcomed to Georgia by the trustees. Such composed a band of Lutheran exiles driven from their homeland by their Catholic ruler, the Archbishop of Salzburg. First they found refuge in England, where in 1733 the trustees agreed to transport them to the colony and to equip them as ordinary settlers. Led by a nobleman, the Baron von Reck, they arrived in Georgia in 1734, there to establish a settlement, Ebenezer, on a small tributary of the Savannah River. Other Germans, however, especially the peace-loving Pietists, did not respond to the appeal of a military outpost, and although a few Moravians came in 1735 their aversion to war soon led them to move to Pennsylvania.[31]

Not all the settlers brought to Georgia were sent by the trustees: the latter made arrangements which allowed men of means to secure tracts up to five hundred acres, provided they transport ten servants to the colony; after four years of labor each servant was entitled to a twenty-acre farm. Since the cost of transporting and maintaining a servant was relatively high (£20) the trustees allowed such masters to borrow the money from the trust on condition that it be repaid within three years. And if the master had not peopled his five hundred-acre tract after ten years it should revert to the trust.

With Oglethorpe in command the first band of colonists—thirty-five families or 130 settlers—embarked from England in September 1732. Well supplied with provisions (they stopped at Madeira and took on board five tuns of wine—an indication of unusual affluence) their good ship *Ann* carried them without mishap to Charleston, where, as prospective defenders of the southern frontier, they received a most cordial welcome. When they later reached the Savannah River Oglethorpe made good use of his military knowledge by selecting an easily defended site on a high bluff. Since the trustees had not sought profit from the expedition they had provided for the emigrants so amply that only two of them died during the voyage. Soon the colonists were constructing their first town, Savannah—erecting a palisade, clearing land, and building log houses; working in gangs under Oglethorpe's martial

---

[31] The best short work is James R. McCain, *Georgia as a Proprietary Province* (Boston, c. 1917); the best state history is E. Merton Coulter, *A Short History of Georgia* (Chapel Hill, 1933). See chapters 1–8.

PLAN OF SAVANNAH, GEORGIA, 1734

This shows the land already cleared and laid out, with public mill, guesthouse, public oven, well, public store, fort, parsonage, palisades, and houses beginning to be built.

discipline and supported by provisions supplied by the trust, all with the understanding that at the end of the year they were to receive land and livestock and to work for themselves thereafter.

Early life in Georgia exhibits an illustration of a planned economy under a paternalistic government in which the workers had no part. In order to keep settlement compact, grants of land in excess of five hundred acres were outlawed, settlers were not allowed to sell, rent, mortgage, or lease their small farms (their fifty acres included a town lot sixty by ninety feet), nor could such farms be divided by inheritance; the whole passed to the eldest son. Freed servants who could not immediately become independent farmers were allowed to work at wages fixed by the trust—8d. a day for men and 6d. a day for women. By virtue of the scarcity of labor and small landholdings, grain and cattle farming became the first mainstay of the colony. The trust did not conduct the trade in farm products (this was opened to private merchants) although it did establish and operate the necessary saw- and gristmills. By October 1741 the workers sent by the trust had been allotted 41,600 acres of land, and importers of about 560 servants had received 28,185 acres. Between 1733 and 1740 the trust transported 915 English settlers and 606 foreign Protestants.[32]

Endeavoring to introduce staple commodities that might be exchanged in England for manufactured goods the trustees encouraged the production of wine, silk, and naval stores. They sent over a skilled botanist to instruct the inhabitants in the art of silk culture, required that two mulberry trees be planted on each acre of land allotted, and gave bounties to the producers of raw silk. So also the trustees collected the English bounty on naval stores exported from the colony and remitted the money to the producers in Georgia. In order to preserve friendly relations with the Indians (which Oglethorpe had taken pains to establish at the start), fur traders were strictly regulated by the trustees, who prohibited the importation of rum, fixed the prices of trading goods and furs, required that the traders renew their licenses every year, and designated the areas and trails that could be used. Lest the settlers be drawn away into the forest traffic the trustees forbade any trader to employ servants; each trader had to operate single-handed, under penalty of a fine of £8. One purpose governed all these economic regulations: the settlements should be kept compact and enterprise should remain on a small scale; by this means the colony would consist of a concentrated force of self-sustaining farmer-soldiers.[33]

[32] See again H. L. Osgood, *American Colonies in the Eighteenth Century*, Vol. III, pp. 34–74.

[33] See again E. B. Greene, *Provincial America*, chapter 15.

Like earlier attempts to shape colonial development from England the plans of the Georgia trustees retarded the growth of the province and provoked intense opposition among the settlers. Fundamentally the difficulty arose from the land and labor policy of the trust. The poorer elements became dissatisfied—the servants because they received only a mere twenty acres, and younger sons of proprietors because they could not share in the inheritance of their fathers' lands. The small farmers considered their fifty-acre farms inadequate; moreover, since the landowners could not alienate their land they could not use it as a credit base and consequently could not borrow needed capital. The prospect of a yearly quit-rent of 2s. for each fifty acres was equally displeasing. To the fur traders the ban on rum and servants seemed an unnecessary means of curtailing profits. The larger enterprisers could not obtain all the land or laborers they wanted: in order to acquire the maximum five-hundred-acre tracts they were obliged to import ten servants at a cost of £200. They could not purchase Negroes, and white servants were not attracted to a colony where their freedom dues amounted to only twenty acres of land. Both the large and small proprietors were excluded from the government which seemed to them a despotism of absentee trustees who imposed unpopular policies through the agency of the governor, a military dictator. Owing to the cost of acquiring land and servants the experiments in wine and silk production failed, while the richest lands of Georgia, admirably suited to rice cultivation, could not be exploited because the hot climate and malaria-carrying insects precluded the utilization of white labor. Only by importing slaves could large enterprisers hope to compete with the rice plantations of South Carolina.

About 1737 discontent with the regime of the trustees became acute. The poor settlers left the colony in large numbers, thus diminishing the inadequate labor force. The landed proprietors now complained so loudly of their lot that the trust sent an investigator to the colony. Nothing less than the abandonment of the principal policies of the trust would satisfy the malcontents: they demanded the privilege of importing Negroes, a reduction of the quit-rents, complete freedom in disposing of their farms, the right to elect local officers, and the opportunity of acquiring more land. Although the trustees stoutly opposed these demands they were forced to make concessions gradually until by 1750 their whole regime had been overthrown. The land grant to a freed servant was increased in 1742 to fifty acres; the farmers were conceded the right to sell and otherwise dispose of their lands; the law of inheritance was changed so as to give all sons and daughters equal shares; the maximum limit for plantations was raised from five hundred to two thousand acres; the importation of rum was permitted (in response to a vote of the House of Commons) and in 1749 the introduction of Negro slaves was authorized. These changes enabled large enterprisers, many of whom soon came in from South Carolina, to acquire and consolidate small holdings that had been prepared for cultivation, to obtain an adequate dependent labor force, and thus to perpetuate the large plantation in the economy of Georgia. In the meantime but little progress had been made toward self-government; in 1751 the trustees granted an assembly—not, however, a law-making body but merely an agency through which the property owners could voice their demands and discontents. For the trustees the end was now in sight. Dismayed by the trend of affairs in the colony and the failure of their principal plans they relinquished their rights to the king in 1751. Georgia took its place in the ranks of the royal colonies, ruled thereafter by an elected assembly and by a governor and council appointed by the king, while the growth of a class of large landowners rapidly brought the colony within the circle of the plantation aristocracy of the South.[34]

The economic trend in early Georgia has a significance broader than that of purely local interest. The trustees had deliberately tried to develop an economy of small farms, to prevent the monopolization of land, and to provide an economic basis of independence for a body of once impoverished people. The outcome demonstrated the impracticability of the program; the underlying conditions in America fostered the growth of large enterprise and the concentration of property ownership in a relatively few hands. In this respect Georgia epitomizes the tendency in all colonies toward economic inequality—toward the progress of capitalistic economy.

[34] See again L. H. Gipson, *The British Empire before the American Revolution,* Vol. II, chapter 6.

## BIBLIOGRAPHICAL NOTE

Works Previously Cited: The following references apply to Georgia: G. Bancroft, *History of the United States,* II, ch. 42; *Pageant of America,* I, ch. 15; J. Winsor (ed.), *Narrative and Critical History of America,* V, ch. 6.

Special Studies for Advanced Students: For the student making special studies the following are useful as reference works: G. D. Bernheim, *History of the German Settlements in . . . North and South Carolina* (Philadelphia, 1872); C. K. Bolton, *Scotch Irish Pioneers* (Boston, 1910); Lucian J. Fosdick, *French Blood in America* (New York, c. 1906); Charles A. Hanna, *The Scotch-Irish* (2 vols., New York, 1902); Herrmann Schuricht, *History of the German Element in Virginia* (Baltimore, 1898); John W. Wayland, *The German Element in the Shenandoah Valley* (Charlottesville, Va., 1907).

Sources: An important collection of documents on immigration is being prepared by Professor M. W. Jernegan. V. H. Todd has edited *Christoph von Graffenried's Account of the Founding of New Bern* (Raleigh, 1920). On Georgia see A. B. Hart (ed.), *American History Told by Contemporaries*, II, pp. 110–127, and W. MacDonald (ed.), *Documentary Source Book of American History*, no. 27.

MAPS: D. R. Fox, *Harper's Atlas*, p. 11; C. O. Paullin, *Atlas of the Historical Geography of the United States*, plate 60; W. R. Shepherd, *Historical Atlas*, pp. 189–194.

# XVI

# THE GROWTH OF AMERICAN CAPITALISM

In an address in 1932 former President Coolidge expressed his opinion that the unemployed would be put to work again when somebody could make money by hiring them—a statement which expresses the essence of the American capitalist society as it has developed from early beginnings in colonial times. During the eighteenth century, particularly, the history of the colonies was notable for the growth of capitalist enterprise. The central features of early American capitalism were the ownership of the means of production and transportation (land, tools, shops, buildings, machines, warehouses, ships, etc.) by private individuals—merchants, master artisans, landowning farmers, and planters—and the existence of a class of dependent laborers—wage-earners, slaves, servants, and tenant farmers—who did not share in the ownership of the means of production. Capitalist enterprise functioned through the employment of the dependent workers by the owners of land and capital goods who claimed in consequence a part of the commodities produced by joint use of capital and labor. In the simplest form of capitalist economy, the share of the owners consisted of farm produce and manufactured articles. With the growth of enterprise, the owners obtained more of such "consumers' goods" than they themselves could consume, with the result that they desired to convert their surpluses into capital goods of some durable form.[1]

A first step necessary in the process of converting surplus consumers' goods into capital was to sell them for hard money or its equivalent—a fact which explains the great value attributed to coin and bullion, since they were a non-perishable form of wealth, inexpensively stored and transported, and in such universal demand that they might at any time be converted into any other kind of property. More particularly the owners of money could use it to pay the wages of workers engaged in producing machines, buildings, ships, etc. In reality this practice meant the conversion of the surplus farm and manufactured products received by the capitalists into the labor of those who pro-

[1] Special attention is called to a very important chapter (22 on mercantilism) by J. F. Rees in *The Cambridge History of the British Empire*, Vol. I.

duced capital goods. Such capital goods belonged of course to the capitalists and, when used in new production, augmented their stock of income-producing property. Capital, therefore, displayed a tendency to multiply and to enlarge the income of its owners, while the earnings of the dependent workers did not increase proportionately.

Three principal types of colonial enterprise may be differentiated, although the lines dividing them were by no means hard and fast.

In the first category we find the southern planters, whose labor force was composed of servants and slaves, whose gains consisted, in the first instance, of surplus tobacco, rice, and indigo or their equivalents in other products, and whose investments were made in additional slaves, implements of production, buildings, and lands. Comparable to the southern planters were the landed magnates of New York; only the employment by the latter of tenants instead of slaves and the collection of interest and rents in grain and livestock instead of plantation produce differentiated such magnates from the planters. In the same category belonged the large independent farmers in the northern colonies who employed several servants. Obviously the farmer would not have employed servants if their labor, when applied to his capital, had not yielded a return above the cost of purchasing and maintaining them.[2]

Quite distinct from the rural capitalists was the merchant capitalist of the towns. As a shipowner he employed wage-earning sailors and received his return on his invested capital in the form of freight payments; in the fur traffic he invested in trading goods and trading posts, hired traders to whom he paid wages, and profited so greatly by reason of a dominant position that he may be regarded as the employer of the Indians, whose return for their labor probably did not exceed that obtained by Negro slaves. The key to the position of the merchant capitalist, however, is to be found in his relations with the small farmers within his trading area. Here was a class sprung from poor immigrants, freed servants, younger sons without property, and once independent proprietors who had been dispossessed and obliged to start anew. Although it was relatively easy for the poor farmer to secure a small piece of land, yet he could not cultivate it without capital, and that, ordinarily, he did not possess. The town merchants, however, from their surplus earnings, were ready to extend credit, either long-term loans which enabled the farmer to provide himself with land, tools, buildings, and livestock, or short-term credit for the purchase of store goods such as cloth, notions, and utensils. In thus supplying the farmer the merchant became entitled to several re-

[2] See again J. T. Adams, *Revolutionary New England*, chapters 7–8, 10.

turns; freights on goods imported in his vessels, warehouse charges, insurance premiums, profits or commissions on goods sold, and interest on loans. These payments had to be made by the debtor farmers in the form of produce; hence they were required to deliver their surplus to the merchant or his country agents in order to discharge past debts and to obtain fresh credit for the purchase of the next year's supply of store goods.[3]

Once a farmer had become a debtor he discovered that the odds were heavily against him. His class consisted of unorganized producers who could not exert any influence over the prices of the goods they bought and sold. Each year after harvest they had great supplies of produce which temporarily flooded the market and sent prices to their lowest level during the year. At such times the merchants made their purchases or received the produce of their debtors, thereby obtaining at low cost a maximum share of the farmer's output. On the other hand the prices paid by the farmers were not subject to seasonal fluctuations. Interest charges of course did not vary at all; transportation costs remained practically stationary and even the prices of store goods were fairly constant. By selling high and buying low the merchant acquired a considerable share of the farmers' surplus which he was able to sell at a handsome profit, thereby gaining new funds for investment.[4]

Similarly the cyclical movement of prices worked against the debtor farmer. When depressions came the price of his produce dropped drastically and yet the credit charges against him did not change and the prices of transportation and store goods did not fall in proportion. At such times all his surplus was needed to pay his debts and often it did not suffice for that, so he was compelled to go deeper into debt. When his credit had been exhausted and his surplus would not pay existing debts his merchant creditor commonly foreclosed and took possession of his farm—an action whereby the creditor acquired the permanent improvements which the farmer had added to the land. In this manner the holdings of the merchant were enlarged and the trend toward the concentration of capital was intensified.

The acquisition of a large part of the agricultural surplus by the merchants had another important effect; it slowly developed a class of propertyless workers forced off the farms because the meager profits of farming would not sustain all the sons and daughters of the

[3] C. P. Gould, "The Economic Causes of the Rise of Baltimore," in *Essays in Colonial History Presented to C. M. Andrews.*

[4] Leila Sellers, *Charleston Business on the Eve of the American Revolution* (Chapel Hill, 1934), is a careful study of the economy of the Lower South.

family on the land or enable its head to give them the training and capital necessary for an independent status. Many of these surplus workers found employment as wage-earners in industry but most of them took up land of their own. The latter—as propertyless farmers —were obliged to borrow capital, thus gradually extending the scale of business carried on by the merchants and providing new employment for their accumulated capital. The small profits of agriculture meant further that the debtor farmers did not receive an income sufficient to justify intensive improvements on their land; instead they were compelled to "mine" the soil of its resources and its fertility, with the result that agriculture in the older areas was soon menaced by the competition of newly opened and more fertile lands—a pressure which enlarged the ranks of pioneers who migrated to the West.

In the third category of capitalist enterprise were included the various industries which employed wage-earners: such were the fishery, lumbering, flour milling, iron manufacturing, shipbuilding, the production of naval stores, hat making, sugar refining, and the manufacture of rum.[5] In all these industries the manufacturing capitalists steadily increased their stocks of invested capital and the number of employed hands. Their profits in the first instance assumed the form of a share of the commodities produced by the labor of their workers —a surplus that was in part converted into money and then invested in additional capital goods.

Colonial capitalism had many distinguishing characteristics. As a common rule the owners of capital goods controlled and managed the enterprises in which they were concerned, since large-scale corporations had not yet come into vogue. The class of such owners was relatively large, considering all the planters, independent farmers, master artisans, merchants, and small traders. Yet there were marked differences among the capitalists and the trend toward the concentration of capital set the most affluent apart in a superior category. The mass of the people, as servants, tenants, wage-earners, debtor farmers, or slaves, remained in a dependent condition. There was not as yet a visible specialization of capitalist function: the town merchant invested in ships, lands, buildings, industries, insurance, and mortgages, and the large planter was also often a trader, land speculator, manufacturer, and money-lender. On the whole the merchants occupied the strongest position. Manufacturing employers were cramped by high wages of workmen while the planters suffered both from England's restrictions upon their trade and from the relative inefficiency of slave

[5] Virginia D. Harrington, *The New York Merchant on the Eve of the Revolution* (New York, 1935), is a detailed study of the mechanisms of northern business.

labor. Inasmuch as the merchants made their profits from their dealings with the farmers and because nine-tenths of the people were engaged in agriculture the economy of the colonies offered well-nigh unlimited opportunities to the merchant class.[6]

## PLANTATION ECONOMY

The trend toward the concentration of capital operated with full force in the southern colonies where the soil and climate afforded staples in great demand in Europe. With the fall in the price of tobacco in Virginia and Maryland after 1660 the larger enterprisers with capital extended their plantations and labor force, thereby cutting costs and driving small producers to the wall, so that by 1700 the plantation dominated the economy of the tidewater area. Two new crops, rice and indigo, supported large-scale capitalist farming in South Carolina and Georgia during the eighteenth century.

In 1694–96, when rice was first successfully cultivated in South Carolina, the demand for the product in Europe and the resulting high prices yielded the planter a return of 40 per cent on his labor and investment. The crop required a considerable capital outlay in that the cultivated fields had to be flooded two or three times during the growing season: this was accomplished by damming a river and erecting a reservoir above the fields, which were enclosed by a levee; water was then admitted through an upper gate in the levee, and when the fields had been sufficiently flooded it was drained off through a lower gate. Another method employed after 1758 which utilized the tides brought into cultivation the rich swampy lands along the principal rivers. The rising tide forced the river water onto the rice fields through the levee gates; drainage was possible whenever the tide was out. This method, however, proved to be expensive: floods occasionally broke the levees or they were undermined by alligators or muskrats, thus effecting drainage at the wrong time, while hurricanes occasionally drove salt water onto the fields, thereby making them sour and unproductive until after they had been bleached for several years. After the introduction of Negro slavery in Georgia (1750) rice plantations developed rapidly, largely under the auspices of South Carolina planters.[7]

Because of the tedious labor required (hoeing, harvesting by sickle,

[6] Gertrude S. Kimball, *Providence in Colonial Times* (Boston, 1912), a broad study, discusses business interests in chapter 7.

[7] A. S. Salley, *The Introduction of Rice Culture into South Carolina* (Columbia, S. C., 1919).

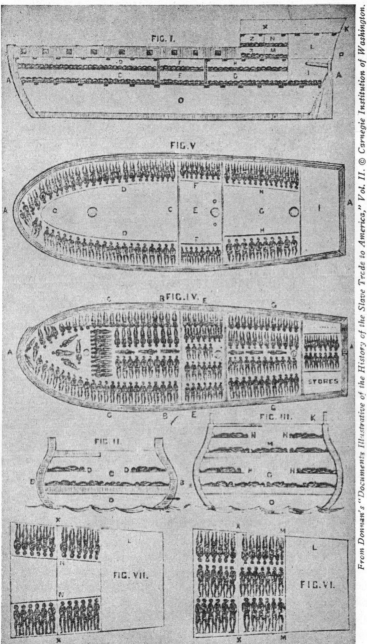

PLAN OF THE *BROOKES*, A SLAVE TRADING VESSEL OF THE EIGHTEENTH CENTURY

threshing by hand flail, and winnowing, sifting, and polishing the grains) and by virtue of the malarial condition of the swamp lands, slave labor was particularly necessary in the rice fields, since long residence in the jungles of Africa had made the Negro immune to malaria, while the white worker was highly susceptible to the disease. As a heavy, low-priced product (2d. or 3d. a pound in America) rice could be cultivated only along the rivers which afforded cheap transportation to Savannah or Charleston, whence vessels carried it to England and Europe. It was placed on the enumerated article list in 1705, with the result that the cost of shipment through England deprived the colonies of one of their markets, Portugal, and Parliament was forced to yield concessions in 1730, 1735, and 1737 by allowing rice exported from South Carolina, Georgia, and North Carolina to be shipped directly to points in Europe south of Cape Finisterre. Exports from Charleston (in barrels) increased from 3,000 in 1713 to 100,000 in 1724 and 125,000 in 1775. The growth of the plantation in South Carolina is indicated by the fact that after 1708 the Negro and white populations increased at the ratio of three to two.

Indigo supplemented rice in South Carolina after 1742. This product was introduced from the West Indies by Miss Eliza Lucas and cultivated under her supervision on an estate of her father, then governor of Antigua.[8] When it was found that South Carolina could not subsidize the new industry, Parliament in 1748 provided for a continuing bounty to producers of 6d. a pound. Due to the decline of indigo production in the West Indies there was a brisk demand for the Carolina product: its price in England ranged from 3s. to 6s. a pound, netting profits of 33 to 50 per cent to the planters and enabling them to bring the uplands of the interior under cultivation. The dyestuff was a bluish substance extracted from the indigo leaf by fermentation and pressed and cut into cubes—a process so disagreeable, even repulsive, that only slave labor could yield such handsome profits.

Although in its early stages the large plantation was efficient enough to crowd out the small producers yet in the long run it tended to become unprofitable—a trend clearly discernible in the tobacco area. During the eighteenth century the price of tobacco did not rise, whereas the costs of production advanced considerably. True, there was an enlarged production of tobacco; England's yearly imports from America consisted of 28,000,000 pounds in 1700–10 while in 1771–75 England and Scotland together received annually 102,000,000 pounds. Accompanying this growth in production was a large increase

[8] The standard biography is Harriott H. Ravenel, *Eliza Pinckney* (New York, 1902).

in the slave trade: in Virginia, Negroes composed 43 per cent of the population in 1756 as against 24 per cent in 1724; in North Carolina 26 per cent in 1767 as against 22 per cent in 1754; and 29 per cent in Maryland in 1755 as against 18 per cent in 1712. Yet despite such increases in production and in the labor force there are many evidences to show that tobacco growing became less and less profitable due to two primary causes: soil exhaustion and the mounting burden of fixed charges and debt. Both of these causes are traceable to the methods of trade upon which the planters had to depend.[9]

In 1764 a merchant wrote that "the African trade in Virginia must soon be at an end, for the people will not soon pay for the slaves they have already bought." With the progress of rice and indigo in the lower South the demand for slaves boosted their price, and in consequence the tobacco planters were obliged to pay a larger share of their profits to slave traders. Whereas the price of slaves in 1650 had been about £20 a head, it had risen to £25 in 1700, to £30 in 1741, to £40–£60 in 1750 and to £50–£80 in the 1770's. Since slave importations averaged about 3,500 in the years 1715–70, it is apparent that in the eighteenth century the planters had to pay, due to higher prices alone, from £20,000 to £100,000 or more a year.

The slave trade was but one part of a commercial system that frequently did not function for the planters' benefit. It will be recalled that the Navigation Acts required that tobacco should be exported to Europe, its chief market, by way of Britain; that imports to the colonies should pass through Britain; and that only British ships should be employed in the trade. These acts obliged the planters to deal with British merchants, who employed three methods in their colonial business. The wealthy tidewater planters commonly consigned their tobacco to merchants in England who sold it for them and remitted the proceeds to the colonies. Supplementing this method was the factorage system, whereby the merchant hired an agent in the colony to collect tobacco from the smaller planters and to deliver the goods sent from England in return. Then, with the growth of small farms in the interior, the merchants established stores which supplied the farmers with English goods on credit and collected tobacco in payment. With respect to the fundamental relations between farmer and merchant these three methods tended toward a common result.[10]

---

[9] See again L. C. Gray, *History of Agriculture in the Southern United States*, Vol. I, chapters 5, 12–13, 18–20.

[10] Charles C. Crittenden has written a scholarly history of *The Commerce of North Carolina, 1763–1789* (New Haven, 1936). See chapters 1–8.

As it has been previously explained, a planter who consigned his tobacco to England assumed the chief risks of the trade, whereas the merchant occupied a protected position. From the proceeds of a consignment which the latter sold several charges had to be deducted before the planter received anything. Such were the English import duties (6½d. a pound), the freights and insurance on the shipment to England, and the merchant's commission (2½ per cent of the gross proceeds), unloading, trucking, and warehouse fees, a charge for giving bond for the payment of import duties, and an assessment for maintaining a parliamentary lobby of the merchants; moreover the planter had to bear the loss arising from waste and shrinkage. All these charges were of a fixed character and the customs and earnings of the merchants constituted a first claim against the proceeds. In time of war the merchants insured their freight earnings, thus doubling freight rates and greatly increasing the sum deducted from the proceeds before the planters received a penny.[11]

If trade conditions were good and tobacco prices were high the planters secured a substantial profit but when depressions occurred the price of tobacco often fell so low that all the proceeds were consumed by the English charges, and if those charges exceeded the proceeds the planter became indebted to the merchant for the deficit. Several severe and protracted depressions (1703–13, 1720–34, and 1756–65) plunged the planters so deeply in debt that they were never able to extricate themselves. As debtors they were obliged to consign their future crops to their creditor merchants—an arrangement which gave birth to the tradition in Virginia that a delegation of the merchants "would meet annually and settle the price of tobacco for the year, . . . and at the same time have a similar understanding as to the profits of their merchandise, which was often 100 per cent of the prime cost." [12]

The planters also complained that the goods shipped to America by the merchants were of poor quality, that they were carelessly packed and damaged en route, and that orders were improperly or only partially filled. The debts contracted for slaves and merchandise during depressions took a heavy toll of the planters' surplus in better times. Writing in the 1730's Sir Robert Walpole said that the planters were reduced almost "to a state of despair by the many frauds that have been committed in that trade, by the heavy duties which the

[11] E. Donnan, "Micajah Perry," *Journal of Economic and Business History*, IV (Nov. 1931).

[12] For a good account of Virginia's trade see Leonidas Dodson, *Alexander Spotswood* (Philadelphia, 1932), chapter 4. T. J. Wertenbaker's *Norfolk* (Durham, N. C., 1931) is one of the best histories of a colonial town. See chapter 2 (trade).

importers of tobacco are obliged to pay . . . , and by the ill usage
they have met with from their factors and correspondents here in
England, who from being their servants are now become their lords
and masters."

Because of the slender profits of agriculture the planters could not
invest in improving and conserving their land, with the result that
soil exhaustion rapidly undermined the older plantation areas. The
high cost of slaves and their character as workers also impaired plantation economy which, by failing to utilize fertilizers, crop rotation,
and deep-soil plowing, rapidly reduced the yield per acre: in Maryland it had fallen, by the end of the eighteenth century, from four
thousand to two thousand pounds of tobacco. Although in Virginia in
1700 "soil wastage was everywhere evident and barren fields that
would not grow crops profitably," yet the burden of fixed charges—
slaves and debts—remained unchanged, thus cutting the planters'
profits to the bone.[13]

In hope of extricating themselves from their plight the planters
advocated many abortive remedies. After 1700 they secured colonial
laws which levied high import duties on slaves, with the object of
protecting the older plantations adequately supplied with labor against
their rising competitors. Such a duty of £5 was levied by Virginia in
1710. The English government, ever desirous both to extend tobacco
production and to promote the slave traffic, consistently opposed all colonial acts designed to curtail the importation of Negroes. Thus the
Virginia act of 1710 was disallowed by the Privy Council and in 1731
the Crown ordered colonial governors not to sign any bills which
levied duties upon imported slaves.

Of similar intent was another scheme: that of curtailing tobacco
production by legal means. When tobacco prices fell to ruinous levels
during depressions the assemblies of Virginia and Maryland passed
laws which limited the number of plants that could be grown on each
plantation and provided for the destruction of all inferior tobacco.
Such acts, however, could not be enforced because they penalized the
planter who complied and benefited the "chiseler"; moreover, it was
impossible to induce all producing areas to coöperate; curtailment in
one place led to expansion elsewhere so that the supply and price of
tobacco were not materially altered. Crop restriction was also opposed
by the small planters who paid officers' fees, taxes, and quit-rents in
tobacco at a fixed number of pounds: hence they refused to curtail

[13] An especially important study is Avery O. Craven, *Soil Exhaustion as a Factor
in the Agricultural History of Virginia and Maryland, 1606–1860* (Urbana, c. 1926).
See chapters 1–2.

the quantity of tobacco money which they minted on their farms. In Maryland (1727–30) the small farmers refused to consent to restrictive schemes unless the quantity of tobacco which they were obliged to pay to the proprietor was correspondingly reduced. Lord Baltimore vetoed the latter proposal, realizing that a mere reduction of the amount of tobacco grown in the colony would not necessarily raise the price; he might merely receive a smaller quantity of tobacco which, when sold in England, would yield less money than a larger quantity. Virginia could not act without the coöperation of Maryland and therefore the whole plan fell through.[14]

Next the colonists appealed to England for relief when in 1732 they presented a petition, *The Case of the Planters of Tobacco in Virginia,* which requested that the heavy fixed charges collected in London be reduced. The import duties should be cut from 6½d. to 4d. a pound, the government should provide warehouses where tobacco could be stored without bond until the duties had been paid, and no duty should be collected on tobacco reëxported. Sir Robert Walpole, then chief minister of England, favored reduction or abolition of the import duties in order to prevent smuggling—a practice, incidentally, which lowered the price of tobacco and cut down the planters' proceeds from shipments which paid the duties. Walpole's scheme failed, due to political opposition and to the antagonism of the tobacco merchants, and the old abuses of the trade continued.[15]

The planters also endeavored to reduce their debts by legal action. In 1708 Maryland enacted a law that debtors without property might declare bankruptcy and escape punishment for debt. This act was disallowed by the Privy Council when English merchants objected that it permitted a planter to assign his lands and slaves to friends or relatives and by feigning bankruptcy to defraud his creditors. A comparable act of Virginia in 1749 allowed the planters to pay debts with depreciated Virginia currency: a debt of £100 in English money might be paid with £125 in Virginia money, even though the latter was not actually worth the former. The English government responded in 1754 by instructing the governor not to sign bills which allowed the planters to pay debts in Virginia currency at a fixed evaluation in English money. All colonial acts which scaled down debts were disallowed by the Privy Council; after 1710 the royal governors were instructed to see that courts were held fre-

---

[14] P. H. Giddens, "Trade and Industry in Colonial Maryland, 1753–1769," *Journal of Economic and Business History,* IV (May 1932).

[15] St. George L. Sioussat, "Virginia and the English Commercial System, 1730–1733," *Report,* American Historical Association, 1905, Vol. I.

quently so that English creditors might conveniently collect their "just dues," and in 1732 Parliament made the lands and slaves of the planters liable for debts.

The reforms sought by the planters—crop restriction, changes in the marketing system, lower import duties, reduction of debts and curtailment of the slave trade—were opposed by English interests which had the support of the imperial government; consequently the planters were obliged to look elsewhere for enduring relief. The most successful planters, who had made profits during good times, found two ways out of the distress of their class. First, they developed a real-estate business in the newer parts of their colonies, acquiring huge tracts of land which they leased to tenants or sold to small farmers.[16] When Robert Carter died in 1752 he possessed 300,000 acres of land, an area too vast to be cultivated by even his large force of a thousand slaves. William Byrd II held eighty thousand acres in 1744; Charles Carroll in Maryland between 1740 and 1765 acquired improved tracts ranging from five to ten thousand acres; Daniel Dulany, also in Maryland, obtained large holdings in Frederick County; in the years 1714–22 Governor Spotswood built up a vast estate in Spotsylvania County, Virginia. The profitableness of such acquisitions is indicated by the fact that land values in Maryland rose threefold between 1730 and 1760.

In the first stage of land speculation the planter ordinarily did not sell his tracts but rather imported tenants (Germans, Scotch-Irish, and settlers from the northern colonies) whom he supplied with tools, seed, and livestock, receiving rent in tobacco, grain, and other produce —an income which obliged him to assume the role of merchant. The rents received by Daniel Dulany in 1764 included fifty thousand pounds of tobacco. In leasing land the speculator often hoped merely to develop it and to pay expenses until a rise in values permitted sales at a profit.

The more efficient planters also found a way out of their difficulties by operating additional plantations on newer, more fertile soil and by diversifying production, so that southern economy became increasingly self-sufficing. The industrial development of the plantation exhibits three general stages. First, the individual estate produced a variety of things for its own use: cattle, sheep, hogs, horses, wheat, corn, rye, cotton and woolen clothing and coarse shoes for the slaves, certain farm implements and utensils, cooperage stock, bricks, soap, candles, salt, beer, and wine. The workers employed were indentured

[16] Halsted L. Ritter's *Washington as a Business Man* (New York, 1931) is an introductory study.

servants or slaves trained as carpenters, coopers, weavers, brick makers, brewers, sawyers, blacksmiths, etc. In the second stage of development the plantation sold a surplus of such products in its neighborhood: to smaller farmers and freed servants and to shipowners who purchased cereals and meats. Then came the final stage when a regular export trade was conducted. Staves, hoops, and headings were exported to the West Indies; thither also went flour, bacon, pork, and livestock; in 1755 Virginia's exports included 200,000 bushels of corn and 40,000 bushels of wheat.[17]

Despite this trend toward diversification the industrial opportunities of the plantation area were limited. The employment of slaves as artisans operated to prevent free craftsmen from migrating to the South, since the social status of their trades was degraded by slavery. Moreover, slave labor—deprived of incentive—was generally inefficient, while the purchase of slaves required a long-term investment that was avoided in the North by the employment of free wage-earners. When slaves were hired by their owners to employers the wage rate was necessarily high because it had to provide not only for the maintenance of the worker but also for a payment to the owner which would cover the principal and interest on his investment. As an industrial force slave labor also lacked the mobility and adaptability attainable when an employer might bargain with a laborer who was free to go where he pleased and who could be discharged at will. Only the scarcity of free wage-earners in the South (a scarcity induced largely by slavery itself) made it profitable for employers to utilize slave artisans as a labor force.[18]

### THE PROGRESS OF INDUSTRY

During the eighteenth century the economy of the middle colonies and New England was shaped largely by their commerce with Britain. They continued to purchase great quantities of manufactured and other European goods from England: by 1770 their imports amounted to £1,410,000 a year. Yet the northern colonies had not succeeded in developing domestic staples like tobacco which could be sent to England in payment for their large volume of imports: only a few native products—fur, ship timber, whale products, and lumber —were available as direct returns. Thus in 1770 the visible exports from the northern colonies had a value of only £178,000 and the

[17] See again M. W. Jernegan, *Laboring and Dependent Classes in Colonial America*, pp. 3–23.
[18] See again U. B. Phillips, *American Negro Slavery*, chapter 5.

nominal balance of trade against them amounted to £1,232,000. It is true that the unfavorable trade balance was not so great as these figures indicate because they do not include one very important export from the northern colonies—the ships which were built there and sold to English merchants. Even so, however, the value of imports greatly exceeded the value of the exports sent directly from the northern colonies to England.

Their lack of staples marketable in England had two profound effects on the northern colonies. First, it compelled them to engage in diversified production in order to satisfy as many of their wants as possible. Their agriculture afforded wheat, Indian corn, oats, rye, barley, cattle, sheep, swine, horses, mules, vegetables, fruits, and dairy products, while their domestic industries supplied them with coarse woolen and linen cloth, shoes, furniture, implements, household utensils, candles, soap, paper, glass, hats, sugar, beer, fish, flour, lumber, rum, cooperage stock, ships, saddles, earthenware, ironware, and woodenware. Secondly, the Northerners were obliged to engage in a complex trade in order to dispose of their surplus products in such a way as to provide them with purchasing power in England. The markets available for this surplus included the southern colonies, the West Indies, Africa, the Wine Islands, southern Europe, Newfoundland, Canada, Nova Scotia, and the interior fur trading areas; in each case the exports from the northern mainland were exchanged for commodities that could be used as remittances to England: coined money, bullion, sugar, indigo, dyewoods, ginger, cottonwool, rice, tobacco, naval stores, furs, wine, and bills of exchange. By virtue of these external trades the merchants of the northern colonies not only acquired the means of completing their payments for imports from England but also obtained excess profits from their marketing, shipping and credit services which explain the accumulation of capital in the northern commercial towns.[19]

Northern agriculture did not change materially after 1700 except for the rapid expansion of the settled area: the products raised and the methods of farming were the same as those previously described. In industry, however, the eighteenth century witnessed considerable progress in the form of diversification, specialization, and improved techniques. Household manufacturing, it is true, remained the backbone of industrial production, although it advanced to a more ma-

[19] Robert E. Peabody, *Merchant Venturers of Old Salem* (Boston, 1912), tells the story of Richard Derby, merchant. See chapter 1. See also E. Edelman, "Thomas Hancock, Colonial Merchant," *Journal of Economic and Business History*, I (Nov. 1928).

ture stage. In the frontier regions the family carried on a primitive form of production simply to supply itself with such articles as furniture, leather goods, utensils, soap, candles, fuel, and food products. A slightly more advanced community employed the services of traveling artisans who worked on materials supplied by the farmer:

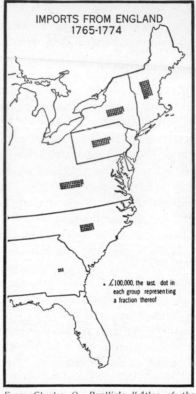

From Charles O. Paullin's "Atlas of the Historical Geography of the United States." © Carnegie Institution of Washington. Reprinted by courtesy of the American Geographical Society of New York.

among such artisans were masons, weavers, carpenters, and candle-makers. A third stage occurred when the family produced a surplus of manufactures which were at first exchanged in the neighborhood for other local products. Then, as an area became well settled, with improved transportation facilities, the farmers produced for general sale, more or less as employees of merchant manufacturers. Thus in the seaboard areas the latter supplied the farmers with flax, wool, and cotton which their families spun and wove into cloth—a form of capitalist production, since the merchants owned the raw materials and paid the farmer-workers a wage. This advanced stage of household manufacturing attained in the northern colonies by 1775 resembled the domestic system in vogue in England at the close of the six-

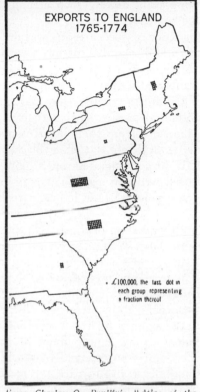

EXPORTS TO ENGLAND
1765-1774

£100,000, the last dot in each group representing a fraction thereof

From Charles O. Paullin's "Atlas of the Historical Geography of the United States." © Carnegie Institution of Washington. Reprinted by courtesy of the American Geographical Society of New York.

teenth century, when her merchant capitalists became interested in colonization as a means of extending their markets.[20]

A similar evolution brought the small settled artisan within the circle of capitalist production. In the simplest form of handicraft industry, common to new settlements, a craftsman worked in his own

[20] L. H. Gipson's *The British Empire before the American Revolution* is especially good on economic themes. See Vol. II, chapter 3 (tobacco), pp. 165–185 (South Carolina), chapters 7–9 (sugar islands), chapter 10 (Africa); Vol. III, chapters 8 (iron), 10 (fishery), 11 (British colonial system).

shop, using his own tools with which he fabricated raw materials brought to him by the farmers of the neighborhood. This stage of production for local custom on advance orders was soon followed by a second stage in which the artisan purchased raw materials and manufactured goods for general sale which he displayed at his shop or sold to peddlers. Most important among such artisans were blacksmiths, hatmakers, shoemakers, weavers, tailors, saddlers, and wheelwrights. In colonial times the work of such artisans was not fully specialized: a shoemaker was also a tanner and a currier, a weaver a cloth dresser and a dyer, and a blacksmith a tool maker. Although employers of journeymen or servants and owners of their own tools, these settled craftsmen were not capitalists because they did not employ enough hands to receive substantial profits, so that their income was derived chiefly from their labor, not from their investments. The capital possessed by such artisans was not large: a blacksmith worked at a "bloomery" or small forge, operated by a power-driven bellows, where he manufactured wrought-iron goods; an estate of a leading Boston weaver in 1696 included four looms, a fulling mill, and two dye furnaces.

Ordinarily the small workshop of the artisan did not expand into a large industrial plant, largely because the owner did not possess capital sufficient to sustain production for distant markets which required payments for material and wages before the finished goods could be sold. As the chief possessors of capital the merchants played the principal part in the organization of large-scale production. At first they contracted with the artisans for the wares they produced—a practice virtually equivalent to the employment of the latter as wage-earners. Thus the merchant who received livestock from the farmers hired butchers to slaughter it and to pack the meat products for the market. Inasmuch as the merchants were the owners of the raw material and had control over the marketing processes, they were able to reap the profits arising from the spread between production costs and the sale price of manufactured wares.[21]

For those industries which had advanced beyond the handicraft to the mill stage and which required expensive plants and machinery, the artisans could not provide the necessary capital: that had to be obtained from merchants, large landowners and European investors. In order to establish mills, ironworks, distilleries, breweries, furnaces, etc., the promoters organized partnerships or companies. This method allowed a successful artisan to contribute a share of the capital and to

[21] See again J. R. Commons, *History of Labor in the United States*, Vol. I.

assume control of production, while the merchant investors took charge of financial and marketing operations.

What were the capital requirements of colonial industry? A saw-mill, with water wheel and dam, which cut a thousand feet of boards daily, cost between $500 and $1,000. By 1765 flour mills (with a producing capacity of between a hundred and two hundred bushels a day) included besides the mill proper a storehouse or grain elevator, screens for cleaning wheat, a bolting house, ovens, and a cooper's shop. "Most of the merchant mills in the central colonies were covered by substantial structures, usually of stone, two or three stories high. . . . The wheels were protected from ice and weather by being enclosed in the building itself." Ironworks consisted of blast furnaces for smelting the ore, refining forges at which a tilt hammer operated by water power fashioned bar iron, and slitting mills and plating mills equipped with rollers and cutters which worked the iron bars into rods, flat iron, and sheeting. Two iron establishments in the late colonial period—the Principio works in Maryland and the Peter Hasenclever works in New Jersey—represented an investment of $250,000 each: the latter consisted of six blast furnaces, seven forges, a stamping mill, three sawmills, and a gristmill. At New York in 1767 one company operated a linen factory which contained fourteen looms. The famous Stiegel glass plant at Mannheim, Pennsylvania, was so large that it was related "that a coach and four could turn around within the brick dome of its melting-house." In the Carolina naval stores industry tar kilns were constructed which had a capacity of 960 barrels; as early as 1664 a tile kiln in New York cost $25,000. The equipment of a brewery (a malt cellar, storehouse, and horses for operating the malt mill) required an outlay of between $1,000 and $3,000, while the equipment of a Trenton, New Jersey, tannery in 1778 included sixty-four vats, two water pools, a bark house, a currying shop and skin dresser's shop, and facilities for making leather breeches.[22]

Judged by modern industrial plants these colonial enterprises seem small enough, yet when it is considered that a colonial artisan, in a lifetime of labor, ordinarily did not accumulate more than $500, it is apparent that the capital outlays were considerable for the time. Whence came such capital? Foreign investors contributed a part: the Principio ironworks was an English concern, while German capital founded the Stiegel glass plant and the Hasenclever ironworks. Otherwise the capital was advanced by colonial enterprisers whose

[22] See again V. S. Clark, *History of Manufactures in the United States, 1607–1860*, chapters 1–9.

initial profits were derived from investments in land and commerce. A schedule of prices drawn up in Maryland in 1775 indicates the profits of trade: a merchant should not sell imported goods wholesale for more than 112.5 per cent above their prime cost, nor at cash retail prices in excess of 130 per cent, while retail credit prices should not exceed 150 per cent. Land rents in New England in 1720–30 yielded a return of between 6 and 8 per cent. Such gains explain the growth of mercantile fortunes in the North. When Thomas Amory, Boston merchant, died in 1728 his estate exceeded $100,000; in 1737 Peter Faneuil owned English securities worth at least $75,000. Such foreign investments by a Boston merchant prince show that colonial fortunes were accumulating at a faster rate than the opportunities for traditional colonial investments in land and shipping—a trend that continued unabated between 1725 and 1775, and that explains in part the flow of colonial capital into industrial enterprises. Merchants of Philadelphia found an outlet for their surpluses in the iron industry, not only in works located in Pennsylvania but also in Virginia and Carolina. So common were investments in flour that many mills were known as merchant's mills. The employment of butchers, meat packers, cloth workers, and shipwrights by the merchants who provided the raw materials afforded additional capital outlets. At Newport a leading Jewish merchant, Aaron Lopez, turned to the manufacture of spermaceti candles. Rope walks, rum distilleries, the fur trade, and the fishery also gave employment to the excess accumulations of the merchant class. Benjamin Franklin invested in paper mills and printing establishments: in 1733, he wrote, "I sent one of my journeymen to Charleston, . . . where a printer was wanting. I furnished him with a press and letters, on an agreement of partnership, by which I was to receive one-third of the profits of the business, paying one-third of the expense." [23]

Large-scale production afforded a high rate of profit by virtue of operating economies and a more effective control over markets and prices. The pioneer glass manufacturer of New Jersey accumulated an estate of approximately $150,000; similarly the Stiegel glass works for a time earned $13,000 a year. In 1705 the income of a Pennsylvania sawmill was £400, only a third of which was necessary to pay maintenance and labor costs. Of the flour industry V. S. Clark says that the miller "usually remained a local magnate, whose home assumed with increasing affluence something like manorial dignity." A Philadelphia cloth manufacturing society earned profits of 41 per

[23] Joseph S. Davis, *Essays in the Earlier History of American Corporations* (2 vols., Cambridge, 1917), gives the best discussion of the corporation in the eighteenth century.

cent during the first two years of operations (1775–76). Wherever possible industrial promoters endeavored to establish monopolies. The merchants and flour millers purchased or received grain when prices were low, attempted to obtain all local supplies, held flour from the market at dull seasons, and sold when prices were high. In the 1760's the spermaceti candlemakers formed an association in order to fix the prices of candles and raw materials (which they purchased through a single agent) and to prevent the "setting up of any new spermaceti works." Conditions of employment also favored the owners of industries: Clark states that "many colonial iron-masters ruled with almost feudal sway over a neighborhood settlement of their laborers and country people." When a sawmill was erected it frequently became the nucleus of a settlement where the owners established a store and a gristmill to serve at first the lumbermen-employees and later the farming community which developed on the cleared land. After 1720 industrial promoters in Boston, Philadelphia, and New York organized societies for the employment of the poor: workhouses were erected and skilled artisans were engaged to instruct children in the production of yarn, thread, cordage, bagging, and cloth. The products belonged to the promoters: "the idea was well fixed in the popular mind that the employment of children in such arts served the general welfare and that the profit of their labor, even when unremunerated, properly belonged to the person who undertook the burden of their instruction."

### THE PROBLEM OF SURPLUS CAPITAL

It is notable that the colonial enterprises which assumed large proportions—the fishery, lumbering, flour milling, shipbuilding, etc.—afforded surpluses in excess of colonial needs and that other industries such as the textile, iron, and leather manufactures did not produce enough goods to meet the colonial demand.[24] Why, then, did some industries expand beyond the requirements of American consumption while others lagged behind? Primarily because the "surplus" industries yielded commodities which in the course of external trade were exchanged for English manufactures of the type not produced in sufficient abundance in the colonies. This industrial evolution was not wholly the outgrowth of natural conditions: it was shaped in large measure by English colonial policy, which dictated that the colonies should buy English manufactures, paying for them with staple commodities that could not be produced conveniently and

[24] On the whaling industry the best recent account is Elmo P. Hohman, *The American Whaleman* (New York, 1928), chapter 2.

cheaply in England; therefore the colonies should not develop industries in competition with those of the mother country. However, there was a class of products which England did not desire either to obtain from or sell to the colonies: such were fish, meats, cereals, flour, lumber, bread, and rum: consequently she placed no restraints upon the production or sale of such articles in America. On the other hand she restrained the colonial production of leather goods, woolens, hats, and ironware—all major products of her own export industry. This twofold policy of encouraging some colonial enterprises and of restraining others explains why the favored ones produced in excess of colonial needs while the progress of the others was arrested; also why the surpluses of the favored industries had to be exchanged for English manufactures of the sort which the colonies were not encouraged to produce.[25]

By a long train of measures England sought to retard the growth of colonial industries. The Woolen Act of 1699 prohibited the exportation of American wool, woolen yarn, and woolen cloth from any colony—a restriction which denied to colonial producers an extensive market needed to support large-scale enterprise. When Pennsylvania passed an act to encourage shoemaking the Board of Trade in 1706 recommended that it be disallowed on the ground that "it cannot be expected that encouragement should be given by law to the making any manufactures made in England . . . , it being against the advantage of England." About the same time the Board rejected a suggestion for producing sailcloth at New York because it would "be more advantageous to England that all hemp and flax of the growth of the plantations should be imported hither, in order to the manufacturing of it here." Whenever a colonial assembly levied duties on English goods imported with the object of giving tariff protection to colonial industries such acts were speedily disallowed by the Privy Council. Similarly the colonial governors were instructed by the Crown not to sign any bills which discriminated against English manufactures in the colonies or which aimed to foster competing industries there. Of this latter policy the authority on the subject, E. B. Russell, states: "Largely as a result of the government's determined attitude in the matter, comparatively few laws for this purpose were enacted in the plantations." Comparable to the Woolen Act was the Hat Act of 1732, which prohibited the exportation of American-made hats from the colony in which they were produced and which restricted

[25] C. M. Andrews, *The Colonial Background of the American Revolution* (New Haven, 1924), in chapter 2 discusses economic aspects of British policy in terms of political factors.

each hatmaker to two apprentices—another safeguard against large-scale production in the colonies.[26]

As early as 1710 the iron manufacturers of England complained of growing competition from the colonial iron industry. The latter developed rapidly from that date until by 1750 numerous furnaces, forges, and mills were operating in New England, the middle colonies, Virginia, and Maryland. When the first large shipments of colonial bar iron entered England in 1735 the product proved to be of such excellent quality that English ironmakers became involved in an acrimonious controversy over the fate of the colonial industry. One group—the ironmasters, who smelted native ores into pig iron—insisted that colonial pig iron be excluded from England by high import duties and went farther to urge that the whole colonial iron industry be suppressed. Allied with this group were the owners of English mines and forests (charcoal then being used in smelting ores). On the other side were the iron manufacturers who desired an abundant supply of cheap pig and bar iron which they might fashion into nails, tools, and other iron wares. The iron manufacturers therefore sought to encourage the production of pig and bar iron in the colonies by admitting it into England duty free, but at the same time they demanded that the colonists should not be allowed to work their crude iron into finished products. Allied with the iron manufacturers were the merchant shipowners who foresaw many weighty cargoes for their vessels in the transportation of crude iron from America to England and of iron manufactures from England to the colonies. The woolen industry sided with the iron manufacturers on the assumption that colonial exports of crude iron would provide the colonists with buying power for English cloth, thus retarding the growth of the woolen manufactures in America.[27]

After a long struggle between the ironmasters and the iron manufacturers the latter triumphed when Parliament in 1750 passed the famous Iron Act, which removed all duties on colonial pig iron imported into England and on colonial bar iron shipped to London. Nor were the colonies to develop iron manufactures; after June 24, 1750, the erection of three types of ironworks was prohibited; slitting mills which cut iron for nails, plating forges which made sheet iron, and steel furnaces which produced blister steel for tools. Such works

[26] Sir William J. Ashley defends British colonial policy in his *Surveys, Historic and Economic* (London, 1900). See essays on commercial legislation and American smuggling.

[27] Arthur C. Bining's *British Regulation of the Colonial Iron Industry* (Philadelphia, 1933) is a splendid study.

already established were not to be destroyed; only new ones were proscribed.

The purpose of the English measures against colonial manufactures—to outlaw enterprises which could profit by the economies of large-scale production—was generally realized. Extensive plants could not be concealed from the king's officials, and colonial investors (a cautious class) would not put their money into forbidden enterprises that might be suppressed overnight with the penalty of a fine. The English acts therefore diverted colonial capital from advanced manufactures and intensified the problem which had long confronted the northern colonies—that of finding adequate means of paying for imported goods.[28]

It will be recalled that the bounties on colonial naval stores granted by Parliament in 1705 were intended to provide the northern colonies with exports to England. The industry, however, took root in Carolina, fostered by the generous premiums paid to importers of colonial supplies: £4 a ton for pitch and tar; £3 a ton for resin and turpentine; £6 a ton for hemp; and £1 a ton for masts, yards, and bowsprits. Under the impetus of the bounties, pitch and tar shipped from the Carolinas, 1705–18, amounted to 134,000 barrels a year; from New England, 86,000 barrels. The exports from New England were not produced there but came originally from Carolina; however, the effect of this trade was to provide New England with additional returns. During four years, 1725–29, when the bounties were discontinued, the colonial trade fell off so abruptly that Parliament restored certain of the bounties in 1729 at a reduced rate: £2 4s. a ton for tar and £1 a ton for pitch. The yearly exports for the period 1763–75 were approximately twice as large as those for the years 1730–50; the bounties paid by England were as follows: from 1730 to 1750, about £17,000 a year; from 1750–63, about £24,000; and from 1763–75 about £34,000. Yet despite the substantial growth of naval stores exports they failed to provide the northern colonies with adequate exports to England: when the industry was at its height in 1770 the year's unfavorable trade balance against those colonies amounted to £1,230,000.[29]

Ships built in America and sold to English merchants supplied additional purchasing power for English imports—a value not accounted for in the estimates of colonial exports, since such vessels were not entered in the English custom records from which such estimates have been compiled. The colonial shipbuilding industry made steady progress throughout the eighteenth century—a trend explained

[28] See again E. Lipson, *Economic History of England*, Vol. III, chapter 4.

by the fact that American vessels could be constructed at costs 20 to 50 per cent below those prevailing in England. So severe was the competition of the colonial industry that in 1724 the shipbuilders of the Thames district in England, complaining that it was ruining their business, petitioned the government for protection. But despite the emigration of skilled shipwrights to America England did not interfere with the colonial industry: her merchants needed cheap vessels and the colonists obtained purchasing power for English manufactures by providing them. By 1775 30 per cent of the vessels in England's merchant marine were of American construction and 75 per cent of the commerce of the colonies was served by colonial ships. New England remained the center of the industry: in 1772 she produced 68 per cent of all colonial-built vessels as against 10 per cent constructed in Pennsylvania, 8 per cent in New York, and 14 per cent in the southern colonies. Important as such vessels were as an invisible export to England, even so they made but a slight impression on the unfavorable balance of trade: in 1763–66, when that balance against the northern colonies stood at £1,000,000 a year, the value of vessels annually built for sale in New England, Pennsylvania, and New York was only £80,000.

Despite the encouragement given by England to colonial shipbuilding and naval stores, the staple exports of the northern colonies consisted of commodities that could not be marketed in England. Of the value of the exports of New England, 1763–66, the fishery contributed 52 per cent, lumbering 14 per cent, and agriculture 7 per cent; for New York the figures were: farm products 80 per cent and lumber 10 per cent; for Pennsylvania, farm products 80 per cent and lumber 5 per cent. Such commodities, by and large, had to be sold in intermediate markets in order to supply the Northerners with buying power for English goods.

One trade in which the northern colonists did not participate during the seventeenth century—the slave traffic—afforded after 1715 a new outlet for colonial products and additional employment for colonial ships.[30] Newport, Boston, New York, and other towns sent forth vessels laden with rum to purchase slaves in Africa, then to make the famous middle passage to the West Indies and there to dispose of their cargoes, chiefly for commodities marketable in England, and partly for molasses to be returned to the northern colonies as raw

[29] J. Williams, "English Mercantilism and Carolina Naval Stores, 1705–1776," *Journal of Southern History*, I (May 1935).

[30] A brief sketch of the slave trade appears in W. E. B. DuBois, *The Suppression of the African Slave-Trade* . . . (New York, 1896), chapters 1–4.

material for more rum. So important was this heady beverage in the trade that rum distilleries sprang up rapidly in New England (there were sixty-three of them in Massachusetts in 1750 and about thirty in Rhode Island). By 1771 the colonial slave traders employed between sixty and seventy vessels, each capable of transporting sixty-five Negroes—an investment equal to about a fourth of England's stake in the traffic. When a slaver sailed for Africa from a colonial port its value (including cargo and supplies) was about £1,000; after sixty-five Negroes had been transported the owners derived a profit of 33 per cent over and above all costs of the voyage and a depreciation allowance of a third of the value of the vessel. Such handsome profits explain the readiness of colonial merchants to engage in the traffic: of Peter Faneuil of Boston the New England historian, W. B. Weeden, asks: "Did Peter slap his fair round belly and chuckle when he named the snow *Jolly Bachelor?* or was it the sad irony of fate that his craft deliberately designed to be packed with human pains and echo with human groans should in its very name bear the fantastic image of the luxury-loving chief owner? If these be the sources of profit and property, where is the liberty of Faneuil Hall, where the charity of good Peter's alms?" [31]

The growth of the slave traffic intensified the dependence of the northern colonies upon their commerce with the Caribbean region as the principal outlet for their surplus capital and products. Prior to 1700, the northern colonies had traded chiefly with the British West Indies; afterward, however, the British islands did not afford adequate markets for northern produce: population and production increased much more rapidly on the mainland than in the islands—and at a time when English policy induced the Northerners to produce an export surplus of fish, lumber, provisions, and work animals. An additional market therefore became necessary, and this the northerners found in the French West Indies—Guadeloupe, Martinique, and Santo Domingo, also producers of sugar, molasses, and rum.[32]

The trade which ensued greatly benefited the northern colonies but its effect upon the British sugar islands was not so happy. As a more efficient producing area the French colonies were able to undersell the British islands and thus to curtail the profits of the British planters. Established nearly a half century after the British plantations, the French sugar industry had the advantage of newer, more

[31] David D. Wallace, *The Life of Henry Laurens* (New York, 1915), devotes chapter 6 to the slave trade. See also E. Donnan, "The Slave Trade into South Carolina before the Revolution," *American Historical Review*, XXXIII (July 1928).

[32] H. C. Bell, "The West India Trade before the American Revolution," *American Historical Review*, XXII (Jan. 1917).

fertile soils and the benefit of the efficiency and enterprise of energetic planters unburdened by heavy fixed charges and wasteful methods. The British plantations, on the other hand, had been sadly reduced by a long process of exploiting the land for the sake of immediate gain. It was the ambition of the British planter to live luxuriously in England—a practice which diverted the earnings of his class from plantation improvements to extravagant living, while such absenteeism necessitated the employment of overseers who commonly "mined" the soil for the sake of quick profits. In the French islands the plantations were generally smaller and operated by their owners, who reinvested their surplus in plantation improvements, took pains to conserve the soil, and managed their estates with that care, prudence, and economy for which French farmers are famous.[33]

Because the French plantations had to be developed under the shadow of the established English sugar industry the French government encouraged them with privileges which the British planters did not enjoy. Whereas the latter had to ship their sugar first to British ports their French competitors were allowed to export directly to their best European markets without the added charges of visiting a French port. In order to meet the costs of local government the British planters were obliged to pay heavy duties on their sugar exports; France on the other hand supported her colonial governments from national revenues, with the result that the island duties on French sugar exported were only a fourth of those collected by England. By virtue of these many advantages the French islands could sell sugar and its products from 25 to 30 per cent cheaper than Barbados and the Leeward Islands; they could also pay higher prices for northern products which were seeking wider markets. France could not supply her sugar islands with the necessary provisions, nor could her fur trading settlements in North America do so. Neither did France desire to buy West Indian molasses and rum: the French people did not like the taste of molasses, and rum was discriminated against in order to protect the French producers of wine and brandy. For these reasons France allowed her sugar colonies to obtain provisions, lumber, and work animals from the northern colonies in exchange for molasses and rum, and English colonial vessels were permitted to carry on the trade.[34]

As early as 1710 the planters of the British islands demanded pro-

---

[33] Two significant articles are C. M. Andrews, "Anglo-French Colonial Rivalry: the Western Phase," *American Historical Review*, XX (April, July 1915).

[34] Frank W. Pitman, *The Development of the British West Indies, 1700–1763* (New Haven, 1917), is the best analysis of West Indian economy.

tection against their French competitors. When England and France were locked in a fateful struggle was it not intolerable that the sugar colonies of England should be undermined by a trade through which her own colonies provisioned the French plantations, thereby enlarging the supply of sugar and depressing its price? Did not the northern colonial merchants sell their products in the British West Indies and obtain money there which was used to buy sugar and molasses from the French planters? And did not the Northerners relabel French sugar as British sugar and then ship it to England, thus depriving the British planters of the home market especially reserved for them? What a nefarious traffic was this which strengthened France's hold upon the sugar trade at the expense of England! Not only were the British planters concerned; the British merchants had a vast stake in the islands—a huge investment built up through loans to the debtor planters, a profitable commission business in London, and a fleet of vessels which carried products to and from the West Indies. If the British sugar industry fell it would drag down with it one of the most prosperous branches of England's overseas trade.[35]

In a campaign of self-protection the whole West Indian interest, planters and merchants, brought pressure upon the English government through a powerful parliamentary lobby, and after a long agitation secured the Molasses Act of 1733. Designed to impoverish the French West Indies, this statute imposed extremely high duties on foreign sugar, molasses, and rum imported into the English colonies (the molasses duty was 6d. a gallon.) The spokesmen of the northern colonies protested bitterly: the act, by lowering the prices of the northern staples and raising the price of sugar, molasses, and rum, would curtail the profit of colonial trade or destroy it altogether. Molasses and rum were ingredients in the slave trade, the fur trade, the Newfoundland trade, and the fishery: if the northern colonies could not obtain cheap rum they would lose those all important sources of profit and employment. And for what? Merely to protect the indolent, inefficient planters of the British West Indies! [36]

Obviously the Molasses Act involved the British empire in a serious contradiction. The northern colonists, not permitted to manufacture in competition with English industry, were encouraged to produce a

[35] Lowell J. Ragatz, *The Fall of the Planter Class in the British Caribbean, 1763–1833* (New York, c. 1928)—an outstanding book—devotes chapters 1–3 to West Indian society, agriculture, and trade.

[36] On the political influence of the West Indies see Lillian M. Penson, *The Colonial Agents of the British West Indies* (London, 1924.) For a briefer statement see L. M. Penson, "The London West India Interest in the Eighteenth Century," *English Historical Review*, XXXV (July 1921).

surplus of fish, lumber, provisions, and rum—products which had to be sold in outside markets in order to procure purchasing power for English goods. Yet the Molasses Act would have destroyed one of the necessary markets for that surplus. Two parts of the British empire were out of balance: the sugar islands were not keeping pace with the northern colonies, and when the issue became acute England prepared to sacrifice the northern farmers, fishermen, lumbermen, and merchants to the sugar planters and the English merchant-investors concerned in the West Indies. The Northerners presumably were neither to manufacture for themselves nor to sell their crude products where they could obtain purchasing power for English manufactures. How then could colonial investors find new outlets for their surplus capital?

The critical issue thus raised was evaded for twenty-five years by smuggling on a grand scale. The Northerners regarded the Molasses Act as grossly unjust, ignored it completely, and continued the foreign West Indian trade with unabated vigor.[37] Colonial labor and capital therefore continued to flow into shipbuilding, shipping, lumbering, agriculture, the fishery, distilleries, and all the trades dependent upon rum. Instead of resolutely enforcing the act the English government in 1739 offered a concession to the planters by permitting the exportation of sugar directly from the West Indies to points in Europe south of Cape Finisterre. But this availed little, because the best sugar markets were in northern Europe. Meanwhile, as the French plantations and the northern colonies continued to prosper in their unlawful partnership, the British planters repeatedly demanded the suppression of the trade which sustained their rivals. And when they forced the issue after 1758 they helped to precipitate the Revolutionary War.

[37] William S. McClellan, *Smuggling in the American Colonies* . . . (New York, 1912), is a good, compact discussion.

## BIBLIOGRAPHICAL NOTE

WORKS PREVIOUSLY CITED: J. T. Adams, *Provincial Society*, chs. 2, 8–9; H. J. Carman, *Social and Economic History of the United States*, I, ch. 3; E. Channing, *History of the United States*, II, pp. 491–526; H. E. Egerton, *Short History of British Colonial Policy*, Book II, chs. 5–6; E. B. Greene, *Provincial America*, chs. 16–17; H. Heaton, *Economic History of Europe*, chs. 14–16; A. C. Flick (ed.), *History of the State of New York*, II, chs. 7–9; Emory R. Johnson *et al*, *History of the . . . Commerce of the United States*, I, chs. 6, 9–11; R. McFarland, *History of the New England Fisheries*, chs. 5–6; W. B. Weeden, *Economic and Social History of New England*, I, pp. 365–410, ch. 11; II, chs. 12–16, pp. 665–691.

SOURCES NEWLY CITED: Guy S. Callender's *Selections from the Economic History of the United States* (New York, n. d.) is highly valuable. See chapters 1–3 and note particularly the discriminating introductory essays. The anonymous *American Husbandry* (2 vols., London, 1775) gives an inside view of colonial agricultural techniques. The first two volumes of *A Documentary History of American Industrial Society* (10 vols., Cleveland, 1910–11), edited by U. B. Phillips under the title *Plantation and Frontier, 1649–1863*, contain much material on the eighteenth-century plantation. Elizabeth Donnan (ed.), *Documents Illustrative of the History of the Slave Trade* (4 vols., Washington, 1930–35), is a collection of great importance. Two well-known statements of mercantilism are Joshua Gee, *The Trade and Navigation of Britain Considered* (London, 1767), and William Wood, *A Survey of Trade* (London, 1718).

SOURCES PREVIOUSLY CITED: E. L. Bogart and C. M. Thompson (eds.), *Readings in the Economic History of the United States*, chs. 2–4; H. S. Commager (ed.), *Documents of American History*, I, no. 30; J. F. Jameson (ed.), *Privateering and Piracy*, pp. 290–586; W. MacDonald (ed.), *Documentary Source Book of American History*, no. 28 (Molasses Act).

# XVII

# COLONIAL SOCIETY

FROM Europe, and particularly from England, came the cultural traits which contained the germs of American society. The transplanted customs and ideals which survived in America were those best suited to the new environment; and they in turn were modified by it. Occupations, primitive contacts with nature, and the economic organization of society: such influences shaped the mold and spirit of colonial life. If there was diversity of manners and customs traceable to racial, religious, geographical, and class differences, so also—and more important—there were fundamental similarities arising from psychological and physiological traits common to all people, from the common inheritance of Christian morality, and from an economic organization that cut across racial, religious, and geographical lines.[1]

## THE COLONIAL FAMILY

The most important element in colonial society, the family, gave a dominant tone of domesticity to the age. It was the unit of production and business enterprise, the means of perpetuating the race, and the chief agency of human association. Often containing as many as twenty or thirty people (counting servants and odd relatives), the family was a large unit primarily because of the numerous children that swarmed about the home. Families of ten or twelve children were considered common; those of twenty or twenty-five were not regarded as phenomenal. Patrick Henry was one of nineteen; John Marshall the first of fifteen. Not all the children survived; in Pennsylvania it was estimated that four in ten died before the age of sixteen. A New England versifier paid tribute to Mrs. Sara Thayer, who died in 1751:

> Also she was a fruitful vine,
> The truth I may relate

[1] Charles A. and Mary R. Beard's *The Rise of American Civilization* (2 vols., New York, 1930) is a stimulating synthesis. See Vol. I, chapter 4.

> Fourteen was of her body born
> And lived to man's estate.
>
> From these did spring a numerous race,
> One hundred thirty-two;
> Sixty and six each sex alike
> As I declare to you.
>
> And one thing more remarkable,
> Which I shall here record:
> She'd fourteen children with her
> At the table of the Lord.

An observer of North Carolina in 1760 wrote: "the necessaries of life are so cheap and so easily acquired, and the propagation being unrestricted, that the increase of people there is inconceivable, even to themselves." Oglethorpe advertised in 1732 that a husband, wife, and child over seven could earn six times as much in Georgia as in England. At any rate, economic productivity explains the rapid growth of population and the custom of early marriage. Girls in all the colonies were commonly married when sixteen or eighteen (occasionally when only thirteen or fourteen); young men became husbands more often "under twenty years than above." Such early marriages enabled parents, while still young and adaptable, to become adjusted to each other and to the wear and tear of little children. Nor did youth have to contend with the psychological strain of abstinence when the urge of sex was strong.[2]

As the custodian of property the family played an important economic role. Marriage portions, dowries, marriage settlements, and inheritance figured prominently in family affairs in all the colonies. Due to the property aspects of marriage the early Protestant reformers considered marriage primarily as a civil contract and authorized that the wedding ceremony be performed by civil magistrates. Such was the practice in the middle and New England colonies during the seventeenth century; not until 1692 was marriage by clergymen legalized in Massachusetts. In the eighteenth century, when religious ceremonies became common, the minister acted as an agent of the state. The Anglican Church in the South affirmed the principle of marriage by the clergy, but due to the union of church and state, the clergyman acted as a representative of the civil government as well as of the church. In all the colonies the disposition of

---

[2] Arthur W. Calhoun, *A Social History of the American Family* (3 vols., Cleveland, 1917–1919), though not a definitive work, contains much interesting information, with intelligent comments. See Vol. I.

THE ABBOT HOUSE, ANDOVER, MASSACHUSETTS. BUILT IN 1675.

THE GRISWOLD HOUSE, GUILFORD, CONNECTICUT.
ERECTED BEFORE 1760.

A ROOM IN THE SAMUEL WENTWORTH HOUSE, PORTSMOUTH,
NEW HAMPSHIRE. PANELING DONE ABOUT 1710.

A ROOM IN A HOUSE IN ALMODINGTON, MARYLAND.
PANELING DONE ABOUT 1750.

property by marriage settlement or inheritance was regulated by civil law; fundamentally marriage was a civil rather than a religious institution.[3]

Since marriage involved a transfer of property, either immediate or in the future, the consent of parents—as the owners of the property concerned—was necessary to a match. Thus custom in all the colonies required that a young man secure the permission of his father and of the father of the young lady of his choice before he began his suit—a custom reinforced by laws which voided marriages entered into without parental consent. Such parental authority, however, was not unlimited: in New England the civil authorities might overrule parental objections made on capricious or unjustifiable grounds. In order to assure parental consent all the colonies condemned secret marriages and required that advance notice be given and that a wedding ceremony be performed. Families of the lower middle class gave notice by having banns thrice published in church; the wealthier folk obtained marriage licenses from governors or ministers, paying fees which the poor could not afford. In Pennsylvania the issuance of a minister's license required two men of good repute to certify that the bridegroom was free to marry; they in turn became liable for damages if he could not legally perform his part of the contract. The rustic wedding in Pennsylvania, which took place in church or in the bride's house, was followed by many a bucolic joke and an all-night celebration given over to feasting and dancing. "Whoever stole off to get some sleep was hunted up, dragged out on the floor, and the fiddler ordered to play, 'Hang on till tomorrow morning.' " [4]

Among upper-class groups there prevailed an acute awareness of the property status of wooer and wooed. An important New Englander wrote of his daughter: "she may stay here long 'ere she meet with a better [match] unless I had more money for her than I can now spare." Certainly few of the upper class "married beneath them"; practical considerations kept a tight rein on romantic fancies. "Where passion and affection sway, that man is deprived of sense and understanding." A suitor of Nancy Shippen, belle of Philadelphia in 1781, lamented that a girl "who has all the advantages of a good education must be married in a hurry and given up to a man she dislikes." Due to the class limitations of courtship the wealthy families became closely related by intermarriage. In 1767 the relatives of Abram De

---

[3] C. L. Powell, "Marriage in Early New England," *New England Quarterly*, I (July 1928).

[4] C. M. Andrews, *Colonial Folkways* (*Chronicles of America*, New Haven, 1919), chapters 1–5, 8.

Peyster of New York included Van Cortlandts, Beekmans, Livingstons, De Lanceys, Philipses, Schuylers, Stuyvesants, Jays, Roosevelts. So also the first families of Virginia—the Carters, Balls, Fitzhughs, Lees, Washingtons, Stuarts, Ludwells, and Corbins—were bound together by ties of marriage. Since the number of prospective husbands among the upper class was limited, the young ladies did their utmost to make themselves attractive in order to charm as many eligible young men as possible and thus to have a wide range of choice. Washington's condemnation of loveless marriages indicates that the romantic ideal survived despite pecuniary handicaps.

Among artisans and small farmers parents considered, not so much the property assets of a prospective mate (although that was not to be scorned), as his or her industry and efficiency as a provider or housewife. Franklin [5] voiced the contempt of this class for mercenary marriages in a "jingle" written in 1721:

> A swarm of sparks, young, gay, and bold
> Loved Sylvia long, but she was cold, . . .
> At last came Dulman, he was old,
> Nay he was ugly, but had gold.
> He came and saw and took the hold,
> While t'other beaux their loss consoled.
> Some say, she's wed; I say she's sold.

Theoretically the husband was lord and master of the family, but numerous references to housewives in *Poor Richard's Almanac* suggest that not all women were meek and submissive. Unquestionably the personal status of women was rapidly improved in colonial America—a fact explained by their high economic value and by their relative scarcity. As cook, seamstress, nurse, laundress, baker, teacher, cloth maker, and supervisor of household production the colonial woman was indispensable in rural economy, her value being attested by the high price of women indentured servants. One writer estimated that a wife and child earned as much as a man. "A good husband," said a commentator on New Hampshire, "with his wife to attend the cattle and make butter and cheese will be profitable, for maids they are soon gone in this country." Throughout colonial times immigration brought to America more men than women; consequently wives were at a premium. So scarce were women in Virginia in 1619 that the Virginia company sent over a shipload of marriageable girls who were disposed of to the planters at the rate of 120 pounds of tobacco each. Oglethorpe wrote of a settlement in Georgia:

[5] A brilliant interpretation is Bernard Faÿ, *Franklin, the Apostle of Modern Times* (Boston, 1929), the best biography for the general reader.

"there is now in this place . . . above 700 men more than there are women. Most of these would marry if they could get wives." In view of the prevailing scarcity, every woman was supposed to marry: an act of Maryland provided a woman must forfeit land inherited if she did not marry within seven years. And a woman who could not "get a husband" was deemed deficient indeed; hence the odium and even disgrace attached to spinsterhood. Similarly, widows and widowers re-married quickly; one man in Pennsylvania proposed to a young lady the day his wife died and remarried within a week. Third and even fourth marriages of bereaved husbands and wives were common in all the colonies.[6]

> Luke, on his dying bed, embraced his wife
> And begged one favor: swear my dearest life,
> Swear if you love me, never more to wed. . . .
> Anne dropped a tear. You know my dear, says she,
> Your least desires have still been laws to me;
> But from this oath, I beg you'd me excuse
> For I'm already promised to J[ohn] H[ughes].

Although colonial women did not attain equality with men, it is certain that they gained a better status than they had enjoyed in Eu-rope. Employments out of doors conferred personal freedom upon girls of the farm; the ideal of maidenly seclusion could not be ad-hered to. A. W. Calhoun, social historian of the American family, states: "If a young man took it into his head that his betrothed should not be free and gay in her social intercourse, he would run the risk of being discarded, incur the reputation of jealousy, and find it very difficult to get married." In the southern and middle colonies the scarcity of women enabled "maid servants of good honest stock" to "choose their husbands out of the better sort of people." A jealous servant in Maryland disparaged a successful rival:

> What if as planter's wife you go
> Nature designed you for the hoe.

Wertenbaker believes that the handicap of poor, degraded men in finding wives acted as a selective factor to improve the race. Mittel-berger, observing eighteenth-century Pennsylvania, was struck by the fact that a wife could not be compelled to do anything against her will, that her husband could not box her ears, and that he might be punished at law for maltreating her. The New England colonies also provided penalties for the ill usage of wives: Plymouth enacted "that

[6] Alice M. Earle, *Colonial Dames and Goodwives* (Boston, 1895), is an entertaining account.

every married woman shall be free from bodily correction or stripes by her husband." [7]

The economic status of women is evident in laws governing property. Widows received either a third or a half of the estate of husbands who died without making wills—a rule which acknowledged the claim of the wife to property produced by joint effort. Connecticut, a colony conservative in family matters, reversed in 1723 its rule which gave husbands complete control over real estate inherited by their wives: a new law prescribed that such property was not to be alienated without the wife's consent. As early as 1675 a marriage contract in Virginia gave the wife full power over the property bestowed upon her by her father. In the middle and southern colonies widows whose husbands had died intestate became administrators of the family estate. The experience of women with the practical affairs of shop or household and their training in industry, economy, and thrift qualified them to serve as managers of the family business or estate: many widows carried on as shopkeepers, merchants, shipowners, innkeepers, farm and plantation operators, printers, editors, and workers in the household crafts. Such careers employed women in all the colonies. Widows without independent estates commonly remarried or lived with relatives; there were few opportunities available to women as wage-earners.[8]

Despite the improved status of women in the colonies, their station in life was determined primarily by the position of their husbands or fathers. Thus women of the poorest families, compelled to work in the fields, stood at the bottom of the social scale. Such was the lot of the many women pioneers, and, according to William Byrd, of the wives of the small farmers in North Carolina. Crèvecoeur states that German farm women "often share . . . the most severe toils of the field." An observer of early Virginia said of women servants: "Yet some wenches that are nasty, beastly, and not fit to be so employed [in household work] are put into the ground." The words "dirty" and "soiled" indicate the opprobrium associated with work in the fields. One of the surest signs of the social advancement of a family was the exemption of its womenfolk from such toil. In middle-class circles the wife, as mistress of the other dependents of the family (the children and servants), confined her activities to work within the household. Such being women's approved function, there was in all the

[7] Carl Holliday, *Woman's Life in Colonial Days* (Boston, 1922), a sentimental eulogy, contains many good quotations.
[8] Elisabeth A. Dexter's *Colonial Women of Affairs* (Boston, 1924) is a "study of women in business and the professions in America before 1776."

colonies before 1740 a strong opposition to literary education for girls; they should rather be trained in the household crafts and the practical arts of family management. An ideal housewife was described by John Dunton, a visitor to New England in 1686: "Her pride was to be neat and cleanly, and her thrift not to be prodigal, which made her seldom a non-resident of her household."

The women of the upper class occupied themselves chiefly with planning the work of the home and with supervising the domestic servants, although they also performed lighter duties such as baking, nursing, and sewing. Upper-class girls, exempt from common toil and not yet prepared for the responsibilities of management, were disciplined by training in fancy needlework, drawing, music, refined manners, and care of the person. All such attainments, being decorative rather than utilitarian, indicated that the aristocratic lady, exempt from menial work, belonged to a family of superior status.[9] The intellectual training given to upper-class girls was superficial; at the end of the colonial period James Franklin said that southern ladies "seldom read or endeavor to improve their minds"—a remark that bears out the earlier comments of William Byrd: "We supped at nine and then prattled with the ladies." "Our conversation with the ladies was like whip-syllabub, very pretty but nothing in it." Dr. Shippen's ideal for his daughter was to make her "one of the finest women in Philadelphia."

Occupying a dependent position in society, the colonial women were particularly prone to improve their status by emulating the upper class. Of a visit to his overseer a planter wrote in 1772: "I was sorry to see his wife act the part of a fine lady in all her wearing apparel, with at least two maids besides her own girl to get dinner and wait upon her; but this I do suppose she did to show respect. . . ." An English traveler in the Revolutionary period noted a zest for fashion among American women, both rural and urban, and was impressed by the fact that an innkeeper's daughter "went regularly three times a week seven miles to attend the lessons of one de Grace, a French dancing master, who was making a fortune in the country."

The place of children in colonial society was determined largely by the value of their labor on the farm and in the shop.[10] Boys sowed seed, weeded fields, combed wool, shelled corn, sawed and chopped wood, fed the pigs, watered horses, picked berries, gathered vegetables, made brooms, and ran errands; the girls helped in all the tasks

[9] Mary S. Benson, *Women in Eighteenth-Century America* (New York, 1935) is an interesting, informative, scholarly study.
[10] See again Alice M. Earle, *Child Life in Colonial Days.*

about the house. The Reverend Francis Higginson wrote of New England in 1629, "Little children here by setting of corn may earn much more than their own maintenance"—a condition that continued throughout colonial times, as indicated by the traffic in child indentured servants and by the custom of binding poor children to enterprisers who employed them at a profit in workshops. Describing the German settlers in 1789 an observer said: "Upon the birth of a son, they exult in the gift of a plowman or waggoner; and upon the birth of a daughter they rejoice in the addition of another spinster or milkmaid to the family." The high death rate among colonial children meant that the weak and sickly perished; those who survived were generally able to perform the required labor. In 1737 a Dr. Brickell noted that the children of North Carolina were "seldom or never troubled with rickets, and many other distempers that the Europeans are afflicted with, and you seldom see any of them deformed in body."

The customs governing the inheritance of property reflected the diversity of colonial society.[11] The small farmers and artisans believed that each child should receive an equal share of the family estate—a principle which recognized that the labor of the child conferred a claim to the accumulated property. Moreover, equal inheritance was an incentive to labor during childhood. The merchant families also divided estates among the children: dowries, settlements, and inheritances induced intermarriage within this class, thereby multiplying business contacts, reducing competition, and bringing to one family the assistance, in time of need, of other mercantile houses. On the other hand, the wealthy landed families, whose eminence rested upon a large ancestral estate, favored both the principle of primogeniture, which preserved the estate intact in the possession of the eldest son, and the law of entail, which vested the title to a property in a future heir, thus preventing its sale or alienation by the family. Primogeniture and entail did not become prominent in America until large estates developed which were cultivated by tenants, servants, or slaves; on such estates the children of the owner did not work; consequently they had no claim to the family property, nor was an assured inheritance needed as a spur to child labor within the family. Primogeniture, however, was unpopular in the colonies because social development had not gone far enough to provide the younger sons with honorable, well-paid positions in an army, navy, church, or civil service, in business, or in the legal and learned professions. Hence

[11] Richard B. Morris, *Studies in the History of American Law* (New York, 1930), is a significant though technical treatment. See chapters 1-3.

among the colonial aristocracy it was customary to provide subsidiary plantations for the younger sons—a practice which gave the landed interest a strong bent toward expansion.[12]

The law of inheritance governing the estates of landowners who died without making wills illustrates the foregoing observations. Massachusetts in 1641 provided for equal inheritance, except that the eldest son was granted a double portion; Connecticut in 1699 enacted that all children should share equally in the family estate. The Georgia trustees were forced to abandon primogeniture and to allow all sons and daughters to share alike. The Dutch brought from Holland to New Netherland the custom of equal inheritance. In the eighteenth century several colonies (Virginia, Maryland, Pennsylvania, the Carolinas, New York, and Massachusetts) permitted landowners to will estates by the rule of primogeniture; similarly, lands could be entailed by will in all the southern colonies and in Pennsylvania and New York.[13]

## THE OUTLOOK ON LIFE

Of the influences that shaped the colonial way of life none had greater force than the determination of the people not to relapse into savagery but to maintain a European standard of living. That ideal necessitated unremitting labor which contact with a primitive environment rendered doubly onerous. Moreover, social betterment depended upon thrift and saving, since the standard of living could be raised only by means of the accumulation of capital so necessary to improved efficiency of production. To the mass of farmers and workers life meant incessant toil; similarly, members of the upper class, possessed of relatively small fortunes, could achieve superiority in society only by that vigilant attention to the details of business through which the accumulation of capital was effected. The hard conditions of life fostered a stern moral code, the essence of which was the condemnation of everything deemed to have a weakening, injurious effect upon oneself and one's neighbors. Health, strength, stamina, endurance, and vitality: such were the desiderata of colonial morality. "If thou would'st live long," said Poor Richard, "live well; for folly and wickedness shorten life." [14]

High among the approved virtues ranked the habit of industry.

[12] R. B. Morris, "Primogeniture and Entailed Estates in America," *Columbia Law Review*, XXVII.

[13] C. M. Andrews, *The Connecticut Intestacy Law* (New Haven, 1933—Connecticut Tercentenary Commission, no. 2).

[14] See again E. Eggleston, *The Transit of Civilization*, chapter 4.

Crèvecoeur noted with approval "that restless industry which is the principal characteristic of these colonies"; an act of Massachusetts condemned "divers loose, vain and corrupt persons . . . [who] insinuate into the fellowship of the young people . . . , drawing them both by night and day from their callings, studies and honest occupations." Of sleep Poor Richard said:

> Nature needs but five,
> Custom gives us seven,
> Laziness takes nine,
> And wickedness eleven.

Since waste destroyed the fruits of industry, thrift and saving were properly in order. Among Poor Richard's maxims the exhortations to economy are numerous: "All things are cheap to the saving, dear to the wasteful"; "Silks and satins put out the kitchen fire"; "Too much plenty makes mouth dainty"; "Spare and have is better than spend and crave"; "A fat kitchen makes a lean will"; "Many dishes, many diseases." So also Franklin commended the utility of honesty, observing that "there being in the world a number of rich merchants, nobility, states and princes who have need of honest instruments for the management of their affairs . . . no qualities . . ." are "so likely to make a poor man's fortune as those of probity and integrity." [15]

The code of sexual morality also condemned all practices considered injurious to the individual and the race. A. W. Calhoun states that the "Puritan emphasis on sexual restraint was of a piece with the general gospel of frugality so appropriate among a class of people trying to accumulate capital in an age of deficit." The New England colonies imposed various restrictions on unmarried men with the object of protecting community morality by keeping bachelors under surveillance or by forcing them to marry or to depart. Womanly modesty everywhere held a high place among the virtues: Dr. Brickell observed of North Carolina: "the women are very shy in their discourses, till they become acquainted": a traveler wrote in 1745 of American girls: "their dress is neat and clean, and not much bordering on the ridiculous humor of the mother country, where the daughters seemed dressed up for a market." In rural communities, where women were somewhat unprotected in their associations, the canon of modesty was particularly imperative. Southern society fostered among men of the upper and middle classes an attitude akin to chivalry, in

[15] The most important literary work of the colonial period is *The Life of Benjamin Franklin Written by Himself* (ed. John Bigelow, 3 vols., Philadelphia, 1905).

From Abbott's "The Expansion of Europe." © F. S. Crofts & Co.

THE INDUSTRIOUS AND THE LAZY APPRENTICE

One of the series of drawings entitled *Industry and Idleness*, executed by William Hogarth in 1747.

view of the necessity of protecting the ladies of the plantation in the presence of servants and slaves.[16]

The training of youth reveals the prevailing moral tone. John Adams wrote to his wife in 1774: ". . . make your children *hardy*, *active*, and *industrious;* for strength, activity and industry will be their only resource and dependence." Little children were not sheltered from the rigors of nature: "Josiah Quincy at three years was taken from his warm bed, winter and summer, carried to the cellar kitchen, and dipped three times in water just from the pump." Winter life in icy rooms had a toughening effect. Numerous children in crowded quarters, busy parents, and the natural distaste of youth for steady work made obedience a cardinal virtue. Teach your child to obey, said Poor Richard, and you may teach him anything. Cotton Mather made his children sensible that " 'tis a folly for them to pretend unto any wit or will of their own . . . my word must be their law." Slaveowners demanded filial obedience on the assumption that "he that cannot obey cannot command." A colonial book of etiquette instructed children thus: "Never sit down at the table till asked. . . . Ask for nothing; tarry till it be offered thee. . . . Sing not, hum not, wriggle not. Spit nowhere in the room but in the corner. When any speak to thee, stand up." [17]

Religious teaching enforced the parental discipline—particularly through the fear of damnation: violators of the fifth commandment would certainly go to the wrong place. Children were told what to do, not coaxed or argued with, and the rod reinforced religious instruction. "Love well, whip well." A whip used in rural Pennsylvania consisted of a piece of leather about six inches in diameter, fastened to a pliable handle. Among educated people in New England, stern parental discipline induced intellectual precocity; some children were taught reading at three and Latin at six! In accordance with Calvin's teachings the Puritan colonies provided severe punishments for children who should curse or smite their parents or be guilty of "stubborn or rebellious carriage."

Two conceptions of life contended for mastery in colonial times. One, a materialistic outlook, assumed that life evolved in response to external forces of environment and social organization; man's struggle with nature and his material necessities shaped his ideas and habits; so also man, through the conquest of nature, might lighten

---

[16] See again T. J. Wertenbaker, *The First Americans*, chapter 8.

[17] T. H. Johnson, "Jonathan Edwards and the 'Young Folks' Bible" (*New England Quarterly*, V, Jan. 1932), discusses attitudes toward sex education of youth.

his burdens on earth. The second—a religious or spiritual conception —affirmed that life moved in response to a divine will; God, an ideal being governing an ideal universe, had foreordained man's destiny; hardship and misfortune chastened man and attuned him to the divine purpose; morality was not a reflection of man's experience but an unchanging decree of God: "the moral law is written on the tablets of eternity." Divine revelation and inspiration were the light of the world. Man could not change his fate through the conquest of nature or the reorganization of society; he must conform to the divine will as recorded in the Scriptures. Nor was man a mere physical mechanism, a product of material forces, but a creature made in the image of God, possessing an immortal soul and destined for eternal life.

In a society as diverse as that of the colonies religion was compounded of numerous ideas.[18] Many forces of nature, not understood by the unlearned, were attributed to a supernatural power. A hard life, in which pain, sickness, hardship, accidents, loss, and death were frequent and beyond control, was more easily borne when such afflictions were regarded as the will of God, who would one day reward the sufferer. A New Englander wrote of his wife: "She would sometimes say to me that bearing, tending and burying children was hard work, and that she had done a great deal of it for one of her age . . . yet would say it was the work she was made for and what God in his providence had called her to, and she could freely do it all for Him." The belief in heaven and hell gave an intensely personal quality to religion; so also attitudes of fear and reverence instilled in youth persisted, often in the recesses of the mind, throughout life. Moreover, some religious sects taught the submission of dependents to their superiors, who were invariably identified with an important church. On the other hand, the New Testament, condemning as it did the rich and exalting the poor and downtrodden, contained the seeds of social revolution; equality before God might also mean equality on earth.[19] To the sensitive, the beauty and order of nature and the feeling that life was essentially good were proof of the existence of a benevolent God. Some embraced mysticism, seeking by prayer and meditation to become suffused with a sense of peace and oneness with God; others inclined toward deism, a creed which denied revelation and the divine

[18] For a view of the influence of American environment see Peter G. Mode, *The Frontier Spirit in Christianity* (New York, 1923).

[19] Thomas C. Hall, *The Religious Background of American Culture* (Boston, 1930), finds the clue to colonial religion in the dissenting tradition of pre-Reformation times.

inspiration of the Scriptures, but accepted the view of a benevolent God, whom man should worship by doing good to one's fellow men.[20]

Despite the religious inheritance of the colonists, their preoccupation with practical concerns, their day-long labor in field and shop, and the necessity of subduing nature in order to mitigate the rigors of life: all these influences strengthened the materialistic conception of life.[21] New Englanders gained a reputation as shrewd traders and investors; travelers in the middle colonies noted that the religious impulse there was at a low ebb (Christian sects tended "to wear themselves out"; "religious indifference becomes prevalent"). Jernegan says that the "main energies and thoughts" of most of the southern planters "were centered on material gains." Of the American farmer Crèvecoeur wrote: "He conceives no other idea of a clergyman than that of a hired man; if he does his work well, he will pay him the stipulated sum; if not he will dismiss him and do without his sermons, and let his church be shut up for years. But notwithstanding this coarse idea, you will find his house and farm to be the neatest in all the country; and you will judge by his wagon and fat horses, that he thinks more of the affairs of this world than of those of the next." In keeping with this materialistic outlook was an engrossing interest in all things useful. Even Cotton Mather aspired to "enkindle" in his children "a mighty desire of being useful in the world." "Sometimes," wrote Crèvecoeur, "I delight in inventing and executing machines, which simplify my wife's labor. I have been tolerably successful that way." Franklin, the most significant American of the eighteenth century and a utilitarian *par excellence,* directed his scientific thought to the improvement of material conditions; he once apologized for making a mathematical study which had no utility.[22]

As in other societies, the colonists faced the problem of harmonizing the need of individual achievement and self-expression with the necessity of coöperation, association, and the social control of property. Individualism, a vital force generated by private ownership of the means of production and by the resulting scheme of individual enterprise in farming, trade, and industry, was intensified by the desire to acquire more capital, and diffused throughout the population by reason of the widespread ownership of land, which conferred upon a

[20] Herbert M. Morais, *Deism in Eighteenth Century America* (New York, 1934), is the best study of this aspect of religious thought.

[21] I. Woodbridge Riley, *American Philosophy: The Early Schools* (New York, 1907), an important pioneer work, discusses idealism, materialism, Puritanism, realism, and deism.

[22] Paul L. Ford, *The Many-Sided Franklin* (New York, 1899), is an analysis of Franklin's thought and personality rather than a narrative of his career.

multitude of small producers the boon of independence and self-directed activity. Crèvecoeur put it thus: "Here the rewards of his [the farmer's] industry follow with equal steps the progress of his labor; his labor is founded on the basis of nature, self-interest, can it want a stronger allurement. . . . As farmers they will be careful and anxious to get as much as they can, because what they get is their own." Some manifestations of the prevailing individualism were the authority of parents and masters over children, servants and slaves; the ideal of individual improvement, morally and intellectually (note Franklin's efforts toward self-education and moral perfection); and the emphasis placed by religion on the salvation of individual souls. Individualism was naturally strongest among big property owners who had the greatest opportunity to exercise their managing talents and to direct the labor of others; on the other hand, there was no scope for initiative among slaves and but little among servants and wage-earners, since such workers carried out the commands of their masters.[23]

Necessity forced the small farmers to coöperate with one another; unable to command dependents, they were obliged to exchange services among themselves. Pioneers occasionally migrated in companies for the sake of protection, association, and mutual assistance in opening roads and fording streams. House-raisings, huskings, quilting parties, road and bridge building, funerals, the erection of schools and churches—all called forth the coöperative labor of the settlers. In early New England the ideal of community life was particularly strong. On the voyage of 1630 John Winthrop told his fellow emigrants that "they must be knit together in this enterprise as one man, they must rejoice and mourn together, labor and suffer together, 'always having before our eyes our commission and community in the work'" (P. G. Miller). In another vein Poor Richard said: "He that drinks his cider alone, let him catch his horse alone."

The amusements of the common folk reflect the coöperative spirit. Boys indulged in various sports: racing, coasting on sleds, street games, hunting, fishing, trapping. Samuel Sewall condemned April Fools' Day jokes, first practiced in Boston in 1708: "What an abuse of precious time; what a profanation!" Many rural pastimes combined pleasure and utility: such were the "drive" (to clear the neighboring woods of wolves and bears), the house raising, the log rolling, and the deer hunt. At the country fairs, held in Pennsylvania twice a year,

[23] One of the most influential interpretations of American society is F. J. Turner's "The Significance of the Frontier in American History," reprinted in *The Frontier in American History*, chapter 1.

spring and autumn, the rural folk transacted business, consorted with friends and relatives and enjoyed many a rustic diversion. At the side show one saw the polar bear, the camel, the tightrope walker, the juggler, the puppet show, and the musical clock. Foot races, wrestling matches and target shooting contests engaged the young men of prowess; the chief attractions for all were quarter-mile horse races.[24] Apart from the Sabbath, holy days were not observed; the economic creed of Protestantism condemned such "waste" of time in an age of scarcity. Except among the Germans even Christmas was just another day. Thanksgiving in New England, not only a religious observance but also a week-long harvest festival celebrated by feasting, afforded relaxation after the toil of summer. Church services, Thursday lectures, town meetings, and training days also brought the New Englanders together; in the South the ever-popular folk dances (jigs, square dances, the Virginia reel) bore witness to a vigorous community spirit.

The regulation of private property by law imposed another restraint upon individualism.[25] "Particular estates," wrote John Winthrop, "cannot subsist in the ruin of the public." All the colonies resorted to social control, particularly in time of calamity or depression. Laws governing interest rates, forbidding the exportation of needed products, regulating coinage, weights, and measures, offering bounties and other public aid to encourage new industries (mining, cloth making, iron manufacturing), prohibiting monopolies (except of limited duration, for the introduction of new enterprises), providing for the inspection of commodities, and authorizing deferred payment of debts due—all such acts swell the bulk of colonial statute books. In early Massachusetts, efforts to regulate wages failed because workmen "would either remove to other places where they might have more, or else being able to live by planting and other employments of their own, they would not be hired at all." Although many regulatory acts served the interests of particular groups, even so they asserted in theory the right of public control of property.

Nor was the head of the family a law unto his individualistic self. Pennsylvania in 1683 decreed that persons in charge of young children who failed to instruct them in reading and writing should pay a fine of £5 for each child. The New England colonies adopted similar

[24] John A. Krout, *Annals of American Sport* (*Pageant of America*, XV, New Haven, 1929), chapter 1.
[25] Lewis J. Carey, *Franklin's Economic Views* (Garden City, N. Y., 1928), is a satisfactory recent discussion. See also W. A. Wetzel, *Benjamin Franklin as an Economist* (Baltimore, 1895).

acts, enforced by county courts, sheriffs, and grand juries; parents who defied the law were fined or otherwise punished. Massachusetts in 1668 provided that men delinquent in the care of their families should be classed as idle persons and "subject to the house of correction." Due to the prevailing sense of social responsibility and of human solidarity, such acts were necessary because a family head who ignored his duties thereby imposed a burden upon the community.[26]

Life in the colonial towns also exhibited a lively spirit of coöperation. Five urban centers may be classed as major commercial towns: Boston, Philadelphia, Newport, New York, and Charleston. In 1774 Charleston was the only "city" in the South; Philadelphia, with a population of nearly 40,000, had gained first rank in the colonies; New York (25,000 to 30,000) was on the upgrade; Boston, with 20,000, was stationary or declining; Newport, with 12,000, was feeling the competition of Providence. Other port towns of local commercial importance, with populations of less than 12,000, were Salem, New Haven, Providence, Perth Amboy, Newcastle, Baltimore, Richmond, Wilmington (North Carolina), and Savannah. There were also small country towns tributary to the commercial centers—the many villages of New England, Albany, Burlington, Princeton, Trenton, Germantown, Chester, Lancaster, Norfolk, etc. Annapolis, Maryland, and Williamsburg, Virginia, deserve notice as political and social capitals rather than as commercial centers.

The major commercial cities and many of the minor towns operated markets, daily, weekly, or semi-weekly, to which the farmers of the vicinity brought produce for sale to traders and to the townspeople. The rules for the Boston market provided in 1696 that produce must be offered to the householders before traders could buy. New York had six markets in 1774; that of Philadelphia, then described as the best regulated in North America, was "raised upon pillars and covered over for a quarter of a mile in length." Market days broke the monotony of the farmer's life with a taste of town associations and a sojourn at the tavern at the end of the day's bargaining.

The common problems of the towns called forth common efforts. In early times police protection was a community responsibility shared by all able-bodied men. The smaller New England towns utilized trainbands in which all males over sixteen were liable for guard duty at night. In Philadelphia, prior to 1751, all householders were required to serve in the night watch. It became the practice for wealthy men to pay the

[26] Henry B. Parkes, "New England in the Seventeen-Thirties," *New England Quarterly*, III (July 1930).

constable 6s. a year for exemption from duty. Two defects in this custom, pointed out by Franklin,[27] had appeared by the 1740's: the wealthier inhabitants paid no more for protection of their property than the less wealthy, and the constables often employed shiftless, incompetent substitutes. In 1751 a regular, paid watch was established, the cost being assessed against the inhabitants according to property holdings. "In 1772 the watch was instructed to patrol the streets from 10 P. M. to 4 A. M. and call out the time of night and the state of the weather."

By 1775 the leading towns had made some progress toward the paving of streets. An observer said of Philadelphia in 1774: "The streets are all straight, and well paved, about thirty-six . . . feet wide, with foot paths on every side, raised a little above the carriage way, and laid with bricks for the conveniency of the foot passengers." New York's streets (built of "large pebble stones" and made to slope toward a gutter in the middle of the street) were described in 1774 as "ill paved, irregular and too narrow," although they impressed John Adams as "vastly more regular and elegant than those of Boston."

Franklin was an American pioneer in devising city fire protection. At Philadelphia he organized a company of thirty volunteers who equipped themselves with leather buckets and bags and baskets (for removing articles from burning houses), whereupon other companies were soon formed "till they became so numerous as to include most of the inhabitants who were men of property." Later, the companies raised money for the purchase of engines, hooks, and ladders. New York in 1772 had eleven fire companies and engines, with a force of 163 men organized under a fire chief. Every householder had to pay a shilling a year for each chimney of his dwelling, the money being used to have the chimneys swept once a week. "And when a fire happens, a premium is always allowed to the captain and his men who can first make their engines play upon the fire." By 1775 the fire menace in New York and Philadelphia was well under control.[28]

Little progress was registered in other municipal activities. Philadelphia installed street lamps in 1751; New York in 1775 was the only town which regularly cleaned its streets. Elsewhere, trash and ashes were dumped in vacant lots; hogs roamed about in search of garbage; at Charleston, buzzards were welcomed and protected as

[27] A familiar, journalistic, readable biography is Phillips Russell, *Benjamin Franklin, the First Civilized American* (New York, 1926). S. G. Fisher, *The True Benjamin Franklin* (Philadelphia, 1899), is solid, well-rounded, and compact.

[28] Carl Bridenbaugh, *Cities in the Wilderness*, the best study of colonial towns, will be published in 1938.

scavengers. For water supply, reliance was placed upon "pumps sunk at convenient distances in the streets." No house had a bathroom or running water. The impurities of water from wells or streams help explain the vogue of taverns and homemade drinks. New York was erecting a central pumping system, with a reservoir and conduits, when the Revolution cut short the work.

The American town-dweller's relish for clubs, fraternal orders, and other societies appeared in colonial times, a strong urge of that sort manifesting itself after 1710. A Masonic lodge existed in Philadelphia in 1715; by 1770 the order—which included Franklin and Washington among its members—was well represented in the principal seacoast towns. Other clubs, formed along national, professional, or craft lines and avowing the pursuit of knowledge as their aim, brought gregarious spirits together once a week for an evening's comradeship in taverns or private homes. Most of such clubs seem to have forsaken their high aims and to have yielded to the delights of conviviality and good fellowship.

> Boy, bring a bowl of china here,
> Fill it with water cool and clear:
> Decanter and Jamaica right,
> And spoon of silver, clear and bright
> Sugar twice fin'd, in pieces cut,
> Knife, sieve and glass, in order put,
> Bring forth the fragrant fruit and then
> We're happy till the clock strikes ten.

Despite numerous economic or class conflicts, colonial society was held together by strong integrating forces.[29] Religious toleration, made possible largely by the scarcity of labor and vast open lands, diminished Old World tensions among Christian sects. Wealthy groups practiced in business the virtues of industry and thrift which were taught to the lower orders; there were no idle rich, and no gulf between upper-class social theory and practice. Widespread ownership of land—the squatter ideal—diffused the spirit of acquisitive individualism throughout the population. It was easy to convince oneself that personal success and the pursuit of self-interest best served society as a whole: did not the frontier welcome the dispossessed; was not the lot of the common man better in America than in Europe: was not failure due to the defects of the man who fell by the wayside? The standards of the upper class penetrated to the lower classes,

---

[29] A. M. Schlesinger's *New Viewpoints in American History* (New York, 1922) discusses some of the major problems of American society. See chapters 1–7.

binding all with the cement of emulation. "How many poor men, common men, and mechanics," queried a Philadelphia "democrat" at election time in 1776, "have been made happy within this fortnight by a shake of the hand, a pleasing smile, and a little familiar chat with gentlemen who have not for these seven years past condescended to look at them."

The colonial outlook may be described as an expression of a middle-class psychology which exalted industry and thrift and which exposed both a core of utilitarianism overlaid with religious tradition and a spirit of individualism, tempered by coöperation and association. It was an outlook which took economic inequality for granted: how, indeed, might the small property owner become a large owner if the latter were legislated out of existence? [30]

The literature of the eighteenth century, largely a product of the upper middle class, expressed the prevailing sense of social integration. Serenity, zest for life and faith in progress were its distinguishing traits. John Adams wrote in 1765: "I always consider the settlement of America with reverence and wonder, as the opening of a grand scheme and design in Providence for the illumination and the emancipation of the slavish part of mankind all over the earth." Confidence, optimism and a sense of an historic mission were the fruits of such an attitude. "Americans," wrote Crèvecoeur, "are the western pilgrims, who are carrying along with them the great mass of arts, sciences, vigor and industry which began long since in the east; they will finish the great circle." The processes of social growth and construction turned men's thoughts from the past to the future; said a traveler in 1794: "Every first settler in a new country labors less for the present than for the future; less for himself than for posterity; and it is this honorable consciousness that invigorates his toil, cheers his solitude, and alleviates his privations." Colonial society, moreover, called into play the energies of youth: ability, prowess and initiative were not sacrificed to mediocrity and inertia entrenched in aged authority. Washington at twenty-two and George Rogers Clark at twenty-five commanded in the West; Patrick Henry argued the "parson's cause" at twenty-seven; Franklin composed a philosophical work at eighteen; Jefferson wrote the Declaration of Independence at thirty-three; Hamilton became Secretary of the Treasury at thirty-two.[31]

[30] See again V. L. Parrington, *The Colonial Mind*, Book II, chapter 1.
[31] For suggestive essays on American society see Albert F. Pollard's *Factors in American History* (New York, 1925).

## Social Problems

The felicity portrayed by promoters of settlement and by writers of the upper middle class is only a part of the picture of colonial life. Many families lived so close to poverty that misfortune reduced them to destitution. Hence arose the problem of caring for the impotent poor—the aged, the blind, the sick, the lame, and the insane. Moreover, there was a class of able-bodied poor: idlers, misfits, tramps, troublemakers, and criminals. The presence of such undesirables is accounted for in part by the English practice, authorized by Parliament in 1662 and 1717, of shipping rogues, vagabonds, and beggars to the colonies. Many of these immigrants had acquired a distaste for work which did not forsake them in the New World.

The principles of poor relief introduced into America were those with which the colonists had been familiar in England. After the dissolution of the English monasteries the burden of caring for the poor was assumed by the state, the work being assigned to the localities and the funds obtained through taxes levied on the property owners. All these features characterized the poor relief systems devised in the colonies. The assemblies acknowledged the public duty of caring for the poor and made the taxpayers of each locality responsible. Plymouth adopted such an act in 1642, Virginia in 1646, Connecticut in 1673, Massachusetts in 1692. In New England, where the town was the unit of administration, the town meeting provided specific regulations which were executed by the selectmen, tithingmen, or overseers of the poor; in the southern colonies the parish was the administrative unit, governed by the vestry—a group of twelve men, chosen after 1676 by the freeholders, and empowered to assess and collect parish taxes, to care for the poor, and to preserve religion and morality. Two of the vestrymen served as church wardens—the "executive arm" of the vestry in discharging its duties.

In New England the simplest mode of poor relief was for each family to care for a destitute person during part of the year. Thus Hadley, Massachusetts, voted in 1687 that a widow should be sent "round the town" to live two weeks with each family "able to receive her." Some of the poor, not wholly incapacitated, were given money from the town treasury and allowed to live alone. The most common practice followed by the smaller towns before the Revolution was the "putting out" system. The selectmen paid a householder who agreed to provide food and shelter for a destitute person; the town generally supplied clothing and medical care. Doctors who served the poor received payment from the town. In the larger settlements almshouses soon appeared; Boston had one in 1660. Prior to 1712 it housed criminals as well as the "honest poor," so great was the stigma attached to poverty. After 1712 efforts were made to realize the "primitive and pious design" of the almshouse, i. e., "the relief of the necessitous, that they might lead a quiet, peaceable and godly life there." [32]

Convinced that all able-bodied poor could find work, the New Englanders wasted little sympathy upon vagabonds and sturdy beggars. Such idlers were either bound out as indentured servants, whipped out of town, or clapped into jail. As the number of the able-bodied poor increased, the costs of confining them in prison (or the house of correction) led to the construction of workhouses. Massachusetts in 1699 provided for the erection of such institutions and authorized the confinement of idlers, tramps, "common pipers, fiddlers, runaways, stubborn servants or children, common drunkards, common night-walkers, pilferers, wanton and lascivious persons, . . . common railers or brawlers such as neglect their callings. . . ." The town provided materials and tools with which the inmates were required to earn their living. Connecticut erected a colony workhouse in 1727; the Boston workhouse began to function in 1729. Whipping supplied discipline and the incentive to work.

A specialization of function was evident in the system of poor relief at the end of the colonial period.[33] The almshouse cared for the "honest poor," the workhouse employed idlers and minor offenders, the prison housed criminals, and the hospital domiciled the sick. Insane asylums had not yet appeared. The care given to the insane poor is suggested in a vote of Braintree in 1689: the town agreed to pay for the erection of a house seven feet long and five feet wide where a man might "secure his sister and good wife Witty, being distracted. . . ."

The prudential New Englanders used prevention as well as relief in dealing with the poor. A master of a vessel who imported immigrants into Massachusetts had to give bond that they would not become a public charge; thus it was hoped "to prevent the importation of poor, vicious and infirm persons." Should an inhabitant bring servants into a town, he must agree to maintain them if they became "diseased, lame or impotent." Again: a householder who received

---

[32] See again M. W. Jernegan, *Laboring and Dependent Classes in Colonial America*, pp. 175–209.

[33] This illustrates one principle of American social development presented in D. R. Fox's charming essays, *Ideas in Motion* (New York, 1935).

outsiders must give notice of their presence; if they seemed likely to become a public burden, they were "warned out" of the town and deported if they would not go willingly. Since each town had to care for its own poor, destitute strangers were speedily returned to their home localities.

Poor relief in the southern colonies may be illustrated by the practices of Virginia, where drifters, runaway servants, and delinquent family heads raised problems akin to those of the northern colonies. The vestries in Virginia disposed of the able-bodied poor, destitute orphans, and the illegitimate children of indentured servants by binding them to masters as apprentices or servants. Almhouses, hospitals, and workhouses do not appear in the parish records; the impotent poor were placed in private homes, the parish supplying clothing and paying the householder the costs of maintenance. Outlays for poor relief, as in New England, varied from 9 per cent to 33 per cent of all expenditures for local purposes. These early forms of relief are the antecedents of modern orphan asylums, poorhouses, public hospitals, widows' pensions, free medical service, and insurance against accidents, unemployment, sickness, and old age.

Criminal tendencies in the colonial population also bear witness to social maladjustments. From England the early settlers brought those conceptions of wrongdoing and those forms of punishment which gave a rough uniformity to the legal practices of all the colonies. Certain crimes were commonly regarded as serious enough to incur the penalty of death. Such were murder, treason, piracy, and acts of sexual perversion. The codes of New England in 1664 also imposed the death penalty for denying the true God, for invading a town, for giving false evidence with the intent of taking a person's life, and—in the case of children over sixteen—for the unprovoked cursing or smiting of parents. Pennsylvania in 1718 prescribed the death penalty for arson, infanticide, burglary, murder, and the malicious mutilation of a person. After the colonies issued paper money they soon added counterfeiting to the list of capital crimes.

Other serious offenses were punished by imprisonment, branding, whipping, compulsory labor, or heavy fines.[34] In this category were theft, burglary, highway robbery, sexual immorality, forgery, serious profanity, and habitual drunkenness. In seventeenth-century New England, women guilty of repeated moral lapses were whipped or occasionally forced to wear the scarlet letter; after 1720, whipping was resorted to only for serious offenders. The law of Pennsylvania

[34] Alice M. Earle, *Curious Punishments of Bygone Days* (New York, 1907)—a readable sketch.

provided, after 1720, that a person thrice guilty of adultery should receive twenty-one lashes, serve seven years in prison, and be branded on the forehead with the letter A; thieves and housebreakers might be branded with the letter T; a fourth offense of serious profanity incurred a fine of £5 and two months of labor, while the culprit became liable to twenty-one stripes every three months for seven years. Five crimes were punishable by branding in Pennsylvania in 1767.

Minor offenses, such as occasional drunkenness and Sabbathbreaking (including unnecessary labor and travel) drew fines and short prison sentences. In colonies with established churches, attendance at divine service was required by law, but only persistent violators were fined; in most places the churches were not large enough to accommodate the whole community at one time.[35] The New England colonies fined persons guilty of owning or playing cards and of disporting themselves at such time-consuming games as shuffleboard, ninepins, and billiards. The Puritans also outlawed lotteries and games of chance. As late as 1717 two dancing masters were ordered not to practice their art in Boston; however, the ban did not extend to folk dances. Among the minor iniquities condemned by the Pennsylvania code of 1682 were stage plays, masques, bullbaiting, and cockfighting.

The New England Puritans, never idealistic regarding human nature, adopted at the start a strict legal code and proceeded to enforce it. The Massachusetts court of assistants considered 286 cases between 1636 and 1644. On the whole the criminal record of colonial New England makes a good showing. After 1692 the death penalty was inflicted for only two crimes—piracy and murder; the white inhabitants of Connecticut, between 1663 and 1775, were involved in but twelve murders, only five of which were premeditated. Sexual irregularities exceeded all other classes of offenses three to one; the number of illegitimate births doubled, trebled, and even quadrupled in the various towns between 1730 and 1770. Other frequently committed offenses included drunkenness, Sabbathbreaking, non-attendance at church, and breach of the peace. A marked increase of heavy drinking occurred in eastern Massachusetts after 1700 and extended to the western counties and to Connecticut after 1725. The number of tavern licenses in many New England towns doubled or trebled between 1700 and 1730 and increased sixfold or eightfold between 1700 and 1770.[36]

---

[35] Alice M. Earle, *The Sabbath in Puritan New England* (New York, 1902), is light reading.

[36] H. B. Parkes, "Morals and Law Enforcement in Colonial New England," *New England Quarterly*, V (July 1932).

In accordance with William Penn's humanitarianism, Pennsylvania in 1682 adopted an extremely mild criminal code which inflicted the death penalty for only one crime—murder. Such liberalism, together with lax enforcement of the law, did not suffice for the province: in 1697 Penn referred to scandalous things done in Philadelphia, "openly committed in defiance of law and virtue: facts so foul, I am forbid by common modesty to relate them." The attractions of Pennsylvania for runaway servants, convicts, and other outcasts account in part for the conditions described by Penn. Beginning in 1701 the criminal law was made progressively severe: branding, whipping, and mutilation were frequently resorted to against stubborn criminals and the number of crimes punishable by death was increased to sixteen by 1767. Between 1683 and 1715 only three serious criminal cases came before the Pennsylvania council; the court records of the years 1715–45 indicate that twenty-three persons were sentenced to death; in the period 1745–75 such sentences numbered at least 112. As a board of review and pardons the council often changed the penalty from death to banishment from the colony. Of the 112 offenders just mentioned only sixty-one were executed.[37]

In all the colonies indentured servants frequently ran afoul of the law. Since they received but a bare subsistence they were tempted to steal; ordinarily not permitted to marry, they were driven to sexual irregularities. The latter problem was particularly acute in the southern colonies, where a number of servants and slaves lived together in comparative isolation. If a servant woman became the mother of an illegitimate child, her efficiency as a worker was temporarily lessened; moreover, the master had to care for the child, and since such children were born free, the master could not command their future labor, as he could in the case of slaves. In grappling with this problem, the southern colonies first enacted that a servant mother should compensate her master with additional service. But this law did not check the evil: it "put a premium on immorality and there seem to have been masters base enough to profit by it." The servant codes respecting illegitimate children were modified after 1660 so as to incorporate the following principles. If the master were not responsible, he was entitled to additional service; if he were responsible, his servant was to be sold by the parish and the sale money used for the support of the child; if the father were known, he was held liable for such support. In any case the mother was fined or flogged.

The early court records suggest that crime and moral lapses were

[37] L. H. Gipson, *Crime and Its Punishment in Provincial Pennsylvania* (Lehigh University, Bethlehem, Pa., 1935).

most common among the lower classes. But such an inference should be guarded against because the upper classes were frequently able to keep their offenses out of the courts. Servants, tenants, and wage-earners had little recourse against their masters; the slaves had none. The offenses of dependents were punished severely; those of the masters often received no legal notice. Similarly, a person of means might make a financial settlement out of court, whereas the poor had to be punished through the legal agencies that authorized whipping, branding, and prison sentences.

Negro slavery constituted another exception to the happy conditions portrayed by writers of the middle class.[38] Estimates of the total slave population after 1700 are unreliable, due to inadequate statistics for the tobacco colonies. In South Carolina the number of slaves increased from 32,000 in 1724 to 90,000 in 1765—representing about 69 per cent of all inhabitants in each year. Connecticut had 6,500 slaves in 1775 as against thirty in 1720; Massachusetts had more than 5,000 in 1775 as against 550 in 1708; Rhode Island's total rose from 3,077 in 1749 to 3,668 in 1774. By 1750 the Negroes in Pennsylvania numbered about 11,000; in New York, after the mid-century, slaves accounted for a seventh of the population.

Slavery came into being in the colonies by virtue of force and custom, without the sanction of positive law; originally the line between slave and indentured servant was indistinct. Not until about 1660 did Virginia recognize slavery by law; after that year each colony enacted a slave code, patterned after the laws of the West Indies, where legal regulations were first adopted. Such codes presumed that every Negro was a slave; emancipation by individual masters was so rare that free Negroes formed an extremely small group. As misfits sharing the stigma attached to their race which exposed them to abuse and exploitation, they held an unprotected, degraded place in society.[39]

Four purposes may be discerned in the colonial slave codes. First, the law safeguarded the master's property right in the slave. Children of a slave woman became the property of her owner. If any freeman injured, stole, or killed a slave, the offender was required to satisfy the owner with double or treble damages. The slave could not leave his master's premises without a permit or unless accompanied by a white person. Fugitives could be arrested by anyone who

[38] Two surveys by a Negro historian are Benjamin Brawley, *A Social History of the American Negro* (New York, 1921), chapters 1-4; and *A Short History of the American Negro* (New York, 1919), chapters 1-4.

[39] John H. Russell, *The Free Negro in Virginia, 1619-1865* (Baltimore, 1913).

encountered them, whereupon they were to be advertised and returned to their owners. Both in Africa and on some plantations slaves were branded as a means of identification.

Secondly, the slave codes aimed to protect the personal property of the master. A slave guilty of theft might be punished by death or by severe whipping; similarly, trading with slaves was made unlawful on the assumption that a slave would sell only his master's property. Owners were commanded to search the slave quarters for stolen goods.

Thirdly, other acts placed the slave in utter subordination to the master as a means of enforcing work and discipline. The owner committed no offense if he killed or maimed a slave; he could punish at his discretion; he might work the slave fourteen or fifteen hours a day; if a slave struck a white person he might be imprisoned or severely whipped. The slave could not sue or testify in court or otherwise secure legal redress of grievances. The law also forbade the sale of liquor to slaves without the master's consent.

A fourth object of the slave codes was to prevent insurrections. Thus the laws decreed that three or more slaves were not to assemble unless with the owner's permission, ordered that slaves should not be kept on plantations unless white persons were in residence, required that slaves remain indoors at night after curfew, commanded owners to search the slave huts for weapons, and forbade the slaves to beat drums or blow horns.[40]

The punishments prescribed for the misdeeds of slaves resembled those for other crimes, with whipping the most common penalty. Court records do not disclose the extent of slave offenses, since masters ordinarily inflicted punishments without trial; the slave could not pay fines, and prison sentences were rare, due to the cost of maintenance and the loss of the slave's labor. The most dangerous, intractable slaves, guilty of arson, murder, or insurrection, were hanged, broken at the wheel, burned at the stake, or deported. Thus Massachusetts in 1681 ordered one slave burned and another hanged—both convicted of arson.

Although the treatment of slaves varied with the temperament of the master, it is certain that most of them endured a hard lot. They enjoyed no protection against a vicious owner; even the considerate master insisted upon full subservience. John Taylor of Caroline,

[40] J. C. Ballagh, *A History of Slavery in Virginia* (Baltimore, 1902), is an outstanding study of the legal aspects of slavery. See also the introductions to material on the various colonies in Helen T. Catterall (ed.), *Judicial Cases Concerning American Slavery and the Negro* (4 vols., Washington, 1926–36).

urging liberal treatment in 1809, said that "a stern authority, strict discipline and complete subordination must be combined . . . to gain any success at all."

Numerous insurrections bear witness to maladjustments among the slaves.[41] Revolts in Virginia occurred or were plotted in 1663, 1687, and 1709—none, however, of serious proportions. Despite the fact that conspirators in South Carolina in 1720 were punished by hanging, burning at the stake, or deportation, an important insurrection broke out there in 1739. A score of slaves armed themselves by robbing a store and set out for Florida, gathering recruits and murdering whites as they advanced. A white force, assembled when the alarm was sounded, finally attacked the fugitives and captured all but ten. This plot cost the lives of twenty-one whites and forty-four Negroes. In New Jersey a slave accused of plotting an insurrection in 1734 met death on the gallows. A band of slaves in New York (1712) set fire to a house at night and killed citizens as they rushed to the scene. After the revolt had been suppressed by soldiers, twenty-one participants were executed, one being sentenced "to be burned with a slow fire, that he may continue in torment for eight or ten hours." Again, at New York in 1741, charges that a gang of slaves had set fire to several houses and had perpetrated several robberies led the supreme court to ferret out the culprits, who were also suspected of plotting an insurrection. Four white persons implicated were hanged, twenty-nine Negroes were hanged or burned at the stake, and eighty Negroes were deported. Only when forced confessions implicated people of "known credit, fortune and reputation" did the hysteria subside.

In Pennsylvania—where slave insurrections did not threaten—were uttered the first emphatic protests against slavery. In 1688 four men in the Mennonite settlement at Germantown took a public stand against bringing "men hither to rob or sell them against their will." During the next seventy years opposition to slavery found expression among individual Quakers until in 1758 the yearly meeting registered a formal protest.[42] Foremost among the Quaker opponents was John Woolman (1720–72), originally a New Jersey tailor, whose religious mysticism and humane spirit moved him to devote his life to crusades in behalf of peace, the poor, the Indians, and the slaves. After a visit to Virginia in 1746 to observe slavery he wrote: "I saw in these southern provinces so many vices and corruptions increased by this trade and way of life, that it appeared to me as a dark gloominess

[41] See again U. B. Phillips, *American Negro Slavery.*
[42] On this theme see Stephen B. Weeks, *Southern Quakers and Slavery* (Baltimore, 1896), chapter 9.

hanging over the land." He condemned slavery in his famous *Jour-nal* (1774) and in an essay, *Some Considerations on the Keeping of Negroes* (1754). Partly in response to his labors, the Philadelphia yearly meeting of the Quakers in 1776 disowned members who refused to free their slaves. Among the New England Puritans early protests against slavery had been voiced by John Eliot and Samuel Sewall. By 1775 men of strongly democratic tendencies in the middle colonies and New England (artisans and small farmers) regarded slavery with disfavor. Emancipation came in these states between 1775 and 1800, while the Northwest Ordinance of 1787 forbade the extension of slavery into the territory north of the Ohio River.

## BIBLIOGRAPHICAL NOTE

WORKS PREVIOUSLY CITED: J. T. Adams, *Revolutionary New England*, ch. 3; P. A. Bruce, *Institutional History of Virginia*, I, Part I, chs. 3–5; L. C. Gray, *History of Agriculture in the Southern United States*, I, ch. 22 (slaves); A. C. Flick (ed.), *History of the State of New York*, IV, ch. 9 (woman's status); E. W. Spaulding, *New York in the Critical Period*, ch. 2; E. R. Turner, *The Negro in Pennsylvania*, ch. 5; T. J. Wertenbaker, *Norfolk*, ch. 1; C. G. Woodson, *The Negro in our History*, chs. 3–4.

SOURCES: WORKS NEWLY CITED: Three readable, informative travel accounts are Andrew Burnaby, *Travels through the Middle Settlements of North America* [1759–60] (ed. Rufus R. Wilson, New York, 1904); Peter Kalm, *Travels into North America* (2 vols., London, 1772); and Gottlieb Mittelberger, *Journey to Pennsylvania in the Year 1750* (trans. C. T. Eden, Philadelphia, 1898). The American Bookshelf editions (ed. Mark Van Doren) contain *Samuel Sewall's Diary* [1675–1724] (1927) and William Byrd's *A Journey to the Land of Eden and Other Papers* (1928). Carl Van Doren has edited a convenient handbook, *Benjamin Franklin and Jonathan Edwards, Selections from their Writings* (New York, c. 1920). The American Writers Series (ed. H. H. Clark) includes *Benjamin Franklin* (ed. F. L. Mott and C. E. Jorgenson, New York, c. 1936)— a discriminating selection from Franklin's writings, with excellent Franklin bibliography. Franklin's *Autobiography* and J. Hector St. John de Crèvecoeur's *Letters from an American Farmer* are available in Everyman's Library editions. Every student should become familiar with Franklin's *Poor Richard's Almanac* (various editions).

MAPS: C. O. Paullin, *Atlas of the Historical Geography of the United States*, plates 40, 60–61, 156–157, 159 (colonial towns).

# ☆ XVIII ☆

## CULTURE AND RELIGION

### THE COLONIAL CHURCHES

THE most prominent feature of religion in the English colonies was the dominance of Protestantism; in every colony the Roman Catholics formed only a small minority. A few dwelt in Virginia, New York, and New Jersey; where they were most numerous—in Maryland and Pennsylvania—they numbered between but four and seven thousand in 1756. Always exposed to the animosity inherited by Protestants from Old World religious strife, the colonial Catholics were further weakened by the Anglo-French wars—by the identification of their faith with the cause of the principal enemy of the English settlers.[1]

The Protestant Reformation, which popularized the idea that man might commune with God without the medium of a priest, emphasized in thought and religion those forces of individualism which early capitalism fostered in the economic sphere. Rejecting the authority of any single ecclesiastical hierarchy, the Protestants divided into numerous sects: many interpreters meant many interpretations. Moreover, the Protestant sects gave expressions to social distinctions—to the interests and outlooks of the various classes. Class differences fostered diversity in religion, while changes within the class structure affected established sects.

Three tendencies are evident in early American Protestantism. Some churches, like the Anglican, expressed the aristocratic spirit of an upper class in control. They vested authority in the clergy and the most wealthy parishioners, favored formal services, frowned upon religious emotionalism, and tended to emphasize external observances rather than the inner spiritual life of the individual. Another upper-class tendency was the effort to establish a church by law and to force it upon all the people, irrespective of individual belief.[2]

A second Protestant trend, which may be described as democratic

[1] The best introduction, popular, scholarly and attractive, is William W. Sweet, *The Story of Religions in America* (New York, 1931).

[2] Luther A. Weigle, *American Idealism* (*Pageant of America*, X, New Haven, 1928), chapters 2–4.

or popular, is manifest in such churches as the Baptist, the Methodist (after 1750), and the German Pietist sects like the Moravians and the Mennonites. These churches, dominated by middle-class groups, emphasized the right of individual judgment (soul liberty) as against ecclesiastical authority, favored informal services, stressed an inner spiritual life as against mere outward conformity, and lodged control in the body of believers rather than in a priestly caste or an oligarchy of wealthy laymen. Believing firmly in freedom of conscience, these popular churches resisted all efforts to impose by law a religion not wanted by the people themselves.

A third group of churches included the Quaker, the Presbyterian, the Dutch Reformed, the Lutheran, the German Reformed, and the Congregational. In the eighteenth century they exhibited an inner conflict between aristocratic and democratic tendencies. Originally composed of middle-class groups, these churches became divided in America partly because some of the members rose into the upper class, whereas the majority remained in their former circumstances. The upper-class groups generally stood for the aristocratic principles just mentioned; the lower middle-class elements adhered to the democratic ideas of the popular churches.

Throughout colonial times the Baptist Church retained its democratic character. Its creed affirmed that each man might commune directly with God and thus know religious truth at first hand; hence it rejected the office of priest and the authority of ecclesiastical officials. Only true believers should belong to the church—that is, those who had been converted or awakened by God to a spiritual life. Baptism should follow conversion, and because conversion visited only the mature, infant baptism was held to be ineffectual. Some Baptists accepted the doctrine of predestination; others believed that salvation might be attained through faith and good works. Religion being a relationship between God and each individual, the state should not interfere in matters of conscience. After 1650 the American Baptists regarded immersion as the correct mode of baptism. In keeping with their democratic beliefs they adopted the congregational form of church organization, vesting all power in the church members. After 1707 the Baptist congregations of the middle colonies coöperated through an association which held its meetings in Philadelphia.[3]

The expulsion of Roger Williams from Massachusetts (he may be regarded as the first outstanding American Baptist) illustrates the position of this radical sect in early times. The Baptists were objec-

[3] Albert H. Newman, *A History of the Baptist Churches* . . . (New York, 1904), is the most satisfactory treatment.

tionable to established churches because they opposed the union of church and state and because their doctrine of baptism seemed dangerous to those Protestants who believed that each child should be brought under the discipline of the church through the agency of infant baptism. In 1644 Massachusetts ordered the expulsion of Baptists; six years later two Baptists from Rhode Island were fined and expelled from the Bay colony, while another, Obadiah Holmes, who refused to pay a fine, was given thirty lashes. Due to such persecution the Baptists became strongest in those colonies which rejected state coercion in religion—Plymouth, Rhode Island, New Jersey, Pennsylvania, and Delaware. In the eighteenth century they were generally tolerated, though frequently in conflict with Puritans and Anglicans over the question of paying taxes for the support of an established church.

Many of the German and Swiss settlers in the colonies belonged to churches which espoused democratic ideals. Such churches were offshoots of German Pietism—a movement of the seventeenth century in protest against formalism that had crept into the two principal churches, the Lutheran and the German Reformed. The early Pietists organized private societies devoted to Bible study and prayer and designed to promote personal holiness. The chief sects which emerged —the Mennonites, the Moravians, and the Dunkers—resembled the English Quakers and Baptists. Drawing their strength from the German peasantry, these radical groups emphasized the worth of the common man, affirmed that salvation might be achieved through personal piety, rejected external authority in religion, believed in direct communion between God and man, resisted social inequality, and some were even inclined toward an agrarian type of communism. They seemed a threat to privileged classes, since they opposed tax-supported churches, military service, the use of force, slavery, severe punishments, and oaths of allegiance to the *status quo*. They settled where peace and toleration prevailed, principally in Pennsylvania.[4]

By 1640 the Congregational churches of Massachusetts had fallen under the control of conservative groups, although democratic tendencies survived among the people. The men who shaped the early religious policy had belonged to the upper middle class in England; in the colony they composed the local upper class. Consequently, they established a conservative church which was ruled by the clergy and an oligarchy of influential laymen. Only members of an approved congregation could vote or hold office in the general government; all

[4] Lucy F. Bittinger, *German Religious Life in Colonial Times* (Philadelphia, 1907), is a readable survey of the external aspects of pietism.

inhabitants must attend the Puritan services; all must contribute toward the support of the church, either voluntarily or through public taxes.[5] Moreover, the creed of Puritanism gave great influence to the clergy. Man, who was born and lived in sin, could not effect the salvation of his soul; that was a gift of God to the elect. And God would indicate those of his creatures to whom he had granted salvation. The sign of election was a spiritual awakening or conversion which inspired one to forsake sinful ways and to live a godly life. Only after such a conversion might one be admitted to membership in the church and become a partaker of communion. In this process the clergy had a threefold role. They were God's instrument to awaken the soul—to prepare sinful man for his conversion or calling; they then examined the convert to determine whether he had received a true calling and was entitled to church membership, and they strengthened the members in their determination to live in the manner which God required of the elect. The use of political authority to assure religious uniformity and the influence of the clergy were essentially conservative features of Puritanism; democratic features were the selection of the minister by the congregation, the congregational plan of church organization, and the mystical ideal of conversion which meant that salvation required an inner experience of the individual—not mere conformity to an established system.[6]

In the seventeenth century the conservative principle triumphed in the official policy of the Massachusetts church. This outcome is explained in part by the expulsion of the radicals—Roger Williams, Anne Hutchinson, and other mystics who exalted the spiritual experience of the individual as against the authority of the clergy and the state. Then came the persecution of the Quakers. About 1656 Quaker missionaries entered Massachusetts, preaching their doctrine of the inner light (direct inspiration) which was so obnoxious to orthodox leaders because it avowed that the people did not need a trained ministry for spiritual guidance. Quaker doctrines also irked the governing class because they diffused among humble folk a sense of their importance by virtue of their presumed kinship with God. Accordingly, the General Court ordered that Quakers be banished on pain of death if they returned—a law which resulted in the execution in 1659–60 of four intractable missionaries who refused to stay in exile. The early purges in Massachusetts placed in control of the churches men

[5] Perry G. Miller, *Orthodoxy in Massachusetts, 1630–1650* (Cambridge, 1933), supersedes all other studies of the origins and nature of Congregationalism in the Bay Colony.

[6] Herbert W. Schneider's *The Puritan Mind* (New York, c. 1930) presents in modern form a concise analysis of New England Puritanism.

who looked askance at a personal, emotional type of religion in which the persecuted mystics had indulged. Meanwhile, the increasing wealth of the upper class strengthened the trend toward formalism in the Puritan church.[7]

In 1662 this trend received further recognition when the clergy of Massachusetts and Connecticut adopted the "halfway covenant." The issue then considered was the admission of the children of the church founders as church members. Many of the second generation did not experience a conversion; were they to be excluded from membership, thus losing the privilege of having their own children baptized? The clergy decided to admit all children of members to a sort of half membership, reserving full membership (i. e., the privilege of communion) to those who have been converted. Afterward, the clergy tended to emphasize observance of the church discipline and an outward moral life as tests of election. This outcome was conservative in that inheritance and family connections were favored at the expense of the spiritual life of the individual. Conservative people disapproved of excessive religious fervor: it might find expression in an uncouth manner and it might evoke the sort of radicalism that unsettled the status quo by questioning the moral foundations of property and government.[8]

After 1684 the interference of the English government in the affairs of Massachusetts threatened to undermine the Puritan church, since England insisted upon equal privileges for Anglicans and the toleration of dissenters. Hence the new royal charter of 1691 outlawed religious tests for voting and promised liberty of conscience to all Christians except papists. But Puritanism was not crushed. The new property qualifications for voting left the Puritans in control of elective offices, since they were the largest body of property owners. In 1692 the General Court again enacted that all taxpayers must contribute toward the support of the Congregational churches. In the years 1690–1720 the chief spokesmen of orthodoxy were Increase Mather and his son, Cotton Mather—both men of essentially conservative views. Somewhat prone to morbid introspection and ambitious to be the prophet of his age, Cotton Mather was doomed to disappointment. Mistrustful of the common man, too self-centered to be a popular leader, and yet too much given to middle-class religious fervor to appeal to conservative laymen who were growing

[7] Perry G. Miller, "The Marrow of Puritan Divinity," *Publications*, Colonial Society of Massachusetts, XXXII, 247–300.

[8] Perry G. Miller, "The Half-way Covenant," *New England Quarterly*, VI (Dec. 1933).

complacent in the accumulation of wealth, he failed to satisfy either the democratic or the aristocratic parties. Now that Britain appointed the governor of Massachusetts, the clergy no longer exerted their former influence in the executive councils, and Cotton Mather's ambitions to be a power behind the throne were likewise frustrated. His abilities and temperament did not fit him for the leadership to which he aspired, although he taxed his strength to exhaustion, wrote voluminously and became the most widely read author in the colonies.[9]

In order to strengthen the power of the clergy Cotton Mather and other orthodox ministers proposed in 1705 a church organization along Presbyterian lines. The churches of each county were to form an association and to set up a council composed of the ministers and important laymen. Each county council in turn was to send delegates to a general colonial conference, which was to examine and license candidates for the ministry, to ordain, install and dismiss ministers, and to hear appeals from the congregations and the county councils. Designed to impose a uniform doctrine and discipline on all the people, this new plan (called the Consociation) aimed to strengthen the clergy, who were to control the general council; the rule of the many in the various congregations was to give way to the rule of a few at the top. Connecticut adopted the scheme in 1708 (the Saybrook Platform) by authorizing each church to join an association, whereupon the congregations so affiliated became the established churches of the colony. In Massachusetts two factors thwarted the plan. The British government opposed it, fearing to enlarge the power of anti-British, anti-Anglican ministers in a colony none too loyal to the Crown. And the local democratic elements protested. In 1717 appeared the *Vindication of the Government of the Churches of New England*, written by the minister of Ipswich, the Reverend John Wise—a vigorous democrat whose father had been an indentured servant. Wise argued that church government by the congregation was the true principle of New England Puritanism, declaring that "an aristocracy is a dangerous constitution in the church of Christ" and that the "end of all good government is to cultivate humanity and promote the happiness of all." [10]

With the failure of the Consociation movement in Massachusetts the conservative Puritans utilized the General Court to control the congregations. This the General Court did by authorizing the establish-

[9] Ralph and Louise Boas, *Cotton Mather, Keeper of the Puritan Conscience* (New York, 1928), is excellent. Among earlier studies Barrett Wendell, *Cotton Mather* (New York, 1891), is especially recommended.

[10] Williston Walker, *A History of the Congregational Churches* . . . (New York, 1904), is a brief, factual survey.

ment of new churches, by removing objectionable ministers, by settling contests among rival candidates for a pastorate, and by enforcing
laws for the public support of all churches. Such legislation perpetuated the old conflict between dissenters and the orthodox church. By
absorbing Plymouth Colony in 1691 Massachusetts assumed jurisdiction over numerous Quakers and Baptists settled there. Both sects
protested vigorously against paying taxes to support Puritan ministers, the less numerous Baptists accepting the leadership of the more
influential Quakers. When such protests to the Massachusetts authorities proved fruitless, the Quakers appealed to the British government
through English Quakers who were influential in the Whig party,
then in power in England. Such political pressure induced Massachusetts in 1731 and 1734 to exempt the Quakers and Baptists from paying taxes for the support of the Puritan ministers.[11]

The Presbyterian Church gained a foothold in the colonies largely
through the work of Francis Makemie, a missionary who, arriving in
1683, traveled through the settlements from New York to South
Carolina. The first American presbytery, established in 1708, bore
witness to his labors. Since the American congregations were independent of the Presbyterian Church in Scotland and Ulster they were
obliged to provide their own ministers—a task to which they proved
unequal after the Scotch-Irish immigrants began to arrive in large
numbers in 1714. Accordingly, frontier communities commonly lacked
a settled ministry and were prone to neglect religion. Presbyterianism was conservative in that its church organization vested large
authority in the presbytery or district council of elders and ministers;
moreover, it rejected the doctrines of the inner light and salvation
through personal effort, adhering instead to the idea of predestination which affirmed the unworthiness of ordinary men in the sight
of God. On the other hand the mass of the Scotch-Irish settlers, in
their demands for land and political rights, exhibited a strongly democratic spirit. The Presbyterians were most numerous in Pennsylvania
and in the western parts of Virginia, Maryland, South Carolina, and
North Carolina.[12]

Similar to the Presbyterian Church in organization, creed and internal divisions were two other Calvinist churches—the Dutch Reformed and the German Reformed. The latter had thirty churches

[11] *Church and State in Massachusetts, 1691–1740*, by Susan M. Reed (Urbana,
1914), emphasizes the relation of the dissenters to the orthodox church. This story is
continued in Jacob E. Meyer, *Church and State in Massachusetts, from 1740 to 1833*
(Cleveland, 1930)—a detailed monograph.

[12] For the special student Charles A. Briggs, *American Presbyterianism* (New York,
1885), is the best work.

in Pennsylvania in 1750. The Dutch Reformed Church had been the official church of New Netherland until disestablished by the English after they took over the province in 1664. Ruled by the aristocratic families of New York and northern New Jersey, the Dutch Reformed churches remained under the jurisdiction of the mother church in Holland, where ministers were ordained before they were sent to the colonies.[13] The Lutheran Church, first introduced by the Swedes on the Delaware, grew very slowly until the great influx of the Germans after 1730. By 1750 the Lutherans were supporting forty churches in Pennsylvania. Although the Lutheran Church was a state church in Germany and in the Scandinavian kingdoms, the American Lutherans, as a minority without much political influence, objected to being taxed for the support of any non-Lutheran church and thus strengthened the movement for religious liberty in the colonies.

In the eighteenth century the American Quakers did not display the fervor that had characterized them before 1700. After England granted toleration in 1689 the colonies ceased to attract dissenters animated by religious zeal. In Rhode Island, New Jersey, and Pennsylvania, where the Quakers were most numerous, they were not driven to extremes by persecution. Meanwhile, many Quakers had grown wealthy; moreover, children commonly did not feel the ardor of their once persecuted parents. In eastern Pennsylvania many Quaker merchant families became quite conservative, inclining toward a comfortable way of living, to decorous manners, and to formality in religious worship. Sharing political power through their control of the assembly (to 1757) they betrayed a complacency that generally comes to those long in office. The more conservative Quakers owned slaves, consented to increasingly harsh punishments for criminals, and forsook the early ideal of non-resistance, although they continued to adhere to the forms of their religion and to oppose persecution and appropriations for the defense of the frontiers.[14]

In Massachusetts, Virginia, North Carolina, and Maryland, where the Quakers belonged to the small farmer-artisan class, contests with state churches weeded out the indifferent and kept alive religious zeal. Among such Quakers opposition to oaths, tithes, military service, social inequality, and slavery remained active. The democratic organization of the church enabled the various elements to work together

[13] E. T. Corwin, *A History of the Reformed Church, Dutch* (New York, 1905), is a convenient manual.

[14] Rufus M. Jones, *The Quakers in the American Colonies* (London, 1911), ranks high among religious histories. See also his *The Later Periods of Quakerism* (2 vols., London, 1921), Vol. I.

with reasonable harmony. Each congregation governed itself through its weekly and monthly meetings; hence the majority controlled. The quarterly meeting—a gathering of the people themselves, not an assembly of church officers—provided social life and religious fellowship. And the yearly meetings (the New England Quakers met at Newport; those of the middle colonies and the South at Burlington or Philadelphia) did not attempt to dictate to each congregation. These meetings heard reports of persecutions, provided relief for Friends in distress, and sustained missionary work. Quakerism thus afforded religious freedom to the individual; congregations of radical tendencies were not severely repressed by conservative elements; instead the latter coöperated to protect all Quakers from persecution and to support missionaries who labored among the Indians and the slaves.

By a series of laws, 1619–64, Virginia established the Anglican as the official church of the colony. Maryland followed in 1692, New York in 1693, North Carolina in 1701 and 1715, South Carolina in 1704 and 1706, and Georgia in 1758. But the strength of Anglicanism in these colonies varied greatly. The Church was established in only four counties in New York; in 1775 its communicants numbered only one in fifteen of the population of the province. North Carolina then had only six Anglican churches; Georgia in 1769 had only two. The influence of the Anglicans was declining in Virginia before the Revolution; in Maryland they were a small minority; the condition of the Church was most flourishing in South Carolina.

After 1685 the Anglican churches in America were under the jurisdiction of the Bishop of London. Unable to visit the colonial parishes, he sent thither his personal representatives (called commissaries) who inquired into conditions, advised the clergy, and undertook to improve the morale of communities and to promote religious education by building up schools and parochial libraries. Although the commissaries did not possess the bishop's power to confirm church members or to ordain ministers, in exceptional cases they could discipline and even suspend unworthy rectors. The best-known commissaries were Thomas Bray (Maryland), noted for his work in establishing numerous parish libraries, and James Blair (Virginia), instrumental in securing a royal charter for the Anglican College of William and Mary (1693).[15] By virtue of the colonial charters many royal governors claimed the power of selecting the clergy—a claim successfully disputed by the church members. Except in Maryland, where the governor or proprietor exercised the appointing power, selections were made commonly by the vestry—a board of twelve men who repre-

[15] Daniel E. Motley, *Life of Commissary James Blair* (Baltimore, 1901)—a brief sketch.

sented the most wealthy parishioners. Since the vestry also controlled the finances of the parish church it became the center of gravity. Home rule by the vestry, the isolation of churches, and the weakness of external authority gave American Anglicanism an independence somewhat suggestive of Congregationalism.[16]

The Anglican clergyman usually received the use of a house and a glebe or farm, together with a salary from parish taxes plus wedding and funeral fees. In New York, although other means were tried, salaries were provided through voluntary contributions; in South Carolina dissenters were taxed, not directly, but through custom duties. In fifty years the people of North Carolina paid taxes sufficient only to support two ministers for one year! Except in South Carolina the Anglican clergy did not exhibit much religious zeal. Security of tenure, lax discipline, and small incomes all contributed toward a complacency to be expected of a church sustained by law rather than by the fervor of its members. All the Anglican clergy had to be ordained by the Bishop of London—a rule which hindered the recruiting of Americans; hence a large majority were Englishmen. Frequently those who came to the colonies were the unaspiring who had been unable to obtain better places at home. Nor was the spiritual ardor of the Church of England particularly high. In Virginia and Maryland the clergy brought discredit upon the Church by their fondness for horse racing, fox hunting, and other worldly pleasures. The urge to uplift was weak, since the clergy ministered chiefly to people already at the top of the social scale.

Nor was it deemed desirable to agitate members of the lower classes, particularly the slaves. Six colonies between 1664 and 1706 enacted laws declaring that the conversion of slaves did not make them freemen. The planters were lukewarm or hostile to religious instruction for Negroes, partly because Christianity and membership in the owners' church might inculcate ideas of equality and independence, partly because attendance at remote services interfered with work on the plantations. A Presbyterian minister in 1756 deplored "the almost universal neglect of many thousand of poor slaves . . . who generally continue heathens in a Christian country." "It is too manifest to be denied," wrote a Quaker missionary in 1765, "that the life of religion is almost lost where slaves are very numerous; and it is impossible it should be otherwise, the practice being as contrary to the spirit of Christianity as light is to darkness."[17]

[16] Arthur L. Cross, *The Anglican Episcopate and the American Colonies* (New York, 1902), traces the relations between the colonies and the Church of England.

[17] M. W. Jernegan, "Slavery and Conversion in the American Colonies." *American Historical Review*, XXI (April 1916).

One remedy proposed for the weakness of the Anglican Church in America was to establish a resident bishop vested with the power to confirm members and to ordain and discipline ministers. Prelates and colonial officials in England pressed this plan in the years 1710–13, when the Tories (strict Anglicans) were in control. The strengthening of the Anglican Church in the colonies might bind them more closely to Britain by fostering attitudes of obedience to the Crown, since the Anglicans at home stood for the submission of the people to the royal power. However, the Whigs regained control in 1714 and the scheme was dropped. Then the Whig policy of encouraging foreign Protestants to settle in the colonies further lessened the influence of Anglicanism. Nor did the Whigs care to antagonize the colonists by taxing them for the support of an Anglican bishop at a time when their assistance was needed against the French. Non-Anglicans in America opposed the plan; so also did most of the Anglicans, who were satisfied to have their local churches governed by the leading families of their neighborhoods.

In 1701 William III chartered the Society for Propagating the Gospel in Foreign Parts (the S.P.G.)—a small organization dominated by prelates of the Anglican Church. Its purpose was to support missionaries in the colonies for the conversion of Indians, slaves, and non-Anglicans among the white settlers. Accordingly, the S.P.G. centered its efforts upon those regions without an established Anglican Church—particularly upon the middle colonies and Rhode Island. But the society accomplished little. It lacked popular support, as indicated by its small yearly income (£1,000 to £1,500—obtained chiefly from high churchmen), and for this reason it could sustain only a few missionaries. Due to the dearth of enthusiasm among Anglicans for missionary hardships, the agents assigned to the Indians soon left the frontiers and sought a more pleasant life in the settlements. The failure of a missionary sent among the Iroquois in 1704 frustrated plans to use the S.P.G. as a means of combating the political influence of the French Jesuits on the northern frontiers. By virtue of the opposition of the planters to the conversion of slaves little could be accomplished in that direction. The mass of the colonists were either confirmed in a particular faith or indifferent toward religion. Despite the efforts of the S.P.G. Anglicanism steadily lost ground as a popular religion in eighteenth-century America.[18]

[18] E. B. Greene, "The Anglican Outlook on the American Colonies," *American Historical Review*, XX (Oct. 1914).

## THE GREAT AWAKENING

In the 1730's occurred a stirring revival, the Great Awakening—the first spontaneous outburst of popular feeling in American history. Cutting across racial and denominational lines, it affected the mass of the small farmers and artisans, bearing witness to their class solidarity and to their antagonism toward aristocratic influences. Opposed by the Anglican clergy and welcomed by the Baptists, the Great Awakening split the Presbyterian, Congregational, and Dutch Reformed churches into conservative and popular factions. This American movement was only one aspect of a worldwide protest against the complacency, formalism, authoritarianism, and lack of emotional fervor that had come to characterize most of the Protestant churches. From German Pietism a wave of religious zeal swept over Europe after 1700; in England John and Charles Wesley launched the Methodist movement in an effort to infuse new life into complacent Anglicanism.[19] In America the lack of churches in many settlements had caused a neglect of religion which was favorable to an emotional reaction when once the people living in comparative isolation were subjected to the spell of eloquent evangelists.

The Great Awakening exhibited many democratic features, the most important being the conception of salvation popularized by Jonathan Edwards, graduate of Yale College and Congregational minister at Northampton, Massachusetts. Edwards adhered to the Calvinistic view that man was steeped in sin and that a spiritual awakening was God's sign to those whom he had predestined to salvation. By portraying vividly the torments of hell, Edwards aroused in his hearers a dread of sin and a longing for purification that blossomed in a joyful sense of God's presence in the soul. Not wealth or social status but one's individual experience was the condition of salvation. Now it so happened that such a conversion was most likely to visit humble, uneducated people; its effect therefore was to diffuse among the common folk the belief that they were the chosen of the Lord—and thus to intensify their dissatisfaction with an inferior place in society.[20]

The Great Awakening also enabled the common man to participate in the church services, even though such activity took the form of wailing, shouting, rolling on the ground, praying, singing, and leaping in

[19] James Laver, *Wesley* (New York, 1933), is an admirable brief summary.

[20] The best study of Edwards's ideas is Arthur C. McGiffert, *Jonathan Edwards* (New York, 1932); the most readable biography is H. B. Parkes, *Jonathan Edwards* (New York, 1930); the best older study is Alexander U. G. Allen, *Jonathan Edwards* (Boston, 1889).

ecstasy. No longer was religion a monopoly of a few educated, conservative clergymen. The evangelist who aroused the people addressed them in the language they knew. He spoke to the heart rather than to the intellect; he held services in fields and groves where all might attend. Rank, formality, and exclusiveness had no place among a company of worshippers equal in the sight of God.

The Great Awakening popularized the idea that the truth was to be found by each person in the Bible—not in man-made laws, sermons, or creeds. Authorities who violated the divine law did not merit respect; institutions contrary to the Scriptures were deemed invalid: here were the seeds of revolution. Every congregation should govern itself, since each member had received in full the divine benediction. And because any person might be revealed as one of God's elect, all (including Indians and slaves) were entitled to dignified and humane treatment.[21]

One precursor of the revivalists was Theodore Frelinghuysen, a Dutch Reformed minister educated in Germany, where he had fallen under the influence of Pietism. Taking a pastorate in the Raritan valley he traveled in the 1720's a circuit of four churches, championing a strict morality and the doctrine of spiritual rebirth. Opposed by the conventional ministers of the Dutch Reformed Church, he coöperated with Presbyterian revivalists. A pioneer evangelist among the Presbyterians was William Tennent, who arrived in Philadelphia from Ireland about 1717 and soon undertook to supply ministers for the Scotch-Irish settlers near the frontiers. To carry out this purpose he established a log college (1736) at his farm between Philadelphia and New York, where he trained zealous young preachers and inspired them with the new evangelism. His son Gilbert, who became a co-worker with Frelinghuysen, carried forward at New Brunswick the work in northern New Jersey.[22] In 1740 Gilbert visited Boston, where his preaching moved a conservative minister to describe him as "impudent and saucy" and to lament that in the "dreadfullest winter I ever saw, people wallowed in the snow night and day for the benefit of his beastly braying." Even before this the younger Tennent had become the most powerful revivalist in the middle colonies. Meanwhile, in the Connecticut valley Jonathan Edwards, dismayed by the moral laxity of the age, was calling sinners to repentance and a righteous life, combining in his utterances the qualities of poet, mystic, and

---

[21] See again H. L. Osgood, *American Colonies in the Eighteenth Century*, Vol. III, pp. 407–450.

[22] Charles H. Maxson, *The Great Awakening in the Middle Colonies* (Chicago, 1920), is a concise, informative study.

stern Calvinist. Although he remained at Northampton, his influence extended so widely through his sermons and writings that he reawakened all New England to the dangers of hell-fire and sin.[23]

English Methodism contributed to the American revival the greatest evangelist of the age. In 1739 George Whitefield arrived at Philadelphia, whence he visited New York, Charleston, Savannah, and New England. At Northampton he was cordially received by Jonathan Edwards and in Pennsylvania by the Tennents. Already known as the foremost preacher of Britain, Whitefield attracted immense and eager audiences wherever he spoke. Not intellectual in his discourses, he spoke on the simple themes of sin, repentance, and regeneration, swaying thousands of humble folk by his superlative oratory. A tireless worker, he did more than anyone else to spread the spirit of revivalism and to keep it alive.[24]

The most important result of the Great Awakening was the division of the churches into parties which corresponded roughly to existing social classes. The Presbyterians in 1741 divided into the "old lights" and the "new lights"; the Congregationalists into orthodox and separatist. Not until 1758 was the breach closed in the Presbyterian Church. Of the Congregationalist separatists, some eventually returned to the old churches, some formed independent congregations, and many joined the Baptists—the sect which benefited chiefly by the revival in New England. The revivalists insisted that salvation and church membership depended upon conversion; they received as ministers untrained laymen who had been particularly moved by the divine spirit; they supported itinerant preachers and desired to receive them into the existing churches; they favored soul-stirring sermons and emotional demonstrations by the laity. The anti-revivalists (most of the educated ministers, the well-to-do parishioners, and the professors at Yale and Harvard colleges) stressed the fine points of theology and adherence to creeds and church discipline, favored dignified, decorous, unemotional services, recognized only ordained ministers, and protested vehemently against receiving itinerant preachers and their "rabble" followers into the churches.

Other effects of the revival may be noted briefly. It intensified the religious criticism of slavery, gave a short-lived impetus to missionary work among the Indians, and strengthened the humanitarian spirit, as evinced by Whitefield's work in founding an orphans' asylum in

[23] M. H. Mitchell, *The Great Awakening* (New Haven, 1934—Connecticut Tercentenary Commission, no. 26).

[24] The most recent biography is Albert D. Belden, *George Whitefield, the Awakener* (Nashville, c. 1930); the most complete is Luke Tyerman, *The Life of the Rev. George Whitefield* (2 vols., New York, 1876-77).

Georgia. Four new colleges grew out of the movement: Princeton (Presbyterian), Brown (Baptist), Rutgers (Dutch Reformed), and Dartmouth (Congregationalist). The opposition among dissenters to established churches received a fresh stimulus, while defiance of authorized institutions prepared men's minds for the next act of resistance—the American Revolution.[25]

## THE EDUCATION OF YOUTH

In colonial times the pursuit of knowledge exhibited two phases. The organized schools trained the youth in the body of existing knowledge; outside the schools, learned and ingenious men speculated anew about nature and the destiny of man. However, both the formal instruction of the schoolroom and the creative intellectual life outside were affected by similar influences, five of which should be understood.[26]

First, the colonists started with the cultural heritage of Europe. They brought with them the European conceptions of the natural world—a strange mixture of folklore, superstition, and scientific truth —and thereafter they were continually affected by cultural currents emanating from the Old World. To New England alone before 1650 came about a hundred and thirty men (most of them ministers) who had been educated in the universities of Europe and Britain. A few colonists maintained close connections with the centers of thought overseas, importing books and scientific apparatus and reporting to European correspondents their observations of natural phenomena in America. The Royal Society of London, incorporated in 1662 and devoted to scientific inquiry, numbered among its correspondents such men as John Winthrop, Jr., and Cotton Mather in New England, William Byrd and John Mitchell of Virginia, and Benjamin Franklin and David Rittenhouse of Pennsylvania. Harvard College, founded at Cambridge (then Newtown) Massachusetts, in 1636, was originally conceived of as a refuge for English Puritans in exile, as a center to which the English Puritans might send their sons, and as a means of preserving the Puritan flame which Charles I sought to extinguish in the English universities. Supported in part by benefactions from English sources, drawing its teachers from England, and shaped by the course of English politics, Harvard retained its inter-

[25] F. I. Carpenter, "The Radicalism of Jonathan Edwards," *New England Quarterly*, IV (Oct. 1931). Wesley M. Gewehr's *The Great Awakening in Virginia, 1740–1790*, an excellent study, emphasizes the social aspects of the revival.

[26] Intellectual trends are ably summarized in I. Woodbridge Riley, *American Thought* (New York, 1923).

national character until the Puritans, seizing power in England, no longer needed their "university in exile" after 1650.[27] In Virginia, the College of William and Mary was established in 1693 in order to train the southern youth in the ideals of the Church of England.

Foremost among the cultural influences inherited from Europe was the religious impulse. The medieval union of education and religion had not been dissolved when the colonies were founded. To the colonial clergy more than to any other group belonged the task of preserving and fostering learning in the New World. Most Prot estant sects held that an educated ministry was necessary that the Scriptures might be fully understood by men competent to read the original records in Hebrew and Greek; moreover, it was appropriate that the clergy investigate the mysteries of nature and thus be qualified to explain the ways of God to man. Religion also had its part in the education of youth. The Calvinists believed that all should be taught to read in order that they might know the sources of divine truth; children should be reared in the true faith; and the virtues of obedience, industry, and honesty should be inculcated through religious schools. The major sects, both Protestant and Catholic, accepted private property as a sacred institution; two of the Ten Commandments enjoin respect for property rights.[28]

Long before 1600 European thought had manifested a practical, utilitarian bent, as scientific inquiry sought to master the forces of nature in order to lighten men's burdens on earth. To enlarge production and to increase the physical comforts of life: such was the underlying aim, which also dominated the training of the youth of the lower and middle classes, whose education as apprentices taught the skills of craft and trade. To the colonial farm boy or girl incessant contacts with tools, materials, plants, animals, and the soil—a continual preoccupation with the processes of production—gave an education that was extremely practical and concrete.

The environment of the New World strengthened the practical, secular, utilitarian influence in thought at the expense of theology. Concern with the physical aspects of society was imperative since the colonists had to provide in a short time a material equipment (houses, buildings, fences, clearings, roads) which Europe had been generations in acquiring. Moreover, the strange aspects of life in America intensified the curiosity of men about the natural world: the

[27] S. E. Morison, *The Founding of Harvard College* (Cambridge, 1935), combines broad knowledge, keen scholarship, and literary charm.

[28] Harvey G. Townsend, *Philosophical Ideas in the United States* (New York, 1934), finds in idealism the key to American philosophy.

contrast between the familiar and the strange is always a potent stimulus to inquiry. There were new plants, soils, minerals, climates, animals, and trees to be observed and utilized—new routes of travel, new seas, ocean currents, lakes, rivers, and harbors to be mastered; even the heavens wore a strange aspect. Animals and plants brought from Europe developed surprising characteristics. Probably every colonist encountered some manifestation of nature that seemed to him strikingly novel—hurricanes, comets, electrical storms, eclipses, heavy snows, clouds of insects or birds, intense heat, bitter cold. Many an intelligent man employed his idle hours in the study of the new nature—the ways of the bee, the migration of birds, the strange face of the seasons, the movements of the stars, the habits of the beasts of the forest. The strongest voice the colonist heard was the voice of nature, and for many years it spoke in unfamiliar accents. It is not surprising, then, that the first American scientists occupied themselves with descriptive botany, zoölogy, geography, and astronomy and with native curiosities among natural phenomena.[29]

Colonial education reflected the class standards of Europe, where the higher learning was closely identified with the higher classes. Exempt from physical toil, the children of the well-to-do needed an intellectual discipline to provide that regularity, application, and restraint, without which leisure and wealth are likely to lead to deterioration. Difficult subjects like Latin, Greek, and mathematics had a high disciplinary value and hence were especially esteemed by the upper-class groups. Higher education also furnished the fortunate with intellectual adornments which set them off from the poor; correct literary usage, an approved accent, the use of Latin or Greek phrases, a knowledge of ancient literature—all served to distinguish the gentleman from peasants and workers. Assuming that superior intellect was the basis of their supremacy, the upper classes emphasized the training of the mind and pursued those studies, like the law and the military arts, which reinforced the economic and military bases of political power. Cultural activities also gratified one's curiosity and esthetic sense and provided an agreeable employment for the leisure hours of the upper-class gentleman.[30]

Since members of the lower classes were disciplined by poverty and toil, and because they enjoyed but little leisure, the studies deemed appropriate for them were of a useful rather than a decorative char-

---

[29] Edwin E. Slosson, *The American Spirit in Education* (*Chronicles of America*, New Haven, 1921), chapters 1–5.

[30] Merle Curti, *The Social Ideas of American Educators* (New York, 1935), is an excellent study. See chapter 1.

acter. Book learning consisted only of reading, writing, and arithmetic; in addition the poor should acquire physical strength and the skills of artisan or laborer. To masters and employers it seemed equally desirable that the lower classes be trained in the habits of obedience, industry, and honesty.

The most significant influence on education was exerted by the colonial middle class. A desire to emulate the upper class induced the middle class to pursue some studies of a decorative, disciplinary, and esthetic nature; and yet, because the middle class was not exempt from work, it was forced to concern itself largely with the gainful arts and professions—with business, the law, medicine, agricultural improvements, and the skilled trades. Middle-class education therefore combined the useful and the ornamental: as Franklin put it, the preferred studies were the *most* useful and the *most* decorative. "Write with the learned, pronounce with the vulgar," advised Poor Richard. From the middle class came the demand for extending educational opportunities among the people, and because the lower class followed the lead of the middle class, popular education in the colonies aimed to prepare the individual for a useful, gainful life and to confer upon him some of the cultural advantages previously associated with the upper class.

The most distinctive feature of American educational history is the growth of the system of public schools. To New England goes much of the credit for this evolution—a fact explained by many circumstances. The New England colonies, products of an intellectual movement in England, were founded in order to preserve a cultural ideal. Accordingly the Puritan leaders imposed religious unity and erected compact settlements in order to achieve coöperation and cultural solidarity. Since education was permeated with the religious spirit, the New Englanders (except in Rhode Island) could act together in education as a single public body and bring to bear upon the school the concentrated resources of the community.[31] In the middle colonies, religious differences made it impossible for the people to develop one system of public education; religious diversity bred educational diversity. In the southern colonies, the strong economic impetus to emigration resulted in a similar religious diversity; and, moreover, settlements were so dispersed that the localities lacked the concentration of people and resources necessary for the effective support of schools. The advantage of New England's unity becomes apparent when the religious aspect of early education is considered.

[31] Thomas G. Wright, *Literary Culture in Early New England* (New Haven, 1920), is a group of incisive, penetrating essays (for the advanced student).

When the colonies were established there were few state-supported public schools in Europe; most instruction, directly or indirectly, was under the influence of the various churches. Accordingly, the first schools erected in America were established and supported by religious groups. Elementary schools taught reading, writing, church doctrine, and rules of conduct; ministers often served as teachers; and the subject matter of instruction was drawn largely from the Bible. Early textbooks, like the hornbook and *The New England Primer*, abound with religious allusions.

> Young Obadias
> David, Josias
> All were pious.

A colony like Massachusetts or Connecticut, where the people adhered to one creed, could develop a unified public, state-supported religion, whereas other colonies that contained many sects could not act together through the state. In Pennsylvania and New Jersey the Quaker objection to the union of church and state imposed a special obstacle to religious instruction through public (political) agencies.

One other factor influenced education in New England.[32] In most towns the class distinctions were not so marked as to induce the upper-class groups to provide separate schools for their children. In the South, however, with its sharply drawn class lines, the wealthy planters did not want their children to associate with the poor; hence all the youth could not readily be brought together in a single school. Virginia acted upon the assumption that education was a private, not a public, responsibility. The wealthy planters who had to pay for the schooling of their sons in private schools did not care to support public schools for the poor, and since servants, workers, poor farmers, and slaves did not control the colonial governments, they could not provide a system of public schools for themselves.

Between 1635 and 1645 the principal towns of New England, excepting in mainland Rhode Island, made provision for the public support of a local schoolmaster. Massachusetts, caught in an economic depression in 1642, endeavored to foster home industry by requiring that parents and masters teach their children and apprentices to read and to master a trade; if a parent failed, the child might be apprenticed to a master who would give the proper instruction. Then in 1647 Massachu-

[32] S. E. Morison's *The Puritan Pronaos* (New York, 1936) embodies the latest researches into the intellectual life of seventeenth-century New England. Especially recommended.

setts ordered that each town of fifty families provide a schoolmaster to teach the children to read and write. This extremely important act permitted the town to pay the schoolmaster through either a tax levy or tuition fees collected from the parents. Unfortunately, many of the poorer towns preferred to pay a fine of £5 rather than support a schoolmaster; hence the act did not have the colony-wide effect which its authors intended. The act was copied by Connecticut and in part by New Hampshire and Plymouth Colony. Rhode Island, as a colony, made no move to establish schools because public religious instruction seemed to savor of that coercion in matters of conscience to which Roger Williams and his followers objected.[33]

When the Dutch controlled New Netherland they established a group of public schools which by 1664 had been extended to nearly all the towns in the colony. But inasmuch as these schools were under the control of the Dutch Reformed Church, the English, while not forcing Anglican instruction upon the Dutch, did not care to entrust all elementary education to the Dutch Church, and consequently did not provide for the public support of schools after 1664. In Maryland an opposite set of factors thwarted the development of a public school system which English officials sought to build up after 1696. In this case failure was due largely to the effort to foster Anglican schools in a colony composed mainly of Catholics and dissenters. Pennsylvania, New Jersey, North Carolina, and Virginia did not establish many elementary public schools; in South Carolina an act of 1712 authorized optional grants for the support of teachers in the parishes.

Outside New England, the lack of public instruction compelled reliance upon private schools, of which there were two principal types —those maintained by religious bodies and those supported by well-to-do families. By 1800 the Quakers had established between sixty or seventy schools; in New York the Society for Propagating the Gospel gave Anglican instruction, especially to the poor. Other sects active in supporting schools were the Dutch Reformed Church and the Presbyterian Church. In the plantation area the planters joined together to hire a schoolmaster and to provide a schoolhouse. Some southern schools received endowments from philanthropic men which provided a little free schooling for poor children. In the religious schools the poor were given free instruction; only parents who could afford to pay were charged tuition fees. Outside rural New England

[33] See again M. W. Jernegan's definitive studies of early education in *Laboring and Dependent Classes in Colonial America*, pp. 59-171.

free education lost caste by virtue of its identification with poverty. Most private schools in the plantation South, when conducted by the local minister, inculcated the beliefs of the Anglican Church.[34]

In considering the meager facilities of colonial schools it should be remembered that the home, the farm, and the shop had a high educational value. There the child learned how to avoid injury, how to do the practical things that sustain life, how to get along with associates; from his elders he learned a thousand lessons taught by the experience of the race. In the elementary schools there was no marked class influence on the subjects taught; nor did the American environment alter the course of instruction. Reading, writing, arithmetic, and rules of conduct were the foundations of all education, both vocational and cultural, serviceable alike in America and in Europe, to rich and poor, to children destined to be farmers, artisans, or gentlemen of leisure. The most important trend in elementary education appeared in New England after 1690—the result of demands that facilities be extended so as to serve all the people. As the settled areas of the towns increased, families remote from the local school petitioned that the town be divided into districts and that their tax money be used to support a new school near at hand. The creation of such district schools kept education close to the people, although the instruction was often of poor quality and the school term only a month.

In the field of secondary education, American experience led to a sharp break with the past.[35] At the start the colonists attempted to duplicate the Latin grammar schools of England, which provided a thorough training in Latin for young gentlemen and students for the ministry. In 1647 Massachusetts enacted that each town of a hundred families maintain such a grammar school. However, the Latin curriculum proved unsuited to the needs of the colonists; and not every town cared to support a school for a few prospective ministers. Accordingly, the Latin grammar school was supplanted after 1750 by the academy—a private school which retained Latin and Greek as the backbone of the curriculum but also emphasized English composition and literature, mathematics, modern languages, and philosophy (including natural science). The academy, well suited to American needs, took root in all the colonies. It retained the instruction necessary for clergymen; it emphasized the disciplinary and decorative studies

---

[34] Two outstanding texts are Ellwood P. Cubberley, *Public Education in the United States* (Boston, 1934), and Edwin G. Dexter, *A History of Education in the United States* (New York, 1922).

[35] Elmer E. Brown, *The Making of Our Middle Schools* (New York, 1921), is the standard work.

suitable to young gentlemen; and it imparted some knowledge useful in business and the professions.[36]

As the number of wealthy families increased after 1700 a host of private schools appeared, established by enterprising schoolmasters who offered polite instruction to ladies and gentlemen, either in small refined classes or in the home. Such schools taught higher mathematics, geography, Latin, Greek, letter-writing, French, philosophy, and civil government, while special studies of practical value included mechanics, optics, drawing, gauging, astronomy, navigation, fortification, and gunnery. Shorthand was recommended to gentlemen for "dispatch in what they would write for their own memory, and [for] concealing what they would not have lie open to every eye." Fencing and swordsmanship were presented as honorable attainments of young gentlemen, while the youth of both sexes were urged to achieve refinement through dancing (minuets and cotillions), instrumental music (the flute, violin, spinet, and harpsichord), psalmody, French (increasingly popular after 1763), and horsemanship ("an art justly admired and courted as a part of polite education"). We learn that one object of education was to enable youth to enter "the stage of life with advantage and to make an amiable figure in the world." One music master taught by the methods of "the organist of his majesty's chapel," and shorthand was reputable because "many of the nobility, gentry, ministry, etc. [of England] have taken pains to learn it." There were also private schools giving instruction in reading, writing, and arithmetic to children of the well-to-do, thus exempting them from attending the public schools. Another type of private school, designed for aspiring tradesmen, taught the three R's, spelling, and merchants' accounts.[37]

Excepting a little public or private assistance given to poor candidates for the ministry, the colonial college served the youth of the upper and upper middle classes. This explains in part why higher instruction resisted change more effectively than the utilitarian branches of education. One mark of such conservatism was the continued dominance of the religious influence on the curriculum. Of the nine colleges established in colonial times, three were founded by the Congregationalists: Harvard (1636), Yale (1701), and Dartmouth (1769); two by the Anglicans: William and Mary (1693) and King's College, now Columbia (1754); one by the Presbyterians—the Col-

[36] C. K. Shipton, "Secondary Education in the Puritan Colonies," *New England Quarterly*, VII (Dec. 1934).

[37] For other books on education see J. T. Adams, *Provincial Society*, pp. 341–342.

lege of New Jersey, now Princeton (1747); one by the Dutch Reformed Church—Queen's College, now Rutgers (1766); and one by the Baptists—Rhode Island College, now Brown (1764). The only institution not under sectarian auspices was the "Academy," established at Philadelphia in 1749.

Higher education is best illustrated by the history of Harvard, the most important of the colonial colleges. Its purpose was to train ministers, to educate young gentlemen, to sustain the Puritan faith and to preserve learning, good manners, and Christian morality in the wilderness. To this end students and teachers lived in the same building, under a fixed discipline, studying, dining, and worshipping together. All the decencies and comforts of life which the times afforded were deemed necessary for the gentleman scholars.[38]

The college students received preparatory training from the Latin grammar schools or through private instruction from ministers. The main entrance requirement was the ability to speak, write, and translate Latin, since the college textbooks were written and classroom instruction given in that tongue. The early curriculum consisted of logic, rhetoric, Greek, Hebrew, ethics, and metaphysics. After his freshman year the student became a sophomore, one who was doing his "sophomes" or exercises in logical disputation. Then he became a junior sophister (one sufficiently adept in logic to take part in public disputations); then a senior sophister. Each tutor taught all subjects; there were no "courses," credits, or written examinations; promotion came upon the tutor's certification of the capacity and application of the student. At the end of the four-year term the seniors had to take open examinations ("sitting solstices"), when they might be examined in every subject of the curriculum "by all comers." At commencement (which centered in the conferring of the B.A. degree) the great men of the colony assembled early in July to listen to orations, to hear the students debate propositions printed on a thesis sheet, and to partake of a great feast. To Cambridge thronged a multitude of country folk, pleasure seekers, sharpers, and riffraff who gave to the occasion something of the character of a modern football game, Fourth-of-July celebration, and county fair.

The student for the ministry commonly remained in residence three years after commencement, reading in theology and philosophy "on his own," whereupon he received the M.A. degree and assumed a place of great prestige in his community. Undergraduates were sub-

[38] S. E. Morison's *Harvard College in the Seventeenth Century* (2 vols., Cambridge, 1936) is the definitive work. For a delightful summary of Professor Morison's researches see chapters 1–6 of his *Three Centuries of Harvard* (Cambridge, 1937).

ject to a strict routine of study, prayers, lectures, and recitations which, together with four meal hours and two periods for relaxation, occupied the day from five in the morning till nine at night. Freshmen lived in abject subjection to all superiors, both upper students and faculty. The natural exuberance of youth often broke out in nocturnal excursions and practical jokes, which were generally tolerated on the theory that "a wild colt often makes a good horse." The flogging of culprits, practiced before 1700, gave way to ear-boxing; that in turn passed out about 1765. Since all students were ranked and given privileges according to the social position of their families, an effective punishment was to lower an offender's college status. In 1772 the college adopted an alphabetical classification; social ratings were then causing too much jealousy and envy among the elite of the province.

Despite the innate conservatism of higher education, it too responded to the trend away from theology toward secular interests.[39] In the late 1690's Harvard's hospitality toward general literature and philosophy as against Puritan dogma moved many strict Puritans to support a new, orthodox college in Connecticut, founded by Harvard graduates in 1701 and named in 1718 at the suggestion of Cotton Mather, leader of the Puritan old guard, in honor of Elihu Yale, a rich merchant benefactor. In the eighteenth century the college curriculum placed increasing emphasis upon mathematics, science, literature, and French. A similar non-sectarian influence appeared in the founding of the Medical College of Philadelphia (1765), soon followed by the establishment of a medical department at King's College in 1767. Benjamin Franklin in 1749 published a plan for higher education, proposing a non-sectarian institution devoted to useful and ornamental studies, of which he deemed the most essential to be English, mathematics, astronomy, geography, history, politics, logic, and morality; the languages, ancient and modern, should be required only when needed in professional training. The general student might choose languages as electives, but not to the neglect of "English, arithmetic, and the other studies absolutely necessary." Franklin's ideas bore some fruit when the Philadelphia Academy was chartered in 1754 as a non-sectarian institution, although the prestige of Latin won it a larger place than Franklin had intended.[40] The launching of the College of Rhode Island (Brown) further weakened the theologi-

[39] J. J. Walsh, "Scholasticism in the Colonial Colleges," *New England Quarterly*, V (July 1932).
[40] Thomas Woody (ed.), *Educational Views of Benjamin Franklin* (New York, 1931).

cal influence in education. Although a Baptist school, its charter granted equal opportunities to the youth of all denominations, guaranteed liberty of conscience, permitted the recruiting of teachers and officers (except the president) from all Protestant elements, banned sectarianism from the general curriculum, and decreed that "the public teaching shall in general respect the sciences."

## THE NATURAL WORLD

The colonial period registered notable progress in scientific inquiry. The early settlers came steeped in fears and superstitions drawn from the ancient stock of mythology and folklore. Primitive man had interpreted the natural world in terms of his own welfare: whatever inflicted injury, pain, or illness he deemed evil; whatever induced health, contentment, strength, and prosperity he deemed good. The Christian concept of a single, just God raised the problem of evil; how could the manifold torments and misfortunes that afflicted mankind be reconciled with a God who was both good and all-powerful? The most popular solution of this problem was the conception of Satan—the master evil spirit who had led a host of angels in a revolt against God's rule in heaven, had been hurled with his cohorts into hell, and had thereafter devoted himself to wreaking vengeance upon God by corrupting His creature, man. Another idea affirmed that God kept evil spirits in chains, occasionally lengthening the chain so that the evil ones might torment those deserving divine punishment. Thus there were evil spirits to torment the wicked, and emissaries of Satan who sought to injure the chosen of God.[41]

The concrete evidences of the activity of evil spirits included accidents that befell man, misfortunes, human suffering, and aberrations of nature. To Cotton Mather thunderbolts that struck churches seemed necessarily the work of Satan; superstitious mariners readily attributed stormy weather to evil spirits. Unfortunately, the manifestations of evil extended beyond natural occurrences that all could witness; apparitions, dreams, and delusions of deranged minds were believed to reveal authentic evidences of the powers of darkness—a fact which gave a wider scope to Satan's genius than would have been the case had all his "actions" been subject to tests applied by sane observers. The Devil also operated by taking possession of people (witches), through whom he inflicted torments upon those faithful to the Lord.

Between 1647 and 1662 fourteen people were hanged as witches in

[41] See again Edward Eggleston, *The Transit of Civilization.*

Connecticut and Massachusetts. Then the interest abated until about 1681, when the ministers of Massachusetts revived it. The colony had suffered many afflictions and people were drifting away from the old faith; clearly Satan was at work in the land. In 1684 Increase Mather published *An Essay for the Recording of Illustrious Providences*, wherein he recited various instances of witchcraft—a work prepared at the suggestion of the Puritan divines. Cotton Mather further stimulated interest by studying a "bewitched" child at Boston and by charging in a book, *Memorable Providences* (1689), that the denial of witchcraft was "a dangerous stroke" to "settle men in atheism." Obviously, the belief in evil spirits exalted the power of the ministers, since the people must rely upon the church to protect them against Satan. In March 1691 began the witchcraft delusion at Salem, instigated by some young girls who probably had been unstrung by weird stories they had heard from West Indian slaves. The girls, giving signs of mental derangement, accused neighbors right and left of bewitching them. A wave of hysteria engulfed the village; when it subsided in 1692 twenty persons had been hanged for witchcraft and fifty-five others had confessed their "guilt." Eventually the hysterical accusers (who had at first named as witches only old, poor, unattractive women) began to implicate important people, whereupon the governor and the special trial court of seven judges stopped proceedings, emptied the jails and pardoned those who had confessed. The belief in witchcraft prevailed in the other colonies, but only in New England did executions occur—a fact which suggests the exceptional influence of the Puritan clergy.[42]

Witchcraft was only one superstition entertained by the colonists. Among prevalent notions were the ideas that the earth was the center of the universe, that different stars exerted influence over particular persons, plants, and animals, that comets were signs of impending calamity, that earthquakes were caused by winds imprisoned within the earth, that insects were generated by decaying matter, and that migratory birds wintered on the moon or in the bottoms of rivers. Hogs should be slaughtered during the waxing of the moon or they would shrink and be poor; brushwood should be cut during the waning of the moon so that it would not grow again. "The moon in the wane, gather fruit for to last." Snakes hypnotized animals; water could be detected by moving a forked willow branch over the earth (if water were present, the stick would bend downward). Unlucky days, signs, and charms had a great vogue. A bird's entering a room,

[42] George L. Kittredge's erudite *Witchcraft in Old and New England* (Cambridge, 1929) places the Salem episode in its general historical setting.

a dog's barking all night were portents of approaching death; a cock's crowing at ten o'clock at night foretold a morning rain; horse-shoes and brooms placed at doors would keep out witches.

The study of science did not dispel all such popular notions, but during colonial times the groundwork was prepared for the rapid progress to come. When the colonies were founded most scientific inquiry was motivated by religious objectives—to understand God's mysteries and to demonstrate the reality of the world of spirits. The method employed was medieval scholasticism—the process of thought that applies evidence and inductive logic to religious principles, with the purpose of coming at new conclusions consistent with Scriptural premises. Increase and Cotton Mather collected accounts of natural curiosities and monstrosities in order to reinforce their views of Satan's influence and of God's providence.

At the close of the colonial period science was freeing itself from the restrictions of religion. American conditions favored a science that was practical—that would serve the profit motive in industry, ship-ping, and agriculture; hence the emphasis placed upon plant study, astronomy, surveying, mapmaking, mathematics, chemistry, physics, and medicine. In a sense the process of settlement was a continuation of the great achievements of geographical discovery: new observations of nature, new adjustments to the hard material facts of life had to be made on an ever-extending scale. Hence the American experience proved especially receptive to the inductive, experimental study of nature developed by Copernicus, Galileo, Bacon, Newton, Kepler, and Boyle. By testing and measuring with instruments of precision one drew conclusions from the evidences of the senses, not from past revelations of God to man, and such conclusions might or might not harmonize with prevailing religious conceptions.[43]

The line between revealed religion and experimental science cannot be drawn too sharply, however, because some ministers conducted experiments, used the observational method, kept accurate records of findings, exploded superstitions, and accepted new ideas. Increase and Cotton Mather championed inoculation for smallpox when colonial doctors opposed the innovation.[44]

The leading man of science in the seventeenth century was Governor John Winthrop, Jr., of Connecticut (1606–1676). Convinced that manufactured goods were the basis of a mature civilization and

[43] Holland Thompson, *The Age of Invention* (*Chronicles of America*, New Haven, 1921), chapter 1.
[44] Henry R. Viets, *A Brief History of Medicine in Massachusetts* (Boston, 1930), is admirable.

acutely aware of New England's difficulty of buying them from England, Winthrop concluded that New England's salvation lay in the development of home industries and mining. His interest in chemistry, astronomy, and mining were largely those of an industrial promoter. As an astronomer he predicted the discovery of a fifth satellite to Jupiter, although unable to prove his theory due to inadequate instruments. The foremost colonial botanist, John Bartram, a Quaker farmer of Pennsylvania (1699–1777), was drawn to plant study by his love of nature. Not content merely to classify plants, he established a botanic garden near Philadelphia, where he conducted experiments in hybridization and grew many exotic plants sent by friends in Europe. His religious ideas were probably responsible for his expulsion from the Quaker society into which he was born. He traveled the frontiers extensively in search of new seeds, bulbs, and roots for his garden. As a lover of nature he worked chiefly alone, for he found that most Americans had little interest in pure science and that they were prone to exploit rather than to worship nature. Among other contributions he explained the formation of limestones and marbles along lines which geologists now accept.

The first creative scientist in academic circles was John Winthrop, professor of mathematics and natural philosophy at Harvard between 1738 and 1779. As the son of a Boston merchant, Professor Winthrop was in touch with that element among the colonial capitalists which was turning from Puritan dogma to science, and his appointment was viewed with misgivings by the theologians. He established the first laboratory of experimental physics in an American college, using the best available scientific apparatus to demonstrate the laws of heat, light, and mechanics, and in 1751 he introduced the study of calculus at Harvard. He made observations of sunspots, studied electricity, and proved that earthquakes are the result of natural forces, not of divine anger. In 1761 he led an official expedition to Newfoundland to observe the transit of Venus over the sun. His scientific contributions were printed in the *Transactions of the Royal Society*—the main channel of publication for the papers of colonial scientists.[45]

An outstanding thinker like Benjamin Franklin was also a symbol of a broad movement in which a host of lesser figures were taking part. Franklin's early life as a printer—his practice of applying handwork to ideas—explains in large measure the practical cast of his thought. No activity satisfied him so much as scientific inquiry—a mistress who did not have to be flattered and cajoled as did the human

---

[45] T. Hornberger, *Science and the New World* (San Marino, Calif., 1937), is an excellent brief résumé.

beings through whom he sought to accomplish his useful aims. His experiments that proved the identity of lightning and electricity established his international renown as a scientist. The invention of the Franklin stove (which sent the heat into the room instead of up the chimney), of the lightning rod, and of a clock having only three wheels and two pinions, all testify to the practical nature of his work and to the simplicity and economy of his devices. One of his most interesting studies demonstrated that northeast storms on the Atlantic move against the wind. In keeping with his honesty, clarity of thought, and desire to serve his fellow men he dispelled obscurity and mystery from the subjects of which he wrote.[46]

When the colonial period ended the practice of medicine had made but slight progress. The first colonists commonly regarded disease as the work of supernatural agencies. Plagues and severe distempers were caused by evil spirits; common ailments and disturbances were God's means of punishing or purifying the soul. Many people therefore resorted to the ministrations of the clergy as an antidote to illness and pain. Home remedies, the chief reliance of the household, were efficacious largely because, by lessening the patient's fears, they aided natural processes of recuperation. John Winthrop, Jr., advised this cure for ague: "Pare the patient's nails when the fever is coming on; and put the parings into a little bag of fine linen . . . ; and tie that about a live eel's neck, in a tub of water. The eel will die and the patient will recover." Particularly defective were the care given women at childbirth and the treatment of children's diseases; hence the high death rate among young women and infants. Once a person had survived childhood illnesses and had reached the age of twenty he had become so hardened that he could look forward to a ripe old age.[47]

Many doctors came to the colonies in the seventeenth century, some trained in medical centers of Europe and Britain. The physicians of the second generation were educated in the colonies as apprentices or students of individual practitioners—a training inferior to that of Europe—with the result that medical competence declined noticeably after 1670. The failure of the colonies to impose standards and supervision upon the profession opened the door to a variety of quacks, who flourished by virtue of the dread of pain which makes the ignorant so susceptible to easy cures. Even the most competent physicians had

[46] See the sketches of early scientists in the *Dictionary of American Biography*, particularly Carl Becker's essay on Franklin.

[47] E. Eggleston, "Some Curious Colonial Remedies," *American Historical Review*, V (Jan. 1900).

little to offer: bleeding was the sovereign remedy, even though the patient might actually need a blood transfusion. Many doctors believed in witchcraft, explaining their failures by the intervention of evil spirits. After 1700 medical students from the colonies sought education in Paris, London, and Edinburgh, thereby raising the level of technical competence, and in the 1760's two medical schools were founded in Philadelphia and New York. Although the colonists showed a common-sense appreciation of the effects of unhealthful sites and of contact with diseased persons, they had no knowledge of bacteria, antiseptics, or most antitoxins. Internal surgery had to wait upon anesthetics, not discovered until after colonial times. The state of colonial medicine is illustrated by the views of Dr. Benjamin Rush (1745–1813), professor at the Philadelphia Medical College, and probably the foremost physician of his day. Believing that all diseases arose from the excessive excitability of the blood vessels, he advocated bleeding as the universal cure. Although he freed himself from denominationalism, his early religious background often cropped out in his use of theological arguments to support his medical theories.[48] Since the Bible affirmed that man was made in the image of God, many pious people believed that to experiment on the human body or to modify natural processes was darkly iniquitous.

## THE COMMUNICATION OF IDEAS

In the seventeenth century the ground was being prepared for the growth of an American culture through the adaptation of the English cultural heritage to the frontier environment. However, most colonists then lived in comparative isolation, and it was not until after 1700 that new facilities of communication sprang up to foster and give expression to a slowly emerging culture.[49] In the process of Americanization the colonial towns played the decisive role of radiating centers of trade and thought. The merchants of each town strove to improve their land and sea transportation facilities in order to dominate as wide a market as possible. This urge led to the building and improving of roads, over which flowed an increasing stream of traffic.

Prior to 1700 most travelers journeyed by sea. Roads were little

[48] Nathan G. Goodman, *Benjamin Rush* . . . (Philadelphia, 1934) gives in full the story of a varied public career. James T. Flexner, *Doctors on Horseback* (New York, 1937), though dealing mostly with the postcolonial period, describes earlier conditions.

[49] An admirable introduction to this theme is Michael Kraus, *Intercolonial Aspects of Culture on the Eve of the Revolution* (New York, 1928).

more than paths marked on trees through the forest, compelling the overland traveler to go by horseback or on foot. In 1704 Madam Knight took five days to reach New Haven from Boston, travel at night being exceedingly difficult.. However, by 1770 roads had assumed a more modern aspect. A main highway, in fairly good condition—particularly in summer—ran from Boston via Providence, New York, Philadelphia, and Jamestown to Charleston, while first-class roads extended thirty or forty miles inland from the principal port towns. At mid-century the first traveler's guidebook had been published (1732); milestones marked the main roads; and rivers were being crossed by ferries, toll bridges, and an occasional free or public bridge. In 1754 a certain James Wells opened a regular semi-weekly stage and boat line between New York and Philadelphia (extended to Annapolis in 1757); a second line between New York and Philadelphia began to operate in 1760; a third advertised a four-day journey from New York to Boston in 1775. Over the improved dirt roads freight wagons passed to and fro; wealthy folk were jostled onward in their private carriages; the common people rode horseback; the poorest straggled along on foot.[50]

Along the highways life came to a rude but lusty focus at the welcome inns. There the weary traveler found shelter for himself and his horse; there his travel-sharpened appetite made endurable the coarse food and strong drink; there on cold days he warmed himself before the open fire. There, too, he might find fellow travelers with news of distant parts or native inhabitants to regale him with the lore of the district. High and low mingled together with a democratic, inquisitive familiarity. The guests often slept four in a room, men and women together, chance companions of the road. In the South the scarcity of inns obliged the traveler to seek the freely given hospitality of private homes. Coffeehouses, fashioned on the London model, appeared about 1700 in the larger port towns, to become centers of news, business dealings, and good fellowship. At the ordinary tavern one might meet many an eccentric fellow, drawn thither by the lure of the bottle, by lively arguments over politics and religion, and by the opportunities for gambling afforded by the bowling alley and the billiard table.[51]

One figure who paused at the country inn—the post rider—played an important if humble part in binding the colonies together. In the

[50] A History of Travel in America, by Seymour Dunbar (4 vols., Indianapolis, c. 1915), is a useful, interesting, well-illustrated compilation. See Vol. I, chapters 1–9.
[51] Alice M. Earle, Stage Coach and Tavern Days (New York, 1900); Edward Field, The Colonial Tavern (Providence, 1897); Elsie Lathrop, Early American Inns and Taverns (New York, 1926).

early days letters were carried by travelers or entrusted to sea captains; official papers were sent by special messengers or borne from
town to town by local officials. Legally, the regulation of mails was a
function of the colonial governments, which gradually established
colony-wide postal services—Massachusetts in 1677, Pennsylvania in
1683. The assemblies fixed the postal rates and designated the places
(taverns as a rule) where letters should be posted and delivered. In
1691, when the English government desired a greater wartime efficiency of communication with the colonies, William III granted to
Thomas Neale a twenty-year monopoly of the postal business in
Massachusetts, Pennsylvania, and New York. Neale chose Andrew
Hamilton as his deputy—an efficient lawyer who organized a regular
service between Portsmouth, New Hampshire, and Philadelphia,
even though postal rates were still fixed by the individual colonies.
Neale, finding his monopoly unprofitable, surrendered it in 1707,
whereupon Parliament in 1710 ordered that the postal service be
placed under the English post office. Not until 1732 did Virginia
come into the general American system.[52]

The imperial postal administration was notable for Franklin's term
as deputy-postmaster (1753–75), when he instigated three important
reforms. He strove to increase the speed, aiming to cut the Boston to
Philadelphia run from three weeks to six days, introducing shorter
routes, road markings, and day and night riding. He advocated lower
postal rates, and when he secured reductions in 1765 the volume of
business and postal revenues increased as he had anticipated. He also
urged that regular charges be assessed against newspapers in the
mails. Previously, publishers had paid the riders a bonus; and moreover, since publishers were often postmasters they were able to exclude the papers of their rivals from the mails. Franklin's objections
to such irregularities bore fruit in 1758 when the British government
ordered that all newspapers be admitted to the mails at prescribed
rates. At the onset of the Revolution the patriots immediately seized
control of the postal service, so essential had it become to American
unity.[53]

The principal agency for the expression of an American point of
view was the provincial press. As early as 1638 a printing press was
brought to Cambridge, Massachusetts, there to be operated in connection with Harvard College, feeding New England with Puritan

[52] William Smith, *The History of the Post Office in British North America, 1639–
1870* (Cambridge, 1920), devotes chapters 1–4 to the thirteen colonies. See also
W. Smith, "The Colonial Post Office," *American Historical Review,* XXI (Jan. 1916).
[53] Wesley E. Rich, *The History of the United States Post Office to the Year 1829*
(Cambridge, 1924), contains three precise, complete chapters on the colonial service.

tracts, catechisms, sermons, statutes, broadsides, poems, and copies of English books. By 1715 eight presses existed in the colonies: six in New England, one in New York, and one in Philadelphia. Boston's priority as a publishing center explains the appearance there in 1704 of the first American newspaper, *The Boston News-Letter*. Between 1713 and 1745 twenty-two new papers were launched, seven in New England, ten in Pennsylvania (including three published in German), and five in the South. Excepting Delaware and New Jersey, every colony had at least one newspaper by 1765.

*The Boston News-Letter*, a weekly, appeared as a "tiny four-page, two-column folder," offering a meager fare of local items (such as shipping notices) and of European news. In 1719 Andrew Bradford printed at Philadelphia *The American Weekly Mercury*—soon to be followed at Boston by James Franklin's *New England Courant* (1721), now noted for its publication of the youthful Benjamin Franklin's attacks on Puritan orthodoxy shortly before he migrated to Philadelphia, where in 1729 he bought *The Pennsylvania Gazette*. At this time editors were hearing the call of culture; poems, essays, and reprints of English articles now kept company in the papers with news items, local and foreign. Advertisements, informative if often flowery, revealed that advertisers had not yet learned how to capitalize fear, sex, and snobbishness. After 1750 the press devoted more and more space to politics and to sensational happenings such as crimes and accidents; letters from eminent men, signed with classical *noms de plume*, presented their thoughts on the issues of the day; in 1754 appeared the first American cartoon—Franklin's picture of a snake (symbol of the colonies) divided into eight parts, with the caption, "Unite or Die." In the South, papers like *The Virginia Gazette* and *The South Carolina Gazette* (in the latter Franklin had an interest) equaled the northern papers in range and quality.[54]

Although these early papers had each but a small subscription list, they were handed about from reader to reader until worn out, and moreover they were exchanged freely among the various editors, so that an outstanding article was likely to be reprinted throughout the colonies. Native writers now found a vent for their thoughts—a condition indispensable to the growth of American culture. Without the provincial press one can scarcely envisage the unified action of the

[54] Brief surveys of the colonial press appear in Willard G. Bleyer, *Main Currents in the History of American Journalism* (Boston, c. 1927), chapters 1–3; James M. Lee, *History of American Journalism* (Boston, 1917), chapters 1–6; and George H. Payne, *History of Journalism in the United States* (New York, 1920), chapters 1–8.

Revolutionary era—that upsurge of American sentiment which bore out the early fears of Governor Berkeley that learning fostered "disobedience and heresy" and that printing divulged "libels against the government."

Before the colonial press could play its part in the Revolution it had to be freed from the shackles of British control. Where there were vested interests menaced by new ideas, the privileged classes strove to silence the dissenting voice. Thus, in the early eighteenth century, royal governors and clergymen of influence (especially in Massachusetts) kept a tight rein on journalistic utterance, by direct or indirect means.[55] In 1733 Peter Zenger, a German printer at New York, published in *The New York Weekly Journal* a series of articles written by Lewis Morris (formerly chief justice of the province) which attacked the royal governor, William Cosby. When Zenger was arrested on the charge of false and scandalous libel, the Morris faction employed as his counsel the eighty-year-old Nestor of the American bar, Andrew Hamilton of Philadelphia. In a masterly plea Hamilton proved that the statements printed by Zenger were true and persuaded the jury to find him innocent. Previously juries had decided only whether the accused had published the statements complained of, whereupon the judges decided whether they were libelous or not. Hamilton's success in inducing the jury to decide that the articles were not libelous went far to deprive the judges (Cosby's friends, in this case) of that all-important power and thus set an important precedent for the freedom of the press. Channing states that by reason of the Zenger victory the American newspapers "kept alive and directed the forces of liberty and finally brought about the inevitable separation from the mother country sooner than it would otherwise have occurred."

Newspapers reached readers of all classes; the almanac was addressed primarily to the farmer. *Poor Richard's* was but the leader of a numerous company. After 1750 the almanac became a small magazine which kept the enterprising farmer informed about scientific discoveries (particularly in agriculture and astronomy), told him the year's tale of the moon, stars, and seasons, instructed him through maps, bits of worldly wisdom, and notices of important events, entertained him with jokes and stories, and enriched his culture with portraits, poems, and essays. Circulating by the thousands, read and reread from cover to cover, the almanacs expressed the practical,

[55] Clyde A. Duniway, *The Development of Freedom of the Press in Massachusetts* (New York, 1906), is a pioneer study in censorship.

homespun quality of life on the farm and the rural zest for self-improvement.[56]

In the path of the newspaper and the almanac followed the literary magazine. In 1741 Franklin launched *The General Magazine,* the first or second to be published, significant because it was addressed to "all the British plantations in North America" and because it reprinted American articles and reviewed American publications (the birth of book reviewing in the colonies). In his prospectus Franklin promised to print important political documents, news briefs, "select pieces of poetry," and "essays, controversial, humorous, philosophical, religious, moral or political." With the object of printing things of enduring value, in order—as Washington later put it—"to preserve the liberty, stimulate the industry and meliorate the morals of an enlightened and free people," the numerous magazines which appeared after 1741 (usually published by a printer-editor and priced at about a shilling a copy) were addressed to the elite and supported by only five hundred to fifteen hundred subscribers. This fact explains why most such magazines expired after a year or two, although *The Massachusetts Magazine* and *The New York Magazine* each lasted eight years. Discussions of economic issues (especially the currency) and of education, religion, temperance, prison reform, and slavery animated many an essay written in the strain of the Addison-Steele *Spectator Papers,* while uncertain native bards contributed verses in the manner of Milton, Pope, or Dryden.[57]

The scarcity of books in colonial times gave unusual importance to libraries, private, semi-public, and public. In the South the Society for Propagating the Gospel did useful work in providing parochial libraries, Thomas Bray managing to establish one in nearly every parish in Maryland after he became commissary in 1696. South Carolina founded a general library in 1700, requiring by law that it be open to the public. In 1731 Franklin induced some of his tradesman and artisan friends to pool their slender resources and to buy books for their common use—a practice soon copied by other communities. The largest private collections, like those of Cotton Mather and William Byrd II, contained as many as four thousand volumes. Each college steadily added to its store of treasures; well-to-do students built up personal libraries; and privately owned books circulated almost as freely as the gossip of the neighborhood. To such institutions as the

[56] G. L. Kittredge, *The Old Farmer and His Almanac* (Boston, 1904), is interesting reading.

[57] The best general introduction is F. L. Mott, *A History of American Magazines, 1741–1850* (New York, 1930); the most detailed analysis is Lyon N. Richardson, *A History of Early American Magazines, 1741–1789* (New York, 1931).

Newport, New York, and Charleston libraries (all active after 1754) Franklin attributed in part that "enlightened sentiment" so essential to the defense of American liberties.

Indicative of the forces of unity was the genesis of the first important intercolonial society of learned men. As early as 1727 Franklin had taken part in organizing the Junto Club at Philadelphia—a society of young artisans who composed, read, and discussed papers on philosophical and practical themes—and so successfully that Franklin called the club "the best school of philosophy, morality and politics that then existed in the province." With the model of European learned societies before him, Franklin and other "virtuosi or ingenious men residing in the several colonies" organized in 1744 an American academy, which in 1769 was reorganized as the American Philosophical Society. Although destined for a later career of distinction, the Society was significant before 1775, not because of its scientific accomplishments, but as a symbol of the increasing integration of American life.

Meanwhile the common people were slowly fashioning an American language. "Colleges and books," says Emerson, "only copy the language which the field and work-yard make." First of all the Indians enlarged the common speech. One might visit the *wigwam*, there to see the *medicine man*, the *sachem*, the *squaw*, and the *papoose*, to smoke the *pipe of peace*, with the *tomahawk* lying idle, to trade *wampum* and *firewater* for the skins of *raccoon*, *moose*, and *opossum*, and to eat *squash*, *hominy*, *hickory* nuts, *pawpaws*, and *succotash*. The *paleface* might attend a *powwow* just before the *big chief*, covered with *war paint*, took to the *warpath*. Or perhaps in *Indian summer* one might receive *moccasins* from an *Indian giver*. In the settlements of the Dutch the *Yankee* visitor might take a *sleigh* ride to the home of a *boss* or *patroon*, where one dared not *snoop*, and where one might eat *cookies* or *waffles* and hear tales of *spooks* or *Santa Claus*. The French *voyageurs* crossed *portages* and *prairies*, encountering *gophers* and *braves* that were not *bogus*, hiding their treasures in a *cache*, far away from a *bureau*.[58]

From the English vocabulary the colonists coined many Americanisms, either by forming new terms from familiar words or by giving an old word a new meaning. One might set out from a *back-street* or a *back-lane* in a town, round a *bluff* or *cliff*, traverse *barrens*, *bottoms*, and a *hollow*, ascend the *foothills*, pass through a *water gap*, cross a *watershed* and reach a *clearing* in the *back country*, surrounded by *underbrush* where a *log house* near a *salt lick* domiciled a *squatter* adept

---

[58] An important work of scholarship and literary charm is H. L. Mencken, *The American Language* (4th ed., New York, 1936). See chapters 1–3.

at *logrolling,* who had a *corncrib* and a *hog wallow* frequented by *razor-backs.* Inside the cabin one might be served *hoecake, sweet potatoes, eggplant, roasting ears, mush, apple butter, clingstone* peaches, *johnny-cake,* and *popcorn.* Outside one encountered the *garter snake,* the *bull-frog,* the *ground hog,* the *copperhead, bluegrass,* the *lightning bug,* the *June bug,* the *muskrat.* In summer the *back settler* feared the *prickly heat;* in winter he made a *beeline* from *bobsled* or *snowplow* to a fire of *pine knots* and *backlog.* The established settler might have a *frame house* covered with *shingles,* employ a *hired girl, advocate* or *oppose* a cause, *dicker* or *negotiate* with a *mossback, deed* his land at a *land office* or *camp meeting,* watch his wife make a *crazy quilt,* or see his son *shin up* a *pitch pine.* If a *hired man* should *fly off the handle* or *go on the warpath* and be unable *to whitewash* himself or *to face the music,* he might be told *not to darken one's door again* and be compelled *to take to the woods.*[59]

## THE REFINEMENT OF TASTE

In his *Conduct of Life* Emerson observes that genius creates manners and artistic forms, that the upper class adopts and utilizes them, and that the common people follow the example of the upper class. He also remarks that men of genius arise largely from the middle class. In the colonial period, when the American middle class produced few artistic geniuses, the American upper class looked to European genius and to English upper-class standards for guidance in the art of living. Consequently, with respect to manners and elegant pursuits, early American culture was derivative, imitative, provincial.[60]

Inasmuch as imaginative power and technical perfection are the secrets of great achievements in the arts, the lack of such genius in the colonies explains their cultural shortcomings. The activities of the educated colonists, centering in business, public affairs, and religion, assumed a practical or a theological cast. When the first cares of life are over, wrote Franklin, we shall begin to think of the embellishments. The colonies produced no masters of the most creative arts—no outstanding poets, dramatists, sculptors, or composers. In literature, practical concerns largely absorbed the energies of the most original minds: witness the excellent discussions of the public issues of the day. Historical writing (not the most original art form) appealed to many learned gentlemen and divines who became competent practitioners. The colonies had no native theater or virtuosi of the concert stage;

---

[59] Richard H. Thornton, *An American Glossary* (2 vols., Philadelphia, 1912), is the great pioneer collection of Americanisms.

[60] See again J. T. Adams, *Provincial Society,* chapters 3, 5, 6, 10–11.

their painters for the most part were copyists rather than creators; their architecture (excepting that of the farmhouse, designed for the new environment) followed English models; their higher craftsmen —furniture makers, glaziers, etc.,—drew inspiration from Europe; their fashions in dress and refined conduct came from over sea.

Colonial painters produced three principal types of pictures—portraits, landscapes, and historical scenes. The religious impulse in art was weak, due partly to the Calvinistic belief that things divine should be apprehended by the mind, not pictured to the senses. Since most patrons of art were upper-class families, the chief demand was for portraits that would preserve family traditions, celebrate the virtues of the subject portrayed, and clothe the artistocratic figure in graceful forms.[61]

All the leading colonial painters arose from the middle class—sons of artisans, preachers, shopkeepers. The first artists of note came to America from Europe: such were Gustavus Hesselius (1682–1755), who emigrated from Sweden to Delaware in 1711, and John Smibert of Edinburgh (1688–1751), who settled at Boston in 1730. Soon, however, American-born artists appeared, young artisans often self-taught, able to eke out a bare living with paintbrush if they traveled in search of patrons. In 1760 Benjamin West of Pennsylvania (1728–1820) arrived in Italy to initiate foreign study by aspiring American artists—an example followed by Charles W. Peale of Maryland (1741–1827) at London and by Gilbert Stuart of Rhode Island (1755–1828), also at London. Three Americans—Stuart, West, and John Singleton Copley of Boston (1738–1815)—remained long in London, where cultural atmosphere and artists' fees were more appealing than in America. West eventually became court painter to George III, executing many historical scenes in a stilted, classical style now out of date. Copley and Stuart achieved high distinction as portrait painters; the work of other colonial artists, though precise, faithful, and pleasing, was generally formal, conventional, and uninspired.[62]

The origins of the American theater appear in amateur performances given privately in the southern colonies. The first records of professional companies relate to Charleston (1703) and New York (1704). Early plays were presented in taverns, warehouses, and court-

---

[61] Samuel Isham, *The History of American Painting* (New York, 1936), is the standard authority. See chapters 1–2.

[62] Frank J. Mather *et al*, *The Spirit of American Art* (*Pageant of America*, XII, New Haven, 1927), chapter 1. See also William Dunlap's *The History of the Arts of Design in the United States* (1834), an important pioneer work, which has been corrected in a new edition by F. W. Bayley and C. E. Goodspeed (3 vols., Boston, 1918). See Vol. I.

rooms, but in the 1730's makeshift theaters were being erected, rude, unadorned, barnlike. In 1750 Mr. and Mrs. Lewis Hallam of London arrived in America with a competent English company—to remain for twenty years, playing not only at New York, Philadelphia, Annapolis, and Williamsburg, but also at such places as Hobb's Hole and Port Tobacco. Their career was notable for a season at New York (1753–54), when they gave twenty-one performances of standard English plays. In 1766 the first permanent theater, the Southwark, was built in Philadelphia; in 1767 the first play written by an American, Thomas Godfrey's *The Prince of Parthia*, was offered to the Philadelphia public. The early dramas were either ephemeral pieces which sounded loudly the note of love, or the classical English plays of Congreve, Steele, Addison, and Shakespeare (including *The Tempest*, *King Lear*, *Hamlet*, and *Romeo and Juliet*). After 1750 the colonial aristocrats frequented the theater quite regularly, its class character being indicated by a resolve of the Continental Congress in 1774 "to discourage . . . shows, plays and other expensive diversions." Although the Puritan conception of the theater as a "house of Satan" kept it out of colonial New England, the Quaker opposition to plays had subsided sufficiently to permit the Hallams to perform in Philadelphia in 1754.[63]

Concerts and noteworthy musicians were non-existent before 1715. Apparently the first recitals and concerts given in Boston, New York, and Charleston came in the 1730's: by 1750 they had become a regular feature of life in the larger towns. Thereafter interest was sustained by select organizations such as the Orpheus Club of Philadelphia (founded in 1759) and the celebrated St. Cecilia Society of Charleston, organized in 1762. Francis Hopkinson's "My Days Have Been So Wondrous Free," written in 1759, was probably the first musical composition of a native American. Since the colonists had not attained individual excellence in music, the soloist was overshadowed by group performances, choral or orchestral. The principal instruments then employed were the violin, viola, bass viol, 'cello, flute, French horn, harpsichord, spinet, organ, guitar, and pianoforte. Such group performances must have been of very uneven quality, although the trend was probably toward greater precision.[64]

[63] Three excellent histories of the early stage are: Arthur H. Quinn, *A History of the American Drama . . . to the Civil War* (New York, 1923), chapter 1; George C. D. Odell, *Annals of the New York Stage* (8 vols., New York, 1927–36), Vol. I, Book I; and Arthur Hornblow, *A History of the Theatre in America* (2 vols., Philadelphia, 1919), Vol. I, chapters 1–6.

[64] John T. Howard, *Our American Music* (New York, 1931), is the most valuable

Puritanism limited musical expression in seventeenth-century New England to psalm singing, unaccompanied by organ or other instruments. The effect of many untrained voices seems to have been pretty bad, even though the various psalms were sung to about only a half-dozen tunes. To one sensitive hearer it seemed that the congregation was singing five hundred different tunes at once; another remarked, "We used frequently to have some people sing a note or two, after the rest had done." Many efforts after 1700 to achieve vocal harmony gave psalmody a more sedate character. In the 1740's the hymns of Isaac Watts became immensely popular with people responsive to the Great Awakening, although the psalms—now accompanied by bass viol or flute—remained triumphant in the more formal churches. Outside of religious circles, ballads and other secular music had won good repute by 1750; then the Revolution gave birth to a host of marching songs (e. g., "Yankee Doodle") and new ballads celebrating the deeds of military heroes.[65] At Bethlehem, Pennsylvania, founded in 1741, the Moravians established a musical center which soon became famous for its performances of German religious music, particularly the works of Johann Sebastian Bach.

Although the mode of living of the poorer farmers (as described in chapter XII) did not change materially during the eighteenth century, that of the upper class was almost completely transformed. In architecture the most striking feature was the construction of the new mansions of the aristocracy. After 1720 English books on architecture, and after 1740 English plans of houses, were followed, often literally, by colonial builders. That many colonists used wood when brick and stone were in vogue in England did not alter the style of construction. Despite numerous variations in the designs of the houses, three principal types were evident. The rich merchants of New England and of the middle colonies built town dwellings and country or summer houses (the latter often fifteen miles or so from their places of business)—houses commonly rectangular, three stories high, with dormer windows lighting the third-floor rooms, with chimneys at each end, and with either a pitched roof or a roof slanting on all sides from a railed platform on top. In the plantation area a common type of house exhibited a square central section (the family's living quarters); on each side, separate or joined to the main dwelling, were wings contain-

work on the early history of music. O. G. Sonneck, *Early Concert-Life in America, 1731–1800* (Leipzig, 1907), is a careful and detailed, if not very readable, account.

[65] J. H. Kouwenhoven, "Singing in New England," *New England Quarterly*, VI (Sept. 1933).

ing kitchen, pantry, office, and carriage house. At Charleston, South Carolina, many planters had town houses, built adjacent to one another, with principal rooms above the ground floor, a balcony at the front or street, and at the rear a veranda overlooking a private garden.[66]

Most of the later colonial mansions adhered to the Georgian style of architecture that reigned in England after 1720. Designed to be as durable as possible, the mansion expressed the desire of the owner to give permanence to his superior social status and to perpetuate it in his descendants, thus indicating a society of fixed class lines. Naturally the mansion also satisfied the esthetic sense and the demands of health (high sites) and of comfort (summer retreats). Moreover, an expensive dwelling proclaimed the owner's wealth to the world; its size (guest chambers and servants' rooms) and its decorative (non-utilitarian) features signified his mastery of the services of other people. Externally, the lines and proportions gave an impression of solidity and stateliness; inside, high ceilings, spacious rooms, and numerous windows denoted that the owner did not live a cramped existence. The interior effect was one of elegance rather than of easy comfort—an effect attained by means of graceful stairways, polished floors, delicately carved doors, doorways, and mantelpieces, by colored tapestries or figured paper hung on the walls, and by paneling and woodwork painted in light colors or treated so as to bring out the texture of fine woods. Outside one would find flower beds, shrubs, groves, lawns, walks or drives lined with trees, fish ponds, and perhaps a bowling green or a "Roman" temple.[67]

Had one been able to step from a room in the house of a well-to-do colonist in 1670 into a room of a mansion of 1770, the difference would have been startling. In place of the straight, somber, heavy pieces of the early period, one would have found light, polished, and gracefully curved furniture. To a large extent the use of mahogany after 1725 explains the change, for here was a strong, lustrous wood capable of producing objects both sturdy and graceful. Other woods commonly used included oak, pine, maple, and cypress. By 1775 colonial cabinet-makers had attained a high degree of skill, although they copied English models, particularly the work of Chippendale, whose influence prevailed between 1760 and 1775.

[66] The most outstanding work is Fiske Kimball, *Domestic Architecture of the American Colonies and of the Early Republic* (New York, 1927).

[67] Thomas E. Tallmadge, *The Story of Architecture in America* (New York, c. 1927), gives a brief résumé of the colonial period in chapter 2. Harold D. Eberlein,

In the colonial mansion of 1770 one would have observed elegant furnishings in the parlor or drawing room. The easy wing chair, the Windsor chair, introduced from England and popular after 1725, numerous straight-back chairs with rush, leather, or upholstered seats, tall, graceful candle stands, the circular tea table, a settee or sofa that did not invite lounging—all these bespoke a rather stiff refinement. As a rule there were small rugs on the floor, "Turkey carpets" used as table covers, portraits, engravings, and prints on the walls, a mirror over the fireplace, and embroidered or painted fire screens that were fastened to slender posts and might be raised or lowered. A common type of desk, reaching nearly to the ceiling, consisted of a bookcase, the desk proper (with a slanting lid that opened outward to rest on pulls), and a chest of drawers. Only a few hall or "grandfather" clocks were made before 1800 but a mantel clock or a wall clock served as well. Near the colored tiles of the fireplace stood the coal tongs and the warming pan, which, with the andirons, might be of polished brass.[68]

The dining room contained a mahogany table with straight-back chairs to match—accommodations sufficient, perhaps, for twenty guests. A built-in corner cupboard displayed the family chinaware (of oriental designs, in subdued colors) and held the silverware and linen. Forks were then a mark of gentility; ivory-handled knives were fashionable; and silverware served many a purpose, as described earlier by William Fitzhugh: it "gives myself the present use and credit, is a sure friend at a dead lift or is a portion for a child at my decease." Silver serving dishes and candlesticks, glass bowls and goblets, and linen tablecloths and napkins gave a tone of authentic elegance—an effect enhanced by graceful side tables of the "piecrust," "dish-top," or "drop-leaf" design.

At night one retired to a well-appointed chamber where stood the high, massive, carved four-poster, covered perhaps with a hand-woven bedspread of intricate pattern, and enclosed by a canopy and curtains of damask, chintz, or silk. Gauze protected the sleeper from the ravenous mosquito. Other furnishings included linen sheets, hair or feather mattresses, feather pillows, and woolen blankets. In early times personal articles were stored in boxes, later in chests, and finally in highboys. The highboy, distinctively American, was a chest of drawers graced usually with delicately carved shell ornaments and brass handles, and raised two or three feet above the floor by a frame of four or

*The Architecture of Colonial America* (Boston, 1927), is a popular, well-illustrated outline.

[68] L. V. Lockwood, *Colonial Furniture* (2 vols., New York, 1913), is the foremost treatment.

six legs. For a dressing table one used a lowboy—a single drawer, resting on a frame and furnished with a mirror and a dressing box. Objects of art such as one found in the rooms below might also decorate the bedrooms.[69]

Polite society required elegant attire. The ladies and gentlemen of town and tidewater evinced a deep interest in fashion, adopting the upper-class modes of London almost as soon as they appeared there. Many a London tailor or dressmaker was kept busy filling orders placed by the colonial elite through their English correspondents. "Whatever goods you may send me," wrote Washington to his London agent, "let them be fashionable." Colonial dress reached its peak of elegance, richness, and profusion in the years 1740–75, when delicate decoration, flowered and checked patterns, and varied colors (scarlet, blue, maroon, rose, gold, silver, and claret) held sway.

For the most select occasions the gentlemen of that day wore a suit of velvet or satin (breeches and a long decorated coat reaching to the knee), a satin or velvet waistcoat of a different color, silk stockings, and low shoes of black kid. Lace ruffles at the neck and sleeves, coat buttons covered with cloth to match the suit, silver shoe buckles set with sparkling stones: all such finery, together with powdered wig and ornamented sword, denoted in the wearer, not effeminacy, but mastery, showing that he did not engage in physical toil and was thus able to satisfy his common wants through the labor of others.[70]

The colonial lady's apparel in 1760 included petticoats, richly embroidered and brocaded gowns of silk or satin billowing from a tight waist, silk stockings, shoes covered with silk or satin, hoods of velvet or silk, lace caps with ribbons, kid or silk gloves, and jeweled ornaments for the hair, neck, ears, and hands—costumes that reflected dignity, poise, and self-restraint, even though now they might appear none too comfortable. It was fashionable for the upper-class lady to keep her skin "delicately white, smooth and soft," for then everyone would know that all her time was given to refined pursuits. The children of the upper class were dressed in clothes patterned after those of the adults—a means of training the young aristocrat in those rigid manners and disciplines deemed necessary by people of wealth and leisure in order both to avoid individual deterioration and to overawe social inferiors. For out-of-doors wear, for traveling, and for indoor occupations the ladies and gentlemen had outfits less costly than those

[69] Marion Harland (Mary V. H. Terhune), *Some Colonial Homesteads* (New York, 1897), describes many well known upper-class dwellings.
[70] Elisabeth McClellan, *Historic Dress in America, 1607–1800* (Philadelphia, 1904), is the best study of early costume.

for social functions, yet even so such common apparel also served the purpose of establishing one's social superiority by a conspicuous display of wealth.

Perhaps all the diversions of the upper class did not signify an increased refinement of taste, but at least they denoted the enjoyment of means and leisure. The colonial aristocrat was much given to entertaining: one might expect to find guests at his table at any of the four meals of the day. The formal dinner had a great vogue. At the close of a sumptuous repast the gentlemen remained in the dining room, there to imbibe many a glass of wine (Madeira was the aristocratic drink) and to converse at ease over their pipes of tobacco, neither cigars nor cigarettes having yet come into use. The ladies, having retired to the drawing room, entertained themselves until the gentlemen rejoined them for a game of whist or a round of dancing to the strains of a stringed orchestra engaged for the occasion. When gentlemen enjoyed only their own company they resorted freely to the card table or the billiard cue, playing commonly for sizable stakes. One observer at Wilmington noted that "an intolerable itch for gambling prevailed in all companies." The IOU and the cardsharper were not unknown, and more than one scion of the aristocracy dissipated his patrimony at the gambling table.[71]

For diversion out of doors the colonial gentlemen turned to fishing, hunting, fencing, horse racing, and an occasional game of cricket. In 1674 a tailor was fined in Virginia for participating in a horse race—a sport then deemed suitable only for gentlemen. Southern fox hunters imported foxes from England; the devotees of the race track imported blooded stallions and mares, making a business of breeding, trading, and racing thoroughbreds. In the summer young gentlemen of the North might go boating to some near-by cove, there to partake of a picnic dinner, and return at night in jovial spirits. So also it was proper to drive in one's carriage to some picturesque spot, refreshing oneself at a fashionable tea house along the way. The evening promenade graced the social life of the larger towns. At New York sleighing became very popular in the winter. Late in the day a party of twenty or thirty would set out, four to a sleigh, drive to an inn, and enjoy a festive supper.

From such pastimes sprang many select societies. Jockey clubs became prominent in the southern and middle colonies—clubs of sportsmen who arranged rather elaborate programs, particularly on Long Island, in New Jersey and in the South, where three- or four-year-olds and fillies (pacers and runners, for trotters had not yet been intro-

[71] See again C. M. Andrews, *Colonial Folkways*, chapters 3–7, 9.

duced) ran on race tracks or on the greensward for money prizes or trophies. The dancing club or "assembly" sponsored parties at which the stately minuet was performed, as well as informal jigs, reels, marches, hornpipes, and country dances. There were also hunting clubs (e. g., the Gloucester Hunt of Philadelphia), fishing clubs, and miscellaneous societies, like the Friday Night Club at Newport, evidently a company of epicures. After 1750 many aristocrats from Carolina and Pennsylvania summered at Newport, where the climate suggested that of Italy. There a succession of diversions occupied the visitors, who sought to regain health or to escape the heat of regions farther south.[72]

The young ladies, excluded from most of the daytime pursuits of the gentlemen, devoted some of their leisure hours to study, learning to write gracious "epistles," to read "with elegance and propriety," and to speak with correct diction. Other polite pursuits included painting on glass, working with wax, drawing with pencil, and painting with water colors. Fancy needlework of a dozen intricate varieties produced decorative objects which signified that the aristocratic lady was exempt from ordinary tasks—the mark of superior affluence. One teacher advertised that French, "when taught agreeable to its native purity and elegance," was "acquired with becoming ease and gracefulness, as renders it truly ornamental." French dancing masters, Parisian milliners, and French hairdressers (adept at making "hair cushions for ladies") were generously patronized after 1760. At sixteen the young lady's polite education was sufficiently advanced to warrant her formal introduction to the "world of fashion."

[72] Carl Bridenbaugh, "Colonial Newport as a Summer Resort," *Rhode Island Historical Society Collections*, XXVI (Jan. 1931).

## BIBLIOGRAPHICAL NOTE

Works Previously Cited: B. Adams, *Emancipation of Massachusetts*, chs. 3, 5, 7–11; E. Channing, *History of the United States*, II, pp. 423–490; H. J. Eckenrode, *Church and State in Virginia*, ch. 3; E. Eggleston, *Transit of Civilization*, chs. 1–3, 5; J. Fiske, *New France and New England*, I, chs. 5–6; E. B. Greene, *Provincial America*, chs. 6, 18; M. L. Greene, *Religious Liberty in Connecticut*, chs. 4–11; A. C. Flick (ed.), *History of the State of New York*, II, ch. 1; III, ch. 2; G. Kimball, *Providence in Colonial Times*, chs. 8–10; S. E. Morison, *Builders of the Bay Colony*, chs. 4, 6–8, 11; H. L. Osgood, *American Colonies in the Eighteenth Century*, I, pp. 293–326; II, pp. 3–48; III, pp. 407–490; P. Smith, *Age of the Reformation*, chs. 12–13; T. J. Wertenbaker, *The First Americans*, pp. 139–188, 237–282.

Sources: Two excellent source books of American literature are: R. E. Spiller (ed.), *The Roots of National Culture* (New York, 1933), pp. 62–237; and H. R. Warfel, R. H. Gabriel, and S. T. Williams (eds.), *The American Mind* (New York, 1937), Part I. The Jameson *Original Narratives* series includes

George L. Burr's edition, *Narratives of the Witchcraft Cases* (New York, 1914).
K. B. Murdock, *Selections from Cotton Mather* (New York, c. 1926), contains
bibliography and excerpts from Mather's writings, particularly the *Magnalia
Christi Americana*. The ever interesting *Diary of Cotton Mather, 1681–1724* is
published in the *Collections* of the Massachusetts Historical Society, 7th Series,
VII, VIII (Boston, 1911–12). *Jonathan Edwards*, in the American Writers
Series (ed. C. H. Faust and T. H. Johnson, New York, c. 1935), gives the most
important writings of Edwards. The earliest known copy (1727) of *The New
England Primer* is edited by P. L. Ford (New York, 1909). Robert F. Seybolt's
*The Private Schools of Colonial Boston* (Cambridge, 1935) contains interesting
newspaper advertisements. For religious topics the best guide is Peter G. Mode,
*Source Book and Bibliographical Guide for American Church History* (Menasha,
Wis., 1921). See also A. B. Hart (ed.), *American History Told by Contempo-
raries*, I, pp. 467–517; II, pp. 35–65, 255–276.

BOOKS ON AMERICAN LITERATURE: Inasmuch as many of the ideas of colonial
writers have been discussed in this text in connection with the problems and
issues which engaged their thought, there has not been included a formal discussion of literature as such. For those who desire to study literary tendencies,
the following books are the most important: Moses C. Tyler's *A History of
American Literature* (2 vols., New York, 1879) treats the colonial period to
1765 with thoroughness, emphasizing individuals rather than social forces. Barrett Wendell, *A History of American Literature* (New York, 1900), explains
colonial writings in terms of English tradition—i. e., the survival in the colonies of the Elizabethan temperament of spontaneity and enthusiasm. *The Cambridge History of American Literature* (ed. W. P. Trent, J. Erskine, S. P. Sherman, and Carl Van Doren, 3 vols., New York, 1917) consists of able essays by
leading scholars. See Vol. I, chs. 1–9. Very useful. V. L. Parrington's *The Colonial Mind* is an outstanding study from the democratic point of view. Charles
Angoff's incisively written *A Literary History of the American People* (2 vols.,
New York, 1931) dismisses most of the literature of the colonial period as
trivial, criticizing Moses C. Tyler's work for its excessive praise of early writers.
V. F. Calverton, *The Liberation of American Literature* (New York, 1932),
interprets literary expression in terms of economic influences and uses early writers to illustrate his views of the class character of colonial society. Two well-
written surveys by able scholars not hostile to Puritanism are Bliss Perry, *The
American Spirit in Literature* (*Chronicles of America*, New Haven, 1918), chs.
1–2; and S. T. Williams, *The American Spirit in Letters* (*Pageant of America*,
XI, New Haven, 1926), chs. 1–2. Percy H. Boynton, *A History of American
Literature* (Boston, c. 1919), is an outstanding brief text. See chs. 1–5.

# XIX

# THE STRUGGLE FOR LAND AND CURRENCY

THE social upheavals of the seventeenth century had not resolved the underlying conflicts of interest which separated various groups within the colonies. After 1700 the growth of commerce and of plantation economy had greatly increased the wealth and power of the colonial aristocracy, while at the same time the extended immigration from abroad enlarged the class of farmers and workers who formed the backbone of the democratic party. The conflict between aristocratic and democratic forces therefore continued with unabated vigor, revolving around the issues of land, currency, and the control of the colonial governments.[1] In South Carolina, prior to 1720, the two parties faced a common enemy in the absentee proprietors who ruled those colonies in the narrow spirit of self-interest, thereby imposing restraints which retarded the advancement of all groups. The latter united in revolutionary action to overthrow the proprietary government in 1719, but once the common enemy had been defeated the latent antagonisms between the aristocratic and democratic parties transformed the struggle into an internal conflict.

## THE OVERTHROW OF THE CAROLINA PROPRIETORS

Five different parties were concerned in the South Carolina revolution of 1719. Far removed from the province, the proprietary board after 1700 was composed in the main of indifferent and inferior men who cared little about the welfare of the inhabitants, regarding them merely as a source of income. To sell land at a high price and to exact quit-rents indefinitely; to take as much as possible from the province and to give as little in return: such was the ambition of the absentee proprietors; such were their policies which provoked the popular revolt.

With the progress of rice cultivation after 1695 the large planters acquired a predominating influence within the province. Plantation economy forced a rapid growth of the settled area until by 1720 it ex-

[1] W. E. Dodd, "The Emergence of the First Social Order in the United States," *American Historical Review*, XL (Jan. 1935).

tended a hundred and fifty miles along the coast. But as plantations moved southward they encroached upon the lands claimed by the Spaniards at St. Augustine and their Indian allies. In this situation the rice planters were at a grave disadvantage: their Negro slaves might turn against them when the Spaniards and the Indians attacked, while their servants and slaves who escaped found refuge and protection at St. Augustine. What the planters desired most was an aggressive policy of defense, including the establishment of frontier settlements of Protestant farmers who would shield the planters from the double menace of slave insurrection and Indian attack. When the proprietors failed to provide for such defenses, the planters were not merely antagonized; they felt it necessary to control the colonial government in order to act for themselves.

In this contest the planters were supported by the small farmers, who were equally eager for assistance from the proprietors and desirous also of obtaining lands which the proprietors granted with a niggardly hand. Yet when Indian war came, the farmers—receiving no aid from the proprietors—were obliged to finance the war themselves and at the same time to pay tribute in the form of quit-rents. Somewhat similar was the plight of the Charleston merchants who engaged in the western fur trade. Confronted now by the competition of the French in Louisiana, the English fur traders felt the need of a strong government to support them in the wilderness. However, the proprietors, indifferent as usual, refused to contribute funds for frontier troops and forts or for presents and diplomatic missions to the Indian tribes.[2]

The fifth party involved was the British government. It was imperative, first of all, that the southern frontier be adequately defended against the French and Spaniards. Not only would a conquest of South Carolina deprive Britain of the western fur traffic and the growing rice trade; it would also bring the French and Spaniards so close to Virginia as to imperil the more important tobacco trade. Moreover, the Acts of Trade and Navigation must be enforced, and piracy—which had taken a new lease of life in the Carolinas—must be suppressed. So inefficient had the proprietors proved in protecting England's commercial interests in the southern region that the Board of Trade had recommended repeatedly since 1700 that the Crown assume control of the government of the two colonies. In view of these interests it is understandable how the planters, small farmers, and fur traders of South Carolina combined with the British government to accomplish the overthrow of the proprietary regime.

[2] See again H. L. Osgood, *American Colonies in the Eighteenth Century*, Vol. II, pp. 347–384.

The power exercised by the proprietors before 1719 also explains the cause of the revolt. At Charleston there existed a party of officials appointed by the proprietors—the governor, the councillors, the secretary, the chief justice, the marshals, the receiver-general, and the surveyor-general—who held the reins of government and ruled in the proprietary interest. Of the councillors the inhabitants complained that they were wholly subservient to the proprietors "and think themselves obliged to carry everything they can in favor of the lords proprietors' intentions and advantage." The elected assembly of the province was a veritable shadow, restricted by the proprietors on three sides—by the negative vote of the council, by the veto of the governor, and by the veto of the proprietors in London. The inhabitants insisted that when the governor signed an act it should stand as if approved by the proprietors; an additional proprietary veto tended "to the great confusion of their administration, contrary to any power given them by the charter."

Even the elected house (or Commons House of Assembly) was not immune from the proprietary influence. Prior to 1716 the election of deputies had been held in Charleston, but with the establishment of remote plantations the assembly in 1716 enacted that elections be held in the respective precincts, "apportioning members according to the largeness of each parish." This act the proprietors rejected and substituted a new electoral scheme whereby the freemen were summoned to two bodies, there to vote "by subscribing their names to lists of representatives to the major part of whom the freemen are generally strangers," thus "giving room for faction, corruption, and tumultuous meetings, and to the great expence of time, travel and money to the freemen."

The judicial system of South Carolina seemed to the inhabitants equally autocratic. The proprietors had not established county courts for the administration of local justice; instead they made Charleston the sole judicial center, presided over by their chief justice—a virtual dictator who performed the functions of the county courts and of the courts of king's bench, exchequer, and common pleas and from whose decisions there was no appeal except to himself. He named attorneys, took fees at his discretion, forced the inhabitants from remote parts to attend courts at Charleston, and delayed suits "in order to multiply his perquisites"; he held himself beyond the control of the assembly, asserting that he was accountable only to the proprietors, and when the inhabitants appealed to them for relief their appeals were ignored.[3]

[3] Edward McCrady, *History of South Carolina under the Proprietary Government*, chapters 14–31.

And how had the proprietors used their extensive powers for the benefit of the colony? They had not erected a single mission, church, school, or college: the youth of the country "by imbibing irreligion for want of due education" were in danger of becoming "as barbarous as the native savages." The proprietors had not done anything in recent times to people the colony or "so much as contribute one penny toward the raising of forts and fortifications." Nor had they conferred titles of nobility upon colonists who merited them but instead had offered them for sale—"a procedure so mean" that decent men would not accept the honor.

An early conflict over religion taught the colonists that they had a better friend in the English government than in the proprietors. Freedom of worship having been extended by an act of 1696 to all Christians except Roman Catholics, the assembly, probably packed by the governor, Sir Nathaniel Johnson, a resolute Anglican, enacted in 1704 two laws which established the Anglican Church, taxed even the dissenters for its support, and required members of the elected house to take an oath to conform to the Anglican faith. The dissenters thus excluded sent an agent to England, where they enlisted the aid of the Bishop of London, of whose diocese South Carolina was a part—a later act of the colony having deprived him of some of his ecclesiastical power in the province. Believing that the Church Acts would retard the growth of the colony and its commerce with England, the Board of Trade espoused the cause of the dissenters, whereupon the proprietors yielded and agreed to the repeal of the offensive acts, although they had refused concessions until this official pressure was brought to bear. A new act now established the Anglican Church, provided for its support by all taxpayers, and allowed the laymen of each parish to select the minister, vestrymen, and churchwardens. The dissenters had won a major victory in the removal of the religious test for officeholding, and a precedent for resisting the proprietary power had been established.

While this controversy was in progress the colony was called upon to defend itself during Queen Anne's War; then in 1715 a destructive Indian War ravaged the frontier and penetrated to the heart of the colony. A southern tribe, the Yamassees, incited by the Spaniards at St. Augustine, launched a surprise attack upon the border settlements, massacred two hundred whites, and forced the other farmers to flee into Charleston. Under the leadership of Governor Craven, and with the aid of troops from North Carolina and Virginia, the South Carolinians drove the Yamassees back. Meanwhile appeals to the proprietors brought no aid except one hundred and fifty small arms; later the colonists complained that during the two and a half years of "that unhappy time" the proprietors "took no more notice of us than if they had abandoned the province," acting apparently on the assumption that "if the inhabitants were destroyed the country might be settled by a better people." Forced to shoulder the financial burden of the war without assistance from the proprietors the colony became so deeply involved in debt that its credit by 1719 was exhausted.[4]

Depredations of pirates were also attributed to proprietary neglect. In 1718 a notorious pirate, one Teach or Blackbeard, seized several ships trading to the province and took as prisoners several important South Carolinians; thence he proceeded to North Carolina and there committed further acts of piracy, "with the governor's connivance." And instead of punishing such crimes the proprietors "according to their wonted supineness and negligence took no notice of the same."

On the western frontier other distressing events occurred; in May 1715 the French prevailed upon the Alabama Indians to murder the South Carolina traders within their midst, and following this the French erected a fort, New Toulouse, at Mobile. Next they occupied the Spanish fort at Pensacola, thus surrounding South Carolina on the south and west, strengthening their influence among the Indians and giving force to the charge that they intended to seize the English colony. Again the South Carolinians besought the proprietors for protection; again without avail.

The struggle for land ultimately precipitated the revolt. After the Yamassees had been driven out of their country the assembly enacted that their lands should be settled by British Protestants and thereupon five hundred immigrants were encouraged to come to the province. The proprietors, however, reserved the whole Yamassee tract for themselves, and reversing the land policy of the local government, refused to confirm the titles of the newcomers or to refund their purchase money. The latter, "by sickness contracted by their often removings and spending all their substance they brought to begin their settlements," were reduced to such "want and poverty that they are daily . . . perishing and those that have anything left [are] removing off the province to the great weakening of the same."

Before 1718 the proprietors had allowed the governor and council to dispose of land, only to find that exorbitant grants were made—and in such an underhand manner that the records of titles and quit-rents soon fell into a state of utter confusion. Accordingly, in September 1718 the proprietors decreed that no additional lands be surveyed or granted "to any person whatsoever without our consent and approbation be

[4] See again V. W. Crane, *The Southern Frontier*, chapter 7.

first obtained." Once more the interests of the planters were to give way to those of the proprietors.

In 1719, when a Spanish invasion threatened and Governor Robert Johnson called out the militia, the colonists used the occasion to march upon Charleston and to seize control. A newly elected assembly transformed itself into a revolutionary convention, took charge of the province in the name of the king, and sent an agent, Colonel John Barnwell, to England. The cordial reception which he received gave color to the charge that the revolt had been instigated by British officials. The Crown now assumed the powers of governing South Carolina and dispatched Sir Francis Nicholson thither as the first royal governor. The rights of the proprietors to seven-eighths of the land were finally purchased for the Crown in 1728–29 at a price of £22,500. One proprietor, Lord Carteret (later Lord Granville), refused to sell and retained his claim to the soil. The dominating parties in the revolution were the large rice planters and the English merchants, both of whom regarded the proprietors as an obstacle to the progress of the colony.[5]

### The Struggle for Land

North Carolina, having failed to participate in the revolt of 1719, remained under the proprietary government until 1728, when it too joined the ranks of the royal colonies by reason of the surrender of the proprietary rights. The Crown in 1729 became the owner of ungranted lands; it now appointed the governor, councillors, and other executive and judicial officers of the northern province. Primarily interested in the growth of settlement as a means both of increasing the colony's trade with England and of extending the naval stores industry, British officials pursued a liberal policy in disposing of ungranted lands. To speculative promoters huge tracts were sold at less than a penny an acre on condition that the grantee establish one settler to each two hundred acres received; if lands were not thus settled within a given time they were to revert to the Crown. Likewise the British government liberally bestowed small tracts upon *bona fide* settlers and readily confirmed the claims of squatters after they had established farms. One object of this lenient policy was to extend the chain of English settlements westward and thus to hold the interior against the French. In order to obtain money for the governor's salary and for other costs of administration the Crown insisted that all lands which it granted pay

[5] See again Justin Winsor (ed.), *Narrative and Critical History of America*, Vol. V, pp. 316–327.

a yearly quit-rent—a measure which gave the governor a special interest in the collection of such revenues.

Second in influence to the Crown were certain large landowners who acquired immense holdings in North Carolina. In 1744 the Privy Council ordered that Lord Granville's proprietary estate should consist of a tract extending from sea to sea between the Virginia border and the line of 35° 34': within this area he was entitled to receive the quit-rents.[6] After the other proprietors had surrendered their land claims in 1728–29 the British government granted large tracts to certain London merchants, the foremost of whom was Henry McCulloch: he and his partners received nearly a million and a half acres during the early 1730's. Their plans included the utilization of the pine barren land for the production of naval stores and the selling or renting of the better farm lands to settlers whom they transported to the colony. Land speculation thus offered a field of investment for the surplus capital of the English merchants and at the same time promised an expansion of trade. In 1739 McCulloch was appointed supervisor of the royal revenues and land grants in North Carolina; later, in 1752, his influence was strong enough to secure the appointment of one Arthur Dobbs, an Irish gentleman, as governor. Also a large-scale land speculator, Dobbs, in the 1730's had secured three hundred thousand acres in the southern part of the province, where he had established seven hundred colonists.[7]

Another group of speculators had been active after 1729—wealthy residents of the colony who had obtained land by means of "blank patents" which were issued and signed by the governor in advance of surveys, thus conferring a general claim to unspecified areas. By this method the Moore and Moseley families and other rich speculators obtained title to a half million acres and by 1750 all the good farming lands except in the back country near the mountains had been patented.

From the neighboring colonies a large stream of small farmer pioneers poured into North Carolina during the eighteenth century and occupied the lands of the piedmont region. Too poor to buy land outright or to go to the seat of government on the coast in order to get titles from the governor and council, such settlers as squatters came into conflict with the claims of the large speculators. They expressed their aspirations in the elected house of the legislature, and since the large

[6] Beverley W. Bond's *The Quit-Rent System in the American Colonies* (New Haven, 1919), a book of fundamental importance, is technical and detailed; the general student should read an article: B. W. Bond, "The Quit-Rent System in the American Colonies," *American Historical Review*, XVII (April 1912).

[7] See again H. L. Osgood, *American Colonies in the Eighteenth Century*, Vol. IV, chapters 5, 9, 11.

landowners controlled the council the conflicts between Assembly and council generally revolved around the issue of land. Nor did the small farmers care to pay quit-rents to either Lord Granville or the king.[8]

During the term of Governor Gabriel Johnston (1734–52) the quit-rents were responsible for the most heated conflict within the colony. Johnston insisted that the rents be paid promptly at a few designated places, that arrears be collected, and that payments be made in full at the rate of 4s. sterling per hundred acres. The Assembly on the other hand demanded that the rents be collected at the individual farms, that arrears be overlooked, that payments be made in produce instead of money, and that when such produce was tendered it should be given a higher monetary value than its mere market price. Unable to get his bills passed the governor dissolved several assemblies and when the two parties agreed upon compromise measures they were disallowed in England. The upshot of the controversy was the complete disorganization of the quit-rent system. Collections virtually ceased, the receiver-general grew indolent and indifferent, the rent rolls were kept in a slipshod fashion, and the deficit became so great that the governor's salary was not paid for thirteen years after 1740. As the menace from France on the western frontiers was increasing at this time Britain did not harass the small farmers of the interior; they were even favored as against the large landowners of the seaboard area, and in consequence the conflict between the frontiersmen and the eastern speculators over land patents and other related issues outranked the contest with Britain over the quit-rents.

The land question also played a decisive role in the rather complicated politics of Pennsylvania.[9] In a general way the province after 1720 was divided into two antagonistic sections. In the eastern counties of Bucks, Chester, and Philadelphia lived the wealthy merchants and farmers who composed a conservative party which controlled the elected assembly. In this alliance the Quakers furnished the political leadership, while the Germans, a group inexperienced in government, provided support at the polls. Sharing similar religious beliefs and united by opposition to the proprietary land system, the eastern Quakers and German Pietists strove to make the assembly superior to the governor representing the Penn family, while at the same time they used their legislative power to withhold protection desired by the set-

---

[8] See again L. H. Gipson's *British Empire before the American Revolution*, Vol. II, pp. 143–163.

[9] See two works by W. R. Shepherd: *History of Proprietary Government in Pennsylvania* (New York, 1896) and "The Land System of Pennsylvania," *Report*, American Historical Association, 1895.

tlers on the western frontiers—a stand dictated by the Quakers' aversion to war and by their dislike of paying taxes for the benefit of other people.[10]

On the frontiers the Scotch-Irish rapidly became the dominant group. Encouraged at first to come into the province by the Penns in order to buy land and to build up a party against the anti-proprietary Quakers, the Scotch-Irish increased so prodigiously that by 1750 they constituted a third of the population. But as settlers they disappointed the Penns; although they pretended they would buy land "not one in twenty" had "anything to buy with." As early as 1726 it was estimated that there were fifty thousand Scotch-Irish squatters on the frontiers; in 1730 Penn's agent, James Logan, wrote: "I must own, from my experience in the land office, that the settlement of five families from Ireland gives me more trouble than fifty of any other people." Moreover, these "poor but presumptuous people" refused to pay quit-rents to the proprietary family. Equally spirited was their opposition to the eastern Quakers who refused to grant public money for frontier defense; in addition many of the eastern conservatives were speculators who, demanding more for their lands than did the proprietors, viewed the squatters with unbounded contempt. The poorer German settlers on the frontier, finding themselves at odds with their wealthier countrymen of the eastern counties, accepted the political leadership of the aggressive Scotch-Irish. The interior fur trade contributed another cause of antagonism between east and west as the Germans at Lancaster broke in upon the monopoly of trade in the Susquehanna region previously held by Philadelphia merchants. And with the founding of Baltimore in 1729 the Scotch-Irish and German pioneers were able to export their surplus produce by way of the Susquehanna River, thereby lessening their dependence upon Philadelphia and accentuating the cleavage between the sections within the province. Eastern Germans and Quakers against western Germans and Scotch-Irish, and both parties against the proprietor: such was the alignment of political forces until the close of the French and Indian War.[11]

Prior to 1757 the Quakers retained control of the province but their unwillingness to provide for frontier defense finally induced Britain to threaten to enact a parliamentary statute to exclude them from the assembly. They parried this threat in 1757 when several of them withdrew and allowed a non-Quaker majority to assume control. The critical issue at this time was: should the assembly tax the ungranted lands

[10] See again H. L. Osgood, *American Colonies in the Eighteenth Century*, Vol. IV, chapter 6.

[11] See again E. Channing, *History of the United States*, Vol. II, chapter 9.

of the Penns? To raise money for defense and to force a more rapid disposal of the proprietary lands (a proposal agreeable to both speculators and small farmers)—such were the purposes of the assembly in contending that the Penns should "give a part to save the whole and not only save it but render it of double or treble value." The assembly also desired to appoint the assessors of lands, to tax the proprietor's income from quit-rents, and to allow the settlers to pay the rents in depreciated currency. To all these measures the Penns objected strenuously: they would consent to the taxation of their lands which netted an income, but, in the words of W. T. Root, "to impose a tax on the vast areas of unlocated and unsurveyed lands appeared to them subversive of the principles of right." [12]

Over these issues raged one of the sharpest legislative battles of colonial times. After being thwarted by the governor in the sessions of 1755–58 the representatives carried the day in 1759 when they induced him to violate his instructions and sign a bill which taxed the ungranted proprietary lands and allowed the assembly to name the assessors. Governor Denny received a legislative gift of £1,000 and a promise that the province would compensate him if his assent should cost him the £5,000 bond he had given to enforce the proprietors' instructions. In spite of the refusal of the assembly to make any appropriations for the war unless he agreed to the tax; in spite of the fact that pressure had been brought to bear upon him by General Amherst, Denny was dismissed by the Penns, who likewise called upon the Crown to disallow the law. In 1760 agents of the province in England agreed to a compromise which excluded the ungranted, unsurveyed land from taxation, provided that surveyed but unimproved lands be taxed at the same rate at which similar lands owned by private persons were taxed, gave the Penns a voice in the selection of assessors, and required that quit-rents be paid according to contracts. However, the assembly refused to ratify this agreement or to repeal the tax of 1759. Then when Indian war again ravaged the frontiers in 1763 the assembly declined to grant defense money except upon its early conditions. Once more a deadlock ensued as the governor vetoed the land tax; no defense funds were voted and the frontier was left to shift for itself. Organizing themselves as the "Paxton Boys," the frontiersmen took up arms, killed some Indians, and then descended upon Philadelphia, demanding relief. This turn of events enabled the governor to extract defense money from the assembly without consenting to the debated tax. So indignant now were the representatives that they sent Benjamin Franklin to

[12] See again W. T. Root, *Relations of Pennsylvania with the British Government*, chapter 7.

England with a petition praying that the Crown assume the powers of the proprietor on the assumption that it was necessary "to fly from petty tyrants to the throne." [13]

Inasmuch as the eastern counties controlled the assembly during this conflict its history demonstrates that the wealthier, conservative groups were the chief opponents of the proprietary land system. Many of the easterners favored the proprietary land tax merely as a means of shifting the defense burden to the proprietors from themselves. Land speculators on the other hand had a twofold motive. They desired to make it unprofitable for the Penns to withhold vast tracts from the speculative buyers, and they hoped to force the Penns to charge higher prices for lands they sold to settlers in competition with private speculative offerings. With regard to the frontier settlers, their main interest for the time was in adequate defense.

The farmers of New Jersey outdid even their Pennsylvania neighbors in opposing an unpopular land system. When in 1702 the numerous and weakly organized proprietors of New Jersey surrendered to the Crown their rights to govern the province they retained possession of the soil, and the English government thereafter attempted to enforce their claims as landlords by decreeing that only they could extinguish Indian titles and that all the settlers should pay to them the required quit-rents. Essentially land speculators, the proprietors parceled the province among themselves, each laying claim to large tracts and carrying on an individual land office business. Politically they were united; they controlled the governor's council and the courts and used their power to enforce their rights as overlords. Before 1747 they enjoyed the backing of the British government, made effective through its agent, the royal governor.[14]

The settlers who occupied the hilly parts of New Jersey west of Newark (for the most part they were of Dutch, English, and Scottish stock) took up unsurveyed land, justifying themselves with the frontier philosophy that the land belonged to him who would use it. They ignored the proprietors by buying their titles from the Indians, by refusing to pay quit-rents, and by cutting timber on lands which the proprietors reserved for themselves. In this conflict the frontiersmen could count upon assistance from the established, more prosperous farmers in Elizabethtown and Monmouth County—settlers who also resisted the proprietary claims, contending that since they had origi-

[13] An exceptionally good study is Charles H. Lincoln, *The Revolutionary Movement in Pennsylvania* (Philadelphia, 1901), chapters 1–4.

[14] See again H. L. Osgood, *American Colonies in the Eighteenth Century*, Vol. IV, chapter 5.

nally derived their titles from the Duke of York they were exempt from quit-rent payments to the New Jersey overlords. And because the farmers dominated the assembly and the militia the proprietors could not depend upon them for protection of their interests; accordingly they were forced to rely upon the council and the courts. The struggle over land therefore assumed a legal character as the proprietors sought by court actions to evict trespassers and the latter directed their attack upon lawyers, judges, and jails.[15]

In 1745 a certain Samuel Baldwin was arrested for cutting trees on a proprietary tract. His neighbors rallied to his defense and forcibly removed him from jail, whereupon some of the rioters were arrested. They too were soon freed by mob violence, the frontier settlers now being well organized under their chosen leaders. The governor who had to deal with these riots was Jonathan Belcher—previously a vigorous opponent of the rural democracy of Massachusetts. Although Belcher "was surpassed by none in his love for the rich and powerful" (Osgood), at the same time as a New Englander he had little sympathy for quit-rents. Accordingly he did nothing to suppress the unrest or to punish the rioters. Nor did the assembly act, except to offer pardons. Inasmuch as legal actions against the farmers invariably evoked new riots, the proprietors finally appealed to England for protection. The Board of Trade favored the use of British troops to quell the revolt but the Privy Council decided to send a commission of inquiry and to arrange for a legal settlement of the proprietors' claims. However, before such steps could be taken the French and Indian War compelled the proprietors to abate their zeal against the farmers in order to enlist their support for the war, while the rioters found a new outlet for their fighting energies. Meanwhile the rioters for nearly a decade had successfully sustained one of the most important of the colonial rebellions against a narrow, semi-feudal land system.

Even New England with its freedom from proprietary overlords and quit-rents did not escape the prevalent controversy over land.[16] During the seventeenth century the Puritan land system had been reasonably conducive to social integration. The title to the lands of Massachusetts, Connecticut, and Rhode Island was vested by the charters in the colonial legislatures and they in turn made initial township grants to small bodies of settlers called town proprietors. Usually the Indians' claim to the land was first extinguished—not by individuals but by the authority of the colonial governments. In disposing of lands

<hr>

[15] See again L. H. Gipson's *British Empire before the American Revolution*, Vol. III, chapter 6.
[16] See again J. T. Adams, *Revolutionary New England*, chapters 6–8, 10.

the legislatures did not require a money payment but they did impose conditions in order to provide for group settlement conducive to defense, coöperation in economic pursuits, and a common social and religious life. The townships (usually eight or ten square miles) were laid out by the colony, while the town proprietors were required to keep the bounds well marked.[17]

At the outset the proprietors composed the main body of working settlers; hence the township was originally a democratic institution. When the proprietors met together they formed the town meeting, and there they decided upon the utilization and disposition of the land. Each proprietor received a home lot (from two to five acres) located near the village common where the church, school, minister's residence, and town market were placed. Surrounding the common lay the planting and mowing fields; these were divided into small plots which were distributed among the proprietors by lot. The ungranted land belonged to the proprietors in common: pasturage, timber lands affording wood and stone, undivided arable and mowing fields, and waste and swamp lands. In order to build up the community the proprietors attracted outsiders by granting them small plots and by permitting them to attend and participate in the town meetings. Thus there occurred a division between the proprietors and non-proprietors or newcomers, but as long as the former constituted the majority the cleavage was not important. The proprietors continued to exercise alone the right of granting land, but they permitted the newcomers to vote for the selectmen who managed the town's public affairs. Moreover, in the early days the proprietors apportioned lands on a fairly equal basis: although the wealthiest settlers received more land than their poorer neighbors the former got disproportionately small shares—an arrangement necessary to prevent dissatisfaction in the initial period of extreme hardship and privation.[18]

The gradual influx of newcomers sharpened the competition for the ungranted lands as they became increasingly valuable. Then there appeared a pronounced antagonism between the original proprietors or their heirs and the non-proprietors. In the later apportionments of the commons the proprietary party insisted that it alone had the right to give title to land, whereas the non-proprietors urged that the whole body of inhabitants possessed that power. And in granting individual lands the proprietors now tended to assign tracts on the basis of indi-

---

[17] Lois K. Matthews [Rosenberry], *The Expansion of New England* (Boston, 1909), has a good factual discussion in chapter 4.

[18] Roy H. Akagi's *The Town Proprietors of the New England Colonies* (Philadelphia, 1924) is a monograph of unusual merit and importance.

vidual wealth. Thus the town of Lancaster resolved in 1653 "that in the second division and so through all other divisions of land the matter shall be drawn as near to equality of men's estates as we are able to do": to him that hath shall be given. Similarly the town proprietors began to deny to non-proprietors the privilege of using the commons for grazing purposes or as sources of timber and stone. And bit by bit the wealthier townsmen purchased the small plots of their poorer neighbors so that by 1715 the process of accumulation was propelling the landless outward toward the frontiers. At the same time it supplied the proprietary class with surplus funds which they could use for speculating in wilderness lands.

The growth of a class of propertyless farmers in conjunction with the rise of a class of wealthy men who had surplus capital but who did not desire to leave their established homes—this twofold evolution forced a change in the New England method of creating new towns. After 1725 Massachusetts, Connecticut, and New Hampshire, instead of granting townships to *bona fide* settlers, sold them to speculative promoters. Thus Connecticut in 1737 sold six townships at public auction, each purchaser being allowed to buy one of about fifty proprietary rights in a township at a minimum cost of between £30 and £60. Massachusetts went farther in 1762 when she disposed of ten large tracts at prices ranging from £380 to £3,200, and allowed a single purchaser to acquire an entire township. Because the colonial governments had an interest in settling the frontiers for protection against the French and Indians the speculative purchasers were required to establish a certain number of families within a given time (forty within four years, for instance) and to provide them with a minister, church, and school.[19]

After such purchases had been made (usually on the partial payment installment plan), the speculators operated land offices in eastern towns like Boston, whence they sent their agents on sales missions, not only throughout New England, but to the other colonies and to England as well. Many of their customers were non-pioneering investors who bought titles with the hope of a profitable resale. Among the most noted of the speculators were Josiah Willard of Massachusetts and James Fitch and Roger Wolcott of Connecticut. It soon appeared that grants had been made far in excess of the potentialities of settlement; consequently the speculators were unable to fulfill the prescribed conditions respecting the establishment of families on their lands: however, the colonial governments commonly granted generous extensions. Two principal results issued from the new land system. The early New

[19] Lois K. M. Rosenberry, *Migrations from Connecticut prior to 1800* (New Haven, 1934—Connecticut Tercentenary Commission, no. 28).

England ideal of community solidarity and the use of land grants to promote compact settlement gave way to unregulated competition for individual holdings, while on the frontiers isolated farms replaced the integrated towns common to the seventeenth century. Secondly, the frontier farmers viewed the speculators as their natural enemies who withheld land from cultivation, waged war against squatters, forced the price of land upward, controlled town governments as absentee voters, and failed to contribute toward the defense and welfare of the new communities. The most important legacy of speculation was this sharpened antagonism between seaboard wealth and frontier poverty.[20]

## CURRENCY CONFLICTS

Equal in importance with the colonial struggles over land titles was a series of dramatic conflicts over currency—contests to determine the prices which the farmers should receive for their produce. Such prices in turn determined whether debtors should remain in a dependent state and perhaps eventually lose their improved lands through foreclosure or whether they should achieve financial independence and security. The peculiar weakness of the farmers arose from the fact that the prices of their produce fluctuated widely whereas their debts remained fixed; hence when prices went down all their surplus might be required to satisfy their creditors. The farmers therefore desired to keep prices at high levels and they concluded that the best means of doing this was to obtain a large supply of money. For opposite reasons the creditors favored a "sound" or contracted currency.

The monetary expedients adopted by the colonies prior to 1700 had not solved the basic problem of currency supply; the unfavorable balance of trade continually drained them of the gold and silver coin and bullion which they obtained from Europe and the West Indies.[21] The resulting lack of a metallic money compelled them to issue paper currency—a natural culmination of financial practices long in vogue. Since the beginnings of settlement the colonists had used personal promissory notes as a medium of exchange—notes that circulated from hand to hand upon endorsement until they fell due and were paid by the issuer. Similarly at an early date the colonial treasurers issued such notes promising to pay to the holder a certain sum when taxes voted by the assembly had been collected: by this means the colony could obtain funds, say in January, when tax money would not be available

[20] C. K. Shipton, "The Shaping of Revolutionary New England," *Political Science Quarterly*, L (Dec. 1935).
[21] See again C. P. Nettels, *The Money Supply of the American Colonies*, chapter 10.

until December. The next development occurred in Massachusetts in 1690 when the legislature itself issued the promissory notes in anticipation of tax collections. Such notes or bills were now printed in a form similar to modern paper money and they circulated in the same manner, without individual endorsement. During the years 1700–15 New York, New Jersey, all the other New England colonies, and the two Carolinas printed such bills of credit, while Pennsylvania followed in 1723, Maryland in 1733, Virginia in 1755, and Georgia in 1760. In most colonies the bills were issued originally to raise money for war expenditures and ordinarily they circulated only a year or so until the colony retired them by buying them from their owners with the tax money that had been collected. Although not generally made legal tender they were supposed to represent a certain amount of silver: 8s. in bills for one ounce of silver was the most common rating. Issued in relatively small amounts before 1710, this paper currency did not depreciate materially even though never actually redeemable in silver on demand.[22]

Bills of credit proved to be such a satisfactory currency substitute that the colonists desired to use them in time of peace. However, the termination of Queen Anne's War meant that the bills outstanding would be withdrawn within a short time and that new issues would not be needed for public expenditures; hence a new method of putting bills into circulation and a form of security other than taxes had to be devised. By this time also the farmers began to realize that a large volume of bills of credit would raise prices and lessen their debt burdens. These facts explain the growing popularity of "land banks." It was now proposed that the colonial governments issue a large sum in bills (say £50,000) and lend them to the farmers on the security of their land, up to half of its assessed value. The farmer should then retire the loan in twenty yearly installments and also pay an interest charge to the colony of 5 per cent on the principal due—an income which might enable the colony to dispense with taxes. In short, the colony should use its property assets as a credit base, issue notes thereon, lend to farmers needing money, and use the interest received to support the colonial governments.

A little experience with land banks made the colonial merchants suspicious of them. When land was the security behind the bills there was practically no limit to the amounts that could be issued and therefore no effective barrier against depreciation. In addition the land banks modified the credit relations between farmer and merchant. A farmer

---

[22] Kathryn L. Behrens, *Paper Money in Maryland, 1727–1789* (Baltimore, 1923), is a satisfactory technical study.

who could borrow from a land bank might obtain enough money to pay his debts and thus gain greater freedom in buying supplies and selling his crops; as a debtor he could deal only with his merchant-creditor. Contrariwise, when ordinary bills of credit based on taxes were issued, the merchants usually obtained the money in the first instance (by selling supplies to the colony); then they could lend it to the farmers. Should the farmers first secure the credit their bargaining power with the merchants would be greatly improved; similarly if the merchants obtained the bills in the first instance they could lend on terms profitable to themselves. And another thing: the common legal rate of interest for land bank bills was only 5 per cent whereas the farmers had to pay a much higher charge for credit obtained from the merchants. Finally, if the farmer could not repay his loan from the colony he could expect more lenient treatment than from a private creditor.[23]

In order to make bills of credit completely effective the debtors endeavored to force creditors to accept them as legal tender, and accordingly many acts were passed to that effect. But since the legal tender principle menaced British creditors they appealed to the Crown for protection as early as 1706, whereupon an imperial currency policy was formulated. The royal governors were permanently instructed not to sign acts which declared bills of credit legal tender or which provided for the issuance of bills unless they were accompanied by acts levying taxes for redeeming them within a restricted period. Nor were the governors to sign any extraordinary measures affecting British trade unless they contained clauses suspending their enforcement until the king's consent had been given. And when paper currency laws were enacted contrary to these instructions they were commonly disallowed by the Privy Council. On the currency issue, therefore, colonial creditors could depend upon Britain to protect them against colonial debtors.

Paper money first became a subject of controversy in South Carolina. The expenses of wars waged by the province against the Spaniards and the Indians between 1703 and 1715 were met largely by bills of credit backed by taxes. But such taxes were not collected in amounts sufficient to retire the bills at the times designated and accordingly they were retained in circulation. Moreover, a land bank authorized in 1712 added £32,000 of bills to the colony's stock of currency and by 1715 the total volume outstanding was about £74,000. Later issues caused depreciation: an ounce of silver was worth 8s. in bills in 1710 as against

[23] See again C. J. Bullock, *Essays in the Monetary History of the United States*, Part I, chapter 4; Part II, chapters 1–2; Part III, chapters 1–2.

27*s*. in 1720 and 36*s*. in 1730. Inasmuch as the South Carolina bills were made legal tender they had a pronounced effect upon the relations between creditors and debtors.[24]

The merchants of Charleston and the wealthier rice planters formed a creditor party which controlled the governor's council—their instrument for resisting further currency issues. Against them were arrayed the less affluent planters and the small farmers—a debtor party determined to use its control of the Commons House of Assembly (the lower house) to evade tax payments for the redemption of outstanding bills and even to force new issues upon the colony. The antagonism between the creditor council and the debtor assembly became so intense in the late 1720's that a complete legislative deadlock ensued. When the council rejected new currency issues demanded by the assembly the latter refused to assent to bills of any other character, whereupon the colony approached the brink of anarchy as existing laws of a temporary nature expired without substitute legislation being passed. Finally in August 1731 a compromise provided that no new issues should be made —on condition that the existing quantity of bills remain in circulation, £7 in paper being rated as worth £1 sterling. Thereafter the creditors, the council, and the royal governor held the debtors in check, partly by the exercise of their legislative vetoes and partly by controlling the membership of the lower house in such a manner as to deprive the frontier debtor districts of the full representation to which they were entitled.

The most acrimonious conflict over the currency broke out in Massachusetts in the late 1730's.[25] The province had issued large quantities of paper money after 1713, and because the bills of other New England colonies also gravitated to Boston, the currency became superabundant and rapid depreciation ensued: in 1730 bills supposed to equal an ounce of silver were worth only two-fifths of an ounce. When Governor Belcher in 1733 assented to acts which emitted £106,000 in additional bills the British government instructed him not to consent to future issues in excess of £30,000 a year and to see to it that all outstanding bills were not reissued or allowed to circulate after the date originally set for cancellation. These orders meant that by 1742 most of the paper would be withdrawn, with disastrous effects upon prices and debts. Determined not to permit such a currency contraction the debtor farm-

---

[24] W. Roy Smith's *South Carolina as a Royal Province* (New York, 1903), an important study devoted principally to land and financial questions, is best suited to the advanced student.

[25] The foremost work on eighteenth-century finance is Andrew M. Davis's *Currency and Banking in the Province of Massachusetts-Bay* (2 vols., New York, 1900, 1901). It is too technical for the general reader.

ers devised a means of issuing bills which would not be subject to the governor's veto.

This was the famous land bank of 1740 which proposed to print £150,000 in bills to be lent to farmers on land mortgages at 3 per cent interest, with provision for repaying the principal in twenty equal yearly installments. Beginning operations in September 1740 the bank issued £49,250 in bills to about a thousand subscribers—bills without legal authorization which had to depend upon popular support for their effectiveness. That, however, seemed assured, since the mass of the farmers were heavily in debt to the merchants, whom they denounced as "griping and merciless usurers" bent upon building up "vast estates" and making themselves "lords of manors." "Hundreds of thousands are due to them." Without such currency relief the yeomen would surely sink to the status of laborers or tenants and the marchants would "swallow up" thousands of families.[26]

Styling the land bankers as the "needy, idle and extravagant," and charging that the "rabble" would transform "this province noted for trade" into "a habitation of rude rustics," the leading merchants combined, refused to accept any of the newly issued bills and launched a bank of their own for emitting bills to be redeemed in silver after fifteen years. In Governor Belcher they had a determined ally who said of the debtor farmers that they "are grown so brassy and hardy as to be now combining in a body to raise a rebellion." In fact the farmers did organize a march upon Boston in 1741, where they dominated the elections and chose a new set of councillors hostile to the merchants. Belcher, however, dissolved the House of Representatives (which was overwhelmingly pro-land bank), jailed the ringleaders, removed justices of the peace and officers of the militia who were sympathetic to the popular cause, refused to allow attorneys to plead before the council unless they were on the right side, and rejected the new councillors who had been nominated by the general assembly in 1741.

In danger of being engulfed by the popular tide the merchants appealed to Britain for protection and obtained immediate aid when Parliament in 1741 extended to the colonies a statute called the Bubble Act, which outlawed joint-stock companies operating without special authority from Parliament. Although enacted in 1720 this statute had been construed afterward as not applying to the colonies; now, however, it was not only made to apply but also broadened so as to include land banks. With one stroke Parliament made all the transactions of

[26] J. C. Miller, "Religion, Finance, and Democracy in Massachusetts," *New England Quarterly*, VI (March 1933).

the Massachusetts land bank illegal and forced it to wind up its affairs.[27]

The participants in the bank were at once exposed to ruin. As an illegal institution it could not enforce the contracts it had made or recover loans it had extended to its members. Yet each individual subscribed was held individually responsible for all the debts of the bank (or compelled to make good all the bills it had issued). Now it so happened that many of the subscribers were insolvent; hence the solvent participants had to redeem all outstanding bills. So bitter had the conflict grown that the merchants who had been forced to accept the bills were determined to make the subscribers pay to the last farthing. The upshot was a series of lawsuits which harassed the land bankers for nearly twenty years and which ruined many. Foremost among these was one of the bank directors, Samuel Adams, father of the Revolutionary leader. In 1757 two notices appeared simultaneously in the Boston press. One announced a public auction sale of the estate of Samuel Adams, the elder; the other was a notice from the son warning that the sale was illegal and that he would prosecute anyone who trespassed on his father's estate. The embittering of the relations between local creditors and debtors and a legacy of rural antagonism to Parliament's authority—such were the offspring of the Massachusetts land bank episode.

After 1740 Rhode Island became the principal scene of strife between debtors and creditors. There the small farmers who dominated the elected assembly for many years had the wealthy merchants of Newport at their mercy, since the farmers elected the governor as well as the deputies and moreover the governor did not possess the veto power, nor were Rhode Island's acts subject to the royal disallowance. The democratic spirit for which the colony had always been noted expressed itself largely in the paper money crusade; in fact democracy and inflation were kindred spirits in colonial times: let the people have money as well as votes.

So firm was this faith among the Rhode Islanders that between 1710 and 1750 they created nine land banks, the total currency issues of which amounted to £465,000. As a rule the farmers did not bother to pay their loans obtained from land banks; instead, when the payments were well in arrears, they would create another bank and borrow its bills in order to pay their old debts. New banks were also created to supply additional bills for the farmers to borrow. Meanwhile the

[27] See again W. B. Weeden, *Economic and Social History of New England*, Vol. II, pp. 473-491.

colony continued to issue tax-supported bills for public purposes and then failed to pay the taxes when due. In 1740 the paper in circulation amounted to £340,000 and when by 1750 the total had reached £525,000, depreciation had gone so far that bills supposedly worth an ounce of silver were actually worth only about an eighth of an ounce. Although Rhode Island did not make its bills legal tender yet so strong was the pressure of popular sentiment and so prone were rural judges to require creditors to accept them that in effect they circulated as lawful currency.

About 1730 the Newport merchants began to oppose additional issues, arguing that the farmers were deliberately striving to multiply the bills in order to wipe out private debts, that new loans would be obtained by debtors whose land was already mortgaged to the limit, that the interest rates which the farmers were supposed to pay were unreasonably low, and that the time allowed for the payment of such loans was too long. To these arguments the debtors replied that the merchants, by charging exorbitant prices for their goods, had obtained most of the old bills and had sent them to Boston in the course of trade. In 1730-31, when Governor Jenks attempted to veto a new land bank act the assembly successfully maintained that he did not possess the veto power, and when the merchants appealed to Britain for protection the Crown refused to act because Rhode Island's bills were not legal tender. Encouraged by such success the land bankers set up four new banks between 1733 and 1744 and in so doing nearly drove the merchants to distraction. After they had failed to exclude the debtors from the assembly by raising the property qualifications for voting (meanwhile the depreciation of the currency had greatly extended the franchise by increasing the nominal value of all property) and when in 1750 the debtors were on the point of creating a new bank, the merchants made a last desperate appeal to Britain. Ruin, they said, would visit them if the Assembly continued its reckless conduct.

The British government at last decided to take a hand. Due largely to the exigencies of King George's War the Crown had permitted the New England colonies to issue large quantities of paper but the resulting depreciation had wrought havoc with property rights and trade. Now when the war was over it was deemed necessary to stabilize New England's currency; hence in 1751 Parliament passed the Currency Act in response to the pleas of the Rhode Island and other merchants. This statute prohibited the New England colonies from erecting new land banks and from making bills of credit legal tender; it also required that outstanding bills be retired at the time appointed in the act of issue. In the future only bills backed by taxes could be issued: those emitted for ordinary purposes of government should be retired within two years and those issued for military emergencies should not run for more than five years. Inasmuch as this act sounded the death knell of New England land banks it intensified the opposition of rural debtors to Parliament's authority.

## TIDEWATER VERSUS FRONTIER

After 1720 the social cleavage in Virginia, Maryland, North Carolina, and South Carolina assumed a sectional as well as a class character, due to the rough division of those colonies into two antagonistic areas—the seaboard or tidewater and the piedmont or back country.[28] Separated from the interior by the line of the falls of the southern rivers, the seaboard area was distinguished by its large plantations, its highly stratified society, and the supremacy of its slaveholding aristocracy which ruled through the established governments. As a frontier region of small farms varying from fifty to two hundred acres, the back country had not yet become socially stratified; rather it expressed the informal and democratic spirit of laboring farmers among whom slavery was insignificant. And since they were cut off from direct access to the ocean they were forced to rely upon diversified farming and household manufacturing, their chief exports consisting of cattle driven overland to port towns like Baltimore and Richmond—a trade which enabled them to buy essential manufactures such as firearms, ammunition, notions, and ironware.

A host of interests divided these interior farmers from the tidewater aristocracy. As a debtor group they clamored for cheap paper money with which to pay their debts to eastern merchants and planter capitalists—a demand which explains the opposition of the aristocracy to currency inflation. Sorely in need of roads and bridges which they were too poor to construct by themselves, the frontiersmen called upon the colonial governments for assistance, only to find that the aristocracy refused to tax itself for such improvements. A similar opposition met their demands for frontier defense against the Indians, and as squatters they ran afoul of the land claims of the seaboard speculators. They strongly favored the system of small farms and the division of property equally among all children, whereas the tidewater planters preferred the law of primogeniture which awarded the whole ancestral estate to the eldest son. Recognizing that slavery was the basis of the power of their planter enemies the frontiersmen readily criticized that institution

[28] See again F. J. Turner, *The Frontier in American History*, chapters 2–3 (important).

and thereby not only provoked the planters to justify slavery as inherently right but also to deride the small farmers as shiftless and inefficient. And over taxation raged many a fierce battle as the back country, objecting to poll taxes, either insisted upon shifting the burden to the vast landholdings of the planter class or demanded heavier levies upon slaves. As Baptists, Quakers, Methodists, or simply as people indifferent to religion, the frontiersmen also objected strenuously to the parish taxes required by law for the support of the Anglican Church.[29]

In view of such fundamental differences of interest and outlook the control over government was a primary concern to both parties. Not only was the aristocracy determined to retain its mastery over the governor's council; it also sought to curb the influence of the back country in the elected assembly. The tidewater originally obtained control of the lower houses because it was the area first settled; then when the back country was peopled it had to appeal to the tidewater for representation. The South Carolina planters retained power by granting six or eight representatives to each of the coast counties and by allowing only one or two to the western counties. In Virginia the aristocracy erected more counties in the east than in the west and gave each two representatives, even though the tidewater counties were far less populous than those of the piedmont. In 1710 Governor Spotswood remarked that some of the western counties in Virginia were ninety miles in length and inhabited by three times as many people as some of the eastern counties, while in 1780 Jefferson wrote that "19,000 men below the falls give the law to more than 30,000 living in other parts of the state." So also in South Carolina: as late as 1790 the back country complained that the governing class included only a fifth of the white people. The blame for unequal representation may be laid in part to the British government, which feared the leveling tendencies of the interior and reserved to the royal governors the power of apportioning seats in the assembly—a power they used to perpetuate the existing inequalities.[30]

To the tidewater aristocracy it seemed equally imperative that local governments in the back country should be in "proper" hands—that justices of the peace should render correct decisions and that sheriffs

[29] Henry R. McIlwaine, *The Struggle of Protestant Dissenters for Religious Toleration in Virginia* (Baltimore, 1894), treats this theme briefly. See also Stephen B. Weeks, *Church and State in North Carolina* (Baltimore, 1892, 1893).

[30] Charles H. Ambler's excellent *Sectionalism in Virginia* . . . (Chicago, 1910) sketches the colonial conflict in chapter 1. See also William A. Schaper, "Sectionalism in South Carolina," *Report*, American Historical Association, 1900, Vol. I, a standard work.

should duly execute the judgments of the courts. Since such officers were appointed by the governors and councils the interests of the aristocracy were not seriously neglected. Moreover, the excessive size

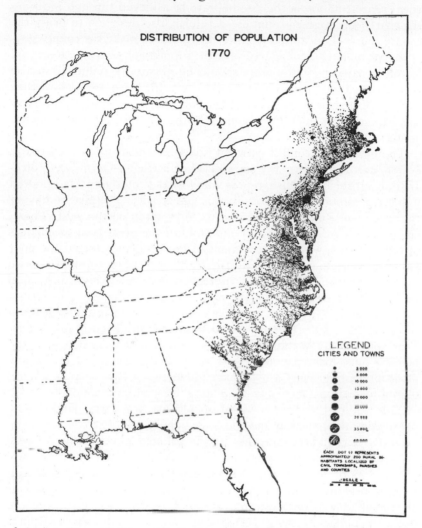

DISTRIBUTION OF POPULATION
1770

LEGEND
CITIES AND TOWNS

of the interior counties worked a hardship upon poor farmers who had to choose between a journey of thirty or forty miles to the county courts or adverse judgments for failure to attend. Nor did the large counties provide adequate police protection to the farmers against cattle thieves and other lawless elements. Above all, the highest provincial courts of appeal were located on the seacoast and were presided over by the very aristocrats who were the oppressors of the interior farmers.[31]

In resisting such conditions the back country at first petitioned for equal representation in the assembly, to be achieved through reducing the size of the western counties—a reform also designed to bring the county courts closer to the frontier farms and to make the county governments more efficient agencies for the suppression of crime. Fees paid to courts, lawyers, and officers should be drastically reduced; so also the sheriffs should not be permitted to steal the tax money which they collected. In short local government ought to promote the welfare of the back country, not merely protect the interests of the seaboard aristocracy.

The most bitter conflict between tidewater and frontier occurred in North Carolina. After 1763 a stream of settlers—Germans, Scotch-Irish, English, and Welsh, representing most Protestant sects—poured into the piedmont from Pennsylvania and western Virginia, occupying the area from Raleigh on the east to Morganton on the west. There, eking out a bare existence, they ran afoul of the great land speculators of the seaboard, whose engrossment of the best lands forced the poor pioneers either to cultivate unfertile tracts or to pay a substantial price to the magnates. The poll tax, moreover, bore relatively much more heavily on the poor than on the rich. A trade depression gripped the colony after 1763; money was scarce or non-existent in the back country, since the paper currency issued to finance the French and Indian War was rapidly withdrawn from circulation. This meant that the farmers must make payments with their produce, and due to the low prices prevailing many a poor man found that all his surplus was required for land payments, taxes, officers' fees, and private debts.

Meanwhile, the aristocracy of merchants and large landowners, dominating the governor and the council, held complete control of the executive and judicial branches of the colonial government. Closely allied to the eastern aristocracy was a rising upper class in the back country—agents of the former, such as surveyors, lawyers, and debt collectors; local merchants and land speculators; and, most conspicuous of all, the officials of the western counties. First came the justices of the peace, appointed by the governor and council, usually the wealthiest men of the back country, who composed the county court, which decided most cases at law, levied parish and county taxes, and was in fact almost the only unit of local government. Next in influence was the county sheriff, appointed by the governor from a panel of three nomi-

[31] St. George L. Sioussat, *Economics and Politics in Maryland, 1720–1750* (Baltimore, 1903), has a brief discussion of social conflicts.

nees prepared by the county justices, and usually assisted by a host of deputies in collecting taxes and executing the orders of the county court. The official party also included a number of clerks, registers, and lawyers who lived by the fees they collected for registering deeds, witnessing papers, and tying and untying the official redtape.

Supported by the governor and council, and free from local restraints, the western officials acted about as they pleased in upholding the *status quo*. It is evident that they interpreted the colony's fee laws to allow the taking of three or four fees when the farmers thought they were entitled to only one, and that the sheriffs kept their tax accounts secret and pocketed part of the tax money collected. When the poor farmers could not pay their debts or the high fees and taxes, the county courts ordered the sale of their property; and in the face of a depressed price level the local upper-class elements were able to buy or acquire such foreclosed property for a trifle and thus improve their style of living.

In 1765 a preliminary outbreak occurred against one George Selwyn, a large land operator, and his surveyor, John Frohock, who attempted to evict settlers in Mecklenburg County who refused to pay the high prices Selwyn asked for land. Three years later the farmers of Orange County formed an association, the Regulators, pledging to pay only legal taxes and legal fees and to act together under majority rule.[32] The local upper-class party, charging that the Regulators were taking the law into their own hands by usurping the functions of the officials and thus seeking to overthrow the government, immediately gained the backing of Governor Tryon and the provincial council. Thus fortified, the officials sought to suppress the uprising by jailing a few leaders, whereupon the Regulators stormed the jails, released their friends and began to threaten their enemies with violence. Governor Tryon, while promising to investigate grievances and to punish lawbreaking officials, betrayed much antagonism toward the Regulators and their methods. Seeking to overawe them he led an armed expedition into their country in 1768, but by avoiding fighting and punishments he quieted them for a time with more promises of reform.

An election in 1769 gave the Regulators control of the provincial assembly. But popular hopes for legal reforms ended abruptly in November when Governor Tryon dissolved the house for its opposition to British policies—an action which served notice that the Regulators could not depend upon the assembly to defend them against Tryon and the council. Meanwhile, the elements in power refused to

[32] The best account is J. S. Bassett, "The Regulators of North Carolina," *Report,* American Historical Association, 1894.

yield. To the Regulators the trials of accused officials appeared a farce: juries were packed; the justices declared their friends and allies innocent, or if technically guilty, fined them a penny; orders for the sale of debtors' property continued apace. Convinced that the courts and officers were adamant, the Regulators resorted to more direct action. They raided jails to free their imprisoned leaders; they assembled at the county courts and intimidated the justices; they whipped their enemies, drove them away, and burned their houses and stables.

In response to such activities Governor Tryon raised a small army which consisted of the eastern aristocrats, the officials, and soldiers recruited through bounties. On May 16, 1771, this force fell upon a large body of poorly armed and unsuspecting Regulators at the Alamance River, routing them after a battle of two hours. Seven Regulator leaders were summarily executed. Tryon's course received the hearty approval of the British government, which however recommended amnesty for the surviving leaders. The movement collapsed completely, since the Regulators had not sought an overthrow of government and were unwilling to fight on. Hundreds of them migrated to Tennessee; the others submitted. When the American Revolution broke out the remaining Regulators still regarded the eastern aristocrats as their chief enemies, and because the latter joined the Revolutionary party, many of the Regulators adhered to the British cause.[33]

[33] "North Carolina as a Royal Province," by Enoch W. Sikes, *The South in the Making of the Nation*, Vol. I, pp. 441–462.

## BIBLIOGRAPHICAL NOTE

SOURCES: The Publications of the Prince Society contain Andrew M. Davis's edition of *Colonial Currency Reprints, 1682–1751* (4 vols., Boston, 1910–11) —the best collections of sources on paper money. For a more convenient selection see A. M. Davis (ed.), *Tracts relating to the Currency of Massachusetts Bay, 1682–1720* (Boston, 1902).

# XX

# SELF-GOVERNMENT AND IMPERIAL CONTROL

FROM the preceding chapters it is evident that the growing economic value of the colonies to Britain and their habit of acting contrary to her interests constantly magnified the problem of imperial control. The ensuing conflicts raised the central issue of government and statecraft— the problem of authority. Were the colonies helpless dependencies of Britain or were they virtually independent countries? And if dependencies, where did the power of governing them rest? Where did sovereignty reside in the British state?

## THE POWER OF PARLIAMENT

The political struggles in seventeenth-century England between king and Parliament were decided for the future by the Revolution of 1688, which demolished the doctrine of the divine right of kings and demonstrated conclusively that in a profound conflict the forces identified with Parliament were far more powerful than the Crown. After that momentous victory Parliament slowly and gradually, yet remorselessly and irresistibly, extended its power in all directions. The Bill of Rights of 1689 denied to the king for all time the privilege of dispensing with laws or of suspending their enforcement, and it also prohibited the maintenance of a standing army without Parliament's consent. By the Toleration Act of 1689 the religious liberties of the English Protestants were safeguarded against royal encroachments, while a Mutiny Act, also of 1689, necessitated that the king call Parliament into session every year. Through statutes of 1692, 1694, and 1696 Parliament assumed control of national finances by authorizing public loans, by chartering the Bank of England, and by regulating the coinage—acts previously within the sphere of the king's prerogative. The Triennial Act of 1694 and the Septennial Act of 1716 deprived the sovereign of the right to dispense with parliamentary elections, the first act requiring that they be held at least once in three years, the second specifying seven years. Particularly significant was the Act of Settlement of 1701 by which Parliament decreed that the British crown should be worn only by Protestants and designated that after the death of Anne (soon to succeed William III) it should pass to the Electress Sophia of Hanover, a granddaughter of James I. For the future the sovereign must be a member of the Church of England; he or she could not marry a Roman Catholic or involve England in war in behalf of foreign possessions without Parliament's consent. Judges were no longer removable at the sole command of the king. Finally in 1720 Parliament assumed the once royal prerogative of chartering joint-stock companies.[1]

The character of the sovereigns who ruled between 1702 and 1760 contributed largely to the growth of Parliament's power. Queen Anne (1702–14) was a listless, meek woman of mediocre talents; wholly incompetent to deal with great issues of state, she was dominated by friends and ministers who represented the powerful parties of the day. Then followed the reign of George I (1714–27), a king imported from Hanover, whose ignorance of the English language caused him to ignore the meetings of his ministers, leaving to them the business of government while he occupied himself with unimportant foreign affairs. His successor, George II (1727–60), also born in Hanover, was a timid, pedantic man whose indifference to England and whose interest in Hanover prompted him to give Parliament a free rein. Thus it happened that during these reigns the gains of the Revolution of 1688 assumed the form of parliamentary supremacy over the sovereign.[2]

Since it was undesirable to resort to revolution in order to control the monarchy the task of Parliament after 1688 was to devise some machinery by which it might dictate the course of policy from day to day. One step toward this end was taken during the reign of Queen Anne when Parliament practically deprived the sovereign of the veto power. Earlier, in 1694, William III had begun the practice of mollifying Parliament by choosing ministers who represented the majority of its members—a custom which rapidly developed into the principle of ministerial responsibility or the right of the majority party in the House of Commons to designate and remove the king's advisers, thereby enabling Parliament to dominate the executive branches of the government. Later, after Robert Walpole became the chief financial minister in 1721, he so distinguished himself from his colleagues as to set a precedent for the office of Prime Minister and he also established the idea of cabinet solidarity—the principle that officials who opposed

[1] See again G. B. Adams, *Constitutional History of England*, chapters 15–16.
[2] An engaging study of British politics, 1710–35, is Frederick S. Oliver, *The Endless Adventure* (2 vols., London, 1931). Charles Grant Robertson, *England under the Hanoverians* (New York, 1911), is an attractive survey.

the policy of the majority of the ministers should resign. It is true that Parliament's power was often only nominal—that influential ministers like Walpole kept control by bribing members and by manipulating elections and that in consequence a small circle of men dictated to Parliament rather than submitted to its freely formed judgments. Yet this technique of manipulation acknowledged the theoretical supremacy of Parliament as expressed by Blackstone in the 1750's: "So long therefore as the English constitution lasts we may venture to affirm that the power of Parliament is absolute and without control." [3]

Ordinarily the members of Parliament did not originate or frame legislation pertaining to the colonies; most commonly English merchants or other special groups appealed first to colonial officials for a certain action, whereupon the latter would draft a bill for Parliament's consideration. Because the Whig party (representing the merchant class) held power during most of the time between 1689 and 1760 the laws then enacted were designed as a rule to promote the interests of that class. Thus one series of acts aimed to protect the investments of the merchants in the colonies: the Coin Act of 1708, the statute of 1731 which made the lands and slaves of planters liable for debt, the extension to the colonies of the Bubble Act in 1741, and the Currency Act of 1751. A second group of laws were intended to increase colonial exports both in order to provide raw materials for English industry and to supply the colonies with purchasing power for English goods. In this category belong the naval stores Bounty Acts (1705, 1729), the acts placing rice (1705) and copper ore, beaver skins, and other furs (1722) on the enumerated article list, a White Pine Act of 1711 which reserved for the use of the royal navy certain trees on ungranted lands in New England, New York, and New Jersey, and the indigo bounty act of 1746. Other statutes provided for the protection, regulation, or promotion of colonial trade: the Navigation Act of 1696, a statute canceling the monopoly of the Royal African Company (1698) and another dissolving the company (1750), the act for the suppression of colonial piracy (1700), a law of 1708 designed to promote England's trade with Spanish America, the Molasses Act of 1733, and the acts of 1730, 1735, 1737, and 1739 permitting the plantation colonies to ship sugar and rice to points in Europe south of Cape Finisterre. Similarly the Woolen Act (1699), the Hat Act (1732), and the Iron Act (1750) sought to curtail manufacturing in the colonies. Of more particular interest was a statute of 1699 which regulated the English fishery at Newfound-

---

[3] Edward Jenks, *Parliamentary England* (New York, 1903), is a good, brief, readable introduction to the development of the cabinet.

land. Two facts emerge from this legislation: the extension of Parliament's activity and its preoccupation with issues of industry and trade.[4]

The need for parliamentary legislation touching the colonies came to light in 1705 when they were freely violating the queen's proclamation of 1704 which regulated the value of foreign coin. The Attorney-General of England then pointed out that the proclamation could not be enforced because it carried no penalties; in addition he insisted that the sovereign, single-handed, could not create new offenses for which punishments could be inflicted. This meant that the sovereign, acting alone, could not exert any real power in the sphere of policy—that Parliament must act in order to authorize those penalties necessary for the enforcement of new decrees. Accordingly, in 1708 Parliament passed the coin act which gave legal force to the queen's proclamation of 1704. Since this action was taken at the time when Parliament deprived the sovereign of the veto power it helped to establish the principle of parliamentary supremacy over the colonies; the sovereign could not act without Parliament's approval whereas Parliament could in effect act without the sovereign's. Two other cases reveal the altered status of Parliament and the king. Prior to 1700 Parliament had had no part in either the founding of colonies or the revocation of charters. Now, however, in 1729 it authorized the transfer to the Crown of the rights of the Carolina proprietors and in the 1730's it appropriated large sums of money toward the establishment of Georgia.

Because most parliamentary statutes were designed for Britain they could not be applied to the colonies, where local conditions required special legislation. Hence there existed a distinction between the realm (England, Wales, and after 1707 Scotland) and the dominions (Ireland and the colonies). A statute of the realm did not apply to the colonies unless it was expressly stated in the law that it should so apply, unless it was extended to the dominions by special parliamentary action, as in the case of the Bubble Act, or unless it was adopted by one of the colonial legislatures. Inasmuch as both Parliament and the colonial assemblies exercised the lawmaking power, a rather indefinite distinction between internal and external legislation was allowed to develop. Parliament generally confined itself to the regulation of the external affairs of the colonies (trade, currency, etc.) and permitted the colonial assemblies to legislate for domestic concerns. At best, however, such a distinction was a bit nebulous, since laws regulating trade and debts had important bearings upon local groups while most domestic issues like Indian relations, religion, and the administration of justice might

[4] Mary T. Blauvelt, *The Development of Cabinet Government in England* (New York, 1902), is a concise, lucid outline for the general reader.

readily affect groups outside the colony. Yet the acts passed by Parliament before 1763 were so generally confined to external affairs as to confirm the view of the colonists that domestic legislation was reserved exclusively to the colonial assemblies. On the other hand Parliament assumed that it had full power over both the external and the domestic concerns of the colonies—that it might legislate on any subject and that its statutes would always take precedence over acts of colonial legislatures. From these conflicting conceptions arose a serious misunderstanding between England and the colonies over the limits of Parliament's authority.[5]

## The Agencies of Colonial Administration

Throughout the eighteenth century the executive administration of the colonies was performed in the name of the sovereign—a practice which kept alive the fiction of the royal prerogative which the Revolution of 1688 and the subsequent growth of Parliament had in reality dispelled. To enforce British statutes in the colonies, to apply general principles to special situations, and to provide a corps of officials who could safeguard Britain's interests in America: such was the task of British colonial administration. Due to its preoccupation with the legislative needs of Britain proper and to the difficulty of legislating in detail for subjects three thousand miles away, Parliament could only lay down general rules of policy and then permit executive officers to make detailed applications in day-to-day administration. Nor did Parliament create a special executive machinery for governing the colonies; instead the regular executive agencies of Britain assumed that task. The colonies were esteemed by England primarily for their trade; and because such trade was inseparably tied up with all British commerce it seemed desirable to govern them through the same agencies which regulated British affairs. Moreover, since colonies were valuable to England chiefly as sources of revenue it was imperative that they be supervised at a minimum cost; hence the utilization of the established executive departments for colonial administration.[6]

To American students the problem of imperial government becomes intelligible when one understands its similarity to the problem of federalism in the history of the United States. How might a central government regulate the concerns common to all the colonies or states;

---

[5] Charles H. McIlwain, *The High Court of Parliament* (New Haven, 1934), is an acute study of parliamentary supremacy.

[6] For an excellent résumé of imperial relations see C. M. Andrews, *The Colonial Background of the American Revolution*, chapter 1.

how might disputes among the members of the empire or the federal union be resolved? In the colonial-imperial phase the central government of England conducted all diplomatic negotiations with foreign states, declared and waged war, made treaties of peace, supervised commerce, collected custom duties and quit-rents, regulated currency, managed and disposed of the royal lands, provided naval protection, maintained an army and a postal service, heard appeals from colonial courts, and reviewed legislation enacted by the colonial assemblies. Thus Parliament and the Crown exercised those general powers over the colonies which are now exercised by the President, the Congress, and the federal judiciary over the states.

Among the most important British officials who had a hand in managing the colonies was the Secretary of State for the Southern Department. As the director of Britain's diplomatic relations with France and southern Europe he issued declarations of war, raised armies, conducted military campaigns, and negotiated treaties of peace. Because the numerous wars with France and Spain always involved the colonies he played an important part in colonial administration, acting through the royal governors who were chosen by him (except during the years 1752–61) and were therefore primarily his representatives, responsible to him for colonial defense and military operations. He countersigned their commissions and instructions, transmitted special orders to them, and required that they inform him of events in their colonies. Only once, however, did a secretary infuse vigor into the conduct of colonial affairs: that occurred during the years 1757–61 when William Pitt prosecuted the successful campaigns of the French and Indian War. Otherwise the office failed to provide effective imperial control, for three reasons. First, the ordinary tenure of a secretary was too brief: thirteen ministers served between 1696 and 1724 and nine between 1748 and 1768, so that the incumbent usually did not hold office long enough to become familiar with the remote colonies. Secondly, the minister who enjoyed the longest term (the Duke of Newcastle, 1724–48) had little interest in colonial matters. Finally, the diplomatic and military duties of the office were so onerous as to preclude serious consideration of the details of colonial administration.[7]

The overseas trade of the colonies, coupled with the fact that war and defense against France and Spain called principally for maritime operations, explains the role of the British navy in American waters. After 1708 the management of the navy was entrusted to the

[7] See again L. H. Gipson's *British Empire before the American Revolution*, Vol. I, chapters 1–3, 5.

Admiralty, a board of high officials who formed general policies and executed them through subordinate bureaus such as the Navy Board, the Transport Board, the Victualling Office, and the Navy Pay Office. Acting in close touch with the Secretary of State, the Admiralty and its various offices directed the movements of the navy, appointed naval officers and employees, provided guard-ships for the protection of the coasts of the colonies, supplied convoys and licenses to merchantmen in time of war, issued letters of marque and reprisal to privateers, and issued commissions to vice admiralty officials in America. To the Admiralty also fell the tasks of suppressing piracy, of inspecting colonial naval stores and paying the bounties due, of enforcing the Acts of Trade and Navigation, and of providing transports and convoys for expeditions against the colonies of France and Spain.

Far less important than the Admiralty was the War Office headed by the Secretary at War, whose duties were of a routine nature—since plans of campaign were mapped out by the Secretary of State and the commander-in-chief of the army. The recruiting, inspection, quartering, and payment of the troops constituted the chief duties of the Secretary at War. Thus two of his subordinate officers were the Paymaster of the Forces and the Paymaster of Guards and Garrisons, while independent of the War Office was the Ordnance Board in charge of artillery, engineers, and fortifications. In the thirteen colonies the principal task of the War Office before 1756—to look after four companies of British troops stationed at New York—was performed in a scandalously inefficient manner. The French and Indian War however imposed the great burden of organizing and equipping the British forces in America, whereupon the War Office developed into a department of major importance.[8]

The financial operations of the British government exhibit the reality of Parliament's power after 1688. The Treasury department, descended from the medieval Exchequer, was managed by a board of high officials consisting of the First Lord of the Treasury (usually the Prime Minister), the Chancellor of the Exchequer (the financial leader of the House of Commons) and three Junior Treasury Lords. They supervised the collection of all revenues and the payment of all moneys appropriated by Parliament, making such disbursements through treasury warrants countersigned by the Board. Since Parliament could not foresee every trifling expenditure that might become necessary it was obliged to give the Treasury Board a large measure of discretion in

[8] See again *The Cambridge History of the British Empire*, Vol. I, chapters 14, 21 (important).

meeting irregular claims arising from emergencies. This power, coupled with the authority to withhold payments in cases involving error or peculation, enabled the Treasury officials to exert a decisive influence in colonial administration, for such irregularities and emergencies arose most frequently in the far-away colonies and moreover the outcome of important colonial policies often depended upon the granting or withholding of funds. Most of the money appropriated by Parliament was released by the Treasury to designated spending departments but even so the Treasury Board acted as a sort of court of appeal in cases of an extraordinary nature.[9]

An influential board under the Treasury—the Commissioners of the Customs—supervised the collection of import and export duties and helped to enforce the Navigation Acts. These commissioners also advised other departments on all phases of commercial policy and drafted special instructions to the royal governors to guide their actions with reference to trade and revenue. In the colonies the Customs Board was responsible for the collection of the Virginia tax of 2s. on each hogshead of tobacco exported, the plantation duties on enumerated articles shipped to other colonies (act of 1673), and the duties levied by the Molasses Act of 1733. The act of 1673, which provided for erecting customhouses in the colonies, required the Customs Board to maintain the necessary collectors and searchers. The colonies were then (1683) grouped into districts in charge of a Surveyor of the Customs; after 1720 there were two such surveyors, one presiding over the West Indies and the mainland south of Delaware Bay, the other over the remaining colonies and Newfoundland. A second group of officers—naval clerks—entered and cleared vessels in colonial ports, examined ships' papers, and kept records of the cargoes, voyages, tonnage, ownership, etc., of vessels engaged in colonial trade.[10]

The Crown also claimed a host of other revenues in the colonies: quitrents, forfeitures, escheats, fines for violation of the Navigation and other acts, license fees, and a share of prize goods and money and of property recovered from wrecks. The duty of collecting this money was assigned, after 1679, to the Surveyor and Auditor-General of the king's revenue in America—an officer under the Treasury Board whose deputies in the colonies collected and remitted the funds and forwarded accounts for his scrutiny. First to hold this office was William Blath-

[9] See again W. T. Root, *Relations of Pennsylvania with the British Government*, chapters 1–6, 11.
[10] Bernard Holland, *Imperium et Libertas* (London, 1901), interprets the imperial relationship as a constitutional problem. See chapter 1.

wayt, probably the most influential figure in colonial administration during the years 1679–1706.

Another important body of officials under the Treasury Board—the Commissioners of the Mint—not only managed England's coinage system but also gave advice pertaining to colonial currency policy. The most famous of these commissioners, Sir Isaac Newton, outlined the monetary principles which England applied to the colonies after 1700.

Separate from the executive boards such as those for the Treasury and the Admiralty were the Attorney-General and the Solicitor-General who assisted in drafting charters, parliamentary statutes, and royal decrees and gave opinions to guide officials on the legal side of colonial relations. They also served as representatives of the Crown in preparing and prosecuting cases in the English courts.

When it is recalled that the first five cabinet positions created in the United States government after 1788 were those of the Attorney-General and the Secretaries of State, War, the Treasury, and the Navy, the bearing of imperial administration on American federalism becomes self-evident. And there is another parallel: in colonial times the English Privy Council exercised a function similar to that later assumed by the Supreme Court of the United States.[11]

Before the Puritan Revolution of the 1640's the Privy Council had been a powerful body of the king's chief ministers who acted as a unit in framing and executing official policies. After 1700, however, the influence of the Council declined, partly because the great executive commissions like the Admiralty assumed their special tasks of administration and partly because a new council of ministers—the cabinet— took form as a means of rendering the chief officials responsible to Parliament rather than to the king. The Privy Council therefore became increasingly an honorary body which either ratified ministerial acts in the king's name or supervised minor interests that did not fall within the jurisdiction of the main executive departments. With reference to the colonies the Council received petitions and complaints, disallowed colonial laws, heard appeals from colonial courts, appointed the royal governors and councillors, put the seal of approval to the commissions and instructions of the governors, and settled disputes among royal agents in the colonial service. It issued orders-in-council or royal decrees which, having the force of law, elaborated parliamentary statutes or applied to the colonies established English legal principles in cases where Parliament had not provided specific legislation.

The Privy Council did its work as a committee of the whole, assum-

[11] See again E. B. Greene, *Provincial America*, chapters 11–13.

ing special names for particular business. Thus it acted as a committee for plantation affairs when it disallowed or approved colonial laws and as a separate committee for hearing appeals from the colonial courts. When it received a petition or complaint it called upon the appropriate executive department for a recommendation, which as a rule it ratified offhand, although in rare instances such "representations" were ignored. Generally speaking it was merely a registering, not a deliberative, body.[12]

Apart from special agents in America who served under the executive departments—collectors of customs, naval clerks, commanders of naval vessels, etc.—the Crown made its will effective through a group of officials whom it placed over each royal colony. Such were the governor, the councillors, the secretary, the attorney-general, the receiver-general, the surveyor-general, and the justices of the supreme court. The appointment of these officials gave England great control over the executive and judicial branches of the colonial governments—a fact that explains in part why Virginia was made a royal province in 1624, New Hampshire in 1679, New York in 1685, Massachusetts in 1691, New Jersey in 1702, the Carolinas in 1719–29, and Georgia in 1751. Only Pennsylvania-Delaware and Maryland survived as proprietary governments in which a proprietor exercised the appointive powers, but inasmuch as the proprietors were bound to enforce parliamentary statutes and were restrained from approving any colonial acts contrary to English law, their governments functioned very much like those of royal provinces. Connecticut and Rhode Island retained their early privilege of electing their governors and lesser officials and hence exercised more autonomy than any of the other thirteen colonies.[13]

Each royal governor received both a commission approved by the Privy Council which vested in him the general powers of his office and a long set of instructions which recited in minute detail what acts he should perform or shun. Though legally such instructions were "private orders of the king," they "were in fact a composite draft, showing the handiwork of nearly every prominent official who had to do with the colonies" (Andrews). As the guardian of all English interests in his colony the royal governor also received numerous letters, special instructions, and orders from the various executive departments. Generally the temper of such executive control was ultra-conservative. British officials high and low frowned upon innovations, adhered to the

[12] The detailed, scholarly work of Edward Raymond Turner, *The Privy Council of England in the Seventeenth and Eighteenth Centuries* (Baltimore, 1927, 1928), is best suited to the advanced student.

[13] C. M. Andrews, *Connecticut and the British Government* (New Haven, 1933—Connecticut Tercentenary Commission, no. 1.).

same policies decade after decade, and viewed the colonies as tributary to all groups in England which had an economic stake in America.

## The Colonial Administration at Work

Because the principal executive departments acted more or less in isolation and because they regarded the colonies as a side issue, some machinery was necessary to keep the latter under constant surveillance and to draw together the many threads of imperial administration. After 1696 this task fell to the Board of Trade—a commission of eight active and eight honorary members charged with the duty of making the colonies profitable to England and of assuring that their trade show a balance in her favor. As ardent mercantilists the eight active members (representatives of the English merchants) performed the actual work of the Board, often meeting as frequently as four times a week. They drafted the commissions and instructions of the royal governors, examined applicants for posts in the colonial service and recommended appointments, heard complaints from the colonies, conducted investigations, gave information and advice to the executive departments, to Parliament, and to the Privy Council, and drafted decrees, letters, and statutes. After considering colonial laws they recommended to the Privy Council that such acts be approved or disallowed; they corresponded regularly with the colonial governors, receiving official reports and transmitting special instructions; and they kept a library of newspapers, statutes, customs records, maps, documents, legislative proceedings, and treaties—the most extensive collection of material pertaining to the colonies.[14]

The personnel of the Board (a secretary, a dozen or more clerks, and after 1718 a special legal adviser) acted in a systematic manner. As a rule matters were placed before the Board by English merchants, by executive departments, by colonial governors, by Parliament, or by petitioners in the colonies. Thereupon the Board assembled pertinent information from interviews with interested parties, from colonial officials and from other government offices; then after securing legal counsel it framed a representation which urged that either Parliament, the Privy Council, or one of the executive departments take a recommended action. If the proper authority complied the Board informed the colony of the decision and endeavored to put it into effect. Quite obviously the Board did not have the power of decision; it was merely an investigating and advisory body. But inasmuch as of all agencies in

[14] Oliver M. Dickerson, *American Colonial Government, 1696–1765* (Cleveland, 1912), is the standard work on the Board of Trade.

England it possessed the most knowledge of the colonies its recommendations were generally approved—except when they called for sizable outlays of money.[15]

The history of the Board of Trade exhibits four well-marked phases. Between 1696 and 1725 it met regularly, considered a vast amount of business, and labored diligently to make the colonies subordinate to England, particularly by placing them under royal governors. During the next period, 1725–48, the Board became a prey of politics; indifferent members were appointed who were interested chiefly in their salaries (£1,000 a year); hence indolence and inefficiency were the rule. A revival occurred in 1748 when the Earl of Halifax assumed the presidency and endeavored to elevate the Board to the rank of an effective, independent department of state. However, after his retirement in 1761 a relapse ensued and the Board grew increasingly feeble until it expired in 1784.

The power of the Privy Council and the Board of Trade to approve or disallow colonial laws was gradually extended until after 1730 it applied to all the colonies except Connecticut and Rhode Island. A colonial act might be disallowed on the ground that it was contrary to a parliamentary statute, to the common law, to a colonial charter, or to a governor's instructions. A careful examination of the act in question usually preceded the exercise of the royal disallowance and even then the latter was used sparingly: of 8,563 colonial laws only 469 are recorded as disallowed. The scaling down of debts, the inflating of colonial currency, discrimination against English trade and shipping, the fostering of colonial manufactures, the injuring of other colonies, the usurpation of the powers of the royal governors, and encroachments upon the rights of minority groups—such were the measures denied to the colonial legislatures by the royal disallowance.[16]

The complexity of English administration and the lack of integration among the executive departments aggravated the inherently difficult task of governing settlements three thousand miles away. Despite the numerous activities of the Board of Trade it never became a fully effective colonial office, primarily because it lacked the authority to decide and to enforce. "The Lords of Trade," said Governor Belcher of Massachusetts, "are not very mighty lords; nor are they able to administer life or death," while Governor Pownall remarked that "even the

[15] Mary P. Clarke, "The Board of Trade at Work," *American Historical Review*, XVII (Oct. 1911).

[16] An excellent survey is Elmer B. Russell, *The Review of American Colonial Legislation by the King in Council* (New York, 1915). The best brief discussion is C. M. Andrews, "The Royal Disallowance," *Proceedings*, American Antiquarian Society, N. S. XXIV (Oct. 1914).

meanest . . . officers in the plantations looking up solely to the *giving power*, will scarce correspond with the *directing;* nay, may perhaps make court to the one by passing over the other." Similarly, the division of authority among several agencies often resulted in confusion: as the Earl of Shelburne put it in 1763: "it frequently happened that contradictory orders were given by different officers on the same points, and more frequently in affairs of difficulty and delicacy no orders were given at all, the responsibility of both officers being set aside by each having it in his power to throw the blame on the other." As early as 1721 the Board of Trade complained that too many agencies had to do with the colonies, "from whence it happens that no one office is thoroughly informed of all matters relating to the plantations, and sometimes orders are obtained, by surprise, disadvantageous to your Majesty's service."

Another weakness marred the Board of Trade: of all its members none had ever resided in the colonies; accordingly they did not share the American outlook or possess first-hand knowledge of conditions in the colonies. In 1701 William Penn suggested that former governors be appointed to the Board, arguing that they would "supply the rest with that knowledge their experience has given them, that they who have never been in those parts of the world, cannot, though otherwise oracles, comparably understand." The Board, it is true, endeavored to overcome its lack of American experience by consulting persons who had lived in the colonies or who were authorized to present the colonial point of view.[17] To this end most of the colonies maintained agents in London to look after their interests at Whitehall. Such a colonial agent, somewhat comparable to a lobbyist, was appointed, paid, and instructed by the assembly to answer complaints, to protest against unwanted measures and in general to make known colonial desires. "In and out of the colonial offices he passed, encountering the armies of clerks, minor officials, and members of committees, attending hearings in the hope of furthering the interests of the colonies, keeping a watchful eye on bills and debates in Parliament, writing voluminous letters to his lawyers, and to his American correspondents." [18] Although the Board of Trade almost invariably consulted these colonial agents when framing a policy, even so the bulk of its information came from British merchants and royal officials; consequently the Board generally saw things through British eyes and acted without sufficient regard for

---

[17] James J. Burns, *The Colonial Agents of New England* (Washington, 1935); E. P. Tanner, "Colonial Agencies in England during the Eighteenth Century," *Political Science Quarterly*, XVI (March 1901).

[18] M. Appleton, "Richard Partridge: Colonial Agent," *New England Quarterly*, V (April 1932).

colonial interests. Many agents like Jeremiah Dummer (Massachusetts), Richard Partridge (Rhode Island), and Benjamin Franklin exerted much influence, yet at best they could only protest and retard action; in matters of primary importance interested groups in England usually had their way.[19]

Not all the policies recommended by the Board of Trade were officially adopted. Occasionally it ran against vested interests, as in its campaign to vacate the colonial charters it encountered the opposition not only of proprietary families like the Penns and the Calverts but also of the great English chartered companies which feared that the attack upon the colonial charters might also spread to them. Again, many of the plans urged by the Board (particularly with reference to colonial defense), called for large expenditures which neither Parliament nor the Treasury would authorize. In such cases the Board might appeal to the colonial assemblies for funds, but the latter felt perfectly free to ignore such requests. In fact, the unwillingness of Britain to spend money on the colonies was the primary cause of inefficient administration.

In 1721 the Board of Trade presented a plan for more effective imperial control. It proposed that all the colonies be converted into royal provinces to be ruled by a single governor-general who would be represented in each colony by a deputy-governor. The governor-general should be subordinate to the Board of Trade, which in turn should be converted into a first-class executive department with full powers of decision and action. However, it was not until Halifax became president of the Board that any reforms were made. Then in 1752 it received the right to appoint the colonial governors and to receive all their ordinary correspondence. But the Board lost the appointing power in 1761 and control over colonial correspondence in 1766.[20]

A final gesture toward effective administration was made in 1768 when the Crown created the office of Secretary of State for the Colonies. Probably designed as an independent department coördinate with the other great executive branches, this office failed to bear its intended fruit, for three reasons. First, the colonies had been so long habituated to lax administrative methods that they could not now be subjected to rigorous control. Second, the colonial secretaries were chosen for political reasons, not because they were especially qualified. Finally, the powers of the new secretary were not sharply defined, nor was his

[19] B. W. Bond, "The Colonial Agent as a Popular Representative," *Political Science Quarterly*, XXXV (Sept. 1920).

[20] A. H. Basye, *The Lords Commissioners of Trade and Plantations* (New Haven, 1925), is the best survey of the later history of the Board of Trade (1748–1782).

relationship to other officials made sufficiently clear, with the result that even during the Revolutionary crisis the colonial administration faltered as ministers debated whether the Colonial Secretary was merely the head of the Board of Trade or whether he had full jurisdiction over the colonies as an official coördinate with the other secretaries of state.[21]

Conditions in the colonial civil service also contributed to the ineffectiveness of imperial control. All sorts of considerations dictated colonial appointments: bribery, party politics, friendship, family relationship—nearly anything except merit. No civil service tests existed; training for colonial administration was unknown. Appointments that paid past personal or party debts implied that appointees need not slave at their work, else where was the reward? Hence it was deemed proper for an officeholder to draw his salary and enjoy life in England while a deputy performed his duties in America. And since such deputies received but a pittance from their principals they were forced to accept bribes in order to piece out a living. Of bribery in the customs service Governor Bernard of Massachusetts observed in 1764 that "if conniving at foreign sugars and molasses and Portugal wines and fruits be reckoned corruption, there never was, I believe, an uncorrupt customs house officer in America until within twelve months." Inadequate compensation made it difficult to obtain competent men to occupy subordinate posts; some deputies could not prepare an intelligible report. Far removed from effective supervision many an agent found it easier to live well by complying with colonial wishes than to undergo poverty for the sake of duty. And why not, when bribery, corruption, and favoritism were the accepted means by which the Whig statesmen manipulated Parliament itself? Even well-paid and conscientious colonial officials were often rendered ineffectual—thwarted by colonial opposition. Such resistance encountered by colonial governors and judges sheds additional light upon the weakness of imperial administration.[22]

### Royal Governors versus Colonial Assemblies

Fundamentally the antagonism between the colonists and royal officials in America arose from differences of economic interest—because the merchants and other groups in England, through Parliament and the Crown, strove to direct colonial development and to utilize colonial resources for their own profit, whereas the colonists stubbornly resisted such exploitation. And since each side had to rely upon government

[21] A. H. Basye, "The Secretary of State for the Colonies, 1768–1782," *American Historical Review*, XXVIII (Oct. 1922).

[22] See again J. T. Adams, *Revolutionary New England*, chapters 1–2.

in America to promote its interests, the struggle for control increased with the growing productivity of the colonies. Who should own land? In whose interest should commerce and industry be regulated? By whom should taxes be paid? Who should provide for defense? And who should have the final word about currency and debts? English groups depended upon the royal governors and other officials; the colonists resisted through their elected assemblies. The ensuing contest seemed on the surface to range the assemblies against the king, but back of the king stood Parliament and behind it the English merchants, while behind the assemblies stood the colonial farmers, planters, and merchants.

In a rough way the three branches of colonial government resembled those of England: the royal governor occupied the place of the king, the governor's council that of the House of Lords, and the elected assembly that of the House of Commons. As in English politics the House of Commons became the center of gravity, so also the colonial assemblies strove for supremacy over the royal governors. England, on the other hand, sought to maintain her executive power over the colonies unimpaired and therefore insisted that the governor exercise those powers of which the king, as ruler of England proper, had been deprived. However, colonial leaders, familiar with the fight made by Parliament against the king, claimed its victories for their own assemblies. Thus an English official, Robert Quary, observed in 1703 that the Virginia legislature insisted that it was "entitled to all the rights and privileges of an English Parliament." Obviously, if the colonists made good this claim their assemblies would come to dominate the royal governors in the same manner that Parliament had triumphed over the king.[23]

By 1700 the colonial assembly had won two privileges of the utmost importance: the right to assent to laws and taxes and the right to initiate legislation; hence it could make its demands known and refuse to grant money for the support of government unless they were met. Moreover, the colonists had learned what the English House of Commons had discovered long before: that the executive might nullify parliamentary privileges by manipulating the legislature and that many other liberties were necessary in order to ward off such executive encroachments. First, the members of the legislature must enjoy freedom of debate, the privilege of electing their speaker, and the right to frame their course of action. Secondly, the executive must not determine the membership

[23] Frederic A. Ogg, *Builders of the Republic* (*Pageant of America*, VIII, New Haven, 1927), chapter 1.

of the elected house. In case of disputes arising from elections the members themselves should decide which contestant had the better title; otherwise the executive might manipulate elections in such a way as to pack the house with his own partisans. Nor should any officeholder appointed by the king occupy a seat in the House of Commons. So also elections should be held at prescribed intervals, lest the king keep in office indefinitely a set of members friendly to himself. Thirdly, the sessions of the legislature should be held independently of the sovereign's will. The members should assemble frequently and their meetings should not be adjourned, prorogued, or dissolved except with their consent. Finally, in cases of acute conflict between the legislature and the executive, the latter should give way. Such were the powers and rights which the English House of Commons had won from the sovereign by 1710 and to which the colonial assemblies laid claim during the eighteenth century.[24]

That the assemblies enjoyed a few parliamentary privileges England conceded without protest. Thus when contests over seats arose from elections the assemblies were allowed to decide the issue. Occasionally royal governors attempted to usurp this power, but the assemblies stood firm and successfully asserted their rights. One such contest drew from the Board of Trade an instruction to Lord Cornbury, governor of New Jersey, that he would "do well to leave the determination about elections of representatives to that house, and not to intermeddle therein." Similarly, England did not deprive the assemblies of the privilege of free discussion or the right to choose their own mode of procedure. And as a rule the assemblies met frequently (at least once a year, with a few exceptions); in fact the Massachusetts charter of 1691 definitely provided for annual elections and sessions at fixed dates. The possession of such privileges gave color to the colonial contention that the assembly was in effect a miniature House of Commons. That, however, English officials would not admit; they insisted instead that the colonial governments resembled municipal corporations and that the legal position of the assembly was akin to a municipal council, entirely subordinate to the powers of Parliament.[25]

Accordingly Britain denied to the assemblies certain rights which Parliament exercised openly after 1688. Inspired by the English Triennial Act of 1694 the assemblies periodically passed laws which required

---

[24] Mary P. Clarke, "Parliamentary Privilege in the American Colonies," in *Essays in Colonial History Presented to C. M. Andrews.*

[25] Attention is again called to H. L. Osgood, *The American Colonies in the Eighteenth Century;* each of its four volumes contains lengthy discussions of imperial administration and local politics.

that new elections be held every two, three, or five years. This issue arose in New York, the Carolinas, New Hampshire, and Virginia when the long continuance in office of representatives friendly to the governor made the assemblies unresponsive to colonial needs; as the New York assemblymen put it in 1737: "in some counties even their very representatives have become their greatest grievance." The British government, however, insisted that the power of calling new elections belonged to the royal governors; consequently they were instructed to veto all triennial acts, and whenever such measures were approved by governors they were disallowed by the Privy Council. Governor Montgomerie of New Jersey explained the secret of Britain's attitude when he said that his predecessors "could not have carried on the public business so quietly and successfully as they did, if they had been obliged to call a new assembly every three years."

The colonists also endeavored to put into effect a clause in the English Act of Settlement of 1701 which excluded officeholders appointed by the king from membership in the House of Commons. In 1713 Governor Spotswood of Virginia demonstrated the need for such legislation when he secured the passage of an act which created forty new offices, each with a large yearly stipend, explaining that he would distribute them among the burgesses and thereby control their votes. Since similar practices prevailed in Massachusetts, South Carolina, Maryland, and New York the assemblies of those colonies enacted laws at various times providing that appointees of the governor should not hold seats in the elected house. Opposing such measures as an infringement upon the governor's appointing power, Britain even went so far in 1770 as to disallow a New York act which excluded royal judges from the assembly.[26]

Most conflicts between governor and assembly involved privileges which Parliament exercised in fact although actions were performed in the name of the king. For instance: the early power of the king to reject speakers elected by the House of Commons became after 1688 a matter of mere form as the king automatically ratified the action of the house. In the colonies the royal governors endeavored to make this power really effective by rejecting as well as approving the speakers chosen by the assembly, whereas the colonists insisted that the governor, like the king, should simply register approval. The governors' instructions generally conferred the power both to reject and to approve. A contest on this issue went against the assembly in New Hampshire, and when the Massachusetts House of Representatives successfully defied

---

[26] See again W. Roy Smith, *South Carolina as a Royal Province* (section 2, on government).

two governors a clause was inserted in a supplementary charter of 1725 which definitely vested the governor with the power in question.

Before 1688 the king created new electoral districts in England and determined the number of representatives for each; after 1688, however, this power was never exercised and eventually it was assumed by Parliament itself. So also the colonial assemblies claimed the right to erect new electoral districts and to apportion seats; contrariwise, English officials asserted that the governor's right to issue writs to the sheriffs calling for new elections conferred the power to determine representation—to which the colonists objected that such power enabled the governor to give undue weight to districts favorable to the Crown. When the North Carolina Assembly forced a governor to yield on this issue its law governing representation was disallowed; in New Hampshire the assembly was defeated by the governor. In 1767 the Crown instructed all the royal governors not to sign "any law . . . by which the number of the assembly shall be enlarged or diminished." [27]

In the political struggles of seventeenth-century England the king had possessed great influence over Parliament by virtue of his control over its meetings. His power of prorogation enabled him to end a session; his power of dissolution allowed him to terminate the life of a particular Parliament, whereupon a new election had to be held. Although these powers continued to be exercised after 1688 in the king's name, in fact the decisions were made by Parliament itself. As the representative of the king in the colonies the royal governor was authorized by his commission to prorogue and dissolve the assembly. The power of prorogation (the governor could prorogue to any time or place) was used to bring refractory delegates to terms or to delay action when passions ran high. On the other hand the governor exercised the right of dissolution when, utterly at odds with an assembly, he hoped to secure a more tractable house through another election. However, as the antagonisms between England and the colonies deepened before 1775 dissolution lost its effectiveness because a new assembly was generally as hostile as the old. The frequent use of the power of dissolution after 1763 indicated a revolutionary crisis, just as the dissolution of Parliament by Charles I in 1629 and by Charles II in 1681 foreshadowed the English Revolutions of 1642 and 1688.

As a part of the colonial legislature the governor possessed the right to propose legislation desired by groups in England. But since his recommendations, when contrary to colonial interests, were generally ineffective, he was obliged to exert his legislative influence through the

[27] E. B. Greene, *The Provincial Governor* . . . (Cambridge, 1898), is a standard study of the constitutional relations between England and the colonies.

veto power, with which he was vested by the king's commission "to the end that nothing may be passed or done . . . to the prejudice of us, our heirs and successors." Unlike the modern American veto, that of the royal governor was final: a bill could not be passed over his negative by a special vote of the legislature. His instructions told him what sort of bills to oppose; in general they were the kind to which the royal disallowance was applied. If, contrary to his instructions, he failed to veto an important bill his disobedience might cost him his office or work a forefeiture of his bond. A compromise between the veto and the royal disallowance was the suspending clause which provided that a doubtful act should not go into effect until the king's approval had been given. Just as Parliament deprived the sovereign of the veto power in 1707 so also the colonial assemblies resorted to many ingenious devices in order to nullify the power of the royal governors.[28]

Of the privileges enjoyed by Parliament after 1688 three—free discussion, the determination of contests for seats, and control over procedure—were accorded to the colonial assemblies. Two powers which Parliament made effective by statute—the regulation of elections and the exclusion of royal appointees from the elected house—were denied to the colonies, while five other functions which the king did not in fact perform in England after 1707—the rejection of the speaker, prorogation, dissolution, the creation of new electoral areas, and the veto—remained a part of the royal prerogative in America. But even so the governors' power over the colonial assemblies was not absolute because they possessed the same weapon that Parliament had used to wrest concessions from the king—the right to levy taxes and to grant supplies.

The instructions of the royal governor stated the salary to which he was entitled and enjoined him from receiving other emoluments from the colony. However, except in the case of Georgia (where the Crown paid the salaries of executive officials), the governor had to depend upon colonial revenues for his means of support. And only in two colonies did there exist a permanent fund for this purpose: in Virginia, the revenues from the 2s. tax per hogshead on tobacco exported; in North Carolina, the uncertain quit-rents. The governors of New York, New Jersey, Massachusetts, South Carolina, and New Hampshire, on the other hand, had to rely for their income upon temporary grants from the assembly—a dependence which enabled the assembly to coerce the governor by withholding his salary until he had assented to measures which it desired. By this method the governor could be forced to

---

[28] Leonard W. Labaree, *Royal Government in America* (New Haven, 1930), is an outstanding study of British colonial policy as revealed in the workings of imperial administration.

violate instructions that directed him to veto designated bills. And in order to keep the governor permanently in a state of subordination these five assemblies habitually limited the salary grants to a single year. Of the representatives of New York it was remarked in 1741 "that if a governor will not blindly consent to their bills, however unreasonable or contrary to instructions, they will starve him into compliance." [29]

Endeavoring to break this financial power of the assembly the Crown as early as 1703 instructed the governors to secure permanent appropriations for the salaries of all executive officials. But since the assemblies understood the issue perfectly they steadfastly refused to comply. After a long contest in New York, 1710-15, Governor Hunter surrendered and accepted the principle of the annual grant. A similar controversy occurred in Massachusetts during the term of Governor Burnet (1728-29), whose predecessors had labored in vain to place the salary on a permanent basis. Citing the practice of Parliament in granting the king a fixed income for the duration of his reign, Burnet insisted that the governor should enjoy a similar privilege; otherwise he would be a mere creature of the assembly. The latter rejected the analogy: unlike the king, the royal governor was generally a stranger serving a brief term who had little personal interest in the province; only his financial dependence on the assembly gave assurance of his good conduct. Since Burnet would not accept a grant for a single year he had to finance himself during his short stay in office. His successor, Jonathan Belcher (1730-41), yielded to the assembly. Even the Board of Trade later admitted the hopelessness of its case when in 1755 it ordered the governor of New York to accept temporary grants without further protest.

Not content with reducing upon the governors' legislative power, the assemblies, like the House of Commons, used their control over the purse to usurp many executive functions, insisting that certain conditions be met before appropriation bills were sanctioned. Thus the assemblies extended their sway over financial matters by stating in detail how money was to be spent, by appointing provincial treasurers (except in New Hampshire, New Jersey, and Georgia), by naming collectors of the revenues levied by the colonies (as distinct from Crown revenues), and by setting up committees to supervise the spending of money appropriated.[30] Similarly the assemblies usurped much

[29] See again E. Channing, *History of the United States*, Vol. II, pp. 282–366.

[30] For a detailed study of party organization and legislative committees see Ralph V. Harlow, *The History of Legislative Methods in the Period before 1825* (New Haven, 1917), chapters 1–3.

of the governor's power over Indian affairs by appointing their own agents to transact such business. In the military sphere the governor's power as commander of the colony's armed forces was controlled in various ways: appropriation acts dictated when and where troops were to be used; legislative committees took charge of the management of military operations; and the assemblies determined appointments by withholding officers' pay. All these powers of the legislature issued from the primary power of taxation as asserted by the Massachusetts assembly in 1692: "no aid, tax . . . or imposition whatsoever" shall be "levied on any of their majesties' subjects or estates, but by the act and consent of the governor, council and representatives of the people assembled in general court."

To the colonists the outcome was pleasant indeed; the people's money, declared a Pennsylvania publication of 1759, "is never so well disposed of as in the . . . purchase of good laws." When colonial autonomy was at stake it mattered little that the assembly's power over the purse resulted in coercion and even bribery and that it placed the governors in an intolerable situation by making them responsible to two hostile parties—to British officials who issued their instructions and to colonial legislators who appropriated money. If the governor was a corruptionist like Fletcher or Cornbury he could get a good price for violating the king's orders; if, like Burnet, he was uncompromisingly faithful to the king he usually ran afoul of the assembly and accomplished little. Even the most effective administrators (from Britain's point of view)—honest, tactful, and able men like Hunter, Spotswood, and Shirley had to make many concessions contrary to their instructions.[31] All which explains the steady growth of the assembly's powers —a trend particularly marked during the years of war, 1744–63. Of Massachusetts the Board of Trade observed in 1757: "Almost every act of executive and legislative power, whether it be political, judicial or military, is ordered and directed by votes and resolves of the general court, in most cases originating in the house of representatives." The Privy Council complained in 1745 that the assembly of New York had assumed control of practically the entire executive branch of the government; of South Carolina Governor Glen remarked in 1748 that "the people have the whole of the administration in their hands"; while Governor Lewis Morris said of New Jersey that there was a strong "inclination . . . in the meanest of the people (who are the

---

[31] Outstanding studies of colonial governors are Alice M. Keyes, *Cadwalader Colden* (New York, 1906); George A. Wood, *William Shirley* (New York, 1920); Leonidas Dodson, *Alexander Spotswood*; Everett Kimball, *Public Life of Joseph Dudley*.

majority and whose votes make the assembly) to have the sole direction of all the affairs of the government."

The extension of the influence of the assemblies over the royal governors magnified the importance of the courts as the last line of defense for Britain's interests in America. Not only did the trial and punishment of violators of British laws determine the effectiveness of colonial administration; all rules for individual cases could not be prescribed in detail by a general statute; hence many decisions had to be left to the discretion of judges. But the manner in which judges decided doubtful points of law and evidence determined whether British policies were to be actually enforced or ignored. For these reasons both Britain and the colonists desired to dominate the courts.[32]

The English theory of law, derived from the Middle Ages, defined the king as the fountain of justice. Accordingly, he appointed the judges, established courts, and prosecuted criminals on the assumption that crime was a breach of "the king's peace" and an affront to his dignity. English history, however, had demonstrated before 1688 that judges are human beings, swayed by their associates and superiors and that the king's power of appointment often placed justices in office who merely registered his desires. Accordingly, Parliament in 1701 endeavored to make the judges independent by depriving the king of his power to remove them at will so that he might pack the courts with his satellites.

The earlier principle of the king's control of justice was extended to the colonies before the Revolution of 1688. The royal governors, as agents of the king, were commissioned to erect courts and to appoint the judges—both the local justices of the peace (who were also judges of the county courts) and the justices of the superior courts of appeal. Moreover, the governor and council served as the highest appellate court within a colony—not in criminal cases but in civil suits involving sums in excess of £50, £100, or £300. Final appeals in both civil and criminal cases could be made to the Privy Council. Acting under orders from the governor, the attorney-general of a royal colony prosecuted cases for the king in the higher courts.[33]

Four major issues arose in the contest between the assemblies and Britain over the control of colonial justice. One question was: should the governor or the legislature erect the necessary courts? During the

[32] George A. Washburne's *Imperial Control of the Administration of Justice in the Thirteen American Colonies, 1684–1776* (New York, 1923) is the most complete study of this theme.

[33] A. M. Schlesinger, "Colonial Appeals to the Privy Council," *Political Science Quarterly*, XXVIII (June and Sept. 1913).

early colonial period the assemblies had exercised this power and thereafter they insisted that the governor could not act alone. Although a few special courts were created by executive order, the assemblies generally made good their contention; hence the main judicial structure of the colonies rested upon laws to which they had given their consent.

A second controversy involved the jurisdiction of the courts. The colonists generally desired to make the county courts supreme, partly because the judges were neighbors of suitors and therefore inclined to favor them in contests with outsiders, partly because local justice saved the expense of travel to courts far away. For opposite reasons British merchants and landlords desired to enlarge the powers of the central or superior courts—to grant to them original jurisdiction in order to save the cost of attending numerous county courts and to widen their appellate jurisdiction as a means of protection against decisions influenced by local pressures. In this controversy the British government favored the central courts and therefore consistently disallowed colonial acts which extended the jurisdiction of the county courts.[34]

The appointment and removal of judges occasioned the third—and most active—conflict. The tendency of British policy was to give the governor the power to dismiss judges at will, thus enabling him to appoint new men who were properly respectful of British interests. Claiming the same power that Parliament had exercised in 1701—that of protecting judges against summary dismissal at the mere pleasure of the executive—the assemblies of New York, Pennsylvania, and North Carolina passed bills between 1759 and 1761 which provided that judges should hold office during good behavior. Such measures, however, were either vetoed by the governor or disallowed; and in 1761 general instructions sent to all the governors ordered that they veto any acts which regulated judicial tenure and that, when appointing new judges, they reserve the executive's right to dismiss them at his pleasure.

Even then, however, the assembly was not helpless: if a governor removed colonially minded judges and appointed unpopular successors it might withhold their salaries, force to resign, and compel him to respect its desires. Once again the assemblies claimed a power exercised by Parliament after 1688; once more the Board of Trade objected, arguing that to grant permanent tenure to judges would "lessen that just dependence which the colonies ought to have upon the government of the mother country."

During colonial times only sixty-seven cases were appealed from

[34] O. P. Chitwood, *Justice in Colonial Virginia* (Baltimore, 1905), is a lucid analysis, for the advanced student.

American courts to the Privy Council; hence that phase of judicial control did not seriously antagonize the colonists. The rules governing such appeals had a restraining effect: in case an appellant failed to secure a reversal of a colonial decision he was obliged to bear the expense of the appeal and to pay any damages incurred by the appellee. The cost of transporting witnesses to England, the delays involved, and the uncertainty of the outcome deterred such appeals except when a litigant had a strong sense of the justice of his cause.[35]

In the administration of the colonies prior to 1763 British officials adopted two contradictory policies: they conceded to the assembly the right to vote taxes and to make appropriations but they also denied that it possessed the status and the other privileges of the English House of Commons. The colonies, however, tended to duplicate English experience in that the elected house used its control over the purse in order to establish its supremacy over the executive; hence it became evident that its financial power conflicted with the theory that it was an inferior body. Two alternatives therefore confronted British officials: they might limit the financial independence of the assembly, or they might acknowledge that as the master of the governor it was in effect supreme. When, after 1763, they chose the first alternative they forced the political issue of the Revolutionary War.

[35] H. D. Hazeltine, "Appeals from Colonial Courts to the King in Council," *Report*, American Historical Association, 1894.

## BIBLIOGRAPHICAL NOTE

WORKS PREVIOUSLY CITED: G. Bancroft, *History of the United States*, II, chs. 28, 31, 41; III, chs. 1–3; G. N. Clark, *The Later Stuarts*, chs. 6, 8–9, 12; C. J. H. Hayes, *Political and Cultural History of Modern Europe*, I, ch. 10; A. C. Flick (ed.), *History of the State of New York*, II, ch. 5; III, chs. 1, 4; N. D. Mereness, *Maryland as a Proprietary Province*.

SOURCES: Orders in council on important issues are contained in *Acts of the Privy Council of England, Colonial Series* (ed. W. L. Grant and James Munro, 6 vols., Hereford, 1908–12). The orders are arranged chronologically, for the period 1613–1783. A most important collection. Another highly important collection is Leo F. Stock's edition of the *Proceedings and Debates of the British Parliaments respecting North America* (3 vols., Washington, 1924–30). *Royal Instructions to British Colonial Governors* (ed. by L. W. Labaree, 2 vols., New York) is also of primary value. A political classic, Jeremiah Dummer's *A Defense of the New England Charters* [1721] is reprinted in Vol. I of J. Almon, *A Collection of the Most Interesting Tracts . . . on the . . . American Colonies . . .* (2 vols., London, 1766). Thomas Pownall, *The Administration of the Colonies* (4th ed., London, 1769), discusses constitutional problems of empire in a spirit friendly to the colonies, from the point of view of a colonial governor. Two works which give insight into the problems of a colonial governor are: C. H. Lincoln (ed.), *Correspondence of William Shirley* (2 vols., New

York, 1912), and Gertrude S. Kimball (ed.), *The Correspondence of the Colonial Governors of Rhode Island* (2 vols., New York, 1902–03). See again A. B. Hart (ed.), *American History Told by Contemporaries*, II, pp. 127–224.

STUDIES USEFUL TO THE SPECIAL STUDENT: Among detailed, technical studies the following are useful to the special student: Arthur G. Dorland, "The Royal Disallowance in Massachusetts," (Kingston, Ontario, 1917); Edgar J. Fisher, *New Jersey as a Royal Province, 1738–1776* (New York, 1911); Percy S. Flippin, *The Financial Administration of . . . Virginia* (Baltimore, 1915); William H. Fry, *New Hampshire as a Royal Province* (New York, 1908); Charles L. Raper, *North Carolina, A Study in English Colonial Government* (New York, 1904); Charles W. Spencer, *Phases of Royal Government in New York, 1691–1719* (Columbus, 1905); Henry R. Spencer, *Constitutional Conflict in Provincial Massachusetts* (Columbus, 1905); David D. Wallace, *Constitutional History of South Carolina from 1725 to 1775* (Abbeville, S.C., 1899). Consult also the list of special works at the end of chapter 7 dealing with the government of individual colonies.

☆ XXI ☆

## BRITAIN CONQUERS NEW FRANCE

THE rivalry between Britain and France for supremacy in North America which continued with full force after 1713 determined the later course of colonial development. While war was in progress Britain had to grant concessions to the colonies as the price of their necessary coöperation; hence she failed to enforce many of the oppressive features of her colonial system. But once she had expelled France from North America she attempted a vigorous enforcement of her imperial policies. Victory, however, came too late; the colonists had become so accustomed to acting as they pleased that they could not then be effectively repressed. In short, the French conflict fostered an American spirit of independence; British success inspired efforts to curb the colonies; and that in turn drove them to revolt.

### PEACE AS A PRELUDE TO WAR

After the Peace of Utrecht one sentiment dominated the principal powers of Europe: let there be peace; let the nations recover from the exhaustion of war and seek in industry and commerce the strength to sustain them when the conflict should be renewed. Bitter dynastic hatreds and economic rivalries remained; innumerable points of friction kept Europe in a threatening state of "universal combustion." In the shifting diplomatic alignments of the time three constant factors were at work: the enmity between France and Britain, the intense antagonism between Britain and Spain, and the accord between Spain and France. Once the Hanoverian dynasty had been established in Britain (1714) the Whig statesmen desired at all costs to avoid a general war lest it give the signal for an internal revolution which would put a Catholic Stuart upon the throne—not an imaginary menace, since two uprisings did occur and until 1748 France championed the Stuart cause. To consolidate the gains of Queen Anne's War (which had added £300,000 to Britain's favorable trade balance), to restore commerce with France, always one of Britain's best customers, and to strengthen her grip on colonial trade: such motives lay behind the British desire for peace. "Trade," said Robert Walpole, "is the main riches of the nation and enhances the value of our lands." Dominant in English politics between 1721 and 1739, Walpole labored to keep France and Spain apart, refused to force a war with France, and played one power against another in his effort to prevent a European combination aimed at Britain. Material well-being for the nation was the end which he pursued with easygoing, unruffled assurance, with unwearied patience, and with a cynical disregard for abstractions and ideals. "We have one minister," wrote a contemporary, "that does everything with the same ease and tranquillity as if he were doing nothing." [1]

France too desired nothing so much as an interval of peace. Confronted by Austria on the Continent and by Britain on the seas and ruled now by a boy king (Louis XV was only five when he succeeded his grandfather in 1715) the French willingly joined the concert of Europe to maintain the balance of power and embraced the British policy of peaceful penetration in the colonial sphere. During the regency of Philip, Duke of Orleans (1715–23), who valued peace abroad and pleasure at home, France combined in 1717 with Britain and Holland to form the Triple Alliance which became the Quadruple Alliance when Austria entered in 1718 and the Quintuple Alliance when Spain joined in 1720. By such coöperation the powers maintained the peace of Europe until 1733. [2]

In the meantime America had lost none of its attraction as a source of riches to European investors and speculators; both Britain and France indulged in frenzied financial schemes inspired by the American dream. France had its Mississippi Company, fathered by John Law in 1717, given at first a monopoly of the trade of Louisiana and the beaver trade of Canada and then allowed to absorb other companies until it virtually monopolized the commerce of France. Acting in harmony with Law's companion national bank (which issued France's paper currency), the Mississippi Company took charge of the mint and the collection of the nation's taxes. Britain had its South Sea Company, now holding the assiento and, as rumor affirmed, about to fall heir to the silver mines of Peru. In 1720 Parliament gave this company official sanction by authorizing it to manage the national debt. Both companies promised such fabulous dividends to stockholders that a speculative craze drove the price of shares to ten times their par values; then in 1721 both bubbles burst; stock prices declined to almost nothing and thousands of investors were

[1] George R. Sterling Taylor's *Robert Walpole and His Age* (London, 1931) is a well-rounded, readable survey of society and politics.
[2] See again *The Cambridge History of the British Empire*, Vol. I, chapters 11, 15–18.

ruined. In England the crash resulted in placing Walpole in power
while Law was forced to leave France. Both episodes demonstrated
that schemes of colonial exploitation were now uppermost in the
public mind.

The long interval of peace after 1713 did nothing to remove the
causes of strife between France and Britain; in fact each nation
seized the opportunity to extend its power in America, thereby in-
tensifying instead of allaying the underlying antagonisms.[3] During
the 1720's and 1730's the Board of Trade repeatedly recognized
the menace of French competition and urged aggressive measures
to combat the French influence in Newfoundland and Nova Scotia
and on the New York and Carolina frontiers. But since a strong
forward policy meant war with France the more drastic recommendations of the Board were ignored by Walpole and his fellow ministers. And because both France and Britain avoided war in order
to gain greater strength, peace merely postponed the time of reckoning. The English accused the French of "pushing into an universal
commerce as the way of coming at their darling scheme of universal
dominion"; in 1740 the Duke of Newcastle declared: "From what
I can see France will sooner or later dominate Europe, and perhaps
America also."

After 1713 France compensated herself for the loss of Nova Scotia
and Newfoundland by erecting Fort Louisbourg on Cape Breton
Island. Spending money lavishly upon this stronghold she rapidly
made it the most powerful fortress in America. Favored by an Atlantic harbor open during the winter it became the focus of vigorous
activities, naval, commercial, and diplomatic, by which France strove
to safeguard Canada and to exert a preponderating influence in Nova
Scotia, upper New England, and the northern fishery. Moreover, in
time of war French privateers from Louisbourg could prey upon
the fishing boats and trading vessels of New England, thereby undermining the prosperity of Massachusetts.[4]

Determined to achieve the mastery of the northern fishery the
French removed their settlers from Placentia to Cape Breton Island
and continued to pursue the codfish so aggressively that their loss
of Newfoundland had little effect. Meanwhile, the British fishery at
Newfoundland had declined, weakened and disorganized by Queen
Anne's War and torn by the rivalries between the resident settlers
and the fishermen of western England who desired to conduct the
fishery from English ports. In 1718 the Board of Trade estimated

[3] See again G. M. Wrong, *The Rise and Fall of New France*, Vol. II, chapters 24–27.
[4] William Wood, *The Great Fortress* (*Chronicles of Canada* series, Toronto, 1915).

that England's annual income from the Newfoundland fishery had diminished by £314,000 since 1644—a loss attributed to the inefficiency of the fishermen settled on the island; consequently the Board recommended that they be removed to Nova Scotia and that the fishery be carried on exclusively from England. However, the profits of the London merchants who supported the settlers told in the long run and the latter were not removed; instead they became so important that Britain finally accepted the settlement as inevitable and sanctioned it in 1729 by establishing a civil government at the island. Newfoundland proper was not a subject of dispute between Britain and France, but the fishery was; and because by 1740 it yielded Britain between £225,000 and £300,000 annually it was a prize well worth holding against the French.

A more pressing dispute between the two powers involved Nova Scotia, a province which Britain esteemed, not for its fur trade, now shrunk to trifling proportions, but for its forests capable of producing the best of masts and other naval stores and for its fishery, the finest in America. After 1710 Britain allowed the French settlers either to leave or to remain; having neither purchasers for their lands nor vessels in which to leave the Acadians had to stay. The British occupied Annapolis and established there a governor and four companies of fifty soldiers; otherwise the inhabitants of Nova Scotia were French (between 2,500 and 12,000), concentrated in three settlements: one in the south near Annapolis and two in the north near the Basin of Minas and Chignecto Bay. Failing to erect other forts or to bring in non-French settlers, the British allowed the Acadians to retain their property, to adhere to their Roman Catholic faith, and to trade with Cape Breton, Quebec, and France. Nor did Britain exact quit-rents or levy taxes.[5]

France in the meantime, still hoping to control the region, exerted her influence from Louisbourg, whose officials encouraged the Acadians to remain and to adhere to the French interest. The boundary of the province provoked controversy as France contended that she had ceded only the peninsula south of the Bay of Fundy, while the British claimed all the peninsula north to Cape Breton and all the mainland north of the St. Croix River. From the resident Indians (the Micmac and Malecite tribes, closely allied with the Abenakis of Maine—a tribe bitterly hostile to New England) France could count upon unwavering support. The political mentors of the submissive, inarticulate Acadians were Jesuit priests who acted in con-

[5] J. B. Brebner, *New England's Outpost* (New York, 1927), treats the English rule of the Acadians as a political problem.

cert with French officials at Louisbourg to incite the Indians and the settlers against the British with the object of preventing their fishing off the coast. So also the Jesuits instructed the Acadians not to take an oath of loyalty demanded by Britain which would have pledged them to bear arms against their countrymen in Canada. So firm was the resistance on this score that when an oath was finally taken by the Acadians in 1730 it was so ambiguous as to be wholly ineffectual.

The weakness of Britain's rule in Nova Scotia prompted the Board of Trade to call repeatedly for drastic measures. It recommended that the Acadians be removed from the province and replaced by Protestant settlers, that new forts be erected, that four regiments and a warship be added to British defenses, and that a tract of 200,-000 acres of timber land be reserved for the royal navy. But because of the expense involved and the desire of the Whig ministers for peace with France the proposals of the Board were long ignored.[6]

By 1715 land speculation and settlement on the New England frontier had replaced the earlier interest in the fur trade. As the New Englanders advanced up the Kennebec and Penobscot Rivers they encroached upon the hunting lands of the Abenakis, thereby threatening them with extinction. The governor of Canada, promising ammunition and supplies to the Indians if they would drive the English from the eastern frontier, influenced them through Jesuit priests, particularly Père Râle, in charge of a mission at Norridgewock on the Kennebec. In New England Indian missionary work had practically ceased; moreover, the haughty, superior attitude which the New Englanders displayed at the council fire enraged their forest neighbors. In June 1722 the Abenakis, incited by the French, attacked the English settlements on the Kennebec; in July Governor Shute of Massachusetts declared war. Only New Hampshire and Massachusetts participated in the expeditions which proceeded up the Penobscot and Kennebec Rivers, destroyed the Jesuit missions there, killed Père Râle, and drove the Indians inland more than a hundred miles from the coasts of New Hampshire and Maine. So weakened were the Abenakis by Râle's war that eastern New England thereafter was exempt from attack, and settlement moved rapidly toward the interior.[7]

To the west of New England the Anglo-French conflict revolved around the fur trade. After 1713 the French resumed their advance in the Great Lakes country, reoccupying strategic sites previously abandoned and constructing new forts and trading posts. Two routes

[6] See again F. Parkman, *Half-Century of Conflict*, chapters 9-24.
[7] See again J. T. Adams, *Revolutionary New England*, chapters 11-13.

led from Montreal, the metropolis of the fur trade, to the great West. One traversed the Ottawa River and Georgian Bay to the northern end of Lake Huron; there it divided, one branch leading to Sault Ste. Marie and Lake Superior, the other to Michilimackinac and Lake Michigan. On northern Lake Superior the French established a fort, Kaministiquia, which commanded the country adjacent to the northern shore; to the southwest, in Chequagemon Bay, they erected Fort La Pointe which gave access to the upper waters of the Mississippi and also served the traders who frequented the lands of the Chippewa south of Lake Superior. From Michilimackinac the French *voyageurs* entered Green Bay (at the foot of which stood Fort La Baye); thence the route followed the Fox and Wisconsin Rivers to Fort Marin at the junction of the Wisconsin and the Mississippi. Here again the route divided: on the upper waters of the Mississippi were several small forts, while south of Fort Marin the traders paddled down the Mississippi to Fort de Chartres near the French settlements of Cahokia and Kaskaskia in the Illinois country. From Michilimackinac the *voyageurs* also traversed Lake Michigan to its southeastern end, where Fort St. Joseph on the St. Joseph River dominated the surrounding region, and to the southwestern end, where a fort on the Chicago River was the key to the Illinois River route to the Mississippi.[8]

The second and more important route led from Montreal by way of the St. Lawrence and Lake Ontario to the western end of Lake Erie. There the settlement at Detroit commanded the lands of the Ottawa between Lakes Erie and Huron and gave the French control of the southern entrance to Lake Huron as well as a second approach to Lakes Superior and Michigan. The Maumee River, flowing into the western end of Lake Erie, opened the way to the Ohio valley where the French had Fort Miami on the Maumee and forts Quiatanon and Vincennes on the Wabash. It was this lower lakes route which became the scene of Anglo-French rivalry for the interior trade.

The organization of the French fur trade exhibited the common features of early merchant capitalism. Wealthy merchants of Montreal imported from France the trading goods required and sold them on credit to interior traders called *bourgeois* who in turn employed *voyageurs* or *engagés*—men versed in woodcraft and adept in navigating canoes and bargaining with the Indians. The *bourgeois* usually had their *engagés* in debt; moreover they supplied the Indian

[8] See again L. P. Kellogg, *The French Regime in Wisconsin*, chapters 14–20.

on credit, taking in payment the furs with which they in turn paid their debts to their Montreal creditors. In order to reduce the frauds incident to the trade the French government required that the *bourgeois* buy licenses (and at a high price) and submit to the regulations imposed by the commander of the fort in their sphere of operations. Usually a favored company held the exclusive right of buying all furs exported from Canada—a privilege which enabled the company to keep prices at low figures. This monopoly, plus the licensing system, meant that the interior traders could not pay high prices to the Indians, thereby creating an opportunity for English interlopers to cut in by overbidding the French concessionaires.[9]

After 1713 the New York fur trade divided into three branches. The Iroquois continued to bring furs to Albany, encouraged to do so by acts of the New York Assembly, 1714–17; and yet this source of supply steadily decreased until by 1725 only 17 per cent of the furs reaching Albany were brought thither by the Indians. The aggressive advance of the French in the Ohio and Mississippi valleys convinced the more enterprising Albany traders that they too must go directly to the west. By 1716 they were journeying to Lake Ontario in quest of furs; during the 1720's Governor Burnet of New York advocated direct penetration and sent out trading parties each year; in 1725–27 the New Yorkers constructed a post and fort, Oswego, at the mouth of the Onondaga River on Lake Ontario. Fearing that this direct trade would alienate the Iroquois, many of the Albany men opposed it at the start, but it proved such an effective answer to French expansion that by 1725 68 per cent of the furs arriving at Albany were brought in by the western traders. The French met the English advance by erecting a post and fort at Niagara (1716, 1726) to protect their stake in the Ontario region.

Recognizing the fur trade as a grand prize of North America the Board of Trade in 1721 urged that Britain adopt aggressive measures to detach the interior Indians from their alliance with France.[10] British traders should be encouraged to take Indian wives and to live among the tribes; Anglican missions should be established as a counterweight to the Jesuits, who were now regarded as political agents of France; forts should be erected on Lakes Erie and Ontario; the good will of the Indians should be secured by presents and treaties of alliance; the fur trade should be so regulated as to eliminate

[9] See again H. A. Innes, *The Fur Trade in Canada*, pp. 84–192.

[10] See again H. L. Osgood, *American Colonies in the Eighteenth Century*, Vol. III, pp. 363–404, 491–539; Vol. IV, chapters 14–17.

those incessant frauds which angered the Indians; and monopolies should be avoided in order to enable British traders to overbid the French. These elaborate plans, however, were not adopted by the Crown (the expense was too great); hence the only concrete evidence of British advance between 1713 and 1740 was Fort Oswego.

Albany also obtained interior furs through a trade with Montreal made possible by the cheapness of English dry goods—particularly strouds, "a coarse woolen blanketing." Fifteen per cent of the furs entering Albany in 1725 were sent from Montreal in payment for such English merchandise. Although this traffic seemed an easy way of tapping the profits of the French fur trade it was strongly opposed by Governor Burnet and the Albany expansionists on the ground that it did not challenge the French influence among the Indians and that at any time it might be destroyed by France. The New York Assembly therefore passed laws (1720–27) to prohibit the sale of English goods to Canada; however, New York importers and London merchants who supplied the Canadians with traders' goods protested to the Privy Council and in 1729 secured the disallowance of the restraining acts. Nor did the French government suppress this traffic with the ancient enemy.[11]

Although both France and Britain claimed supremacy in the Great Lakes country and demanded that the other withdraw; although the competition of the interior traders of the two nations was sharpened year by year; and although the Board of Trade recommended strong measures against France, nevertheless the rival claims were not pressed to the point of war, largely because the home governments favored peace and economy. Meanwhile the Iroquois were losing their earlier status of middlemen for the English; now, about 1740, many Albany magnates were buying lands from the Six Nations and promoting settlement in the eastern part of the Mohawk valley. Numerous frauds in such land deals estranged the Iroquois from the British cause: in 1744 Governor Colden of New York lamented that the "Indians . . . will on no occasion trust an Albany man."

The progress of the French colony, Louisiana, shaped the relations between Britain and France on the southern frontier.[12] So great were the capital outlays needed for the development of the Mississippi valley that the French government had to offer generous

[11] Peter Wraxall's *An Abridgement of the Indian Affairs* . . . *transacted in the Colony of New York* [1678–1751] (ed. C. H. McIlwain, Cambridge, 1915), contains an excellent introduction on the northern fur trade.

[12] For a good introductory survey, brief, accurate, well-written, see Albert Phelps, *Louisiana* (Boston, 1905), chapters 1–4.

privileges and monopolies to enterprisers in the new colony. Thus between 1712 and 1715 Louisiana was held as the private domain of one Antoine Crozat; in 1717 John Law's Mississippi Company received the province along with the right to govern it and a monopoly of its trade. Because an underlying object was to supply France with rice, tobacco, silk, and indigo, large estates were granted to promoters who hoped at first to people them with emigrants from Switzerland, the Palatinate, and the Low Countries. But this scheme failed: John Law himself was able to send only two hundred and fifty Palatines to his estate on the Arkansas River instead of the nine thousand he intended to transport thither. Hence the promoters had to rely principally on slave labor; in 1745 Negroes accounted for 36 per cent of the population. Rice became the principal product of the province; tobacco and indigo cultivation made moderate progress; experiments with silk and cotton failed. Four centers of settlement existed in 1745: at New Orleans (founded in 1718), at Natchez, at Natchitoches on the Red River, and in the Illinois country. The latter, an offshoot of Canada but annexed to Louisiana in 1717, produced wheat, Indian corn, and livestock. In 1731 the Mississippi company surrendered its political rights to the king and thereafter Louisiana, like Canada, was governed as a royal province.[13]

Wedged in between Louisiana and the English colonies were four important Indian tribes: the Chickasaws and Choctaws, adjacent to Louisiana, and the Cherokees and Creeks, on the Carolina-Georgia frontier. The French controlled the Choctaws and the English the Cherokees; both wooed the other tribes, the English more successfully. Two policies of the French favored the English. First, the Mississippi Company used its monopoly of the fur trade to exploit the Indians by exacting exorbitant prices for traders' goods, thus driving the red men into the arms of the South Carolina traders. In 1731 Charleston exported 250,000 deerskins. Secondly, the agricultural program of Louisiana called for the removal of the Indians from desirable planting lands. Fearing such deportation the Natchez tribe in 1729 massacred two hundred and fifty French settlers, thereby inaugurating the Natchez wars which until 1750 imposed a severe drain upon the infant colony: in 1745 it could boast of only 3,200 white settlers and 2,000 Negro slaves.[14]

[13] N. M. M. Surrey, *The Commerce of Louisiana during the French Regime* (New York, 1916), is a comprehensive, technical study, for the special student.
[14] Justin Winsor's *The Mississippi Basin* (Boston, 1895) treats the Anglo-French conflict with emphasis upon Louisiana. Very useful.

Britain's greatest defensive effort between 1713 and 1740—the establishment of Georgia—indicated that war with Spain (which would involve the southern colonies) was more imminent than war with France. Britain claimed the land south to a line midway between the thirtieth and thirty-first parallels; the Spaniards in Florida denied that Britain was entitled to Georgia and demanded that she evacuate all posts south of St. Helena Sound, near Beaufort, South Carolina. Charging that the Spaniards assaulted British vessels along the coast, that they incited the slaves of South Carolina to revolt (a dangerous uprising occurred there in 1739), that at St. Augustine they harbored runaway Negroes and servants, and that they induced the Indians to attack Georgia, Britain made vigorous preparations for war. In 1738 Oglethorpe returned to America from England, bringing a newly formed regiment and a commission as commander of the forces of Georgia and South Carolina. After stationing most of the regiment on the Altamaha River, Oglethorpe visited Charleston whence he journeyed westward to secure the alliance of the Creeks in the impending struggle.[15]

The strife on the Florida frontier was primarily a by-product of a commercial conflict between Britain and Spain which culminated in war in 1739. The trade concessions which Britain had forced from Spain in Spanish America had only whetted the appetite of British merchants for a larger share of the silver of Mexico and Peru. It will be recalled that in 1713 the South Sea Company had obtained a thirty-year monopoly of the slave trade with the Spanish colonies and the right to send each year one vessel of five hundred tons (one thousand tons, after 1716) with a cargo of general merchandise for sale at Porto Bello. The company might employ British ships in the slave trade and transport silver and other Spanish products directly from Spanish America to Britain, and in British ships. Otherwise all British vessels and traders were excluded from the Spanish colonies and all legal commerce had to be carried on by way of Spain. These concessions did not appease Britain because they left intact the main features of Spanish policy which closed the Spanish Indies to British merchants; Spain in turn was irked because the concessions, wrung from her by force, threatened to wreck her whole colonial system.

After 1713 the South Sea Company concentrated on the general trade in merchandise rather than on the traffic in slaves, stationing its "annual ship" off the coast of Porto Bello where it was frequently restocked with manufactured goods brought by trading sloops under

[15] See again V. W. Crane, *The Southern Frontier*, chapters 8–13.

the cover of night.[16] The value of a single cargo sent out in 1717 was £256,800. Moreover, when the company dispatched vessels with slaves to the Spanish colonies it sent along forbidden merchandise which was received on the sly and sold by its agents in such towns as Havana, Vera Cruz, Porto Bello, Cartagena, and Buenos Aires. Private British merchants at Jamaica joined in this illegal trade so that after 1713 British shipping "abounded in Spanish waters." Spanish officials used two methods to drive out the British smugglers: they arrested and imprisoned British traders in Spanish towns and confiscated their goods; and they stationed guard-ships in the Caribbean which seized British vessels laden with such products as dyewoods, indigo, and silver. Since these commodities were also obtained from the British islands many innocent British vessels were taken by the *guarda-costas*, to the intense exasperation of British merchants who raised the issue of the freedom of the seas. As the House of Commons put it in 1738: "It was the undoubted right of British subjects to sail their ships in any part of the seas of America." Although the British retaliated by seizing Spanish vessels, the Spaniards were the more active: in 1738 Britain's losses from such depredations exceeded Spain's by £95,000.

The interest in the Spanish American trade was shared by all British merchants because it afforded a large part of the nation's bullion supply. And because a bullion shortage in the 1730's was deemed the principal cause of currency troubles and a stagnation of British trade, the mercantile interests demanded strong measures against Spain, for which they prepared public sentiment by circulating tales of atrocities inflicted upon British traders by the Spaniards. A certain Captain Jenkins, who claimed that Spanish officials had cut off one of his ears, stirred up a wave of hysteria by exhibiting his affliction and relating the cruelties he had suffered. Walpole wanted peace, but his plan of pacification was defeated by the South Sea Company and the merchants. Rumors that France had joined the Spaniards in an alliance whereby France would receive commercial privileges in Spanish America and help Spain expel the British traders—such reports intensified the excitement in England. In May 1739 Spain suspended the English held assiento; in October the British merchants, Parliament, and the Whig ministers forced Walpole to consent to war.[17]

---

[16] Richard Pares, *War and Trade in the West Indies* (New York, 1936), is excellent on the Anglo-Spanish conflict.

[17] V. L. Brown, "The South Sea Company and Contraband Trade," *American Historical Review*, XXXI (Oct. 1925); E. Donnan, "The Early Days of the South Sea Company," *Journal of Economic and Business History*, II (May 1930)—technical.

## THE CONFLICT RESUMED

Once more aiming at the conquest of the Spanish Indies Britain captured Porto Bello in November 1739 and then sent an expedition of eight thousand men against Cartagena. But when disease took a toll of half the British force this grand design collapsed in May 1741. Another expedition under Admiral Anson rounded Cape Horn to the Pacific and repeated Drake's exploit of plunder but did not conquer Spain's western settlements. By 1742 Britain's failure in the Spanish Indies was overshadowed by a general European war which had broken out in November 1740. The Austrian Emperor, Charles VI, had died in October, leaving the vast Hapsburg possessions to his daughter, Maria Theresa. In May a new sovereign, Frederick II, had ascended the throne of Prussia; in November he despoiled the inheritance of Maria Theresa by invading the Austrian province of Silesia. Since Austria had long been Britain's counterweight to French influence on the Continent, France took the side of Prussia. In 1742–43 British diplomacy secured support for Austria from Holland, Russia, and Saxony; in 1743 France openly allied herself with Spain, still at war with Britain; and in 1744 Britain declared war against France.[18]

Only one event, the British conquest of Louisbourg, gives significance to the War of the Austrian Succession in America—an achievement provoked by French efforts to seize Annapolis in Nova Scotia and by the desire of the merchants of Massachusetts to protect their trade and fishery against the onslaughts of the French. Prodded by the merchants, Massachusetts voted £50,000 for the expedition and obtained cannon from New York, provisions from New Jersey and Pennsylvania, troops from the other New England colonies, and three naval vessels from Britain. The chief promoter of the project, Governor William Shirley of Massachusetts (one of the better royal governors), feared the menace of Louisbourg to New England; the leader of the colonial forces, William Pepperrell of Kittery Point, Maine, one of the richest men in the colonies, had large investments in northern lands and in the fishery; the British commander, Sir Peter Warren, allied by marriage to the New York De Lanceys, had landholdings in the Mohawk valley. The religious enthusiasm engendered by the Great Awakening found vent in this crusade against the Catholic foe: Pepperrell was a pillar of the Congregational Church; and the war preparations were blessed by

[18] The seventh volume of the *Cambridge Modern History* devotes chapters 3 and 4 to the Anglo-French conflict.

the New England clergy with sermons and prayers. On March 24, 1745, the expedition of four thousand men and nearly a hundred vessels sailed from Boston; on June 15 Louisbourg surrendered after a forty-nine-day siege during which nine thousand cannon balls were poured into the town. Great rejoicing in Britain and New England greeted the news of success; Pepperrell was made a baronet, the first American-born colonist to be so favored.[19]

Shirley now raised a force for the conquest of Quebec, but naval aid promised by Britain did not materialize; instead the Crown in 1747 ordered the disbanding of the troops. France made two imposing but abortive efforts to recover Louisbourg in 1746–47. Much to the disgust of the New Englanders Britain restored the prize to France in 1748 in order to regain for the British East India Company the post of Madras in India which the French had taken during the war. But Britain did send large sums of money to the New England colonies to enable them to redeem the now sadly depreciated paper currency which they had issued to finance the expedition. By the Treaty of Aix la Chapelle (1748) all conquered territories were returned to their former possessors and the points of conflict remained as in 1740.

The center of strife now shifted to the area of present-day Ohio, western Pennsylvania, and West Virginia—a region of crucial importance, the key to the control of the interior.[20] The shortest route from Canada to Louisiana traversed the Ohio country via the Maumee, Great Miami, and Wabash Rivers; hence the French believed that the security of their whole American empire depended upon their possession of this pivotal territory. In like manner the mastery of the interior, by 1748, had become indispensable to the British, in view of the peculiar economy of their seaboard colonies. Not only was settlement rapidly pressing westward in Pennsylvania and Virginia; the capitalists of those colonies needed new fields for the investment of their surplus capital, due to the contraction of opportunities for investment in commerce, the relative unprofitableness of tobacco cultivation, and the refusal of Britain to permit the colonies to develop manufacturing industries. The needed outlets for excess capital had been found by Pennsylvania merchants and Virginia planters in speculation in western lands; in 1768 an observer said of Philadelphia that "It is almost a proverb in this neighborhood that 'Every great fortune made here within these fifty years has been

[19] George A. Wood, *William Shirley*, an excellent study, devotes chapters 9–19 to war problems.
[20] See again C. W. Alvord, *The Illinois Country*, chapters 7–11.

by land.'" In the process of land speculation and the financing of indigent settlers colonial promoters hoped to utilize the Ohio valley fur trade: not only would it provide profits to meet the costs of erecting forts to hold the interior against the French; it would also afford those contacts with the Indians necessary for acquiring title to their lands.[21]

Pennsylvania traders had penetrated beyond the mountains in the 1720's; Virginians followed in the 1730's. New York's preoccupation with her Oswego trade and South Carolina's preoccupation with the far southern trade left the Ohio region open to the Pennsylvanians and Virginians, between whom a heated contest for supremacy ensued. Pennsylvania had a shorter route to the Ohio but the provincial assembly, dominated by the Quakers who always strove to avoid Indian wars incident to the fur trade and settlement, did not give adequate backing to the Pennsylvania expansionists. In Virginia, on the other hand, land speculation had become such a primary concern that the colonial government pursued a more vigorous forward policy. At a conference held at Lancaster, Pennsylvania, in 1744 the Iroquois ceded to Virginia all their lands within that province (lands which they claimed as overlords of weaker tribes, particularly the Delaware and Shawnee). Then, in order to overcome Pennsylvania's advantages in the West, a group of Virginia gentlemen organized the Ohio Company; among them were such representatives of the planter aristocracy as Thomas Lee, Thomas Nelson, George Fairfax, Lawrence and Augustine Washington and, later, George Mason and Governor Robert Dinwiddie. That one of the original promoters was John Hanbury, a London merchant, indicates that English capitalists were also looking to the Ohio valley as a field of investment. Because settlement was the principal object of the company it obtained from the king in 1749 a grant of 200,000 acres on both sides of the Ohio between the Monongahela and Great Kanawha Rivers, together with a promise of 300,000 acres more if a hundred families were settled upon the first tract within seven years. Immediately thereafter the company imported a large stock of goods for the Indian trade and dispatched to the West one Christopher Gist, who traversed large parts of present-day Ohio, Kentucky, and West Virginia as well as western Maryland and southwestern Pennsylvania in his search for lands best suited to settlement. The company also erected a trading house on the Potomac opposite the mouth of Will's Creek (now the site of Cumberland, Maryland) and

[21] Louis K. Koontz, *The Virginia Frontier* (Baltimore, 1925), emphasizes the role of Washington.

in 1752 it negotiated an Indian treaty which authorized the construction of a fort at the forks of the Ohio.[22]

For more than a decade the British traders had been strengthening their influence among the Ohio valley Indians by virtue of their ability to overbid the French in the fur trade. In 1741 France adopted a new commercial policy: all traders' licenses were revoked and thereafter the interior posts were leased by the government to individuals on a monopoly basis. The merchant princes of Montreal purchased such leases, but at rates so high as to oblige them to charge extortionate prices for the goods which they supplied to the natives. Exempt from such payments, and exposed to more vigorous competition, the British traders offered better bargains. When the disaffection of the Indians had become critical the governors of Canada prepared to protect the monopolists by force. First, in 1749, an expedition under Céloron de Blainville was sent from Canada to assert France's claim to the upper Ohio. Taking the route of Lake Erie, the Allegheny, the Ohio, the Great Miami, and the Maumee, Blainville's party deposited at the mouth of each important river a lead plate inscribed with the French claim. Next, in 1752, the French destroyed an English fort, Pickawillany, in what is now Miami County, Ohio; then in 1753 a newly arrived governor of Canada, the marquis Duquesne de Menneville, dispatched a second expedition which erected Fort Presque Isle on Lake Erie and Fort le Boeuf on French Creek and took possession of Venango, a British trading post, at the junction of French Creek and the Allegheny River.[23]

When the news of this advance reached Governor Dinwiddie he sent young George Washington to demand that the French withdraw (1753). Washington as yet did not belong to the inner circle of the Virginia aristocracy but he was already one of its most trustworthy agents. He journeyed as far as Fort le Boeuf only to have the French ignore his demands. Dinwiddie immediately retaliated by sending Captain William Trent with a small force to erect a fort at the forks of the Ohio. No sooner was the work under way than a stronger French force expelled the Virginians and thereupon erected Fort Duquesne. Dinwiddie, having raised a small body of troops, again dispatched Washington with orders to drive out the French. Near a place called Great Meadows in the Alleghenies Washington encountered and defeated a French force; then he retreated to

---

[22] In Charles H. Ambler's *George Washington and the West* (Chapel Hill, 1936) there is a careful narrative of the beginnings of the French and Indian War. See chapters 1–7.

[23] G. A. Wood, "Céloron de Blainville and French Expansion in the Ohio Valley," *Mississippi Valley Historical Review*, IX (March 1923).

Great Meadows and hurriedly erected Fort Necessity, which the French attacked and captured in July 1754. Virginia and Canada were now at war.[24]

The replacement of New York by Virginia as the challenger of French supremacy requires an explanation. After 1713 the western problem occasioned a factional strife in New York over two alternatives of policy. One course of action, which may be styled the anti-French program, entailed large expenditures for frontier defense and unceasing efforts to retain the Iroquois as allies in war. The second or neutrality policy, which aimed to preserve peace with Canada, involved the neglect of frontier defenses and an indifferent attitude toward the Iroquois. Advocates of neutrality were the New York and Albany merchants, headed by James De Lancey, who carried on the trade with Montreal. In alliance with them were land speculators, particularly the Livingstons, active in the Mohawk valley: their method of buying land from the Iroquois and of occupying more than they bought made it difficult to propitiate the Six Nations as the anti-French policy demanded. The neutrality party could count upon the political support of the residents of other parts of the province who, having no interest in the frontier, wished merely to avoid expenditures for defense and war.

The anti-French policy derived its impetus from the British government's insistence that New York play a leading role in winning America from France; hence the royal governors, especially William Burnet and George Clinton, were its principal sponsors. The traders who operated at Oswego also inclined toward the anti-French camp; because they traversed the Iroquois country they desired to conciliate the Iroquois in all ways consistent with their trade. The most effective advocate of this policy, William Johnson, an Ulsterman, had settled on the Mohawk valley frontier, where he engaged in the fur trade and by reason of his fair dealings won the unlimited confidence of the Six Nations, even being "adopted" by the Mohawk tribe. His residence, Mount Johnson, became the center of his rather dubious diplomacy, which consisted largely of warning the Iroquois that France was seeking their destruction.[25]

During King George's War the neutrality party had frustrated Governor Clinton's plans for war against the French; and although Clinton made Johnson the Indian agent of the province, the opposi-

[24] See again E. Channing, *History of the United States*, Vol. II, chapters 18–19.
[25] The best biography is Arthur Pound, *Johnson of the Mohawks* (New York, 1930). A briefer, popular narrative is Flora W. Seymour, *Lords of the Valley* (New York, 1930).

tion was so strong in the Assembly that he could accomplish little and was obliged to finance the Oswego garrison and Indian negotiations from his own pocket: when he was forced to resign in 1750 the province owed him £7,000 for his outlays. At several abortive conferences held between 1745 and 1753 the Iroquois eloquently

From Adams and Vannest's "The Record of America." © Charles Scribner's Sons.

WHERE THE FRENCH AND INDIAN WAR BEGAN

voiced their wrongs: their lands were being filched by speculators and the great English father did nothing to protect them from the French. Meanwhile the traders from Virginia and Pennsylvania did not pursue a policy of neutrality; by inciting the Indians against the French they inspired the latter to send out the Blainville expedition and to erect the Lake Erie-Ohio River forts. This show of strength so impressed the Indians that most of them now sided with France. In the impending war the Iroquois were certain to be involved, and yet New York had done nothing for their protection. Their disgust with Britain's indecision had created a crisis on the New York frontier by the end of 1753.[26]

[26] A. H. Buffinton, "The Policy of Albany and English Westward Expansion," *Mississippi Valley Historical Review*, VIII (March 1922).

To meet this situation the Board of Trade issued a call for a general colonial congress designed to induce the Indians south of the Great Lakes to cease intertribal warfare and to join Britain against France. Hence in June 1754 representatives of New York, Pennsylvania, Maryland, and the New England colonies met the Iroquois at Albany. Particularly important were the delegations of Pennsylvania (Benjamin Franklin was its leader) and of New York (headed by William Johnson and Governor De Lancey). Unfortunately Virginia, the pivotal colony, did not participate. The Iroquois again aired their grievances, such as British land frauds, the defenseless New York frontier, and the invasion of their country by Pennsylvania and Virginia traders. The delegates framed a report which denounced the French, acknowledged the grievances of the Iroquois, recommended the construction of new forts, and advised that the limits of the seaboard colonies should extend only to the mountains. Since the congress had no power to raise money it could only urge (and quite futilely) that the colonial assemblies give effect to its plans. The congress also adopted a plan of colonial union drafted by Franklin which proposed that a president for all the colonies be appointed by the king to act with a grand council of delegates chosen by the assemblies, each colony to be represented in proportion to its financial contributions. This super-government was to have charge of all British interests in the West—Indian treaties, trade, defense, and settlement; and the president was to bear a relation to the council similar to that of a royal governor to a colonial assembly. None of the colonies accepted Franklin's plan or the general recommendations of the congress: none wished to surrender to an outside body both the power of taxation and control over the development of the West. More particularly, the Albany plan would have thwarted the Ohio Company, now dominant in the government of Virginia.

Upon learning of Washington's defeat at Fort Necessity British officials ceased considering their own plans of colonial union and dispatched a force of two regiments to Virginia under the command of Edward Braddock, an aged general, brave and headstrong—a firm disciplinarian who had learned on the battlefields of Europe what he considered the entire art of warfare.[27] Through the influence of John Hanbury and the Ohio Company, Braddock's force landed in Virginia instead of Pennsylvania, thereby necessitating an unduly long march through the wilderness to Fort Duquesne, the first objective of the expedition. Exposure, sickness, and the strain

[27] T. W. Riker, "The Politics behind Braddock's Expedition," *American Historical Review*, XIII (Oct. 1907).

of building wilderness roads for army supply had exhausted Braddock's men by the time they arrived within seven miles of Fort Duquesne, where on July 9, 1755, a force of nine hundred French and Indians sheltered by trees inflicted a decisive defeat in a day's fighting. Braddock perished and the British survivors fled until they reached Fort Cumberland in Maryland. All supplies were lost so that the whole campaign had to be abandoned. The Indians, having now chosen France as the stronger party, ravaged the frontiers of Virginia and Pennsylvania far and wide. "The undeclared war of 1755 had not gone well for Britain."

The continued opposition of the French settlers in Nova Scotia to Britain's authority evoked drastic measures against them in the autumn of 1755. After restoring Louisbourg to France, Britain had strengthened her hold upon the province by establishing in 1749 twenty-five hundred settlers at Halifax—a force which had increased to four thousand by 1752. The French residents (now numbering about nine thousand) occupied a strategic position, since Nova Scotia lay athwart the British route to Louisbourg and Canada, both of which Britain was at last determined to conquer. Hence a part of the campaign of 1755 had been the seizure of a French fort, Beauséjour, at the northern part of the Bay of Fundy. Having succeeded there in June, Britain gained undisputed control of Nova Scotia which she perpetuated in the autumn by deporting more than six thousand Acadians to her colonies south of New Hampshire. Although this action was taken when France and Britain were still nominally at peace, its extreme harshness signified that North America was no longer large enough to accommodate two such bitterly hostile powers.[28]

Colonial rivalry was the underlying cause of the Seven Years' (or French and Indian) War, officially declared in May 1756. That it grew into a general European conflict is explained in the main by the hatred of Austria for Prussia, a legacy of Prussia's seizure of Silesia during the preceding war. When Austrian diplomats after 1748 effected a combination against Prussia, the latter countered with an alliance with Britain—a bargain which assured Prussia of financial backing and gave Britain a powerful ally against France. No longer seeking territorial dominance in Europe but rather striving for supremacy in America, France joined hands with Austria, the power which had long opposed her designs of European conquest. Thus in the spring of 1756 was consummated the Diplomatic Revo-

[28] Arthur G. Doughty, *The Acadian Exiles* (*Chronicles of Canada* series, Toronto, 1916).

lution by which those ancient enemies, the French Bourbons and the Austrian Hapsburgs, united in opposition to Prussia and Britain.

In America the plans of campaign revolved around Fort Duquesne and Quebec, or the control of the Ohio valley and Canada.[29] Britain's determination to conquer the latter brought into prominence three approaches to the north: the sea route to the St. Lawrence, guarded for France by Louisbourg; the path of the Richelieu River and Lake Champlain, where France had forts at Ticonderoga and Crown Point; and the Great Lakes-St. Lawrence route, which the French commanded through Forts Niagara and Frontenac on the south-western and northeastern sides of Lake Ontario. Until 1758 the for-tunes of war frowned upon the British; the French destroyed Fort Oswego in 1756, repulsed a large expedition sent against Louisbourg in July 1757, captured Fort William Henry on Lake George in the following August, and maintained their prestige among the upper Ohio valley Indians, particularly the Delaware and Shawnee, whose raids upon the Virginia-Pennsylvania frontier drove the British set-tlers to or beyond the Allegheny Mountains.[30]

These reverses brought into power the resolute and energetic William Pitt, who, as Secretary of State for the Southern Depart-ment, 1757–61, directed Britain's successful campaigns for the con-quest of Canada. Exhibiting unlimited self-confidence ("I believe," he said, "that I can save this nation and that no one else can"), he purged the army of the corrupt spoils system, chose the ablest com-manders he could find, and inspired the nation with his own zeal for empire. Convinced that "when trade is at stake you must defend it or perish," he concentrated upon America as the decisive theater of the war, at the same time subsidizing Prussia in order to keep France occupied in Europe.[31] Success greeted his first efforts in 1758 when British forces, by conquering Louisbourg, Fort Duquesne (re-named Fort Pitt), and Fort Frontenac, opened the way to Canada. The campaign of 1759 involved a threefold attack: one expedition was to take Fort Niagara and sever Canada from the West; a second, under General Jeffrey Amherst,[32] was to proceed northward by way

[29] The most elaborate study of military operations is *A History of the British Army* (13 vols., London, 1899–1930) by the Hon. Sir John W. Fortescue. Volume II covers the years 1713–63.

[30] Julian S. Corbett, *England in the Seven Years War* (2 vols., London, 1907), is a standard, intensive study of naval and military strategy, politics, and warfare.

[31] For the general reader the best biography is Basil Williams, *The Life of William Pitt* (2 vols., London, 1914).

[32] Two satisfactory biographies stress the military aspect: Laurence S. Mayo, *Jeffrey Amherst* (New York, 1916), and John C. Long, *Lord Jeffrey Amherst* (New York, 1933)

of Lake Champlain; and the third, a combined land and sea force under General James Wolfe, was to advance upon Quebec from the East. The first expedition took possession of Niagara but could not advance down the St. Lawrence; Amherst seized Ticonderoga and Crown Point but had to halt for the winter on Lake Champlain; hence Wolfe's force was compelled to act alone. Tense was the situation during the winter following Wolfe's success in September as both the conquered and the conquerors, cooped up in Quebec, awaited reinforcements from Europe. But in 1759 Britain had shattered the French navy, and the fleet which arrived in May 1760 confirmed the victory of Wolfe. Montreal fell in September and all Canada lay prostrate before Britain's arms.[33]

Britain's relation to war underwent a decisive change as the result of the accession of George III in 1760. Both education and inclination prompted this ambitious, headstrong king to assert his right to rule in fact as well as in name. And since he had been born and bred in England and "gloried in the name of Briton"; because his conventional moral virtues commended him to the powerful English middle class; and because the Hanoverian dynasty was now safely established upon the throne and reinforced by forty-five years of kingship, George III found circumstances favorable to his design of breaking the power of the great Whig families which had ruled continuously since 1715. Pitt was now the chief symbol of Whig influence, and because his power stemmed from the war, George III was determined to restore peace as the means both of ousting Pitt and of gaining the sovereign power. The Achilles' heel of Pitt's policy was the expensive and unpopular practice of subsidizing Prussia; in opposition to this policy George III built up a peace party which forced the great war minister to resign. Meanwhile, France and Spain in 1761 had entered into treaties which renewed the Bourbon family compact: one agreement provided that if France and Britain were at war in May 1762, Spain would aid France. Urging an attack upon Spain but thwarted by George III, Pitt resigned in October 1761 rather than remain in office without power. Nevertheless Britain was forced to declare war against Spain in January 1762 and to prolong the conflict another year—during which she conquered the French

---

[33] On this famous engagement see Parkman's masterly narrative, *Montcalm and Wolfe* (2 vols., Boston, 1884); Frederick E. Whitton, *Wolfe and North America* (Boston, 1929), an attractive, reliable account of military campaigns; and William Wood, *The Fight for Canada* (London, 1904), a well-informed description of the conquest which glorifies Pitt and Wolfe. Biographies are: Arthur G. Bradley, *Wolfe* (London, 1895)—a brief sketch; and William T. Waugh, *James Wolfe* (Montreal, 1928), which incorporates the latest information.

sugar island, Martinique (she had already taken Guadeloupe in 1759), and occupied Havana and Manila, thereby gaining control of Cuba and the Philippine Islands.[34]

During the negotiations for peace Britain held Canada, Guadeloupe, and Martinique, but because France would rather continue the war than surrender all three colonies, and because George III insisted upon peace, the question arose: should Britain retain Canada or the two sugar islands? Over this issue raged a spirited public debate. Those who urged the retention of Guadeloupe and Martinique argued that their trade was much greater than Canada's: in 1761 the exports of Guadeloupe to Britain exceeded those of Canada more than fortyfold. Similarly, the two islands would increase the markets of Britain's northern mainland colonies, encourage them to continue to produce provisions, lumber, etc., supply them with buying power for British goods, and divert them from manufacturing in competition with British industries. Should France be expelled from Canada, the mainland colonies—no longer in need of Britain's protection—would break away from the mother country. Island colonies were generally secure dependencies because they could never successfully defy a naval power like Britain. And if France lost Guadeloupe and Martinique her naval strength in the Caribbean would be annihilated.

The advocates of Canada urged that its retention would give Britain control of the North American fur trade and greatly enlarge the market for British manufactures, since the northern colonies adjacent to Canada were now surpassing the British West Indies as purchasers of European goods. If Canada and the Ohio valley were restored to France, the English colonies, hemmed in at the mountains, would have to turn to manufactures in order to support their expanding populations. Moreover, the mainland settlements now needed protection from French onslaughts as the condition of their prosperous development. Nor was a revolt of the thirteen colonies likely; local rivalries and jealousies would keep them apart, and Britain could always subdue them by virtue of her mastery of the sea. Finally, the vast extent of Canada would add immeasurably to Britain's prestige in the eyes of the world.[35]

The decision to retain Canada was shaped by three influences. First, British planters and investors in the old British sugar islands did not wish to admit Guadeloupe and Martinique into the empire,

[34] Lewis B. Namier, *England in the Age of the American Revolution* (London, 1930), treats English society and politics, 1760–63.

[35] W. L. Grant, "Canada versus Guadeloupe," *American Historical Review*, XVII (July 1912).

fearing that they would flood the British sugar markets and ruin the British plantations. Secondly, British merchants regarded the fur trade of Canada as a prize of the first magnitude. And thirdly, the mainland colonies, having spent so much blood and treasure in winning Canada, could not be condemned indefinitely to the horrors of war by returning their conquests to the enemy. The conflict in America had reached the point where it could be resolved only by the expulsion of the French.

The Treaty of Paris of 1763 awarded Canada to Britain, as well as the territory west to the Mississippi. Spain ceded Florida to Britain as the price for the restoration of Cuba and the Philippines, while France compensated Spain for the loss of Florida by giving her that part of Louisiana west of the Mississippi and a small strip of land east of the mouth of the river. Britain and Spain were now the premier colonial powers of the world.[36]

## The Decentralized Empire

The imperial crisis which precipitated the American Revolution issued directly from the French and Indian War. Having expelled France from North America, Britain no longer needed to make political concessions to the colonies in order to secure their assistance against the French; hence she was free to enforce those parts of her colonial system which had previously been neglected. Secondly, the conquest of Canada and the Ohio valley imposed upon Britain the task of governing the whole interior; and in shaping a western policy she antagonized powerful interests in the colonies which were bent upon exploiting the newly won territories. Finally, the war exposed many deep-seated conflicts between Britain and the colonies and demonstrated that the latter were prone to ignore British interests and to evade imperial restrictions. Animosity and mistrust were the results.[37]

One of the most bitter conflicts between the colonies and the mother country arose from the wartime commerce which the former carried on with Canada and the French West Indies—a trade that in British eyes wore the treasonable aspect of giving aid to the enemy. Not only were French military and naval forces furnished with indispensable provisions; equally important, such colonial exports to the enemy made it difficult for British forces to obtain necessary supplies except

[36] W. R. Shepherd, "The Cession of Louisiana to Spain," *Political Science Quarterly,* XIX (Sept. 1904).

[37] Eugene I. McCormac, *Colonial Opposition to Imperial Authority during the French and Indian War* (Berkeley, 1911), is an excellent brief analysis.

at high prices. A similar trade with the French West Indies during King George's War had been blamed by a British admiral for the failure at that time of Britain's naval operations in the Caribbean. Moreover, it was charged that the northern colonies, by trading with the French sugar islands, forced down the price of sugar, molasses, and rum, thereby rendering unprofitable the British plantations in the West Indies. The French sugar obtained by the northern traders was disguised as British sugar and sent to Britain where it deprived the British planters of the home market especially reserved for them.[38]

When at the outbreak of war Britain prohibited all commerce between her subjects and the French, the mainland colonies engaged in an indirect trade whereby they used the Spanish and Dutch islands as depots for the goods which they sold to or received from Guadeloupe, Martinique, and Santo Domingo. In this case neutral vessels made the direct exchanges with the French. In order to stamp out such traffic Parliament in 1757 prohibited the exportation of all provisions (excepting fish, roots, and rice) from a British colony to any place except Britain, Ireland, or other British colonies. With the same object an English admiralty court promulgated the Rule of 1756, which declared that neutrals could not carry on in time of war a trade which was legally closed to them in time of peace. France, of course, regularly excluded the Dutch and Spaniards from the peacetime trade with her colonies; however, due to Britain's naval superiority, she opened her ports to neutrals as a means of continuing her commerce when at war. The Rule of 1756 said in effect that Britain could regulate the trade of other nations with France.[39]

The merchants of the thirteen colonies exhibited much ingenuity and boldness in evading Britain's anti-French statutes and decrees. For one thing, the merchants obtained licenses from colonial governors which authorized their vessels to proceed under a "flag of truce" to the French islands in order to effect an exchange of prisoners of war. Thus colonial ships could transport cargoes of provisions under the shelter of such licenses, which were issued so profusely (especially by the governors of Rhode Island and Pennsylvania) that a more or less open traffic in them developed, as they multiplied and fell in price. Other colonial vessels, having cleared for British ports, traded with the French colonies and then visited British

---

[38] G. L. Beer, *British Colonial Policy, 1754–1765* (New York, 1907), is of primary importance. See chapters 1–9.

[39] Kate Hotblack, *Chatham's Colonial Policy* (London, 1917), is an able, intensive study of the years 1739–65.

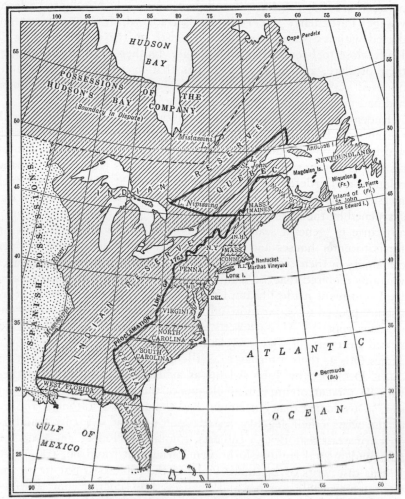

British and Spanish possessions after the Treaty of Paris, 1763, and
the organization of British territory under the Royal Proclamation of
October 7, 1763. Besides authorizing the "Proclamation Line," the
Proclamation of 1763 created the three British provinces of Quebec,
East Florida, and West Florida.

ports, where they purchased fraudulent papers which indicated a legal voyage. Particularly important was a trade which the colonists conducted with a Spanish port, Monte Cristi, on the northern shore of Haiti, close to French Santo Domingo. Thither the French brought their produce, and in such quantities that in 1760 more than four hundred vessels unloaded cargoes of sugar, although the little town had had no commercial importance before the war.

Endeavoring to enforce her prohibitions against commerce with the enemy, Britain made use of the royal navy to capture vessels which were abusing the flag of truce, attempted to enforce the Molasses Act as a means of excluding French products from the mainland colonies, and ordered her subjects not to trade at Monte Cristi. Such measures angered the colonial merchants, whose antagonism was sharpened by the introduction into the colonies at this time of writs of assistance or general search warrants which authorized customs officials to enter houses and ships, to break down doors, and to open containers in their search for smuggled goods. Because special search warrants required that the name of the informer be given and because local sentiment made life unpleasant for such informers, writs of assistance proved to be far more effective. They were first issued by the superior court of Massachusetts in 1755; when they had to be renewed in 1760 the Bay merchants banded together and employed James Otis as their attorney to challenge the legality of the writs in court. Described by John Adams as a "flame of fire" who attacked with "a torrent of impetuous eloquence the terrible menacing monster," Otis denied that Parliament had the power to authorize the use of the writs (their legality rested upon a statute of 1662) and asserted instead that British subjects, colonists included, possessed certain fundamental rights which even Parliament could not take away. In this case writs of assistance violated the subjects' right to be free from unreasonable searches and seizures. The superior court affirmed the legality of the writs, but in the meantime Otis had crystallized public indignation against them and had inaugurated the constitutional debate of the Revolutionary era by denying that Parliament possessed unlimited power over the colonies.[40]

The methods used by Britain to finance the war in America also provoked friction within the empire. Because the British colonists on the mainland outnumbered the French settlers by about fourteen to one, Britain possessed a tremendous military advantage over France, provided of course that her colonists could be welded into an effec-

[40] E. Hickman, "Colonial Writs of Assistance." *New England Quarterly*, V (Jan. 1932).

tive army. Having decided to employ colonial troops (as in previous wars), British ministers were confronted by two questions: what should be the relation between the colonial troops and British regulars in America and how could the colonists be made to share the expenses of the war? The first question was answered by subordinating colonial forces to British commanders, thus providing for centralized military operations as directed by the ministry in Britain. Although this method produced many rivalries and antagonisms between colonial officers and British commanders it did not produce nearly so much enmity as that evoked by the means of financing the colonial forces. Due to the cost of the war on the Continent Britain felt unable to pay all the expenses of the colonial campaigns. Between 1748 and 1754 British officials had proposed that Parliament tax the colonies for imperial defense; however, since the colonists were strongly opposed to such levies, this plan had to be abandoned in order to secure colonial coöperation during the critical years of war. In consequence, Britain resorted to the "requisition system"—a scheme whereby each colonial assembly was called upon to furnish a prescribed quota of men and money as its contribution to the war.

As developed by Pitt the requisition system obliged the assembly to vote the money for recruiting, clothing, and paying the wages of the colonial troops; Britain in turn supplied the necessary provisions, tents, arms, and ammunition. Moreover, in order to encourage the assemblies to provide their quotas, Parliament reimbursed the colonies for part of their outlays of the previous year. All told the colonies in this manner received from Britain about two-fifths of the money they spent for recruiting, clothing, and paying their own troops. To British officials this plan seemed fair and generous, especially when the benefits to America from the war were taken into account, hence they expected an equally generous response from the colonies and were sorely exasperated when it was not forthcoming.[41]

Of the colonial attitude the British commander-in-chief in America, Lord Loudoun, said in 1757: "it is the constant study of every province here to throw every expense on the Crown and bear no part of the expense of this war themselves." Three sources of colonial opposition may be distinguished. Some colonies (New Hampshire, Georgia, North Carolina) considered themselves so poor that they could not afford to meet the British requisitions. In New Jersey and Pennsylvania, where the Quakers were powerful, their aversion to war expressed itself in resistance to military appropriations. Generally, the

[41] Hubert Hall, "Chatham's Colonial Policy," *American Historical Review*, V (July 1900).

residents of the seaboard area who were not concerned in the fur trade or in western land speculation had little interest in the frontier and were unwilling to be taxed for its defense—an attitude particularly strong in Rhode Island, Delaware, and New Jersey, since those colonies did not possess claims to the territory around which the conflict revolved. Each colony, fearful that it might contribute more than its share, delayed action in order to see what its neighbors would do; the failure of one then provided an excuse for the remissness of the others. Moreover, the assemblies refused to fill their quotas unless they believed that the money would be spent for their particular advantage. Thus British plans for the conquest of Louisiana in 1762 had to be abandoned because the colonies failed to provide their quotas, so indifferent were they to that faraway country. Only Massachusetts, Connecticut, and New York responded effectively throughout the war: the general failure of the requisition system is apparent from the fact that those three colonies contributed seven-tenths of all the troops raised in America.[42]

Even when the assemblies complied with Britain's requests the delay involved often hampered military operations. "The sloth of the colonies," wrote General Amherst, "in raising their troops and sending them to their rendezvous makes it impracticable for me to move the troops on so soon as I could have wished." Nor did the quality of the colonial soldiers satisfy British officers: as General Forbes put it in 1758, the forces from Pennsylvania and Virginia, excepting a few of their principal officers, were "an extreme bad collection of innkeepers, horse jockeys and Indian traders . . . a gathering from the scum of the worst people . . . who have wrought themselves up into a panic at the very name of Indians." Most grievous of all the features of the requisition system was the use made of it by the colonial assemblies to wrest political concessions from the royal governors and the proprietors as the price of military grants—a practice that in British eyes seemed as reprehensible as trade with the enemy.[43]

Contests over the currency illustrate the wartime tactics of the assemblies. Unwilling to tax themselves to meet the immediate costs of the war the colonists again issued paper money in large amounts and the resulting depreciation increased the old tension between debtors and creditors. Virginia now became the principal scene of conflict; there the struggle over currency and debts bore witness to the im-

[42] See again W. T. Root, *Relations of Pennsylvania with the British Government*, chapter 10.
[43] Stanley M. Pargellis, *Lord Loudoun in America* (New Haven, 1933), is an able study of problems facing the British army in America, 1756–58.

pending bankruptcy of the tobacco planters, caught as they were in the grip of British merchant capitalism. In 1748 Virginia enacted a law which provided that debts might be paid in Virginia currency (foreign coin or tobacco) at the rate of £125 Virginia money for each £100 sterling due. When the British merchants complained that £100 sterling was worth £140 in Virginia currency the province in 1755 passed a new act which authorized judges to decide the sterling value of the Virginia currency that was tendered in payment of debts. This act evoked two objections from the merchants: first, the judges might overvalue Virginia currency, thereby defrauding British creditors; secondly, Virginia's currency was steadily depreciating, so that a remittance of £100 might lose ten or fifteen per cent of its value between the time a court acted and the time the creditor received the money. The currency issue was intensified at this time (1755) when Virginia issued its first paper currency and made it legal tender in payment of debt. Depreciation followed: in 1757 it took £135 in Virginia paper currency to buy £100 sterling; in 1759 the ratio was 140:100; in 1762 it stood at 165:100. Yet despite the demands of British creditors that they should not be compelled to accept such depreciated paper at more than its sterling value, the assembly refused to provide money for the war except in the form of legal tender paper currency. On the other hand, after the conquest of Canada had satisfied Virginia's military ambitions, the assembly refused to grant money for the war on the ground that such grants would increase the supply of paper currency. Britain thus had either to accept new currency issues or to forego colonial military aid. The exigencies of the war forced her to accept legal tender paper—a concession that embittered British creditors and impelled them to insist upon an anti-paper currency policy as soon as peace deprived the assemblies of their powers of coercion.[44]

The money question became a crucial issue in Virginia in connection with the famous "parson's cause." Prior to 1755 the Anglican clergy of the province had received their salaries in tobacco, each stipend consisting of 17,280 pounds. When poor crops afflicted the colony in 1755 and 1758 the price of tobacco rose to the unusual figure of $5\frac{1}{2}d.$ a pound—an increase occasioned in part by the depreciation of Virginia's currency. Had the clergy been paid their salaries in tobacco, the 17,280 pounds to which each was entitled would have amounted to £400. However, the assembly in 1758 passed an act which provided that salaries, dues, and fees might be paid in money

[44] *Virginia and the French and Indian War,* by Hayes Baker-Crothers (Chicago, 1928), stresses imperial defense as a political issue.

at the rate of 2*d*. for each pound of tobacco due, an arrangement that reduced the salaries of the clergy to £144 each. The clergy objected strenuously, arguing that they had been paid in tobacco when its price was low; now when the price was high they ought to receive a compensating benefit. They were joined in their opposition to the "twopenny act" by the British merchants; consequently word arrived in Virginia in 1760 that the act had been disallowed. The clergy, having generally received £144 in money rather than £400 in tobacco, were now entitled to sue for the balance due to them under the former law. Among the suits that followed one gained especial prominence.[45] The Reverend James Maury of Fredericksville sued the vestrymen of his parish; the latter employed Patrick Henry as their attorney. Since the legal technicalities favored the minister, Henry directed his attack against the royal disallowance, asserting that Britain and the colonies were bound together in a mutual compact which neither party could violate without dissolving it. The disallowance of the "twopenny act" was such a manifest piece of tyranny that the colonists must defend their rights. In response to Henry's oratory the court awarded the minister damages of one penny—a thinly disguised defiance of Britain's authority over the colony.

Thus during the French and Indian War two notable attacks upon British merchant capitalism gave evidence of a critical situation within the empire. Speaking for the merchants of New England James Otis repudiated the supreme authority of Parliament which underlay the British acts restraining the commercial opportunities of the northern colonies; speaking for the Virginia planters Patrick Henry voiced their dissatisfaction with the Privy Council, that final guardian of British investments in America.[46] Restraints upon trade which menaced the profits of the colonial merchants; debts which consumed the profits of the southern planters: those two features of British mercantilism had at last evoked an opposition so determined as to indicate the approach of a revolutionary crisis.

[45] A. P. Scott, "The Constitutional Aspect of the 'Parson's Cause,'" *Political Science Quarterly*, XXXI (Dec. 1916).
[46] A standard biography is M. C. Tyler, *Patrick Henry* (Boston, 1887). For a popular account see George Morgan, *The True Patrick Henry* (Philadelphia, 1907).

### BIBLIOGRAPHICAL NOTE

Works Previously Cited: W. C. Abbott, *Expansion of Europe*, I, chs. 30, 32; G. Bancroft, *History of the United States*, II, chs. 39–40, 43; II, chs. 3–5, 7–20; H. J. Eckenrode, *Church and State in Virginia*, ch. 2 (Parson's cause); J. Fiske, *New France and New England*, I, chs. 7–10; A. J. Grant, *The French Monarchy*, II, chs. 16–18; C. J. H. Hayes, *Political and Cultural History of*

*Modern Europe*, 1, ch. 9; G. B. Hertz, *The Old Colonial System*, chs. 1–2; A. T. Mahan, *Influence of Sea Power upon History*, chs. 6–8; J. H. Schlarman, *From Quebec to New Orleans*, pp. 160–347; A. Shortt and A. G. Doughty (eds.), *New France*, Vols. I and II in the *Canada and Its Provinces* series; J. Winsor (ed.), *Narrative and Critical History of America*, V, chs. 1, 7–8; G. M. Wrong, *Conquest of New France*, chs. 4–11.

SOURCES NEWLY CITED: The *Sir William Johnson Papers* have been edited in eight handsome volumes by James Sullivan and A. C. Flick (Albany, 1921–33). The first three volumes relate to the Anglo-French conflict. For the Albany plan of union see A. H. Smyth (ed.), *The Writings of Benjamin Franklin* (10 vols., New York, 1905–07), III, pp. 197–226. Gertrude S. Kimball (ed.), *Correspondence of William Pitt* (2 vols., New York, 1906), pertains to the years 1757–61. S. M. Pargellis has edited an important set of documents, *Military Affairs in North America, 1748–1765* (New York, c. 1936), selected from the Cumberland papers in Windsor Castle. *Colonial Captivities, Marches and Journeys* (ed. Isabel M. Calder, New York, 1935) throws interesting sidelights on the Anglo-French conflict. See also *The Journal of Jeffrey Amherst* (ed. J. C. Webster, Toronto, 1931).

SOURCES PREVIOUSLY CITED: H. S. Commager (ed.), *Documents of American History*, I, nos. 31–32; A. B. Hart (ed.), *American History Told by Contemporaries*, II, Part V; W. MacDonald, *Documentary Source Book of American History*, nos. 29–30.

MAPS: D. R. Fox, *Harper's Atlas*, pp. 14–15; C. O. Paullin, *Atlas of the Historical Geography of the United States*, plates 41, 161; W. R. Shepherd, *Historical Atlas*, pp. 130–133, 136.

# XXII

## THE REVOLUTIONARY CRISIS

HAVING expelled the French from North America in 1763, Britain proceeded to consolidate her new territories and to strengthen her colonial system, long weakened by concessions to the colonies in return for their assistance against the French. The measures adopted after the war exposed a crisis in British mercantilism, indicated alike by antagonisms among commercial groups within Britain and by irreconcilable conflicts between British merchants on one side and colonial merchants and planters on the other. Because the colonies had copied the English methods of business enterprise they tended rapidly to duplicate the merchant capitalism of the mother country—with the result that mercantilistic tendencies took shape in America and clashed violently with British mercantilism. Both Britain and the colonies operated through expanding economies, the essential features of which were the accumulation of surplus capital by merchants and planters and the investment of such surpluses in a manner that opened new areas for exploitation and created new employments for the poor, the unemployed, and the dispossessed. Two fundamental conditions had to be met if eighteenth-century mercantilism was to function successfully: first, both British and colonial capitalists must protect those enterprises in which they had previously invested; second, both groups needed new fields of exploitation in which they could utilize their newly acquired profits.[1]

The central fact governing such investments in America was Britain's policy of prohibiting the development of colonial manufactures that would compete with the products of her own industry. Necessarily this policy greatly limited the opportunities for investment in the colonies, since it confined colonial and British enterprisers to non-manufacturing pursuits. Prior to 1760 there had been three general outlets in North America for the surplus capital of British and colonial investors. First, the tobacco, rice, and indigo plantations had attracted British investments in the form of merchants' loans to planters and had also absorbed colonial capital through the purchase of lands

---

[1] A brilliant, original interpretation is L. M. Hacker, "The First American Revolution," *Columbia University Quarterly*, XXVII (Sept. 1935).

and slaves. Secondly, the northern economy, revolving around the fishery, lumbering, grain and cattle farming, shipbuilding, and the manufacture of rum, flour, bread, cooperage stock, and crude iron had employed the vessels and other capital of the northern merchants and had enabled them to accumulate new capital to invest in lands, warehouses, trading goods, ships, mills, mortgages, and short-term loans. Thirdly, the fur trade and investments in western lands afforded outlets when plantation economy and northern enterprises were insufficient to absorb the surplus of new capital.[2]

By 1750–60 several tendencies had become apparent in colonial economy. Tobacco production, due to soil exhaustion, the burden of debt, heavy fixed labor costs, and the restraints of the British Acts of Trade, had reached the limits of expansion; in the late 1750's the demands for currency inflation in Virginia as a means of reducing the debt burden and the complaints of the planters against the British colonial system revealed that opportunities for investment of British and colonial capital in tobacco production had ceased to be attractive. After 1763 George Washington, one of the most efficient of the Virginia planters and one of the most unsparing critics of British merchant capitalism, shifted his principal economic activities from tobacco to wheat, flour, plantation manufactures, and investments in western lands. Similarly, by 1760 the commerce of the northern colonies and the economy on which it rested had reached a point where its expansion, depending upon the foreign sugar colonies, threatened Britain's investments in her own sugar islands. Clearly the commercial opportunities within the empire were not sufficient to support both the British merchants and their vigorous colonial rivals. With respect to the fur trade and western land speculation, British and colonial interests had acted in concert prior to 1760, a fact explained by the presence of the common enemy, France. Once the French had been removed, the vast interior awaited exploitation. But since both British and colonial capital could not find adequate outlets in plantation production, in colonial manufacturing, and in imperial commerce, a crucial question arose: should colonial investors or British investors reap the profits of the available enterprises, including the fur trade and the development of the West?[3]

[2] A. M. Schlesinger, "The American Revolution Reconsidered," *Political Science Quarterly*, XXXIV (March 1919).

[3] The passages from W. E. H. Lecky's *History of England* bearing on the Revolution have been edited by J. A. Woodburn as *The American Revolution* (New York, 1929).

## THE WESTERN PROBLEM

By 1730 most of the vast unoccupied land west of Pennsylvania, Maryland, and the southern colonies had come under the direct control of the British government. The land policy which Britain then pursued reflected the purposes of British merchant capitalism. The Crown did not seek to obtain a revenue for itself through land sales and quit-rents; instead the object was to increase British trade. This was to be accomplished by opening the land to *bona fide* settlers who would enlarge the supply of colonial commodities from which British merchants made their profits. Accordingly, British policy provided for free grants of small farms to actual settlers, and large tracts were given to speculative promoters like the Ohio Company on condition that they establish a prescribed number of families on their land. Otherwise the Crown objected to large grants to speculators who intended merely to acquire great holdings without contributing anything to the peopling of unoccupied areas. Little effort was made to collect the quit-rents nor were other conditions imposed upon land grants which would have stunted the growth of settlement. If, in the northern colonies, the use of certain lands was restricted for the production of naval stores, the object was to provide those colonies with commodities to support their commerce with Britain. And ever since 1700 the Crown had manifested an inflexible opposition to the creation of new proprietary colonies—partly because the proprietary land system generally retarded settlement and therefore curtailed the profits which British merchants made by trading in colonial produce. The proprietary system was allowed to continue in Pennsylvania partly because, in that exceptional instance, the liberal land policy of the Penns led to rapid settlement and increased production and trade with Britain.[4]

Prior to 1763 the necessity of opposing France and Spain in North America had reinforced Britain's policy of extending settlement as rapidly as possible, since the English colonist was a soldier as well as a farmer. Thus Britain's efforts to occupy Georgia and Nova Scotia reflect the Spanish-French menace; so also the Crown was careful to respect the land rights of Indians like the Iroquois whose assistance Britain needed against the French. Later, land policy became an instrument by which the British strengthened their hold in the upper Ohio valley. In 1754 Governor Dinwiddie of Virginia offered land bounties in that region to colonial soldiers and in the same year the

[4] C. W. Alvord's *The Mississippi Valley in British Politics* (2 vols., Cleveland, 1916) is one of the most outstanding studies of the colonial period. Very important

Crown instructed Dinwiddie to grant tracts west of the Alleghenies up to a thousand acres; by 1757 two million acres had been so granted.[5]

After 1760 several factors gave a new slant to Britain's attitude toward the West. First, now that France and Spain had been expelled from the territory east of the Mississippi, Britain no longer needed to encourage settlement as a defense measure. Secondly, the region into which colonial pioneers were now penetrating lay west of the mountains. Would settlements there serve British commerce; were not the Westerners going beyond the reach of British merchants? Thirdly, migration to the West constituted a threat to the established seaboard area. British merchants now had a substantial investment in the tobacco plantations; if the people moved West, would not the tobacco industry be ruined and the debts which the planters owed to British merchants be shuffled off? Fourthly, investors in England were affected by a new speculative craze; one colonist, George Croghan, when visiting England, found his associates there "land crazy." [6] If money was to be made from Britain's newly won territories, certainly British investors should have a substantial share. Moreover, the North American fur trade was now in Britain's possession, and the British merchants who proposed to exploit it looked askance at settlers who would drive the Indians away and destroy the fur-bearing animals. Finally, a new British land policy might be made to protect Britain's established commerce. The French and Indian War had shown that the Acts of Trade and Navigation were but poorly enforced—largely because colonial officials were paid from legislative appropriations and consequently were not dependent upon the Crown. But if the king's lands in America might be made to yield more revenue through sales and quit-rents a fund could be obtained which would make colonial officials independent of legislative support and therefore attentive to the commands of their new paymaster, the British Crown.

Such being the factors involved, it was natural that British land policy should now aim to protect the North American fur trade and to regulate the settlement of the West in such a manner that British investors would have an opportunity to make profits, that existing British investments in the seaboard area would not be wiped out by sudden population shifts, and that the Crown would obtain a revenue

[5] Justin Winsor's *The Westward Movement* (Boston, 1897), a detailed factual survey of events, 1763–98, is valuable as a reference work.

[6] Albert T. Volwiler, *George Croghan and the Westward Movement, 1741–1782* (Cleveland, 1926), is a detailed study of one of the central figures in western trade, Indian affairs, and land speculation.

for the support of colonial officials, thereby enabling them to function more effectively in Britain's interest. Each of these objectives entailed a much more cautious disposal of unused lands than that characteristic of the period of the Anglo-French conflict when the settlers were occupying a region easily accessible to British traders. A more cautious land policy in turn required that the western lands be severed from the thirteen colonies and incorporated into new provinces, the governments of which would be thoroughly subservient to British interests. Hence British colonial officials (Lord Halifax in 1757 and the Earl of Shelburne in 1767) proposed that new royal colonies be erected in the West.[7]

To many colonial capitalists no enterprise seemed more attractive than investments in western lands. The region which now beckoned to the colonial promoters was that of present-day West Virginia, southern Ohio, and Kentucky. Not only were important merchants like Thomas and Samuel Wharton of Pennsylvania interested; so also were leading planter families of Virginia such as the Washingtons and the Lees. The Ohio valley, an excellent wheat country, appealed to the more enterprising planters who were shifting production from tobacco to wheat. Washington now expressed his desire to "increase our export of wheat, gently lead our people off from tobacco, as well as render a vast extent of back country useful to trade." [8] Colonial speculators organized numerous companies, seeking to obtain title to far-reaching areas upon part of which they might establish settlers whose labor would enhance the value of the land which the company retained for future sale. By this means, also, the promoters hoped to obtain choice tracts as their personal estates. In the meantime a company might engage in the fur trade until settlement matured; thus the company might increase its capital and also establish contacts with the Indians preparatory to removing them from its grant. Foremost among such speculative ventures were the Loyal Company, a company of New Yorkers for establishing a colony of New Wales, the Company of Military Adventurers, the Illinois Company, the Wabash Company, the Mississippi Company, and the Susquehannah Company.[9] The proposed land acquisitions of these corporations varied from 200,000 to 12,000,000 acres; the great West inspired great visions.

[7] Clarence E. Carter, *Great Britain and the Illinois Country, 1763–1774* (Washington, 1910), is a thorough, detailed critique for the advanced student.

[8] Paul L. Haworth, *George Washington: Farmer* (Indianapolis, 1915), has been republished (1925) as *George Washington: Country Gentleman*.

[9] J. P. Boyd, "Connecticut's Experiment in Expansion: the Susquehannah Company," *Journal of Economic and Business History*, IV (Nov. 1931).

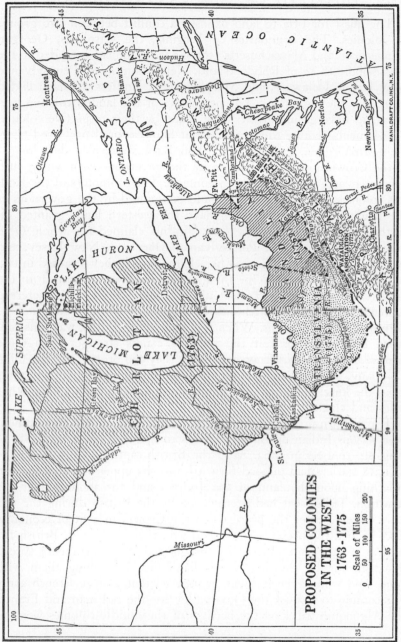

Based on "*Atlas of American History.*" © *Harper & Brothers.*

PROPOSED COLONIES IN THE WEST: 1763–1775

The quest for title to land exposed a conflict between two groups of colonies. The boundaries of Virginia, the Carolinas, Georgia, Connecticut, and Massachusetts (the landed colonies) extended to the Mississippi; those of Rhode Island, New Hampshire, Pennsylvania, New Jersey, Delaware, and Maryland (the landless colonies) ended at or near the mountains. The promoters of the landed colonies preferred to have grants in the West made by their respective colonial governments because their influence at home assured preferred treatment. In Virginia, for instance, although the western lands belonged to the Crown, grants were made by the governor—with whom such promoters as a rule had friendly contacts. The promoters of the landless colonies, fearful that they would be ignored by the governors of the landed colonies, desired to have the western lands granted directly by the Crown.[10] Since only Virginia claimed the whole Ohio valley the promoters of Pennsylvania, Maryland, New Jersey, and New York were united against her claims, which they attacked in two ways. First, they sought for their companies direct grants from the king; secondly, if such grants could not be procured, they preferred to have the West divided into new colonies which would not be dominated by Virginians. When the issue of land titles was thus confused the Virginians felt the need of claims stronger than those created by a royal governor and hence they too organized (the Ohio Company, the Mississippi Company) and petitioned for direct grants from the king, knowing that such grants took precedence over other titles and claims.[11]

The western problem was projected before the British government by a serious Indian uprising, Pontiac's conspiracy, which ravaged the English frontiers in 1763. After the British captured Fort Duquesne in 1758 settlers had pressed forward into the upper Ohio valley, encroaching upon the land of the Indians and threatening their destruction. Tribes that had been wooed by the British during the war were angered after the peace when the Crown, in a fit of economy, discontinued the presents which had won their good will. British fur traders (at the time practically unregulated by government) spread dissatisfaction by cheating the Indians and debauching them with rum. And when French agents whispered that a large French army was coming to recover the Ohio valley for the red man and France, the Algonquin tribes on the borders of the middle colonies went on

[10] A brief sketch of western trade and land interests appears in Max Savelle's *George Morgan, Colony Builder* (New York, 1932).

[11] C. W. Alvord, "Virginia and the West," *Mississippi Valley Historical Review*, III (June 1916).

the warpath and drove the English settlers from all the frontier posts
except Fort Pitt and Detroit. Due to a conference between British
agents and the southern Indians in 1763 the latter were pacified and
did not enter the conspiracy. Before the revolt was suppressed by
British regulars and colonial troops late in 1763 it had convinced
British statesmen that a new policy was needed for regulating the fur
trade, the settlement, and the defense of the West.[12]

In October the British government issued the Proclamation of 1763
—a highly important state paper drafted by the Earl of Shelburne
when president of the Board of Trade. It provided that for the time
being colonial settlement was not to extend westward beyond a line
running through the sources of the rivers flowing into the Atlantic.
Colonial governors were not to authorize surveys or issue patents for
any land west of this line—nor for any other land to which the Indian title had not been extinguished. Drafted in order to pacify the
Indians, the Proclamation of 1763 was regarded by Shelburne as a
temporary measure that would give Britain time in which to form a
permanent western policy. Its immediate effects were to remove the
western lands from the control of the colonial governors and to compel colonial land speculators to appeal directly to the king for desired
grants.

In 1767 Shelburne, now Secretary of State for the Southern Department, proposed that the western country be opened to settlement
and that three new colonies be established: at Detroit, on the Ohio, and
in the Illinois country.[13] A change in the ministry which occurred soon
afterward transferred colonial administration to the Earl of Hillsborough, who occupied in 1768 the newly created post of Secretary of
State for the Colonies. Hillsborough rejected Shelburne's proposals
of 1767 and advised instead that new colonies should not be erected
and that the flow of settlement westward should be carefully regulated, arguing that the interior would drain population from the seaboard and that new settlements should be placed under the military
rule of the British commanders of the western posts as a means of
avoiding colonial insubordination. In conformity with Hillsborough's
program, Britain in 1768 adopted the idea of an Indian boundary
line to be located periodically with the consent of the Indians concerned. For the future the title to Indian lands should be purchased
by the imperial government; settlement should proceed under the

---

[12] Francis Parkman's *The Conspiracy of Pontiac* is a fascinating narrative.

[13] The standard biography is Lord Fitzmaurice, *Life of William Earl of Shelburne*
(2 vols., 2d ed., London, 1912). See also R. A. Humphreys, "Lord Shelburne and
British Colonial Policy, 1766–1768," *English Historical Review*, L (April 1935).

supervision of British agents; the boundary should be moved westward gradually; and white settlers were not to cross the existing line.[14] By 1770 the line had been located as follows: "Beginning at Lake Ontario, it bent westward so that it opened up for settlement the upper waters of the Ohio as far as the mouth of the Great Kanawha; thence it turned south and east, closing for settlement the back country of the southern colonies" (Alvord).

Hillsborough's policy and the boundary line of 1768 thus dealt a hard blow to Virginia's efforts to dominate the West. Only a small area was now opened to settlement, which was to proceed directly under the Crown, thus making it possible for the speculators of the middle colonies to secure land at Virginia's expense. Foremost among such speculators were Samuel Wharton and William Trent, Pennsylvania merchants and spokesmen in the late 1760's for a group of "suffering" fur traders who had lost much property during Pontiac's conspiracy. Since 1763 the suffering traders had been asking Britain for a large piece of land in the West. Failing in that quarter they had attended a conference at Fort Stanwix in 1768 where they persuaded the Six Nations to cede to them a large tract in what is now West Virginia. And when this area was opened to settlement by the boundary line of 1768 the suffering traders applied to the Crown for a confirmation of the cession, proposing that it form the basis of a new colony, Vandalia. Many men of influence in England were induced to back the Vandalia project and Benjamin Franklin acted as agent for the promoters at court. Lord Hillsborough opposed the scheme, but his successor in the colonial office, Lord Dartmouth (1772), approved. However, the forces behind Hillsborough, acting through the Board of Trade, effectively thwarted the Vandalians at Whitehall, so that in 1774 the project was still hanging fire.[15]

The year 1774 brought a major development in Britain's western land policy—the Quebec Act. With the object of reserving the lands north of the Ohio and west of Pennsylvania as an Indian country and fur trading area, this act annexed this territory to the province of Quebec and thereby removed it from the influence of the settlers and speculators of Virginia and the middle colonies. Virginia's position was now desperate. Excluded from the country north of the Ohio by the Quebec Act and on the point of being excluded from West Virginia and Kentucky by the Vandalia project and the Indian boundary

[14] M. Farrand, "The Indian Boundary Line," *American Historical Review*, X (July, 1905). The best recent study is Thomas P. Abernethy, *Western Lands and the American Revolution* (New York, 1937)—important.

[15] Louis P. Kellogg's *The British Regime in Wisconsin and the Northwest* (Madison, Wis., 1935) is an able survey. See chapters 1–8.

line, the Virginians were forced to act aggressively in defense of their western claims.[16]

Fortunately for the Virginians their governor, Lord Dunmore, stood behind the speculators and pioneers. Himself a speculator who hoped to make his fortune from western lands, Lord Dunmore had ignored Britain's policies by making grants in the Vandalia tract and in the country west of the boundary line. The Virginians were now ready to occupy Kentucky, Daniel Boone having led the way in 1769. Realizing in 1774 that, in the face of the Vandalia project, Virginia needed to defend her claims in the West, Lord Dunmore instigated a war against the Shawnee in the neighborhood of Wheeling, defeated them and wrung from them the right of Virginia pioneers to hunt in Kentucky. In Dunmore's War the Shawnee were isolated; their overlords, the Six Nations, had already granted to Britain the lands occupied by the Shawnee south of the Ohio and west to the Tennessee River (Treaty of Fort Stanwix, 1768). The Iroquois, by sacrificing the Shawnee and their lands, evidently hoped to divert the whites to the country south of the Ohio and thus to preserve intact their own territory in the Mohawk valley.[17]

The landed interest in the colonies received another shock from Britain when the Crown in 1774 promulgated new regulations for the disposal of ungranted lands in Virginia, New York, North Carolina, South Carolina, New Hampshire, Georgia, Florida, and throughout the West. Previously, fertile lands had been occupied by colonists in irregular parcels, thus leaving uneven tracts in between, which the farmers adjacent often appropriated without ceremony. The usual quit-rent of 2s. a hundred acres had not been excessive and great quantities of land had been given away by the Crown. Now the king ordered that for the future all grants must be surveyed in regular lots (minimum, one hundred acres; maximum, a thousand); the quit-rents exacted for such lands should amount to 4s. 2d. a hundred acres (twice the rate prevailing in Virginia); governors were not to make further gifts of land; and all tracts should be sold at auction to the "best bidder" at a price not less than 6d. an acre. Thomas Jefferson objected to these new regulations on the ground that "the ac

---

[16] Alfred L. Burt, *The Old Province of Quebec* (Minneapolis, 1933), is a thorough study of the period 1760–91, emphasizing economic influences. R. Coupland's *The Quebec Act* (Oxford, 1925) is a study in British efforts to conciliate the French Canadians.

[17] On settlement west of the southern colonies see Archibald Henderson, *The Conquest of the Old Southwest* (New York, 1920)—well written, in a romantic strain; and Constance L. Skinner, *Pioneers of the Old Southwest* (*Chronicles of America*, New Haven, 1919).

quisition of lands being rendered difficult, the population of our country is likely to be checked"—an indictment which he included in the Declaration of Independence.

British land policy as finally formulated in 1774 declared a virtual embargo on colonial expansion in the West. It closed to speculators and settlers the territories north of the Ohio and south of Virginia, it opened only a small tract in western Virginia, it subjected all ungranted lands in the East to rigorous and hampering conditions of purchase, and it deprived the landed colonies of their claims to the interior. Even the Vandalia speculators had not gained approval for their project, and despite the powerful forces making for westward expansion in Virginia that colony was denied independent access to the West.[18] The restrictive policy applied to the thirteen colonies did not mean, however, that British investors and speculators were being ignored. After 1763 the Crown conferred numerous large tracts upon merchants, army officers, and wealthy landowners (all residents of Britain), such tracts being located in Canada, Nova Scotia, Florida, and Prince Edward Island—regions accessible to British trade and not likely to produce commodities that would compete with the products of industries in which British investors had a large stake. By opening these areas Britain created speculative opportunities for her own investors while opposing the schemes of colonial promoters to develop the trans-Allegheny West.

Britain's regulation of the fur trade north of the Ohio River exhibited the same tendencies which made her land policy odious to the thirteen colonies. The furs of this region were regarded in England as its most valuable form of wealth—a resource that Britain must monopolize in order to provide new outlets for the capital of her merchants and in order also to render the Indians dependent upon herself as the means of controlling their movements in peace and war.[19] More particularly, the British must prevent the French traders who remained in the Northwest from diverting the fur trade down the Mississippi to Spanish New Orleans. After the conquest of Canada British merchants replaced the French capitalists at Montreal; then Pontiac's conspiracy gave the British Canadians a further advantage by disrupting the fur trade of Pennsylvania and New York. Although the traffic was less important to the middle colonies than land specula-

[18] Justin Winsor, "Virginia and the Quebec Bill," *American Historical Review*, I (April 1896).

[19] Wayne E. Stevens, *The Northwest Fur Trade* (Urbana, 1928), is an excellent analysis of the economics of the fur trade and of the political influence of the British fur traders. See also W. E. Stevens, "The Organization of the British Fur Trade, 1760–1800," *Mississippi Valley Historical Review*, III (Sept. 1916).

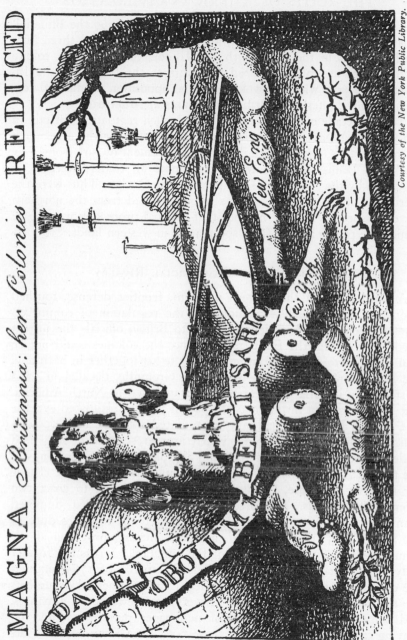

MAGNA *Britannia: her Colonies* REDUCED

BRITAIN WEAKENED BY OPPRESSIVE MEASURES AGAINST HER COLONIES (1768)

tion it remained a worth-while source of profit: in 1767 the Philadelphia firm of Baynton, Wharton, and Morgan employed three hundred boatmen in the trade with the Illinois country. Each colony with western aspirations desired to dominate the trade and the Indians—a purpose which provoked colonial opposition to imperial regulations in the interest of British merchants at Montreal.

After a decade of experimentation with such regulations Britain in the Quebec Act of 1774 proclaimed a new policy for the area north of the Ohio. Its object was to divert the movement of furs from New York and Pennsylvania to Montreal; hence all traders were to be regulated by the governor of the province of Quebec. Thus were the merchants of the thirteen colonies to be excluded from the northern fur trade, precisely in the manner that colonial promoters were to be denied the profits arising from speculation in western lands.[20]

### ANGLO-COLONIAL COMMERCIAL RIVALRY

A third phase of the western problem, frontier defense, touched upon two related issues—taxation and the regulation of commerce. Pontiac's conspiracy had demonstrated to British officials the urgent need of protecting the frontiers, and since the colonies could not be counted upon to support a large army or to act together in harmony, the British ministry, headed by George Grenville, decided in 1763 to station an imperial force of ten thousand men in North America. But Britain was not in the mood to pay in full the estimated expense of £350,000 a year; she had now accumulated a debt of £130,000,000 which cost the nation £4,500,000 yearly in interest; and she staggered under oppressive taxes, those on land amounting to four shillings in the pound. Arguing that the colonists should bear part of the charge for their own defense, Grenville induced Parliament to enact two momentous statutes. The first—the Sugar Act of 1764—imposed many new taxes on colonial trade and reduced the molasses duty of the act of 1733 from 6*d.* to 3*d.* a pound, making provision at the same time for efficient collection of the new tax, whereas the former duty had yielded next to nothing. The Stamp Act of 1765 required the colonists to pay stamp duties on legal and commercial documents (to the dismay of merchants and lawyers), on newspapers, almanacs, and pamphlets (to the distress of newspaper publishers), and on playing cards and dice. From all these taxes the Crown hoped to de-

---

[20] Victor Coffin's *The Province of Quebec and the Early American Revolution* (Madison, Wis., 1896), a technical study of Britain's problems in governing Canada after 1760, emphasizes the importance of the fur trade.

rive a revenue of about £100,000 to defray nearly a third of the cost of frontier defense.[21]

The Sugar Act and the Stamp Act at once focused the attention of the colonists upon their long-standing commercial conflicts with Britain. The colonies now supplied British capitalists with income from three principal sources: the general commerce and shipping of the empire, investments in the British sugar islands, and manufacturing industries in England sustained by colonial markets. But because the colonial merchants had to resort to similar enterprises they constantly menaced their British rivals—partly by obtaining a large share of the profits of imperial commerce and partly by trading with the foreign sugar colonies, thus undermining British investments in the British islands. Britain's interests therefore dictated that the colonies should be regulated in such a manner as to protect her West Indian investments, to strengthen her manufacturing industries, and to safeguard the profits of her merchants in colonial trade. These objectives were to be realized in two ways: by imposing new restrictions upon colonial commerce and by enforcing more rigidly the existing Acts of Trade. The importance of such a policy is indicated by a report of the Duke of Newcastle in 1766 that the trade of Britain was declining in every part of the world except America.[22]

Of the new measures adopted after 1760 one group of acts aimed to extend further aid to British manufacturers. Bounties were now offered to stimulate production in the colonies of hemp and flax, raw materials needed by British cloth-workers and rope-makers. The Sugar Act added to the enumerated article list a new group of products desired by British manufacturers—whale fins, hides, skins, raw silk, potashes, pearl ashes, coffee, pimiento, and cocoanuts. The Sugar Act also tightened the hold of British manufacturers on the colonial market: first, by removing most of the drawbacks previously allowed on European goods passing through England to the colonies, thereby increasing their prices so that they could be undersold by British products; secondly, by placing new duties on other competing goods such as oriental silks and calicoes, foreign linens, and French lawns. Finally, an act of 1774 carried forward the prohibitions on colonial manufactures by prohibiting the exportation from Britain to the colonies of tools used in linen, cotton, silk, and woolen manufactures.

[21] C. E. Carter, "The Significance of the Military Office in America, 1763–1775," *American Historical Review*, XXVIII (April 1923).

[22] An intensive, highly important study is Arthur M. Schlesinger, *The Colonial Merchants and the American Revolution* (New York, 1918). Very valuable.

These measures also promised to aid British merchants in that they tended to center colonial trade in England and therefore assured that the freights, commissions, profits, and interest charges involved would go to British firms. Similarly, acts of 1766–67 required that non-enumerated articles bound for parts of Europe north of Cape Finis-terre should first pass through a British port. A major clause of the Sugar Act was designed to protect British merchants in the colonial wine trade. Prior to 1763 the colonial merchants had imported great quantities of wine from Madeira, the Canaries, and the Azores. Now, however, all such wines imported from the Wine Islands were to pay in the colonies a duty of £7 a tun, whereas wine imported from Brit-ain was to pay only 10s. a tun. Were such duties efficiently collected, wines exported by British merchants from London to the colonies might compete with wine brought from the Wine Islands by colonial merchants.[23]

Both the Sugar Act and the Stamp Act contained a further threat to colonial business. This was the rule that the taxes collected in America were to be remitted to the British exchequer and disbursed by order of Parliament. Once more the old problem of returns raised its head. The colonial merchants argued that such remittances would deprive them of specie or its equivalent in buying power for English goods and thus make it impossible for them to pay for needed im-ports, since their "returns" to England had never been adequate, even when they had not had to make remittances of tax money to the Crown. It is true that the tax money was to return to the colonies for the army, but it would come back in the form of English goods which would be exchanged for colonial products and colonial currency needed by the army. If the Crown should contract with British mer-chants to supply the army, they would obtain the money in England, invest it in English goods, and thereby strengthen their hold upon colonial trade. In other words Britain might deprive the colonial mer-chants of their means of buying English goods, transfer such buying power to English merchants, and drive the colonial merchants from their customary trade.

In 1773 the British government made its most open move to favor British merchants when Parliament in effect gave the East India Company a monopoly of the colonial trade in tea. A discussion of this measure appears in chapter XXIII.[24]

Five clauses in the Sugar Act extended protection to British in-

[23] See again G. L. Beer, *British Colonial Policy, 1754–1765*, chapters 10–14.
[24] M. Farrand, "The Taxation of Tea," *American Historical Review*, III (Jan. 1898).

vestors in the British West Indies. The English colonists were prohibited from importing rum from a foreign sugar colony; they must now pay an added duty of £1 2s. a hundredweight on all white sugar which they bought from the foreign islands; a new duty of 6d. a pound was placed upon foreign indigo which they purchased; foreign coffee was subject to a duty of £2 19s. 9d. a hundredweight; and foreign molasses to a duty of 3d. a gallon. All these taxes were designed to raise the colonial price of foreign West Indian products in order that the British planters might obtain higher prices for their products.

Hand in hand with these duties and trade restrictions came a series of measures for the strict enforcement of all British regulations, old and new. The Grenville ministry, 1763–65, ordered that absentee officials should take themselves to the colonies and perform their duties in person rather than through low-paid and inefficient deputies; it authorized anew the use of writs of assistance; and it put British naval vessels in American waters to the task of enforcing the Acts of Trade. Parliament in 1764 decreed that customs officials who made seizures and arrests with good cause could not be sued for damages by colonists who were not proved guilty as charged; the burden of proof as to whether duties had been paid or whether goods were of foreign origin was placed upon the accused; and an act of 1764 authorized the erection of a general vice-admiralty court for all the colonies, with the provision that penalties arising from violation of the acts of trade might be recovered in any colonial admiralty or vice-admiralty court, thus removing trials from the neighborhood of the defendant. Next came the Townshend Acts of 1767, strengthening the admiralty courts and reorganizing the American customs service, whereupon the king immediately appointed an American Board of Commissioners of the Customs whose authority extended over all British North America. With energies concentrated upon a single task and with virtually complete powers, this board set about vigorously to enforce the British Acts of Trade.[25]

Before 1763 British customs and trade laws had not seriously injured the colonial merchant class, such acts having not been rigidly enforced—and that because Britain was unwilling to pay for enforcement and shrank from raising the necessary funds by taxing the colonies. But the time had now come to be done with such weakness; hence the decision of 1763 to maintain an army in America and to tax the colonists for its support. (Incidentally the army might be used to enforce the Acts of Trade.) Although Parliament in 1766 re-

[25] See again E. Channing, *History of the United States*, Vol. III, chapters 1–4.

pealed the Stamp Act and lowered the molasses duty of the Sugar Act from 3*d*. to 1*d*., the principle of taxing the colonies for the army remained, since the other duties of the Sugar Act were not removed. Then in 1767 Parliament extended the principle by levying new taxes (the Townshend duties) to be paid in the colonies on imported tea, paper, glass, painter's colors, and lead. The money thus raised was to go to the support, not only of the army, but also to pay expenses of colonial government and the administration of justice; thus might Britain enjoy a revenue independently of the colonial assemblies and free its American agents of their dependence upon the colonists for their pay.[26] The land ordinance of 1774 promised more revenue for this purpose. And when the colonial merchants warred against the Sugar Act, the Townshend duties, and the British customs agents, the Crown in 1768 transferred the army from the West to the East and prepared to crush opposition with military force.

The efficiency of the new enforcement policy contrasted sharply with the lax conditions prevailing before. Between 1767 and 1770 the number of British customs agents in Philadelphia was trebled and new revenue cutters were added to the coast patrol. Channing estimates that in seven years, 1768–74, the colonists paid £200,000 in taxes to the British customs service; British levies collected in America rose from less than £2,000 a year before 1763 to £30,000 a year after 1767. And all this for the purpose of making colonial trade profitable to British merchants at the expense of their American competitors who paid the taxes.

The relation between taxation and enforcement appeared also in the Quartering Act of 1765, which required the colonists to supply additional funds for the support of the imperial army. For that part of the forces stationed within any colony its assembly was to provide barracks, "certain necessary utensils," salt, vinegar, rum or beer, and part of the money to pay the costs of transportation. Since New York was the gateway to the interior the Quartering Act imposed upon that province a disproportionately large share of this extra expense, much to the annoyance of the New Yorkers, who contended that they should not be so penalized simply because the army crossed their territory en route to the West. After 1767 the same problem confronted Massachusetts when royal troops were moved to Boston.[27]

Meanwhile, Britain had adopted a new Currency Act of 1764 in

---

[26] C. M. Andrews, "The American Revolution: an Interpretation," *American Historical Review*, XXI (Jan. 1926).

[27] George E. Howard's *The Preliminaries of the Revolution, 1763–1775* (New York, 1905) is one of the less distinguished volumes of the *American Nation* series.

order to protect the investments of her merchants in the colonies. During the French and Indian War Virginia had issued £250,000 in bills of credit which were declared legal tender in payment of private debts, old and new. As the value of such bills in terms of English money declined, British merchants complained that they diminished debts due in sterling money "of certain and fixed value" by permitting payments to be made in a currency "of a local, uncertain value." Not even the bills of the Bank of England or exchequer notes issued by the British government were legal tender. In 1764 the Board of Trade condemned colonial paper currency as a device whereby colonial debtors could defraud their creditors, and Parliament thereupon forbade the issuance of legal tender bills and ordered that all such bills emitted during the war should be retired at the time appointed by the act of issue. Should any governor sign an act for legal tender currency he should pay a fine of £1,000, lose his post, and be forever barred from offices of trust. The Currency Act of 1764 extended to all the colonies the provisions of the Currency Act of 1751, which the Board of Trade deemed to have had a salutary effect in New England.

## THE PLIGHT OF THE COLONIES

Had all the acts on the British statute books after 1763 been rigidly enforced their cumulative force would undoubtedly have crushed the colonies. Let us consider first the region north of Maryland, where the producers of fish, lumber, and farm commodities were steadily enlarging their output and therefore in need of expanding markets, and where the merchants required an extended field of investment for their surplus capital. Prior to 1763 the foreign West Indies and the Wine Islands had afforded two such necessary markets and outlets. The Sugar Act, however, burdened the trade with both regions and tended to raise the prices of the products involved—particularly of rum and molasses, ingredients in nearly every important branch of colonial commerce. Restraints upon trade made shipowning unprofitable and not only depressed the colonial shipbuilding industry but also induced shrewd merchants to sell vessels previously acquired. More particularly the Sugar Act made it difficult for the Northerners to obtain their customary means of buying in England, while the payment of tax money to Britain promised to deprive them of a large part of such remittances as remained.[28] Since colonial com-

[28] F. B. Wiener, "The Rhode Island Merchants and the Sugar Act," *New England Quarterly*, III (July 1930). See also B. M. Bigelow, "Aaron Lopez, Merchant of Newport," *New England Quarterly*, IV (Oct. 1931).

merce revolved around the import trade from Britain, anything which reduced the buying power of the colonial merchants for British goods threatened to dislocate all their other trades. When in 1773 Britain endeavored to give the British East India Company a monopoly of the colonial tea trade the denial of profits to colonial merchants was beyond question. The general effect of Britain's measures, if enforced, would have been to raise the price of all imported goods (the Townshend duties taxed imports even from Britain) and to reduce the prices of colonial exports; losses sustained by colonial producers and merchants through being compelled to buy dear and sell cheap were to provide the gains of British merchants and the tax revenues of the Crown. And if foreign commerce became inadequate and unprofitable, what could the northern colonies do? They were not allowed to develop manufacturing industries and they were to be excluded from the fur trade and the development of the West. In place of the growth long characteristic of the colonies, British policy now threatened repression, contraction, and decay.[29]

Nor did the prospects of the tobacco colonies appear in a happier light. As the profits of the tobacco industry vanished the energetic planters had turned to the production of new commodities—fish, grain, and livestock; they had tried to check the importation of slaves; they had fostered home manufacture of textiles and leather goods; and they had invested in western lands. Yet each of these activities inspired hostile orders from Britain. The slave trade was to remain open and unhampered; home manufactures were not to expand; the markets for southern grain and livestock in the foreign islands were to be curtailed; and the West was to be closed to Virginia speculators. The planters should continue to produce tobacco, even though forced to use inefficient slave labor on exhausted lands, to stagger under an oppressive burden of debt, and to market their crops through creditor-merchants who took the cream of the profits. British policy decreed that the tobacco planters remained wedded to a declining productive system, faced with the certain prospect of economic bondage.[30]

By 1763 the contradictions in mercantilism had become self-evident. If the colonies were to buy more in goods and services from Britain than they sold to her, the deficit could be cared for in only a

[29] C. M. Andrews, *The Boston Merchants and the Non-Importation Movement* (Cambridge, 1917), is an excellent résumé.

[30] See chapter 1 of an admirable study by Isaac S. Harrell, *Loyalism in Virginia* (Philadelphia, 1926).

few ways. Gold and silver might have been used to settle the adverse balance, but the supply in the colonies was not adequate. The other alternative was to sell goods to the colonies on credit. But this solution had its dangers: first because the interest charges ensuing increased the demands on the colonies and enhanced their unfavorable balance of trade; secondly, because the increasing debt burden required an expanding economy if it were to be carried successfully by the debtors. But the investments of British creditors created an interest in established enterprises that might be destroyed by the development of new and competing enterprises. And if new enterprises were retarded, if expansion were stopped, the burden of fixed debts which pressed upon old enterprises would become unbearable, since the debts themselves had been created on the assumption that an expanded production would provide for future payment. Clearly, by 1763 the colonies had to expand in order to prosper, and yet Britain sought to restrain their manufactures, their foreign trade, and their westward settlements, seeking thereby to protect her own commerce, industry, and investments in the tobacco-sugar areas, and to reserve the West as a field for British enterprise. Such enterprises as Britain proposed to leave free to the colonists would have yielded little beyond a subsistence living and the means of paying their sterling debts. Mercantilist tendencies had previously created critical situations but the colonists had escaped because British acts had not been enforced. Now, however, when Britain taxed the colonists for an army and prepared to use it to keep them in an economic strait jacket, a reckoning was at hand.[31]

In a conflict so profound as the American Revolution the interests of all classes were vitally affected by the issues at stake. In some way or other every man's fortune felt the impact of British policies, and for the most part the effect was injurious. A common foe across the sea drew the colonists together, and yet within colonial society were cleavages as deep as those which separated the colonies from the mother country—class divisions that common opposition to British policies could not efface. In the words of Carl Becker, the American Revolution "was the result of two general movements; the contest for home-rule and independence, and the democratization of American politics and society." In order to account for this dualism two questions must be considered: what factors worked to unite the colo-

[31] H. E. Egerton, *The Causes and Character of the American Revolution* (Oxford, 1923), attributes American resistance to the English settler's opposition to an inferior status within the empire.

nial classes against British rule, and what counter-forces arrayed class against class?

A large section of the upper class in America objected strenuously to the lot assigned to them by Britain after 1763. Many southern planters, thoroughly aroused against Britain's dominance of their trade, complained that the British merchants paid unduly low prices for their crops and sent them inferior European goods, poorly packed and shipped and priced excessively high. In the face of such conditions the debt burden had become insupportable: as Jefferson put it, "these debts had become hereditary from father to son, for many generations, so that the planters were a species of property annexed to certain mercantile houses in London." Accepting Jefferson's estimate that the debts of Virginia amounted to £2,000,000 sterling, it is safe to assume that a yearly interest charge of 6 per cent or £120,000 was enough to absorb the income of the planters after all other fixed costs had been deducted. "With their plantations, slaves, and sometimes their furniture and ungrown crops mortgaged beyond their actual value, it seemed in 1775 that nothing less than virtual repudiation could save them" (Carman). The planters, however, were not repudiationists; their status as property owners inculcated a strong sense of the sanctity of private contracts. But when Britain increased the difficulty of debt payment there was no alternative except to resist. The attempted closing of the West to planters' investments threatened to cut off a principal source of income by which they previously had carried their debt burdens, while the new British taxes increased the price of imported goods without adding a penny to their income. The Crown's refusal to permit restrictions on the slave trade also antagonized those planters who were overstocked with now unprofitable workers. For these various reasons the planters raised a voice of protest against Britain's rule. Among them were George Washington, Thomas Jefferson, Benjamin Harrison, Richard Blair, Edmund Pendleton, Richard Henry Lee, Francis Lightfoot Lee, George Mason, Edmund Randolph, Peyton Randolph, James Madison, and Thomas Nelson of Virginia, Charles Carroll and Thomas Johnson of Maryland, and Edmund Rutledge, John Rutledge, Arthur Middleton, Rawlins Lowndes, and Charles C. Pinckney of South Carolina. Among such planters two groups may be distinguished. One, represented by Thomas Jefferson, consisted of agriculturists whose investments and activities were centered upon their plantations and who relished the life of a country gentleman; the second, represented by George Washington, was composed of planters who were also businessmen—merchants, moneylenders, investors in western lands, and promoters of industrial enterprises.[32]

From a large body of colonial merchants came an equally spirited resistance. Their grievances against Britain included the restraints upon their commerce, their exclusion from the northern fur trade and western land speculation, the prohibitions against colonial manufactures, the added burden of taxes, the new measures to enforce the British colonial system and the tendency of these measures to reduce their profits and increase the difficulty of paying debts due to England. (Such debts of Pennsylvania in 1765 amounted to £300,000.) In short, British measures imperiled the existing investments of the colonial merchants and closed new outlets for their surplus capital. The chief merchant opponents of British measures were John Hancock, James Bowdoin, and Elbridge Gerry of Massachusetts, John Langdon of New Hampshire, Jonathan Trumbull and Roger Sherman of Connecticut, Stephen Hopkins, William Ellery, Samuel Ward, and Moses Brown of Rhode Island, Alexander MacDougall, Isaac Sears, and John Lamb of New York, Isaac Pemberton, Thomas Mifflin, Robert Morris, Samuel Wharton, Thomas Wharton, and George Clymer of Pennsylvania, and Henry Laurens, Gabriel Manigault, and Christopher Gadsden of South Carolina. Somewhat akin to the merchants were the New York aristocrats, with their threefold interests in land, commerce, and the fur trade, whose opposition to Britain was voiced by Philip Livingston, Stephen Van Rensselaer, Philip Schuyler, Gouverneur Morris, Robert Livingston, and Lewis Morris.

Many members of the professional class, who were affiliated with the aristocracy by ties of marriage and business or property ownership, directed the campaign against Britain on the legal and intellectual plane. Among them were John Witherspoon, president of Princeton college, George Wythe, professor of law at the College of William and Mary, Dr. Benjamin Rush of Pennsylvania, and an able group of lawyers which included or was to include John Adams and James Otis of Massachusetts, John Jay and Alexander Hamilton of New York, and James Wilson, John Dickinson, and James Smith of Pennsylvania.[33]

[32] Burton J. Hendrick, *The Lees of Virginia* (Boston, 1935), a vigorous, fascinating study of a family, is highly recommended to the general reader. Edward S. Delaplaine, *The Life of Thomas Johnson* (New York, 1927), is too detailed for the general reader, considering the importance of the subject.

[33] Gilbert Chinard's *Honest John Adams* (Boston, 1933) is a good modern study, though not equal to the same author's biography of Jefferson. For older standard

The small farmers who composed the backbone of the colonial democracy also had their reasons for resisting Britain's encroachments. All restraints on colonial trade which curtailed markets meant lower prices for the farmers' surpluses, just as British taxes increased the cost of their purchases, while British currency policy now made it impossible for debtors to obtain cheap currency in the form of land bank loans. The Currency Act of 1764 required that the colonists tax themselves to redeem immediately the bills of credit issued during the war—debts which in 1763 amounted to £750,000. Once currency contraction had taken place private debts incurred when money was plentiful and cheap became more burdensome, since payments had to be made in a scarce and dear currency. Franklin in 1766 informed British officials that the restraints on paper money were one of the principal causes of colonial disaffection. If a debtor farmer lost his land through foreclosure, the difficulty of obtaining a new farm was now enhanced, thanks to Britain's new western program and the land ordinance of 1774; hence the land policy of the Crown benefited speculative holders of large estates in the East at the expense of the small farmers and their large and none too affluent families. In the southern colonies the unpopular quit-rents and taxes for the support of the Anglican Church were associated with the oppressions of the British government. The colonial yeomen now controlled the elected house of the legislature in New Jersey, North Carolina, and the New England colonies, while in the South Carolina, Pennsylvania, and Virginia assemblies, although under-represented, they were able to assert their demands.[34] Their leading spokesmen were Samuel Adams of Massachusetts, Patrick Henry and Thomas Jefferson of Virginia, and George Clinton of New York.

Even the unprivileged workers in the towns and the tenants on large estates felt the heavy hand of Britain's rule. The gulf between the small landowning farmers and unprivileged tenants, and workers, skilled, semi-skilled, and unskilled, was not wide. All performed rough and heavy labor, all felt oppressed by the upper class, whether they were debtors, employees, servants, or tenants, and all were imbued with the democratic ideal of the dignity of man. Parrington in his *Colonial Mind* relates an incident showing the antagonism between the working farmers and the aristocratic governor of Massachusetts, Joseph Dudley. "One December day in 1705, as he was

biographies consult John Quincy Adams and Charles Francis Adams, *The Life of John Adams* (2 vols., Philadelphia, 1874), and John T. Morse, *John Adams* (Boston, 1887).

[34] E. Francis Brown's *Joseph Hawley* (New York, 1931) is an admirable study of a Massachusetts radical.

driving along a country road with high snowdrifts on each side, he met with two loads of wood. The chariot coming to a stop, Dudley thrust his head out of the window and bade the carters turn aside and make way for him: but they were inclined to argue the matter in view of the drifts. Words were multiplied, and one of the carters cried . . . 'I am as good flesh and blood as you . . . you may go out of the way.' In a rage the governor drew his sword and struck at the fellow, who snatched the sword away and broke it. . . . He arrested both carters and threw them into jail. . . . They were of good yeoman families, yet the matter hung on for nearly a year before they were discharged from their bonds." [35]

When yeomen could experience such treatment from a royal governor, it is evident that unprivileged workers and tenants were even more at the mercy of their masters. Not that the latter were the British government, but the king's officials in America were the symbol of prerogative, power, and privilege, and in conflicts between workers and masters Britain generally used its power to maintain the authority of the owning class. Hence the unprivileged workers, oppressed by a sense of political and social discrimination, degraded by an economic status derived from and maintained by Britain, and aflame with anti-British feeling, were prepared to remonstrate against any British measures which intensified their unhappy lot.[36]

The British acts of 1763–65 fell upon the colonies when in the midst of an economic depression. Wartime prosperity had been sustained by British military expenditures in America, by privateering, and by the inflation of colonial currency. When all these artificial factors were removed after 1762, trade dwindled, prices declined, and unemployment gripped the towns. The new British taxes and trade restrictions levied a toll upon a shrunken colonial trade that could only mean further impoverishment to the working class, dependent as it was upon the industries that served external commerce. More particularly the artisans resented both the British restrictions upon colonial manufactures and Britain's currency policy which denied to the colonies a money and credit structure necessary to sustain industrial activity. In denouncing Britain's restraints upon colonial manufactures and paper money Benjamin Franklin voiced the protests of the artisan class, of which he himself was the greatest product. A writer in a Boston paper of April 29, 1765, lamented that a "colonist

[35] Quoted from the 1929 edition, p. 126, by permission of the publishers, Harcourt, Brace and Co., New York.

[36] A pioneer work analyzing class relationships is Carl Becker's penetrating study, *The History of Political Parties in the Province of New York, 1760–1776* (Madison, Wis., 1909).

cannot make a button, a horseshoe, nor a hobnail, but some sooty ironmonger or respectable button-maker of Britain shall bawl and squall that his honor's worship is most egregiously maltreated, injured, cheated, and robbed by the rascally American republicans." Nor could the colonial workers look with favor upon Britain's new land policy which retarded the movement of surplus farmers and workers into unoccupied areas. As Franklin wrote in 1751: "It is the multitude of poor without land in a country, . . . who must work for others at low wages or starve. . . ." All the British measures adopted after 1760 tended toward a common result: to curtail those industries dependent upon the foreign commerce of the colonies, to deny to the American workers employment in new industries, and to increase the host of landless workers competing for employment in a restricted economy. It is not surprising, then, that such men as Isaac Sears and John Lamb of New York and Paul Revere of Boston could lead the workers in opposition to British rule—and in alliance with outraged farmers of the middle class.[37]

Although the farmers and workers and the colonial upper class had many common grievances against Britain, in other respects the two groups were antagonistic. With respect to paper money the colonial merchants and the more prosperous planters looked with disfavor upon the demands of the colonial debtors, while colonial landlords and speculators were frequently at war with tenant farmers and squatters. Moreover, the employers and owners of large property dreaded the specter of mob rule, fearing that if the lower classes gained control of the colonial governments they would become imbued with a spirit of insubordination, repudiate debts, and seize and redistribute large estates. The merchants, moreover, had long enjoyed certain benefits within the British empire—the protection of the British navy, access to all the markets of the empire, the right to employ their vessels in imperial trade, British support of the slave traffic, and the backing of British diplomacy in disputes with foreign states. Such advantages were not to be surrendered lightly—especially when the destruction of Britain's authority would expose the upper class to mob rule and deprive the colonial merchants of Britain's protection against currency inflation and the repudiation of debts.[38]

In such circumstances the colonial aristocracy found itself in a difficult position. A few merchants like John Hancock perceived that

[37] See again C. A. and M. R. Beard, *Rise of American Civilization*, Vol. I, chapter 5.
[38] See three stimulating, well-written essays, *The Spirit of '76*, by Carl Becker, J. M. Clark, and W. E. Dodd (Washington, 1927).

there was an irreconcilable conflict between British profits and colonial profits, and accordingly waged a persistent war against British rule. However, the majority of the disaffected merchants and planters desired to retain the advantages of the empire and at the same time to free themselves from its shackles of restraint. When it became apparent after 1774 that such advantages could be had only at the cost of British taxes and trade restrictions, a large number of the merchants and planters decided that the restraints outweighed the advantages. Interested primarily in the growth of their influence and fortunes through continued colonial expansion, such members of the upper class were forced to recognize that American development had to be freed from the blight of British mercantilism.

But not all members of the colonial upper class joined the revolutionary movement; others remained firm in their attachment to Britain. At the head of the loyalist party stood the royal governors, the most prominent of whom was Thomas Hutchinson of Massachusetts.[39] As the son of a New England merchant prince Hutchinson inherited an ample fortune which enabled him to devote himself to politics, serving as a multiple officeholder under the Crown before he became royal governor in 1770. Upon his friends, relatives, and dependents he conferred minor royal offices, thus creating a pro-British party animated alike by his own reverence for large property, aristocracy, and British institutions and by his hostility to the political demands of the lower classes. Perceiving the exposed position of the colonial aristocracy, he concluded that it could best be protected from the "mob" by British force. "I wish the good of the country," he wrote, "when I wish to see some further restraint of liberty rather than the connection with the parent state should be broken; for I am sure such a breach must prove the ruin of the colony." When it is recalled that after 1768 the colonists paid £30,000 a year in British taxes for the support of the royal officials in America it is evident that there was a breach between the payers and receivers that was not easily closed.

In Pennsylvania and Maryland the position of the proprietary governors and their officers, emissaries, and employees was analogous to the status of the British officials in the royal colonies. Both the Penn and the Calvert families enjoyed the full support of the British government; the attack in England on the proprietary governments had long since subsided. An estimate that the lands in possession of

[39] James K. Hosmer defends the loyalist view in his *Life of Thomas Hutchinson* (Boston, 1896).

the Penn family were now worth £1,000,000 suggests a reason why the Penns should desire to maintain the connection with Britain, whence their title to this princely estate was derived. Nor were the quit-rents and other revenues of the proprietors an income to be willingly surrendered. A recent study by C. A. Barker shows that in 1766 the income of Lord Baltimore from Maryland amounted to £12,500, and that £12,000 went to a hundred and fifty officials of the colony whom he appointed. Since the exports of Maryland were then valued as between £175,000 and £225,000 a year, the proprietary system meant a drain of between 12 and 14 per cent of the purchasing power of the Maryland farmers. "And as more than half of all the income controlled by the proprietary element was concentrated in the hands of the lord proprietor and half a dozen high officials, the preponderance of privilege is evident." [40]

Moreover, the land policy of the Crown as formulated in 1774 was highly beneficial to Baltimore and the Penns. Neither had claims to the land severed from the old colonies by Britain, while the Crown's restrictions on settlement in the Ohio valley and the new conditions imposed upon the sale of unoccupied royal lands would have forced upward the price of ungranted lands still in possession of the Penn and Calvert families. A like good fortune would have visited the holders of large tracts in the area east of Quebec and the Indian boundary line. Among the great speculative holders whose lands would have risen in value through Britain's policy of restricting the area open to settlement were some of the most prominent loyalists. Sir William Pepperrell had an estate stretching for thirty miles along the coast of Maine; Sir John Johnson (son of Sir William Johnson, who died in 1774) had title to fifty thousand acres in the Mohawk valley; [41] the Philipse family in New York possessed lands to the extent of three hundred square miles; Sir James Wright claimed an estate in Georgia later valued at $160,000; and there were besides these the vast domains of Lord Fairfax (over five million acres) and of Lord Granville, one-third of North Carolina. British land policy also promised to benefit the substantial, employing, non-debtor farmers of the seacoast area: first by minimizing the competition of newer lands of the interior; secondly by increasing the force of landless workers who could be hired at low wages. And when

[40] C. A. Barker, "Property Rights in the Provincial System of Maryland," *Journal of Southern History*, II (Feb., May 1936).

[41] M. G. Walker, "Sir John Johnson, Loyalist," *Mississippi Valley Historical Review*, III (Dec. 1916).

the British army created a cash market for the farm products of the seacoast area, another potent factor influenced the attitude of this class.

An important section of the merchant class likewise remained loyal to Britain. There were those of ultra-aristocratic temper who feared the mob spirit and the debtor's cry for cheap money more than they feared British restrictions. Particularly was this true of those merchants who were contractors with the Crown for supplying the British army in America, those whose established trading contacts were within the empire, those who were factors of British mercantile firms, and those who did business for British merchants on a commission basis. The merchants of New York usually did not trade with Britain in an independent capacity but rather bought and sold for British correspondents. Other New Yorkers were deeply involved in trade with Montreal. The loyalist group among the New York merchants was particularly strong, represented by members of such families as De Lancey, Bayard, Van Cortlandt, Smith, Cruger, and Walton.

In the professional classes the most prominent loyalists were lawyers and Anglican clergymen. In Massachusetts the wealthy and aristocratic Daniel Leonard, a defender of the British constitution and the class system which supported it, manifested dismay at the democratic trend in America. "It would . . . be the highest degree of impudence and disloyalty," he wrote, "to imagine that the king, at the head of his Parliament, could have any but the most pure and perfect intentions of justice, goodness and truth, that human nature is capable of." The richest man in Pennsylvania, Joseph Galloway, another loyalist attorney (who derived a large income from the legal business of the proprietary land system), led the seaboard aristocracy in opposition to the Philadelphia mechanics and the back-country farmers. The outstanding loyalist of Connecticut, Jared Ingersoll, was also a lawyer.[12] As to the Anglican clergy: not only were many of them Anglo-Americans, trained in loyalty to the king and imbued with respect for authority; in the southern colonies they were menaced by the anti-British democracy, which aimed to abolish the taxes which supported the Anglican Church. In the 1760's the income of the Anglican clergy in Maryland amounted to £8,000 a year. The most outspoken Loyalist among the Virginia clergy, Jonathan Boucher, declared that existing social and political institutions were divinely ordained and lamented that "the laboring classes, instead of

[12] L. H. Gipson, *Jared Ingersoll* (New Haven, 1920), an excellent biography, gives a full account of pre-Revolutionary events in Connecticut.

regarding the rich as their guardians, patrons and benefactors, now look upon them as so many overgrown colossuses whom it is no demerit in them to wrong." [43]

Although the small farmers as a whole did not entertain loyalist sympathies, there was an important exception. In the Carolinas the yeomen and squatters of the back country were first of all enemies of the planter-merchant aristocracy, and since the aristocracy was predominantly anti-British, many of the frontiersmen looked upon Britain —the enemy of their enemies—as a friend. Moreover, the back country of South Carolina was not yet sufficiently settled to make British land policy a serious menace to land-hungry farmers. Finally, the naval stores industry—an important source of income to Carolinians who occupied the sandy, pine-bearing lands beyond the plantation area—was threatened by a rupture with Britain which promised to cut off the British bounties that sustained production in the Carolinas.[44]

From the standpoint of economic issues a broad line may be drawn to separate the colonists who remained loyal to Britain from those who became hostile. Those whose business, investments, and income were menaced by Britain's measures pertaining to land, currency, taxation, trade, and manufacturing enlisted in the opposition, while those whose property would have been protected or enhanced in value by British measures enlisted in the loyalist ranks. And since Britain's policies, in their total effect, meant restriction and contracting opportunity, they antagonized those colonists who were concerned primarily with American expansion; on the other hand, those who stood to gain generally had vested interests that would have been served by a rigid maintenance of the *status quo*. This division meant that the more enterprising and aggressive men joined the struggle against Britain, whereas the most satisfied, conservative and inert remained loyal to the Crown—a fact which explains why the colonial upper class contributed so many more vigorous leaders to the Revolution than to the British cause. And because the mass of the colonists aspired to a better life that could be attained only through an expanding economy, Britain's policies of contraction and repression endangered a much larger part of the democracy than they benefited. Thus British measures, when imposed upon the economy and social structure of the colonies, evoked widespread unrest and inspired a group of able men from the

[43] *Reminiscences of an American Loyalist, 1738–1789: being the Autobiography of the Reverend Jonathan Boucher* (ed. Jonathan Bouchier, Boston, 1925).

[44] *Essays in Honor of William E. Dodd* (ed. Avery Craven, Chicago, 1935) contains a significant study by Philip Davidson, "The Southern Backcountry on the Eve of the Revolution."

upper class to lead the popular resistance to a menace that Franklin once described as "grievous tyranny and oppression." [45]

[45] Carl Becker's *The Eve of the Revolution* (New Haven, 1918) is an outstanding volume in the *Chronicles of America* series.

## BIBLIOGRAPHICAL NOTE

SOURCES NEWLY CITED: S. E. Morison, *Sources . . . illustrating the American Revolution, 1764–1788* (Oxford, 1923), is a valuable collection, made with discrimination. See pp. 1–148. Three volumes of documents on the British in the Illinois country have been edited by C. W. Alvord and C. E. Carter, all published at Springfield, Ill. They are: *The Critical Period, 1763–1765* (1915); *The New Regime, 1765–1767* (1916); and *Trade and Politics, 1767–1769* (1921). *The Grenville Papers* (ed. William J. Smith, 4 vols., London, 1852–53) include George Grenville's correspondence and his "diary of memorable transactions" during his administration (Vols. II, III).

For other sources, works previously cited, maps, etc., see references in the bibliographical note for chapter XXIII.

# XXIII

# THE IMPERIAL CONFLICT

## THE COLONIES OPPOSE THE STAMP ACT AND THE TOWNSHEND ACTS

SPEAKING in the House of Lords in 1766 on the repeal of the Stamp Act the Duke of Grafton said: "If . . . America is not sufficiently taxed, there are other means by which they may be taxed don't tax them universally. By that means you join them when you should keep them asunder." This advice was amply justified by the storm of opposition which had greeted the Stamp Act in the colonies. Each of the other British measures of 1763–65—the Sugar Act, the Currency Act, the Quartering Act, the Proclamation of 1763 and the new enforcement decrees—affected directly only particular classes and sections. The Stamp Act, however, struck a blow at many groups; hence it became the focus of discontent, a symbol of the iniquities of the British government. More particularly it antagonized four influential and vocal parties: the lawyers, the printer-editors, the merchants, and the planters, constituting as it did a direct levy on the income of all. Seldom in American history have the newspapers been so united behind a single cause as in 1765–66. To most men of the upper class and to the democracy alike the Stamp Act meant a challenge to political liberty. Should Britain collect taxes directly from the colonies, it would be only a matter of time until all the colonial governments might be supported by parliamentary levies. Then the assemblies would lose the power of coercing royal officials and thus of undoing British policies; then Britain might control the economy and the resources of the colonies in a manner most beneficial to British merchants and investors; then all the threatened oppressions of British mercantilism which the colonies had previously evaded by ignoring parliamentary statutes and by bending royal officials to their will would become effective. Unless the colonists were to be squeezed as in a vise they must retain that power over taxes and expenditures which was the means of enforcing economic policy.[1]

[1] S. G. Fisher's *The True History of the American Revolution* (Philadelphia, 1902) and *The Struggle for American Independence* (2 vols., Philadelphia, 1908) portray

How was the well-nigh universal opposition to the Stamp Act to be made effective? Those members of the upper class most friendly to Britain—men like Joseph Galloway—favored dignified petitions and remonstrances. The more disaffected planters and merchants were willing to use stronger measures. In the northern colonies some lawyers and merchants refused to use the stamps; the courts were closed; business requiring stamps was not transacted. In the South the planters gave a forecast of the later doctrine of nullification by ignoring the law and doing business without the stamps. In the commercial towns, merchants promised not to import British goods (the non-importation agreements), and artisans and farmers pledged themselves to foster the production and use of American articles. New York led in this movement; Philadelphia and Boston followed; by the summer of 1765 colonial orders for British goods were cut by £600,000. The merchants complained that the Sugar Act deprived them of their means of getting hard money; the Currency Act forbade new issues of legal tender paper money; trade was stagnant; where then could the towns obtain more money, without which the Stamp Act would ruin their already prostrate commerce? On the other hand, critics of the non-importation agreements asserted that the merchants used them to unload on the colonists their accumulated stocks, charging "high prices for old, moth-eaten goods which couldn't have been sold but for the patriotic fervor." [2]

The most radical merchants and the artisans and laborers in the towns were not content with mere petitions and non-resistance. Instigated by radical leaders and by the most anti-British merchants, the farmers and workers formed loose societies, called Sons of Liberty, whereby they gave vent to both their hatred of the British ruling class and their opposition to the new British measures, to which they attributed the unemployment and impoverishment of the postwar depression. Two demonstrations occurred in Boston in the summer of 1765. First a band of townspeople hanged in effigy the stamp distributor and then burned the image on the wreckage of a demolished stamp office; twelve days later another throng swooped down upon the homes of a customs officer and of Lieutenant-Governor Hutchinson and seized and burned records, particularly those pertaining to violation of the Acts of Trade. The "real authority of the government is at an end; some of the principal ringleaders in the late riots walk the streets with impunity; no officers dare attack them; no

the Revolution as conflict with many ugly features, not as a polite disagreement among gentlemen.

[2] See again *The Cambridge History of the British Empire*, Vol. I, chapters 22–23.

attorney-general prosecute them, and no judges sit upon them"—thus Hutchinson described the unruly spirit of the Boston people. Similar occurrences took place in North Carolina, Charleston, Newport, and New York.[3]

The small farmers and planters expressed their dissatisfaction chiefly through the elected assembly. Those of Virginia first sounded the "alarm bell to the disaffected" in May 1765 when the House of Burgesses adopted a series of resolves which declared that the colonists were entitled to the rights and liberties of English subjects and therefore should not be taxed except through their own representatives. Patrick Henry, mindful of his victory in the parsons' cause over the Anglican clergy and British currency policy, spoke so ardently that the speaker warned him against treason. In Massachusetts, the House of Representatives—spurred on by James Otis, then the legal spokesman of the merchants in arms against the Sugar Act—issued a circular letter to all the colonies urging them to send delegates to a conference at New York. Nine colonies complied, and in October twenty-nine representatives assembled in the city hall at New York, there to adopt a declaration of rights and grievances, and to petition king and Parliament for a repeal of the Stamp Act on the ground that the colonists, as British subjects, could be taxed only by their representatives in their own assemblies.

The most telling weapons used by the colonists were the non-importation agreements, which struck the British merchants at a time when trade was bad. The latter clamored for repeal of the Stamp Act, asserting that one hundred thousand workmen were unemployed in Britain because of the breach in American trade. But how could Parliament back down without losing face? Many members of the House of Lords feared the "mob" spirit in the colonies and insisted that Britain must crush it at all costs. The colonists were not really opposing the Stamp Act; their object, said Lord Sandwich, was to determine "whether by resistance they can get themselves loose from other acts more disagreeable and detrimental to them." But if the Stamp Act were not repealed what would be the consequence to Britain? The Duke of Grafton gave the answer: "An increase of poor rates. A diminution of the revenues of excise. A loss of the great debt from America to England."[4]

The British merchants triumphed in 1766 when Parliament repealed the Stamp Act, and—in order to assert Britain's supremacy—

---

[3] See again J. T. Adams, *Revolutionary New England*, chapters 14–18.

[4] W. T. Laprade, "The Stamp Act in British Politics," *American Historical Review*, XXXV (July 1930).

passed the Declaratory Act which affirmed that Parliament possessed the power to enact laws to bind the colonies in all cases whatsoever. As a concession to British manufacturers and merchants concerned in the trade of the northern colonies, Parliament also modified the Sugar Act. The molasses duty was lowered from 3*d.* a gallon to 1*d.* a gallon and now made to apply to molasses from the British islands as well as from foreign sources. Since the northern colonies had complained that the Sugar Act made it difficult for them to buy British goods, the lowering of the molasses duty meant a slight sacrifice of the British West Indian interest to that of the British merchants and manufacturers who supplied the markets of New England and the middle colonies. Meanwhile, the principle of raising a revenue in the colonies by parliamentary taxes was stoutly reaffirmed.[5]

Throughout the colonies the news of the repeal of the Stamp Act evoked spirited rejoicing. In the excitement the Declaratory Act was ignored; the colonial remonstrants felt that by their opposition they had forced Parliament to retreat. The grievance that had united the colonies vanished; there remained only the acts which had previously not been rigidly enforced or which were of local or restricted application. The merchants gave up the non-importation agreements; the Sons of Liberty subsided; trade resumed its course; and peace seemed at hand. But it was only a respite—for in 1767 came another series of measures which stirred anew all the elements of discord.

The debates in Parliament on the Stamp Act had disclosed a widely held opinion that the colonies were determined to shake off the Acts of Trade and Navigation. In repealing the Stamp Act the British ruling class—the wealthy landowners and merchants—had had no intention of encouraging the unruly temper of the colonists; rather there was manifested a stiff determination to assert Britain's unqualified right to rule. The opportunity came in 1767, when the Chancellor of the Exchequer, Charles Townshend—a veritable embodiment of the hard attitude of the ruling class toward the colonies—was called upon to draft the fiscal measures of the government. Intent upon reducing British taxes by making more efficient the collection of duties levied on American trade, Parliament in 1767, by substantial majorities, passed a group of acts which Townshend had prepared. One authorized the superior courts of the colonies to issue writs of assistance, thus giving specific legal authority to those general search warrants so hateful to colonial merchants. A second created the American Customs Board, previously described in chapter XXII. These two measures

[5] H. L. Osgood, "The American Revolution," *Political Science Quarterly*, XIII (March 1898).

were an effective answer to those colonial merchants who continued to protest against British commercial restrictions after the Stamp Act had been repealed.[6]

During the Stamp Act controversy a Maryland attorney, Daniel Dulany, an ultra-conservative, had written an essay in which he had drawn a nice distinction between internal taxes (stamp taxes, land taxes, poll taxes) and external taxes, or duties on imports and exports. Dulany had also intimated that although it was improper for Parliament to lay internal taxes upon the colonies, external taxes had been in force for more than a century and therefore Parliament had the right to levy them. This distinction gained great popularity among men of the colonial upper class who desired to preserve the imperial connection and at the same time to ward off further parliamentary encroachments. To Townshend such a distinction was nonsense, but if the colonists were foolish enough to prefer external to internal taxes, very well, let them have the external kind. Accordingly, the Townshend Acts levied duties on paper, glass, lead, painters' colors, and tea exported from Britain to the colonies. Designed to raise £40,000 for the support of colonial governors, judges, customs officers, and the British army in America, these duties were to be collected in colonial ports—an arrangement designed to prevent the smuggling of such commodities from foreign countries which would certainly have resulted had the duties been collected in Britain.

Another one of the Townshend Acts singled out the Assembly of New York for special punitive treatment, that province having been previously selected by General Gage as the headquarters of British troops in the colonies. When the Assembly refused to provide all the army supplies called for by the Quartering Act of 1765, great was the indignation in Britain. Accordingly, Parliament in 1767 ordered the legislative "privileges" of the Assembly suspended until compliance was duly made. This action informed the colonies that their assemblies were simply creatures of Britain which Parliament might change or destroy at will. Granted this assumption, the right of the colonists to tax and govern themselves became a repudiated fiction.[7]

The hostility bestowed upon these new measures rivaled that which had greeted the Stamp Act. Leading Bostonians complained that the

[6] The works of Claude H. Van Tyne, which emphasize political and intellectual factors and lean toward the British-loyalist point of view, include *The American Revolution* (New York, 1905)—see chapters 1–4; *The Causes of the War of Independence* (Boston, 1922); and *The War of Independence* (Boston, 1929)—see chapters 10–12, 15–17.

[7] The political ideas of the period are admirably stated in Charles E. Merriam's *A History of American Political Theories* (New York, 1928), chapters 1–2.

new revenue officers had come "to plunder our trade and drain the country of its money"; in Charleston a conservative merchant, Henry Laurens, compared such officers to the "miscreants who were driven out of the temple by Jesus with a scourge of small cords." From the quiet of his country estate a Pennsylvania conservative, John Dickinson, issued a series of *Letters from a Farmer in Pennsylvania*, which carried the taxation argument of the colonial upper class a step farther. Perceiving in the Townshend duties a means of wresting from the assemblies their real power by depriving them of their control of the purse, Dickinson abandoned the early distinction between internal and external taxes and introduced a new criterion. What was the *purpose* of a British levy? Was it to regulate trade? If so, the colonists could accept it. But the Townshend duties were levied on British exports to America; such duties could not benefit any commercial group within the empire; hence they were not intended to regulate trade but merely to raise a revenue. If the colonial assemblies were to retain a semblance of power they could not concede that Parliament had the right to levy even an external tax merely for revenue. In addition, Dickinson pointed out that the Stamp Act aimed to raise money for the defense of only the thirteen colonies, whereas the Townshend duties embraced Florida and Canada, so that the old colonies were "to be drained of the rewards of their labor, to cherish the scorching sands of Florida and the icy rocks of Canada and Nova Scotia, which never will return to us one farthing that we send to them." [8]

The colonial merchants again resorted to the non-importation agreements as the most effectual means of compelling Britain to repeal the Townshend Acts. Boston led the way in March 1768; New York followed in April; and the Philadelphia merchants, under pressure from the city populace and the other towns, reluctantly joined in March 1769. The import trade of Boston was cut in half, while Philadelphia's purchases from Britain dropped from £441,000 in 1768 to £134,800 in 1770. When the Virginia Assembly was dissolved by the governor the burgesses met privately in May 1769 and agreed not to import the dutied articles, British luxuries, or slaves. In Charleston the merchants were forced to fall in line by coercion from the city workers led by the anti-British merchant, Christopher Gadsden. Throughout the plantation area non-importation agreements could not be strictly enforced because the trade with Britain was not centered in a few ports. Meanwhile, individual citizens banded into

[8] The best biography is Charles J. Stillé, *The Life and Times of John Dickinson* (Philadelphia, 1891).

associations, pledging themselves to boycott British wares and to purchase American-made goods. The whole movement revealed that,
when the conditions of their foreign trade became unfavorable, the
colonies were compelled to divert their surplus labor and capital to
manufacturing pursuits. Many colonial leaders, among them Washington and Franklin, saw in non-importation a means of fostering
American manufactures as an escape from the thraldom of British
mercantilism.[9]

Once again the mechanics of the towns, in alliance with the most
anti-British merchants, resorted to direct action. In Philadelphia, fifty
pipes of Madeira wine were seized from the king's officers who had
sequestered them as smuggled goods; in Newport some of the townspeople burned a British revenue ship which had taken two vessels
charged with illegal trade; in Boston, Providence, and New York
the wrath of the populace, expressed in personal assaults and coats of
tar and feathers, visited British customs agents and informers who
exposed illegal traders. Such acts brought to Boston harbor in 1768
the *Romney*, a British man-of-war. Then, in June 1768, arrived
John Hancock's sloop, *Liberty*, bearing a cargo which included Madeira wine. The British customs searcher who went aboard was imprisoned in the cabin, there to hear "a hoisting out of goods"; soon
afterward the customs officials ordered the seizure of the *Liberty* by
the *Romney*. That done, the townsmen attacked the customs officers
and their houses, forcing them to flee to Castle William for safety.
Immediately they called upon the British ministry for military protection, and in October 1768 two regiments of British regulars en-
camped in Boston. The Townshend Acts and the Sugar Act, with its
tax of £7 a tun on wine imported by the colonies from Madeira, had
created a situation akin to war.[10]

The issue, however, was not forced at the time because in 1770
Parliament repealed all the Townshend duties except the threepence
tax on tea. A new Prime Minister, Lord North, servant of the British
ruling class and of George III, effected the repeal because he and his
colleagues believed it unwise for Britain to tax her own goods sold
abroad—not because the non-importation agreements had driven the
British merchants to demand the removal of the duties. The British
merchants were now prospering by a trade revival sustained by war
in Europe and by good harvests in England; their commerce with
the tobacco and sugar colonies was not seriously curtailed; and the

[9] See again A. M. Schlesinger, *The Colonial Merchants and the American Revolution.*
[10] John Fiske, *The American Revolution* (2 vols., Boston, 1891), finds in the political ambitions of George III the cause of the Revolution.

non-importation agreements of the northern towns did not become fully effective until 1769—and even then there was much evasion. Moreover, it appeared now that the disaffected colonial merchants, farmers, planters, and artisans were bent upon overthrowing the whole British colonial system; where would such treason end if Britain again supinely gave way? At the suggestion of George III Parliament readily retained the tea duty in order to assert Britain's right to tax the colonies. The partial repeal of the Townshend duties seemed to moderate men in America a concession that justified peace. Boston merchants strove to preserve the non-importation agreements until the tea tax and all the duties of the Sugar Act had been repealed, but the other commercial towns resumed trade and Boston had to follow, lest her near-by rivals engross her former commerce.

Despite the confusion of British politics after 1763, a consistent, unyielding attitude toward the colonies was exhibited: they must be kept in economic subordination to those powerful interests which profited from colonial commerce and investments oversea.[11] It mattered little whether the king's influence were strong or weak, or whether one or another faction of the Whig party held office: British merchants and landowners successfully asserted their purpose of extending and perfecting the colonial system which served their interests so well. The apparent concessions offered to the colonies were also made for the benefit of groups in Britain. Neither Parliament nor the king had demonstrated any intention of abandoning mercantilism in order that colonial economy might expand and function in the interest of a large majority of the colonial farmers, artisans, and merchants.

## THE RISE OF COLONIAL DEMOCRACY

During the first period of opposition to British measures (1763–66) there had been substantial agreement among the different classes in the colonies. The Stamp Act had menaced both the conservative merchants whose business was carried on within the British empire (the fair traders) and the anti-British merchants who dealt with foreign countries or colonies (the smugglers or free traders). In the towns the unskilled workers and artisans—the oppressed, the unemployed, and the employees of the free traders—were ripe for action that would assert their political importance and at the same time give vent to their hatred of the British ruling class and its agents in America, to whose measures was attributed the depression of 1763–65.

[11] Lewis B. Namier, *The Structure of Politics at the Accession of George III* (London, 1929), is an intensive analysis of the composition of Parliament.

Deeming it desirable that the colonies present a mass opposition to the Stamp Act, even men of conservative temper, although condemning violence, gave approval to popular demonstrations. Thus in New York many merchants acted with the mechanics as Sons of Liberty; in Boston the popular agitation was directed by such moderates as John Adams and James Otis. Since the principal targets of the populace in 1765 were the stamp distributors, the colonists of the upper class did not at once feel endangered by the outbursts of popular feeling. However, the Stamp Act demonstrations let loose forces not easily controlled. For the first time the mechanics, hitherto denied any influence in politics, became aware of their latent power.[12] When resisting British measures the spokesmen of the colonial upper class had been compelled to speak for all the colonists; they could not with propriety assert the right of a small minority to be free from parlia mentary restraints; hence they had spoken in terms of the rights and liberties of every man, of every British subject. Such appeals made the unprivileged workers politically conscious. If Parliament did not have the right to tax the colonists without their consent, then why should workers in America be denied the vote and thus be taxed by the assemblies without *their* consent? As John Adams put it: the Stamp Act controversy filled the minds of the people with sentiments of liberty—liberty that could mean freedom from the oppressions of the colonial aristocracy as well as freedom from British rule.

In the agitation against the Townshend Acts, the demonstrations of the city workers assumed a new character. Those merchants who traded chiefly with Britain did not object to the Townshend measures which aimed to suppress illegal trade with foreign ports; in fact the suppression of colonial smuggling promised to benefit such fair traders. The free traders, however, were violently opposed to the Townshend Acts; hence there occurred a sharp division within the merchant class. In New York, for instance, the unwillingness of the pro-British merchants to oppose the Townshend acts delayed the adoption of a non-importation agreement but this was finally agreed to as a protest against other British measures, particularly the Currency Act of 1764. Even then many merchants proceeded to evade the non-importation agreement, whereupon the free traders again turned to direct action and stirred the mechanics to assaults upon their pro-British rivals. Such attacks raised fears among men of wealth that unbridled mechanics might launch a social revolution that would transfer property and political power to the lower middle classes. Thus frightened for

[12] See again Carl Becker, *History of Political Parties in the Province of New York.*

the security of their own goods and persons many conservative men looked to British officials and troops for protection.[13]

After 1768, when the British troops arrived in Boston to defend the king's officials and the pro-British merchants, the leaders of the mechanics adopted new tactics. In 1770 John Adams wrote that endeavors "had been systematically pursued for many months, by certain busy characters, to excite quarrels, rencounters, and combats, single or compound, between the inhabitants of the lower class and the soldiers, and at all risks to enkindle an immortal hatred between them." Such efforts bore fruit on the evening of March 5, 1770, in the form of the Boston Massacre. A group of boys and young men threw snowballs at a sentry stationed before the customs office in front of the State House; a band of soldiers rushed to his aid; a crowd which quickly assembled assaulted two of the troopers; musket shots answered the attack; five of the townspeople were killed and several others wounded, among them apprentices, shipwrights, a mulatto laborer, a sailor, a ropemaker, and a tailor.[14]

> Unhappy Boston! See thy sons deplore
> Thy hallow'd walls besmeared with guiltless gore.
> While faithless P[resto]n and his savage bands
> With murd'rous rancour stretch their bloody hands
> Like fierce barbarians grinning o'er their prey,
> Approve the carnage and enjoy the day.

Acting-Governor Hutchinson, under pressure from the popular elements, removed the troops—previously quartered in the town proper —to Castle William in the harbor. In the ensuing trial of the soldiers accused of firing into the crowd, two privates were convicted of manslaughter and the charge against the officer in command of the guard was dismissed. The removal of the troops quieted the nerves of the Boston people, while in all the towns the news of the partial repeal of the Townshend duties, the rescinding of the non-importation agreements, and the revival of prosperity occasioned a lull in the storm of opposition (1771–73).

During this "interval of calm" one man—Samuel Adams of Massachusetts, the first organizer of American democracy as a political force—did more than anyone else to keep alive the flame of colonial discontent. His hostility to the wealthy merchants of Boston and to the British government probably arose from their part in destroying

[13] A. P. Peabody, "Boston Mobs before the Revolution," *Atlantic Monthly*, LXII.
[14] R. S. Longley, "Mob Activities in Revolutionary Massachusetts," *New England Quarterly*, VI (March 1933).

the Massachusetts land bank of 1740, which had all but ruined the fortunes of his father. After graduating from Harvard College, he had forsaken the practice of law and devoted himself to politics, living an abstemious life animated by hatred of aristocracy and faith in the common man. To the management of the colony's affairs he proposed to bring the spirit of the New England town meeting. On two counts he opposed British rule: first, because he regarded Britain as the sponsor of the colonial aristocracy; secondly, because he believed that the British colonial system exploited the colonists for the benefit of the British upper class.[15]

In politics Adams's major achievement was the welding of the small farmers and the town workers into a democratic party. His experience with the land bank made him as one with the hard-pressed farmers who demanded currency relief; as an associate in Boston of tradesmen and mechanics he won their confidence and support. His first task was to free these plain people from their awe of their social and political superiors—to arouse among them a sense of their own importance. This he accomplished largely by attacking the royal officials and judges, and by tearing away the veil of secrecy from government so as to expose the aristocrats as actuated by selfish motives, thereby divesting them of noble traits and reducing them to the level of ordinary men. For this his enemies labeled him a character assassin.[16]

His second task was to arouse the people to action. That meant banding them together in order that the weakness of individuals might be transfused into collective strength. In newspapers he published many articles, written under different names and in various literary styles so as to suggest that a host of colleagues labored at his side. He used a Boston political society, the Caucus Club, as a training school for political leaders; in the town meeting and in the provincial assembly he instigated resolutions and speeches which appealed to democratic impulses and emphasized the oppressions of British rule. Then in 1772 he induced the Boston town meeting to select a committee of correspondence to state the rights and grievances of the colonists, to communicate with other towns in the province, and to request them to draft replies. Gradually the towns fell in line, appointing their own committees, until by 1773 the democracy of Massachusetts was prepared for quick, united action under his com-

[15]An excellent, scholarly study by John C. Miller, *Sam Adams* (Boston, 1936), is an intensive analysis of early propagandist activities.

[16] R. V. Harlow, *Samuel Adams* (New York, 1923), is a stimulating study in psychology.

mand. Daniel Leonard, the loyalist attorney, described the committees of correspondence "as the foulest, subtlest, and most venomous serpent ever issued from the egg of sedition." [17]

In 1773 Britain played directly into the hands of Samuel Adams and his co-workers when Parliament adopted new regulations for the American tea trade of the East India Company. Mismanagement and corruption had brought the company to the brink of ruin: in the early 1770's its stock dropped to 60, its debts exceeded £1,000,000 and it had on hand 17,000,000 pounds of unsold tea. Due to the Townshend tea tax of 3*d*. a pound, the colonists had boycotted British tea and such a flourishing illegal trade had developed that after 1770 about nine-tenths of the tea consumed in America was of foreign origin and imported duty free. The loss of the colonial tea trade was one cause of the distress of the East India Company; hence Parliament proposed to restore the company's fortunes, in part, by granting it an effective monopoly of the American market. After May 10, 1773, the company (which had previously been compelled by law to sell its tea at auction to merchants in London) was privileged to reëxport tea to America without paying the existing duty collected on imports of tea into England. Only the threepence tax was to burden the company's tea sold to the colonies; thus the tax to be paid by the American consumer was to amount to considerably less than the tax assessed against the English consumer.

Instead of selling the tea to American merchants in London, the East India Company decided to dispose of it through pro-British merchant correspondents in the colonies. Even Governor Hutchinson admitted that the company could sell the tea through its factors "at a much lower price than it could be afforded by particular merchants who purchased it in England"; thus American fair traders who imported tea from England were in danger of losing their business to the company. The free traders, who already had on hand large stocks of Dutch tea, were also due to be undersold, and perhaps ruined. The opponents of the new policy argued that if Parliament, by adjusting duties, could give the East India Company a monopoly of the tea trade, it might grant similar monopolies to other British firms until colonial merchants were driven from American commerce. The opponents of the company also charged that Britain was offering a bribe of cheap tea to induce the colonists to pay the threepence Townshend tax—tempting them "to barter liberty for luxury." [18]

[17] The best of the older biographies is J. K. Hosmer, *Samuel Adams* (Boston, 1885).
[18] A. M. Schlesinger, "The Uprising against the East India Company," *Political Science Quarterly*, XXXII (March 1917).

Once more the disaffected merchants, the city mechanics and the small farmers presented a united front against a common foe. In New York and Philadelphia great popular demonstrations forced the commanders of the East India Company's tea ships to return to England with their cargoes; in Charleston the tea was locked up in a government warehouse, there to remain for three years; at Boston on December 16, 1773, occurred the most decisive action of the pre-revolutionary era when a band of men, disguised as Indians and unidentified to this day, dumped the tea of three vessels into the harbor. This "most magnificent movement of all" followed a series of negotiations between the popular leaders and the royal officials; when the latter refused to send back the tea, Samuel Adams climaxed a demonstration with the cryptic remark: "This meeting can do nothing more to save the country," whereupon the self-invited guests rushed to the Boston Tea Party.

A fateful crisis now confronted Britain. The East India Company had carried out a parliamentary statute; if the destruction of the tea (property worth £15,000) went unheeded, Parliament would admit to the world that its authority over the colonies had vanished. Official opinion in Britain almost unanimously condemned the Boston Tea Party as an act of vandalism and insurrection and gave wholehearted support to the measures by which the North ministry proposed to bring the insurgent colonists to their senses.[19]

The first of these measures, the Boston Port Bill, effective June 1, 1774, removed the British customhouse from Boston and closed the port to all shipping until the town had compensated the East India Company for its tea. An Administration of Justice Act provided that British agents charged with offenses committed when suppressing riots in Massachusetts or when enforcing British laws might be tried in another colony or in Britain. The Massachusetts Government Act gave to the governor the power to appoint the provincial councillors (previously elected by the General Assembly), forbade the holding of town meetings without the governor's consent, and provided that juries should be selected by the sheriffs (appointees of the governor) instead of by the town meetings. In order that the British troops in Boston might be domiciled where they would be needed, a Quartering Act provided that they might be stationed in the town proper; if the barracks there were inadequate, they might be quartered in taverns, alehouses, and unoccupied buildings. These four acts against Massachusetts were accompanied by the Quebec Act (not designed as a punitive measure), which extended the boundaries of Quebec to

[19] See again E. Channing, *History of the United States*, Vol. III, chapters 5–7.

A Satirical View of Colonial Assent to Taxes Levied by Parliament

the Ohio and the Mississippi and among other things granted religious freedom to French Catholics residing in the province.[20]

In one way or another these five acts of 1774 denied all the rights and privileges which the colonists had been demanding since 1763. The Boston Tea Party having been nominally a revolt against the tax on tea, the punitive measures affirmed the power of Parliament to tax the colonies for the support of government in America. In the Boston Port Bill, Parliament asserted unlimited power, not only to regulate commerce, but also to destroy commerce in order to punish all the inhabitants, guilty and innocent alike, of a town wholly dependent upon trade. And what of colonial rights of self-government? The town meeting was made subservient to a royal governor; a colonial charter was altered by Parliament overnight, without allowing the colony concerned to present its case; and an ominous shadow fell over the elected assemblies, since the Quebec Act did not grant a representative legislature to that province. So also the judicial system was to function to England's advantage: royal officials were to choose juries for local trials, while the king's agents in America were to be given immunity from local sentiment through the removal of trials to friendly British courts. At one stroke the Quebec Act swept away the western land claims of Massachusetts and Connecticut and curtailed the area claimed by Virginia. The menace of military rule became more formidable as Britain adhered to the principle of parliamentary taxation for the support of a colonial army and insisted that royal troops be domiciled where they were needed to suppress disorders. More menacing still was the appointment of General Gage, the commander of the king's forces in America, as governor of Massachusetts early in 1774. These measures could mean but one thing to the colonies: the destruction of privileges long enjoyed and the establishment of an arbitrary government upheld by military force.[21]

All the economic and political causes of colonial discontent were heightened by utterances of the clergymen who ministered to the Congregational churches in New England and to the Presbyterian churches of the Scotch-Irish settlers on the frontiers. The Quebec Act, by protecting the property of the Roman Catholics in Quebec, by granting them freedom of worship, and by virtually excluding Protestant settlers from the province, promised to create a bulwark against the extension of the Protestant religions in America. And

[20] G. M. Wrong, *Canada and the American Revolution* (New York, 1935), is a good modern account. See chapters 1–13.

[21] Sir George O. Trevelyan, *The American Revolution* (4 vols., New York, 1899–1907) excoriates the Tory ministers for disrupting the British empire by unjustly goading the colonists to an unwilling revolt.

while Catholicism was to wax strong on the borders of the northern colonies, the various popular churches within those colonies were seemingly to be sacrificed to the Church of England. Since 1748, proposals had been made in Britain for an imperial establishment in the colo-

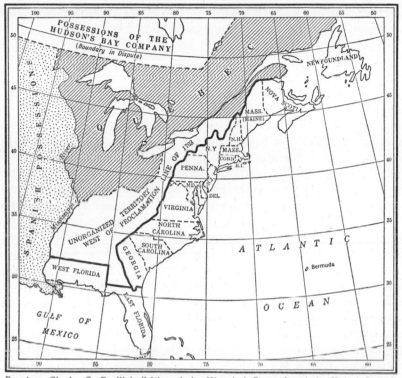

Based on Charles O. Paullin's "Atlas of the Historical Geography of the United States."
© Carnegie Institution of Washington. Reprinted by courtesy of the American Geographical
Society of New York.

THE CLOSING OF THE NORTHWEST TO THE THIRTEEN COLONIES BY
THE QUEBEC ACT OF JUNE 22, 1774

nies of the Anglican Church, to be presided over by an American bishop and supported by parliamentary taxes levied on all the people. Much significance was attached to such proposals when the colonists learned that five Anglican bishops had voted against the repeal of the Stamp Act. Ministers of the Congregational and Presbyterian churches, always prone to discuss political subjects, aroused their parishioners against the Anglican danger. The repeal of the Stamp Act inspired the Reverend Charles Chauncey to preach on the text: "As cold waters to a thirsty soul, so is good news from a far country"; the Boston Massacre elicited from the Reverend John Lathrop a sermon on the theme: "Innocent blood crying to God from the streets of Boston." Such sermons were printed in pamphlet form and widely distributed and read. They revived among radical Protestants the memories of the oppressions of Charles I and Laud and gave religious sanction and fervor to the opposition to British rule: the American cause enjoyed the benediction of the Lord.[22]

## THE MOVEMENT FOR INDEPENDENCE

Of the colonial response in 1774 in defense of Massachusetts, Professor Channing wrote: "Never before in American history, and possibly never before in any history had the waves of sympathetic enthusiasm mounted so high as those which now rolled from South to North and from North to South." The Coercive Acts had placed all the colonies in a position comparable to that occupied by Britain after the Boston Tea Party: either the colonists must surrender abjectly, admitting that they possessed no inherent rights, or they must take an unequivocal stand in self-defense, since it was evident that what Britain did to Massachusetts might be done to all. From Virginia, Philadelphia, Charleston, and Connecticut supplies were sent to Boston; the Virginia burgesses, when the legislature was dissolved by the governor for anti-British expressions, met privately and voiced their sympathy for Boston; everywhere town meetings, committees of correspondence, elected assemblies, and colonial leaders denounced the Coercive Acts—in speeches, resolutions, and pamphlets; while the mechanics of the towns again staged demonstrations and dealt violently with British agents and their partisans among the colonists. At the suggestion of the Virginia burgesses, all the thirteen colonies except Georgia sent delegates to a Continental Congress, which assembled in Carpenters' Hall, Philadelphia, on September 5, 1774. Fifty-five members appeared, some chosen legally by the assemblies, some by extra-legal bodies, and others by the assemblies acting in defiance of royal governors. Although united in opposition to the Coercive Acts, the members divided roughly into two parties: moderates and radicals. Among the moderates were Joseph Galloway and John Dickinson of Pennsylvania, John Rutledge and Henry Middleton of South Carolina, and John Jay of New York; among the radi-

---

[22] Alice M. Baldwin, *The New England Clergy and the American Revolution* (Durham, N. C., 1928), is a superior study. See also C. H. Van Tyne, "The Influence of the Clergy . . . on the American Revolution," *American Historical Review*, XIX (Oct. 1913).

THE BOSTON PORT BILL AS PICTURED BY PAUL REVERE

Lord North, with the Boston Port Bill in his pocket, forces tea upon America, held down by British justice in the person of Lord Mansfield. Boston's petition has been thrown aside in favor of the sword of coercion. France and Spain watch expectantly as Britannia mourns.

cals: Samuel Adams and John Adams of Massachusetts, Richard Henry Lee and Patrick Henry of Virginia, Roger Sherman of Connecticut, Charles Thomson of Pennsylvania, Christopher Gadsden of South Carolina, and Stephen Hopkins of Rhode Island. Two questions divided the parties: What was the extent of Britain's authority over the colonies? And what measures should they adopt in reply to the Coercive Acts? [23]

The moderate party was composed of men of conservative temper who wished to retain the benefits of the British empire and the protection afforded by British rule against the democratic movement in America. They desired also to preserve the old colonial rights of self-government now threatened by British encroachments. In order to accomplish this double purpose, they had evolved a political theory designed to harmonize British and colonial interests. Many of their leading thinkers were lawyers educated in the English Inns of Court (or law schools), where they had been indoctrinated with English constitutional history and the English common law, the principles of which they now asserted. First, they contended that the colonists were entitled to certain constitutional rights of Englishmen which were embodied in Magna Carta, the Petition of Right of 1628, and the Bill of Rights of 1689—rights which transcended the power of government; neither king nor Parliament could usurp them without violating the British constitution. They were guaranteed to the colonies by the colonial charters in the same manner that royal patents, deeds, and warrants conferred individual title to private property. Foremost among such rights was that expressed in the maxim: "a citizen's property may not be taken from him without his consent." Now the colonists, not being represented in Parliament, did not assent to parliamentary taxes; therefore they could be taxed only by their own assemblies. The moderate leaders, however, recognized that Parliament possessed the power to regulate imperial trade; hence a distinction was drawn between right to tax and the power of general legislation. But what if Parliament should encroach upon the civil rights of the colonists? Fearing that forceful resistance to British rule might lead to a democratic upheaval in America, the moderates regarded petitions and remonstrances as the proper means of securing relief.[24]

The radical party consisted of men who disliked British regulations

[23] Allan Nevins, *The American States during and after the Revolution* (New York, 1924), contains a mass of accurate information, admirably classified. On Revolutionary opinion and organization see pp. 1–116.

[24] Charles F. Mullett, *Fundamental Law and the American Revolution* (New York, 1933), is a study in constitutional doctrines.

more than they valued the benefits of empire and more than they feared the dangers of popular rule. The events of the period 1763–74 had demonstrated to such men many weaknesses in the philosophy of the moderates. For one thing, too much reliance could not be placed upon the colonial charters; that of Pennsylvania specifically recognized the right of Parliament to tax the province; in addition Britain claimed the right to modify or to nullify the charters for reasons of which she was the sole judge. As to taxation: British apologists claimed that the colonies were *virtually* represented in Parliament and that the great mass of the English people had no more voice in its deliberations than did the colonists. Clearly a stronger argument than the rights of Englishmen was needed in order to ward off parliamentary taxes. Moreover, there was no valid distinction between taxation and legislation when laws regulating trade also levied taxes. Finally, the tea episode and the Boston Port Bill had demonstrated that the power of Parliament to regulate trade might be more oppressive than the power of taxation.[25]

The radicals did not give up the claim to the civil rights of British subjects; rather they reinforced that claim with the doctrine of the "natural rights of man." There were two principal sources of this doctrine: Calvinist writers of the seventeenth century and a treatise, *Of Civil Government*, written by John Locke to justify the English Revolution of 1688. Locke's argument was as follows: Men originally dwelt in a state of nature, enjoying by virtue of natural law the rights of life, liberty, and property. Civil government had been created by a contract between the people and a ruler in order to preserve these natural rights; therefore if the ruler should deny them to the people, it was their duty to depose him and choose a successor. In this doctrine political sovereignty and property rights were derived, not from the English constitution, but from the people themselves, acting in conformity with the laws of God and nature. The natural rights theory appealed particularly to those colonists who had occupied land without title from the king and who argued that nature intended that land should belong to those who use it.[26]

The radicals in 1774 were not united: a few like Samuel Adams probably desired complete separation from Britain, but the majority desired to remain within the empire—if they could remain on their own terms. To whom then did the colonists owe allegiance? Benjamin Franklin in 1766 suggested the answer which the radicals had

[25] See again V. L. Parrington, *The Colonial Mind*, Book II, Part II.

[26] H. D. Foster, "International Calvinism through Locke and the Revolution of 1688," *American Historical Review*, XXXII (April 1927).

accepted by 1774: that the colonies were not subject to Parliament but only to the king.[27] This theory (which appealed to men who believed that as a result of the British Acts of Trade "the American goose was reserved for British plucking") implied that the colonies were in fact independent states, inasmuch as the king (after the English Revolution of 1688 had established the principle of limited monarchy) could not rule except in coöperation with Parliament; acting alone he could not regulate colonial commerce, currency, and manufactures, or tax, coerce, and punish as the means of enforcement. Thus had Parliament's authority been eliminated, the king, singlehanded, would have been helpless, and all the oppressions of mercantilism which stemmed from parliamentary statutes would have vanished. But if Parliament should insist upon its authority over the colonists and enforce laws which deprived them of their natural rights, then they must resist—by economic pressure, and if need be by force. Such were the views in 1774 of Richard Henry Lee, Roger Sherman, Stephen Hopkins, Christopher Gadsden, John and Samuel Adams, Benjamin Franklin, Thomas Jefferson, George Washington, and Patrick Henry.[28]

Although the most advanced radicals like Samuel Adams had feared the Continental Congress as a potential agency of conciliation, the events of September and October, along with the spirit of indignation which animated the mass of the people, rapidly weakened the moderates and enabled the radicals to have their way. On October 14 they triumphed when the Congress adopted a Declaration of Rights which embodied their constitutional theories. Asserting that the colonists were entitled by the law of nature, the British constitution, and the colonial charters to the rights of life, liberty, and property, this Declaration affirmed that the colonies were not (and could not be) represented in Parliament and that their local assemblies alone possessed the powers of taxation and legislation. However, the colonists would *voluntarily* accept acts of Parliament regulating external trade provided that such acts did not embody any "idea of taxation, external or internal." In line with this position the Congress would not accept the British acts passed since 1763. The Congress also drafted petitions to the king, to the several colonies, to the province of Quebec, and to the people of Britain—petitions in which colonial rights and grievances were vigorously asserted. The Declaration of

[27] V. W. Crane's *Benjamin Franklin* (Baltimore, 1936) is primarily a study of Franklin's political thought. Malcolm R. Eiselen, *Franklin's Political Theories* (Garden City, N. Y., 1928), is a good brief statement.

[28] Randolph G. Adams, *The Political Ideas of the American Revolution* (Durham, N. C., 1922) is an admirable, well-written study.

Rights, by rejecting the authority of Parliament, placed the Congress in a state of virtual rebellion.[29]

But the Congress did not stop with mere resolutions; on October 20 it adopted the momentous Continental Association, by which the members pledged that, unless Britain surrendered, they would not import certain British goods after December 1, 1774, that they would not consume any tea after March 1, 1775, and that they would not export to Britain after September 10, 1775. Article Eleven of the Association provided that the voters of each city, town, or county should select a committee, "whose business it shall be to observe the conduct of all persons touching the association; and when it shall be made to appear to the satisfaction of a majority of any such committee, that any person . . . has violated the association, that such majority do forthwith cause the truth of the case to be published in the *Gazette,* to the end that all such foes to the rights of British America may be publicly known, and universally contemned as enemies of American liberty; and henceforth we respectively will break off all dealings with him or her." Two other articles authorized the local committees to inspect customs entries and "to seize all goods imported contrary to the Association." [30]

Immediately the radicals throughout the colonies, in town meetings, general conventions, and county gatherings, adopted agreements in support of the Association and set up the designated committees. Next the committee members, by house-to-house canvass, called upon the people to join the Association; then followed the publication of the names of non-signers and the use of coercion. The boycott again became effective; outspoken opponents were tarred and feathered; goods seized from persons who violated the Association were burned; in Virginia and the Carolinas the courts were closed when British merchants sued the planters for debt; criticism and force were applied to those who indulged in luxuries, finery, and expensive amusements (all dependent upon trade with Britain); and in the commercial towns the rigid enforcement of the non-importation agreement brought British commerce to a standstill, the imports from Britain to New York falling from £437,000 in 1774 to £1,228 in 1775. Everywhere it was the fashion to use American-made articles as home industries grew by leaps and bounds.

The Continental Association ranks in importance with the Boston

---

[29] C. H. McIlwain's *The American Revolution* (New York, 1923) defends the constitutional theories of the colonial radicals in the light of English precedent.

[30] P. L. Ford, "The Association of the First Congress," *Political Science Quarterly,* VI (Dec. 1891).

Tea Party and the Coercive Acts because it obliged all persons to take an open stand on the issue of resistance. The Congress in effect renounced the authority of Parliament and assumed the power of a sovereign government when it adopted a general policy and created the machinery to enforce it throughout all the colonies. The other non-importation agreements had been local, private, voluntary; the Association was general, public, compulsory. Many of the moderates, continuing to recognize the authority of Parliament and to adhere to their faith in petitions, denounced the action of the Congress as usurpation. Other moderates and the radicals now accepted the Congress as a *de facto* government and joined in acts of coercion in order to destroy the power of Parliament over the colonies. Thus the two parties of the years 1775–76—loyalists and patriots—superseded the loose political groupings of former days.[31]

In eastern Massachusetts the presence of British troops in Boston drove the local committees to accumulate materials of war. So pronounced was the popular hostility to Britain in this quarter during the winter of 1774–75 that General Gage made no attempt to carry out instructions from Britain that he arrest Samuel Adams and John Hancock and ship them to England to stand trial for their lives. Later in the winter, when Gage dispatched small bands of officers to locate the military supplies of the patriots, the opposition they encountered was overwhelming. On April 18, 1775, Gage, ready at last to strike, sent from Boston about a thousand British regulars to take Adams and Hancock at Lexington and to seize the military stores of the patriots at Concord. Adams's chief partner in revolution, Joseph Warren, touched off the signals to arouse the countryside and dispatched William Dawes and later Paul Revere to warn Hancock and Adams. When the British troops reached Lexington they encountered fifty armed colonists. Shots rang out; several of the colonists were killed; and the British pushed on to Concord, where they destroyed a few war materials which the patriots had not removed. On the return march the British met a continuing fire from the now embattled farmers who lined the roadside. Near Lexington a force of fifteen hundred troops joined the harassed soldiers, only to serve as targets on the way to Boston. So widespread was the response of the countryside in this first battle of the Revolution that the British force of twenty-five hundred men suffered losses nearly three times those sustained by the colonists.

The news of Lexington and Concord struck the other colonies like

[31] W. C. Abbott's *New York in the American Revolution* (New York, 1929) is reliable and readable. See chapters 1–7.

an electric shock. The activities of the patriots immediately assumed a military character as the organs of resistance they had already created were devoted to defense.[32] To Washington the choice now lay between slavery and war. Fortunately for the patriots, their revolutionary organization could readily be converted into a war machine. Reaching into most communities were the committees of correspondence, set up in 1773–74, and the committees created to enforce the Continental Association of October 1774. Upon the foundation of the committees of correspondence all the royal and proprietary colonies except Georgia, Pennsylvania, and New York had, by the close of 1774, erected provincial congresses. Patterned after the colonial assemblies, these congresses were formed when royal and proprietary governors dissolved the legal assemblies or refused to call them into session. Determined not to submit to the shelving of representative government, the anti-British leaders of the assemblies of New Hampshire, Massachusetts, North Carolina, Virginia, and Delaware made provision for the elected delegates to meet independently in provincial congresses. In Maryland, South Carolina, and New Jersey the calls for elections were issued by popular meetings in Baltimore, Charleston, and Newark. Not openly revolutionary bodies, the congresses at first confined their activity to protests against the Coercive Acts, to the election of delegates to the First Continental Congress, and to the enforcement of the Continental Association. In Massachusetts, however, the provincial congress, presided over by John Hancock, established a council of safety which made the military preparations that culminated in the engagements at Lexington and Concord.[33]

When the news of the war reached New York and Georgia, the townspeople seized control of the ports of New York and Savannah, whereupon the patriot leaders called upon the electoral districts to send delegates to provincial congresses, which met respectively in May and July 1775. Elsewhere the war gave the signal for the provincial congresses to take over the legislative and financial functions of government. Next they seized the executive powers as the royal and proprietary governors were driven from office. By the end of 1775 all such governors except those of Pennsylvania, New Jersey, and Maryland had been expelled; by July 1776 they too were gone. In Rhode Island and Connecticut, where there were no royal gov-

[32] H. J. Eckenrode, *The Revolution in Virginia* (Boston, 1916), is excellent on political events and conflicts. See chapters 1–5.

[33] Harry A. Cushing, *History of the Transition from Provincial to Commonwealth Government in Massachusetts* (New York, 1896), is a detailed study of the State's politics to 1780, from a legal point of view.

ernors, the patriots converted their established institutions of government into revolutionary agencies. Since the principal task of the provincial congresses after May 1775 was to wage war against Britain they had then become distinctly revolutionary bodies.[34]

At the apex of the revolutionary structure stood the Continental Congress. In January 1775 Britain had ordered the colonial governors to prevent the election of delegates to a second congress; hence they could not be chosen by old legal methods. But the patriot leaders ignored Britain's orders and arranged to have the provincial congresses elect the new delegates. Accordingly, the Second Continental Congress, merely by assembling at Philadelphia in May in defiance of Britain, took another step toward revolution. There was now no evading the issue of war: Lexington and Concord had been fought and the patriot soldiers of Massachusetts were encircling the British troops in Boston. The Second Continental Congress therefore had either to plunge into the war or yield to Britain completely by disowning all Americans who had taken up arms. There was little hesitation. After declaring war in May the Congress in June organized an army into which it incorporated the forces besieging Boston and over which it placed Washington as commander-in-chief. It also adopted a declaration which stated the causes and necessity for taking up arms in defense of American liberty and property, promising that the colonies would disarm "when hostilities shall cease on the part of the aggressors, and all danger of their being renewed shall be removed, and not before."

The patriot party composed of the disaffected merchants, most southern planters, city tradesmen, artisans, and laborers, and the mass of the small farmers and frontiersmen had now completed a revolutionary organization. It may be likened to a pyramid—if one may compare the dynamic with the static. At the base stood the town, parish, and county committees of correspondence; the middle layer consisted of the provincial congresses and their committees or councils of safety; the Continental Congress and its army crowned the structure. As between patriots and loyalists, it may be stated with assurance that, despite the absence of statistics on the subject, an overwhelming majority of the colonists were hostile to British policy in 1775. The number of loyalists was so small that in most places (except in the presence of British troops) they were ruthlessly kept down by mass

---

[34] Two able studies of revolutionary action in Virginia are James M. Leake, *The Virginia Committee System and the American Revolution* (Baltimore, 1917)—thorough, detailed, best suited to advanced students—and Charles R. Lingley, *The Transition in Virginia from Colony to Commonwealth* (New York, 1910)—a lucid, concise monograph.

pressure. Early in 1775, however, patriot sentiment was not united: only a small minority of the leaders then favored immediate separation from Britain; a large majority still hoped that Britain would yield. In July 1775, the conciliationists in the Congress, led by John Dickinson and supported by the conservatives of the town of Philadelphia, secured the adoption of a last humble appeal to the king (the Olive Branch Petition).[35] Such moderate men sought a settlement that would protect colonial interests; they expected Parliament to repeal the Coercive Acts, to withdraw the troops, and to renounce its claim to unqualified supremacy over the colonies. In the meantime, since the conciliationists were unwilling to surrender abjectly to Britain, they were impelled upon a course of resistance that steadily widened the breach. The futility of their hopes was speedily to be demonstrated by the conduct of the British ruling class.

## THE DECLARATION OF INDEPENDENCE

In November 1774 George III declared to Lord North that the New England colonies were "in a state of rebellion" and that "blows must decide whether they are to be subject to this country or independent." Even before 1774 Britain had shown little disposition to humor the colonies; of all the British measures after 1763 only two or three could be construed as concessions. And, in the opinion of British officials, such concessions had merely inflated the colonists with self-importance; not the slightest hint of weakness on the part of Britain could now be permitted. Even the small, uninfluential minority in Britain on whose behalf Edmund Burke addressed his eloquent appeal for conciliation accepted the theory of parliamentary supremacy over the colonies, while the majority was determined not only to assert the theory in words but also to put it into operation.[36] "A minister who had announced as part of his policy, in 1775, the giving up of the idea of parliamentary supremacy could not have held office for a day; a king who had proposed such a thing would have lost his throne" (Channing). In February 1775 the Earl of Chatham (William Pitt) presented to the House of Lords a plan which proposed that an American congress be invited to recognize Parliament's supremacy and to grant a perpetual revenue for the disposal of Parliament, whereupon Parliament would refrain from taxing the colonies. On the first reading of the bill it was rejected. About the same

[35] See again C. H. Lincoln, *The Revolutionary Movement in Pennsylvania.*
[36] An excellent brief biography is John Morley, *Burke* (London, 1879). For a more extended, recent treatment see Robert H. Murray, *Edmund Burke* (Oxford, 1931).

time the House of Commons adopted Lord North's conciliation plan which affirmed Britain's supremacy and promised that if the colonial assemblies would make suitable grants of money each year to Britain, Parliament would not exercise its taxing powers except in acts regulating trade. As this plan made no concession to the colonists on any vital point, it was rejected by every colony, and by the Continental Congress. The latter, in a report of July 31, 1775, stated that the colonies could not safely make gifts without strings attached, lest the money be "wasted among the venal and corrupt for the purpose of undermining the civil rights of the givers" or "diverted to the support of standing armies."

Two measures adopted by Britain in 1775 closed the door to conciliation. In August, George III refused to receive the Olive Branch Petition (on the ground that it was drafted by an illegal, disloyal body) and on August 23 he issued a proclamation stigmatizing the Americans as rebels and ordering that all persons refrain from giving them assistance. Parliament completed the work of repression by an act of December 22, 1775, which prohibited all trade with the thirteen colonies—an act embodying the view of Lord North that because "the Americans had refused to trade with Great Britain, it was but just that they be not suffered to trade with any other nation." [37]

Having accepted the theory that the colonies were bound to Britain, not through Parliament but through the king, the patriot leaders who now perceived that independence was inevitable were forced to direct their attack upon the person of George III. If Parliament actually possessed no authority over the colonies, then independence must be justified by the misdeeds of the king; if he had not acted unjustly, they could not properly renounce his authority. There was little difficulty, however, in preparing a case against George III, especially after he had refused to receive the Olive Branch Petition and had stigmatized the colonists as rebels. Moreover, all British officials in America were nominally agents of the king; consequently any offenses they committed might plausibly be blamed upon him. Late in October 1775 word reached the Continental Congress that a British naval force had burned the town of Falmouth, Maine. In January 1776 the Virginia patriots burned the town of Norfolk, lest it fall prey to Lord Dunmore, who—driven from Williamsburg to a warship—had used naval vessels to ravage the country along the Virginia rivers.

[37] Dora Mae Clark, *British Opinion and the American Revolution* (New Haven, 1930) is a thorough, informative monograph. Fred J. Hinkhouse, *The Preliminaries of the American Revolution as Seen in the English Press, 1763–1775* (New York, 1926), is useful for the special student.

Such actions the patriot leaders were now ready to attribute to a tyrannical king, thereby appealing to the latent democratic sentiments of the mass of the colonists. Among the underprivileged classes smoldered a hatred of aristocracy and royalty that might be quickly fanned into a consuming blaze.

In the winter of 1775–76 one man in particular sensed the public attitude and the need of the hour. This was Thomas Paine, a restless English adventurer in radicalism and idealism, who had come to America with credentials from Franklin in 1774. In January 1776 he published a fifty-page pamphlet, *Common Sense*,[38] written in a rough, vigorous, flamboyant style that drove home with fierce blows the necessity of independence. Ridiculing the idea of hereditary monarchy, he proclaimed that one honest man was worth more to society "than all the crowned ruffians that ever lived." The British ruling class, with the king at the head, lived by exploiting the common people, not only of the colonies, but of Britain as well. It was contrary to nature, he said, that a whole continent should be tributary to an island. In America the goddess of liberty, hunted from other lands, might find a secure abode. The time for separation had come; it was folly for the colonists to avow loyalty while in arms against the king; gather at once, he urged, the ripe fruit of independence, for "now your *rotting time comes on*." [39]

Thousands of copies of *Common Sense* sent throughout the colonies crystallized the conviction then forming in men's minds. New England, at war, needed only allies in order to embrace independence. As early as May 31, 1774, a band of North Carolina frontiersmen gathered at Charlotte, Mecklenburg County, there to resolve that all military and civil commissions "heretofore granted by the Crown, to be exercised in these colonies, are null and void, and the constitution of each particular colony wholly suspended." [40] Then, on February 27, 1776, the North Carolina patriots defeated at Moore's Creek a force of sixteen hundred loyalists, taking nine hundred prisoners, whereupon ten thousand patriots assembled to repel a threatened British invasion. Fired with the war spirit the North Carolina provincial congress on April 12th instructed its delegates in the Con-

[38] Reprinted in Arthur W. Peach (ed.), *Selections from the Writings of Thomas Paine* (New York, c. 1928).

[39] The best of the older biographies, Moncure D. Conway's *The Life of Thomas Paine* (2 vols., New York, 1892), is sympathetic toward Paine. Mary A. Best, *Thomas Paine* (New York, 1927), is a lively, popular biography, written from a liberal point of view. In its defense of Paine it "out-Conways Conway."

[40] This resolution is not to be confused with the so-called Mecklenburg Declaration. For the latter, see A. S. Salley, Jr., "The Mecklenburg Declaration," *American Historical Review*, XIII (Oct. 1907).

tinental Congress to vote for independence. The opposition to Britain having risen to the boiling point in Virginia by virtue of Lord Dunmore's warlike measures, the patriots there on May 15 directed their delegates in the Continental Congress to introduce a motion for separation. During these weeks the Congress itself had moved forward by ordering that the loyalists be disarmed (March 14), by authorizing that privateers be equipped to prey upon British vessels (March 23), by opening American ports to foreign ships (early April), and by advising all the colonies to reject Britain's authority and to erect new governments based upon the people's will (May 10, 15).

On June 7 Richard Henry Lee introduced in the Congress a threefold resolution declaring in favor of independence, foreign alliances, and American federation. The conciliationists headed by John Dickinson postponed a vote, but a committee composed of Jefferson, Franklin, Roger Sherman, R. R. Livingston, and John Adams was named to draft a declaration of independence. On July 1 Lee's resolution was approved by the delegates of nine colonies; on the next day South Carolina, Delaware, and Pennsylvania voiced their assent. Jefferson's declaration was then debated and, slightly modified, was adopted on July 4. New York—the only colony that had not acted—joined its sister states when its provincial congress ratified the Declaration, July 9. Not until August 2 and afterward was it signed by the members of the Continental Congress. One last impetus for separation was the news received at Philadelphia in June that Britain had hired twenty thousand German mercenaries for the American war.[11]

Into the Declaration of Independence Jefferson incorporated the political theories of the most democratic wing of the patriot party. He did not mention Parliament, but allusions to its "pretended legislation" and "unwarranted jurisdiction" implied that the colonists had been bound to Britain solely through the king. They had received their inalienable rights of "life, liberty and the pursuit of happiness" —not from the British monarch—but from "the laws of nature and of nature's God." Their ancestors, presumably, had entered into a contract with the king for the establishment of a just government deriving its powers from the consent of the governed and reserving to the people the right to change that government, should it become destructive of those natural rights it was instituted to preserve. By "a long train of abuses and usurpations" the king had evinced a desire

[11] Herbert Friedenwald, *The Declaration of Independence* . . . (New York, 1904), traces the growth of sentiment in favor of separation and analyzes the Declaration.

to reduce the colonists "under an absolute despotism"; it therefore became their right and duty "to throw off such government, and to provide new guards for their future security." Jefferson next presented a long list of American grievances—which were all attributed to the tyranny of George III. The Declaration then closed with the affirmation "that these United Colonies are, and of right ought to be, free and independent states; that they are absolved from all allegiance to the British Crown, and that all political connection between them and the State of Britain is and ought to be totally dissolved; and that as free and independent states, they have full power to wage war, conclude peace, contract alliances, establish commerce and to do all the acts and things which independent states may of right do." [42]

The Declaration served a purpose beyond that of a public notice of separation; its ideas inspired mass fervor for the American cause. First, by asserting the rights and worth of man ("all men are created equal") it instilled among ordinary folk a sense of their own importance that helped to sustain them at war, inspiring them to struggle for personal freedom, self-government, and a dignified place in society. Secondly, by simplifying the issues of the conflict, the Declaration made it a personal contest—not a protest against lifeless statutes and an abstract Parliament but a struggle against an enemy of flesh and blood—and one who embodied the odious features of European despotism which so many colonists had fled from Europe to escape. Few people in 1776 could have mastered all the issues of the Revolution, but even the simplest mind could grasp the idea of a despotic king. By giving to the common man a personal cause and a personal enemy, the ideas of the Declaration brought the Revolution within the range of popular aspiration and strengthened it with the force of popular emotion.[43]

[42] Carl Becker's *The Declaration of Independence* (New York, 1922) is a fascinating essay—the best of its kind.

[43] John H. Hazelton, *The Declaration of Independence* (New York, 1906), is a detailed critique, for the special student.

## BIBLIOGRAPHICAL NOTE

WORKS PREVIOUSLY CITED: W. C. Abbott, *Expansion of Europe*, II, chs. 34–35; C. W. Alvord, *The Illinois Country*, chs. 12–16; C. M. Andrews, *Colonial Background of the American Revolution*, chs. 3–4; G. Bancroft, *History of the United States*, III–V; P. A. Bruce, *Virginia Plutarch*, I, chs. 9–19; *Cambridge Modern History*, VII, chs. 5–6; H. J. Carman, *Social and Economic History of the United States*, I, ch. 4; H. E. Egerton, *Short History of British Colonial Policy*, Book II, chs. 7–8; G. B. Hertz, *Old Colonial System*, chs. 4–6; A. C.

Flick (ed.), *History of the State of New York*, III, chs. 6–8; *Pageant of America*, VIII, ch. 2; D. D. Wallace, *Life of Henry Laurens*, chs. 8–16; W. B. Weeden, *Economic and Social History of New England*, II, chs. 18–19; B. Williams, *Life of William Pitt*, II, chs. 20–25; J. Winsor (ed.), *Narrative and Critical History of America*, VI, chs. 1–3.

SOURCES NEWLY CITED: Clarence E. Carter (ed.), *The Correspondence of General Thomas Gage* (2 vols., New Haven, 1931, 1933) is a collection of major importance. W. B. Donne (ed.), *The Correspondence of George the Third with Lord North* (2 vols., London, 1867), covers the years 1768–83. See Vol. I to 1775. The Hon. Sir John Fortescue has edited the very important *Correspondence of George the Third* (6 vols., London, 1927–28). The period of these papers is 1760–83. An interesting record is "Debates on the Declaratory Act and the Repeal of the Stamp Act, 1766," ed. H. W. V. Temperley, *American Historical Review*, XVII (April 1912). *The Barrington-Bernard Correspondence* (ed. E. Channing and A. C. Coolidge, Cambridge, 1912) contains Boston-London letters on the imperial problem, 1760–70. A well selected, readable collection is Margaret W. Willard (ed.), *Letters on the American Revolution, 1774–1776* (Boston, 1925). *Letters and Diary of John Rowe, Boston Merchant* (ed. Anne R. Cunningham, Boston, 1903) gives a running account of events, 1759–79. Edmund Burke's *Letters and Speeches on American Affairs* and John Locke's *Of Civil Government* are available in Everyman's Library editions.

SOURCES: PAPERS OF AMERICAN LEADERS: The most important collections of personal material are the following: C. F. Adams (ed.), *The Works of John Adams* (10 vols., Boston, 1850–56); Randolph G. Adams (ed.), *Selected Political Writings of James Wilson* (New York, 1930); J. G. Ballagh (ed.), *Letters of Richard Henry Lee* (2 vols., New York, 1911); J. Bigelow (ed.), *The Complete Works of Benjamin Franklin* (12 vols., New York, 1904); H. A. Cushing (ed.), *The Writings of Samuel Adams* (4 vols., New York, 1904–08); P. L. Ford, *The Writings of John Dickinson* (Philadelphia, 1895); P. L. Ford (ed.), *The Writings of Thomas Jefferson* (11 vols., New York, 1893–1900); C. F. Mullett (ed.), *Some Political Writings of James Otis* (Columbia, Mo., 1929). For Washington's works to 1779 the most complete edition is John C Fitzpatrick (ed.), *The Writings of George Washington* (14 vols., Washington, 1931–36). The next best edition, that of W. C. Ford (ed.), *The Writings of George Washington* (14 vols., New York, 1889–93), covers the period 1748–99.

SOURCES PREVIOUSLY CITED: E. L. Bogart and C. M. Thompson (eds.), *Readings in the Economic History of the United States*, ch. 5, parts 1–2; G. S. Callender (ed.), *Selections from the Economic History of the United States*, ch. 4, part 1; H. S. Commager (ed.), *Documents of American History*, I, nos. 33–66; A. B. Hart (ed.), *American History Told by Contemporaries*, II, Part VI; W. MacDonald (ed.), *Documentary Source Book of American History*, nos. 31–50; *Old South Leaflets*, nos. 2, 68, 156, 179, 199–200, 208, 210, 222; James Sullivan (ed.), *Sir William Johnson Papers*, IV–VIII.

MAPS: D. R. Fox, *Harper's Atlas*, pp. 16–17; C. O. Paullin, *Atlas of the Historical Geography of the United States*, plate 46; W. R. Shepherd, *Historical Atlas*, p. 194.

# XXIV

# THE REVOLUTION WITHIN

DURING the contest for independence the American opponents of Britain divided into two opposing camps: those who pressed for immediate separation and those who wished to postpone the fateful decision. Inasmuch as independence was almost certain to lead to social upheaval in America, many men of conservative temperament feared to release the powerful forces making for internal change. On the other hand those who desired a reconstruction of American society realized that they must first erase the authority of Britain which maintained existing class relationships and the political power of the colonial aristocracy. A cleavage on such a profound issue could not be obliterated by the Declaration of Independence; it persisted afterward, dividing the patriot ranks into contending groups.[1]

For want of a better term one of these groups may be styled the democratic or popular party, keeping in mind that there was then no organization bearing that name. Among the people of this party were the mass of the small farmers and frontiersmen, represented by such leaders as Israel Putnam of Connecticut, John Stark of New Hampshire, Ethan Allen of Vermont, Thomas Person of North Carolina, and Francis Marion and Thomas Sumter of South Carolina. Associated with them were the artisans and laborers of the towns (directed by that resolute democrat, Samuel Adams) and one section of the merchant class—free traders sympathetic toward the popular cause: Hancock and Gerry in Massachusetts, Gadsden in South Carolina, Sears and Lamb in New York, and Stephen Hopkins in Rhode Island. The southern planter class also contributed a few able leaders to the democratic party, notably Jefferson, George Mason, and, before 1777, Patrick Henry and Richard Henry Lee. Particularly important were the lawyers: Luther Martin of Maryland, Joseph Reed and George Bryan of Pennsylvania, William Henry Drayton of South Carolina, Thomas Burke of North Carolina, and John Morin Scott and George Clinton of New York. Towering above all other

---

[1] For an able analysis of this cleavage see C. E. Merriam, *A History of American Political Theories*, chapter 3.

leaders of the democracy were Jefferson,[2] Samuel Adams, and Benjamin Franklin.

The conception of democracy in 1776 included many principles. First of all, man was a dignified being, capable of governing himself in a rational, orderly manner. Realizing that governments in the past had usually been employed for the oppression of the common people, the democracy viewed all government with suspicion, endorsing the view of Tom Paine that "Government, like dress, is the badge of lost innocence." The powers of government should therefore be reduced to a minimum; each man should govern himself, and such social restraints as were necessary should be imposed by the community in which one lived. The farther governmental agencies were removed from the people the less power they should possess; hence a state government should be more important than a federal or national government. In accordance with Franklin's view that property is the basis of virtue ("An empty bag cannot stand upright"), the democrats believed that each individual should be a property owner, preferably of land, thereby assuring him an independent means of livelihood.[3]

In order to check the tendency inherent in government toward tyranny and oppression, two safeguards were necessary. First, the powers of government should be narrowly restricted. All power resided in the people; they must reserve to themselves the rewards of their labor (low taxes) and their rights of life and liberty, permitting government to exercise only such powers as would serve their interests. In their sovereign capacity the people should form constitutions both to confer upon government the powers it might exercise and to reserve to the people their fundamental rights. Secondly, the limited powers of government ought to be exercised by the people themselves through equal representation in the legislature, a liberal suffrage, and the right of the common man to hold office.[4]

Such political conceptions gave great importance to land as the source of wealth and power. The divine order in nature had decreed that the land should be used by man and that it should belong to those who would cultivate it. "All the property," wrote Franklin, "that is necessary to a man, for the conservation of the individual and the propagation of the species, is his natural right, which none can

[2] For the general student the best biography is Gilbert Chinard, *Thomas Jefferson* (Boston, 1929).
[3] Francis W. Hirst, *Life and Letters of Thomas Jefferson* (New York, 1926), is excellent.
[4] Albert J. Nock's *Jefferson* (New York, c. 1926) is an interpretation by a brilliant essayist.

justly deprive him of: but all property superfluous to such purposes is the property of the public, who by their laws have created it, and who may therefore by other laws dispose of it, whenever the welfare of the public shall demand such disposition." In keeping with such ideas the democracy rejected the king's claim to unoccupied lands, opposed the proprietary overlords, and favored the division of great estates into small holdings. But ownership alone was not enough: the husbandman should enjoy also the fruits of his labor, and that might be effected by means of an adequate currency which would keep up the price of the products which he offered for sale. An ample cash income in turn meant that he might pay his debts and avoid losing his land by foreclosure.[5]

In opposition to the democracy of small property owners and expectant property owners stood a conservative party composed of men of large capital which they combined with the labor of dependent workers in such a manner as to obtain abundant incomes for themselves. To this party belonged many of the wealthiest landowners: Benjamin Harrison, Richard Bland, Edmund Pendleton, Thomas Nelson, Edmund Randolph, and George Washington of Virginia, Charles Pinckney, Charles Coatsworth Pinckney, Edward Rutledge, John Rutledge, Henry Middleton, Arthur Middleton, and Rawlins Lowndes of South Carolina, Charles Carroll and Thomas Johnson of Maryland, Samuel Johnston and Richard Henderson of North Carolina, and Robert R. Livingston, Gouverneur Morris, Lewis Morris, James Duane, and Philip Schuyler of New York. The merchant class also contained many conservatives—James Bowdoin of Massachusetts, Roger Sherman and Jonathan Trumbull of Connecticut, the four Brown brothers of Rhode Island (Nicholas, John, Joseph, and Moses), Henry Laurens and Gabriel Manigault of South Carolina, Joseph Hewes of North Carolina, and George Clymer, Thomas Mifflin, Thomas and Samuel Wharton, Robert Morris, and Edward Biddle of Pennsylvania. Outstanding lawyers of the conservative group were Alexander Hamilton and John Jay of New York, James Iredell of North Carolina, and John Dickinson, James Wilson, and George Ross of Pennsylvania.[6]

The conservative philosophy of society assumed that the common people were ignorant, slothful, and incompetent; as individuals, weak; in the mass, rapacious and violent. The natural order of things

[5] A substantial though brief biography is David S. Muzzey, *Thomas Jefferson* (New York, 1918). Of the older biographies, Henry S. Randall's *The Life of Thomas Jefferson* (3 vols., New York, 1858) is the most valuable.

[6] An admirable study of a conservative leader is Frank Monaghan, *John Jay* (New York, 1935).

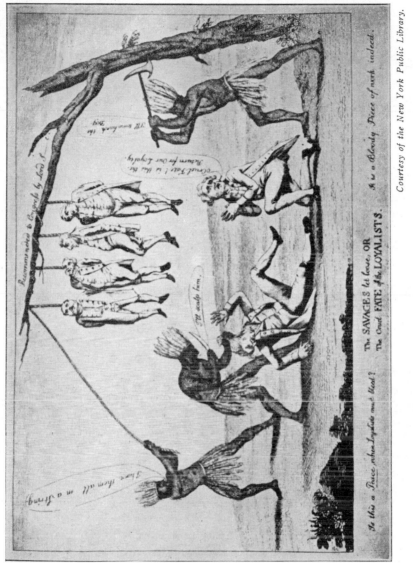

*Courtesy of the New York Public Library.*

A Plea to Britain to Save the Loyalists from American "Savagery"

had decreed that a few able, well-bred, well-educated men should be the custodians of wealth and the repositories of virtue, charged with the duty of preserving order, decorum, and culture in society. To this select few the mass of the people (slaves, tenants, employees, servants, and debtors) should be subservient. At all times the "greed" of the masses should be curbed, lest it lead to attacks upon the persons and property of the upper class. "The mob," wrote Gouverneur Morris in 1774, "begins to think and reason. Poor reptiles! it is with them a vernal morning; they are struggling to cast off their winter's slough, they bask in the sunshine, and ere noon they will bite."

The most conservative men of the upper class believed that popular uprisings should be guarded against with every precaution. Education of the poor should inculcate habits of industry and attitudes of obedience, an established church should teach respect for authority and property, and government should uphold the existing order by protecting the interests of men of wealth. Since in each state the poor outnumbered the rich it was unwise to rely wholly upon state government; a strong central government, equipped with an army, should be empowered to curb the democracy in its efforts to effect a redistribution of wealth, should such a thing be attempted either by state laws or by the use of force. All offices of government should be controlled by the aristocracy; hence the need of high property qualifications for voting and officeholding. Constitutional restraints on majority rule in elected legislatures should give protection against popular laws which threatened to injure the upper class, and taxes for the support of armed forces and state churches should be collected equally from all the people, not from the wealthy in accordance with their ability to pay. For the benefit of creditors a sound or limited currency should be maintained and managed by them in such a manner as to circumvent the scaling down of debts. For similar reasons the courts should not be unduly sympathetic toward debtors, servants, employees, tenants, or anyone disposed to challenge the supremacy of the upper class.[7]

## State Government and Federal Union

On the issue of British rule the democratic elements, unanimous in opposition to king and Parliament, provided the driving force which culminated in independence. On the other hand, the conservatives (who had largely directed the campaign against Britain on legal grounds) were divided. One group, which included Washington,

[7] See again V. L. Parrington, *The Colonial Mind*, Book III.

Carroll, John Adams, Sherman, Trumbull, Thomas Johnson, John Witherspoon, and John Hewes realized that the dangers of British policy exceeded the menace of convulsions within the colonies and acted with the democracy for separation. Excepting pro-British merchants, most of the conservatives of New England, North Carolina, Virginia, Maryland, New Jersey, and South Carolina who joined the revolutionary movement had decided in favor of independence by July 1776. Another group, however, particularly strong in Pennsylvania and New York and represented by James Wilson, Dickinson, Jay, Robert Morris, James Duane, and R. R. Livingston—and in South Carolina by Laurens, Manigault, and John Rutledge—worked to delay independence, fearing that internal upheavals might follow the destruction of British rule. But once the decision for independence had been reached, such conciliationists felt it necessary to take part in the revolutionary movement in order to direct it into what they deemed the proper channels.[8]

Independence erased the authority of the king on which the colonial governments had previously rested, thereby forcing the Americans to establish new state governments on another foundation. And because the Revolution was in part a protest against monarchy and aristocracy, it followed that the will of the people should be declared the source of all political power. The first thing the people had to do was to transform their revolutionary organizations into permanent governments—a task accomplished by means of written constitutions. Even before July 4, 1776, four of the colonies—New Hampshire, South Carolina, Virginia, and New Jersey—had adopted such constitutions. In the autumn and winter of 1776 Delaware, Pennsylvania, Maryland, and North Carolina acted; Georgia and New York followed in 1777; South Carolina formed a new constitution in 1778; and Massachusetts joined the procession in 1780. Rhode Island and Connecticut retained their colonial charters, which they modified by deleting all references to the king. In ten states (Pennsylvania, New York, Virginia, New Hampshire, South Carolina, North Carolina, Delaware, Georgia, New Jersey, and Maryland) the provincial congresses drafted the constitutions, and since the congresses served at the same time as legislative bodies, there was little distinction between the constitution and ordinary law. Not until Massachusetts acted in 1779–80 was a special convention elected which confined itself solely to the task of framing a constitution; and not until then was a constitution submitted to a popular referendum.

[8] See again Allan Nevins, *The American States during and after the Revolution*, pp. 117–630 on political issues and paper money.

In most states the problem of erecting a new government evoked a bitter struggle between the democratic and conservative forces. One section of the democracy stood for three main principles: a liberal franchise, equal representation of all districts in proportion to population, and the supremacy of the popular house of the legislature over the upper house, the executive, and the judiciary. Such was the program of radical democratic leaders like Franklin, Tom Paine, and Samuel Adams. More moderate democratic leaders, including Jefferson, Mason,[9] and R. H. Lee, mistrustful of all government and fearing that an elected lower house might become as tyrannical as an oligarchy of aristocrats, favored a government of limited powers in which the executive, judicial, and legislative branches would keep each other in check. The ultra-conservatives desired to withhold the right to vote from the poor, to give wealthy districts an influence greater than their population alone would warrant, and to provide a strong upper house and an independent executive and judiciary, all three to serve as brakes on the lower house. Radical democrats thus favored popular rule, moderate democrats wanted as little government as possible, and conservatives believed with John Jay that "those who own the country ought to govern it." The radical democrats were small farmers, small tradesmen, artisans, and mechanics; the conservatives were generally the largest property owners; while the moderate democrats were men of liberal sympathies and substantial property, often at odds with the largest property owners and yet not disposed to countenance mob rule or unrestrained attacks upon property rights. In four states (Pennsylvania, North Carolina, Delaware, and Georgia) the new constitutions were essentially democratic, whereas in Virginia, South Carolina, New York, Massachusetts, New Jersey, Maryland, and New Hampshire the conservative influence predominated. The form of government in both Rhode Island and Connecticut after 1776 was democratic, but in Connecticut men of conservative temperament were in control, while in Rhode Island the democratic forces were particularly strong.[10]

Pennsylvania attained the closest approach to pure democracy in its constitution of 1776, adopted by a convention in which delegates from the democratic interior counties outnumbered the representatives of the conservative East by two to one. Its authors (among them Benjamin Franklin) provided for a one-house legislature whose mem-

[9] The best work, Kate M. Rowland, *The Life of George Mason* (2 vols., New York, 1892), consists chiefly of Mason's writings.

[10] See again C. H. Van Tyne, *The War of Independence*, chapters 2, 9–12, and *The American Revolution*, chapters 9, 11, 14.

bers were elected annually by all the taxpayers of their districts. An executive council of thirteen, chosen every three years by the voters, and a president without power took the place of the old proprietary governor and council. Neither the president nor the executive council could veto acts of the legislature or otherwise hamper it. Of the state judiciary a critic of the constitution complained that it was wholly dependent upon the legislators, "who may remove any judge from his office *without trial,* for anything they please to call 'misbehavior.'" So bitter was the opposition of the eastern conservatives like Dickinson and Robert Morris that they organized an anticonstitutionalist party and directed their delegates in the assembly to obstruct the new government in every way. Although the eastern conservatives controlled only a third of the legislature their power was strong enough to bring about a deadlock and a disruption of the new government (December 1776). Only when the Continental Congress threatened to take over the state government did the eastern conservatives agree to coöperate. A new election was held in February 1777 and on March 4 the constitution at last began to function as its authors intended.[11]

The democrats of North Carolina in October 1776 held an election of members to a new provincial congress which was authorized to draft the state constitution. Four seats in five were captured by men of advanced democratic views. A leading conservative, Samuel Johnston (who was burned in effigy after his election defeat), lamented that everyone "who has the least pretensions to be a gentleman is borne down *per ignobile vulgus*—a set of men without reading, experience, or principles to govern them." By the new constitution of December 8 every adult freeman of the state received the right to vote for assemblymen, while the latter were required to possess one hundred acres of land. Any resident who owned fifty acres of land enjoyed the right to vote for state senators, each of whom had to possess an estate of three hundred acres. Although the constitution provided for a governor (elected by the legislature) his powers were only nominal: he could not veto its acts or make important appointments, and his term lasted but one year. One ultra-conservative, William Hooper, contemptuously remarked that the only power given to the governor was the right "to sign a receipt for his salary."[12]

[11] Burton A. Konkle, *George Bryan and the Constitution of Pennsylvania, 1731–1791* (Philadelphia, 1922), a vigorously written biography, surveys Pennsylvania politics through the career of a leading radical. See also P. L. Ford, "The Adoption of the Pennsylvania Constitution of 1776," *Political Science Quarterly,* X (Sept. 1895).

[12] A good brief political account is Enoch W. Sikes, *The Transition of North Carolina from Colony to Commonwealth* (Baltimore, 1898).

The first outstanding example of a conservative constitution was the work of a South Carolina provincial congress in which the seaboard had 144 representatives as against forty for the democratic back country, even though the interior section then contained three-fourths of the white population. The first constitution, probably drafted by the ultra-conservative John Rutledge, remained in force from March 1776 until March 1778, when it was superseded by another, also essentially conservative. The distinguishing features of the second constitution were the senate and the scheme of representation for the lower house. If a senator resided in the district he represented he must own property worth £2,000; if he represented a district of which he was not a resident he must be worth £7,000. Only a man with an estate of £10,000 could serve as governor. Although the legislature possessed much power, it was not a democratic body in that the wealthy eastern aristocracy dominated both the senate and the lower house. In the latter, the lowlands were entitled to 144 seats; the populous upcountry to only fifty-eight. Moreover, the wealthy, aristocratic senate was a check on the lower house, and only residents who owned fifty acres of land received the right to vote. Allan Nevins states that the new government was distinctly "for the rich, well-born lowlanders, who had made it for themselves, and meant to keep it their own."

The provincial congress which in June 1776 adopted the first constitution of Virginia was composed of two delegates from each county and therefore reflected the interests of the small wealthy counties of the seaboard as against those of the larger and more populous counties of the interior. Both the conservatives and the liberal democrats took part in the proceedings: Edmund Randolph, for instance, as president of the congress and George Mason as the chief author of the constitution. Although the legislature was made superior to the governor (whose powers were only nominal), although both the lower house and the senate were elected by all residents who possessed fifty acres, and although the two houses chose the governor, even so the constitution did not establish a popular government. Each county continued to be represented by two delegates, with the result that a small eastern county with a few hundred voters ranked as equal to a large western county containing several thousand. Moreover, the seaboard area obtained a disproportionately large influence in the senate, a fourth of whose twelve members were chosen once a year for four-year terms; and, besides, the senate enjoyed nearly coördinate powers with the lower house. Thus despite the centering of power in the legislature, the tidewater aristocracy remained in control by virtue of the checks on the elected house and the unequal mode of representation; self-government in Virginia continued to mean the rule of the upper class.[13]

Drafted by a trio of conservatives—Jay, R. R. Livingston, and Gouverneur Morris—the New York constitution of 1777 provided for a democratic lower house of seventy members elected by the freemen of the towns and by freeholders worth £20. However, four curbs on the elected house restrained the democracy. The governor, chosen for a three-year term by a restricted electorate, commanded the armed forces and received the power to prorogue the legislature. (All previous state constitutions had provided that the legislature should elect a weak executive—a reaction against the influence exercised by the royal and proprietary governors of colonial times.) The New York senate, which shared coördinate powers with the lower house, was certain to be dominated by wealthy men, a fourth of whom were elected each year for four-year terms by voters who possessed freeholds (clear of debt) worth at least £100 each. A council of appointment consisting of the governor and four senators exercised the appointing power, while a council of revision (the governor, the chancellor, and three supreme court judges) could veto acts of the legislature—and only by a two-thirds vote of each house could such a veto be overridden. In 1790 only one adult male in ten in New York City could vote for governor. The power and nature of the senate gave assurance that it would be the center of gravity in a government dominated by wealthy landowners.[14]

In Massachusetts the conservatives also won a decisive victory. The constitution of 1780 provided for a governor elected by property owners and entrusted with the veto and appointive powers, including the right to appoint judges who were to hold office during good behavior. Although each town was privileged to have a representative in the lower house, no salaries were provided for members, and many poor communities could not afford to send delegates. The senate—an effective check on the lower house—represented the wealthy men of the state. Property qualifications were: for a voter, £60; for a representative, a freehold of £100 or other property worth £200; for a senator, a freehold of £300 or other property worth £600; and for the governor, a freehold of £1,000. Taxation for the support of the Congregational churches remained intact. S. E. Morison has de-

[13] See again I. S. Harrell, *Loyalism in Virginia*, chapters 2–4, and C. H. Ambler, *Sectionalism in Virginia*, chapter 2.

[14] E. W. Spaulding's *New York in the Critical Period* is an admirable study of the social and economic results of the Revolution.

scribed the constitution of 1780 as "a lawyers' and merchants' constitution, directed toward something like quarterdeck efficiency in government and the protection of property against democratic pirates." [15]

While constitution-making was in progress in the states, the Continental Congress was wrestling with the problem of a federal union. Two circumstances forced the Americans to devise a scheme of confederation. First, they had to coöperate in prosecuting the war—on the assumption that they must hang together or they would hang separately. Secondly, the common problems of the states necessitated a permanent machinery for joint action; the American economy of industry, trade, and credit relations cut across state boundaries and involved perpetual contacts with foreign countries, while numerous rival land claims of the states required some agency for the arbitration of disputes. Prior to 1776 Britain had provided the general government to supervise foreign and intercolonial affairs. Now, however, that government had been renounced and a new one had to be erected. The task presented the same difficulty of adjusting local and external interests which had precipitated the Revolution. On the issue of a central authority the Americans divided into two parties which corresponded roughly to the democratic and conservative groups which were contending for mastery within the states. [16]

One of these parties preferred to make the states the center of a federal system, around which a weak general government should revolve as a satellite. Among the small farmers and the southern planters the sentiment in favor of state sovereignty was particularly strong. Remembering that the British government had used its authority to support the British merchants and landlords in their conflicts with American farmers, the agrarian leaders did not intend to create new institutions vested with the old powers of king and Parliament. The program of the democratic-agrarian forces therefore included the following points. A general government should not possess the power of taxation; all levies on the people should be voted by their state legislatures. So also the states must retain control over military forces, lest these be utilized against the people as the British army had been used. Nor should the general government be granted the exclusive power to regulate trade and enact navigation laws; by such measures the commercial class might oppress the farmers. There

---

[15] J. T. Adams's *New England in the Republic* (Boston, 1926) concludes his three-volume history of New England. See chapters 2–4.

[16] C. H. Van Tyne, "Sovereignty in the American Revolution," *American Historical Review*, XII (April 1907).

should be no federal judiciary empowered to set aside the decisions of state courts, nor should state laws be nullified by an external agency in the manner that the British Privy Council had disallowed colonial acts. In the sphere of domestic legislation the states should be sovereign, vested with the power of coining money, issuing bills of credit, and regulating credit relations and property rights. In those states which had western land claims (Georgia, the Carolinas, Virginia, and Connecticut) the state rights sentiment was reinforced by the desire of settlers and land speculators to vest the title to the western lands in the respective state governments which they controlled.[17]

Against the state rights party were arrayed the advocates of a strong central government—merchants, investors, and men of large wealth whose property interests extended over many states. In their opinion the central government should be sovereign over the states in certain fields. It should regulate trade, establish a uniform currency, enact navigation laws, and conduct diplomatic negotiations with foreign nations. Moreover, it should possess an army and a navy and be able to use them to suppress domestic insurrections which might imperil existing property rights. The laws of a general congress regulating currency and debts should take precedence over acts of the states, and a central judiciary should be empowered to reverse the judgments of state courts detrimental to non-resident creditors. No state should exclude the merchants of other states from its trade, and owners of large tracts of land should be protected against settlers who might swarm in from other states and help themselves to farms. In those states without western land claims (especially in Maryland, Pennsylvania, and New Jersey) land speculators preferred that a general government own the western territory in order that the citizens of all states might stand on an equal footing before the grantor of the land. And should the general government take possession of the western lands it would need vigorous powers in order to defend and administer them properly.[18]

In June 1776 the Continental Congress appointed a committee to draft a plan of union. Men of conservative views dominated this committee, whose guiding spirit was John Dickinson. On July 12 he presented a plan of union which proposed to establish a fairly strong central government. The state rights leaders attacked the Dickinson draft

[17] M. M. Jensen, "The Articles of Confederation: A Re-interpretation," *Pacific Historical Review*, VI (June 1937).

[18] On political ideas see Louise B. Dunbar, *A Study of "Monarchical" Tendencies in the United States from 1776 to 1801* (Urbana, 1922).

and because they dominated the Congress they succeeded in modifying it to suit their views. The Articles of Confederation emerged from the debate, ratified by the Congress on November 15, 1777.

Designed to create a "perpetual union," the Articles granted to the general government only limited powers to be exercised by a Congress in which each state was given one vote. No provision was made for an independent executive department or for a permanent federal judiciary, and no agency was created to review or disallow state laws. The Congress could exercise only such powers as were specifically granted to it by the articles; all power not mentioned was reserved to the states. Only by a unanimous vote of all states could the articles be amended. The Congress could not levy taxes; it could only make requisitions upon the states, trusting that they would raise the money. Such quotas were to be apportioned among the states in proportion to the value of lands and buildings legally in private hands. The Congress might enter into commercial treaties and regulate Indian affairs, yet if its acts in those fields conflicted with certain state laws, the latter were to be supreme. Of the powers granted to the Congress, the most important could be exercised only with the assent of the delegations of nine states—that is to say, the power to engage in war, to coin, borrow or appropriate money, to issue bills of credit, and to decide the number of vessels to be acquired for the navy and the number of land and sea forces to be raised. The states retained the concurrent right to issue bills of credit and to coin money, and the sole right to enact laws governing contracts and debts. Moreover, the states could exercise many of the powers granted to the Congress, if they were exercised with its consent: the right to make treaties, to send and receive diplomatic agents, to maintain navies and armies, to engage in war, and to fit out vessels against pirates. In ordinary times the principal military forces should consist of state militias. If a state did not respect its obligations under the Articles there was no legal means of compelling it to conform.

As an embodiment of the revolutionary opposition to the authority of the British Parliament, the Articles of Confederation reserved to the states most of the powers which Parliament had previously claimed. And the powers granted to the Congress were so hedged about that they could not be used by minority groups in control of the general government to the detriment of the people of the states.[19]

The Articles of Confederation were not ratified by all the states—and hence did not become operative—until March 1, 1781. This delay

[19] E. S. Corwin, "The Progress of Constitutional Theory . . ." [1776–87], *American Historical Review*, XXX (April 1925).

was occasioned by a spirited debate in the Congress over the ownership of the western lands. Those promoters of western settlement
who had been seeking land grants from the king prior to 1776 now
became supplicants before the Congress, contending that it superseded the Crown as the proprietor of the West. Two companies of
speculators dominated the scene: the Indiana Company, sponsors of
the Vandalia project; and the Illinois-Wabash Company, a combination formed in 1779. Both companies were vehicles for the promoters of the middle states. Samuel Wharton, George Morgan, and
Benjamin Franklin were leaders in the Indiana Company, which
sought a large tract in present-day West Virginia; Robert Morris,
James Wilson, and George Ross of Pennsylvania and Charles Carroll, Thomas Johnson, and Samuel Chase of Maryland led the
Illinois-Wabash Company, which proposed to operate in the region
north of the Ohio River. Both companies needed confirmation of
their claims, and despairing of obtaining such confirmations from
Virginia, they insisted that Virginia cede her western lands to the
Congress—from which body they hoped to receive favored treatment.
In June and July 1776 Virginia in effect rejected the claims of the
companies and announced that all the lands within her charter limits
should be disposed of through her state government.[20]

Since the Articles of Confederation as finally drafted proposed to
leave the western lands in possession of the states with charter claims,
the landed interest of the middle states worked to prevent ratification
of the Articles. Maryland thereupon refused to ratify until Virginia
ceded her claims. As an inducement to Virginia, New York on February 19, 1780, abandoned its shadowy title to lands west of the present
boundary of the state. The political leaders of New York agreed to
give up the state's claim (derived from Britain's recognition of New
York as the protector of the Iroquois) because the lands reserved to
the state in 1780 offered ample scope for its land speculators. Then
when Virginia was threatened by British troops and hoped to in-
vigorate the defense measures of the Congress, her legislature on
January 2, 1781, ceded to the United States most of the land north of
the Ohio River, with the condition—sponsored by George Mason—
that all existing grants from the Indians to private interests be nullified. Although the Virginia cession cut the ground from under the land
promoters of the middle states, it induced Maryland to ratify the
Articles of Confederation, March 1, 1781. The land companies then
tried to persuade the Congress to reject the Virginia cession, but their

[20] M. M. Jensen, "The Cession of the Old Northwest," *Mississippi Valley Historical Review*, XXII (June 1936).

efforts proved fruitless; the Congress accepted it on March 1, 1784.[21]

Inasmuch as the Articles of Confederation did not become effective until 1781, the Congress acted until then as a *de facto* government, without a definite constitutional basis. The foundations of its authority were twofold: the necessity of waging war and the powers with which its members were vested by their respective state governments. Thus between 1776 and 1781 the general government was a confederation of sovereign states, forced to coöperate by the menace of a common foe.

## THE COSTS OF WAR

To provide the sinews of war was the most urgent task confronting the Congress and the states. That part of the military burden assumed by the Congress in June 1775 included the raising, paying, equipping, and provisioning of a continental army, the appointment of the commander-in-chief and other high officers, the directing of the campaigns of the war, and the apportionment of the expenses of the army among the states on the basis of population (the requisition or quota system). But how was the Congress to raise money in advance of the payment of the state quotas? It could not levy taxes; it could not at first commandeer property (lest it turn the people against the American cause); and it could not obtain adequate funds on loan from men of wealth. Many of the richest men, as loyalists, were unwilling to lend money to the Congress, and their property could be confiscated only by the states. Due to a trade depression in 1775–76, occasioned by Britain's war on American commerce, wealthy patriots were unable to convert commodities into cash, while cautious capitalists feared to lend to the United States when the outcome of the war was in doubt. Should Britain win, all such loans would be repudiated. For similar reasons foreign investors and foreign governments held back; moreover, open support to the Americans might involve a foreign state in war with Britain. The United States had no common currency, either paper or metallic; there were no banks which could extend credit to the government; and the supply of foreign coins and state paper money, thanks to Britain's imperial currency policy, was woefully inadequate for financing an extended war.

In these circumstances the Congress had to issue bills of credit or promissory notes, printed in the form of general currency so that they would circulate without individual endorsements. Such bills had proved serviceable during the earlier wars; and moreover they ap-

[21] Herbert B. Adams, *Maryland's Influence upon Land Cessions to the United States* (Baltimore, 1885).

peased the debtor wing of the revolutionary party which had long clamored for a cheap and abundant currency. They were not redeemable in specie from day to day, but the Congress called upon the states to provide money from taxes for the redemption of the bills at designated times.[22]

All in all the Congress emitted in bills of credit, between June 22, 1775, and November 29, 1779, a sum of $191,500,000. This huge issue was made necessary by the failure of the states to collect the tax money which was supposed to take the bills out of circulation. When such tax money was not paid to the Congress by the states, the old bills remained in use, while money for fresh outlays had to be provided by printing new bills. Prior to September 3, 1779, when the Congress had issued nearly $160,000,000 in bills, the states had provided only about $3,000,000 in tax money for their redemption. Moreover, the states issued notes and bills of their own—$250,000,-000 in all. Since the state and the Congress bills circulated side by side they constituted a uniform currency; each affected the value of the other. The tremendous expansion of the paper currency was not accompanied by an equivalent increase in the supply of silver and commodities; hence the value of the paper currency steadily depreciated. On January 14, 1779, the ratio of silver dollars to paper dollars was 1:8; on May 5 it stood at 1:24; on November 17 at 1:38½.

The superabundance of the Continental bills, their depreciation, and the ability of the Congress after 1779 to borrow money from private sources led to a decision to retire the bills from circulation. Accordingly, the Congress enacted, March 18, 1780, that the states should collect taxes and use the money to redeem the bills at the rate of one silver dollar to forty paper dollars. If a taxpayer were assessed a tax of one dollar (silver) he could pay forty dollars in Continental bills, whereupon they would be sent to the Congress and destroyed. After the redemption period had expired, any bills outstanding were to have no further value. Eventually about $120,000,-000 of the Continental bills were retired in this manner; $71,000,000 remained in circulation. After 1781 remaining bills depreciated to the vanishing point, giving rise to the phrase, "not worth a Continental." Speculators bought them for a song, hoping that in the future the Congress might redeem them at part of their face value.[23]

[22] R. V. Harlow, "Aspects of Revolutionary Finance, 1775–1783," *American Historical Review*, XXXV (Oct. 1929).

[23] An older pioneer work, not too technical or detailed, is Albert S. Bolles, *The Financial History of the United States from 1774 to 1789* (2d ed., New York, 1884).

The paper currency issued by the states consisted of both ordinary bills of credit and interest-bearing treasury notes. All told they amounted to about $250,000,000. The only security behind most of this paper was the promise of the state legislatures to levy taxes for redemption. However, such taxes were not collected (often they were not even assessed), and accordingly the state bills traveled the road of depreciation hand in hand with the Continental bills. After 1780 they were drawn in as tax money at various rates of depreciation: in Georgia and Virginia at $1,000 paper to $1.00 silver, in North Carolina at 800 to 1; in New York at 128 to 1; in Maryland at 40 to 1. Through this mode of redemption the indebtedness of the states represented by the bills of credit was effaced by the end of the war, depreciation having served as a tax upon most of the people through whose hands the bills had passed.[24]

Who benefited by the depreciation of the paper currency? Certainly not the mass of the people—not even the debtor class. In order to maintain the face value of both the state and Continental bills of credit in terms of silver dollars the state legislatures in the years 1775–77 enacted that they pass as legal tender in payment of existing debts. Some states went so far as to provide that the tender of bills to a creditor automatically canceled the obligation. Creditors, however, were not wholly unprotected. In the first place, depreciation caused a rapid rise in the price of commodities; in many cases so much of a debtor's increased income in paper money was required for the purchase of new supplies that he had nothing left for debt payments. Secondly, creditors took advantage of the natural disposition of debtors to defer payment and thus extended loans until collections might be made in a better currency. In other cases poorly paid military service forced men to borrow money to operate their farms while they were away in the army. If a debtor did succeed in clearing himself of debt, the rise in the prices of what he bought often forced him to borrow again. When depreciation became acute the creditors secured laws in 1780–82 which provided that past debts be paid in paper currency of a value in silver equivalent to that which the debtor had received. Thus if a debtor had borrowed in 1776 $100 in paper which was then worth $100 in silver, and if he repaid the debt in 1781 when $100 in paper was worth but one dollar in silver, he must pay $10,000 in the depreciated paper. Finally, by 1781 all the states but South Carolina had repealed their legal tender laws, and South Carolina made it unanimous in 1782.[25]

[24] See again C. J. Bullock, *Essays in the Monetary History of the United States.*
[25] The most detailed of the standard accounts is W. G. Sumner, *The Financier and*

Similarly, the day-to-day operation of the paper currency did not benefit the mass of the farmers, workers, and consumers; instead, those who profited were men skilled in money transactions who devoted all their time to the study of prices and currency values. Merchants who anticipated depreciation raised the prices of the goods they sold; and such prices undoubtedly rose faster than wages and the prices of farm products. Soldiers who received fixed pay in a depreciating currency were particularly hard hit. A conference of New Englanders at Providence in December 1776 warned that "the avaricious conduct of many persons, by daily adding to the price of every necessary and convenient article of life . . . , will be attended by the most fatal and pernicious consequences, as it . . . disheartens and disaffects the soldiers . . . and distresses the poorer part of the community." "The rapid and exorbitant rise upon the necessaries . . . of life," declared the Connecticut legislature in 1776, "is chiefly occasioned by monopolizers, the great pest of society." In order to combat such wartime profiteering the states prepared schedules of prices at which sellers were supposed to part with their goods. But price-fixing failed; either sellers would hoard their commodities if the legal prices were too low or they would evade the law. No government could supervise millions of transactions involving the prices of all commodities. Those persons who did abide by the law merely penalized themselves while "chiselers" grew rich. A conference on price-fixing to which all states but Virginia and New York sent delegates in 1780 finally admitted the hopelessness of the policy and abandoned it as a lost cause.

The ever-prevalent complaints of profiteering and allusions to "sharpers, monopolizers and extortioners" indicate that many traders made a good thing out of the war. Realizing that the currency bubble would one day burst, the shrewdest investors converted their paper profits into some durable form—into land, commodities, mortgage loans, capital goods, and the securities of the state and federal governments, thereby acquiring claims to future incomes to be realized in a better currency. At the end of the war, the investments of the creditor class (as expressed in dollars) greatly exceeded their prewar investments, and the burden of debt, both public and private, was correspondingly increased.[26]

*the Finances of the American Revolution* (2 vols., New York, 1891). For a condensed version see W. G. Sumner, *Robert Morris* (1892).

[26] W. B. Norton, "Paper Money in Massachusetts during the Revolution," *New England Quarterly*, VII (March 1934).

The conversion of depreciated paper into income-producing property is illustrated by the long-term loans floated during the war by the Congress and the states. As early as October 1776 the Congress authorized the sale of long-term securities (similar to government bonds), but until September 1777 purchasers did not respond readily, in part because the Congress could not guarantee the payment of interest and principal. However, after 1777 the United States could borrow from France ($6,353,000, specie value, was obtained between 1777 and 1784) and this money the Congress used to pay the interest on its long-term securities. At the same time occurred the depreciation of the Continental bills of credit. Because these bills could be exchanged for United States securities which now yielded interest in sound money, the demand for the latter became so great that the Congress was able, after September 1777, to dispose of securities amounting to $63,000,000, although the paper it received had a specie value of only $7,684,000. Part of this debt was repaid in 1783–89 from proceeds from the sale of the public lands. In 1790 the total domestic indebtedness of the United States was estimated by Alexander Hamilton as $40,000,000 ($27,000,000 principal and $13,000,-000 unpaid interest). At that time unpaid long term debts incurred by the states exceeded $18,000,000. Since the United States in 1790 provided for the repayment of both the state and federal debts in specie, those investors who had bought government securities in 1777–81 and who retained them until 1790 succeeded in converting depreciated currency into a durable value.[27]

## THE REVOLUTION AND THE LAND

Of all the results of the Revolution none exceeded in importance the transformation of the system of land ownership. The landed aristocracy of colonial times, imported from England with feudal trimmings, went down before the onrush of democracy—a change effected by the confiscation of estates, some of which were characterized by feudal survivals, and by the sweeping away of quit-rents, entails, primogeniture, and the colonial establishments of the Anglican Church. Even slavery felt the impact of the rights of man.

The mainspring of this revolution was the seizure by the states of the ungranted lands in possession of the king. New Hampshire, New York, Virginia, the Carolinas, and Georgia took possession of the

[27] A technical work valuable to the special student is C. J. Bullock, *The Finances of the United States from 1775 to 1789* (Madison, Wis., 1895).

royal acres within their borders, thus freeing themselves from the British land ordinance of 1774 and democratizing the power of land disposal by vesting it in the state legislatures. By obtaining title to the territory north to the Great Lakes and west to the Mississippi, the United States swept away the obstacles to settlement imposed by the Quebec Act and the Indian boundary line, opening the West to farmers and land speculators—at first the area of Kentucky-Tennessee; then the region north of the Ohio and the Southwest.[28]

Proprietary estates also fell into the hands of the states. Pennsylvania took over the ungranted lands of the Penn family—a domain valued at £1,000,000, for the loss of which the state granted the Penns £130,000 "in remembrance of the enterprising spirit of the founder and of the expectations and dependence of his descendants." When Maryland confiscated the lands of its proprietor in 1780, the compensation it provided was so inadequate (£10,000) that the British government paid him an additional £90,000. The only surviving proprietorship in the Carolinas (Lord Granville's estate, a third of North Carolina) also passed into the hands of the state government. Virginia took possession of Lord Fairfax's domain of more than five million acres between the Rappahannock and the Potomac Rivers (the Northern Neck).[29] Originally granted in 1649 by Charles II to Lord Culpeper and a group of his associates as a retreat for English Cavaliers, this estate had been acquired *in toto* by Culpeper's son, from whom it descended to Lord Fairfax. After obtaining a confirmation of his title from the Crown in 1745, Fairfax had surveyors run the "Fairfax line" which connected the head springs of the Rappahannock with the northern branch of the Potomac (1746). The next year Fairfax removed to Virginia and thereafter enjoyed the distinction of being the only British peer among the permanent residents of the colonies. He lived in rustic simplicity at "Greenway Court" (near the site of present-day Winchester, Virginia), occupying himself with his interests as a landed magnate. Despite unproved charges that he was a loyalist during the war he was not molested. The confiscation of his estate (after his death in 1781) was the result, not of his loyalism, but of the revolutionary opposition to feudal survivals.

As the war in America progressed the hatreds of patriots and loyalists for each other deepened, fed by patriot attacks on the civil rights and persons of the loyalists and by their counterattacks upon

---

[28] For western land projects see George H. Alden's *New Governments West of the Alleghanies before 1780* (Madison, Wis., 1897). Consult also F. J. Turner, "Western State Making in the Revolutionary Era," *American Historical Review*, I (Oct. 1895).

[29] J. F. Jameson's *The American Revolution Considered as a Social Movement* (Princeton, 1926) is the best general discussion of themes treated in this chapter.

the patriots.[30] By 1778 the intensity of civil strife had driven the patriots to wholesale confiscation of loyalist property. Moderate loyalists who strove to maintain a neutral stand were harassed on all occasions—by fines for evading militia duty, for harboring members of their families active in the British cause, and for every minor misdeed of which they were accused. New York and South Carolina held them financially responsible for robberies committed in their neighborhoods; they were forced to pay double or treble taxes; they were compelled to receive rents and to sell goods priced in depreciated currency and then to meet their obligations with specie. They lost all offices they had held; professional practice was denied to them; they were boycotted, robbed, and cheated. If they resisted such treatment they exposed themselves to the charge of treason and the confiscation of their property—a punishment ordinarily reserved for those loyalists who joined the king's forces or openly gave them assistance. By such measures moderate loyalists were stripped of their personal property and often driven to overt resistance.[31]

On November 27, 1777, the Congress recommended that the states seize and sell the property of all men who adhered to the king and invest the proceeds in Continental loan certificates. By October 1781 every state except South Carolina had followed this advice, and South Carolina fell into line early in 1782. New Hampshire confiscated the estates of twenty-nine persons; Pennsylvania prepared a "black list" naming 490 loyalists, most of whom had left the state after the withdrawal of the British army from Philadelphia; New York seized the lands of fifty-five loyalists, including those of James De Lancey, Roger Morris, John T. Kemp, and Beverly Robinson. The South Carolina act of 1782 confiscated the property of and banished all men who had openly supported the British or who had proved themselves "inveterate enemies of the state"; those who had accepted the king's protection or had supplied his forces with money were fined 12 per cent of their property. Among the large landed estates lost by the loyalists were those of John Wentworth in New Hampshire, Sir William Pepperrell in Maine, Sir John Johnson in New York, and Sir James Wright in Georgia. At the end of the war five thousand loyal-

[30] The best introductory sketch is C. H. Van Tyne, *The Loyalists in the American Revolution* (New York, 1902). See also M. C. Tyler, "The Party of Loyalists in the American Revolution," *American Historical Review*, I (Oct. 1895).

[31] A. C. Flick, *Loyalism in New York during the American Revolution* (New York, 1901), is one of the best studies of the loyalists. James H. Stark, *The Loyalists of Massachusetts* (Boston, c. 1907) classifies much useful personal information. The bias is pro-loyalist. Wilbur H. Siebert, *The Loyalists of Pennsylvania* (Columbus, 1920), is of interest to the special student. E. Peck, *The Loyalists of Connecticut* (New Haven, 1934—Connecticut Tercentenary Commission, no. 31).

ists asked the British government to compensate them for their lost property, which they valued at £10,000,000. After paring such claims to the minimum Britain awarded them £3,292,000. These losses signify that a large amount of loyalist property passed into the hands of the patriots during the war.[32]

As soon as the war broke out, patriot landowners in the royal and proprietary colonies ceased to pay the quit-rents, which amounted in all to $100,000 a year. Then after appropriating the royal and proprietary lands the state governments abolished the quit-rents altogether; the democratic state now took the place of king and proprietors, substituting for the quit-rents a public tax for the benefit, not of absentee landlords, but of the taxpayers themselves.

In keeping with the attack on semi-feudal survivals was the removal of the two bulwarks of the native landed aristocracy—entails and primogeniture. Jefferson led the assault on both. In 1776 he drafted the Virginia law which permitted landholders to convey entailed property in fee simple—an act which removed entails from nearly three-fourths of the settled lands of the state.[33] South Carolina had already legislated against entails by 1775, Pennsylvania and Georgia acted in 1776 and 1777; North Carolina, Maryland, and New York in 1784 and 1786. Of the southern states only Georgia rejected primogeniture during the Revolution (1777), but Virginia, North Carolina, South Carolina, and Maryland, as well as New York and Massachusetts, fell in line during the years 1784–90. After 1800 the rule prevailed in all states but two that real estate and personal property should be shared equally by all children. North Carolina withheld land from daughters if there were surviving sons; New Jersey allowed only half portions to daughters. Inasmuch as both entails and primogeniture had confined the ownership of large estates in the tidewater area to a few families, they had preserved the rule of the southern aristocracy in the colonial governments. With the division of land equally among direct heirs the economic basis of a landed aristocracy was shattered, as estates had to be sold or divided in order to provide the inheritances of all the children. In the 1830's de Tocqueville explained the democratic trend in the United States partly by the practice of equal inheritance. Only large landed estates which could not be alienated, he believed, could provide the permanence of property necessary for a continuing aristocracy; fortunes dependent

[32] William S. Wallace, *The United Empire Loyalists* (*Chronicles of Canada* series, Toronto, 1914).

[33] See again H. J. Eckenrode, *The Revolution in Virginia*, chapters 6–12.

upon the vicissitudes of trade were too mutable to sustain aristocratic families generation after generation.

The disestablishment of the Anglican Church required the repeal of laws which levied taxes for the support of its ministers and which ordered that all inhabitants attend its services. Because the Anglican Church was a symbol of British authority and because a large percentage of Anglicans and the Anglican clergy were loyalists, the opponents of the establishment, strong in the back country, opened their attack at the outbreak of the Revolution. In their state constitutions of 1776 Maryland and North Carolina stripped the Church of its legal privileges, North Carolina declaring that "there shall be no establishment of any one religious church or denomination in preference to any other." After contests described by Jefferson as the severest "in which I have ever been engaged," the Virginia legislature in 1776 repealed most of the old ecclesiastical laws and exempted non-Anglicans from paying church taxes; in 1779 Anglicans also were relieved. The state constitutions of New York (1777), Georgia (1777), and South Carolina

AN ANGLICAN PRAYER FOR THE KING, AS MODIFIED FOR USE IN THE UNITED STATES

(1778) granted religious freedom and equal privileges to Christians of all sects. Inasmuch as many southern Anglicans like Washington were patriot leaders, the religious contest did not partake of the intensity of the strife between patriots and loyalists, and the outcome was a compromise rather than the destruction of the Anglican Church. The non-Anglican patriots gained religious equality

while the Anglicans retained their Church, with its property intact.[34]

Not content with destroying semi-feudal and aristocratic survivals
in the existing states the democratic leaders took precautions against
their extension into the West. The most crucial action along this line
was taken with reference to the settlement of Kentucky in 1775–76.
In the early 1770's a group of North Carolina merchants and landowners launched a project to establish a great proprietary province
beyond the mountains. Foremost among them was Richard Henderson, a conservative judge of Granville County, whose class affiliations
are indicated by his marriage to the daughter of an English peer. As
a foe of the North Carolina Regulators, Henderson was the victim
of an attack which reduced his home, stables, and crops to ashes. His
interest in the West moved him to employ as his personal scout the
intrepid Daniel Boone, who in 1769–71 explored the wild lands of
Virginia, Tennessee, and Kentucky with an eye to settlement prospects. Then with a group of wealthy North Carolinians, all enemies
of the Regulators, Henderson formed the Transylvania Company,
January 6, 1775. In March the company negotiated a treaty with the
Cherokees, holders of the only surviving Indian title to the region,
purchasing for £10,000 in goods and money some twenty million acres
comprising parts of present-day Virginia and Tennessee and most of
Kentucky (Treaty of Sycamore Shoals). Under Henderson's leadership a band of three hundred frontiersmen built a settlement, Boonesborough, where the promoters erected a proprietorship of the Maryland type, reserving quit-rents, retaining title to the land and sub-
jecting an elected assembly to a proprietary veto, for they "clearly
realized that if they resigned that power, the delegates . . . would
have it in their power to annul the claims and rights of the proprietors" (A. Henderson).[35]

Having acted in defiance of British western land policy, the Transylvania Company evoked the wrath of Lord Dunmore in Virginia,
while its members were denounced by Governor Martin of North
Carolina as an infamous band of "land pirates." When the Revolutionary War was in progress, the Transylvanians turned to the Continental Congress for a confirmation of their claims, sending an agent

[34] Edward F. Humphrey's *Nationalism and Religion in America, 1774–1789* (Boston, 1924), a monograph for the advanced student, discusses church and state in Part
III. See again H. J. Eckenrode, *Church and State in Virginia*, chapters 4–8.

[35] See two articles by A. Henderson: "The Creative Forces in Westward Expansion:
Henderson and Boone," *American Historical Review*, XX (Oct. 1914) and "Richard
Henderson and the Occupation of Kentucky," *Mississippi Valley Historical Review*, I
(Dec. 1914).

in September 1775 to represent them before that body. But the appeal fell on deaf ears; Samuel Adams and Jefferson objected to the proprietary government and quit-rents, Jefferson advising the use of Virginia's charter rights to prevent the establishment of "any arbitrary or oppressive government" in the West. Unsuccessful before the Congress, the Transylvania Company next turned to Virginia, only to have the latter confiscate its lands and to organize Kentucky as a county of Virginia in October 1776. However, the company, in view of its purchase of the Cherokee title, received from Virginia in 1778 a grant of 200,000 acres located between the Green and the Ohio Rivers, south of the present site of Evansville, Indiana.[36]

Virginia's action, along with its success in undermining the claims of the Indiana Company and the Illinois-Wabash Company, sealed the doom of great proprietorships which combined the title to land and the powers of government in a few hands. Instead, the colonization of the West was to proceed through individual land grants to promoters and settlers, to be regulated by governments set up at first by the states with western land claims and later by the United States, and to culminate finally in new commonwealths of the democratic type.

The confiscation of the lands of king, proprietors, and loyalists put the state governments into the real estate business on a large scale. Maryland derived £450,000 from the sale of the lands it confiscated; New York obtained $3,085,000. The disposal of such lands did not establish economic equality among the people because those in the best position to buy were those who already possessed wealth. The state legislatures, however, asserted in theory the principle of equal distribution: in New York, where the sale of tracts in excess of five hundred acres was discouraged, two large estates were divided into 525 farms; North Carolina sold land at 50s. a hundred acres; all the southern states and New York gave land bounties to soldiers; and squatters were given preëmption rights. But despite such liberality, shrewd operators were able to amass huge speculative holdings. In New York, small holdings were acquired through dummy purchases, subsequently to be consolidated into large properties.[37] In New Jersey Governor Livingston charged that state commissioners who sold confiscated property used the proceeds to buy land for themselves and later settled their accounts with the state in depreciated currency

[36] For an antidote to A. Henderson's eulogistic treatment of Richard Henderson see William S. Lester, *The Transylvania Colony* (Spencer, Ind., 1935), a careful study.

[37] A scholarly, technical work by Thomas C. Cochran, *New York in the Confederation* (Philadelphia, 1932), treats finance and land.

which they procured for a trifle. Since Virginia was the grantor of land *par excellence* the fruits of redistribution are best observed in her experience.

Virginia's practice was to sell vacant lands as a means of paying state debts incurred during the war. Acts of 1779 authorized the sale of hundred-acre tracts at the rate of £40 each and provided that the holders of state certificates of indebtedness might exchange them for land. In 1776 the state promised bounties of a hundred acres to Virginians who enlisted in the Continental army; in 1779 the grants were enlarged and offered to those who served under George Rogers Clark and to commissioned and non-commissioned officers. Upon settlers who had, before 1778, occupied land without title, acts of 1777 and 1779 conferred preëmption rights to four hundred acres per family on condition that the settlers remain on the land one year and raise a crop of corn. In 1781 squatters were allowed to purchase hundred-acre tracts for 20s. each and were given two and a half years in which to pay.

Bending these laws to their purposes, promoters obtained great tracts in the West. They purchased at a discount the bounty warrants of soldiers unable or unwilling to migrate; they sent out servants to secure preëmption rights; and they converted state certificates of indebtedness (which represented the values of depreciated currency) into claims upon the land. Estates as large as 140,000 acres came into being. Likewise grants made before the war survived; in 1783 Washington's holdings beyond the mountains amounted to 58,000 acres. Richard Henderson and his partners received 200,000 acres in Kentucky from Virginia and 200,000 acres in Tennessee from North Carolina. By reason of large speculative acquisitions settlers found it difficult to obtain titles (the price of private lands in Kentucky was double the state sale price) and bitter antagonisms ensued, giving birth to reports in 1779 that pioneers were fleeing from speculators to lands held by Spain. Of the abuses of land speculation James Madison wrote, September 8, 1783: "Why did not the assembly stop the sale of land warrants? They bring no profit to the public treasury, are a source of constant speculation on the ignorant, and will finally arm numbers of citizens of other states and even foreigners with claims . . . against the faith of Virginia. Immense quantities have from time to time been vended in this place [Philadelphia] at immense profit. . . . The credulity here being exhausted I am told the land jobbers are going on with their commodity to Boston and other places." [38]

[38] C. H. Laub, "Revolutionary Virginia and the Crown Lands," *William and Mary Quarterly*, 2d Series, XI (Oct. 1931)—technical.

The revolution within the states did not resolve the underlying conflicts between the democratic forces and the upper class, despite their coöperation against the common foe. Several factors account for that coöperation during the war. First, both groups accepted the institution of private property, and since many small property owners hoped to become large owners, no general attack was made upon concentrated wealth *per se*. Again: the ideal of a government of limited powers which appealed to the democracy could also serve the aristocracy; constitutional guarantees of civil rights protected men of fortune as well as ordinary citizens, while the check and balance system safeguarded minorities against majority encroachments. Finally, an economy of small, privately owned farms forced the mass of the farmers (deficient as they were in capital) to depend upon merchants for credit and markets, thus enabling the merchants to accumulate substantial profits. For these reasons the democracy and the upper class could act together, each making gains that perpetuated its influence.[39]

In the sphere of government the democratic forces won some notable victories. The two requirements of political democracy were that the majority should rule within a state and that such a majority should not be curbed by an external government. Through the Articles of Confederation the democratic leaders triumphed by creating a weak central government that could not be used by the conservative elements to stifle the democratic forces when in control of a state. The new state constitutions gave the right to vote for members of the lower house of the legislature to practically all landholders and to small property owners in the towns. The upper house was somewhat democratized in that the senate, elected by property owners, replaced the old royal and proprietary councils, while in most states weak executives, chosen by state legislatures or by a popular electorate, superseded the royal and proprietary governors, who—in theory at least—had possessed extensive powers. In Georgia and Pennsylvania there was no senate to curb the house of representatives.[40] The states which most nearly attained the democratic ideal were New Jersey, Rhode Island, Pennsylvania, and Georgia.

In the economic and social sphere the gains of the democracy consisted principally in the destruction of feudal and aristocratic survivals: the quit-rents, primogeniture, entails, and the establishments of the

[39] An admirable study of the social aspects of the Revolution is Richard F. Upton's *Revolutionary New Hampshire* (Hanover, 1936).

[40] W. R. Smith, "Sectionalism in Pennsylvania during the Revolution," *Political Science Quarterly*, XXIV (June 1909).

Anglican Church. Nor were such vestiges of the past to extend into new settlements. And through military bounties and the sale of confiscated lands at low prices, landowning among the mass of the people was greatly increased.

Most of the gains of the democracy were made at the expense of British interests and the loyalists rather than at the expense of the conservatives who supported the Revolutionary cause. The latter held their own. First, the large landholdings of patriot leaders remained intact, thus preserving the plantation system and slavery and the tenant-occupied estates of the Van Rensselaer, Livingston, and Schuyler families in New York. Large landowners like James Duane, Charles Carroll, Thomas Johnson, Samuel Johnston, and Willie Jones of North Carolina retained their vast possessions. The conservative influence manifested itself in the state governments in two ways: in New York, Massachusetts, and Maryland the democracy was checked by the senate and the governor or by other executive devices which protected the larger property owners; in South Carolina and Virginia the back country was not given full representation in the lower house. At the end of the war the conservatives, though opposed by democratic forces, predominated in New Hampshire, Massachusetts, Connecticut,[41] New York, Maryland, Virginia, and South Carolina.

On the economic front the merchant class benefited through contracts for supplying the army, through wartime privateering, and through the paper profits from currency inflation which were invested partly in government loans later paid in more substantial values. Similarly, the confiscation of royal, proprietary, and loyalist property allowed investors to convert depreciated currency or its equivalent in state securities into warrants for land—a process which favored men of the greatest wealth. By 1791 twenty-one men had acquired claims to 5,432,200 acres in western New York. New commercial fortunes arose upon the ruined businesses of loyalist merchants, while the southern planters freed themselves from the debts they owed to British firms.

At two points, however, the conservative groups in 1783 were exposed to attack. In states where the democracy held control, the legislatures might at any moment enact laws detrimental to merchants, creditors, employers, and large landowners. Secondly, the federal government lacked the power to protect. It could not curb the state legislatures when they overissued legal tender paper money or passed

[41] Richard J. Purcell, *Connecticut in Transition, 1775–1818* (Washington, 1918), is an able analysis of social, economic, and political changes in the state.

laws enabling debtors to evade their obligations. So also the state courts, not subordinate to a federal judiciary, did not offer security to creditors in states where leveling tendencies prevailed. The Congress lacked the power to collect money for the payment of interest and principal on the national debt—a power necessary in order to give value to the securities which wealthy investors had purchased. Likewise, the Congress could not protect American commerce with foreign countries; and as long as the states retained the right to enact tariff laws the Congress could not guarantee that free flow of commodities across state boundaries which was so essential to the merchant class. Finally, should armed revolts against the upper class occur within the states the general government could not assure protection to those attacked. These defects of the Articles of Confederation became evident to the conservative leaders during the years 1783–86. The result was the formation in 1787 of the Federal Constitution, which provided new safeguards against ultra-democratic tendencies within the states.[42]

[42] See again C. A. and M. R. Beard, *Rise of American Civilization*, Vol. I, chapters 6–7.

## BIBLIOGRAPHICAL NOTE

WORKS PREVIOUSLY CITED: G. Bancroft, *History of the United States*, V, ch. 15; VI, chs. 26, 36, 46, 48; H. J. Carman, *Social and Economic History of the United States*, I, ch. 5; C. L. Becker, *Political Parties in the Province of New York*, chs. 10–11; D. R. Dewey, *Financial History of the United States*, ch. 2; A. C. Flick (ed.), *History of the State of New York*, III, chs. 9–10; IV, chs. 4–5; 10; W. B. Weeden, *Economic and Social History of New England*, II, chs. 20–21; G. M. Wrong, *Canada and the American Revolution*, chs. 18–23.

SOURCES NEWLY CITED: A highly important collection is *Letters of Members of the Continental Congress* (ed. Edmund C. Burnet, 8 vols., Washington, 1921–36). A readable collection of sources is R. W. Pettengill (trans.), *Letters from America, 1776–1779* (Boston, 1924). H. E. Egerton (ed.), *The Royal Commission on the Losses and Services of American Loyalists, 1783–1785* (Oxford, 1915), reprints memorials showing effects of the Revolution on the loyalists. See also chapter 1 of Felix Flügel and H. U. Faulkner, *Readings in the Economic and Social History of the United States* (New York, 1929).

SOURCES PREVIOUSLY CITED: G. S. Callender (ed.), *Selections from the Economic History of the United States*, ch. 4, parts 2–3; E. L. Bogart and C. M. Thompson (eds.), *Readings in the Economic History of the United States*, ch. 5, parts 3–4; H. S. Commager (ed.), *Documents of American History*, nos. 67–76; A. B. Hart, (ed.), *American History Told by Contemporaries*, II, chs. 26–27, 30, 33; W. MacDonald (ed.), *Documentary Source Book of American History*, no. 51; S. E. Morison (ed.), *Sources . . . illustrating the American Revolution*, pp. 148–203; *Old South Leaflets*, nos. 2, 173, 206, 209.

# XXV

# WAR AND DIPLOMACY

Six and a half years elapsed between the opening of the Revolutionary War and the surrender of Cornwallis at Yorktown, October 19, 1781. The conflict lasted so long because the British and American antagonists each possessed peculiar advantages which made impossible a speedy triumph by either side.[1]

## Factors in the War

Let us consider first the influences which favored Britain, the foremost of which was her superior commercial and financial strength. By 1775 Britain had achieved supremacy in world commerce and a large favorable trade balance which represented a part of the profits of her merchants and manufacturers. In time of peace such surplus profits were commonly invested in overseas enterprises and in domestic industry. When war came it was the practice of the British capitalists to lend their surpluses to the government—a process which gave the government command of commodities, cash, and credit in foreign lands. Such public loans benefited the merchants in two ways: first, they received interest from the government; secondly, contracts for supplying the armed forces afforded new sources of profit. The leading merchants, said Edmund Burke in 1775, "are kept full fed with contracts and remittances and jobs of all descriptions and are indefatigable in their endeavors to keep the others quiet. . . . They all, or the greatest number of them, begin to sniff the cadaverous *haut goût* of lucrative war."

Britain's financial strength exhibited itself at first in the superiority of its army. In 1775 the British forces in the thirteen colonies numbered about nine thousand men. Some strategists in Britain proposed to subdue the colonies by naval blockades, but since an army was already on the ground and under attack the North ministry decided that it could not be withdrawn without loss of prestige, and hence Britain was committed to a war on land. General Gage's estimate that twenty thousand men were required to subdue New England

[1] See again C. H. Van Tyne, *The War of Independence*, chapters 3–14, 18–23.

necessitated an expansion of the British army, which in 1775 contained only thirty thousand men in far-flung garrisons throughout the empire. Because the iron discipline and the low pay of the army did not appeal to the English people (who disliked militarism to begin with) the enlistment of volunteers failed to provide a desired force of twenty thousand new men; and even the impressment of vagabonds and convicts did not suffice. Accordingly the government sought mercenaries abroad. After a plan to secure Russian troops fell through, Britain contracted in 1775 with the rulers of small German states (Hesse-Cassel, Brunswick, Waldeck, and Ansbach) for eighteen thousand men. By its contract with the Duke of Brunswick, Britain agreed to pay him £7 4s. 4½d. for each soldier he supplied, an equal sum for each of his subjects killed in the war, half this sum for each man wounded, and a yearly subsidy of £11,517 during the war, plus £23,034 a year for two years after the war. The total number of mercenaries obtained before 1781 was about twenty thousand.[2]

Other British forces consisted of American loyalists and the Indians. On several occasions British campaign plans anticipated that uprisings of loyalists would strengthen the king's army—a hope rarely realized. The loyalist forces reached their peak in December 1780 when about eight thousand were attached to the British army at New York. A few loyalist units such as Ferguson's American Riflemen, Lincoln's Queen's Rangers, Tarleton's Legion, and Butler's Tory Rangers did effective work. For two reasons the northern Indians sided with Britain. First, the British monopolized the northern fur trade upon which the Indians were utterly dependent; secondly, the Americans now threatened the Indians' hunting lands, whereas Britain was endeavoring to preserve them against the inroads of settlement.

The discipline, organization and equipment of the British army gave it the initial advantage. The German mercenaries were seasoned soldiers, accustomed to obey orders and not subject to panic when under fire. However, they were poorly paid, indifferent, and unwilling to "fight their hearts out" for a cause. Since the loyalists in most places were a minority their adherence to a British army of occupation raised a serious problem: when the army moved, they could not be left to the vengeance of their neighbors, yet their removal greatly hampered the progress of the troops. Again, since there were more non-combatants than fighters among the loyalists they often impaired the offensive strength of the army by compelling it to defend civilians. As to the Indians: although they were used to harry the frontiers,

[2] See again E. Channing, *History of the United States,* Vol. III, pp. 210–408.

their outrages served chiefly to embitter the Americans. Moreover, the Indians could be counted upon to take to the woods when the war went against the British.

While Britain could rely chiefly upon trained veterans enlisted for the duration of the war, the Americans had to depend upon an improvised army of uncertain composition. The ordinary farmer, who had to keep his farm going, could not remain for long away from home; this meant short-term enlistments, a large turnover in army personnel, and the frequent replacement of seasoned soldiers with raw recruits. Such changes weakened the army because the American volunteer was inexperienced in the art of fighting an organized force in open warfare. The first exposure to gunfire is certain to be a terrible experience to the novice; a series of engagements is usually necessary to harden the soldier against the ever-present danger of panic. Established armies cope with fright by means of the sternest discipline. But such an advantage was denied to the Americans because in 1775 they were intensely individualistic; not accustomed to obeying orders, they regarded their officers as equals whose commands need not be heeded if one's life were at stake.[3] Nor did the American army at the outset possess seasoned officers. Washington, who towered above the others, had earned his reputation in frontier Indian fighting and had not devoted himself to military affairs for a decade. When he took command at Cambridge in 1775 he found such a motley array of citizens that he suggested the uniform of the hunting shirt to give some semblance of order. Of Israel Putnam, the fifth ranking general in June 1775, Beard states that he "insisted on riding at the head of his men at Boston in his shirt sleeves with an old hat on his head as if he were still in the cornfield."

To sustain the war fever at a pitch conducive to recruiting proved to be a task of the first magnitude, especially when the people were not directly menaced by British invasion. Relying chiefly upon volunteers, the states were compelled to offer material inducements: of patriotism Washington said that "a great and lasting war can never be supported on this principle alone. It must be aided by a prospect of interest and some reward." Cash bounties to recruits were increased as the paper money in which they were paid depreciated; slaves who enlisted received their freedom; deserters from the British army were taken into the American ranks. In New England the towns were required to raise quotas of soldiers; when volunteers did not respond, the draft and the hiring of substitutes were resorted to. Two men in

[3] C. K. Bolton, *The Private Soldier under Washington* (New York, 1902), is a brief, careful, realistic study of army conditions.

Connecticut could escape service if they kept one soldier in the field—
a practice which brought many free Negroes into the army. In 1781
Virginia gave three hundred acres of land and a prime Negro slave
or £60 in specie to volunteers. But despite such practices heroic efforts
were needed to keep a Continental army of five thousand men intact. Numerous desertions enhanced the difficulty.[4]

Britain's attack on the import trade of the states curtailed their
normal supply of manufactured goods at a time when American industries were not geared to high-speed production. Throughout the
war there was an acute stortage of clothing, blankets, tents, shoes,
muskets, cannon, powder, and shot. The American stock of gunpowder in April 1775 consisted of the stores seized from government
garrisons; by December the supply was exhausted and for two months
Washington's army besieging Boston had practically no powder at
all.[5] There was no Red Cross, Y.M.C.A., or adequate hospital service
for the relief of the distressed; hence the prevalence of such conditions as those described by General Wayne: "No medicine or regimen
suitable for the sick, no beds of straw to lie on, no covering to keep
them warm other than their own wretched clothing." "Our hospital,
or rather our house of carnage, beggars all description and shocks all
humanity to visit." In 1776 Washington told of the difficulty of operating an army "without any money in our treasury, powder in our
magazines, arms in our stores . . . and by and by, when we shall
be called upon to take the field, shall not have a tent to lie in." General Schuyler testified in 1777 that "our army . . . is weak in numbers, dispirited, naked, in a manner, destitute of provisions, without
camp equipage, with little ammunition, and not a single piece of
cannon." Such conditions persisted until the end of the war.[6]

Britain's naval supremacy gave superior mobility to her army, enabling it before 1778 to move up and down the coast and to occupy
almost at will any American seaport. Philadelphia was easily taken,
though evacuated; at the end of the war the British occupied New
York, Charleston, Wilmington, and Savannah. Between 1776 and
1778 British vessels seized nine hundred American ships and practically ruined New England's fishery. But even the British navy

[4] Louis C. Hatch, *The Administration of the American Army* (New York, 1904),
emphasizes state jealousies as a cause of the ineffective, decentralized conduct of the war.
"The people were often indifferent, the officers captious and quarrelsome, and Congress
inefficient and negligent" (p. 196).

[5] O. W. Stephenson, "The Supply of Gunpowder in 1776," *American Historical
Review*, XXX (Jan. 1925).

[6] John C. Fitzpatrick, *The Spirit of the Revolution* (Boston, 1924), treats neglected
phases of war administration.

could not enforce an effective blockade of the entire coast; armed merchantmen slipped in and out of the ports, maintaining a hazardous trade with Europe and the West Indies which kept the American cause on its feet.[7]

Against the advantages of Britain the Americans possessed one supreme asset—a blended influence of geography, economic organization, and the character of the people. In 1775 there were about 250,000 men of military age in the American population of nearly three million souls. The mass of the people were tough-fibered and inured to hardship and privation. Overwhelmingly anti-British in sentiment, they were determined when fighting for the security of their homes, even if unwilling to enlist for remote campaigns. Adept in the use of firearms, they were masters of guerilla warfare, accustomed to the climate, and familiar with the country they were defending. Courage and hardihood counted for more in the long run than discipline and obedience. Of his men at Valley Forge Washington wrote: "Naked and starving as they are we cannot enough admire the patience and fidelity of the soldiery." Nor should the sacrifices and achievements of the American women be ignored. They plied their spinning wheels and knitting needles, nursed the stricken, tended the farms, worked in the fields, and carried on occupations while their menfolk were away at war. The economic organization of thousands of settlements extending more than a thousand miles along the coast and over three hundred miles into the interior was so decentralized that British control of a single seaport or a river did not give command of a large territory; most communities might eke out an existence in virtual isolation. To hold an area the British were obliged to occupy it with troops; their influence did not then extend beyond their lines, which were constantly exposed to attack; and when they moved they left behind, not a conquered territory, but a defiant people in arms.[8]

Had the British army been able to strike any community at a moment's notice, a permanent conquest might have been effected. But transportation conditions made that impossible; forest trails, roads that at times resembled mudholes, creeks and rivers without bridges, the lack of supply centers and a woeful shortage of wagons, horses, and oxen made troop movements cumbersome in the extreme. The heavier equipment of the British army delayed its advances and en-

[7] C. O. Paullin, *The Navy in the American Revolution* (Cleveland, 1906), a specialized study of naval policy and administration, concludes that the lack of seamen was the chief weakness of the American navy.

[8] Edward E. Curtis, *The Organization of the British Army in America* (New Haven, 1927), describes many of the difficulties encountered by the British.

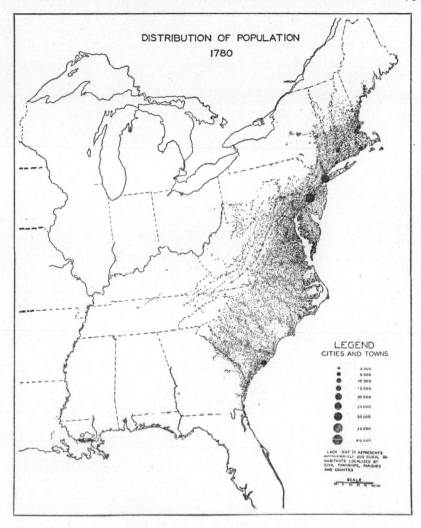

DISTRIBUTION OF POPULATION
1780

LEGEND
CITIES AND TOWNS

abled the American forces, lightly burdened, to elude their pursuers. All the greater were the difficulties of transport when horses, wagons, provisions, gunpowder, and artillery had to be sent from Britain. The uncertainties of transportation made it well-nigh impossible for the British to calculate the time element in campaigns. Since the British ministry directed the war from Westminster, weeks and months elapsed before orders reached officers in America; serious mistakes could not be rectified within a year. The handicaps which now confronted Britain demonstrated how important had been the aid of the once despised colonial forces during the French and Indian War.[9]

The remoteness of the British army from its center of control magnified the responsibility of the officers in command in America. Unfortunately for Britain her generals did not rise to the occasion. Sir William Howe, commander-in-chief from 1775 to February 1778 did not press the war with vigor. Some of his critics attributed his laxity to dissipation and love of luxury; others believed him too friendly to the Americans. Since he had opposed the Coercive Acts and had declared that he would not serve against the colonies, his appointment to the chief command is something of a mystery. As a believer in conciliation he may have reasoned that a savage, destructive war would so antagonize the Americans that they would never afterward feel that sense of loyalty necessary to bind to Britain settlements so dispersed and so remote. At any rate military experts agree that on several occasions Howe let slip the opportunity to deal the American army a crushing blow.[10] His successor, Sir Henry Clinton—who replaced Howe in February 1778—was a mediocre man, while Lord Cornwallis, in command of the southern campaigns, 1780–81, "distinguished" himself chiefly by his surrender at Yorktown.

Britain's naval strength enabled her only to impair—not to destroy—American commerce. The states commissioned a host of privateers which by February 1778 had captured six hundred British vessels. "The damage we have done their West India trade," wrote Franklin in February 1777, "has been estimated by the merchants of London at £1,800,000 sterling, which has raised insurance to 28 per cent, higher than at any time in the last war with France and Spain." The sale of prizes and their cargoes in American ports helped sustain the import trade: one prize sold in Georgia netted £21,138 sterling. Prior to 1780 the southern states, free from invasion, continued normal production, and American blockade runners and European vessels, as neutrals, carried tobacco to northern Europe and rice to the Mediterranean regions. Some of the British West Indian merchants, needing American provisions, connived in illegal trade with the states, while the foreign islands—Dutch St. Eustatius, Danish St. Thomas, and

[9] Francis V. Greene's *The Revolutionary War* . . . (New York, 1911), a concise, well-told story of the military events, emphasizes the elements of strength in the American cause.

[10] Troyer S. Anderson, *The Command of the Howe Brothers during the American Revolution* (New York, 1936), an elaborate critique for the advanced student, criticizes the theory of Howe's Whiggish sympathies for the colonists and explains his failure by the material obstacles encountered in America and by lack of support at home.

French Martinique—served as depots for goods en route to and from Europe.[11] Prior to the autumn of 1777 nearly 80 per cent of the American supply of gunpowder was imported—chiefly from France via the West Indies. The gains of American merchants engaged in privateering are suggested by Franklin's remark in 1779: "The extravagant luxury of our country in the midst of all its distress is to me amazing."

The profits of privateering diverted capital from manufacturing industry and thus retarded its progress during the war, despite the stimuli of the needs of the army, the removal of British restraints on American industry, and the dearth of European goods in the states. Shipbuilders, no longer able to sell to British merchants, went in for the construction of "sharp-prowed, speedy vessels" to serve as privateers. Under the impetus of state bounties, the production of gunpowder yielded about 10 per cent of the quantity used by the American army before the autumn of 1777: 115,000 pounds from domestic saltpetre and 698,245 from imported saltpetre. Powder made at Weymouth, Massachusetts, had the force to drive leaden balls two inches into an oak tree at a distance of eight rods. Philadelphia produced brass and iron cannon, and an arsenal at Springfield, Massachusetts, supplied the army in part with artillery and rifles. The shortage of salt (a necessity previously imported) led the New Englanders to evaporate salt water in shallow pans; the supply thus obtained however was small, as indicated by the price of salt—18¢ a bushel in 1774; $6.00 a bushel in 1781. In 1775 Philadelphia investors organized a company "for promoting American manufactures" which concentrated upon the production of linen, woolen, and cotton cloth; however, homespun continued to be the mainstay of domestic textile production. The shortage and dearness of labor, together with the enemy's menace to mills and factories, deterred cautious capitalists from investing in such enterprises. Thus the Congress had to establish the government munition works at Springfield in 1778. Since most of New England escaped the ravages of war and because its fishery was all but ruined, conditions for manufacturing industries were the most favorable there. Hence the establishment of gun factories or powder mills at Sutton, Andover, Stoughton, Bradford, Waterbury, and North Providence. Due to wartime destruction of old property and of articles currently produced, workshops and mills could not meet the demand for new capital and consumers' goods: in 1781 the states

[11] J. F. Jameson, "St. Eustatius in the American Revolution," *American Historical Review*, VIII (July 1903).

—with respect to their supply of manufactured products—resembled a dry sponge.[12]

The critical events of 1763–75 had brought to the front a group of leaders in each colony, made them known to each other, steeled them in opposition to Britain, and tested their abilities. For one such leader who, like Benedict Arnold, broke under the strain of war, there were a score who stood firm. A country that could produce a general like Washington, a diplomat like Franklin, political leaders like John Adams, Jefferson, and Samuel Adams, and a group of energetic war governors such as Hancock, Trumbull, William Livingston, Thomas Johnson, George Clinton, and Patrick Henry was certainly not deficient in resolute men. Above them all towered the statuesque figure of Washington, determined, patient, persevering, and practical, a man who made concrete knowledge the basis of thinking and who translated thought into action—a completely integrated, fearless personality. His greatest asset was his ability to rise above discouragement and to gain strength by conquering adversity. "Defeat," he said, "is only a reason for exertion. We shall do better next time." [13]

In an accounting of the factors which aided the American cause the assistance received from foreign sources must be given much weight. That will become evident as we review the events of the war.

## The First Phase of the War, 1775–77

When the British fell back from Concord to Boston on April 19, 1775, the farmer militiamen of New England immediately besieged the city. By June the British army numbered ten thousand men and Gage had been joined by Generals Howe, Clinton, and Burgoyne. Occupying a narrow peninsula, the British forces were in effect cooped up on an island, since the besieging Americans held the approaches to the mainland. Boston had little strategic value but both contestants sought an early victory for the sake of prestige. On the night of June 16–17 the Americans occupied the heights of Charlestown north of Boston proper, across the Charles River. Realizing that from such

[12] See again V. S. Clark, *History of Manufactures in the United States to 1860*, chapter 10.

[13] Rupert Hughes, *George Washington* (3 vols., New York, 1926–30), the most extensive and the most readable modern biography, traces Washington's career to 1781. Of many older biographies the best for the general reader is P. L. Ford, *The True George Washington* (Philadelphia, 1896—republished in 1924 as *George Washington*). This is a character study, not a military history. John C. Fitzpatrick's *George Washington Himself* (Indianapolis, 1933) supplements the orthodox biographies with much out-of-the-way information.

positions (Bunker Hill, Breed's Hill) the Americans could bombard
the British forces in the town and harbor, the British generals immediately ordered an attack. After twice repulsing British charges
the Americans had to retreat from Breed's hill when their ammunition gave out, but only after they had inflicted losses three times
those sustained by themselves.[14] The continued siege of Boston, which
lasted until March 1776, imposed severe hardship and suffering on
the townspeople during the winter, since the American army was able
to cut off most supplies from the outside. Meanwhile, the Americans
had so strengthened their position that a British victory could have
been won only at a cost far in excess of any possible advantage. Accordingly, on March 17, 1776, the British evacuated Boston and
moved to Halifax, Nova Scotia, accompanied by nine hundred civilian
loyalists.

British strategists continued to regard New England as the center
of American resistance but, despairing of subduing that stubborn
region by direct conquest, they turned to the plan of dominating New
York, thereby severing New England from outside reinforcements
and supplies. This project entailed the occupation of Manhattan
Island, whence an expedition might ascend the Hudson to join a
companion force from Canada. Having obtained reinforcements in
Nova Scotia, Howe took possession of Staten Island in July 1776.
Washington, in anticipation of Howe's plans, shifted his army from
Boston and occupied Brooklyn Heights which commanded the town
of New York, then confined to the southern tip of Manhattan Island.
But Howe quickly crossed to Long Island, defeated an American
army in front of Brooklyn Heights and compelled Washington to
take refuge on Manhattan Island, north of Harlem.[15] In September
Howe occupied the town of New York. In order to gain mastery of
the Hudson valley he was soon compelled to attack three American
strongholds: Fort Washington at the northern end of Manhattan
Island, Fort Lee across the Hudson in New Jersey, and the territory
about White Plains, a few miles east of the Hudson. A narrow British victory at White Plains, October 28, placed Howe in a position
to menace either New England or the middle states. Accordingly,
Washington divided his army, placing one force in New Jersey between the Hudson and the Hackensack Rivers (to guard Philadelphia)
and leaving another force under Charles Lee in the vicinity of White

[14] Allen French's *The First Year of the American Revolution* (Boston, 1934) is a
detailed history of the military events of 1775.

[15] Charles F. Adams, *Studies Military and Diplomatic* (New York, 1911), contains
four essays which portray Washington as an inferior general saved by Howe's incompetence.

Plains. The British then seized Fort Lee and advanced upon Washington's army in New Jersey, compelling him to call upon Lee for aid. But Lee, ever jealous of Washington, delayed until too late and was finally captured by the British. Greatly outnumbered, Washington's army had to flee, passing through Newark to the Delaware River, which they crossed near Trenton just before Howe's army occupied that town on December 8. When Lee surrendered on December 13 the American cause seemed lost.[16]

By seizing all boats along the Delaware, Washington checked the pursuit of the British at that river. Desirous of a victory to restore the sagging morale of his troops Washington executed the desperate stroke of crossing the Delaware on Christmas night—a surprise movement which enabled his men to defeat the British at Trenton and to take as prisoners over a thousand Hessians (December 26). This victory revived the spirits of the American army and rekindled hope throughout the states. After defeating the British at Princeton, January 3, 1777, Washington went into winter quarters at Morristown, New Jersey, while Howe's retirement to Burlington left most of New Jersey free from British control.[17]

As in the French and Indian War, so also in the Revolution Canada played a decisive role. The Americans desired to acquire the province in order to gain a fourteenth state and to prevent British attacks from the north. Early in 1775 Massachusetts and Connecticut sent expeditions which united (under the command of Ethan Allen) and took Forts Ticonderoga and Crown Point (May 10, 12), valuable for their stores of war supplies and for their strategic location on the route to Canada. This success opened the path for a Continental force under Richard Montgomery which traversed Lake Champlain and entered Montreal, November 12, 1775. About the same time Benedict Arnold led an expedition through the Maine wilderness, via the Kennebec and Chaudière Rivers, arriving before Quebec on November 13 with less than half of his original force of eleven hundred men. Arnold's attack on Quebec having failed, he waited until Montgomery joined him for a combined assault, which the British repulsed on December 31. Arnold, taking command by virtue of Montgomery's death, continued the siege until desertions, sickness (smallpox), and the arrival of a British fleet compelled him to evacuate Canada (June 1776). Sir Guy Carleton, governor-general of Quebec

[16] The military campaigns are given exhaustive treatment in Vol. III of the Hon. Sir John W. Fortescue's *A History of the British Army*.

[17] Louis M. Sears, *George Washington* (New York, c. 1932), is a factual, conventional treatment, heavily weighted on the military side.

"The Yankie Doodle's Intrenchments near Boston, 1776."

"Publish'd as the Act Directs"

and commander of Britain's northern army, pursued Arnold to Lake Champlain. By skillfully contesting Carleton's advance, Arnold held the British from Crown Point till October 14, thus keeping them from the Hudson and saving Washington's army from a northern attack when it was being hard pressed from the south by Howe.[18]

Britain's war strategy in 1777 called for an invasion of the Hudson valley. General John Burgoyne was to lead an army from Canada via Lake Champlain to Albany; a second force under Lieutenant-Colonel Barry St. Leger was to proceed to Albany by way of Lake Ontario and the Mohawk River; and an army from New York was to ascend the Hudson for a junction with Burgoyne. Such maneuvers would either divide the thirteen states at the Hudson (which the Americans still commanded above the northern boundary of New Jersey) or, by engaging American forces in the north, prevent their giving aid to Washington's army against Howe farther south. But there was one flaw in British plans. Burgoyne was not responsible to Howe at New York; instead he was under the orders of the British Colonial Secretary at Westminster, Lord George Germain, an incompetent man, poorly informed of American conditions. In the meantime Howe had decided to move his main army against Philadelphia, hoping that Washington would defend the city and thus expose himself to a pitched battle that would annihilate his army and end the war. Accordingly, Howe notified the army in Canada that he could not give it aid beyond his "endeavor to have a corps on the lower part of Hudson's River sufficient to open the communications by shipping through the Highlands . . . which corps may afterward act in favor of the northern army." Howe's Philadelphia plans received the approval of Germain, who expressed the hope that Howe might return from the Quaker city in time to coöperate on the Hudson. Burgoyne in turn interpreted his orders to mean that he must advance down the Hudson at all costs.[19]

On July 23, 1777, Howe embarked for Philadelphia with sixteen thousand men; on August 25 he arrived at the Head of Elk in Chesapeake Bay. The protracted voyage had enabled Washington to place his forces between the Chesapeake and Philadelphia at Chad's Ford, where the road from the Head of Elk met Brandywine Creek. In the ensuing battle of Brandywine (September 11), Washington was again able to extricate his inferior army intact, but not to turn back the

[18] Justin H. Smith, *Our Struggle for the Fourteenth Colony* (New York, 1907), is a definitive treatment of the role of Canada. See also William Wood, *The Father of British Canada* (*Chronicles of Canada* series, Toronto, 1916).

[19] G. H. Guttridge, "Lord George Germain in Office," *American Historical Review,* XXXIII (Oct. 1927).

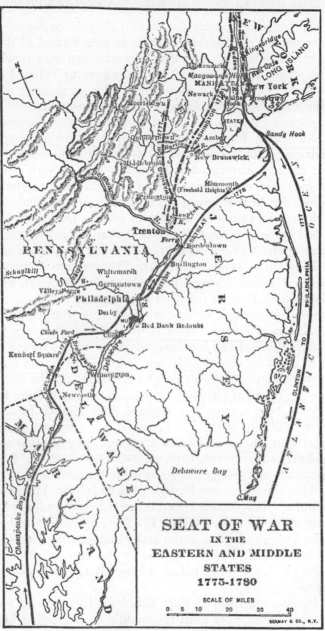

SEAT OF WAR
IN THE
EASTERN AND MIDDLE
STATES
1775-1780

SCALE OF MILES

0  5  10        20        30        40

BORMAY & CO., N.Y.

From "Atlas of American History." © Harper & Brothers.

British, who began the occupation of Philadelphia on September 25. Howe then needed three weeks in order to gain control of the Delaware River. Washington's attack at Germantown was repulsed on October 4, whereupon he retired for the winter to Valley Forge on the Schuylkill, a few miles above Philadelphia—a position which restricted the area from which Howe could obtain supplies.

Having set forth from Canada on June 20, 1777, Burgoyne had little trouble taking Ticonderoga (July 6), after which he advanced to Skenesborough, only twenty miles from the Hudson. But to traverse that distance, through a wilderness whose difficulties General Schuyler increased with every sort of impediment, required three weeks before the British gained Fort Edward on the Hudson (July 30). By this time transportation troubles and the inadequacy of army supplies had become so painfully evident that Burgoyne sent a force of Germans under Colonel Baum to seize American stores of provisions at Bennington (now Vermont). The resolute Indian-fighter, John Stark, rallied the frontiersmen, who dealt the British a decisive defeat that cost them eight hundred men.

Elsewhere the fortunes of war frowned upon Burgoyne. Colonel St. Leger, having collected a force of six hundred European troopers and a band of Indians and loyalists, advanced from Oswego to Fort Stanwix, to which he immediately laid siege. The German settlers of the Mohawk valley came to its relief and fought off the invaders in a savage engagement at Oriskany near the fort. Meanwhile, Benedict Arnold [20] had been sent up the Mohawk with a small force. When about twenty miles from the fort he dispatched a messenger with the false report that Burgoyne had surrendered. The Indians mutinied and plundered their British companions, whereupon St. Leger retreated posthaste to Oswego and returned to Canada.

When Howe departed for Philadelphia he left Sir Henry Clinton in command at New York. The cautious Clinton awaited for reinforcements before he moved up the Hudson; not until October 5 did he take the American forts, Clinton and Montgomery, which guarded the river between the Highlands, and by the time British ships had reached Esopus, sixty miles below Albany, Burgoyne's position had become hopeless.

After Burgoyne arrived at Fort Edward (July 30) he was compelled to wait for supplies until the middle of September before he

---

[20] There are three recent undistinguished biographies, each entitled *Benedict Arnold*; one by Oscar Sherwin (1931); one by Malcolm Decker (1932); and one by Edward D. Sullivan (1932). The best modern analysis of Arnold's character is Charles C. Sellers, *Benedict Arnold* (New York, 1930). See also the article by R. G. Adams in the *Dictionary of American Biography*, Vol. I, pp. 362–367.

could proceed down the Hudson. Meanwhile the fight at Bennington had given the signal for the farmers of New England to join the American army in Burgoyne's path. They responded with such alacrity that the British force was soon outnumbered four to one. The Americans, commanded by General Horatio Gates, occupied Bemis Heights about twenty-five miles below Fort Edward—a site which enabled them to dominate the road along the west bank of the Hudson. Two attacks by Burgoyne having been repulsed (September 19, October 7), the British fell back to Saratoga, where—surrounded by the Americans—they surrendered, October 14. A convention of October 17 permitted Burgoyne's exhausted men (now numbering only 4,880) to go to Boston for embarkation to England on condition that they would not again participate in the American war.[21]

## The United States Secure Foreign Aid

Saratoga ranks as one of the decisive events of the Revolution because it induced France to join the United States in an alliance which contributed greatly to the final victory. Although the peace of 1763 had effected a redistribution of colonial possessions it had not removed the old antagonisms which divided Britain, France, and Spain.[22] After 1762, European capital and labor previously devoted to war sought the channels of trade and oversea investments, thereby prolonging the contest for colonial supremacy. Inasmuch as the three powers adhered to the rule of excluding all foreigners from access to the markets, raw materials, and profit opportunities of their empires, the aggrandizement of one promised to weaken the others, and because imperialism was animated by economic expansion, each state felt it necessary to enlarge its possessions; hence a permanent pacification was impossible. Deprived of Canada and Louisiana, France now concentrated upon her sugar islands, Santo Domingo, Martinique, and Guadeloupe, bringing them to such a high peak of development that she threatened to engross the sugar trade. An estimate of 1766 indicated that France's West Indian commerce exceeded Britain's by 50 per cent and that of the Dutch by 300 per cent. The Duc de Choiseul, France's foreign minister until 1770, proposed to build a new French empire (*La France Equinoxile*) in the region of the Gulf of Mexico and the West Indies, intending, in part, to expel Britain from the trade of

---

[21] Jane Clark, "Responsibility for the Failure of the Burgoyne Campaign," *American Historical Review*, XXXV (April 1930).

[22] James B. Perkins, *France in the American Revolution* (Boston, 1911), thorough, readable, and scholarly, explains American success in terms of French aid.

Spanish America and to divert it to France. Spain, now holding three-fourths of the habitable parts of the Americas and the richest and largest of the West Indian islands, possessed an empire that surpassed her power of control. The British continued to carry on illegal trade with Spanish colonial ports, much to the dismay of the Spanish king, Charles III, the key of whose policy was the preservation of the territory of his empire plus the exclusion of foreigners from its trade and whose animating spirit was hatred of Britain. He denied to the British the right even to navigate the Pacific Ocean, to which the Earl of Chatham replied that "England would sooner consent to give up the Tower of London than to abandon that right." Bitterly resenting Britain's previous conquests of Gibraltar, Minorca, and Florida, the Spaniards, like the French, awaited an opportunity for revenge.[23]

A series of disputes pertaining to the Mediterranean, India, Africa, America, and the West Indies kept the antagonists at swords' points after 1763, Britain and Spain even venturing to the brink of war in 1770. Satisfied with the spoils of 1763, Britain desired peace; France's depleted finances restrained her ambitions; Spain was in a state of chronic unpreparedness. However, some coöperation between the two Bourbon states was maintained as Spain granted commercial privileges to France in Spanish America and France sent engineers to Spanish dockyards to bolster up the Spanish navy.[24]

In her search for new allies France turned her gaze toward Britain's disaffected colonists, to whom after 1762 she dispatched secret agents instructed to fan the flames of discontent, to express the friendly attitude of France, and to get information about the resources, topography, and defenses of the colonies. Realizing that Britain's strength arose from her commerce, to which North America contributed so handsomely, the French saw in a war of revenge the means of gaining that commerce for themselves, thereby weakening their rival and reëstablishing their sorely damaged prestige.

When the American crisis was reached in 1775, both in England and in the colonies the likelihood of French intervention was discussed. The Earl of Chatham likened France to a "vulture hovering over the British empire, and hungrily watching the prey that she is only waiting for the right moment to pounce upon." American sentiment was at first unprepared for a French alliance, due to the hatreds

---

[23] See again *The Cambridge History of the British Empire*, Vol. I, pp. 685–783.
[24] E. S. Corwin, *French Policy and the American Alliance of 1778* (Princeton, 1916), interprets French and Spanish objectives in terms of self-interest and hostility toward Britain.

engendered by the colonial wars, to the dominant Catholicism of France, and to her despotic government. However, the need of foreign military supplies and of the aid of a strong naval power soon overcame such repugnance, which had already been lessened by trade with the French West Indies and by commerce with France at the time of the non-importation agreements. In November 1775 the Congress appointed a secret committee to correspond "with the friends of America"; in the ensuing winter the committee received hopeful assurances of assistance from a French agent, one Bonvouloir; on March 2, 1776, the Congress sent Silas Deane to buy supplies in Paris.[25] One argument in favor of the Declaration of Independence was the necessity of cutting loose from Britain before America could expect substantial foreign aid. In September the Congress decided to appeal to France for a formal recognition of independence and for a treaty of commerce, whereupon Franklin and Jefferson were named to act with Deane in Paris. Jefferson did not serve, his place being taken by Arthur Lee, a young Virginian then in London. The bait offered to France was the commerce of the United States and American aid for a French conquest of the British sugar islands.[26]

Several influences active before 1778 impelled the French king, Louis XVI, to withhold open assistance. His finance minister, Turgot, warned that a war with Britain would bankrupt France; moreover, he discounted the benefits of American commerce, believing that it would continue to center in Britain, regardless of the outcome of the war. On two occasions news of an American defeat cooled the ardor of the French—in October 1776 and a year later when Howe occupied Philadelphia. And yet another thing deterred Louis XVI; France might set a bad example to subject peoples at home and abroad by encouraging the American rebels. Eager "to wound and yet afraid to strike," France proclaimed her neutrality and granted secret aid.

Other forces worked for an open alliance. The foreign minister of Louis XVI, the Comte de Vergennes, an inflexible enemy of Britain, labored incessantly to convince the court that the American war offered France an ideal opportunity to restore her own fortunes by striking down Britain. "She is an enemy," he wrote, "at once grasping, ambitious, unjust, and perfidious. The invariable and most cherished purpose in her politics has been, if not the destruction of France, at

[25] George L. Clark's brief study, *Silas Deane* (New York, 1913), deals principally with the French episode.

[26] C. H. Van Tyne, "French Aid before the Alliance of 1778," *American Historical Review*, XXXI (Oct. 1925).

least her overthrow, her humiliation and her ruin." France must aid
the Americans, argued Vergennes, lest Britain make peace and conciliate them by seizing the French sugar islands and by opening them
to American trade; or, if the colonies should win their independence,
Britain would seek compensation by seizing the French islands. Of
similar views was an influential courtier, merchant capitalist, and versatile man of letters and fashion, Caron de Beaumarchais, whose enthusiasm for the Americans and liberty was exceeded only by his detestation of Britain and his patriotic fervor. With every sort of
argument he urged, even commanded, the king: *"We must aid the
Americans."* [27]

When Deane arrived in Paris he had no official status, since France
had not recognized the United States as an independent country;
hence he had to approach the court in devious ways. The British, following his every move through a highly efficient secret service, asked
that he be expelled from Paris—a request which Vergennes flatly refused.[28] The British found themselves in a dilemma: they did not
care to press France to the point of war and they wanted to discourage
the Americans by minimizing the possibility of French participation;
hence they could not make of French assistance a public issue or a
*casus belli.* To Beaumarchais the French government granted a million livres wherewith he operated a commercial house, Hortalez and
Company, which supplied the Americans with the sinews of war. By
October 1776 Deane had procured clothing for twenty thousand men,
muskets for thirty thousand, and large quantities of gunpowder. "Nor
was this all. Restrictions upon trade were relaxed in favor of American vessels; American privateers were harbored and fitted out, and
their prizes sold in French ports; the construction of ships of war
was carried on under the superintendence of French naval officers"
(Headlam). With the connivance of the government, many French
volunteers sailed for America—idle army officers, bankrupt adventurers, soldiers of fortune, and enthusiastic friends of liberty—seeking
new careers, new opportunities to smite Britain, new excitements.
Most prominent of such volunteers was the Marquis de Lafayette, a
young army officer who longed to exalt France, to abase England, and
to demonstrate his military talents. He joined Washington's army as
a general, serving without pay and giving such a good account of
himself that he won the respect of the great American whom he re-

[27] C. H. Van Tyne, "Influences which determined the French Government to make
the Treaty with America, 1778," *American Historical Review*, XXI (Oct. 1915).
[28] S. F. Bemis, "British Secret Service and the French-American Alliance," *American
Historical Review*, XXIX (April 1924).

garded with a measure of hero-worship.[29] The chief contribution of France before 1778 was the supplying of munitions, without which the American army would have been quite helpless.

On December 18, 1776, Benjamin Franklin arrived in Paris. Quickly realizing that he could not induce the French to join the United States in open alliance until American arms had demonstrated the likelihood of success, he undertook to make himself agreeable to the king, whose caution was now the chief obstacle to French participation. When Franklin perceived that the French people expected him to embody the homespun virtues of "natural" men dwelling in a rustic, Arcadian society, he affected the simplest garb, manners, and style of living and made his plainness conspicuous in a world of finery and luxury. As a democrat, once an artisan, he delighted the urban masses; as the author of Poor Richard's maxims of prudence, thrift, and industry he was adored by the Parisian middle class; as a philosopher and scientist of European reputation he appealed to nobles and intellectuals—followers of Voltaire or Rousseau—who were then riding the crest of the "enlightenment." By flattery, patience, and good will he became the idol of Paris and the symbol of an oppressed people struggling heroically against the ancient enemy of France.[30]

The victory at Saratoga gave Franklin and Deane a trump card. Britain immediately made overtures for peace. Vergennes now pressed with all his might for an alliance, arguing that if France did not enter the war, the Americans would come to terms with Britain and join her in a war for the conquest of the French West Indies. Better, then, to fight Britain with America as an ally than as an enemy. Besides, American success now seemed assured. On February 6, 1778, France and the United States signed two treaties one of commerce and one of alliance. By the latter France recognized the independence of the United States and promised military coöperation until independence became an established fact. France consented to recognize American conquests of British territory on the continent of America in return for American recognition of French conquests of British islands near the Gulf of Mexico. Each party agreed not to make peace without the approval of the other.[31]

Hoping to add Spain's navy to the forces opposed to Britain, Ver-

[29] Louis R. Gottschalk in Lafayette Comes to America (Chicago, 1935) and Lafayette Joins the American Army (Chicago, 1937) demonstrates that Lafayette became a champion of political liberty after his contacts with America.

[30] Bernard Faÿ, The Revolutionary Spirit in France and America (New York, c. 1927), treats cultural relationships, 1770–83, in chapters 1–3.

[31] E. S. Corwin, "The French Objective in the American Revolution," American Historical Review, XXI (Oct. 1915).

gennes redoubled his efforts to unite France and Spain in an anti-British alliance. The Spaniards craved the recovery of Gibraltar, Minorca, and Florida, but they shrank from giving aid to the Americans. They detested the spirit of democracy and republicanism prevalent in the United States and feared that one successful revolt of colonial subjects might provoke rebellion in their own colonies. Besides, the Spaniards looked askance at a powerful American state which was likely to expand westward and encroach upon their territory in Louisiana and Mexico. Accordingly, they informed Vergennes that they must acquire the lands of the Mississippi valley east to the mountains and possess the exclusive right of navigating the Mississippi River. Vergennes desired to placate Spain; he too did not wish to see the United States become a New World colossus; consequently he was willing to concede to Spain the territory west of the mountains and the sole right of navigating the Mississippi. Before entering the war the Spanish king, Charles III, assumed in 1778 the role of mediator between France and Britain, requesting that each power inform Madrid of its conditions for a peace. Britain replied that she could not desist from war until France ceased to aid the Americans; France replied that she could not forsake her treaty engagements. Finally, Charles III became convinced that Britain was acting in bad faith by deliberately delaying peace negotiations while plundering Spanish vessels and colonial territory. In a fit of rage he denounced Britain and signed a treaty of alliance with France, April 12, 1779.[32] By going to war against Britain Spain hoped to recover Gibraltar, Minorca, and Florida. France agreed not to make peace until Spain had regained Gibraltar, and since French approval was now necessary to an Anglo-American peace, France seemingly bound the United States, without its consent, to the Spanish conquest of Gibraltar. This move on the part of Spain, along with her well-known antagonism toward the Americans, made the Spanish-French alliance highly unpopular in the United States.

When the fortunes of the Americans were at a low ebb in February 1781 the Congress instructed John Jay to negotiate a treaty of alliance with Spain, authorizing him to give up the American right of navigating the Mississippi below the thirty-first parallel. Later the Congress was willing even to relinquish the territory west of the mountains. But the war ended soon afterward and Jay did not even

[32] For details of negotiations see French E. Chadwick, *The Relations of the United States with Spain: Diplomacy* (New York, 1909)—a work that overemphasizes racial factors in diplomacy.

disclose his instructions. Spain acted to the end solely in defense of her own interests, not as a champion of the United States.[33]

France's entrance into the war intensified the difficulties of neutral nations engaged in peaceful trade. Vessels sailing to British ports were subject to capture by the French; those bound to France and the United States were liable to seizure by the British. But since Britain was the superior naval power she had the chief advantage. International law in 1779 recognized the right of a belligerent to stop neutral vessels, to search them, and to seize goods belonging to subjects of the enemy. However, a new principle then gaining popularity asserted that goods on neutral vessels should be regarded as neutral and thus not liable to seizure—a doctrine which appealed to states deficient in naval power. As mistress of the seas, Britain adhered to the old rule which permitted the seizure of enemy goods from neutral ships.

Among the European powers, Prussia and the Netherlands were disposed to join France in protests against Britain's war on neutral trade. Frederick the Great, King of Prussia, had become an ardent foe of the British, believing that they had betrayed him, their one-time ally, when dividing the spoils of the Seven Years' War. Like the Spaniards, King Frederick had no love for the Americans, but he was willing to give them indirect aid in order to humiliate Britain. He encouraged France to enter the war by promising that Prussia would not help Britain, and he used his great influence with Russia to induce Catherine the Great to organize a league of neutral states for the protection of neutral commerce. Formed in 1780, the League of Armed Neutrality eventually embraced Russia, Prussia, Denmark, Sweden, the Netherlands, and the German empire. It asserted the principle that neutral ships carried only neutral goods.

Of the members of the new League the Dutch, as the chief shippers of Europe, were the greatest menace to Britain.[34] They took over most of France's foreign commerce; they traded with the United States through their island, St. Eustatius; and they allowed American privateers to operate from Dutch ports. When the Dutch joined the League, December 10, 1780, and thus gained the backing of the other neutral powers, Britain sought a pretext for declaring war, thus depriving the Dutch of their status as neutral shippers. But Britain did not wish to antagonize the other League members, particularly Russia; hence she could not press the issue of neutral rights. How-

[33] See again Frank Monaghan's scholarly and entertaining *John Jay*, chapters 7–11.
[34] Friedrich Edler, *The Dutch Republic and the American Revolution* (Baltimore, 1911), is a standard work.

ever, she had obtained information that the Dutch had been negotiating a treaty with the United States since August 1778. When the Dutch government refused to punish the official who had signed the draft of the proposed treaty, Britain declared war on the Netherlands, December 20, 1780.

Of the financial assistance granted directly to the United States by the enemies of Britain, only that from France ($6,352,000 received on loan between 1777 and 1784) contributed materially to American success. Spain in 1781–82 advanced $174,000, while Dutch bankers did not venture loans ($1,304,000 in 1782–83) until the war had been won.

## THE WAR CONCLUDED

The participation of France and Spain gave the United States the benefit of sorely needed naval power, since in 1779 the combined French and Spanish navies included more than a hundred and twenty ships. In July 1780 Washington wrote that "a decisive naval superiority is the basis upon which every hope of success must ultimately depend." The menace of the French and Spanish fleets deprived Britain of her former ability to move troops at will in America. Britain now had to dissipate her energies in order to guard her own shores against invasion (one such attempt being made by the French and Spaniards in July 1779) and to protect her colonial outposts in the Mediterranean, India, Africa, and Florida. Both France and Spain directed their main attack on the British West Indies, thereby forcing Britain to divert thither a large part of her fleet in order to protect her heavy investments in the islands. American privateers now became more efficient in their raids on British shipping and the British coast by virtue of their free access to French ports. The United States had no navy in the modern sense—only a few vessels; hence American naval engagements did not involve the maneuvering of fleets but rather isolated attacks of a few ships on British merchantmen and their naval convoys.[35] The most sensational combat was fought September 23, 1779, between the American ship *Bonhomme Richard*, commanded by John Paul Jones, and the British frigate *Serapis*, then guarding a Baltic merchant fleet off Scarborough Head. Jones's old, weather-beaten ship overcame the new, well-conditioned *Serapis*, and the Americans then sailed to a Dutch port with their prizes. The refusal of the Dutch to surrender Jones to the British led the latter to renounce all Anglo-Dutch treaties—an important step toward the

[35] A. T. Mahan, *Major Operations of the Navies in the War of Independence* (Boston, 1913), discounts American naval achievements as minor operations.

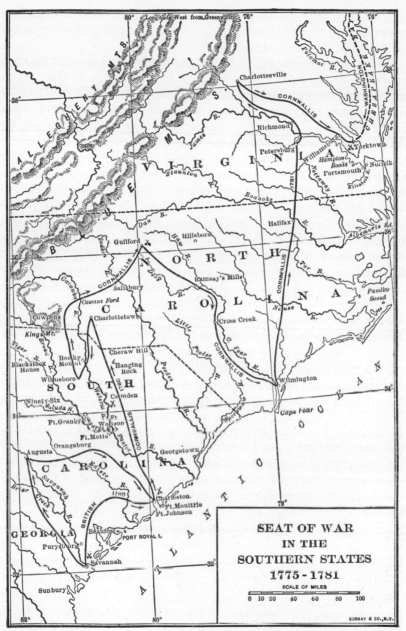

Longitude West from Greenwich

POTOMAC R.

Charlottesville

CORNWALLIS

WASHINGTON

VIRGINIA

Richmond

Williamsbg

Yorktown

Petersburg

Hampton
Roads

Portsmouth

Norfolk

Notaway R.

Elizabeth R.

James R.

Staunton R.

Roanoke R.

Halifax

Albemarle Sd.

ALLEGHENY MTS.

BLUE RIDGE MTS.

Dan R.

Hillsboro

Gullford

Haw R.

Yadkin R.

NORTH

CAROLINA

Salisbury

Ramsay's Mills

Deep R.

Pamlico
Sound

Cowans Ford

Charlottetown

Catawba R.

Cross Creek

Neuse R.

Tar R.

Cheraw Hill

Little Peedee R.

CORNWALLIS

Cowpens

Kings Mt.

Tiger R.

Broad R.

Rocky
Mount.

Hanging
Rock

Peedee R.

Wilmington

Blackstock
House

Winsboro

SOUTH

Wateree R.

Camden

CAPE FEAR R.

Waccamaw R.

Cape Fear

Ninety-Six

Saluda R.

Ft. Granby

Ft. Watson

CONGAREE R.

Ft. Motte

Congaree R.

Georgetown

Augusta

Orangeburg

CAROLINA

Edisto R.

ATLANTIC

Savannah R.

Briar
Creek

Charleston

BRITISH

Ft. Moultrie
Ft. Johnson

GEORGIA

Beaufort

PORT ROYAL I.

Purysburg

Savannah

OCEAN

Sunbury

**SEAT OF WAR
IN THE
SOUTHERN STATES
1775 - 1781**

SCALE OF MILES

0 10 20  40  60  80  100

BORMAY & CO., N.Y.

*From "Atlas of American History."* © *Harper & Brothers.*

Anglo-Dutch War declared in the following year. The damage done to British war transport and supply service was the chief contribution of American privateers and frigates.[36]

The military events of 1778 in America revolved around the naval operations of the French. On April 5 a French fleet of twelve vessels, commanded by the Comte d'Estaing, sailed from Toulon and arrived, July 8, at Delaware Bay, shortly after the British had evacuated Philadelphia. Fearing a French naval attack on New York, the British had decided to station there the army that had occupied the Quaker city—a move which would also release troops for the protection of the British West Indies. Sir William Howe having departed for England in May, the British evacuation of Philadelphia was conducted by Clinton. A section of Washington's army, poorly commanded by General Charles Lee, met Clinton at Monmouth Court House, New Jersey, June 28, in an indecisive battle, after which the British escaped at night and reached New York. The French fleet followed the British thither, but finding the British too strong for an attack, proceeded to New England. A projected assault on Newport (occupied by the British in December 1776) was abandoned by the French, whereupon in November 1778 they sailed to the West Indies. The absence of the French fleet in the Caribbean then permitted the British to undertake the conquest of the southern states.[37]

Since the failure of a British attack on Charleston in 1776, the southern seaboard had escaped the ravages of the war. Hoping that a British army would be greeted by a great uprising of loyalists, the British in 1778 decided to occupy Georgia as the base for a northward advance. On December 29, 1778, the British took possession of Savannah, but combined French and American forces recovered the city in October 1779. Soon afterward, while the French navy was in Europe, Clinton moved seven thousand troops from New York to Charleston and forced the surrender of a small American army under General Lincoln (May 1780). The British thereupon overran Georgia and South Carolina. Compelled to go north to protect New York against Washington's army (again occupying the Hudson above Manhattan Island), Clinton left Cornwallis in command in the South. An American army under General Gates was sent to oppose Cornwallis

[36] *John Paul Jones,* by Phillips Russell (New York, 1927), a lively journalistic account, gives an accurate impression of a "man of action." Mrs. Reginald De Koven's *The Life and Letters of John Paul Jones* (2 vols., New York, 1913) is thorough and scholarly though burdened with details and biased in favor of Jones.

[37] Gardner W. Allen, *A Naval History of the American Revolution* (2 vols., Boston, 1913), treats intensively the engagements in American waters, relating the navy to other phases of the war.

as he advanced to invade North Carolina. The two forces met at Camden, August 16, 1780, where Gates's North Carolina and Virginia militiamen fled the scene and about a thousand of his regulars were killed or captured—a defeat that ended Gates's career as an American commander. However, a regiment of loyalists led by Patrick Ferguson, which had left Cornwallis's army to recruit in the upcountry, was defeated decisively by the Carolina farmers, who stormed the British position at King's Mountain, October 7, 1780, and took or killed about a thousand of the enemy—an engagement significant because it showed that Britain could not count upon the aid of the back country in the conquest of the Carolinas.

General Nathanael Greene, succeeding to the American southern command, reached Charlotte, North Carolina, early in December 1780. Anticipating a British invasion of that state he divided his army into two parts to straddle the British line of advance. The western force, under General Daniel Morgan, won a victory over Tarleton's Tory Legion at Cowpens in the southwestern part of North Carolina (January 17, 1781). Greene and Cornwallis met at Guilford Court House, May 15, 1781, and fought an indecisive battle which obliged Greene to retreat and caused Cornwallis to retire to Wilmington, North Carolina. Greene then moved into South Carolina, where— aided by the upcountry farmers under Sumter, Pickens and Marion— he forced the British to withdraw to Charleston (1781).[38]

The campaign of 1780 suggested to the British that they must occupy Virginia in order to hold the lower South, since Virginia had poured militiamen into North Carolina. Accordingly, in April 1781 Cornwallis marched north from Wilmington to Virginia where he joined other British forces sent from New York by Clinton late in 1780 to ravage the tidewater area. Lafayette, now in command of a small American army in Virginia, succeeded in eluding Cornwallis, while always keeping within striking range. Cornwallis's peregrinations in Virginia finally brought him to the York River, where he took up a position at Yorktown in August 1781.[39]

Two things were necessary for an American victory over Cornwallis—naval control of the Chesapeake and a land attack by a strong army. In December 1780 the Comte de Grasse sailed "with a great armament" from Brest to Martinique, where he joined another French squadron. He then took his whole fleet to the Chesapeake in

[38] For the general student: Francis V. Greene, *General Greene* (New York, 1893); for the special student, George W. Greene, *The Life of Nathanael Greene* (3 vols., New York, 1871).

[39] G. M. Wrong, *Washington and His Comrades in Arms* (*Chronicles of America*, New Haven, 1921).

the summer of 1781, concealing his plans so well that the British admiral in the Caribbean, Sir George Rodney, dispatched only a small fleet in a blind pursuit. Thus De Grasse gained the Chesapeake without opposition.

In the winter of 1779–80, Lafayette had returned to France, there to persuade Louis XVI to send a large army to America. Five thousand strong, a French force under the Comte de Rochambeau arrived, July 10, 1780, at Newport, recently evacuated by the British in order to prosecute the southern campaign. Rochambeau remained idle a year at Newport, but his presence there greatly strengthened Washington's position on the lower Hudson. Sir Henry Clinton at New York was convinced in the summer of 1781 that the American and French armies and navy were preparing an attack on that city; consequently he not only failed to reinforce Cornwallis but even asked the latter to send troops to New York. Instead of attacking Clinton, Washington and Rochambeau slipped away, united at the Head of Elk, ferried down the Chesapeake, and joined Lafayette in a siege of Yorktown. Most of these maneuvers were accomplished while Clinton was preparing for an attack on New York. Meanwhile, a British fleet had met De Grasse's ships at the Chesapeake, September 5. in what proved to be a decisive engagement because the British retired to New York, leaving De Grasse in command of the bay and thus cutting off Cornwallis's communications by sea. When the British at New York learned of Cornwallis's plight they made frantic efforts to get an expedition ready for his relief, outnumbered as he now was by three to one. But the expedition from New York could not reach the Chesapeake until Cornwallis had given up his army of seven thousand men on October 19. As R. G. Adams puts it, Britain for once "failed to muddle through." [40]

Long before the victory at Yorktown, the American frontiersmen beyond the mountains had defeated the British in the contest for control of the Northwest. The Ohio valley was a prize of the first magnitude—an empire in itself, as well as a line of defense of the middle and southern states against inland attacks by the British and their Indian allies. The British, operating from Detroit, incited the Ohio valley tribes to drive out the American settlers in order to preserve the West for the hunt and the British fur trade. A few settlements in the Illinois country—Cahokia, Kaskaskia, and Vincennes—contained small bands of French woodsmen—a people peaceably inclined, yet antagonistic toward Britain and ready to aid the Americans after the

[40] R. G. Adams, "A View of the Surrender of Cornwallis at Yorktown," *American Historical Review*, XXXVII (Oct. 1931).

American-French alliance of 1778. Across the Ohio, the Kentucky country had become, after 1770, a magnet that was drawing pioneers westward from Virginia and North Carolina.

When the Revolution broke out, the pro-British Indians immediately attacked the Kentucky settlements and by the end of 1776 had driven the pioneers to seek protection at three fortified points: Boonesborough, Harrodsburg, and Logan's Fort. Such was the setting for the exploits of a stalwart young Virginian—George Rogers Clark—a pioneer farmer, surveyor, Indian-fighter, and representative of Virginia land promoters who were struggling with Richard Henderson and his North Carolina partners for the mastery of Kentucky. After urging Patrick Henry, governor of Virginia, to provide for the defense of the frontier, Clark was commissioned a major and authorized to organize the Kentucky militia and to undertake the conquest of the Illinois country. Gathering a band of 175 men he occupied Kaskaskia, July 4, 1778, and later secured possession of Cahokia and Vincennes. His plan to seize Detroit was frustrated when Lieutenant-Governor Henry Hamilton (the British "hair-buying general") raised a war party of Michigan and Wisconsin Indians and captured Vincennes in the autumn of 1778. When Clark learned of this counterstroke he took his small force on a harrowing two hundred and thirty mile march in the dead of winter—one of the epics of American heroism—and reconquered Vincennes, February 25, 1779. Thereafter he led the frontiersmen successfully in border warfare, protecting the Kentucky settlements, keeping the British at bay at Detroit, retaining the Illinois country posts, and guarding the southern states against a British attack from the interior. Due largely to his exertions the Americans, in effect, occupied the Northwest at the end of the war.[41]

## BRITISH POLITICS AND THE PEACE

The Revolution differed in one significant respect from the other imperial conflicts in which Britain had participated. In the earlier struggles against Spain, Holland, and France, England had been able to secure allies to aid in defeating a commercial and colonial rival. But in 1775–83 the United States (led by men of English descent) used the old English tactics of forming a coalition against the enemy. The earlier triumphs of Britain now recoiled upon her as her former antagonists, Spain, Holland, and France, joined forces against her,

[41] The most authoritative biography is James A. James, *The Life of George Rogers Clark* (Chicago, 1928). Others are Temple Bodley, *George Rogers Clark* (Boston, 1926), and Frederick Palmer, *Clark of the Ohio* (New York, 1929).

while Prussia, her strongest ally in 1756–61, was also hostile. Britain, the architect of coalitions *par excellence*, was for once bereft of allies.

The political situation within Britain also affected the course of the war. The country remained divided into two general classes: those who ruled through the court and Parliament—the nobles, the squires, the merchants, the prelates of the Anglican Church, and the lawyers —and those who were governed without their consent—the wage-earners, tenants, servants, and small tradesmen. But the ruling classes, acting through the dominant political parties, Whig and Tory, were not united in their attitude toward America. After 1775 the Tory party, led by George III and his personal Prime Minister, Lord North, controlled the government until 1782, representing the most powerful section of the upper class composed of the landed interest, the Anglican Church, and the most conservative merchants.[42] In British politics the Tories insisted upon the right of the rich to rule the poor with a free hand; they regarded the British constitution as the world's best; in foreign affairs they considered Britain invincible. They viewed the mass of the colonists as belonging in the same category with the dependent, unprivileged classes in England. "Sir," said the foremost Tory man of letters, Dr. Samuel Johnson, "they [the colonists] are a race of convicts, and ought to be content with anything we may allow them short of hanging." Should the colonists succeed in their nefarious revolt, their triumph might stir the English masses to demand greater political power and more of the good things of life. Moreover, the Tories, adhering firmly to mercantilism, intended to keep the colonists in the strait jacket of the old colonial system in order to extract maximum profits for the British ruling class. Hence the Tories asserted the supremacy of king and Parliament over America—that is, the right of British merchants and investors to regulate colonial trade, manufactures, currency, and settlement in their own interests. Until 1780 the Tories commanded 260 of the 350 seats in Parliament.[43]

Although George III labored to restore the influence of the monarchy, the methods and policies which he pursued satisfied the more conservative members of the middle class who had once opposed the power of the king. George III acted through Parliament; he did not attempt to dissolve it or to dispense with its statutes; instead he endeavored to control it by giving bribes, offices, titles, and privileges to its members. He defended the Anglican Church, upheld the prin-

[42] There is no outstanding biography of Lord North. Reginald Lucas's *Lord North* (2 vols., London, 1913) may be used by the special student.
[43] See again G. O. Trevelyan, *The American Revolution*.

ciples of mercantilism, and treated the empire as sacred and inde-
structible. Hence he did not encounter the fierce opposition which had
greeted the anti-parliamentary, pro-French, pro-Catholic, and anti-
mercantile policies of James II; in addition, George III's ideal of
popular submission to king and Parliament satisfied the desire of the
ruling class to keep the colonists and the English masses in their place.
Lord North personally disliked the American war and favored conciliatory measures, but to please the king he stayed on as Prime Minister, against his better judgment. George III even threatened to ab-
dicate in 1778 unless Lord North saved him from the humiliation of
a Whig ministry headed by the man he disliked above all others, the
Earl of Chatham.[44]

The Whig party, which held only about a fourth of the seats in
Parliament, was divided into factions. The smaller of these, led by
the Marquess of Rockingham, proposed to give the colonies their independence. This sound, enlightened position was fortified by two
considerations. First, the American war would inevitably draw in
France and Spain; Britain then would be unable to subdue the colonists. Secondly, the old colonial system had outlived its usefulness.
In 1776 Adam Smith published his attack on mercantilism in *The
Wealth of Nations*, arguing that a country would benefit most if it allowed capital and labor to flow, under the spur of competition, into
the most profitable enterprises. Were the Acts of Trade and Navigation repealed Britain would continue to enjoy the trade of America
which was economically most advantageous; only unproductive and
inefficient industries and trades needed the protection of law. Why,
then, said the Rockingham Whigs, should Britain waste her resources
upon a war for the maintenance of an unprofitable colonial system—a
war, moreover, that she could never win?

The main body of the Whigs, followers of Chatham and Shelburne, holding to the theory of parliamentary supremacy, resented
the personal government of George III. They adhered to mercantilism, refused to recognize the independence of the colonies, and
proposed to govern America by conciliation, compromise, and concessions. They would repeal the acts that had precipitated the revolt and
restore the relations existing between the colonies and Britain before
1760. However, the majority of the British ruling class failed to
grant concessions until the Americans had taken a firm stand in favor
of independence. Since the Chatham Whigs emphatically refused to
concede independence, they were forced to endure a war which rapidly

[44] Mary A. Marks, *England and America, 1763 to 1783* (2 vols., New York, 1907),
is a detailed, readable narrative, useful on military operations and British politics.

intensified the antagonisms they hoped to allay, and which eventually placed France in arms against Britain. And because opposition to the French had long been a chief stock in trade of the Chathamites, the participation of France made them even more bellicose than George III.[45]

Little can be said of the attitude of the common people of Britain toward the war, inasmuch as they were not represented in Parliament or heeded by the press. The best index of their sentiments—their refusal to enlist in the army—indicates that they were either indifferent or hostile to the purposes of the ruling class.

As early as November 20, 1775, Parliament authorized negotiations looking toward peace—a commission entrusted to Sir William Howe. Meeting Franklin, John Adams, and Edward Rutledge—special representatives of the Congress—in September 1776 at Staten Island, Howe proposed the redress of American grievances, pardons for the insurgents and the renunciation of the Declaration of Independence, whereupon the American delegation broke up the rather amiable conference by taking a firm stand in favor of separation. In May 1777 Chatham moved in Parliament to end the war on the basis of British concessions but his resolution was defeated, November 20. Then, in order to circumvent the French alliance, Parliament early in 1778 passed two conciliation bills introduced by Lord North. One renounced the right of taxing the colonies except in the regulation of trade; the other authorized the appointment of peace commissioners empowered to arrange an armistice. The tea duty of 1767 was at last repealed. Three British commissioners arrived at Philadelphia in June 1778, just as the British army was evacuating the city. Their proposals to the Congress assumed the restoration of the colonial status, to which that body replied that it could not "consider propositions so derogatory to the honor of an independent nation." Again the negotiations broke down because Britain would not recognize independence and the Americans would not remain colonists.[46]

The disaster at Yorktown placed Britain in a critical position. The war had dragged on six and a half years and yet the prospect of success seemed as remote as ever. With France, Spain, and Holland now arrayed against her, Britain was forced to protect her empire in Africa, India, Ireland, the Mediterranean, and the West Indies—a crushing

[45] The best account of all diplomatic aspects is Samuel F. Bemis, *The Diplomacy of the American Revolution* (New York, 1935).

[46] For a condensed version of S. F. Bemis's work see his important *A Diplomatic History of the United States* (New York, 1936), chapters 2–5.

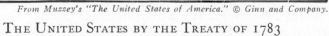

From Muzzey's "The United States of America." © Ginn and Company.

THE UNITED STATES BY THE TREATY OF 1783

burden to assume after the long, expensive war in America. The cost of the war (£12,000,000 a year) had been met largely by government borrowings, with the result that British credit in 1782 showed signs of exhaustion. Due to the interruption of peacetime industry and trade, British investors had placed their surplus funds with the government—a form of investment now ceasing to be attractive as government securities fell in value. Moreover, there was danger that previous investments in war loans might be lost if the national debt grew beyond the government's capacity to pay it from future taxes. As the war continued to take a heavy toll of British trade, the investing or ruling classes realized that peace was necessary, both to safeguard investments in government securities by terminating war expenditures, thus protecting the government's credit, and to restore normal commerce as an outlet for new investments. Accordingly, the House of Commons, February 27, 1782, voted to end the war. On March 20 Lord North resigned, whereupon Lord Rockingham took over the premiership and the task of concluding peace on the basis of American independence. Rockingham died soon afterward and Shelburne became Prime Minister, July 1.[47]

Peace negotiations began in earnest in April 1782 and continued until November 30, when Franklin, Jay, Henry Laurens, and John Adams—named as special negotiators by the Congress—signed a preliminary treaty with the British representative, Richard Oswald. During the negotiations the United States had demanded the territory north to the Great Lakes, west to the Mississippi, and south to Florida, together with the right to navigate the Mississippi. The Americans also wished to continue their fishery adjacent to British territory north of Maine, and they refused to promise to compensate the loyalists for their property confiscated during the war. Spain—conducting independent negotiations with Britain—sought Florida and the land south of the Ohio River and west from the mountains to the Mississippi, hoping thus to gain complete control of the great river and of the Gulf of Mexico. France insisted upon the recognition of the independence of the United States, but otherwise seemed to support Spain's claims to the transmontane West and the navigation of the Mississippi. The British declined to make reparation for American property losses occasioned by the war, insisted that American debts due to British creditors before 1775 be paid, asked com-

[47] Andrew C. McLaughlin, *The Confederation and the Constitution* (New York, 1905), one of the outstanding volumes of the *American Nation* series, devotes chapters 1 and 2 to the peace.

pensation for the loyalists, and refused to give up Canada. Otherwise, the British were inclined to favor the United States at the expense of France and Spain.[48]

While the negotiations were in progress, Jay became convinced that France and Spain were acting in concert to deprive the United States of the territory west of the mountains. He persuaded Franklin to make a separate treaty with Britain—a course which violated the instructions of the Congress that negotiations were to proceed with "the knowledge and concurrence" of France, but which did not violate the American-French Treaty of Alliance, since the preliminary treaty was to be approved by France before it became effective. Spain and France concluded their tentative agreement with Britain in January 1783, and on September 3 the preliminary treaties were signed as final and definitive.

Spain recovered Minorca and Florida (but not Gibraltar), while France received only a few minor concessions. The American treaty acknowledged the independence, freedom, and sovereignty of the thirteen United States. Article Four provided that it "is agreed that creditors on either side shall meet with no lawful impediments to the recovery of the full value in sterling money of all *bona fide* debts heretofore contracted." The Congress was to recommend to the states that they restore the confiscated property of the loyalists, while the people of the United States received the privilege of fishing off Newfoundland and of drying their fish in unsettled parts of Nova Scotia and Labrador. To the United States went the much coveted territory west to the Mississippi. At the northeast the American boundary was to follow the St. Croix River to its source and then proceed due north to the highlands dividing the rivers flowing into the Atlantic from those flowing into the St. Lawrence. Along the highlands the line was to run to the northwesternmost head of the Connecticut River; then down that river to the forty-fifth parallel and along that parallel to the St. Lawrence River; thence through the middle of the St. Lawrence and the Great Lakes to western Lake Superior and through the northwestern point of the Lake of the Woods to the Mississippi. The boundary then followed the Mississippi southward to the thirty-first parallel, along which it proceeded eastward to the Chattahoochee River and down that river to its junction with the Flint River; then straight to the head of the St. Mary's River, and along the St. Mary's to the Atlantic Ocean.

[48] E. Wead, "British Public Opinion of the Peace with America in 1782," *American Historical Review*, XXXIV (April 1929).

And thus in 1783 the United States joined the society of nations. Born of revolution, combining in its complex make-up the conflicting principles of aristocracy and democracy, scorned by the polite of Europe and confronted by a hostile world, this lusty youth now embraced its destiny of building a continental republic through the conquest of nature, for the satisfactions of the many and the aggrandizement of the few.

## BIBLIOGRAPHICAL NOTE

WORKS PREVIOUSLY CITED: W. C. Abbott, *New York in the American Revolution*, chs. 8–11; C. W. Alvord, *The Illinois Country*, chs. 15–16; G. Bancroft, *History of the United States*, IV, chs. 38–40, V, VI; *Cambridge Modern History*, VII, ch. 7; J. Fiske, *American Revolution*, I, chs. 5–7, II, chs. 8–15; S. G. Fisher, *Struggle for American Independence*, I, chs. 25–52; II; G. B. Hertz, *Old Colonial System*, chs. 8 10; A. C. Flick (ed.), *History of the State of New York*, IV, chs. 1–3, 6–8; L. P. Kellogg, *British Regime in Wisconsin*, chs. 9–12; A. T. Mahan, *Influence of Sea Power upon History*, chs. 9–14; *Pageant of America*, VI, chs. 5–10; VIII, ch. 3; J. Winsor (ed.), *Narrative and Critical History of America*, VI, chs. 4–9; VII, chs. 1–2; G. M. Wrong, *Canada and the American Revolution*, chs. 14–15, 17.

SOURCES NEWLY CITED: Jared Sparks has edited two important collections: *The Diplomatic Correspondence of the American Revolution* (12 vols., Boston, 1829–30), containing Franklin, Deane, Adams letters; and *Correspondence of the American Revolution; Being Letters of Eminent Men to George Washington* (4 vols., Boston, 1853). A standard collection is Francis Wharton, *The Revolutionary Diplomatic Correspondence of the United States* (6 vols., Washington, 1889). Jean-Edmund Weelen's *Rochambeau, Father and Son* (New York, 1936) reprints the journal of Rochambeau's son—a description of wartime conditions in America. Frank Monaghan has edited *The Diary of John Jay during the Peace Negotiations of 1782* . . . (New Haven, 1934).

SOURCES: PREVIOUSLY CITED: H. S. Commager (ed.), *Documents of American History*, nos. 69, 74; W. B. Donne (ed.), *Correspondence of George III with Lord North*, II; A. B. Hart (ed.), *American History Told by Contemporaries*, II, chs. 28–29, 31–32, 34–35; *Old South Leaflets*, nos. 43, 47, 86, 97–98, 152.

MAPS: D. R. Fox, *Harper's Atlas*, pp. 18–20; C. O. Paullin, *Atlas of the Historical Geography of the United States*, plate 160; W. R. Shepherd, *Historical Atlas*, pp. 195–196.

# INDEX